PEARSON ALWAYS LEARNING

Macroeconomics A Basic Perspective

Measurement–Analysis–Policy

Where are we–Where do we want to be–How can we get there

Preface and Introduction by Roger W. Mack

Fourth Custom Edition

Taken from:
Macroeconomics, Fourth Edition
by R. Glenn Hubbard and Anthony Patrick O'Brien

Economics: Principles, Applications and Tools, Seventh Edition
by Arthur O'Sullivan, Steven Sheffrin, and Stephen Perez

Principles of Macroeconomics, Tenth Edition
by Karl E. Case, Ray C. Fair, and Sharon M. Oster

Cover Art: Photodisc by Getty Images.

Taken from:

Macroeconomics, Third Edition
by R. Glenn Hubbard and Anthony Patrick O'Brien
Copyright © 2010, 2009, 2008, 2006 by Pearson Education, Inc.
Published by Prentice Hall
Upper Saddle River, New Jersey 07458

Economics: Principles, Applications and Tools, Seventh Edition
by Arthur O'Sullivan, Steven Sheffrin, and Stephen Perez
Copyright © 2012, 2010, 2008, 2006, 2003 by Pearson Education, Inc.
Published by Prentice Hall

Principles of Macroeconomics, Ninth Edition
by Karl E. Case, Ray C. Fair, and Sharon M. Oster
Copyright © 2009, 2007, 2004, 2003, 2002 by Pearson Education, Inc.
Published by Prentice Hall

Pearson Learning Solutions, 501 Boylston Street, Suite 900, Boston, MA 02116
A Pearson Education Company
www.pearsoned.com

Printed in the United States of America

4 5 6 7 8 9 10 V0CR 17 16 15 14 13

000200010271704348

CB

ISBN 10: 1-256-89060-X
ISBN 13: 978-1-256-89060-7

BRIEF CONTENTS

CONTENTS

Chapters 1,3, 4, 8, 9, 10, and 11 were taken from *Macroeconomics,* Fourth Edition by R. Glenn Hubbard and Anthony P. O'Brien.

Chapter 2 was taken from *Principles of Macroeconomics,* Tenth Edition by Karl E. Case, Ray C. Fair, and Sharon M. Oster.

Chapters 5, 6, 7, 12, and 13 were taken from *Economics: Principles, Applications, and Tools,* Seventh Edition by Arthur O'Sullivan, Steven Sheffrin, and Stephen Perez.

PREFACE

Teaching "Principles of Economics" is challenging. Classes are usually composed of students who have varying educational backgrounds, abilities, and desires to understanding economic thinking (as opposed to those merely wishing to pass a class). This text has been designed to avoid intimidation. A major issue in teaching this class is recognizing that students enter with some degree of *subject fear.* The basic theme is the interaction between people's wants and tastes—what they would really like to do—and their budget constraints—what they can do given the economic reality that they reside within. A budget constraint merely expresses the common sense proposition that every dollar spent (exchanged) must somehow be obtained. Thus, budget constraints focus on the sources and uses of people's funds. Economics is basically the study of exchange, what you have and what you are willing to give up for the things you want.

Welcome to a course in Macroeconomics, a course with a perspective much like your own life. While I was teaching this class recently, we discussed fiscal policy, then Congress passed a fiscal stimulus package; we discussed monetary policy, then the Fed created new policies which never before existed; we discussed business cycle theory, then we had a recession! We discussed health care reform and guess what! The current recession, starting December 2007, can be attributed to a number of factors including a sharp downturn in over-valued housing markets, lack of financial institution regulation and oversight, tightening of credit markets, and global interconnectivity of financial institutions and corporations.

Economics, psychology, sociology, politics, anthropology and other branches of social science developed as separate fields of study. In the last part of the 19th century, "political economy" became "economics." Since that time, economics has been frequently defined, as "the study of how scarce resources are allocated to satisfy unlimited wants." As a professional discipline, economics is often regarded as a decision science that seeks optimal solutions to allocation problems.

From the macroeconomics perspective, we are not really interested in the "individual". We are not discussing individual employment or personal income or even a specific person's health or happiness. We are concerned with the general wellbeing of entire economies. We need a formal analysis of what the problem is before we can be confident about policy predictions.

An economy is a social system of production, exchange, distribution and consumption of goods and services of a country. The United States is a market economy. This means the nation's economy is based on capitalism, private property rights and exchange. The system relies on the assumption that market forces, such as supply and demand, basically are the determinants of what is right for a nation's well being. Through policies and different programs, the government creates an environment that affects economic growth and distribution. By using its powers to tax and spend (fiscal policy), it affects the distribution of income and programs. By managing the money supply and controlling the use of credit and interest rates (monetary policy), it attempts to slow down or speed up the economy's rate of growth. While industrial production and GDP seems to be increasing, employment is still close to double the prerecession figure. These issues, which are the focus of this course, are in the news regularly.

Like those issues you consider on a regular basis, we will constantly be looking at three fundamental questions throughout this class. The first question: Where is the present state of the economy? (Where are we?) This represents the measurement issue. The material means to satisfy wants has been a perpetual problem. Before we can discuss or even imagine options for the macro-economy, or even for our own life, we must have a perspective as to where we are now, both in terms of our own life and in terms of the state of jobs, income, prices and purchasing power.

Food and shelter are requirements of human life. Other goods satisfy a range of human desires and give pleasure or utility to individuals. The study of ways that humans deal with these issues and challenges is called "economics." Where have we been, how did we arrive at this point and what are the directions and options from where we are—this is the basis of what is called the 'measurement issue' in macroeconomics.

We will, from the beginning, be discussing Gross Domestic Product (GDP). The total monetary value of all goods and services produced within the economy in a given time period is the basic measurement of the state of the national economy. We will be discussing GDP, both in "real" and "nominal" values. Most of us are more interested in the amount of real goods and services that exist per person in the economy and not in the change in cost or price of that production. We are interested in "real product per capita". We will be looking at GDP per capita as a "measure of growth", as a measure of productivity, but we will also discuss the differences between the size of GDP and levels of societal well-being. We are interested in how changes in GDP affect the prices we pay, the jobs available, and the value of our money and the purchasing power of our income. GDP also affects the real and potential composition of the very goods and services in the economy.

National economic wellbeing or happiness is the subject matter of macroeconomics. We discuss national employment and/or national unemployment rates; nobody is 10.2 percent or 5.1 percent unemployed. We discuss median or average or household income levels. We discuss purchasing power for average or median income workers; rarely are these figures the same as any specific household or individual's income. Our view will be from the perspective of national or regional data and not so much what "goods and services" cost for a specific buyer. We will be interested in general price levels and the real purchasing power of given incomes.

Societies must devise rules or principles that govern how goods are shared or distributed among their members. There exists alternative social and legal as well as social processes that establish the framework of institutions, values, beliefs, knowledge, and infrastructure within which the allocation and distribution of resources takes place. This social framework is the foundation that influences the individuals' perceptions, preferences and responses to the problems of what, how much, how, when and who gets societal goods and services.

If the first question was 'where are we', the second question is centered on where we want to be. What are our goals and dreams? The targets we aim for often determine behavior, the individual and collective decisions of each of us and the societal goals of all of us collectively. Where is it ***we*** want to be? With regard to this issue, we will be dealing with the current state of an economy with reference to the *potential* full-employment, non-inflationary level of that same economy. We will also be discussing alternative goals of happiness, social wellbeing and fulfillment.

What we will be specifically examining will be the goals of full-employment, non-inflationary real growth on real GDP per-capita. But we will also examine the choices and opportunity costs involved with those goals and we will compare and contrast those with social goals of overall wellbeing, targets of income distribution, equity of opportunities and general health and happiness of a society and an economy. These are all dynamic concepts with moving targets, changing social-political objectives and global implications and perspectives. What constitutes the 'good life' will be looked at economically, with reference to inflation and employment as the key issues. Inflation will be seen as a business cycle value above our target goals and unemployment will be viewed as a cycle value below our macroeconomic target goals. The central approach is economic. Models of the aggregate economy are valuable tools both for members of a given society and for policymakers for at least two reasons.

First, such models can help produce forecasts of future inflation, output, unemployment and other variables, which are crucial for forward-looking policy. Second, macroeconomic models can help quantify the amount of uncertainty in making policy choices. Economic thinking can provide insight into several interesting and somewhat controversial public policy issues. In at least some cases, the rigor of economic analysis is missing from much of the public debate on policy issues and hence the quality of public understanding and debate has suffered.

It is acknowledged that many considerations other than those of pure economics are relevant to the policy choices that could or should be made. Conventional economic theories of individual behavior rely on a basic preferences-beliefs-constraint system. That is, people know what they want (have complete and stable preferences) and make the best choices given their beliefs about uncertainties and constraints on time and money.

Most economic analyses are built on two major simplifying assumptions about human nature: first, individuals are assumed to be rational decision makers and second, individuals make decisions that are in their self-interest. The modeling of complex social phenomena often involves simplifying assumptions like these; otherwise, models may quickly become mathematically intractable.

Conveying economic ideas clearly is a very difficult thing to do, and yet it is essential that we succeed because far too much of what passes for debate on national policies is nearly incoherent. Clearly, students and citizens who understand economic principles would be better able to contribute to discussion about national and international economic policy. As a result, we should all expect better policies over time. An economic way of thinking will not necessarily be the decisive input, but must be given considerable weight in any ultimate policy decision.

Economists working today have mostly put behind them the inward-looking reductionism so central of the discipline in the past. Economists are offering insights and evidence about societal decisions, game theory, political economics, behavioral theory and the very organizational basis of human society. Macroeconomics is really the study of what is happening to the economy . . . as a whole, the economy in the large. It is asking; "What policy is available to change cycles into trends?" "What are the effects and trade-offs of each possible policy decision?" "How might the macroeconomy affect the quality of life and level of happiness of its members?" "Why does it matter?"

In general, nothing matters more to the potential future quality of life of a population than the long-run rate of economic growth. Today's governments have powerful abilities to improve economic growth and to promote stabilization of business cycles. Good macroeconomic policy can make almost everyone's life better; bad macroeconomic policy can make almost everyone's life much worse.

Overall, "economic activity" is the pattern of transactions in which goods and services of real useful value—resources, labor, products and activities—are created, transformed, and exchanged. In the United States, if a transaction does not involve something of measurable useful value being exchanged for money, odds are that NIPA (The National Income and Product Account) will not count it as part of "economic activity." It is important to have a base position as to where the economy is and then be able to measure changes from that position. The changes can be either in total output, in the unemployment rate, in the general price level, in average or median income and product distribution or combinations of any or all of these. We will tend to focus in a foundation course on six key indicators of economic activity.

- Real Gross Domestic Product
- The unemployment rate
- The inflation rate
- The growth rate
- The interest rate
- The exchange rate

The first three indicators are directly and immediately connected to a people's material well being. The other three are indicators and controls that profoundly influence the direction health and direction. Real GDP is a key measure for this course. "Real" means purchasing power and corrects 'nominal", current market prices, for changes in the overall price level. "Gross" means that this measure includes the replacement of worn-out and obsolete equipment and structures as well as completely new capital investment and inventory changes. "Domestic" means that this measure counts that economic activity that happens in the United States. "Product" means that real GDP measures the production in America of final goods and services over a given time.

The quality of life is clearly much more than just the total value of goods and services produced within a country. GDP divided by the total population, per capita GDP, or by workers, per worker GDP, can be interesting indicators. But they are imperfect measures of how well the economy produces and distributes those goods and services that people find useful, given their wants and values. GDP measures market value, not user satisfaction. GDP says little about composition of production or distribution. It measures overall market values, not user satisfaction or happiness. GDP says nothing at all as to the distribution of product or income.

In fact, the years between 1930 and 1970 saw the middle income and working classes closed the relative income gap between themselves and the rich. The years between 1970 and the present have seen this gap open wider once again, with the top one percent of the population, by wealth and income level, now controlling over a quarter (25%) of the total income generated in the economy. The 400 wealthiest Americans have an income greater than that of over 150 million Americans combined.

The major reason this recovery has been so anemic seems not to be Europe's debt crisis. It's not Japan's tsunami. It's not Wall Street's continuing excesses. It's not, as some economists tell us, because taxes are too high on corporations and the rich, and safety nets are too generous to the needy. It's not even, as some liberals contend, because the Obama administration hasn't spent enough on a temporary Keynesian stimulus.

The answer is in front of our faces. It's because American consumers, whose spending is 70 percent of economic activity, don't have the income to buy enough to boost the economy—and they can no longer borrow like they could before the crash of 2008. Median family income was $49,600 in 2007. By 2010 it was $45,800—a drop of 7.7%. All of the gains from economic growth have been going to the richest 1 percent—who spend less of their income, no more than half what they take in.

The Fed's latest report shows what is happening. Between 2007 and 2010 (the latest data available) American families' median net worth fell almost 40 percent—down to levels last seen in 1992. The typical family's wealth is their home, not just their stock portfolio—and housing values have dropped by a third since 2006. Families have also become less confident about how much income they can expect in the future. In 2011, over 36% of American families said they did not "have a good idea of what their income would be for the next year." That's up from 31.4% in 2007. But because their incomes and their net worth have both dropped, families are saving less. The proportion of families that said they had saved in the preceding year fell from 56.4% in 2007 to 52% in 2011, the lowest level since the Fed began collecting that information in 1992. The American economy is still struggling because the vast American middle class can't spend more to get it out of first gear.

In 1941 America went to war—a vast mobilization that employed able-bodied adults American, and put money in their pockets. After the war, the GI Bill, sent millions of returning veterans to college. A vast expansion of public higher education, and huge infrastructure investments, such as the National Defense Highway Act were in place. Taxes on the rich remained at least 70 percent until 1981. The result: By 1957, the top 1 percent of Americans raked in only 10.1 percent of total income. Most of the rest went to a growing middle class—whose members fueled the greatest economic boom in the history of the world.

It was once relatively accepted that a student could grasp the basic tenets of almost any discipline by merely studying the text. This is not the case in economics today. Economic ideas are the product of the perspective of the person and the times; they cannot be seen separate and apart from the sociopolitical world that they interpret and hope to understand and explain.

Global politics is also entering a new age. Constitutional democracy has swept through Eastern and Central Europe, Russia, Latin America, Korea, Taiwan and parts of the Middle East and elsewhere. The implications are huge for rich and poor alike. Yet for all its amazing promise, there is much uneasiness. Hundreds of millions of people will not benefit from a new economic order.

"The most significant fact about this (market) system," F.A. Hayek hypothesizes, "is the economy of knowledge with which it operates, or how little the individual participants need to know in order to be able take the right action." Hayek also stated, "The problem addressed by the market system is how to dispense with the need of conscious control and how to provide inducements which will make the individuals do the desirable things without anyone having to tell them what to do." The market system operates with an invisible efficiency that is often not even noticed by the participants themselves as they conduct their life on a daily basis.

Understanding the economic perspective involves the willingness to make an intellectual bet that most of the production and distribution of product and wealth, and a great deal of human social life, is best understood by first examining what situations look like to decision makers as they make choices. The very ability of people to cooperate for a common purpose is an essential competitive advantage. Whereas physical capital is created by changes in materials to create tools that facilitate production, human capital is created by changing ideas and knowledge to give people skills and capabilities to allow them to act in new ways.

Social capital is created when the relationships among people change in ways that facilitate action. The degree of social capital depends the quality of social relationships and organization. Within a few decades, relatively novel technological advances, many organizational innovations, and new ways of behavioral and organizational thinking have transformed both the field of economics and economies. This is partly because capital is not a thing, but rather a set of social relations that belong to a definite historical time and place in human development. To really understand capital, one must therefore decipher its character as a social relation.

From the mid 1700s to the early 1800s it was the steam engines, textile mills, and the Enlightenment that produced the Industrial Revolution. From the later 1800s to the mid 1900s it was largely the spread of electric power, various mass production techniques, and the spread of democracy and private property rights that directed economies and the way people lived. Now it is the Information Revolution that has forged new links between nations, companies, and peoples worldwide. Quick access and use of information, newer techniques of management and new forms of productive organizations guide the current economic era. The idea of good social organization and relations is central in the global competition for mobile financial, physical and human capital.

What has changed is the methods, models, and informational base involved in mutually beneficial actions. Because economics is a social science, involving values and alternative goals. Different people have different views of what makes a free, good, just, or well-ordered society. Debates within economics last longer than they would in a natural science, with rules and laws. The debates are much less likely to end in a clear consensus. Each is an advocate for an economy that harmonizes with their vision of what a society should be and what policy fits that view. They often ignore or explain away those issues that turn out to be inconvenient for their social political views. Unlike the stated objectivity that characterizes most work in the natural sciences, economics has a wide variety of points of view and schools of thought.

Another wrinkle makes economics seem difficult. Natural scientists can always assume the arrow of causality points from the past to the future. Often in economics, people's expectations of what the want in the future means that the arrow of causality often points the other way, from an anticipated desired future state back to the present decisions and policies.

Some economists cite the actions of the government and the lack of regulation as the largest contributing factor to the economic collapse. Others suggest that private market forces, including a prevalence of risk and greed on Wall Street held greater responsibility. A third group suggests that a combination of these factors, added to a rise in individual borrowing and over leveraging, created the problems. The recession officially ended in June 2009 when the economy started to grow again, but the residual effects continue to be felt across the country. Trust in financial institutions remain low, lending remains extremely slow and unemployment high. People are dealing with the loss of their homes, their 401k retirement plans and possible future job loss and foreclosures. The continued economic distress, wealth disparity and disagreement over the role of the government in the United States economy has led to frustration around the nation. Grassroots movements like the Tea Party and Occupy Wall Street protestors offer examples of the frustration Americans feel toward the economy and the role of government and industry in fiscal affairs.

I would like to thank Monika Thomas and Ravjeet Singh, here at DeAnza College, for suggestions and support for this work.

Roger W. Mack, Ph.D.
Mackroeconomics @ G-mail.com
Mack Island
Fall, 2012

INTRODUCTION

"We have two classes of economic forecasters:
Those who don't know...and those who don't know they don't know."
—John Kenneth Galbraith

Macroeconomics—A Basic Perspective

The turn of the century ushered in changes as well as challenges. As in earlier periods, the United States was undergoing profound economic change at the beginning of the 21st century. A wave of technological innovations in computing, telecommunications, and the biological sciences were profoundly affecting how Americans work and play. At the same time, the collapse of communism in the Soviet Union and Eastern Europe, the growing economic strength of Western Europe, the emergence of powerful economies in Asia, expanding economic opportunities in Latin America and Africa, and the increased global integration of business and finance posed new opportunities as well as risks. All of these changes were leading Americans to re-examine everything from how they organize their workplaces to the role of government. Perhaps as a result, many workers, while content with their current status, looked to the future with uncertainty.

The economy also faced some continuing long-term challenges. Disparities in wealth, while not as great as in some other countries, were larger than in many. Environmental quality remained a major concern. Substantial numbers of Americans lacked health insurance. The aging of the large post-World War II baby-boom generation promised to tax the nation's pension and health-care systems early in the 21st century. Global economic integration had brought some dislocation to countries' economies along with many advantages in world markets. In particular, traditional manufacturing industries in some countries suffered setbacks, and our nation had a large and seemingly irreversible deficit in its trade with other countries. The events of September 11, 2001 and the multi-trillion dollar Wall Street uncertainty that followed only added to the mix.

Like those issues you consider on a regular basis, we will constantly be looking at three fundamental questions throughout this class. The first question: Where is the present state of the economy? (Where are we?) This represents the measurement issue. The material means to satisfy wants has been a perpetual problem. Before we can discuss or even imagine options for the macro-economy, or even for our own life, we must have a perspective as to where we are now, both in terms of our own life and in terms of the state of jobs, income, prices and purchasing power.

Food and shelter are requirements of human life. Other goods satisfy a range of human desires and give pleasure or utility to individuals. The study of ways that humans deal with these issues and challenges is called "economics." Where have we been, how did we arrive at this point and what are the directions and options from where we are—this is the basis of what is called the 'measurement issue' in macroeconomics.

We will, from the beginning, be discussing Gross Domestic Product (GDP). The total monetary value of all goods and services produced within the economy in a given time period is the basic measurement of the state of the national economy. We will be discussing GDP, both in "real" and "nominal" values. Most of us are more interested in the amount of real goods and services that exist per person in the economy and not in the change in cost or price of that production. We are interested in "real product per capita". We will be looking at GDP per capita as a "measure of growth", as a measure of productivity, but we will also discuss the differences between the size of GDP and levels of societal well being. We are interested in how changes in GDP affect the prices we pay, the jobs available, and the value of our money and the purchasing power of our income. GDP also affects the real and potential composition of the very goods and services in the economy.

Economics, psychology, sociology, politics, anthropology and other branches of social science developed as separate fields of study. In the last part of the 19th century, "political economy" became "economics." Since that time, economics has been frequently defined, as "the study of how scarce resources are allocated to satisfy unlimited wants." As a professional discipline, economics is often regarded as a decision science that seeks optimal solutions to allocation problems.

From the macroeconomics perspective, we are not really interested in the "individual". We are not discussing individual employment or personal income or even a specific person's health or happiness. We are concerned with the general wellbeing of entire economies. We need a formal analysis of what the problem is before we can be confident about policy predictions.

National economic wellbeing or happiness is the subject matter of macroeconomics. We discuss national employment and/or national unemployment rates; nobody is 10.2 percent or 5.1 percent unemployed. We discuss median or average or household income levels. We discuss purchasing power for average or median income workers; rarely are these figures the same as any specific household or individual's income. Our view will be from the perspective of national or regional data and not so much what "goods and services" cost for a specific buyer. We will be interested in general price levels and the real purchasing power of given incomes.

All societies must devise rules or principles that govern how goods are shared or distributed among their members. There exists alternative social and legal as well as social processes that establish the framework of institutions, values, beliefs, knowledge, and infrastructure within which the allocation and distribution of resources takes place. This social framework is the foundation that influences the individuals' perceptions, preferences and responses to the problems of what, how much, how, when and who gets societal goods and services.

If the first question was 'where are we', the second question is centered on where we want to be. What are our goals and dreams? The targets we aim for often determine behavior, the individual and collective decisions of each of us and the societal goals of all of us collectively. Where is it ***we*** want to be? With regard to this issue, we will be dealing with the current state of an economy with reference to the potential full-employment, non-inflationary level of that same economy. We will also be discussing alternative goals of happiness, social wellbeing and fulfillment.

What we will be specifically examining will be the goals of full-employment, non-inflationary real growth on real GDP per-capita. But we will also examine the choices and opportunity costs involved with those goals and we will compare and contrast those with social goals of overall wellbeing, targets of income distribution, equity of opportunities and general health and happiness of a society and an economy. These are all dynamic concepts with moving targets, changing social-political objectives and global implications and perspectives. What constitutes the 'good life' will be looked at economically, with reference to inflation, employment and purchasing power as the key issues. Inflation will be seen as a business cycle value above our target goals and unemployment will be viewed as a cycle value below our macroeconomic target goals. The central approach is economic. Models of the aggregate economy are valuable tools both for members of a given society and for policymakers for at least two reasons.

First, such models can help produce forecasts of future inflation, output, unemployment and other variables, which are crucial for forward-looking policy. Second, macroeconomic models can help quantify the amount of uncertainty in making policy choices. Economic thinking can provide insight into several interesting and somewhat controversial public policy issues. In at least some cases, the rigor of economic analysis is missing from much of the public debate on policy issues and hence the quality of public understanding and debate has suffered.

It is acknowledged that many considerations other than those of pure economics are relevant to the policy choices that could or should be made. Conventional economic theories of individual behavior rely on a basic preferences-beliefs-constraint system. That is, people know what they want (have complete and stable preferences) and make the best choices given their beliefs about uncertainties and constraints on time and money.

Most economic analyses are built on two major simplifying assumptions about human nature: first, individuals are assumed to be rational decision makers and second, individuals make decisions that are in their self-interest. The modeling of complex social phenomena often involves simplifying assumptions like these; otherwise, models may quickly become mathematically intractable.

Conveying economic ideas clearly is a very difficult thing to do, and yet it is essential that we succeed because far too much of what passes for debate on national policies is nearly incoherent. Clearly, students and citizens who understand economic principles would be better able to contribute to discussion about national and international economic policy. As a result, we should all expect better policies over time. An economic way of thinking will not necessarily be the decisive input, but must be given considerable weight in any ultimate policy decision.

The legal system, private property rights, the existence of markets, organizational structures (corporations, governmental units, etc), religious beliefs, standards of morality and family/kinship relationships are a few examples of elements of the social framework. The matrix of these elements can be structured in almost an infinite number of ways resulting in different approaches to distribution and allocation questions. If we are to study the allocation of resources to competing ends, what is the nature and origin of the ends (goals, objectives)? Individuals have goals. To what extent do different forces in society shape these goals? How do individuals' objectives shape national economic goals?

Different societies have devised sets of institutions and beliefs to allocate resources. Why do individuals value some goods (or services) more highly than others, either for themselves or for others? Are some policies and some outputs more valuable to the functioning of society than others? In some cases traditions, customs and mores guide individual behavior. In other cases, a central authority uses commands to regulate individual choice. Voluntary interaction among the members of society is another alternative. In most cases, societies rely on a mix of culture, tradition, command and voluntary interaction. The interrelationships of economic life with private property rights and a view of justice, ethics, morality, creativity, security and aesthetic values are of concern. Markets reflect all these issues and where we want an economic system with a social and political history and perspective to be is an extremely complex question.

In mid 2012, the economic environment of America is in disarray: the dollar has lost its eminent world position, and both the short-run and long-term outlook for the federal budget is miserable. The Congressional Budget Office (CBO) projects that by 2020 the federal budget will have embarked on an unsustainable path. Federal spending is projected to steadily rise, relative to both revenues and the size of the economy. This will result in steadily rising deficits and debt burdens. The current national debt is over fifteen trillion dollars and the interest on this debt alone requires taxes of one billion dollars a day. Additionally, America's web of housing and financial problems has no simple or quick fix. However, one vital ingredient of progress appears to be on the rise: hope.

It took a long time for the economy's credit problems to build. Businesses and families "leveraged up" with a borrowing and lending boom that went too far. The aftermath is an unwinding process that can't be accomplished overnight. The economic recovery from the 2007-2009 recession has been a slow one in the United States, prompting much grumbling. Recent figures show that many European countries entered new recessions in 2012. The recovery in America is slow, but steady. Since World War II, 10 U.S. recessions have been followed by a recovery that lasted at least three years. This recovery is by far the weakest. This largely is due to the consequence of a housing bust and a grave financial crisis. Credit, the fuel that powers economies, evaporated after September 2008 and a 30 percent drop in housing prices erased trillions in home equity and brought construction to a standstill. The deeply divided U.S. political system has delivered growth-chilling uncertainty. Government spending has traditionally led most recoveries. Following the 1981-82 recession, during Ronald Regan's first term, the economy got a jolt from a 15 percent increase in government spending and investment. This time, state and local government has been slashing spending and jobs. Since June 2009, governments at all levels have slashed 656,000 jobs, the only time government employment has fallen in the three years after a recession. The economy shed over 8.9 million jobs during and shortly after the recession and has created only 4 million during the recovery.

But for American households, what matters most is that this unwinding occur in as orderly a way as possible. If things go well, credit will still be available, more banks won't fail, and the housing market will seek a new equilibrium. Any cooperation toward a solution implies voluntary agreements and a coordinated approach to the problem. Another element in the economic disarray is the demographic projections coming from the Social Security Administration These projections show that the ratio of persons aged 65 or older is steadily rising; these are generally retirees drawing increased amounts of benefits, in relation to those persons 20 to 64, who are generally in the work force paying taxes. With an economic goal of increased productivity (the output per hour of labor) fewer workers actually produce more GDP. They will need to produce greater and greater amounts of GDP. They will to satisfy their own wants and those of the growing number of retirees. Growth in the size of real GDP is even more of an economic goal than it has been.

Lately we've been getting some pretty encouraging news on the economy. It's been a long time coming and is very welcome indeed. There is a return to growth in the job market. The fact that the economy is growing again doesn't mean we're where we ought to be. In particular, the unemployment rate is unacceptably high, creating real hardship for millions of Americans. But, at least we're heading in the right direction. Clearly, the big weight hanging over everyone's heads is jobs. The current high level of unemployment is restraining income and undermining confidence as people worry whether they will have a paycheck in the months ahead. Even those with secure jobs may worry about their finances since debt burdens were near historic highs at the onset of the financial crisis and, since then, equity and house prices have declined sharply.

The economy should gradually pick up steam over the remainder of this year as households and businesses regain confidence, financial conditions improve, Congress makes decisions again after the election and banks increase the supply of credit. Even with moderate growth forecast, the economy will be operating well below its potential for several years. Economists think in terms of what we call the "output gap," which measures the difference between the actual level of GDP and the level where GDP would be if the economy were operating at full employment. The output gap was around negative 6 percent in the first quarter of 2010, based on Congressional Budget Office estimates. That's a very big number and it means the U.S. economy was producing 6 percent less than it could have had we been at full employment. That's equivalent to more than $900 billion of lost output per year, or roughly $3,300 per person.

Estimates are that the potential level of output is increasing roughly 2½ percent a year due to growth in the labor force and increases in productivity. Hence, over the next two years, potential output will increase by about 5 percent. Don't expect the output gap to completely vanish until sometime in 2014. The U.S. economy has shed 8.4 million jobs since December 2007. That's more than a 6 percent drop in payrolls, the largest percentage point decline since the demobilization following World War II. The unemployment rate, which was 5 percent at the start of the recession, rose to over 10 percent in early 2010 and 8.2 percent in late 2012.

In the past, a given level of economic growth produced a more-or-less predictable change in the unemployment rate. Historically, a pattern emerged in which unemployment declined by half as much as the difference in the growth rates of actual and potential GDP. One possibility for this not happening is that the severe recession is fundamentally altering the labor market, shifting jobs away from such sectors as manufacturing, real estate, and finance to other sectors.

This reallocation takes time. Until it is complete, we will see higher levels of unemployment. A second possibility is that the 2011 extended unemployment benefits artificially boosting reported unemployment rates because workers who collect unemployment checks may be saying they are looking for work even if they have given up.

A second possible explanation is that last year's enormous decline in employment was somehow an aberration. In other words, the economy produced roughly the same quantity of goods and services with 4 percent fewer workers, which translates into a 4 percent increase in output per worker. That's a huge rate of productivity growth, well above estimates of the long-term trend in productivity gains that stem from such factors as improved technology.

Those who believe it's temporary point to the unusual nature of this terrible financial crisis and recession. Its severity made employers believe that it would be a long time, if ever, before they would need as many workers as they previously had. The credit crunch may also have caused some to fear that they wouldn't be able to borrow in order to meet their payrolls. Businesses were able to continue to produce the same level of output despite big cuts in their workforces by working their employees harder. We simply can't be complacent when one of every six workers is without a job or is working a schedule that's been cut short. My forecast calls for the unemployment rate to edge down to about 8¼ percent by the end of 2012 and still be about 8 percent by the end of 2013, a very disappointing outlook.

The recession has forced businesses to reexamine just about everything they do with an eye toward restraining costs and boosting efficiency. Strapped by tight credit and plummeting sales, businesses have overhauled the way they manage supply chains, inventory, production practices, and staffing. Shoppers, after hunkering down during the recession, are clearly in a better mood. Over the past few years, they had cut back sharply on outlays for such durable goods as cars and appliances. Now that fear and uncertainty have abated, households are beginning to act on their pent-up demand for these products. And the rebound in the stock market and the stabilization of house prices means that household wealth is growing again, which should give a boost to spending. In a few cases, consumer demand is even feverish, as we see with the new Apple iPad.

Before the onset of the recession, households went on a spending spree, buoyed by easy credit and fast-rising home equity. It was easy to get a loan to buy a car or remodel a home. When the party was over, reveling consumers woke up to a massive hangover in the form of high debt levels, a horrible economy, tight credit, and plummeting home equity. The financial crisis that began in August 2007 has been the most severe of the post-World War II era and, very possibly—once one takes into account the global scope of the crisis, its broad effects on a range of markets and institutions, and the number of systemically critical financial institutions that failed or came close to failure—the worst in modern history. Although forceful responses by policymakers around the world avoided an utter collapse of the global financial system in the fall of 2008, the crisis was nevertheless sufficiently intense to spark a deep global recession from which we are only now beginning to recover.

The financial crisis that began in the summer of 2007 was an extraordinarily complex event with multiple causes. Its immediate trigger was a downturn in the national housing market that followed a long period of rapid construction and rising home prices. The housing slump in turn brought to light some very poor lending practices, especially for subprime mortgages extended to less-creditworthy borrowers. Relative to the global financial system, the market for subprime mortgages was quite small, probably less than 1 percent of global financial assets. How, then, did problems in this market appear to have such widespread consequences? One important reason is that the subprime mortgage market was closely linked to a broader framework for credit provision that came to be known as the shadow banking system. That broader framework, at least as it was structured during the run-up to the crisis, proved deeply flawed.

The innovation underlying the shadow banking system was that it helped provide a wide range of borrowers indirect access to global credit markets. For example, originators of subprime mortgages did not typically retain the loans they made on their own books. Instead, the mortgages were packaged together in complex ways, sometimes with other types of loans, stamped with a seal of approval from one or more credit rating agencies, and sold to investors worldwide, thus—it was thought—broadly dispersing the underlying risks. Credit risks were further dispersed—again, at least in theory—through the use of derivative financial instruments such as credit default swaps.

Importantly, residential mortgage markets were not the only markets caught up in the boom. In part because large flows of capital into the United States drove down the returns available on many traditional long-term investments, such as Treasury bonds, investors' appetite for alternative investments—such as loans to finance corporate mergers or commercial real estate projects—increased greatly in the years leading up to the crisis. These securities too were packaged and sold through the shadow banking system. As we now know, however, neither the investors, nor the rating agencies, nor the regulators, nor even the firms that designed the securities fully appreciated the risks that those securities entailed. Nor were the risks as widely dispersed as thought. For example, many complex securities were held in off-balance-sheet vehicles financed by short-term loans. When investors lost confidence in the underlying securities and pulled their funding, many firms that sponsored the off-balance sheet vehicles found that they were bound by explicit or implicit promises to stand behind the securities. Together with other direct or indirect exposures to risky debt, these commitments left financial institutions dangerously exposed to rising losses.

Critical challenges—both near term and longer term—remain. We have yet to see evidence of a sustained recovery in the housing market. Mortgage delinquencies for both subprime and prime loans continue to rise as do foreclosures. The commercial real estate sector remains troubled, which is a concern for communities and for banks holding commercial real estate loans.

Some of the toughest problems are in the job market. The unemployment rate has edged off its peak, but it is still close to its highest level since the early 1980s. Although layoffs have eased in recent months, hiring remains very weak. By mid 2011 more than 40 percent of the unemployed have been out of work six months or longer, nearly double the share of a year before. This is of great concern, because long spells of unemployment erode skills and lower the longer-term income and employment prospects of these workers.

What about the longer term? The economist John Maynard Keynes said that "...in the long run, we are all dead". If he were around today he might say that, in the long run, we are all on Social Security and Medicare. That brings me to two interrelated economic challenges our nation faces: meeting the economic needs of an aging population and regaining fiscal sustainability. The U.S. population will change significantly in coming decades with the combined effect of the decline in fertility rates following the baby boom and increasing longevity. As our population ages, the ratio of working-age Americans to older Americans will fall, which could hold back the long-run prospects for living standards in our country. The aging of the population also will have a major impact on the federal budget, most dramatically on the Social Security and Medicare programs, particularly if the cost of health care continues to rise at its historical rate. Thus, we must begin now to prepare for this coming demographic transition. The economist Herb Stein once famously said, "If something cannot go on forever, it will stop." That adage certainly applies to our nation's fiscal situation.

Inevitably, addressing the fiscal challenges posed by an aging population will require a willingness to make difficult choices. The arithmetic is, unfortunately, quite clear. To avoid large and unsustainable budget deficits, the nation will ultimately have to choose among higher taxes, modifications to entitlement programs such as Social Security and Medicare, less spending on everything else from education to defense, or some combination of the above. These choices are difficult, and it always seems easier to put them off—until the day they cannot be put off any more. But unless we as a nation demonstrate a strong commitment to fiscal responsibility, in the longer run we will have neither financial stability nor healthy economic growth.

Today the economy continues to operate well below its potential, which implies that a sharp near-term reduction in our fiscal deficit is probably neither practical nor advisable. However, nothing prevents us from beginning now to develop a credible plan for meeting our long-run fiscal challenges. Indeed, a credible plan that demonstrated a commitment to achieving long-run fiscal sustainability could lead to lower interest rates and more rapid growth in the near term.

Many of the challenges facing our economy stem from the extended contraction of the U.S. housing market. In 2006, after a multiyear boom in residential construction and house prices, the housing market reversed course. Housing starts and sales of new homes are now less than half of their respective peaks, and house prices have flattened or declined near twenty percent in most areas. Changes in the availability of mortgage credit have amplified the swings in the housing market. During the housing sector's expansion phase, increasingly lax lending standards, particularly in the subprime market, raised the effective demand for housing, pushing up prices and stimulating construction activity. As the housing market began to turn down, however, the slump in subprime mortgage originations, together with a more general tightening of credit conditions, had served to increase the severity of the downturn. Weaker house prices have in turn contributed to the deterioration in the performance of mortgage-related securities and reduced the availability of mortgage credit.

Consumer spending, the largest single sector of the U.S. economy, continued to increase at a solid pace through much of the second half of 2007, despite the problems in the housing market, but it slowed significantly toward the end of that year. The jump in the price of imported energy, which eroded real incomes and wages, likely contributed to the slowdown in spending, as did the declines in household wealth associated with the weakness in house prices and equity prices.

Slowing job creation is yet another potential drag on household spending. However, the 2008 enacted fiscal (taxing and spending) stimulus package has provided some support for general household spending, although many economists believe that household credit card debt may receive the bulk of the fiscal stimulus monies received by households. The business sector has also displayed signs of being affected by the difficulties in the housing and credit markets. Reflecting a downshift in the growth of final demand and tighter credit conditions for some firms, available indicators suggest that investment in equipment and software has been subdued. The vigor of the global economy has offset some of the weakening of domestic demand.

U.S. real exports of goods and services increased, boosted by continuing economic growth abroad and the lower foreign exchange value of the dollar. Strengthening exports, together with moderating imports, have in turn led to some improvement in the U.S. current account deficit, which likely narrowed (on an annual basis) for the first time since 2001. Although recent indicators point to some slowing of foreign economic growth, U.S. exports should continue to expand at a healthy pace in coming quarters, providing some impetus to domestic economic activity and employment.

To help relieve the pressures in the market for inter-bank lending, the Federal Reserve introduced a term auction facility (TAF), through which prespecified amounts of discount window credit are auctioned to eligible borrowers, and The Fed has been working with other central banks to address market strains that could hamper the achievement of broader economic objectives. These efforts appear to have contributed to some improvement in short-term funding markets.

The projections for economic activity reflect the effects of the financial turmoil on real activity and a housing contraction that has been more severe than previously expected. By mid 2012, projections showed output growth picking up to rates close to its longer-term trend and the unemployment rate edging lower; this reflects the effects of the monetary policy stimulus and an anticipated moderation of the contraction in housing and the strains in financial and credit markets. Information continues to suggest sluggish economic activity in the near term.

Consumer price inflation has increased in substantial part because of the steep runup in the price of energy. Food prices also increased significantly, and the dollar has depreciated. Both overall and core inflation are projected to edge lower. The rate of inflation that is actually realized will of course depend on a variety of factors. Inflation could be lower if slower-than-expected global growth moderates the pressure on the prices of energy.

Additionally, the decline in the foreign exchange value of the dollar has boosted some non-commodity import prices and thus contributed to inflation. However, upside risks to the inflation projection are also present, including the possibilities that energy and food prices do not flatten out or that the pass-through to core prices from higher commodity prices and from the weaker dollar may be greater than expected. Indeed, increases in the prices of energy and other commodities, and general consumer prices, suggest slightly greater upside risks to both overall and core inflation. Should high rates of overall inflation persist, the possibility also exists that inflation expectations could rise. Any tendency of inflation expectations to rise could greatly complicate the task of sustaining price stability and could reduce real economic growth and undermine monetary policy.

A critical task will be to foster objectives of maximum employment and price stability in an environment of downside risks to growth, stressed financial conditions, and inflation pressures. Already changes are being enacted, in 2008, the Federal Reserve Board issued a comprehensive set of new regulations to prohibit unfair or deceptive practices in the mortgage market, under the authority granted by the Home Ownership and Equity Protection Act of 1994. The new rules apply to all mortgage lenders and establish lending standards to help ensure that consumers who seek mortgage credit receive loans whose terms are clearly disclosed and that can reasonably be expected to be repaid.

Accordingly, the rules prohibit lenders from engaging in a pattern or practice of making higher-priced mortgage loans without due regard to consumers' ability to make the scheduled payments. In each case, a lender making a higher-priced loan would have to use third-party documents to verify the income relied on to make the credit decision. For higher-priced loans, the proposed rules would require the lender to establish an escrow account for the payment of property taxes and homeowners' insurance and would prevent the use of prepayment penalties in circumstances where they might trap borrowers in unaffordable loans.

In addition, for all mortgage loans, new Fed regulations address misleading and deceptive advertising practices, require borrowers and brokers to agree in advance on the maximum fee that the broker may receive, ban certain practices by servicers that harm borrowers, and prohibits coercion of appraisers by lenders. The effectiveness of the new regulations, however, will depend critically on strong enforcement. Credit availability has been restricted because some large financial institutions, including some commercial and investment banks and the government-sponsored enterprises (GSEs), have reported substantial losses and write downs, reducing their available capital. Financial institutions' balance sheets have expanded, as banks and other institutions have taken on various assets that can no longer be financed on a standalone basis. Thus, because of this, the capacity and willingness of some large institutions to extend new credit remains limited.

Private payroll employment is falling, with job cuts in construction, auto production and closely related industries accounting for a significant share of the decline. But the demand for labor has also moderated in other industries, such as business services and retail trade, and manufacturing employment has continued on its downward trend. Meanwhile, claims for unemployment insurance have risen somewhat, and jobseekers are experiencing greater difficulties finding work.

Well-functioning financial markets are essential for economic growth and stability. To improve market liquidity and market functioning, and consistent with its role as the nation's central bank, the Federal Reserve has supplemented its longstanding discount window by establishing three new facilities for lending to depository institutions and primary dealers. The lending facilities now in place offer depository institutions and primary dealers two complementary alternatives for meeting funding needs. One pair of facilities—the discount window for depository institutions and the Primary Dealer Credit Facility for primary dealers—offers daily access to variable amounts of funding at the initiative of the borrowing institution. A second pair of facilities—the Term Auction Facility for depository institutions and the Term Securities Lending Facility for primary dealers—makes available predetermined aggregate amounts of longer-term funding on pre-announced dates, with the interest rate and the distribution of the awards across institutions being determined by competitive auction. Although these facilities operate through depository institutions and primary dealers, they are designed to support the broad financial markets and the economy by facilitating the provision of liquidity by those institutions to their customers and counterparties.

Clearly, the U.S. economy is going through a very difficult period. But among the great strengths of our economy is its ability to adapt and to respond to diverse challenges. Much necessary economic and financial adjustment has already taken place, and monetary and fiscal policies should support a return to growth in our economy's long-term prospects. The largest effects of the financial turmoil appear to have been on the housing market, which has deteriorated significantly over the past two years or so. The virtual shutdown of the subprime mortgage market and a widening of spreads on jumbo mortgage loans have further reduced the demand for housing, while foreclosures are adding to the already-elevated inventory of unsold homes. New home sales and housing starts have both fallen by about half from their respective peaks. While home prices drop, slowing in residential construction may continue to be a drag on GDP growth. In particular, a number of factors, including continuing increases in energy prices, lower equity prices, and softening home values, seem likely to further slow consumer spending.

Consumer spending also depends importantly on the state of the labor market, as wages and salaries are the primary source of income for most households. Labor market conditions are disappointing. Employment in residential construction posted substantial reduction, and employment in manufacturing and retail trade also decreased significantly. Employment in services continued to grow.

U.S. exports will likely grow at a healthy pace, providing some impetus to the domestic economy. Financial conditions continue to pose a downside risk to the outlook. Market participants still express considerable uncertainty about the appropriate valuation of complex financial assets and about the extent of losses that may be disclosed in the future. On the whole, despite improvements in some areas, the financial situation remains fragile, and many funding markets remain impaired. Adverse economic or financial news has the potential to increase financial strains and to lead to further constraints on the supply of credit to households and businesses.

The same increase in oil prices that may be a negative influence on growth is also lifting overall consumer prices. Food prices increased rapidly by recent standards, further boosting overall consumer price inflation. Part of this rise may reflect the pass-through of energy costs to the prices of core consumer goods and services, as well as the effects of the depreciation of the dollar on import prices, although some other prices—such as those for some medical and financial services—have also accelerated lately.

Thus far, the public's expectations of future inflation appear to have remained reasonably well anchored, and pressures on resource utilization have diminished a bit. Further, futures markets suggest that food and energy prices will decelerate over the coming year. Furthermore, any tendency of inflation expectations to rise or the Fed's inflation-fighting credibility to be eroded could greatly complicate the task of sustaining price stability and growth in the future. Financial and economic conditions can change quickly. A number of analysts have raised the possibility that fiscal policy actions might usefully complement monetary policy in supporting economic growth over the next year or so.

The United States government used a number of unprecedented monetary and fiscal policy techniques in an attempt to shorten the recession and decrease its severity through stimulus measures. This included a historically large amount of traditional fiscal and monetary stimulus—such as tax cuts, new spending initiatives and interest rate adjustments. The goal of any stimulus is to create easier access to money to increase consumption, investment, government purchases and net exports. If a stimulus is successful, economics can avoid greater falls in demand, deeper economic downturns and can return to a period of economic growth.

Stimulus that comes too late will not help support economic activity in the near term, and it could be actively destabilizing if it comes at a time when growth is already improving. Thus, fiscal measures that involve long lead times or result in additional economic activity only over a protracted period, whatever their intrinsic merits might be, will not provide stimulus when it is most needed. Any fiscal package should also be efficient, in the sense of maximizing the amount of near-term stimulus per dollar of increased federal expenditure or lost revenue. Finally, any program should be explicitly temporary, both to avoid unwanted stimulus beyond the near-term horizon and, importantly, to preclude an increase in the federal government's structural budget deficit. The nation faces daunting long-run budget challenges associated with an aging population, rising health-care costs, and other factors. A fiscal program that increased the structural budget deficit would only make confronting those challenges more difficult.

The American consumer is a very persistent spending machine. It is American consumption growth running at higher than 4 percent annualized—well above its long-term average—that has kept the economy relatively strong as the housing slowdown has subtracted more than a percentage point from growth. Even with a substantial additional drag on the U.S. economy from other areas—inventory liquidation, weakening net exports, and rapidly rising gasoline prices—the American consumer's spending has almost been enough to keep GDP growth in positive territory. But the "credit crunch" finally has stopped the rise in the ability of consumers to consume; they have run out of money and credit!

Durable American consumption growth is an immensely important factor for the world economy. It creates a reliable and persistent source of demand growth that accounts for over 70 percent of U.S. GDP growth and a substantial portion of rising demand for the exports of the rest of the world, including rapidly industrializing economies like China's. The rising elasticity of America's credit system is an important factor to consider in a discussion of the persistent growth of American consumption.

Consumption growth may falter because household savings rates are rising, while household debt levels relative to income are unusually high. Additionally, gasoline prices have risen to a point at which they are subtracting more than 1 percent from disposable income. Consumers have little substitute for gasoline and borrow from other expenditures, mainly services, to continue driving.

The persistence of consumption growth since the early 1980s is even more remarkable in view of the fact that since 1982–85, personal saving as a share of disposable personal income has dropped from a range of 8 to 10 percent to minus 1.3 percent over the previous few years. The most rapid drop in the personal saving rate occurred between 1982 and about 2000, by which time the saving rate had fallen to what was then viewed as a dangerously low 2 percent. After hovering around 2 percent until 2003, the personal saving rate made another swoop down and has been in negative territory since 2003, until 2009, when it rose 3 percent, lowering Consumption expenditures per household. It is, of course, the negative personal saving rate coupled with public sector deficits that has boosted American net borrowing from abroad to about 6 percent of GDP.

That said, a negative saving rate and rising indebtedness to the rest of world have failed to dent the persistent American consumption, due in part to the willingness of foreigners to lend to America at low interest rates the funds necessary for it to keep spending in excess of income. The level of wealth, the accumulated assets of American households, has proven to be an important determinant of spending habits. The breakdown of the usual connection between savings and wealth accumulation has made many casual observers of American consumption behavior uncomfortable over the past twenty-five years.

In opposition to the current trend, the most common way to accumulate wealth is to restrain consumption, boost savings, and thereby acquire assets. The traditional story of the evolution of an American family in the early post-Depression years saw households restrain consumption, save, accumulate financial wealth, and then, perhaps with the help of a loan equal to half the value of the house, purchase the major asset of most traditional American families—the primary residence.

Compare that model with a more contemporary one rising out of the late stages of the recent housing boom. During 2005 and early 2006, so-called subprime lending enabled households with virtually no accumulated assets to borrow 100 percent of the purchase price of residential real estate. Such easy credit led numerous, more adventurous households (many located in California and Florida) to buy multiple speculative real estate units, say, several condominiums, with no money down. These steps were, by the way, totally rational. If a lender is willing to lend 100 percent of the purchase price—even in a risky market—the borrower may as well take up the offer and exercise what amounts to infinite leverage on real estate speculation. Should he be unable to sell the speculatively purchased units, he need only walk away from the loan, leaving the subprime lender to suffer the loss.

Subprime lenders thought that they were invulnerable based upon having sold the subprime mortgages to the credit derivatives market. What tripped them up was the clause in the subprime lending contract specifying that if a borrower failed to make even the first payment on the loan, the loan reverted back to the subprime lender. During 2006, when weakening market conditions in Florida, California, Arizona, Nevada and elsewhere caused many speculative borrowers to walk away from their loans without making even a first payment, subprime lenders were submerged in a cascade of bad paper that pushed many of them out of business.

The contrast between the traditional "save-and-then-borrow-moderately" paradigm and the "borrow-it-all" subprime paradigm illustrates another factor operating on American consumption: American credit markets have become far more elastic, especially over the past decade. While some abuses, such as in the subprime sector, have arisen for American households that have, through rising asset prices, accumulated wealth at an unusual pace without saving, elastic credit markets have provided an important additional degree of freedom that enables most middle-to-upper-income households to maintain spending at a level close to income.

In effect, the elastic credit market has turned the primary asset of American households, residential real estate, into a flexible line of credit. Home equity loans and mortgage equity withdrawal mirroring the rise in the value of residential real estate have contributed to a more stable American spending stream that has persistently risen relative to income. The key reality is that the two major sources of household wealth—financial assets and real estate—have increased in value at an unusual pace.

The other big factor underlying persistent American consumption growth and resultant stable GDP growth has been an unusually rapid pace of wealth accumulation over the past twenty-five years that is not tied to saving, per se. Between 1980 and the end of 2006, the real net worth of American households grew at about 4 percent per year, while overall income grew at about 3 percent per year. As a result, the ratio of household real net worth to annual disposable income rose from about 4.4 to 1 in the early 1980s to 5.7 to 1 by 2006. A peak ratio at about 6 to 1 occurred in 2000 after the spike in the American stock market.

The growth of wealth relative to income at a pace that boosts the wealth-to-income ratio—while personal savings as a share of disposable income is falling from about 8 percent to minus 1 percent—is a remarkable development. The key reality is that the two major sources of household wealth—financial assets and real estate—had increased in value at an unusual pace. The fact that households owned these assets has meant that they are better able to sustain consumption, even when income growth slows or confidence slips. A high wealth-to-income ratio helps to cushion consumption at times when income growth may be reduced or when the inclination to spend a given level of income is reduced by uncertainties such as the Iraq War, Afghanistan, Hurricane Katrina, the 9/11 attacks, and other disasters. U.S. consumption has recovered quickly after these incidents.

What are the sources of exogenous wealth creation—that is, wealth creation not driven by traditional savings and accumulation? Knowing the sources is important because this is the new dominant form of wealth accumulation, that is, that wealth tied simply to the ownership of appreciating assets rather than through restricted consumption and elevated savings. Favorite candidates for the causes of the broad exogenous wealth creation of the past quarter-century are two: the Great Moderation, or the more stable path of the U.S. economy since 1982, in which lower and less volatile inflation has been associated with less volatile growth; and innovations in the credit system that have contributed to the ability of households to manage income and spending decisions with lower holdings of highly liquid savings and more funds invested in less-liquid assets such as equities, bonds, and real estate.

Some circumstantial support for these explanations of exogenous wealth creation come from observing China and India among today's most rapidly growing emerging economies. There, wealth accumulation has, so far, been achieved the old-fashioned way. Households save up to 40 percent of income in order to accumulate assets in a volatile economy with a primitive credit system. Without well-developed government health and retirement systems, households must accumulate assets to provide for old age and medical costs. The credit system into which those assets can be invested is far less developed and far more risky, as the experience in their stock market and credit markets over the past decade has shown.

China's growth rate and inflation rates are both higher and more volatile than those in the United States, contributing to the uncertainty that households in China must manage as they make decisions about savings and consumption. Chinese households want to get richer, and they are saving at an extraordinary rate in order to do so. The saving motive is reinforced by the uncertainty they face, which in turn is tied to economic volatility and poor facilities for wealth storage. The persistent exogenous wealth creation that Americans have been fortunate enough to experience since the early 1980s has not been as available in China or India, although it probably will begin to emerge.

Another insight into American consumption behavior and its relationship with wealth is gained by looking at the period before 1980. During that time, say, between 1960 and 1980, American wealth was growing at a rate of about 3.5 percent a year while income was also growing at a slightly higher rate. The wealth-to-income ratio, which reached about 5 percent in the early 1960s, had fallen to 4.2 percent in the mid-1970s after the massive exogenous shock of a quadrupling of oil prices imposed the equivalent of a heavy tax on American consumers while rendering obsolete much of the American capital stock that had been oriented toward cheap energy. Over the decades, when income was rising faster than wealth, American savings held in a range of 8 to 10 percent, peaking at about 12 percent in the highly uncertain period after the first oil crisis in the second half of the 1970s, when rising inflation and inflation uncertainty penalized growth and increased household concerns about being able to sustain consumption.

In 2012, with the traditionally defined saving rate and saving interest rate, is virtually zero, can exogenous wealth creation and rising elasticity of the credit system contribute to a continuation of consumption spending in excess of income? We do not know the answer, but it seems unlikely that exogenous wealth creation will continue at the extraordinary pace of the past twenty-five years. The pace of productivity growth will provide a clue, with a steady, high level suggesting that exogenous wealth creation may continue, while lower productivity growth may signal declining wealth creation.

The good news about the problems in the financial sector and the larger economy in the United States emanating from the persistent drop in house prices is that these issues will eventually end, and the underlying resiliency of the U.S. economy will reemerge. The bad news about these problems is that they are going to continue for some time. Efforts to address them so far have been somewhat ineffective because they have been aimed at containing a subprime credit crisis, not at containing a rapidly spreading prime-credit, solvency crisis that lead the U.S. economy into recession.

Once we have established some understanding as to where we are as an economy (relative to a level of GDP, employment and inflation) and where we want to be in terms of these same measures (full-employment, real potential GDP), the third question concerns the policy options of how we get from where we are to where we want to be.

What policy tools are available and how specifically should they be used? This is the essence of the understanding of the macroeconomic options and opportunity costs and benefits confronting policy choices in the nation at large. The basic policy choices are national fiscal policies; taxing, spending and transfer payments, and

Federal Reserve monetary policies; expanding or contracting the money supply. Economic theory sometimes infers the incorrect assumption that decision and policy makers have "perfect" information and are capable of quick decisions and immediate policy and behavioral change and impact. This is just not the case when dealing with real decisions and change.

The Federal Reserve is struggling in a two-front war. It is simultaneously battling growing problems in the financial sector and the related problem of a weakening economy in which some inflation pressures have emerged, raising an ominous threat of a bout of stagflation. The Fed, along with central banks in England, Europe, and Canada—with good wishes from the ever-passive Bank of Japan—was establishing measures to enhance liquidity in the banking system. The Fed's "Term Auction Facility" (TAF) aimed initially to supply $40 billion in short-term liquidity directly to all banks (even small regional ones) through a stigma-free auction of term funding, based on a wide set of collateral. The rates were slightly below the Fed's discount rate and were offered for periods up to thirty days, the same as for loans offered at the discount window.

When the sacred benefits of home ownership were threatened during a U.S. election year, one expected a combination of an immense outpouring of blame directed at all quarters, including the Bush administration, Congress, and the Federal Reserve, in addition to greedy subprime mortgage lenders, hedge funds, and the ultimate bugaboo—foreigners.

The TAF constitutes a Fed experiment to improve its ability to manage liquidity flows to the banking system. After the Treasury's sub prime effort, Fed rate cuts, and the creation of a new Fed funding facility (the TAF), the hope and expectation was that financial firms and homebuilders' fortunes might be expected to improve and that this improvement would be reflected in their stock prices. Such was not the case. The Treasury's efforts were judged to be ad hoc, market distorting, and insufficient, while the Fed's efforts, aimed at liquidity problems, failed to address the more serious solvency problems tied to the rising probability of home value losses exceeding $3 trillion.

The underlying cause of the problems in the financial sector is a persistent fall in house prices. That drop in house prices has removed a large part of the elastic credit and wealth appreciation that helped to support consumption during the period of zero savings since the last recession in 2001. Many have contended that it is incorrect to suggest that a housing recession is a necessary condition for a U.S. recession because this time is different. It is true that, normally, a tightening Fed leads to a weakening housing sector, which is part of a recession, not the cause of a recession. But this time it is not different.

The Fed raised interest rates by 400 basis points between June 2004 and June 2006. House prices leveled off in 2005 and began to fall late in 2006. During late 2006 and early 2007, there were repeated episodes of weakness in the housing sector, each of which was deemed the end of the adjustment that was supposed to be confined to based-based lending. However, house prices continued to fall with large enough inventories of unsold homes to suggest that prices would continue to fall until 2010, bringing the total reduction in house prices to around 18 percent.

The U.S. housing stock is worth about $23 trillion, so an 18 percent drop in house prices represents a wealth erasure of $4.14 trillion over a period of a little over two years. That figure represents about a quarter of annual GDP. The total equity capital of U.S. banks, brokers, and finance companies, most of who are exposed to losses and to levered credit markets tied to falling real estate prices, is barely $1 trillion. While their share of total cumulative real estate losses will be only a fraction of the potential $4.14 trillion in losses that would result from a 18 percent drop in house prices, their share of the losses will certainly impair their capital and thereby their lending ability to a substantial extent.

The efforts by the Treasury and the Fed thus far to contain the problems tied to the collapse of the U.S. housing bubble have failed simply because they have been inadequate. The obvious solution to the problems tied to the collapse of the housing bubble is to arrest and then reverse the largest drop in house prices since the Great Depression.

The political complexity of the "solution" to the growing problems facing the U.S. financial sector and the U.S. economy—they grow as house prices continue to fall—is its least attractive aspect. House prices ballooned in the first place because of the massive subsidies that already existed to encourage home-ownership, including full deductibility of mortgage interest expense for most homeowners; favorable tax treatment of home sales; full deductibility of state and local taxes on real estate; preferential lending facilities subsidized by multiple government agencies, including Fannie Mae, Ginnie Mae, the Federal Home Loan Bank System, and the Federal Housing Administration; and others too numerous to mention. Beyond that, a period of very low (under 1 percent) short-term interest rates administered by the Fed was followed by huge capital inflows and a highly elastic credit system that boosted house prices into bubble territory.

So the Fed and Washington's struggling policymakers are left with the unsatisfying option of containing the damage from the housing bust. Given the sharp deceleration of U.S. growth, coupled with troubling signs of higher core inflation, the next step toward containing the damage will be to address the fear that arises as the U.S. recession exacerbates the housing downturn and threatens more acute economic distress among American households.

Unfortunately, the record shows that while election years are high on rhetoric in the face of difficult problems, such as the collapse of the U.S. housing bubble, they are low on solutions. Rather, it probably makes more sense to look for a large housing bailout sometime in 2013. Basically, the compromised loans tied to depreciated housing are auctioned to the highest bidder, many of whom will obtain good bargains. To the extent that auction prices seriously impair the balance sheets of financial intermediaries, taxpayers will likely be asked to fill the hole, probably to the tune of some $500 or $600 billion.

Thus, the current economic situation is both serious and complex. The general objective of this course is to provide a basic introduction and foundation to the meaning and understanding of the macro economy. The intent is to present the tools of economic analysis, the options for policy decisions and a basis for evaluations of goals, policies and societal costs associated with different macroeconomic decisions. More specifically, the goals are:

1. To stimulate an awareness and understanding of the macro economy, nationally and globally.
2. To provide a grasp of the basic principles and analytical tools one must have to think clearly about economic issues. The basic assumption is that analytical concepts, tools and models are most effectively learned when applied in the understanding of actual situations and issues that you encounter in "our real" economic world.
3. To help develop good methods of thinking about economic issues. This involves specific attention to the process of orderly problem solving by:
   - A. Carefully defining the issue or problem.
   - B. Mapping out a stated objective and the main alternative ways of achievement of that objective.
   - C. Careful analysis of the alternative approaches, and use of the appropriate analytical concepts and principles to decide which alternatives or combination of alternatives "best" solves the issue or problem.
   - D. Checking the "solution" reached, both for flaws in reasoning or logic and, where feasible, against experience in similar situations.
   - E. Learning to evaluate and use both qualitative and quantitative evidence when conflicting viewpoints and approaches are encountered.

My years of teaching experience suggest that students tend to enjoy the ideas presented and discussed in a macroeconomics class; they enjoy their heightened ability to understand economic news and its impact on them and the world around them. They seem attracted by the very logic of "an economic way of thinking" and enjoy evaluating the expected impact as well as the social and economic costs of actions and policy alternatives. A key feature of this course is analysis of real world problems and issues such as social happiness, employment, quality of life and their relation to inflation, growth, federal deficits, trade deficits, globalization, general health and overall wellbeing. When students understand the macroeconomic world in which they live, they feel better equipped to deal with those events and decisions that will often determine much of the quality of life they will live.

Roger W. Mack, Ph.D.
Mackroeconomics@G-mail.com
Mack Island
Fall, 2012

CHAPTER 1

Economics:

Foundations and Models

Chapter Outline and Learning Objectives

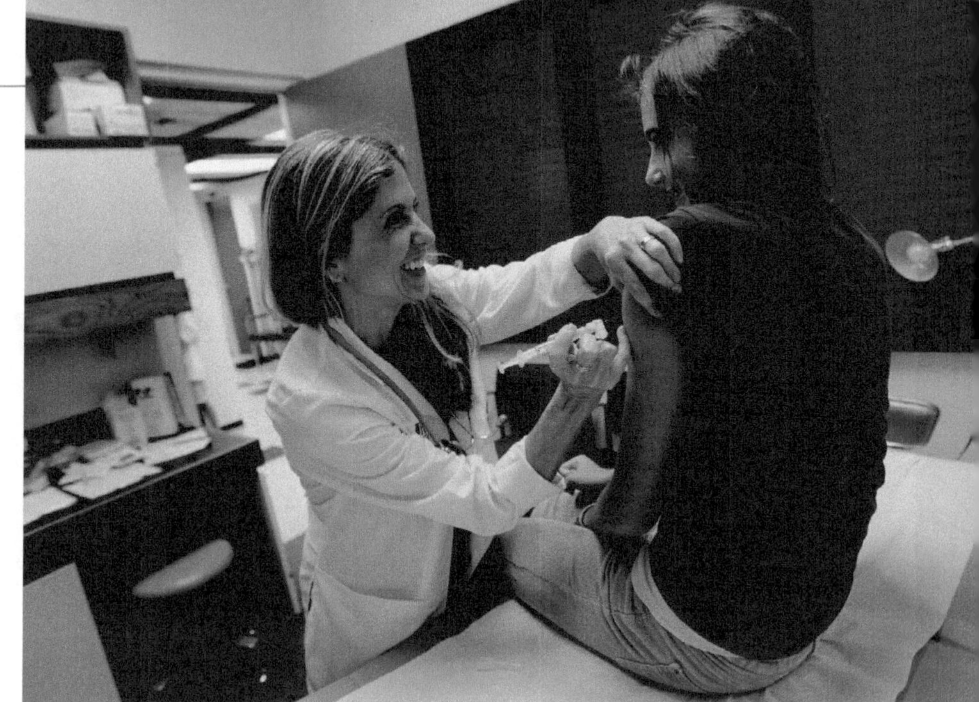

Why Are Some Doctors Leaving Private Practice?

When you visit a doctor's office, you probably don't think of it as a small business, but that's what it is. Like other businesspeople, a doctor hires workers—nurses, physician's assistants, and receptionists—and buys or rents machinery and equipment. A doctor's income represents the profits from his or her practice, or the difference between the revenue received from patients and their health insurance plans and the costs to the doctor of wages, rent, loans, and insurance. For many years, the typical doctor operated his or her practice either alone or in partnership with other doctors. Lately, though, an increasing number of doctors have given up their practices and become salaried employees of hospitals. Although as recently as 2002 more than three times as many medical practices were owned by doctors as by hospitals, by 2008 more medical practices were owned by hospitals.

The movement of many doctors from running their own businesses to being salaried employees of hospitals is due to changes occurring within the U.S. health care system. Soaring health care costs have led many private health care insurers, as well as the federal and state governments, to reduce the payments they make to doctors in return for treating patients. President Barack Obama's package of health care changes, sometimes referred to as "Obamacare," was passed by Congress in 2010 and is being gradually phased in through 2014. The package will result in major changes in how some people will receive health insurance and how doctors will be compensated. Policymakers are also considering changes to Medicare, the federal government program that provides health care to people over age 65, because the costs of the program have been rising very rapidly. Over time, these changes have increased the amount of paperwork doctors must complete in order to be paid for treating patients. This paperwork has raised the costs doctors incur in running their practices, which makes becoming a salaried employee of a hospital more attractive.

Throughout this book, we will see that many policy issues, including changes in the U.S. medical system, involve economics. In fact, knowledge of economics can help you to better understand and analyze many policy issues.

AN INSIDE LOOK on **page 20** discusses how health professionals may be delaying retirement because they are concerned about their finances.

Based on Robert Kocher, M.D., and Nikhil R. Sahni, "Hospitals' Race to Employ Physicians—The Logic Behind a Money-Losing Proposition," *New England Journal of Medicine*, May 12, 2011; and Uwe E. Reinhardt, "Producing More Primary-Care Doctors," *New York Times*, June 10, 2011.

Economics in Your Life

Will There Be Plenty of Jobs Available in the Health Care Industry?

The U.S. Health Resources and Services Administration (HRSA) forecasts that the number of doctors in the United States will increase from about 808,000 in 2010 to 866,400 in 2020. But the HRSA also forecasts that the number of doctors needed to provide patient care will rise from about 805,000 in 2010 to 922,000 in 2020. In other words, this federal government agency forecasts that there will be a shortage of about 56,000 doctors in 2020. The U.S. Bureau of Labor Statistics projects that four of the six fastest growing occupations over the next 10 years will be in the medical field. It would seem that plenty of jobs should be available in health care during the next few years. But the availability of these jobs depends on the reliability of the forecasts. What is the basis for the forecasts on the availability of jobs in health care, and how reliable are the forecasts? As you read this chapter, see if you can answer this question. You can check your answer against the one we provide on **page 18** at the end of this chapter.

In this book, we use economics to answer questions such as the following:

- How are the prices of goods and services determined?
- How does pollution affect the economy, and how should government policy deal with these effects?
- Why do firms engage in international trade, and how do government policies affect international trade?
- Why does government control the prices of some goods and services, and what are the effects of those controls?

Economists do not always agree on the answers to every question. In fact, as we will see, economists engage in lively debate on some issues. In addition, new problems and issues are constantly arising. So, economists are always at work developing new methods to analyze economic questions.

All the issues we discuss in this book illustrate a basic fact of life: People must make choices as they try to attain their goals. We must make choices because we live in a world of **scarcity**, which means that although our wants are unlimited, the resources available to fulfill those wants are limited. You might like to own a BMW and spend each summer in five-star European hotels, but unless Bill Gates is a close and generous relative, you probably lack the money to fulfill these dreams. Every day, you make choices as you spend your limited income on the many goods and services available. The finite amount of time you have also limits your ability to attain your goals. If you spend an hour studying for your economics midterm, you have one hour less to study for your history midterm. Firms and the government are in the same situation as you: They also must attain their goals with limited resources. **Economics** is the study of the choices consumers, business managers, and government officials make to attain their goals, given their scarce resources.

Scarcity A situation in which unlimited wants exceed the limited resources available to fulfill those wants.

Economics The study of the choices people make to attain their goals, given their scarce resources.

We begin this chapter by discussing three important economic ideas that we will return to many times in this book: *People are rational, people respond to incentives, and optimal decisions are made at the margin.* Then we consider the three fundamental questions that any economy must answer: *What* goods and services will be produced? *How* will the goods and services be produced? and *Who* will receive the goods and services produced? Next, we consider the role of *economic models* in analyzing economic issues. **Economic models** are simplified versions of reality used to analyze real-world economic situations. We will explore why economists use models and how they construct them. Finally, we will discuss the difference between microeconomics and macroeconomics, and we will preview some important economic terms.

Economic model A simplified version of reality used to analyze real-world economic situations.

1.1 LEARNING OBJECTIVE

Explain these three key economic ideas: People are rational, people respond to incentives, and optimal decisions are made at the margin.

Three Key Economic Ideas

As you try to achieve your goals, whether they involve buying a new computer or finding a part-time job, you will interact with other people in *markets*. A **market** is a group of buyers and sellers of a good or service and the institution or arrangement by which they come together to trade. Most of economics involves analyzing what happens in markets. Throughout this book, as we study how people make choices and interact in markets, we will return to three important ideas:

1. People are rational.
2. People respond to economic incentives.
3. Optimal decisions are made at the margin.

Market A group of buyers and sellers of a good or service and the institution or arrangement by which they come together to trade.

People Are Rational

Economists generally assume that people are rational. This assumption does *not* mean that economists believe everyone knows everything or always makes the "best" decision. It means that economists assume that consumers and firms use all available information as they act to achieve their goals. Rational individuals weigh the benefits and costs of each action, and they choose an action only if the benefits outweigh the costs. For example, if Microsoft charges a price of $239 for a copy of Windows, economists assume that the managers at Microsoft have estimated that a price of $239 will earn Microsoft the most profit. The managers may be wrong; perhaps a price of $265 would be more profitable, but economists assume that the managers at Microsoft have acted rationally, on the basis of the information available to them, in choosing the price. Of course, not everyone behaves rationally all the time. Still, the assumption of rational behavior is very useful in explaining most of the choices that people make.

People Respond to Economic Incentives

Human beings act from a variety of motives, including religious belief, envy, and compassion. Economists emphasize that consumers and firms consistently respond to *economic* incentives. This fact may seem obvious, but it is often overlooked. For example, according to an article in the *Wall Street Journal*, the FBI couldn't understand why banks were not taking steps to improve security in the face of an increase in robberies: "FBI officials suggest that banks place uniformed, armed guards outside their doors and install bullet-resistant plastic, known as a 'bandit barrier,' in front of teller windows." FBI officials were surprised that few banks took their advice. But the article also reported that installing bullet-resistant plastic costs $10,000 to $20,000, and a well-trained security guard receives $50,000 per year in salary and benefits. The average loss in a bank robbery is only about $1,200. The economic incentive to banks is clear: It is less costly to put up with bank robberies than to take additional security measures. FBI agents may be surprised by how banks respond to the threat of robberies—but economists are not.

In some chapters, the feature discusses a news story or another application related to the chapter material. Read the following *Making the Connection* for a discussion of whether people respond to economic incentives even when deciding how much to eat and how much exercise to undertake.

Making the Connection

Does Health Insurance Give People an Incentive to Become Obese?

Obesity is an increasing problem in the United States. The U.S. Centers for Disease Control (CDC) defines obesity for an adult as having a body mass index (BMI) of 30 or greater. The body mass index measures a person's weight relative to the person's height. (The exact formula is: BMI = (Weight in pounds/(Height in inches)^2) × 703.) A BMI of 30 is equivalent to a person 5'4" being 30 pounds overweight. Obesity is related to a variety of diseases, including heart disease, stroke, diabetes, and hypertension.

The two maps below show the striking increase in obesity in the 15 years between 1994 and 2009. In 1994, in a majority of states the population was between 10 percent and 14 percent obese, and in no state was more than 20 percent of the population obese. By 2009, only in Colorado was less than 20 percent of the population obese, and in about two-thirds of the states, 25 percent or more of the population was obese, including nine states where more than 30 percent of the population was obese.

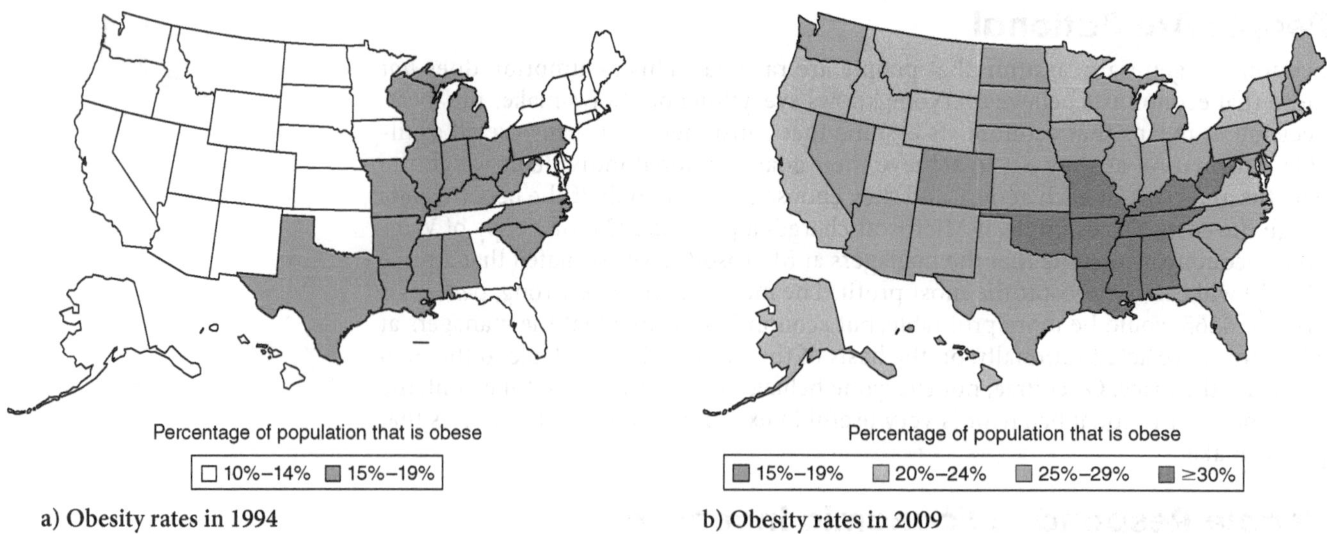

a) Obesity rates in 1994 **b) Obesity rates in 2009**

Data from Centers for Disease Control and Prevention, "Behavior Risk Factor Surveillance System."

Many people who suffer from obesity have underlying medical conditions. For these people, obesity is an unfortunate medical problem that they cannot control. The fact that obesity is increasing, though, indicates that for some people obesity is the result of diet and lifestyle choices. Potential explanations for the increase in obesity include greater intake of high-calorie fast foods, insufficient exercise, and a decline in the physical activity associated with many jobs. The CDC recommends that teenagers get a minimum of 60 minutes of aerobic exercise per day, a standard that only 15 percent of high school students were meeting in 2011. In 1960, 50 percent of jobs in the United States required at least moderate physical activity. By 2010, only 20 percent of jobs did. As a result, the typical worker was burning off about 130 fewer calories per workday.

In addition to eating too much and not exercising enough, could health insurance be a cause of obesity? Obese people tend to suffer more medical problems than do people who are not overweight and so incur higher medical costs. Overweight people with health insurance that will reimburse them for only part of their medical bills or who have no health insurance must pay some or all of these higher medical bills themselves. Overweight people with health insurance that covers most of their medical bills will not suffer as large a monetary cost from being obese. In other words, by reducing some of the costs of obesity, health insurance may give people an economic incentive to gain weight. At first glance, this argument may seem implausible. Some people suffer from medical conditions that can make physical activity difficult or that can cause weight gain even with moderate eating, so they may become overweight whether they have health insurance or not. Some people are overweight due to poor eating habits, and they probably don't consider health insurance when deciding whether to have another slice of chocolate cake or to watch television instead of going to the gym. But if economists are correct about the importance of economic incentives, then we would expect that if we hold all other personal characteristics—such as age, gender, and income—constant, people with health insurance will be more likely to be overweight than people without health insurance.

Jay Bhattacharya and Kate Bundorf of Stanford University, Noemi Pace of University College London, and Neeraj Sood of the RAND Corporation, a research center, have analyzed the effects of health insurance on weight. Using a sample that followed nearly 80,000 people during the years 1989–2004, they found that after controlling for income, education, race, gender, age, and other factors, people with health insurance are significantly more likely to be overweight than are people without health insurance. Having private health insurance increased BMI by 1.3 points, and having public health insurance, such as *Medicaid*, which is a program under which the government provides health care to low-income people, increased BMI by 2.3 points. These findings suggest that people respond to economic incentives even when making decisions about what they eat and how much they exercise.

Based on Centers for Disease Control and Prevention, "Obesity Trends Among U.S. Adults Between 1985 and 2009," www.cdc.gov; Katherine M. Flegal, Margaret D. Caroll, Cynthia L. Ogden, and Lester R. Curtin, "Prevalence and Trends in Obesity Among U.S. Adults, 1999–2008," *Journal of the American Medical Association*, Vol. 303, No. 3, January 20, 2010, pp. 235–41; Jay Bhattacharya, Kate Bundorf, Noemi Pace, and Neeraj Soodin, "Does Health Insurance Make You Fat?" in Michael Grossman and Naci H. Mocan, eds., *Economic Aspects of Obesity*, (Chicago: University of Chicago Press, 2011); and Tara Parker-Pope, "Less Active at Work, Americans Have Packed on Pounds," *New York Times*, May 25, 2011.

Optimal Decisions Are Made at the Margin

Some decisions are "all or nothing": For instance, when an entrepreneur decides whether to open a new restaurant, she either starts the new restaurant or she doesn't. When you decide whether to enter graduate school or to take a job, you either enter graduate school or you don't. But rather than being all or nothing, most decisions in life involve doing a little more or a little less. If you are trying to decrease your spending and increase your saving, the decision is not really between saving all the money you earn or spending it all. Rather, many small choices are involved, such as whether to buy a caffè mocha at Starbucks every day or just three times per week.

Economists use the word *marginal* to mean "extra" or "additional." Should you watch another hour of TV or spend that hour studying? The *marginal benefit* (or, in symbols, *MB*) of watching more TV is the additional enjoyment you receive. The *marginal cost* (or *MC*) is the lower grade you receive from having studied a little less. Should Apple produce an additional 300,000 iPhones? Firms receive *revenue* from selling goods. Apple's marginal benefit is the additional revenue it receives from selling 300,000 more iPhones. Apple's marginal cost is the additional cost—for wages, parts, and so forth—of producing 300,000 more iPhones. *Economists reason that the optimal decision is to continue any activity up to the point where the marginal benefit equals the marginal cost—in symbols, where* MB = MC. Often we apply this rule without consciously thinking about it. Usually you will know whether the additional enjoyment from watching a television program is worth the additional cost involved in not spending that hour studying, without giving the decision a lot of thought. In business situations, however, firms often have to make careful calculations to determine, for example, whether the additional revenue received from increasing production is greater or less than the additional cost of the production. Economists refer to analysis that involves comparing marginal benefits and marginal costs as **marginal analysis**.

Marginal analysis Analysis that involves comparing marginal benefits and marginal costs.

In each chapter of this book, you will see the special feature *Solved Problem*. This feature will increase your understanding of the material by leading you through the steps of solving an applied economic problem. After reading the problem, you can test your understanding by working the related problems that appear at the end of the chapter and in the study guide that accompanies this book. You can also complete Solved Problems on www.myeconlab.com and receive tutorial help.

Solved Problem 1.1

A Doctor Makes a Decision at the Margin

A doctor is considering keeping her office open 9 hours per day rather than 8 hours. The doctor's office manager argues, "Keeping the office open an extra hour is a good idea because your practice will make a total profit of $300,000 per year when the office is open 9 hours per day." Do you agree with the office manager's reasoning? What, if any, additional information do you need to decide whether the doctor should keep her office open an additional hour per day?

Solving the Problem

Step 1: **Review the chapter material.** This problem is about making decisions, so you may want to review the section "Optimal Decisions Are Made at the Margin," which begins on page 7.

Step 2: **Explain whether you agree with the manager's reasoning.** We have seen that any activity should be continued to the point where the marginal benefit is equal to the marginal cost. In this case, that involves a doctor continuing to keep her office open up to the point where the additional revenue she receives from seeing more patients is equal to the marginal cost of keeping her office open an additional hour. The office manager has not done a marginal analysis, so you should not agree with the manager's reasoning. The statement about the total profit of keeping the office open for 9 hours is not relevant to the decision of whether to stay open an additional hour.

Step 3: **Explain what additional information you need.** You will need additional information to make a correct decision. You will need to know the marginal revenue and the marginal cost of keeping the practice open an extra hour. The marginal revenue would depend on how many more patients the doctor can see in the extra hour. The marginal cost would include the additional salary to be paid to the office staff, any additional medical supplies that would be used, as well as any additional electricity or other utilities. The doctor would also need to take into account the nonmonetary cost of spending another hour working rather than spending time with her family and friends or in other leisure activities.

1.2 LEARNING OBJECTIVE

Discuss how an economy answers these questions: What goods and services will be produced? How will the goods and services be produced? Who will receive the goods and services produced?

Trade-off The idea that because of scarcity, producing more of one good or service means producing less of another good or service.

Opportunity cost The highest-valued alternative that must be given up to engage in an activity.

The Economic Problem That Every Society Must Solve

Because we live in a world of scarcity, any society faces the *economic problem* that it has only a limited amount of economic resources—such as workers, machines, and raw materials—and so can produce only a limited amount of goods and services. Therefore, every society faces **trade-offs**: Producing more of one good or service means producing less of another good or service. In fact, the best way to measure the cost of producing a good or service is the value of what has to be given up to produce it. The **opportunity cost** of any activity—such as producing a good or service—is the highest-valued alternative that must be given up to engage in that activity. The concept of opportunity cost is very important in economics and applies to individuals as much as it does to firms or to society as a whole. Consider the example of a doctor who could receive a salary of $100,000 per year working as an employee of a hospital but decides to open his own private practice instead. In that case, the opportunity cost of the physician services he supplies to his own firm is the $100,000 he gives up by not working for the hospital, even if he does not explicitly pay himself a salary.

Trade-offs force society to make choices when answering the following three fundamental questions:

1. *What* goods and services will be produced?
2. *How* will the goods and services be produced?
3. *Who* will receive the goods and services produced?

In some chapters of this book, we will return to these questions many times. For now, we briefly introduce each question.

What Goods and Services Will Be Produced?

How will society decide whether to produce more economics textbooks or more Blu-ray players? More daycare facilities or more football stadiums? Of course, "society" does not make decisions; only individuals make decisions. The answer to the question of what will be produced is determined by the choices that consumers, firms, and the government make. Every day, you help decide which goods and services firms will produce when you choose to buy an iPhone instead of a BlackBerry or a caffè mocha rather than a chai tea. Similarly, Apple must choose whether to devote its scarce resources to making more iPhones or more iPad tablet computers. The federal government must choose whether to spend more of its limited budget on breast cancer research or on repairing highways. In each case, consumers, firms, and the government face the problem of scarcity by trading off one good or service for another. And each choice made comes with an opportunity cost, measured by the value of the best alternative given up.

How Will the Goods and Services Be Produced?

Firms choose how to produce the goods and services they sell. In many cases, firms face a trade-off between using more workers or using more machines. For example, a local service station has to choose whether to provide car repair services using more diagnostic computers and fewer auto mechanics or more auto mechanics and fewer diagnostic computers. Similarly, movie studios have to choose whether to produce animated films using highly skilled animators to draw them by hand or fewer animators and more computers. In deciding whether to move production offshore to China, firms may need to choose between a production method in the United States that uses fewer workers and more machines and a production method in China that uses more workers and fewer machines.

Who Will Receive the Goods and Services Produced?

In the United States, who receives the goods and services produced depends largely on how income is distributed. Individuals with the highest income have the ability to buy the most goods and services. Often, people are willing to give up some of their income—and, therefore, some of their ability to purchase goods and services—by donating to charities to increase the incomes of poorer people. Each year, Americans donate about $300 billion to charity, or an average donation of $2,650 for each household in the country. An important policy question, however, is whether the government should intervene to make the distribution of income more equal. Such intervention already occurs in the United States, because people with higher incomes pay a larger fraction of their incomes in taxes and because the government makes payments to people with low incomes. There is disagreement over whether the current attempts to redistribute income are sufficient or whether there should be more or less redistribution.

Centrally Planned Economies versus Market Economies

Centrally planned economy An economy in which the government decides how economic resources will be allocated.

Market economy An economy in which the decisions of households and firms interacting in markets allocate economic resources.

To answer the three questions—what, how, and who—societies organize their economies in two main ways. A society can have a **centrally planned economy** in which the government decides how economic resources will be allocated. Or a society can have a **market economy** in which the decisions of households and firms interacting in markets allocate economic resources.

From 1917 to 1991, the most important centrally planned economy in the world was that of the Soviet Union, which was established when Vladimir Lenin and the Communist Party staged a revolution and took over the Russian Empire. In the Soviet Union, the government decided what goods to produce, how the goods would be produced, and who would receive the goods. Government employees managed factories and stores. The objective of these managers was to follow the government's orders rather than to satisfy the wants of consumers. Centrally planned economies like that of the Soviet Union have not been successful in producing low-cost, high-quality goods and services. As a result, the standard of living of the average person in a centrally planned economy tends to be low. All centrally planned economies have also been political dictatorships. Dissatisfaction with low living standards and political repression finally led to the collapse of the Soviet Union in 1991. Today, only a few small countries, such as Cuba and North Korea, still have completely centrally planned economies.

All the high-income democracies, such as the United States, Canada, Japan, and the countries of Western Europe, have market economies. Market economies rely primarily on privately owned firms to produce goods and services and to decide how to produce them. Markets, rather than the government, determine who receives the goods and services produced. In a market economy, firms must produce goods and services that meet the wants of consumers, or the firms will go out of business. In that sense, it is ultimately consumers who decide what goods and services will be produced. Because firms in a market economy compete to offer the highest-quality products at the lowest price, they are under pressure to use the lowest-cost methods of production. For example, in the past 10 years, some U.S. firms, particularly in the electronics and furniture industries, have been under pressure to reduce their costs to meet competition from Chinese firms.

In a market economy, the income of an individual is determined by the payments he receives for what he has to sell. If he is a civil engineer, and firms are willing to pay a salary of $85,000 per year for engineers with his training and skills, that is the amount of income he will have to purchase goods and services. If the engineer also owns a house that he rents out, his income will be even higher. One of the attractive features of markets is that they reward hard work. Generally, the more extensive the training a person has received and the longer the hours the person works, the higher the person's income will be. Of course, luck—both good and bad—also plays a role here, as elsewhere in life. We can conclude that market economies respond to the question "Who receives the goods and services produced?" with the answer "Those who are most willing and able to buy them."

The Modern "Mixed" Economy

In the nineteenth and early twentieth centuries, the U.S. government engaged in relatively little regulation of markets for goods and services. Beginning in the middle of the twentieth century, government intervention in the economy dramatically increased in the United States and other market economies. This increase was primarily caused by the high rates of unemployment and business bankruptcies during the Great Depression of the 1930s. Some government intervention was also intended to raise the incomes of the elderly, the sick, and people with limited skills. For example, in the 1930s, the United States established the Social Security system, which provides government payments to retired and disabled workers, and minimum wage legislation, which sets a floor on the wages employers can pay workers in many occupations. In more recent years, government intervention in the economy has also expanded to meet such goals as protection of the environment, the promotion of civil rights, and the provision of medical care to low-income people and the elderly.

Some economists argue that the extent of government intervention makes it no longer accurate to refer to the U.S., Canadian, Japanese, and Western European economies as pure market economies. Instead, they should be referred to as *mixed economies*. A **mixed economy** is still primarily a market economy because most economic decisions result from the interaction of buyers and sellers in markets. However, the government plays a significant role in the allocation of resources. Economists continue to debate the role government should play in a market economy.

Mixed economy An economy in which most economic decisions result from the interaction of buyers and sellers in markets but in which the government plays a significant role in the allocation of resources.

One of the most important developments in the international economy in recent years has been the movement of China from being a centrally planned economy to being a more mixed economy. The Chinese economy suffered decades of economic stagnation following the takeover of the government in 1949 by Mao Zedong and the Communist Party. Although China remains a political dictatorship, production of most goods and services is now determined in the market rather than by the government. The result has been rapid economic growth that in the near future may lead to total production of goods and services in China surpassing total production in the United States.

Efficiency and Equity

Market economies tend to be more efficient than centrally planned economies. There are two types of efficiency: *productive efficiency* and *allocative efficiency*. **Productive efficiency** occurs when a good or service is produced at the lowest possible cost. **Allocative efficiency** occurs when production is in accordance with consumer preferences. Markets tend to be efficient because they promote competition and facilitate voluntary exchange. With **voluntary exchange**, both the buyer and seller of a product are made better off by the transaction. We know that the buyer and seller are both made better off because, otherwise, the buyer would not have agreed to buy the product or the seller would not have agreed to sell it. Productive efficiency is achieved when competition among firms in markets forces the firms to produce goods and services at the lowest cost. Allocative efficiency is achieved when the combination of competition among firms and voluntary exchange between firms and consumers results in firms producing the mix of goods and services that consumers prefer most. Competition will force firms to continue producing and selling goods and services as long as the additional benefit to consumers is greater than the additional cost of production. In this way, the mix of goods and services produced will match consumer preferences.

Productive efficiency A situation in which a good or service is produced at the lowest possible cost.

Allocative efficiency A state of the economy in which production is in accordance with consumer preferences; in particular, every good or service is produced up to the point where the last unit provides a marginal benefit to society equal to the marginal cost of producing it.

Voluntary exchange A situation that occurs in markets when both the buyer and seller of a product are made better off by the transaction.

Although markets promote efficiency, they don't guarantee it. Inefficiency can arise from various sources. To begin with, it may take some time to achieve an efficient outcome. When Blu-ray players were introduced, for example, firms did not instantly achieve productive efficiency. It took several years for firms to discover the lowest-cost method of producing this good. As we will discuss in Chapter 4, governments sometimes reduce efficiency by interfering with voluntary exchange in markets. For example, many governments limit the imports of some goods from foreign countries. This limitation reduces efficiency by keeping goods from being produced at the lowest cost. The production of some goods damages the environment. In this case, government intervention can increase efficiency because without such intervention, firms may ignore the costs of environmental damage and thereby fail to produce the goods at the lowest possible cost.

An economically efficient outcome is not necessarily a desirable one. Many people prefer economic outcomes that they consider fair or equitable, even if those outcomes

Equity The fair distribution of economic benefits.

are less efficient. **Equity** is harder to define than efficiency, but it usually involves a fair distribution of economic benefits. For some people, equity involves a more equal distribution of economic benefits than would result from an emphasis on efficiency alone. For example, some people support raising taxes on people with higher incomes to provide the funds for programs that aid the poor. Although governments may increase equity by reducing the incomes of high-income people and increasing the incomes of the poor, efficiency may be reduced. People have less incentive to open new businesses, to supply labor, and to save if the government takes a significant amount of the income they earn from working or saving. The result is that fewer goods and services are produced, and less saving takes place. As this example illustrates, *there is often a trade-off between efficiency and equity*. Government policymakers often confront this trade-off.

1.3 LEARNING OBJECTIVE

Understand the role of models in economic analysis.

Economic Models

Economists rely on economic theories, or models (the words *theory* and *model* are used interchangeably), to analyze real-world issues, such as those involved with health care. As mentioned earlier, economic models are simplified versions of reality. Economists are certainly not alone in relying on models: An engineer may use a computer model of a bridge to help test whether it will withstand high winds, or a biologist may make a physical model of a nucleic acid to better understand its properties. One purpose of economic models is to make economic ideas sufficiently explicit and concrete so that individuals, firms, or the government can use them to make decisions. For example, we will see in Chapter 4 that the model of demand and supply is a simplified version of how the prices of products are determined by the interactions among buyers and sellers in markets.

Economists use economic models to answer questions. For example, will the United States have a sufficient number of doctors in 2020? For a complicated question like this one, economists often use several models to examine different aspects of the issue. For example, economists at the U.S. Bureau of Labor Statistics (BLS) build models that allow them to forecast future employment in different occupations. These models allow the BLS to forecast how many doctors there are likely to be at a future date. Economists can use different models to forecast the demand for medical services. Together these models can be used to determine whether there will be a sufficient number of doctors in 2020. As mentioned on page 3, economists at the U.S. Health Resources and Services Administration (HRSA) have used models to forecast that there will be a shortage of about 56,000 doctors in 2020.

Sometimes economists use an existing model to analyze an issue, but in other cases, they must develop a new model. To develop a model, economists generally follow these steps:

1. Decide on the assumptions to use in developing the model.
2. Formulate a testable hypothesis.
3. Use economic data to test the hypothesis.
4. Revise the model if it fails to explain the economic data well.
5. Retain the revised model to help answer similar economic questions in the future.

The Role of Assumptions in Economic Models

Any model is based on making assumptions because models have to be simplified to be useful. We cannot analyze an economic issue unless we reduce its complexity. For example, economic models make behavioral assumptions about the motives of consumers and firms. Economists assume that consumers will buy the goods and services that will maximize their well-being or their satisfaction. Similarly, economists assume that firms act to maximize their profits. These assumptions are simplifications because they do not describe the motives of every consumer and every firm. How can we know if the assumptions in a model are too simplified or too limiting? We discover this when we form hypotheses based on these assumptions and test these hypotheses using real-world information.

Forming and Testing Hypotheses in Economic Models

An **economic variable** is something measurable that can have different values, such as the incomes of doctors. A hypothesis in an economic model is a statement that may be either correct or incorrect about an economic variable. An example of a hypothesis in an economic model is the statement that the falling incomes earned by primary care physicians—often referred to as "family doctors"—will result in a decline in the number of physicians choosing to enter primary care in the United States in 2020. An economic hypothesis is usually about a causal relationship; in this case, the hypothesis states that lower incomes cause, or lead to, fewer doctors entering primary care.

Economic variable Something measurable that can have different values, such as the incomes of doctors.

We have to test a hypothesis before we can accept it. To test a hypothesis, we analyze statistics on the relevant economic variables. In our primary care doctor example, we would gather statistics on the incomes of primary care physicians, the number of primary care physicians, and perhaps other variables as well. Testing a hypothesis can be tricky. For example, showing that the number of primary care physicians declined at a time when the average income of these physicians declined would not be enough to demonstrate that the decline in income *caused* the decline in the number of physicians. Just because two things are correlated—that is, they happen at the same time—does not mean that one caused the other. For example, before entering practice, a doctor spends time in a teaching hospital as a resident in his or her field. Teaching hospitals determine how many residencies they will offer in a particular field. Suppose that teaching hospitals decreased the number of residencies in primary care at the same time that the incomes of primary care physicians were declining. In that case, the declining number of residencies, rather than the declining incomes, might have caused the decline in the number of primary care physicians. Over a period of time, many economic variables change, which complicates the testing of hypotheses. In fact, when economists disagree about a hypothesis, such as the effect of falling incomes on the supply of primary care physicians, it is often because of disagreements over interpreting the statistical analysis used to test the hypothesis.

Note that hypotheses must be statements that could, in principle, turn out to be incorrect. Statements such as "Increasing the number of primary care physicians is good" or "Increasing the number of primary care physicians is bad" are value judgments rather than hypotheses because it is not possible to disprove them.

Economists accept and use an economic model if it leads to hypotheses that are confirmed by statistical analysis. In many cases, the acceptance is tentative, however, pending the gathering of new data or further statistical analysis. In fact, economists often refer to a hypothesis having been "not rejected," rather than having been "accepted," by statistical analysis. But what if statistical analysis clearly rejects a hypothesis? For example, what if a model leads to a hypothesis that declining incomes of primary care physicians will lead to a decline in the number of these physicians, but the data reject this hypothesis? In this case, the model must be reconsidered. It may be that an assumption used in the model was too simplified or too limiting. For example, perhaps the model ignored the fact that primary care physicians were moving from owning their own practices to become salaried employees of hospitals, where they would be freed from the responsibilities involved in running their own businesses. This change in how primary care physicians are employed might explain why the data rejected the hypothesis.

In 2010, the BLS analyzed the accuracy of the projections it had made in 1996 of employment levels in 2006. Some projections were quite accurate, while others were less so. For instance, the BLS had projected that 677,917 physicians and surgeons would be employed in 2006, but actual employment was only 633,292, or about 7 percent less than projected. The error with respect to physician's assistants was much larger, with the projection being that 93,485 physician's assistants would be employed in 2006, but employment was actually only 65,628, or about 30 percent less than expected. Analyzing the errors in these projections helps the BLS to improve the models it uses to make projections of occupational employment.

The process of developing models, testing hypotheses, and revising models occurs not just in economics but also in disciplines such as physics, chemistry, and biology. This process is often referred to as the *scientific method*. Economics is a *social science* because it applies the scientific method to the study of the interactions among individuals.

Normative and Positive Analysis

Positive analysis Analysis concerned with what is.

Normative analysis Analysis concerned with what ought to be.

Throughout this book, as we build economic models and use them to answer questions, we need to bear in mind the distinction between *positive analysis* and *normative analysis*. **Positive analysis** is concerned with *what is*, and **normative analysis** is concerned with *what ought to be*. Economics is about positive analysis, which measures the costs and benefits of different courses of action.

We can use the federal government's minimum wage law to compare positive and normative analysis. In 2012, under this law, it was illegal for an employer to hire a worker at a wage less than $7.25 per hour. Without the minimum wage law, some firms and some workers would voluntarily agree to a lower wage. Because of the minimum wage law, some workers have difficulty finding jobs, and some firms end up paying more for labor than they otherwise would have. A positive analysis of the federal minimum wage law uses an economic model to estimate how many workers have lost their jobs because of the law, its effect on the costs and profits of businesses, and the gains to workers receiving the minimum wage. After economists complete this positive analysis, the decision as to whether the minimum wage law is a good idea or a bad idea is a normative one and depends on how people evaluate the trade-off involved. Supporters of the law believe that the losses to employers and to workers who are unemployed as a result of the law are more than offset by the gains to workers who receive higher wages than they would without the law. Opponents of the law believe the losses are greater than the gains. The assessment by any individual depends, in part, on that person's values and political views. The positive analysis an economist provides would play a role in the decision but can't by itself decide the issue one way or the other.

In some chapters, you will see a *Don't Let This Happen to You* box like the one on the next page. These boxes alert you to common pitfalls in thinking about economic ideas. After reading this box, test your understanding by working the related problem that appears at the end of the chapter.

Economics as a Social Science

Because economics studies the actions of individuals, it is a social science. Economics is therefore similar to other social science disciplines, such as psychology, political science, and sociology. As a social science, economics considers human behavior—particularly decision-making behavior—in every context, not just in the context of business. Economists have studied such issues as how families decide on the number of children to have, why people have difficulty losing weight or attaining other desirable goals, and why people often ignore relevant information when making decisions. Economics also has much to contribute to questions of government policy. As we will see throughout this book, economists have played an important role in formulating government policies in areas such as the environment, health care, and poverty.

Don't Let This Happen to You

Don't Confuse Positive Analysis with Normative Analysis

"Economic analysis has shown that the minimum wage law is a bad idea because it causes unemployment." Is this statement accurate? As of 2012, the federal minimum wage law prevents employers from hiring workers at a wage of less than $7.25 per hour. This wage is higher than some employers are willing to pay some workers. If there were no minimum wage law, some workers who currently cannot find any firm willing to hire them at $7.25 per hour would be able to find employment at a lower wage. Therefore, positive economic analysis indicates that the minimum wage law causes unemployment (although economists disagree about how much unemployment the minimum wage causes). *But*, some of those workers who have jobs benefit from the minimum wage because they are paid a higher wage than they otherwise would be. In other words, the minimum wage law creates both losers (the workers who become unemployed and the firms that have to pay higher wages) and winners (the workers who receive higher wages).

Should we value the gains to the winners more than we value the losses to the losers? The answer to this question involves normative analysis. Positive economic analysis can show the consequences of a particular policy, but it cannot tell us whether the policy is "good" or "bad." So, the statement at the beginning of this box is inaccurate.

Making the Connection

Should Medical School Be Free?

The U.S. population continues to increase, which by itself would increase the demand for medical services. In addition, though, the average age of the population is rising, and older people need more medical care than do younger people. So, over time, the number of doctors needs to increase. As mentioned at the beginning of the chapter, the Health Resources and Services Administration (HRSA) estimates that the number of doctors needed to provide patient care will rise from about 805,000 in 2010 to 922,000 in 2020.

Should these medical students have to pay tuition?

Can we be sure that these additional doctors will be available in 2020? The HRSA forecasts that, in fact, there will be a shortage of 56,000 doctors in 2020. The bulk of that shortage is likely to be in primary care physicians, or family doctors. As we will discuss in later chapters, ordinarily we expect that when consumers want more of a product, higher wages and salaries and more job openings will attract workers to that industry. For example, during the U.S. housing boom of the mid-2000s, the number of workers in the building trades—carpenters, plumbers, roofers, and others—increased rapidly. But producing more doctors is a long process. After completing his or her undergraduate education, a doctor spends four years in medical school and then three to five years at a teaching hospital, pursuing a residency in a particular field of medicine. Apparently convinced that hospitals will not train enough doctors unless they get help, Congress contributes $10 billion per year to teaching hospitals, based on the number of residents they train.

Recently, Peter Bach of the Sloan-Kettering Cancer Center and Robert Kocher of the Brookings Institution have proposed that medical schools should charge no tuition. They argue that nearly all students graduate from medical school owing money on student loans, with the average student owing more than $150,000. We might expect that these debts, although large, would not deter students from applying to medical school, because in 2011, the average income of physicians was more than $250,000 per year.

Bach and Kocher argue, though, that the high cost of medical school has two bad outcomes: Some good students do not apply because they either do not want to be saddled with such large debts or because they are unable to borrow sufficient money, and many students avoid going into primary care—where average incomes are $190,000—in favor of specialties such as plastic surgery or anesthesiology—where average incomes are $325,000. Teaching hospitals pay doctors a salary of about $50,000 per year during their residencies. Bach and Kocher propose that hospitals continue to pay residents who pursue primary care but not pay residents who specialize. The money that hospitals would otherwise pay to these residents would be paid to medical schools instead to finance the free tuition. The plan would give residents an incentive to pursue primary care rather than to specialize. Critics of the Bach and Kocher proposal have questioned whether many students capable of being admitted to medical school actually are deterred by medical school tuition. They also question whether many residents who intend to specialize would choose primary care instead, even if specializing means they have to borrow to meet living expenses rather than paying for them with a hospital salary.

Like many other policy debates, the debate over whether changes should be made in how medical school is paid for has positive and normative elements. By gathering data and using economic models, it is possible to assess some of the quantitative claims made by each side in the debate: What role does tuition play in a student's decision about whether to attend medical school? Have tuition increases had a large effect or a small effect on the number of applications to medical school? How do changes in expected future incomes affect the decisions of medical students about which specialty to choose? These are all positive questions, so it is possible to formulate quantitative answers. Ultimately, though, this debate also has a normative element. For instance, some doctors, economists, and policymakers argue that it is important that people living in low-income or rural areas have improved access to health care, so they are willing to support policies that would redirect medical students away from specialized fields and toward primary care. Other doctors, economists, and policymakers believe that medical students who enter specialized fields make a larger contribution to society than do students who enter primary care. A disagreement of this type is unlikely to be resolved by building models and analyzing data because the issue involved is essentially normative.

In 2010, President Obama and Congress enacted the Patient Protection and Affordable Care Act, which made major changes to the U.S. health care system. The changes are being phased in through 2014. Additional changes are likely as policymakers grapple with the rapidly escalating costs of health care. Whether Congress and the president will enact policies intended to increase the number of primary care physicians remains to be seen.

Based on Suzanne Sataline and Shirley S. Wang, "Medical Schools Can't Keep Up," *Wall Street Journal*, April 12, 2010; Uwe E. Reinhardt, "Producing More Primary-Care Doctors," *New York Times*, June 10, 2011; and Peter B. Bach and Robert Kocher, "Why Medical School Should Be Free," *New York Times*, May 28, 2011.

1.4 LEARNING OBJECTIVE

Distinguish between microeconomics and macroeconomics.

Microeconomics and Macroeconomics

Economic models can be used to analyze decision making in many areas. We group some of these areas together as *microeconomics* and others as *macroeconomics*. **Microeconomics** is the study of how households and firms make choices, how they interact in markets, and how the government attempts to influence their choices. Microeconomic issues include explaining how consumers react to changes in product prices and how firms decide what prices to charge for the products they sell. Microeconomics also involves policy issues, such as analyzing the most efficient way to reduce teenage smoking, analyzing the costs and benefits of approving the sale of a new prescription drug, and analyzing the most efficient way to reduce air pollution.

Microeconomics The study of how households and firms make choices, how they interact in markets, and how the government attempts to influence their choices.

Macroeconomics is the study of the economy as a whole, including topics such as inflation, unemployment, and economic growth. Macroeconomic issues include explaining why economies experience periods of recession and increasing unemployment and why, over the long run, some economies have grown much faster than others. Macroeconomics also involves policy issues, such as whether government intervention can reduce the severity of recessions.

Macroeconomics The study of the economy as a whole, including topics such as inflation, unemployment, and economic growth.

The division between microeconomics and macroeconomics is not hard and fast. Many economic situations have *both* a microeconomic and a macroeconomic aspect. For example, the level of total investment by firms in new machinery and equipment helps to determine how rapidly the economy grows—which is a macroeconomic issue. But to understand how much new machinery and equipment firms decide to purchase, we have to analyze the incentives individual firms face—which is a microeconomic issue.

A Preview of Important Economic Terms

1.5 LEARNING OBJECTIVE

Define important economic terms.

In the following chapters, you will encounter certain important terms again and again. Becoming familiar with these terms is a necessary step in learning economics. Here we provide a brief introduction to some of these terms. We will discuss them all in greater depth in later chapters:

- ***Entrepreneur.*** An *entrepreneur* is someone who operates a business. In a market system, entrepreneurs decide what goods and services to produce and how to produce them. An entrepreneur starting a new business puts his or her own funds at risk. If an entrepreneur is wrong about what consumers want or about the best way to produce goods and services, the entrepreneur's funds can be lost. This is not an unusual occurrence: In the United States, about half of new businesses close within four years. Without entrepreneurs willing to assume the risk of starting and operating businesses, economic progress would be impossible in a market system.
- ***Innovation.*** There is a distinction between an *invention* and *innovation*. An *invention* is the development of a new good or a new process for making a good. An *innovation* is the practical application of an invention. (*Innovation* may also be used more broadly to refer to any significant improvement in a good or in the means of producing a good.) Much time often passes between the appearance of a new idea and its development for widespread use. For example, the Wright brothers first achieved self-propelled flight at Kitty Hawk, North Carolina, in 1903, but the Wright brothers' plane was very crude, and it wasn't until the introduction of the DC-3 by Douglas Aircraft in 1936 that regularly scheduled intercity airline flights became common in the United States. Similarly, the first digital electronic computer—the ENIAC—was developed in 1945, but the first IBM personal computer was not introduced until 1981, and widespread use of computers did not have a significant effect on the productivity of U.S. business until the 1990s.
- ***Technology.*** A firm's *technology* is the processes it uses to produce goods and services. In the economic sense, a firm's technology depends on many factors, such as the skill of its managers, the training of its workers, and the speed and efficiency of its machinery and equipment.
- ***Firm, company, or business.*** A *firm* is an organization that produces a good or service. Most firms produce goods or services to earn profits, but there are also nonprofit firms, such as universities and some hospitals. Economists use the terms *firm*, *company*, and *business* interchangeably.
- ***Goods.*** *Goods* are tangible merchandise, such as books, computers, or Blu-ray players.

- ***Services.*** *Services* are activities done for others, such as providing haircuts or investment advice.
- ***Revenue.*** A firm's *revenue* is the total amount received for selling a good or service. It is calculated by multiplying the price per unit by the number of units sold.
- ***Profit.*** A firm's *profit* is the difference between its revenue and its costs. Economists distinguish between *accounting profit* and *economic profit.* In calculating accounting profit, we exclude the cost of some economic resources that the firm does not pay for explicitly. In calculating economic profit, we include the opportunity cost of all resources used by the firm. When we refer to *profit* in this book, we mean economic profit. It is important not to confuse *profit* with *revenue.*
- ***Household.*** A *household* consists of all persons occupying a home. Households are suppliers of factors of production—particularly labor—used by firms to make goods and services. Households also demand goods and services produced by firms and governments.
- ***Factors of production or economic resources.*** Firms use factors of production to produce goods and services. The main factors of production are labor, capital, natural resources—including land—and entrepreneurial ability. Households earn income by supplying to firms the factors of production.
- ***Capital.*** The word *capital* can refer to *financial capital* or to *physical capital.* Financial capital includes stocks and bonds issued by firms, bank accounts, and holdings of money. In economics, though, *capital* refers to physical capital, which includes manufactured goods that are used to produce other goods and services. Examples of physical capital are computers, factory buildings, machine tools, warehouses, and trucks. The total amount of physical capital available in a country is referred to as the country's *capital stock.*
- ***Human capital.*** Human capital refers to the accumulated training and skills that workers possess. For example, college-educated workers generally have more skills and are more productive than workers who have only high school degrees.

Continued from page 3

Economics in Your Life

Will There Be Plenty of Jobs Available in the Health Care Industry?

At the beginning of the chapter, we posed the question "What is the basis for the forecasts on the availability of jobs in health care, and how reliable are the forecasts?" As the U.S. population increases and as the average age of the population rises, it seems likely that there will be an increase in the numbers of doctors, nurses, physician's assistants, and other health care workers. The U.S. Bureau of Labor Statistics (BLS) publishes the most widely used occupational forecasts. Economists at the BLS base these forecasts on economic models. The forecasts can be inaccurate, however. For example, in 1996, the BLS forecast that 93,485 physician's assistants would be employed in 2006, when in fact only 65,628 were. The BLS analyzes errors like these in attempting to improve its forecasts. So, it is likely that the BLS's forecasts will become more accurate over time, but it would be a mistake to expect the forecasts to be exact.

Conclusion

Economics is a group of useful ideas about how individuals make choices. Economists have put these ideas into practice by developing economic models. Consumers, business managers, and government policymakers use these models every day to help make choices. In this book, we explore many key economic models and give examples of how to apply them in the real world.

Reading newspapers and other periodicals is an important part of understanding the current business climate and learning how to apply economic concepts to a variety of real-world events. At the end of each chapter, you will see a two-page feature titled *An Inside Look*. This feature consists of an excerpt from an article that relates to the company or economic issue introduced at the start of the chapter and also to the concepts discussed in the chapter. A summary and an analysis and supporting graphs highlight the key economic points of the article. Read *An Inside Look* on the next page to explore reasons why some health care workers are delaying retirement. Test your understanding by answering the *Thinking Critically* questions.

AN INSIDE LOOK

Doctors Moving Less, Retiring Later

AMEDNEWS.COM

Fewer Physicians Move, a Sign of Career Caution

Physicians changed addresses at a lower rate during the last year than in the previous three years, according to a survey of 253,000 medical offices.

a Each year, SK&A, an Irvine, Calif.-based Cegedim firm that specializes in health care marketing information, compiles a database of 664,600 physicians who work in medical offices. Since 2008, the firm has published a report on the "move rate," which indicates how many physicians are no longer at a given office because they moved, retired or died.

Based on survey answers between March 2010 and March 2011, the firm calculated an 11.3% move rate for its most recent report, marking another year of decline. The move rate was reported as 12.4% in 2010, 15% in 2009 and 18.2% in 2008, according to SK&A.

Experts say the move rate, though an unscientific measure, could reflect the ways in which the economy is keeping physicians from changing jobs or retiring, including financial stress, the medical liability environment and licensure laws.

Physicians "don't seem to be motivated by the factors that in the past have caused a desire to move—a big caseload, a better salary [elsewhere], or a better community with better amenities," SK&A spokesman Jack Schember said.

b SK&A publishes its data for the benefit of pharmaceutical and medical equipment companies who want to sell to physicians, but the figures are one lens through which to view the economy's effect on physician practices.

Mark Doescher, MD, MSPH, director of the University of Washington Center for Health Workforce Studies, said a more stable work force could be good for areas facing a declining number of physicians and other health professionals, mainly outside major cities.

"I do think the down economy has actually caused stability in the work force, which is good for many rural locations," he said. "But when people do retire, we're going to see some difficult times ahead."

c Deane Waldman, MD, a pediatric cardiologist at the University of New Mexico Children's Hospital in Albuquerque and an author who writes about the health care system, cautioned that the SK&A move rate isn't a scientific measurement of physician turnover or retirement.

But he said it makes sense that physicians would be unlikely to change jobs or retire now, given a long list of pressures: uncertainty about health system reform, declining income due to falling reimbursement rates, a constantly shifting medical liability environment, licensing regulations that make it difficult to relocate, and a shortage of physicians that makes it difficult to find someone to take over a practice.

"You add up all the uncertainty, financial losses, change in laws, and it's not surprising people are afraid to make any change at all," Dr. Waldman said.

For those who find a place to go, selling their homes might make it difficult or impossible to leave without taking a financial loss.

A report released May 19 by the Conference Board research group reinforced the difficulty many health care workers face as they reach retirement age. The health industry experienced the largest decline in retirement rates between a 2004-07 survey period and a 2009-10 survey period, according to an analysis of delayed retirement across all industries. Only 1.55% of full-time health care workers age 55 to 64 retired within 12 months of the 2009-10 study period, compared with 3.95% in 2004-07. The health care sector had the lowest rate of retirement, significantly less than the other industries studied.

The SK&A survey found that doctors in some specialties are much more likely to retire or move than their peers. Physicians specializing in aerospace medicine had the highest move rate at 27.9%, and plastic surgeons had the lowest, at 6.3%. Family physicians had an 11.4% move rate.

Source: "Family Physician Can't Give Away Solo Practice," by Gardiner Harris. *The New York Times*, April 22, 2011.

Key Points in the Article

This article discusses the continued decline in the number of physicians who have changed jobs or retired over the past three years. Possible reasons for the decline include the 2007–2009 economic recession, the slow recovery from that recession, the lower insurance reimbursement rates, and the still-uncertain outcome of the reforms to the health care system. A May 2011 report by the Conference Board research group shows that the health care industry had the largest decline in retirement rates from 2004 to 2007 and again from 2009 to 2010, when the industry also had the lowest rate of retirement of all industries surveyed. This decline indicates that changes in the health care industry have many health professionals concerned about their finances as they approach retirement age.

Analyzing the News

a Data compiled by the health care marketing firm SK&A indicates that the rate at which physicians have been changing jobs or retiring (the "move rate") has dropped for the fourth straight year, from a high of 18.2 percent in 2008, the first year the data were collected, to a low of 11.3 percent in 2011. According to the chapter opener on page 3, physicians had for years typically operated their practices on their own or in partnerships with other doctors, but over the past several years, a growing number of physicians have given up their private practices to become salaried hospital employees, and by 2008, more medical practices were owned by hospitals than by the doctors themselves. The figure below illustrates the data. Rising costs and financial uncertainty are thought to be one of the primary reasons that a growing number of physicians have given up private practice for hospital employment, and the "move rate" seems to indicate that a growing number of these physicians are staying put at their hospital jobs, forgoing re-entering private practice or retirement.

b In the 1991 movie *Doc Hollywood*, Michael J. Fox plays a Beverly Hills surgeon who, after causing a traffic accident in a rural community, is sentenced to perform community service at the local hospital. The premise behind the story reflects an ongoing trend of rural communities finding it increasingly difficult to attract medical professionals to their areas. An upside to the decline in job switching and retirement could be more workforce stability in the medical field, especially in these rural areas. Economic uncertainty has kept many of these professionals from retiring or relocating and has therefore been beneficial to the populations in these locations. The upside is likely to be temporary, though, for unlike the typical happy Hollywood ending of the big-city doctor falling in love with the small town, relocation to these areas continues to fall, so when the eventual retirement of these rural physicians ultimately occurs, doctor shortages will likely continue.

c Economic uncertainty, changes in health care laws, and financial concerns have been credited with being partially responsible for not only an increase in physicians giving up their private practices to become salaried hospital employees but also a decrease in the number of physicians either relocating to new jobs or retiring from their practices. This trend seems to indicate that many of those doctors who are continuing to relocate are moving to hospitals rather than new or different private practices. As long as uncertainties remain in the economy and with health care reform, it would not be surprising if physicians remained concerned about their professional and financial futures and worried that this trend will continue.

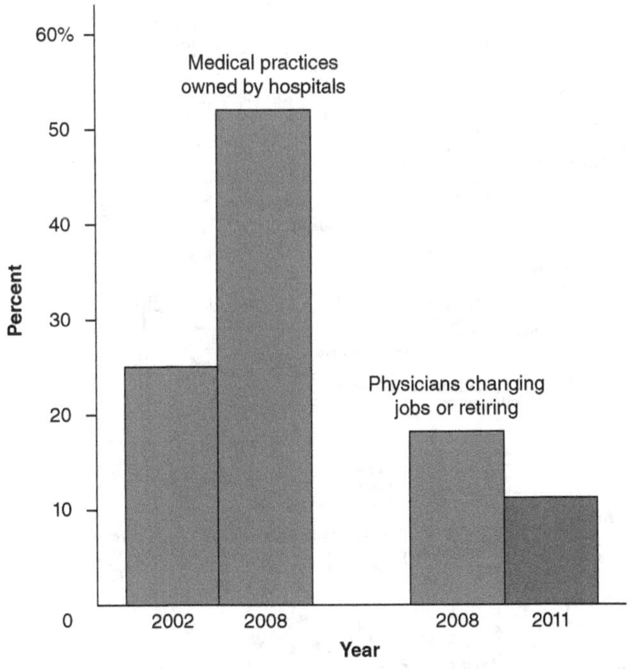

Changes in the ownership of medical practices and changes in the physician move rate.

Data from Robert Kocher, M.D., and Nikhil R. Sahni, "Hospitals' Race to Employ Physicians—The Logic Behind a Money-Losing Proposition," *New England Journal of Medicine*, May 12, 2011; and Uwe E. Reinhardt, "Producing More Primary-Care Doctors," *New York Times*, June 10, 2011. and Emily Berry, "Fewer physicians move, a sign of career caution," June 6, 2011. amednews.com.

Thinking Critically

1. One important economic idea is that people are rational. Explain how this idea relates to the decline in the "move rate" of physicians over the past three years.
2. The article states that in 2009–2010, the health care industry had the lowest retirement rate of all industries surveyed. Suppose you want to develop an economic model to analyze the relationship between the retirement rate of physicians and changes in insurance reimbursement rates. Use information from the article to explain the steps you would take to develop this model.

Appendix

LEARNING OBJECTIVE

Review the use of graphs and formulas.

Using Graphs and Formulas

Graphs are used to illustrate key economic ideas. Graphs appear not just in economics textbooks but also on Web sites and in newspaper and magazine articles that discuss events in business and economics. Why the heavy use of graphs? Because they serve two useful purposes: (1) They simplify economic ideas, and (2) they make the ideas more concrete so they can be applied to real-world problems. Economic and business issues can be complicated, but a graph can help cut through complications and highlight the key relationships needed to understand the issue. In that sense, a graph can be like a street map.

For example, suppose you take a bus to New York City to see the Empire State Building. After arriving at the Port Authority Bus Terminal, you will probably use a map similar to the one shown below to find your way to the Empire State Building.

Maps are very familiar to just about everyone, so we don't usually think of them as being simplified versions of reality, but they are. This map does not show much more than the streets in this part of New York City and some of the most important buildings. The names, addresses, and telephone numbers of the people who live and work in the area aren't given. Almost none of the stores and buildings those people work and live in are shown either. The map doesn't indicate which streets allow curbside parking and which don't. In fact, the map shows almost nothing about the messy reality of life in this section of New York City, except how the streets are laid out, which is the essential information you need to get from the Port Authority to the Empire State Building.

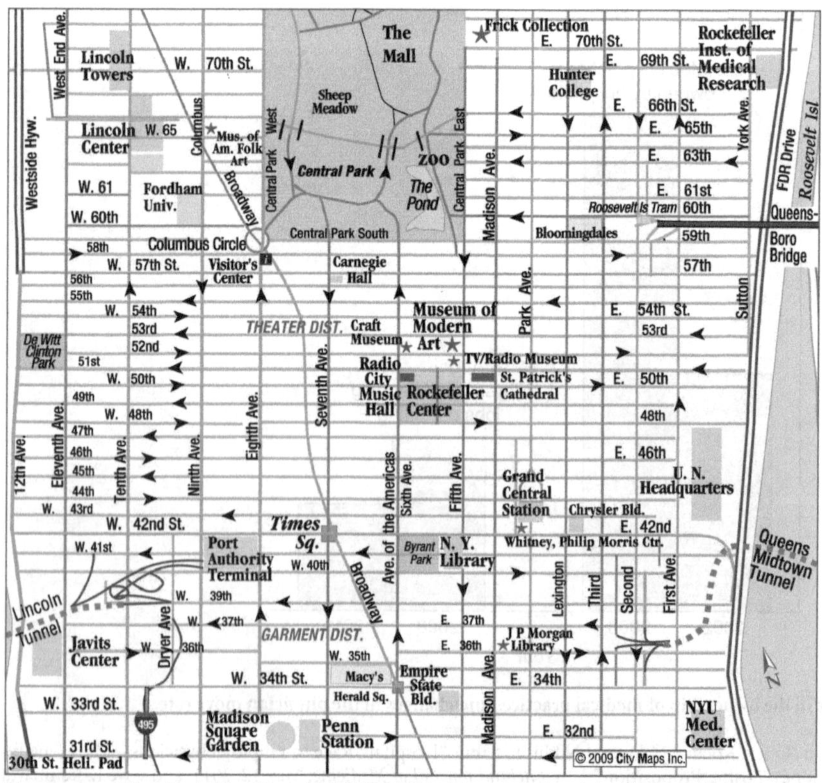

Street map of New York City. Copyright © 2011 City Maps Inc. Reprinted by permission.

Think about someone who says, "I know how to get around in the city, but I just can't figure out how to read a map." It certainly is possible to find your destination in a city without a map, but it's a lot easier with one. The same is true of using graphs in economics. It is possible to arrive at a solution to a real-world problem in economics and business without using graphs, but it is usually a lot easier if you do use them.

Often, the difficulty students have with graphs and formulas is a lack of familiarity. With practice, all the graphs and formulas in this text will become familiar to you. Once you are familiar with them, you will be able to use them to analyze problems that would otherwise seem very difficult. What follows is a brief review of how graphs and formulas are used.

Graphs of One Variable

Figure 1A.1 displays values for *market shares* in the U.S. automobile market, using two common types of graphs. Market shares show the percentage of industry sales accounted for by different firms. In this case, the information is for groups of firms: the "Big Three"—Ford, General Motors, and Chrysler—as well as Japanese firms, European firms, and Korean firms. Panel (a) displays the information on market shares as a *bar graph*, where the market share of each group of firms is represented by the height of its bar. Panel (b) displays the same information as a *pie chart*, with the market share of each group of firms represented by the size of its slice of the pie.

Information on economic variables is also often displayed in *time-series graphs*. Time-series graphs are displayed on a coordinate grid. In a coordinate grid, we can measure the value of one variable along the vertical axis (or y-axis) and the value of another variable along the horizontal axis (or x-axis). The point where the vertical axis intersects the horizontal axis is called the *origin*. At the origin, the value of both variables is zero. The points on a coordinate grid represent values of the two variables. In Figure 1A.2, we measure the number of automobiles and trucks sold worldwide by Ford Motor Company on the vertical axis, and we measure time on the horizontal axis. In time-series

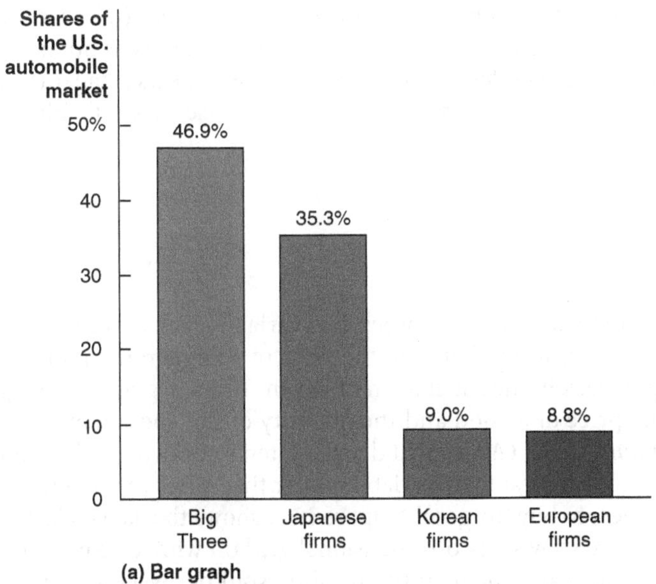

(a) Bar graph

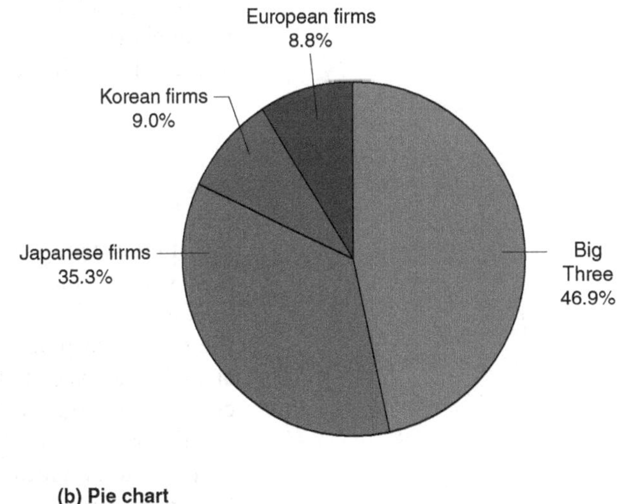

(b) Pie chart

Figure 1A.1 Bar Graphs and Pie Charts

Values for an economic variable are often displayed as a bar graph or as a pie chart. In this case, panel (a) shows market share data for the U.S. automobile industry as a bar graph, where the market share of each group of firms is represented by the height of its bar. Panel (b) displays the same information as a pie chart, with the market share of each group of firms represented by the size of its slice of the pie.

Data from "Auto Sales," *Wall Street Journal*, July 1, 2011.

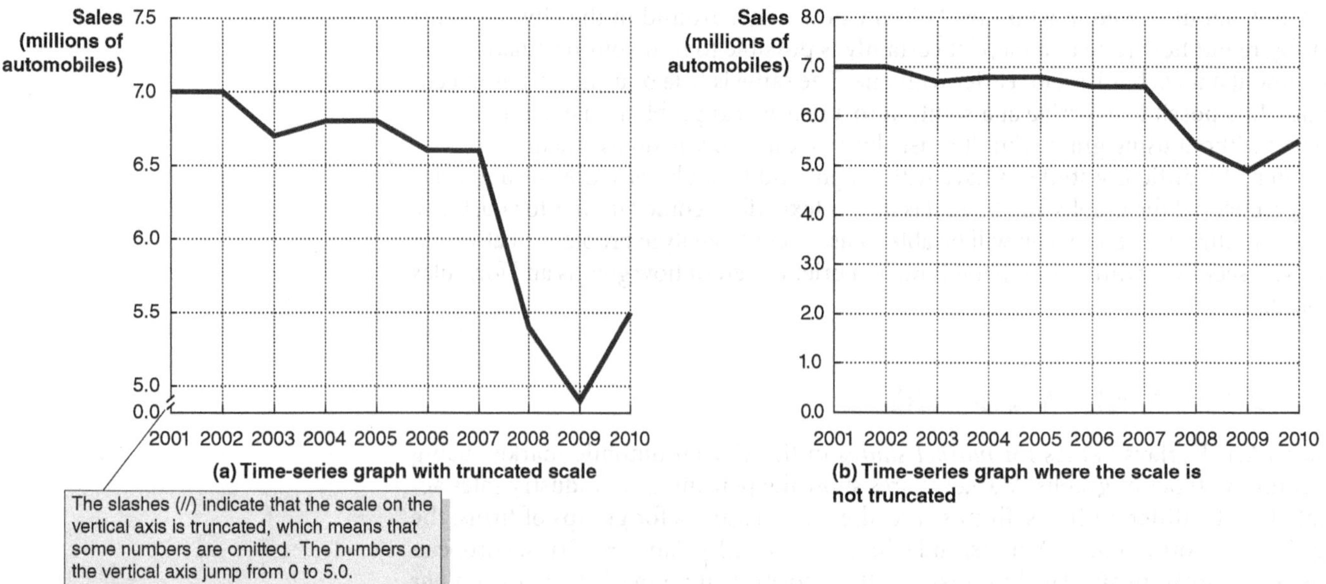

Figure 1A.2 Time-Series Graphs

Both panels present time-series graphs of Ford Motor Company's worldwide sales during each year from 2001 to 2010. Panel (a) has a truncated scale on the vertical axis, and panel (b) does not. As a result, the fluctuations in Ford's sales appear smaller in panel (b) than in panel (a).
Data from Ford Motor Company, *Annual Report*, various years.

graphs, the height of the line at each date shows the value of the variable measured on the vertical axis. Both panels of Figure 1A.2 show Ford's worldwide sales during each year from 2001 to 2010. The difference between panel (a) and panel (b) illustrates the importance of the scale used in a time-series graph. In panel (a), the scale on the vertical axis is truncated, which means it does not start with zero. The slashes (//) near the bottom of the axis indicate that the scale is truncated. In panel (b), the scale is not truncated. In panel (b), the decline in Ford's sales during 2008 and 2009 appears smaller than in panel (a). (Technically, the horizontal axis is also truncated because we start with the year 2001, not the year 0.)

Graphs of Two Variables

We often use graphs to show the relationship between two variables. For example, suppose you are interested in the relationship between the price of a pepperoni pizza and the quantity of pizzas sold per week in the small town of Bryan, Texas. A graph showing the relationship between the price of a good and the quantity of the good demanded at each price is called a *demand curve*. (As we will discuss later, in drawing a demand curve for a good, we have to hold constant any variables other than price that might affect the willingness of consumers to buy the good.) Figure 1A.3 shows the data collected on price and quantity. The figure shows a two-dimensional grid on which we measure the price of pizza along the y-axis and the quantity of pizza sold per week along the x-axis. Each point on the grid represents one of the price and quantity combinations listed in the table. We can connect the points to form the demand curve for pizza in Bryan, Texas. Notice that the scales on both axes in the graph are truncated. In this case, truncating the axes allows the graph to illustrate more clearly the relationship between price and quantity by excluding low prices and quantities.

Price (dollars per pizza)	Quantity (pizzas per week)	Points
$15	50	A
14	55	B
13	60	C
12	65	D
11	70	E

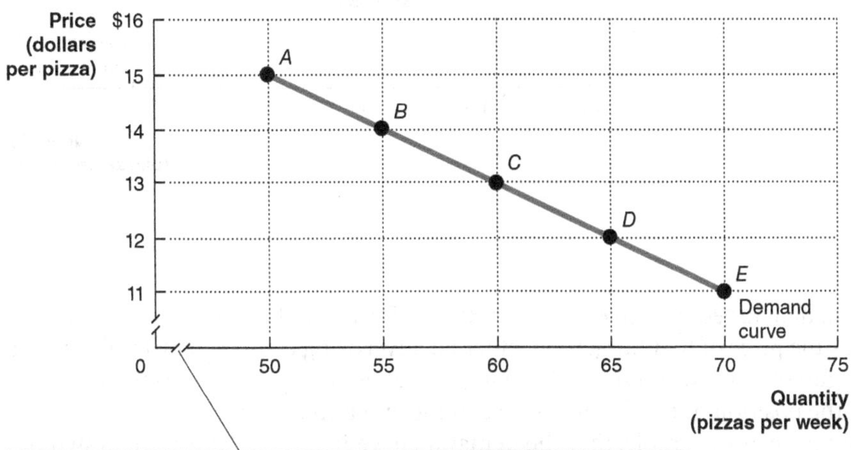

As you learned in Figure 1A-2, the slashes (//) indicate that the scales on the axes are truncated, which means that numbers are omitted: On the horizontal axis numbers jump from 0 to 50, and on the vertical axis numbers jump from 0 to 11.

Figure 1A.3

Plotting Price and Quantity Points in a Graph

The figure shows a two-dimensional grid on which we measure the price of pizza along the vertical axis (or *y*-axis) and the quantity of pizza sold per week along the horizontal axis (or *x*-axis). Each point on the grid represents one of the price and quantity combinations listed in the table. By connecting the points with a line, we can better illustrate the relationship between the two variables.

Slopes of Lines

Once you have plotted the data in Figure 1A.3, you may be interested in how much the quantity of pizza sold increases as the price decreases. The *slope* of a line tells us how much the variable we are measuring on the *y*-axis changes as the variable we are measuring on the *x*-axis changes. We can use the Greek letter delta (Δ) to stand for the change in a variable. The slope is sometimes referred to as the rise over the run. So, we have several ways of expressing slope:

$$\text{Slope} = \frac{\text{Change in value on the vertical axis}}{\text{Change in value on the horizontal axis}} = \frac{\Delta y}{\Delta x} = \frac{\text{Rise}}{\text{Run}}.$$

Figure 1A.4 reproduces the graph from Figure 1A.3. Because the slope of a straight line is the same at any point, we can use any two points in the figure to calculate the slope of the line. For example, when the price of pizza decreases from $14 to $12, the quantity of pizza sold increases from 55 per week to 65 per week. Therefore, the slope is:

$$\text{Slope} = \frac{\Delta\text{Price of pizza}}{\Delta\text{Quantity of pizza}} = \frac{(\$12 - \$14)}{(65 - 55)} = \frac{-2}{10} = -0.2.$$

The slope of this line gives us some insight into how responsive consumers in Bryan, Texas, are to changes in the price of pizza. The larger the value of the slope (ignoring the negative sign), the steeper the line will be, which indicates that not many additional pizzas are sold when the price falls. The smaller the value of the slope, the flatter the line will be, which indicates a greater increase in pizzas sold when the price falls.

Taking into Account More Than Two Variables on a Graph

The demand curve graph in Figure 1A.4 shows the relationship between the price of pizza and the quantity of pizza demanded, but we know that the quantity of any good demanded depends on more than just the price of the good. For example, the quantity

Figure 1A.4

Calculating the Slope of a Line

We can calculate the slope of a line as the change in the value of the variable on the *y*-axis divided by the change in the value of the variable on the *x*-axis. Because the slope of a straight line is constant, we can use any two points in the figure to calculate the slope of the line. For example, when the price of pizza decreases from $14 to $12, the quantity of pizza demanded increases from 55 per week to 65 per week. So, the slope of this line equals −2 divided by 10, or −0.2.

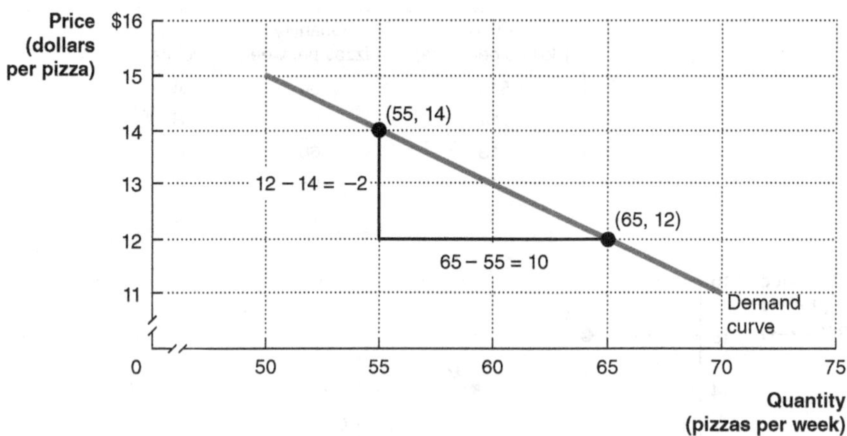

of pizza demanded in a given week in Bryan, Texas, can be affected by other variables, such as the price of hamburgers, whether an advertising campaign by local pizza parlors has begun that week, and so on. Allowing the values of any other variables to change will cause the position of the demand curve in the graph to change.

Suppose, for example, that the demand curve in Figure 1A.4 were drawn holding the price of hamburgers constant, at $1.50. If the price of hamburgers rises to $2.00, some consumers will switch from buying hamburgers to buying pizza, and more pizzas will be demanded at every price. The result on the graph will be to shift the line representing the demand curve to the right. Similarly, if the price of hamburgers falls from $1.50 to $1.00, some consumers will switch from buying pizza to buying hamburgers, and fewer pizzas will be demanded at every price. The result on the graph will be to shift the line representing the demand curve to the left.

The table in Figure 1A.5 shows the effect of a change in the price of hamburgers on the quantity of pizza demanded. For example, suppose that at first we are on the line labeled *Demand curve*$_1$. If the price of pizza is $14 (point *A*), an increase in the price of hamburgers from $1.50 to $2.00 increases the quantity of pizzas demanded from 55 to 60 per week (point *B*) and shifts us to *Demand curve*$_2$. Or, if we start on *Demand curve*$_1$ and the price of pizza is $12 (point *C*), a decrease in the price of hamburgers from $1.50 to $1.00 decreases the quantity of pizzas demanded from 65 to 60 per week (point *D*) and shifts us to *Demand curve*$_3$. By shifting the demand curve, we have taken into account the effect of changes in the value of a third variable—the price of hamburgers. We will use this technique of shifting curves to allow for the effects of additional variables many times in this book.

Positive and Negative Relationships

We can use graphs to show the relationships between any two variables. Sometimes the relationship between the variables is *negative*, meaning that as one variable increases in value, the other variable decreases in value. This was the case with the price of pizza and the quantity of pizzas demanded. The relationship between two variables can also be *positive*, meaning that the values of both variables increase or decrease together. For example, when the level of total income—or *disposable personal income*—received by households in the United States increases, the level of total *consumption spending*, which is spending by households on goods and services, also increases. The table in Figure 1A.6 shows the values (in billions of dollars) for income and consumption spending for the years 2007–2010. The graph plots the data from the table, with disposable personal income measured along the horizontal axis and consumption spending measured along the vertical axis. Notice that the four points do not all fall exactly on the line. This is often the case with real-world data. To examine the relationship between two variables, economists often use the straight line that best fits the data.

	Quantity (pizzas per week)		
Price (dollars per pizza)	When the Price of Hamburgers = $1.00	When the Price of Hamburgers = $1.50	When the Price of Hamburgers = $2.00
$15	45	50	55
14	50	55	60
13	55	60	65
12	60	65	70
11	65	70	75

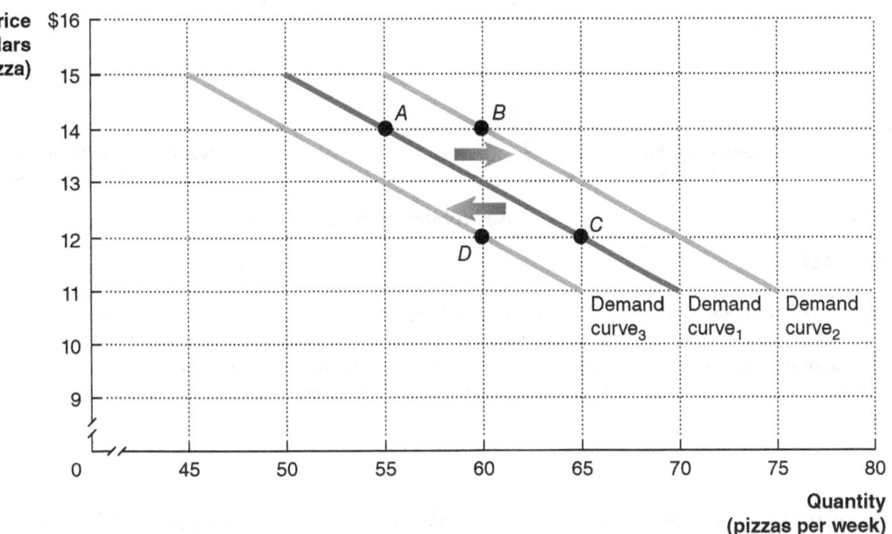

Figure 1A.5

Showing Three Variables on a Graph

The demand curve for pizza shows the relationship between the price of pizzas and the quantity of pizzas demanded, *holding constant other factors that might affect the willingness of consumers to buy pizza.* If the price of pizza is $14 (point *A*), an increase in the price of hamburgers from $1.50 to $2.00 increases the quantity of pizzas demanded from 55 to 60 per week (point *B*) and shifts us to *Demand curve*$_2$. Or, if we start on *Demand curve*$_1$ and the price of pizza is $12 (point *C*), a decrease in the price of hamburgers from $1.50 to $1.00 decreases the quantity of pizza demanded from 65 to 60 per week (point *D*) and shifts us to *Demand curve*$_3$.

Determining Cause and Effect

When we graph the relationship between two variables, we often want to draw conclusions about whether changes in one variable are causing changes in the other variable. Doing so, however, can lead to incorrect conclusions. For example, suppose you graph the number of homes in a neighborhood that have a fire burning in the fireplace and

Year	Disposable Personal Income (billions of dollars)	Consumption Spending (billions of dollars)
2007	$10,424	$9,806
2008	10,953	10,105
2009	11,035	10,001
2010	11,375	10,349

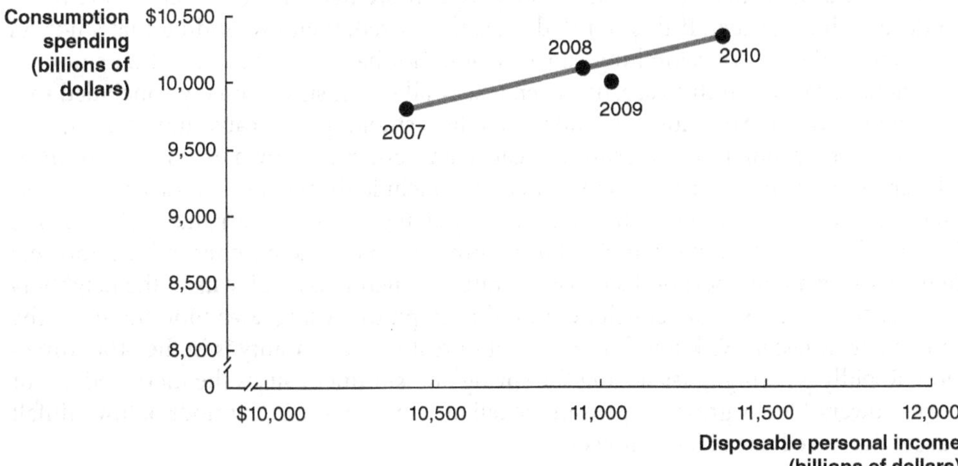

Figure 1A.6

Graphing the Positive Relationship between Income and Consumption

In a positive relationship between two economic variables, as one variable increases, the other variable also increases. This figure shows the positive relationship between disposable personal income and consumption spending. As disposable personal income in the United States has increased, so has consumption spending.

Data from U.S. Department of Commerce, Bureau of Economic Analysis.

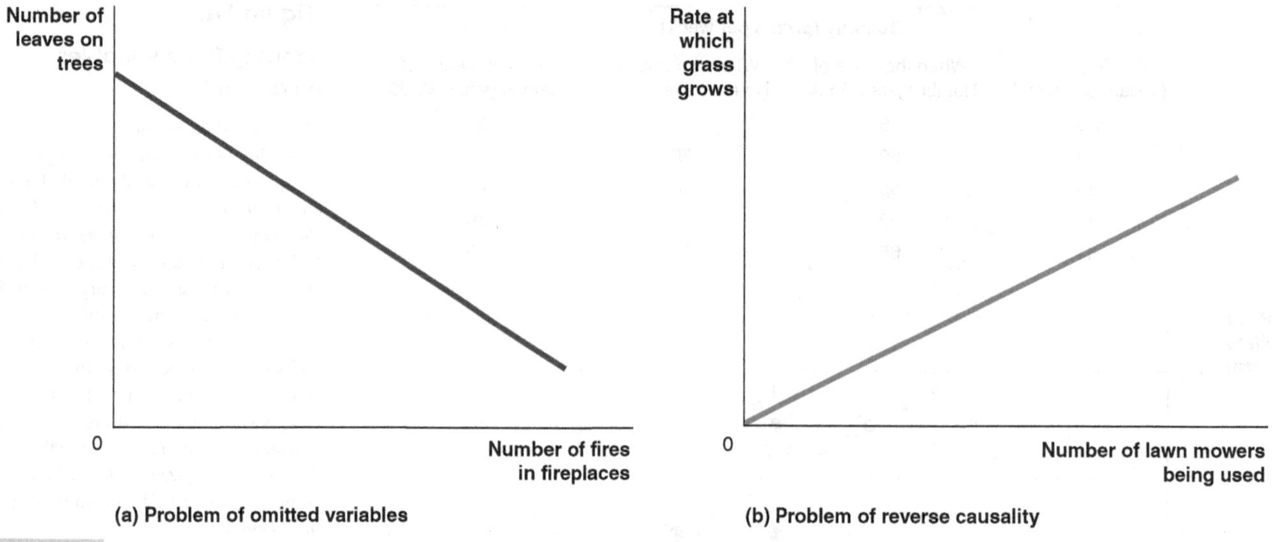

Figure 1A.7 Determining Cause and Effect

Using graphs to draw conclusions about cause and effect can be hazardous. In panel (a), we see that there are fewer leaves on the trees in a neighborhood when many homes have fires burning in their fireplaces. We cannot draw the conclusion that the fires cause the leaves to fall because we have an *omitted variable*—the season of the year. In panel (b), we see that more lawn mowers are used in a neighborhood during times when the grass grows rapidly and fewer lawn mowers are used when the grass grows slowly. Concluding that using lawn mowers *causes* the grass to grow faster would be making the error of *reverse causality*.

the number of leaves on trees in the neighborhood. You would get a relationship like that shown in panel (a) of Figure 1A.7: The more fires burning in the neighborhood, the fewer leaves the trees have. Can we draw the conclusion from this graph that using a fireplace causes trees to lose their leaves? We know, of course, that such a conclusion would be incorrect. In spring and summer, there are relatively few fireplaces being used, and the trees are full of leaves. In the fall, as trees begin to lose their leaves, fireplaces are used more frequently. And in winter, many fireplaces are being used and many trees have lost all their leaves. The reason that the graph in Figure 1A.7 is misleading about cause and effect is that there is obviously an *omitted variable* in the analysis—the season of the year. An omitted variable is one that affects other variables, and its omission can lead to false conclusions about cause and effect.

Although in our example the omitted variable is obvious, there are many debates about cause and effect where the existence of an omitted variable has not been clear. For instance, it has been known for many years that people who smoke cigarettes suffer from higher rates of lung cancer than do nonsmokers. For some time, tobacco companies and some scientists argued that there was an omitted variable—perhaps a failure to exercise or a poor diet—that made some people more likely to smoke and more likely to develop lung cancer. If this omitted variable existed, then the finding that smokers were more likely to develop lung cancer would not have been evidence that smoking *caused* lung cancer. In this case, however, nearly all scientists eventually concluded that the omitted variable did not exist and that, in fact, smoking does cause lung cancer.

A related problem in determining cause and effect is known as *reverse causality*. The error of reverse causality occurs when we conclude that changes in variable X cause changes in variable Y when, in fact, it is actually changes in variable Y that cause changes in variable X. For example, panel (b) of Figure 1A.7 plots the number of lawn mowers being used in a neighborhood against the rate at which grass on lawns in the neighborhood is growing. We could conclude from this graph that using lawn mowers *causes* the grass to grow faster. We know, however, that in reality, the causality is in the other direction: Rapidly growing grass during the spring and summer causes the increased use of lawn mowers. Slowly growing grass in the fall or winter or during periods of low rainfall causes decreased use of lawn mowers.

Once again, in our example, the potential error of reverse causality is obvious. In many economic debates, however, cause and effect can be more difficult to determine. For example, changes in the money supply, or the total amount of money in the economy, tend to occur at the same time as changes in the total amount of income people in the economy earn. A famous debate in economics was about whether the changes in the money supply caused the changes in total income or whether the changes in total income caused the changes in the money supply. Each side in the debate accused the other side of committing the error of reverse causality.

Are Graphs of Economic Relationships Always Straight Lines?

The graphs of relationships between two economic variables that we have drawn so far have been straight lines. The relationship between two variables is *linear* when it can be represented by a straight line. Few economic relationships are actually linear. For example, if we carefully plot data on the price of a product and the quantity demanded at each price, holding constant other variables that affect the quantity demanded, we will usually find a curved—or *nonlinear*—relationship rather than a linear relationship. In practice, however, it is often useful to approximate a nonlinear relationship with a linear relationship. If the relationship is reasonably close to being linear, the analysis is not

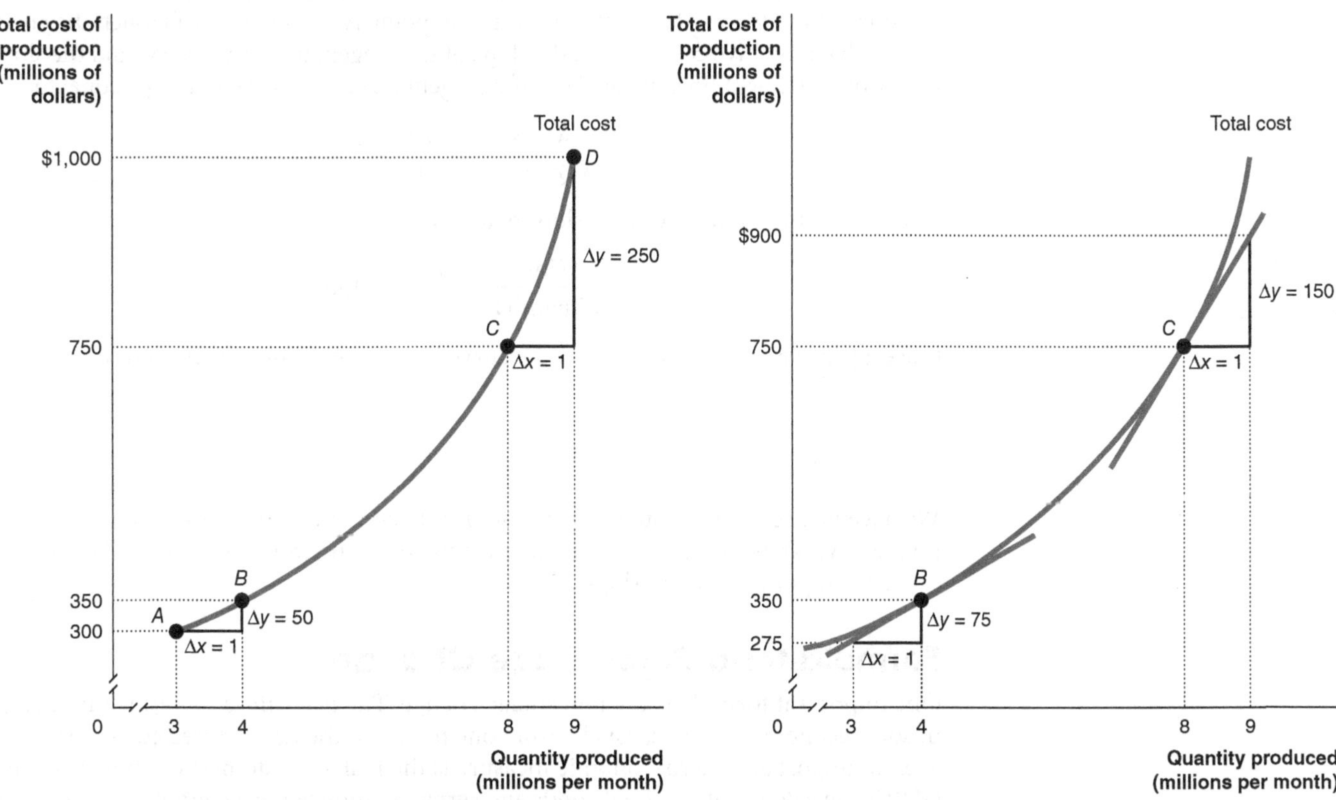

Figure 1A.8 **The Slope of a Nonlinear Curve**

The relationship between the quantity of iPhones produced and the total cost of production is curved rather than linear. In panel (a), in moving from point *A* to point *B*, the quantity produced increases by 1 million iPhones, while the total cost of production increases by $50 million. Farther up the curve, as we move from point *C* to point *D*, the change in quantity is the same—1 million iPhones—but the change in the total cost of production is now much larger: $250 million. Because the change in the *y* variable has increased, while the change in the *x* variable has remained the same, we know that the slope has increased. In panel (b), we measure the slope of the curve at a particular point by the slope of the tangent line. The slope of the tangent line at point *B* is 75, and the slope of the tangent line at point *C* is 150.

significantly affected. In addition, it is easier to calculate the slope of a straight line, and it also is easier to calculate the area under a straight line. So, in this textbook, we often assume that the relationship between two economic variables is linear, even when we know that this assumption is not precisely correct.

Slopes of Nonlinear Curves

In some situations, we need to take into account the nonlinear nature of an economic relationship. For example, panel (a) of Figure 1A.8 shows the hypothetical relationship between Apple's total cost of producing iPhones and the quantity of iPhones produced. The relationship is curved rather than linear. In this case, the cost of production is increasing at an increasing rate, which often happens in manufacturing. Put a different way, as we move up the curve, its slope becomes larger. (Remember that with a straight line, the slope is always constant.) To see this effect, first remember that we calculate the slope of a curve by dividing the change in the variable on the *y*-axis by the change in the variable on the *x*-axis. As we move from point *A* to point *B*, the quantity produced increases by 1 million iPhones, while the total cost of production increases by $50 million. Farther up the curve, as we move from point *C* to point *D*, the change in quantity is the same—1 million iPhones—but the change in the total cost of production is now much larger: $250 million. Because the change in the *y* variable has increased, while the change in the *x* variable has remained the same, we know that the slope has increased.

To measure the slope of a nonlinear curve at a particular point, we must measure the slope of the *tangent line* to the curve at that point. A tangent line will touch the curve only at that point. We can measure the slope of the tangent line just as we would the slope of any other straight line. In panel (b), the tangent line at point *B* has a slope equal to:

$$\frac{\Delta\text{Cost}}{\Delta\text{Quantity}} = \frac{75}{1} = 75.$$

The tangent line at point *C* has a slope equal to:

$$\frac{\Delta\text{Cost}}{\Delta\text{Quantity}} = \frac{150}{1} = 150.$$

Once again, we see that the slope of the curve is larger at point *C* than at point *B*.

Formulas

We have just seen that graphs are an important economic tool. In this section, we will review several useful formulas and show how to use them to summarize data and to calculate important relationships.

Formula for a Percentage Change

One important formula is the percentage change. The *percentage change* is the change in some economic variable, usually from one period to the next, expressed as a percentage. An important macroeconomic measure is the real gross domestic product (GDP). GDP is the value of all the final goods and services produced in a country during a year. "Real" GDP is corrected for the effects of inflation. When economists say that the U.S. economy grew 3.0 percent during 2010, they mean that real GDP was 3.0 percent higher in 2010 than it was in 2009. The formula for making this calculation is:

$$\frac{\text{GDP}_{2010} - \text{GDP}_{2009}}{\text{GDP}_{2009}} \times 100$$

or, more generally, for any two periods:

$$\text{Percentage change} = \frac{\text{Value in the second period} - \text{Value in the first period}}{\text{Value in the first period}} \times 100.$$

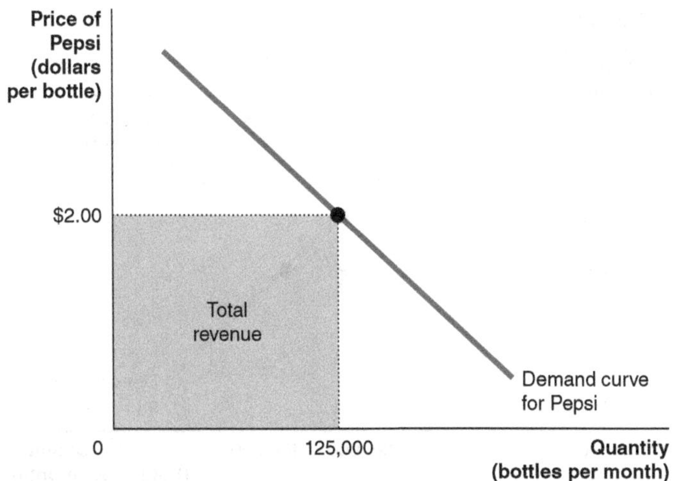

Figure 1A.9

Showing a Firm's Total Revenue on a Graph

The area of a rectangle is equal to its base multiplied by its height. Total revenue is equal to quantity multiplied by price. Here, total revenue is equal to the quantity of 125,000 bottles times the price of $2.00 per bottle, or $250,000. The area of the green-shaded rectangle shows the firm's total revenue.

In this case, real GDP was $12,703 billion in 2009 and $13,088 billion in 2010. So, the growth rate of the U.S. economy during 2010 was:

$$\left(\frac{\$13{,}088 - \$12{,}703}{\$12{,}703}\right) \times 100 = 2.8\%.$$

Notice that it doesn't matter that in using the formula, we ignored the fact that GDP is measured in billions of dollars. In fact, when calculating percentage changes, *the units don't matter*. The percentage increase from $12,703 billion to $13,088 billion is exactly the same as the percentage increase from $12,073 to $13,088.

Formulas for the Areas of a Rectangle and a Triangle

Areas that form rectangles and triangles on graphs can have important economic meaning. For example, Figure 1A.9 shows the demand curve for Pepsi. Suppose that the price is currently $2.00 and that 125,000 bottles of Pepsi are sold at that price. A firm's *total revenue* is equal to the amount it receives from selling its product, or the quantity sold multiplied by the price. In this case, total revenue will equal 125,000 bottles times $2.00 per bottle, or $250,000.

The formula for the area of a rectangle is:

$$\text{Area of a rectangle} = \text{Base} \times \text{Height}.$$

In Figure 1A.9, the green-shaded rectangle also represents the firm's total revenue because its area is given by the base of 125,000 bottles multiplied by the price of $2.00 per bottle.

We will see in later chapters that areas that are triangles can also have economic significance. The formula for the area of a triangle is:

$$\text{Area of a triangle} = \frac{1}{2} \times \text{Base} \times \text{Height}.$$

The blue-shaded area in Figure 1A.10 is a triangle. The base equals 150,000 − 125,000, or 25,000. Its height equals $2.00 − $1.50, or $0.50. Therefore, its area equals 1/2 × 25,000 × $0.50, or $6,250. Notice that the blue area is a triangle only if the demand curve is a straight line, or linear. Not all demand curves are linear. However, the formula for the area of a triangle will usually still give a good approximation, even if the demand curve is not linear.

Summary of Using Formulas

You will encounter several other formulas in this book. Whenever you must use a formula, you should follow these steps:

1. Make sure you understand the economic concept the formula represents.

Figure 1A.10

The Area of a Triangle

The area of a triangle is equal to 1/2 multiplied by its base multiplied by its height. The area of the blue-shaded triangle has a base equal to 150,000 − 125,000, or 25,000, and a height equal to \$2.00 − \$1.50, or \$0.50. Therefore, its area equals 1/2 × 25,000 × \$0.50, or \$6,250.

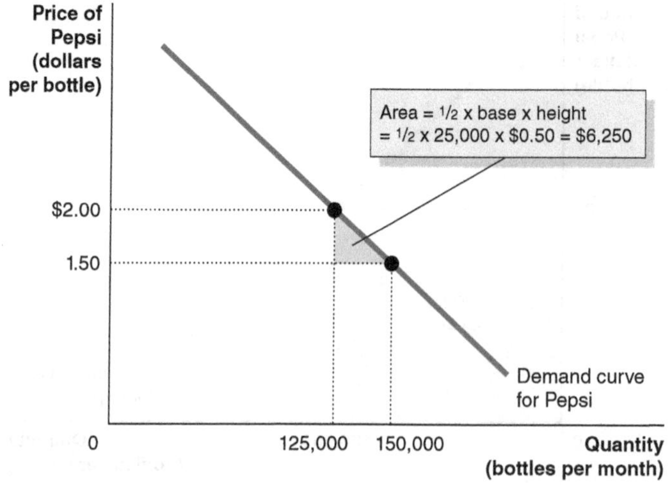

2. Make sure you are using the correct formula for the problem you are solving.
3. Make sure the number you calculate using the formula is economically reasonable. For example, if you are using a formula to calculate a firm's revenue and your answer is a negative number, you know you made a mistake somewhere.

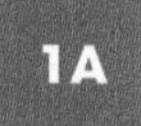

1A Using Graphs and Formulas, pages 22–32

LEARNING OBJECTIVE: Review the use of graphs and formulas.

MyEconLab Visit www.myeconlab.com to complete these exercises online and get instant feedback.

Problems and Applications

1A.1 The following table shows the relationship between the price of custard pies and the number of pies Jacob buys per week:

Price	Quantity of Pies	Week
\$3.00	6	July 2
2.00	7	July 9
5.00	4	July 16
6.00	3	July 23
1.00	8	July 30
4.00	5	August 6

a. Is the relationship between the price of pies and the number of pies Jacob buys a positive relationship or a negative relationship?
b. Plot the data from the table on a graph similar to Figure 1A.3 on page 25. Draw a straight line that best fits the points.
c. Calculate the slope of the line.

1A.2 The following table gives information on the quantity of glasses of lemonade demanded on sunny and overcast days:

Price (dollars per glass)	Quantity (glasses of lemonade per day)	Weather
\$0.80	30	Sunny
0.80	10	Overcast
0.70	40	Sunny
0.70	20	Overcast
0.60	50	Sunny
0.60	30	Overcast
0.50	60	Sunny
0.50	40	Overcast

Plot the data from the table on a graph similar to Figure 1A.5 on page 27. Draw two straight lines representing the two demand curves—one for sunny days and one for overcast days.

1A.3 Using the information in Figure 1A.2 on page 24, calculate the percentage change in auto sales from one year to the next. Between which years did sales fall at the fastest rate?

1A.4 Real GDP in 2008 was \$13,162 billion. Real GDP in 2009 was \$12,703 billion. What was the percentage change in real GDP from 2008 to 2009? What do economists call the percentage change in real GDP from one year to the next?

1A.5 Assume that the demand curve for Pepsi passes through the following two points:

Price per Bottle of Pepsi	Number of Bottles Demanded
$2.50	100,000
1.25	200,000

a. Draw a graph with a linear demand curve that passes through these two points.
b. Show on the graph the areas representing total revenue at each price. Give the value for total revenue at each price.

1A.6 What is the area of the blue triangle shown in the following figure?

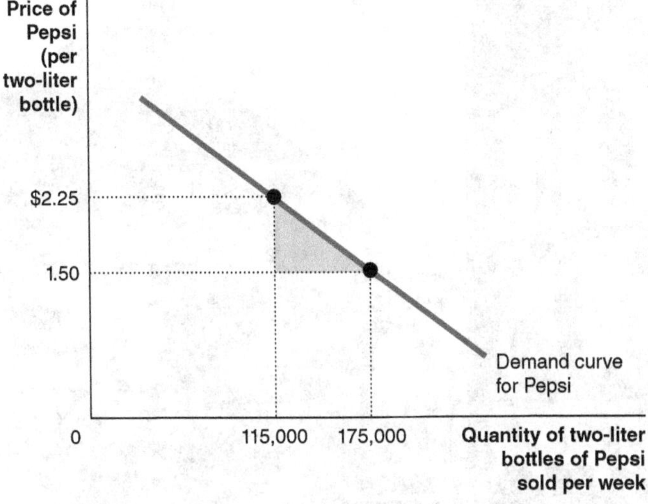

1A.7 Calculate the slope of the total cost curve at point *A* and at point *B* in the following figure.

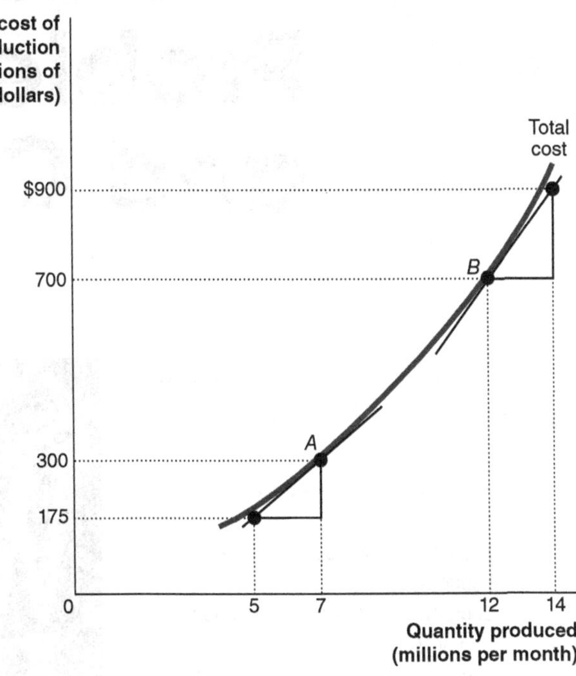

CHAPTER 2

The Economic Problem: Scarcity and Choice

Chapter Outline and Learning Objectives

Every society, no matter how small or large, no matter how simple or complex, has a system or process that works to transform the resources that nature and previous generations provide into useful form. Economics is the study of that process and its outcomes.

Figure 2.1 illustrates three basic questions that must be answered to understand the functioning of the economic system:

- What gets produced?
- How is it produced?
- Who gets what is produced?

This chapter explores these questions in detail. In a sense, this entire chapter *is* the definition of economics. It lays out the central problems addressed by the discipline and presents a framework that will guide you through the rest of the book. The starting point is the presumption that *human wants are unlimited but resources are not.* Limited or scarce resources force individuals and societies to choose among competing uses of resources—alternative combinations of produced goods and services—and among alternative final distributions of what is produced among households.

These questions are *positive* or *descriptive*. That is, they ask how the system functions without passing judgment about whether the result is good or bad. They must be answered first before we ask more normative questions such as these:

- Is the outcome good or bad?
- Can it be improved?

The term *resources* is very broad. The sketch on the left side of Figure 2.1 shows several categories of resources. Some resources are the products of nature: land, wildlife, fertile soil, minerals, timber, energy, and even the rain and wind. In addition, the resources available to an economy include things such as buildings and equipment that have been produced in the past but are now being used to produce other things. And perhaps the most important resource of a society is its human workforce with people's talents, skills, and knowledge.

Things that are produced and then used in the production of other goods and services are called capital resources, or simply **capital**. Buildings, equipment, desks, chairs, software, roads, bridges, and highways are a part of the nation's stock of capital.

Capital Things that are produced and then used in the production of other goods and services.

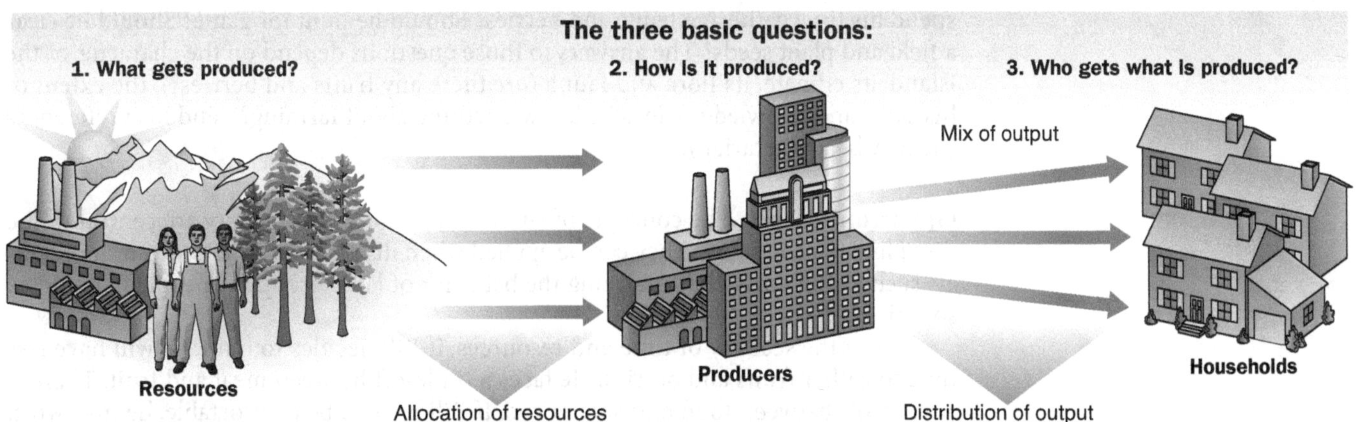

Figure 2.1 The Three Basic Questions

Every society has some system or process that transforms its scarce resources into useful goods and services. In doing so, it must decide what gets produced, how it is produced, and to whom it is distributed. The primary resources that must be allocated are land, labor, and capital.

Factors of production (*or* factors) The inputs into the process of production. Another term for resources.

Production The process that transforms scarce resources into useful goods and services.

Inputs *or* resources Anything provided by nature or previous generations that can be used directly or indirectly to satisfy human wants.

Outputs Goods and services of value to households.

The basic resources available to a society are often referred to as **factors of production**, or simply **factors**. The three key factors of production are land, labor, and capital. The process that transforms scarce resources into useful goods and services is called **production**. In many societies, most of the production of goods and services is done by private firms. Private airlines in the United States use land (runways), labor (pilots and mechanics), and capital (airplanes) to produce transportation services. But in all societies, some production is done by the public sector, or government. Examples of government-produced or government-provided goods and services include national defense, public education, police protection, and fire protection.

Resources or factors of production are the **inputs** into the process of production; goods and services of value to households are the **outputs** of the process of production.

2.1 LEARNING OBJECTIVE

Scarcity, Choice, and Opportunity Cost

In the second half of this chapter we discuss the global economic landscape. Before you can understand the different types of economic systems, it is important to master the basic economic concepts of scarcity, choice, and opportunity cost.

Scarcity and Choice in a One-Person Economy

The simplest economy is one in which a single person lives alone on an island. Consider Bill, the survivor of a plane crash, who finds himself cast ashore in such a place. Here individual and society are one; there is no distinction between social and private. *Nonetheless, nearly all the same basic decisions that characterize complex economies must also be made in a simple economy.* That is, although Bill will get whatever he produces, he still must decide how to allocate the island's resources, what to produce, and how and when to produce it.

First, Bill must decide *what* he wants to produce. Notice that the word *needs* does not appear here. Needs are absolute requirements; but beyond just enough water, basic nutrition, and shelter to survive, needs are very difficult to define. What is an "absolute necessity" for one person may not be for another person. In any case, Bill must put his wants in some order of priority and make some choices.

Next, he must look at the *possibilities*. What can he do to satisfy his wants given the limits of the island? In every society, no matter how simple or complex, people are constrained in what they can do. In this society of one, Bill is constrained by time, his physical condition, his knowledge, his skills, and the resources and climate of the island.

Given that resources are limited, Bill must decide *how* to best use them to satisfy his hierarchy of wants. Food would probably come close to the top of his list. Should he spend his time gathering fruits and berries? Should he hunt for game? Should he clear a field and plant seeds? The answers to those questions depend on the character of the island, its climate, its flora and fauna (*are* there any fruits and berries?), the extent of his skills and knowledge (does he know anything about farming?), and his preferences (he may be a vegetarian).

Opportunity Cost The concepts of *constrained choice* and *scarcity* are central to the discipline of economics. They can be applied when discussing the behavior of individuals such as Bill and when analyzing the behavior of large groups of people in complex societies.

Given the scarcity of time and resources, if Bill decides to hunt, he will have less time to gather fruits and berries. He faces a trade-off between meat and fruit. There is a trade-off between food and shelter too. If Bill likes to be comfortable, he may work on building a nice place to live, but that may require giving up the food he might have produced. The best alternative that we give up, or forgo, when we make a choice is the **opportunity cost** of that choice.

Opportunity cost The best alternative that we give up, or forgo, when we make a choice or decision.

Bill may occasionally decide to rest, to lie on the beach, and to enjoy the sun. In one sense, that benefit is free—he does not have to buy a ticket to lie on the beach. In reality, however, relaxing does have an opportunity cost. The true cost of that leisure is the value of the other things Bill could have produced, but did not, during the time he spent on the beach.

During 2010, more than a dozen cities, including Minneapolis, Los Angeles, and Houston, were actively considering public funding for new football, soccer, and basketball arenas. An important part of that debate was the opportunity cost of the taxpayers' dollars: What else could tax dollars be spent on, and how much value would the alternatives bring to the local taxpayers? Perhaps without the new arena, taxes could be lower. Here the opportunity cost would include the value taxpayers receive from goods and services they would consume with the earnings that are no longer taxed. Most discussions of public expenditures at all levels of government include active considerations of opportunity costs.

In making everyday decisions, it is often helpful to think about opportunity costs. Should you go to the dorm party or not? First, it costs $4 to attend. When you pay money for anything, you give up the other things you could have bought with that money. Second, it costs 2 or 3 hours. Time is a valuable commodity for a college student. You have exams next week, and you need to study. You could go to a movie instead of the party. You could go to another party. You could sleep. Just as Bill must weigh the value of sunning on the beach against more food or better housing, so you must weigh the value of the fun you may have at the party against everything else you might otherwise do with the time and money.

Scarcity and Choice in an Economy of Two or More

Now suppose that another survivor of the crash, Colleen, appears on the island. Now that Bill is not alone, things are more complex and some new decisions must be made. Bill's and Colleen's preferences about what things to produce are likely to be different. They will probably not have the same knowledge or skills. Perhaps Colleen is very good at tracking animals and Bill has a knack for building things. How should they split the work that needs to be done? Once things are produced, the two castaways must decide how to divide them. How should their products be distributed?

The mechanism for answering these fundamental questions is clear when Bill is alone on the island. The "central plan" is his; he simply decides what he wants and what to do about it. The minute someone else appears, however, a number of decision-making arrangements immediately become possible. One or the other may take charge, in which case that person will decide for both of them. The two may agree to cooperate, with each having an equal say, and come up with a joint plan; or they may agree to split the planning as well as the production duties. Finally, they may go off to live alone at opposite ends of the island. Even if they live apart, however, they may take advantage of each other's presence by specializing and trading.

Modern industrial societies must answer the same questions that Colleen and Bill must answer, but the mechanics of larger economies are more complex. Instead of two people living together, the United States has over 300 million people. Still, decisions must be made about what to produce, how to produce it, and who gets it.

Economics in Practice

Frozen Foods and Opportunity Costs

In 2007, $27 billion of frozen foods were sold in U.S. grocery stores, one quarter of it in the form of frozen dinners and entrees. In the mid-1950s, sales of frozen foods amounted to only $1 billion, a tiny fraction of the overall grocery store sales. One industry observer attributes this growth to the fact that frozen food tastes much better than it did in the past. Can you think of anything else that might be occurring?

The growth of the frozen dinner entrée market in the last 50 years is a good example of the role of opportunity costs in our lives. One of the most significant social changes in the U.S. economy

in this period has been the increased participation of women in the labor force. In 1950, only 24 percent of married women worked; by 2000, that fraction had risen to 61 percent. Producing a meal takes two basic ingredients: food and time. When both husbands and wives work, the opportunity cost of time for housework—including making meals—goes up. This tells us that making a home-cooked meal became more expensive in the last 50 years. A natural result is to shift people toward labor-saving ways to make meals. Frozen foods are an obvious solution to the problem of increased opportunity costs.

Another, somewhat more subtle, opportunity cost story is at work encouraging the consumption of frozen foods. In 1960, the first microwave oven was introduced. The spread of this device into America's kitchens was rapid. The microwave turned out to be a quick way to defrost and cook those frozen entrées. So this technology lowered the opportunity cost of making frozen dinners, reinforcing the advantage these meals had over home-cooked meals. Microwaves made cooking with frozen foods cheaper once opportunity cost was considered while home-cooked meals were becoming more expensive.

The entrepreneurs among you also might recognize that the rise we described in the opportunity cost of the home-cooked meal *contributed* in part to the spread of the microwave, creating a reinforcing cycle. In fact, many entrepreneurs find that the simple tools of economics—like the idea of opportunity costs—help them anticipate what products will be profitable for them to produce in the future. The growth of the two-worker family has stimulated many entrepreneurs to search for labor-saving solutions to family tasks.

The public policy students among you might be interested to know that some researchers attribute part of the growth in obesity in the United States to the lower opportunity costs of making meals associated with the growth of the markets for frozen foods and the microwave. (See David M.Cutler, Edward L. Glaeser, and Jesse M. Shapiro, "Why Have Americans Become More Obese?" *Journal of Economic Perspectives*, Summer 2003, 93–118.)

Specialization, Exchange, and Comparative Advantage The idea that members of society benefit by specializing in what they do best has a long history and is one of the most important and powerful ideas in all of economics. David Ricardo, a major nineteenth-century British economist, formalized the point precisely. According to Ricardo's **theory of comparative advantage**, specialization and free trade will benefit all trading parties, even when some are "absolutely" more efficient producers than others. Ricardo's basic point applies just as much to Colleen and Bill as it does to different nations.

Theory of comparative advantage Ricardo's theory that specialization and free trade will benefit all trading parties, even those that may be "absolutely" more efficient producers.

To keep things simple, suppose that Colleen and Bill have only two tasks to accomplish each week: gathering food to eat and cutting logs to burn. If Colleen could cut more logs than Bill in 1 day and Bill could gather more nuts and berries than Colleen could, specialization would clearly lead to more total production. Both would benefit if Colleen only cuts logs and Bill only gathers nuts and berries, as long as they can trade.

Suppose that Bill is slow and somewhat clumsy in his nut gathering and that Colleen is better at cutting logs *and* gathering food. At first, it might seem that since Colleen is better at everything, she should do everything. But that cannot be right. Colleen's time is limited after all, and even though Bill is clumsy and not very clever, he must be able to contribute something.

One of Ricardo's lasting contributions to economics has been his analysis of exactly this situation. His analysis, which is illustrated in Figure 2.2, shows both how Colleen and Bill should divide the work of the island and how much they will gain from specializing and exchanging even if, as in this example, one party is absolutely better at everything than the other party.

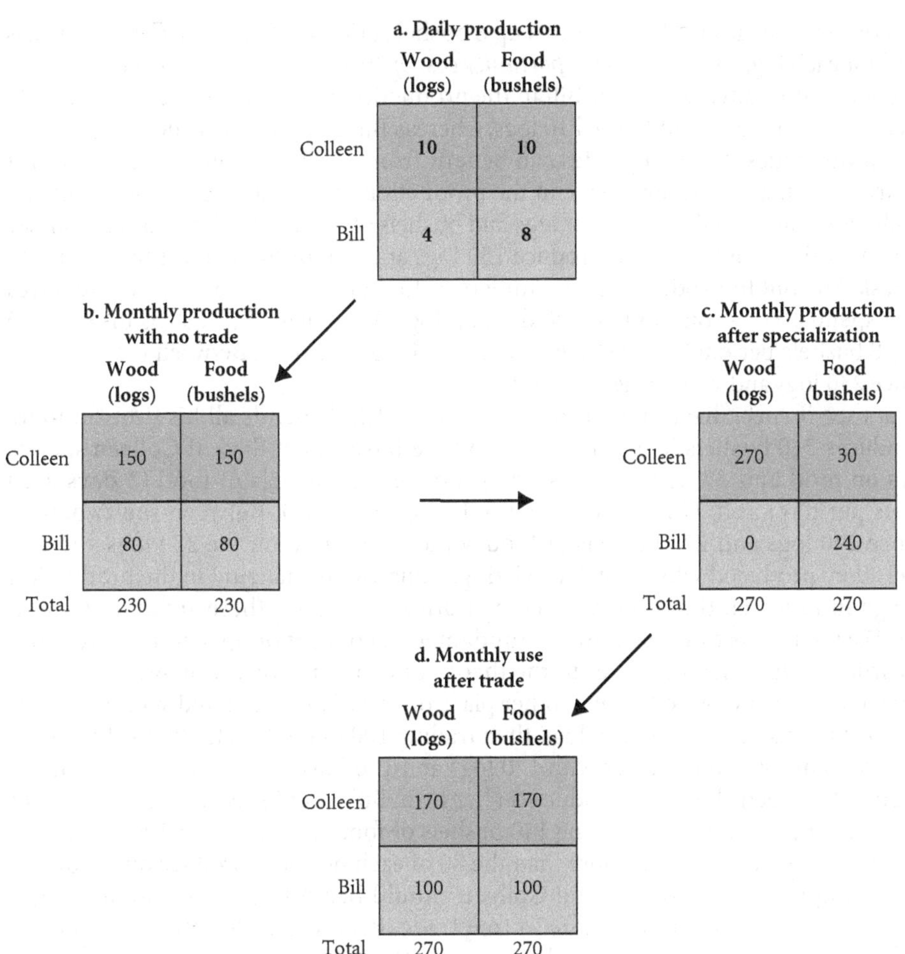

Figure 2.2

Comparative Advantage and the Gains from Trade

In this figure, (a) shows the number of logs and bushels of food that Colleen and Bill can produce for every day spent at the task and (b) shows how much output they could produce in a month, assuming they wanted an equal number of logs and bushels. Colleen would split her time 50/50, devoting 15 days to each task and achieving total output of 150 logs and 150 bushels of food. Bill would spend 20 days cutting wood and 10 days gathering food. As shown in (c) and (d), by specializing and trading, both Colleen and Bill will be better off. Going from (c) to (d), Colleen trades 100 logs to Bill in exchange for 140 bushels of food.

Suppose Colleen can cut 10 logs per day and Bill can cut only 4. Also suppose Colleen can gather 10 bushels of food per day and Bill can gather only 8. A producer has an **absolute advantage** over another in the production of a good or service if he or she can produce the good or service using fewer resources, including time. Since Colleen can cut more logs per day than Bill, we say that she has an absolute advantage in the production of logs. Similarly, Colleen has an absolute advantage over Bill in the production of food.

Absolute advantage A producer has an absolute advantage over another in the production of a good or service if he or she can produce that product using fewer resources.

Thinking just about productivity and the output of food and logs, you might conclude that it would benefit Colleen to move to the other side of the island and be by herself. Since she is more productive in cutting logs and gathering food, would she not be better off on her own? How could she benefit by hanging out with Bill and sharing what they produce?

To answer that question we must remember that Colleen's time is limited: This limit creates opportunity cost. A producer has a **comparative advantage** over another in the production of a good or service if he or she can produce the good or service at a lower opportunity cost. First, think about Bill. He can produce 8 bushels of food per day, or he can cut 4 logs. To get 8 additional bushels of food, he must give up cutting 4 logs. Thus, *for Bill, the opportunity cost of 8 bushels of food is 4 logs.* Think next about Colleen. She can produce 10 bushels of food per day, or she can cut 10 logs. She thus gives up 1 log for each additional bushel; so *for Colleen, the opportunity cost of 8 bushels of food is 8 logs.* Bill has a comparative advantage over Colleen in the production of food because he gives up only 4 logs for an additional 8 bushels, whereas Colleen gives up 8 logs.

Comparative advantage A producer has a comparative advantage over another in the production of a good or service if he or she can produce that product at a lower *opportunity cost.*

Think now about what Colleen must give up in terms of food to get 10 logs. To produce 10 logs she must work a whole day. If she spends a day cutting 10 logs, she gives up a day of gathering 10 bushels of food. Thus, *for Colleen, the opportunity cost of 10 logs is 10 bushels of food.* What must Bill give up to get 10 logs? To produce 4 logs, he must work

1 day. For each day he cuts logs, he gives up 8 bushels of food. He thus gives up 2 bushels of food for each log; so *for Bill, the opportunity cost of 10 logs is 20 bushels of food.* Colleen has a comparative advantage over Bill in the production of logs since she gives up only 10 bushels of food for an additional 10 logs, whereas Bill gives up 20 bushels.

Ricardo argues that two parties can benefit from specialization and trade even if one party has an absolute advantage in the production of both goods. Suppose Colleen and Bill both want equal numbers of logs and bushels of food. If Colleen goes off on her own, in a 30-day month she can produce 150 logs and 150 bushels, devoting 15 days to each task. For Bill to produce equal numbers of logs and bushels on his own requires that he spend 10 days on food and 20 days on logs. This yields 80 bushels of food (10 days × 8 bushels per day) and 80 logs (20 days × 4 logs per day). Between the two, they produce 230 logs and 230 bushels of food.

Let's see if specialization and trade can work. If Bill spends all his time on food, he produces 240 bushels in a month (30 days × 8 bushels per day). If Colleen spends 3 days on food and 27 days on logs, she produces 30 bushels of food (3 days × 10 bushels per day) and 270 logs (27 days × 10 logs per day). Between the two, they produce 270 logs and 270 bushels of food, which is more than the 230 logs and 230 bushels they produced when not specializing. Thus, by specializing in the production of the good in which they enjoyed a comparative advantage, there are more of both goods. We see in this example how the fundamental concept of opportunity cost covered earlier in this chapter relates to the theory of comparative advantage.

Even if Colleen were to live at another place on the island, she could specialize, producing 30 bushels of food and 270 logs, then trading 100 of her logs to Bill for 140 bushels of food. This would leave her with 170 logs and 170 bushels of food, which is more than the 150 of each she could produce on her own. Bill would specialize completely in food, producing 240 bushels. Trading 140 bushels of food to Colleen for 100 logs leaves him with 100 of each, which is more than the 80 of each he could produce on his own.

The simple example of Bill and Colleen should begin to give you some insight into why most economists see value in free trade. Even if one country is absolutely better than another country at producing everything, our example has shown that there are gains to specializing and trading.

A Graphical Presentation of Comparative Advantage and Gains from Trade Graphs can also be used to show the benefits from specialization and trade in the example of Colleen and Bill. To construct a graph reflecting Colleen's production choices (Figure 2.3 [a]), we

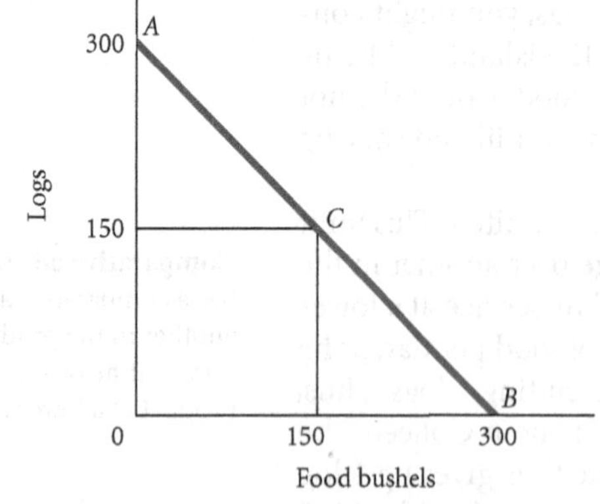

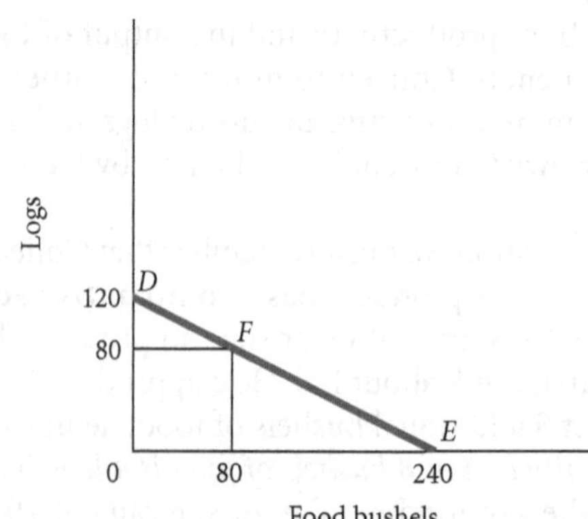

Figure 2.3 **Production Possibilities with No Trade**

The figure in (a) shows all of the combinations of logs and bushels of food that Colleen can produce by herself. If she spends all 30 days each month on logs, she produces 300 logs and no food (point *A*). If she spends all 30 days on food, she produces 300 bushels of food and no logs (point *B*). If she spends 15 days on logs and 15 days on food, she produces 150 of each (point *C*).

The figure in (b) shows all of the combinations of logs and bushels of food that Bill can produce by himself. If he spends all 30 days each month on logs, he produces 120 logs and no food (point *D*). If he spends all 30 days on food, he produces 240 bushels of food and no logs (point *E*). If he spends 20 days on logs and 10 days on food, he produces 80 of each (point *F*).

start with the end points. If she were to devote an entire month (30 days) to log production, she could cut 300 logs—10 logs per day × 30 days. Similarly, if she were to devote an entire month to food gathering, she could produce 300 bushels. If she chose to split her time evenly (15 days to logs and 15 days to food), she would have 150 bushels and 150 logs. Her production possibilities are illustrated by the straight line between *A* and *B* and illustrate the trade-off that she faces between logs and food: By reducing her time spent in food gathering, Colleen is able to devote more time to logs; and for every 10 bushels of food that she gives up, she gets 10 logs.

In Figure 2.3(b), we construct a graph of Bill's production possibilities. Recall that Bill can produce 8 bushels of food per day, but he can cut only 4 logs. Again, starting with the end points, if Bill devoted all his time to food production, he could produce 240 bushels—8 bushels of food per day × 30 days. Similarly, if he were to devote the entire 30 days to log cutting, he could cut 120 logs—4 logs per day × 30 days. By splitting his time, with 20 days spent on log cutting and 10 days spent gathering food, Bill could produce 80 logs and 80 bushels of food. His production possibilities are illustrated by the straight line between *D* and *E*. By shifting his resources and time from logs to food, he gets 2 bushels for every log.

Figures 2.3(a) and 2.3(b) illustrate the maximum amounts of food and logs that Bill and Colleen can produce acting independently with no specialization or trade, which is 230 logs and 230 bushels. Now let us have each specialize in producing the good in which he or she has a comparative advantage. Back in Figure 2.2 on p. 39, we showed that if Bill devoted all his time to food production, producing 240 bushels (30 days × 8 bushels per day), and Colleen devoted the vast majority of her time to cutting logs (27 days) and just a few days to gathering food (3 days), their combined total would be 270 logs and 270 bushels of food. Colleen would produce 270 logs and 30 bushels of food to go with Bill's 240 bushels of food.

Finally, we arrange a trade, and the result is shown in Figures 2.4(a) and 2.4(b). Bill trades 140 bushels of food to Colleen for 100 logs, and he ends up with 100 logs and 100 bushels of food, 20 more of each than he would have had before the specialization and trade.

Colleen ends up with 170 logs and 170 bushels, again 20 more of each than she would have had before the specialization and trade. Both are better off. Both move beyond their individual production possibilities.

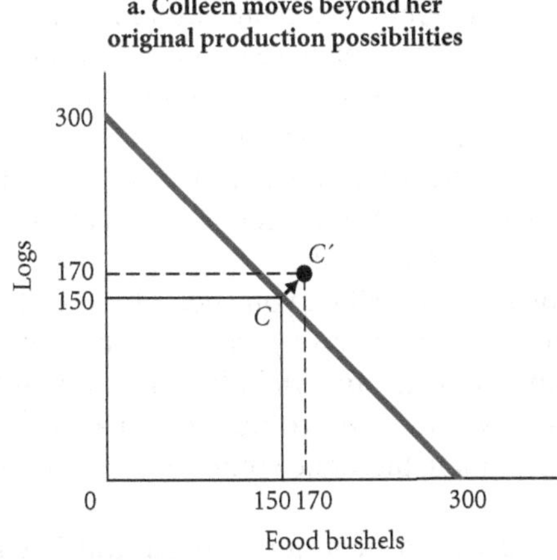

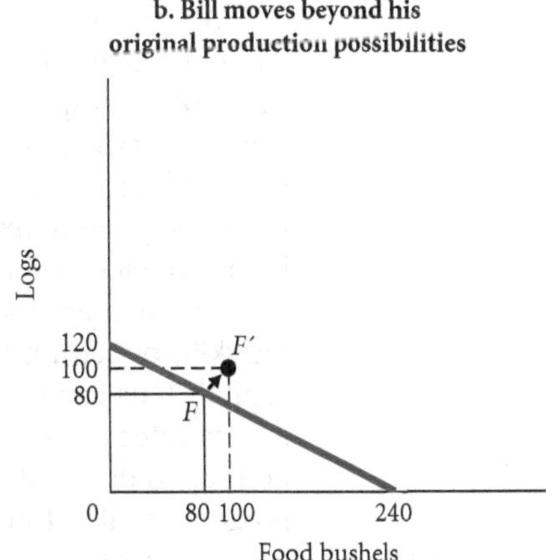

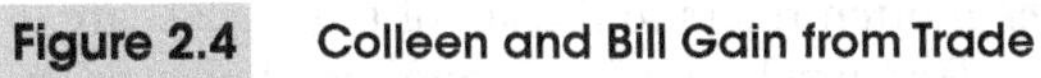
Figure 2.4 Colleen and Bill Gain from Trade

By specializing and engaging in trade, Colleen and Bill can move beyond their own production possibilities. If Bill spends all his time producing food, he will produce 240 bushels of food and no logs. If he can trade 140 of his bushels of food to Colleen for 100 logs, he will end up with 100 logs and 100 bushels of food. The figure in (b) shows that he can move from point *F* to point *F*′.

If Colleen spends 27 days cutting logs and 3 days producing food, she will produce 270 logs and 30 bushels of food. If she can trade 100 of her logs to Bill for 140 bushels of food, she will end up with 170 logs and 170 bushels of food. The figure in (a) shows that she can move from point *C* to point *C*′.

Weighing Present and Expected Future Costs and Benefits Very often we find ourselves weighing benefits available today against benefits available tomorrow. Here, too, the notion of opportunity cost is helpful.

While alone on the island, Bill had to choose between cultivating a field and just gathering wild nuts and berries. Gathering nuts and berries provides food now; gathering seeds and clearing a field for planting will yield food tomorrow if all goes well. Using today's time to farm may well be worth the effort if doing so will yield more food than Bill would otherwise have in the future. By planting, Bill is trading present value for future value.

The simplest example of trading present for future benefits is the act of saving. When you put income aside today for use in the future, you give up some things that you could have had today in exchange for something tomorrow. Because nothing is certain, some judgment about future events and expected values must be made. What will your income be in 10 years? How long are you likely to live?

We trade off present and future benefits in small ways all the time. If you decide to study instead of going to the dorm party, you are trading present fun for the expected future benefits of higher grades. If you decide to go outside on a very cold day and run 5 miles, you are trading discomfort in the present for being in better shape later.

Capital Goods and Consumer Goods A society trades present for expected future benefits when it devotes a portion of its resources to research and development or to investment in capital. As we said earlier in this chapter, *capital* in its broadest definition is anything that has already been produced that will be used to produce other valuable goods or services over time.

Building capital means trading present benefits for future ones. Bill and Colleen might trade gathering berries or lying in the sun for cutting logs to build a nicer house in the future. In a modern society, resources used to produce capital goods could have been used to produce **consumer goods**—that is, goods for present consumption. Heavy industrial machinery does not directly satisfy the wants of anyone, but producing it requires resources that could instead have gone into producing things that do satisfy wants directly—for example, food, clothing, toys, or golf clubs.

Consumer goods Goods produced for present consumption.

Capital is everywhere. A road is capital. Once a road is built, we can drive on it or transport goods and services over it for many years to come. A house is also capital. Before a new manufacturing firm can start up, it must put some capital in place. The buildings, equipment, and inventories that it uses comprise its capital. As it contributes to the production process, this capital yields valuable services over time.

We talked about the enormous amount of capital—buildings, factories, housing, cars, trucks, telephone lines, and so on—that you might see from a window high in a skyscraper. Much of that capital was put in place by previous generations, yet it continues to provide valuable services today; it is part of this generation's endowment of resources. To build every building, every road, every factory, every house, and every car or truck, society must forgo using resources to produce consumer goods today. To get an education, you pay tuition and put off joining the workforce for a while.

Capital does not need to be tangible. When you spend time and resources developing skills or getting an education, you are investing in human capital—your own human capital. This capital will continue to exist and yield benefits to you for years to come. A computer program produced by a software company and available online may cost nothing to distribute, but its true intangible value comes from the ideas embodied in the program itself. It too is capital.

Investment The process of using resources to produce new capital.

The process of using resources to produce new capital is called **investment**. (In everyday language, the term *investment* often refers to the act of buying a share of stock or a bond, as in "I invested in some Treasury bonds." In economics, however, investment *always* refers to the creation of capital: the purchase or putting in place of buildings, equipment, roads, houses, and the like.) A wise investment in capital is one that yields future benefits that are more valuable than the present cost. When you spend money for a house, for example, presumably you value its future benefits. That is, you expect to gain more from living in it than you would from the things you could buy today with the same money. Capital can also be intangible. Consider education that builds skills or knowledge in workers. Clearly education can yield decades of future "benefits" including higher wages. Because resources are scarce, the opportunity cost of every investment in capital is forgone present consumption.

The Production Possibility Frontier

A simple graphic device called the **production possibility frontier (ppf)** illustrates the principles of constrained choice, opportunity cost, and scarcity. The ppf is a graph that shows all the combinations of goods and services that can be produced if all of a society's resources are used efficiently. Figure 2.5 shows a ppf for a hypothetical economy.

Production possibility frontier (ppf) A graph that shows all the combinations of goods and services that can be produced if all of society's resources are used efficiently.

On the *Y*-axis, we measure the quantity of capital goods produced. On the *X*-axis, we measure the quantity of consumer goods. All points below and to the left of the curve (the shaded area) represent combinations of capital and consumer goods that are possible for the society given the resources available and existing technology. Points above and to the right of the curve, such as point *G*, represent combinations that cannot be reached. If an economy were to end up at point *A* on the graph, it would be producing no consumer goods at all; all resources would be used for the production of capital. If an economy were to end up at point *B*, it would be devoting all its resources to the production of consumer goods and none of its resources to the formation of capital.

While all economies produce some of each kind of good, different economies emphasize different things. About 17.1 percent of gross output in the United States in 2005 was new capital. In Japan, capital historically accounted for a much higher percent of gross output, while in the Congo, the figure was 7 percent. Japan is closer to point *A* on its ppf, the Congo is closer to *B*, and the United States is somewhere in between.

Points that are actually on the ppf are points of both full resource employment and production efficiency. Resources are not going unused, and there is no waste. Points that lie within the shaded area but that are not on the frontier represent either unemployment of resources or production inefficiency. An economy producing at point *D* in Figure 2.5 can produce more capital goods and more consumer goods, for example, by moving to point *E*. This is possible because resources are not fully employed at point *D* or are not being used efficiently.

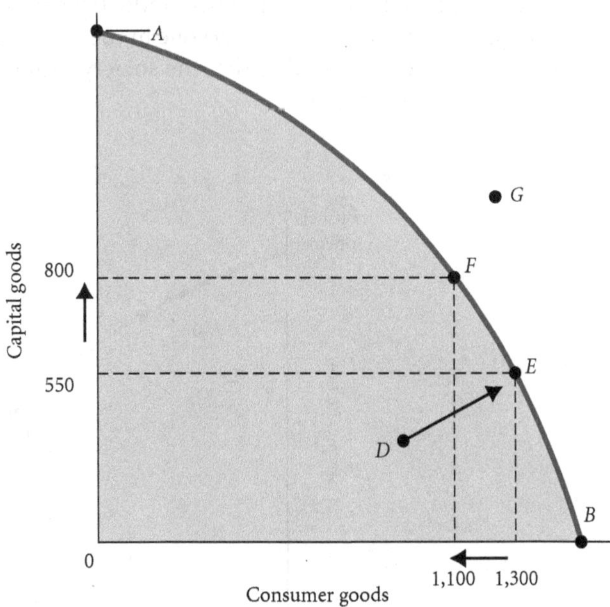

Figure 2.5 **Production Possibility Frontier**

The ppf illustrates a number of economic concepts. One of the most important is *opportunity cost*. The opportunity cost of producing more capital goods is fewer consumer goods. Moving from E to F, the number of capital goods increases from 550 to 800, but the number of consumer goods decreases from 1,300 to 1,100.

Unemployment During the Great Depression of the 1930s, the U.S. economy experienced prolonged unemployment. Millions of workers found themselves without jobs. In 1933, 25 percent of the civilian labor force was unemployed. This figure stayed above 14 percent until 1940. More recently, between the end of 2007 and 2010, the United States lost over 8 million payroll jobs and unemployment rose to over 15 million.

In addition to the hardship that falls on the unemployed, unemployment of labor means unemployment of capital. During economic downturns or recessions, industrial plants run at less than their total capacity. When there is unemployment of labor and capital, we are not producing all that we can.

Periods of unemployment correspond to points inside the ppf, points such as *D* in Figure 2.5. Moving onto the frontier from a point such as *D* means achieving full employment of resources.

Inefficiency Although an economy may be operating with full employment of its land, labor, and capital resources, it may still be operating inside its ppf (at a point such as *D* in Figure 2.5). It could be using those resources *inefficiently*.

Waste and mismanagement are the results of a firm operating below its potential. If you are the owner of a bakery and you forget to order flour, your workers and ovens stand idle while you figure out what to do.

Sometimes inefficiency results from mismanagement of the economy instead of mismanagement of individual private firms. Suppose, for example, that the land and climate in Ohio are best suited for corn production and that the land and climate in Kansas are best suited for wheat production. If Congress passes a law forcing Ohio farmers to plant 50 percent of their acreage with wheat and Kansas farmers to plant 50 percent with corn, neither corn nor wheat production will be up to potential. The economy will be at a point such as *A* in Figure 2.6—inside the ppf. Allowing each state to specialize in producing the crop that it produces best increases the production of both crops and moves the economy to a point such as *B* in Figure 2.6.

The Efficient Mix of Output To be efficient, an economy must produce what people want. This means that in addition to operating *on* the ppf, the economy must be operating at the *right point* on the ppf. This is referred to as *output efficiency*, in contrast to production efficiency. Suppose that an economy devotes 100 percent of its resources to beef production and that the beef industry runs efficiently using the most modern techniques. Also suppose that everyone in the society is a vegetarian. The result is a total waste of resources (assuming that the society cannot trade its beef for vegetables produced in another country).

Figure 2.6

Inefficiency from Misallocation of Land in Farming

Society can end up inside its ppf at a point such as *A* by using its resources inefficiently. If, for example, Ohio's climate and soil were best suited for corn production and those of Kansas were best suited for wheat production, a law forcing Kansas farmers to produce corn and Ohio farmers to produce wheat would result in less of both. In such a case, society might be at point *A* instead of point *B*.

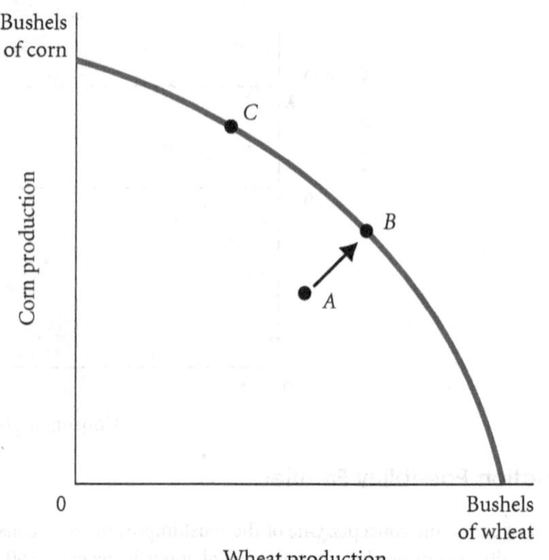

Points *B* and *C* in Figure 2.6 are points of production efficiency and full employment. Whether *B* is more or less efficient than *C*, however, depends on the preferences of members of society and is not shown in the ppf graph.

Negative Slope and Opportunity Cost As we have seen, points that lie on the ppf represent points of full resource employment and production efficiency. Society can choose only one point on the curve. Because a society's choices are constrained by available resources and existing technology, when those resources are fully and efficiently employed, it can produce more capital goods only by reducing production of consumer goods. The opportunity cost of the additional capital is the forgone production of consumer goods.

The fact that scarcity exists is illustrated by the negative slope of the ppf. In moving from point *E* to point *F* in Figure 2.5, capital production *increases* by 800–550 = 250 units (a positive change), but that increase in capital can be achieved only by shifting resources out of the production of consumer goods. Thus, in moving from point *E* to point *F* in Figure 2.5, consumer goods production *decreases* by 1,300–1,100 = 200 units (a negative change). The slope of the curve, the ratio of the change in capital goods to the change in consumer goods, is negative.

The value of the slope of a society's ppf is called the **marginal rate of transformation (MRT)**. In Figure 2.5, the MRT between points *E* and *F* is simply the ratio of the change in capital goods (a positive number) to the change in consumer goods (a negative number).

Marginal rate of transformation (MRT) The slope of the production possibility frontier (ppf).

The Law of Increasing Opportunity Cost The negative slope of the ppf indicates the trade-off that a society faces between two goods. We can learn something further about the shape of the frontier and the terms of this trade-off. Let's look at the trade-off between corn and wheat production in Ohio and Kansas. In a recent year, Ohio and Kansas together produced 510 million bushels of corn and 380 million bushels of wheat. Table 2.1 presents these two numbers, plus some hypothetical combinations of corn and wheat production that might exist for Ohio and Kansas together. Figure 2.7 graphs the data from Table 2.1.

Suppose that society's demand for corn dramatically increases. If this happens, farmers would probably shift some of their acreage from wheat production to corn production. Such a shift is represented by a move from point *C* (where corn = 510 and wheat = 380) up and to the left along the ppf toward points *A* and *B* in Figure 2.7. As this happens, it becomes more difficult to produce additional corn. The best land for corn production was presumably already in corn, and the best land for wheat production was already in wheat. As we try to produce more corn, the land is less well suited to that crop. As we take more land out of wheat production, we are taking increasingly better wheat-producing land. In other words, the opportunity cost of more corn, measured in terms of wheat, increases.

Moving from point *E* to *D*, Table 2.1 shows that we can get 100 million bushels of corn (400–300) by sacrificing only 50 million bushels of wheat (550–500)—that is, we get 2 bushels of corn for every bushel of wheat. However, when we are already stretching the ability of the land to produce corn, it becomes harder to produce more and the opportunity cost increases. Moving from point *B* to *A*, we can get only 50 million bushels of corn (700–650) by sacrificing 100 million bushels of wheat (200–100). For every

Table 2.1

Production Possibility Schedule for Total Corn and Wheat Production in Ohio and Kansas

Point on ppf	Total Corn Production (Millions of Bushels per Year)	Total Wheat Production (Millions of Bushels per Year)
A	700	100
B	650	200
C	510	380
D	400	500
E	300	550

Figure 2.7

Corn and Wheat Production in Ohio and Kansas

The ppf illustrates that the opportunity cost of corn production increases as we shift resources from wheat production to corn production. Moving from point *E* to *D*, we get an additional 100 million bushels of corn at a cost of 50 million bushels of wheat. Moving from point *B* to *A*, we get only 50 million bushels of corn at a cost of 100 million bushels of wheat. The *cost per bushel of corn*—measured in lost wheat—has increased.

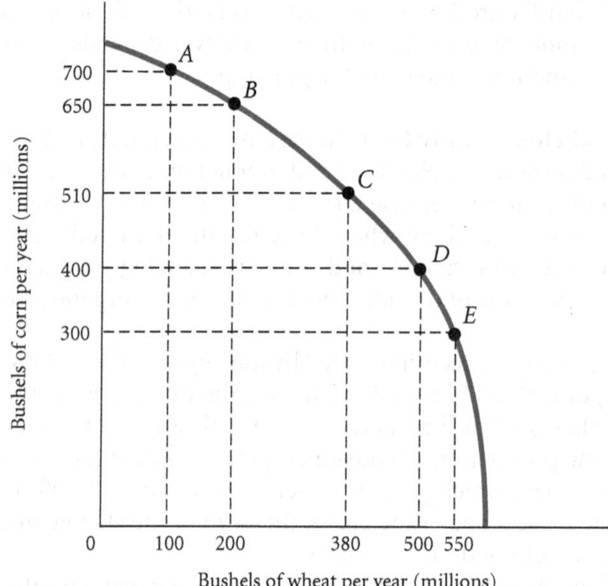

bushel of wheat, we now get only half a bushel of corn. However, if the demand for *wheat* were to increase substantially and we were to move down and to the right along the ppf, it would become increasingly difficult to produce wheat and the opportunity cost of wheat, in terms of corn, would increase. This is the *law of increasing opportunity cost.*

If you think about the example we discussed earlier of Colleen and Bill producing logs and food on an island, you will recognize that the production possibilities described were highly simplified. In that example, we drew a downward slope, *straight line ppf*; to make the problem easier, we assumed constant opportunity costs. In a real economy, ppf's would be expected to look like Figure 2.5.

Although it exists only as an abstraction, the ppf illustrates a number of very important concepts that we will use throughout the rest of this book: scarcity, unemployment, inefficiency, opportunity cost, the law of increasing opportunity cost, economic growth, and the gains from trade.

It is important to remember that the ppf represents choices available within the constraints imposed by the current state of agricultural technology. In the long run, technology may improve, and when that happens, we have *growth.*

Economic growth An increase in the total output of an economy. It occurs when a society acquires new resources or when it learns to produce more using existing resources.

Economic Growth **Economic growth** is characterized by an increase in the total output of an economy. It occurs when a society acquires new resources or learns to produce more with existing resources. New resources may mean a larger labor force or an increased capital stock. The production and use of new machinery and equipment (capital) increase workers' productivity. (Give a man a shovel, and he can dig a bigger hole; give him a steam shovel, and wow!) Improved productivity also comes from technological change and *innovation*, the discovery and application of new, more efficient production techniques.

In the past few decades, the productivity of U.S. agriculture has increased dramatically. Based on data compiled by the Department of Agriculture, Table 2.2 shows that yield per acre in corn production has increased fivefold since the late 1930s, while the labor required to produce it has dropped significantly. Productivity in wheat production has also increased, at only a slightly less remarkable rate: Output per acre has more than tripled, while labor requirements are down nearly 90 percent. These increases are the result of more efficient farming techniques, more and better capital (tractors, combines, and other equipment), and advances in scientific knowledge and technological change (hybrid seeds, fertilizers, and so on). As you can see in Figure 2.8, increases such as these shift the ppf up and to the right.

Table 2.2

Increasing Productivity in Corn and Wheat Production in the United States, 1935–2009

	Corn		Wheat	
	Yield per Acre (Bushels)	Labor Hours per 100 Bushels	Yield per Acre (Bushels)	Labor Hours per 100 Bushels
1935–1939	26.1	108	13.2	67
1945–1949	36.1	53	16.9	34
1955–1959	48.7	20	22.3	17
1965–1969	78.5	7	27.5	11
1975–1979	95.3	4	31.3	9
1981–1985	107.2	3	36.9	7
1985–1990	112.8	NA[a]	38.0	NA[a]
1990–1995	120.6	NA[a]	38.1	NA[a]
1998	134.4	NA[a]	43.2	NA[a]
2001	138.2	NA[a]	43.5	NA[a]
2006	145.6	NA[a]	42.3	NA[a]
2007	152.8	NA[a]	40.6	NA[a]
2008	153.9	NA[a]	44.9	NA[a]
2009	164.9	NA[a]	44.3	NA[a]

[a]Data not available.

SOURCE: U.S. Department of Agriculture, Economic Research Service, Agricultural Statistics, Crop Summary.

Sources of Growth and the Dilemma of Poor Countries Economic growth arises from many sources, the two most important over the years having been the accumulation of capital and technological advances. For poor countries, capital is essential; they must build the communication networks and transportation systems necessary to develop industries that function efficiently. They also need capital goods to develop their agricultural sectors.

Recall that capital goods are produced only at a sacrifice of consumer goods. The same can be said for technological advances. Technological advances come from research and development that use resources; thus, they too must be paid for. The resources used to produce capital goods—to build a road, a tractor, or a manufacturing plant—*and* to develop new technologies could have been used to produce consumer goods.

When a large part of a country's population is very poor, taking resources out of the production of consumer goods (such as food and clothing) is very difficult. In addition, in some countries, people wealthy enough to invest in domestic industries choose instead to invest abroad because of political turmoil at home. As a result, it often falls to the governments of poor countries to generate revenues for capital production and research out of tax collections.

All these factors have contributed to the growing gap between some poor and rich nations. Figure 2.9 shows the result using ppf's. On the left, the rich country devotes a larger portion of its production to capital while the poor country produces mostly consumer goods. On the right, you see the results: The ppf of the rich country shifts up and out farther and faster.

The importance of capital goods and technological developments to the position of workers in less developed countries is well illustrated by Robert Jensen's study of South India's industry. Conventional telephones require huge investments in wires and towers and, as a result, many less developed areas are without landlines. Mobile phones, on the other hand, require a less expensive investment; thus, in many areas, people upgraded from no phones directly to cell phones. Jensen found that in small fishing villages, the advent of cell phones allowed fishermen to determine on any given day where to take their catch to sell, resulting in a large decrease in fish wasted and an increase in fishing

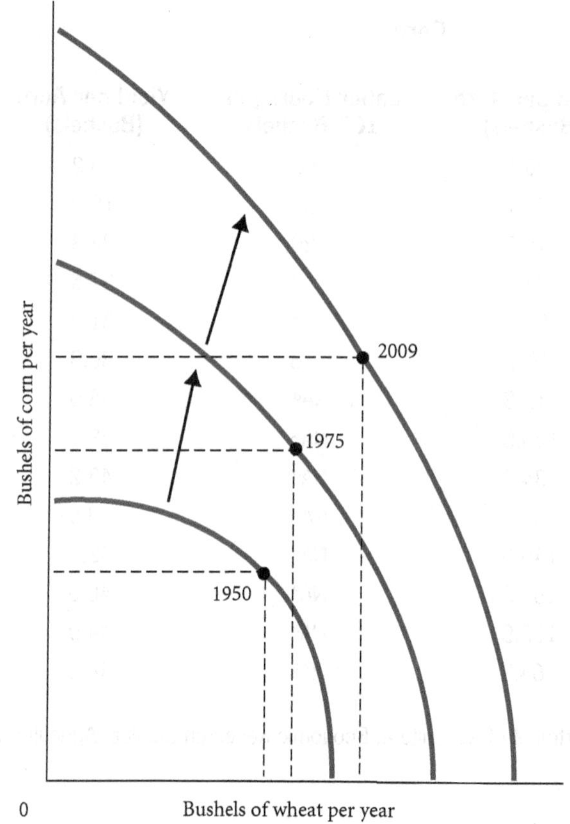

Figure 2.8

Economic Growth Shifts the PPF Up and to the Right

Productivity increases have enhanced the ability of the United States to produce both corn and wheat. As Table 2.2 shows, productivity increases were more dramatic for corn than for wheat. Thus, the shifts in the ppf were not parallel.

Note: The ppf also shifts if the amount of land or labor in corn and wheat production changes. Although we emphasize productivity increases here, the actual shifts between years were due in part to land and labor changes.

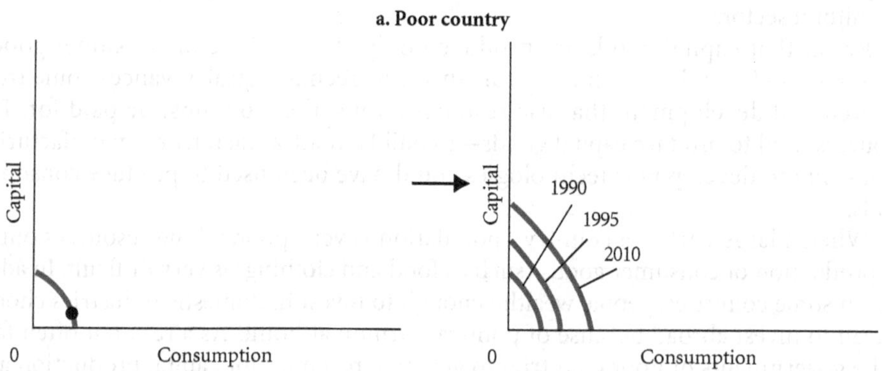

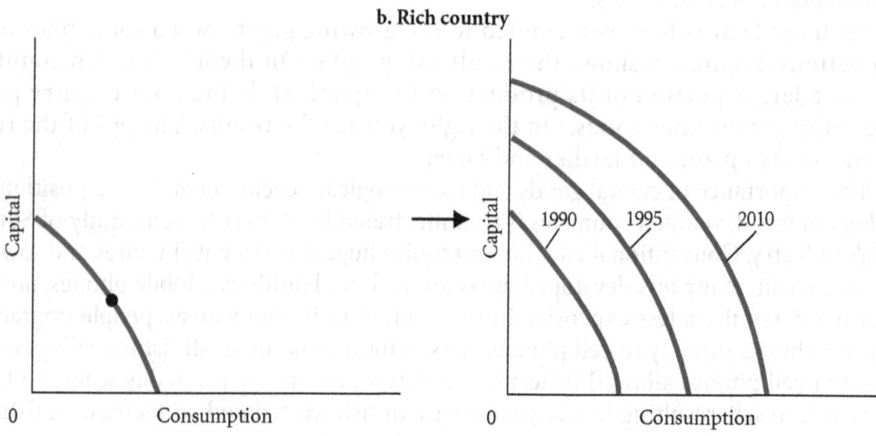

Figure 2.9

Capital Goods and Growth in Poor and Rich Countries

Rich countries find it easier than poor countries to devote resources to the production of capital, and the more resources that flow into capital production, the faster the rate of economic growth. Thus, the gap between poor and rich countries has grown over time.

Economics in Practice

Trade-Offs among the Rich and Poor

In all societies, for all people, resources are limited relative to people's demands. There are, however, quite large differences in the kinds of trade-offs individuals face in rich versus poor countries.

In 1990, the World Bank defined the extremely poor people of the world as those earning less than $1 a day. Among development economists and policy makers, this figure continues to be used as a rough rule of thumb. In a recent survey, Esther Duflo and Abhijit Banerjee, two MIT economists, surveyed individuals living at this level in 13 countries across the world.[1] What did they learn about the consumption trade-offs faced by these individuals versus consumers in the United States?

It should not surprise you to learn that for the extremely poor, food is a much larger component of the budget. On average over the 13 countries, between 56 percent and 78 percent of consumption was spent on food. In the United States just under 10 percent of the average budget goes to food. Even for the poorest consumers, however, biological need is not all determining. The Banerjee and Duflo study finds that in Udaipur, India, almost 10 percent of the typical food budget goes to sugar and processed foods rather than more nutritionally valuable grains. So even at these very low levels of income, some choice remains. Perhaps more interestingly, almost 10 percent of the budget of those surveyed goes to weddings, funerals, and other festivals. In societies with very few entertainment outlets, Banerjee and Duflo suggest we may see more demand for festivals, indicating that even in extremely poor societies, household choice plays a role.

[1] Abhijit Banerjee and Esther Duflo, "The Economic Lives of the Poor," *Journal of Economic Perspective,* Winter 2007, 21(1), 141–167.

profits. The ability of newer communication technology to aid development is one of the exciting features of our times. (See Robert Jensen, "The Digital Provide: Information Technology, Market Performance, and Welfare in the South Indian Fisheries Sector," *Quarterly Journal of Economics*, August 2007, 879–924.)

The Economic Problem

Recall the three basic questions facing all economic systems: (1) What gets produced? (2) How is it produced? and (3) Who gets it?

When Bill was alone on the island, the mechanism for answering those questions was simple: He thought about his own wants and preferences, looked at the constraints imposed by the resources of the island and his own skills and time, and made his decisions. As Bill set about his work, he allocated available resources quite simply, more or less by dividing up his available time. Distribution of the output was irrelevant. Because Bill was the society, he got it all.

Introducing even one more person into the economy—in this case, Colleen—changed all that. With Colleen on the island, resource allocation involves deciding not only how each person spends his or her time but also who does what; now there are two sets of wants and preferences. If Bill and Colleen go off on their own and form two separate self-sufficient economies, there will be lost potential. Two people can do more things together than each person can do alone. They may use their comparative advantages in different skills to specialize. Cooperation and coordination may give rise to gains that would otherwise not be possible.

When a society consists of millions of people, the problem of coordination and cooperation becomes enormous, but so does the potential for gain. In large, complex economies, specialization can go wild, with people working in jobs as different in their detail as an impressionist painting is from a blank page. The range of products available in a modern industrial society is beyond anything that could have been imagined a hundred years ago, and so is the range of jobs.

The amount of coordination and cooperation in a modern industrial society is almost impossible to imagine. Yet something seems to drive economic systems, if sometimes clumsily and inefficiently, toward producing the goods and services that people want. Given scarce resources, how do large, complex societies go about answering the three basic economic questions? This is the economic problem, which is what this text is about.

2.2 LEARNING OBJECTIVE

Economic Systems and the Role of Government

Thus far we have described the questions that the economic system must answer. Now we turn to the mechanics of the system. Here the basic debate concerns the role of government.

On the one hand, many favor leaving the economy alone and keeping the government at bay while others believe that there are many circumstances in which the government may be able to improve the functioning of the market.

In November 2008, President Barack Obama was elected during a period of turmoil in the world economy. In the United States during the month of the election over 700,000 jobs were lost. A year later the unemployment rate was over 10 percent, and even into 2010, more than 15 million were unemployed. At the same time, the banking system nearly collapsed when massive home mortgage defaults led to bankruptcy filings by giants Bear Sterns and Lehmann Brothers. The Federal Reserve System and the Treasury in response took action to save some big banks and big auto companies with the Troubled Asset Relief Program (TARP). While some called it a "bail out," much of the federal expenditure on these troubled institutions was paid back with interest.

In addition, during his first year, President Obama pushed hard for major reform of the health care system, for much stronger government regulation of the financial markets, and for a system designed to more effectively regulate energy consumption and protect the environment.

All of a sudden, the debate is all about the nature of the system. What should the government be doing, and which decisions should be left to the free, private markets? Is it true that the government should save companies or banks in trouble on the grounds that they are "too big to fail"?

Command Economies

Command economy An economy in which a central government either directly or indirectly sets output targets, incomes, and prices.

During the long struggle between the United States and the Soviet Union it was an all or nothing proposition. The Soviet Union had a planned economy run by the government. In a pure **command economy**, the basic economic questions are answered by a central government. Through a combination of government ownership of state enterprises and central planning, the government, either directly or indirectly, sets output targets, incomes, and prices.

While the extremes of central planning have been rejected, so too has the idea that "markets solve all problems." The real debate is not about whether we have government at all, it is about the extent and the character of a limited government role in the economy. One of the major themes of this book is that government involvement, in theory, may improve the efficiency and fairness of the allocation of a nation's resources. At the same time, a poorly functioning government can destroy incentives, lead to corruption, and result in the waste of a society's resources.

Laissez-Faire Economies: The Free Market

At the opposite end of the spectrum from the command economy is the **laissez-faire economy**. The term *laissez-faire*, which translated literally from French means "allow [them] to do," implies a complete lack of government involvement in the economy. In this type of economy, individuals and firms pursue their own self-interest without any central direction or regulation; the sum total of millions of individual decisions ultimately determines all basic economic outcomes. The central institution through which a laissez-faire system answers the basic questions is the **market**, a term that is used in economics to mean an institution through which buyers and sellers interact and engage in exchange.

Laissez-faire economy Literally from the French: "allow [them] to do." An economy in which individual people and firms pursue their own self-interest without any central direction or regulation.

Market The institution through which buyers and sellers interact and engage in exchange.

The interactions between buyers and sellers in any market range from simple to complex. Early explorers of the North American Midwest who wanted to exchange with Native Americans did so simply by bringing their goods to a central place and trading them. Today the Internet is revolutionizing exchange. A jewelry maker in upstate Maine can exhibit wares through digital photographs on the Web. Buyers can enter orders or make bids and pay by credit card. Companies such as eBay facilitate the worldwide interaction of tens of thousands of buyers and sellers sitting at their computers.

In short:

> Some markets are simple and others are complex, but they all involve buyers and sellers engaging in exchange. The behavior of buyers and sellers in a laissez-faire economy determines what gets produced, how it is produced, and who gets it.

The following chapters explore market systems in great depth. A quick preview is worthwhile here, however.

Consumer Sovereignty In a free, unregulated market, goods and services are produced and sold only if the supplier can make a profit. In simple terms, making a *profit* means selling goods or services for more than it costs to produce them. You cannot make a profit unless someone wants the product that you are selling. This logic leads to the notion of **consumer sovereignty**: The mix of output found in any free market system is dictated ultimately by the tastes and preferences of consumers who "vote" by buying or not buying. Businesses rise and fall in response to consumer demands. No central directive or plan is necessary.

Consumer sovereignty The idea that consumers ultimately dictate what will be produced (or not produced) by choosing what to purchase (and what not to purchase).

Individual Production Decisions: Free Enterprise Under a free market system, individual producers must also determine how to organize and coordinate the actual production of their products or services. The owner of a small shoe repair shop must alone buy the needed equipment and tools, hang signs, and set prices. In a big corporation, so many people are involved in planning the production process that in many ways, corporate planning resembles the planning in a command economy. In a free market economy, producers may be small or large. One person who hand-paints eggshells may start to sell them as a business; a person good with computers may start a business designing Web sites. On a larger scale, a group of furniture designers may put together a large portfolio of sketches, raise several million dollars, and start a bigger business. At the extreme are huge corporations such as Microsoft, Mitsubishi, and Intel, each of which sells tens of billions of dollars' worth of products every year. Whether the firms are large or small, however, production decisions in a market economy are made by separate private organizations acting in what they perceive to be their own interests.

Often the market system is called a free enterprise system. **Free enterprise** means the freedom of individuals to start private businesses in search of profits. Because new businesses require capital investment before they can begin operation, starting a new business involves risk. A well-run business that produces a product for which demand exists is likely to succeed; a poorly run business or one that produces a product for which little demand exists now or in the future is likely to fail. It is through free enterprise that new products and new production techniques find their way into use.

Free enterprise The freedom of individuals to start and operate private businesses in search of profits.

Proponents of free market systems argue that free enterprise leads to more efficient production and better response to diverse and changing consumer preferences. If a producer produces inefficiently, competitors will come along, fight for the business, and eventually take it away. Thus, in a free market economy, competition forces producers to use efficient techniques of production. It is competition, then, that ultimately dictates how output is produced.

Distribution of Output In a free market system, the distribution of output—who gets what—is also determined in a decentralized way. The amount that any one household gets depends on its income and wealth. *Income* is the amount that a household earns each year. It comes in a number of forms: wages, salaries, interest, and the like. *Wealth* is the amount that households have accumulated out of past income through saving or inheritance.

To the extent that income comes from working for a wage, it is at least in part determined by individual choice. You will work for the wages available in the market only if these wages (and the products and services they can buy) are sufficient to compensate you for what you give up by working. Your leisure certainly has a value also. You may discover that you can increase your income by getting more education or training. You *cannot* increase your income, however, if you acquire a skill that no one wants.

Price Theory The basic coordinating mechanism in a free market system is price. A price is the amount that a product sells for per unit, and it reflects what society is willing to pay. Prices of inputs—labor, land, and capital—determine how much it costs to produce a product. Prices of various kinds of labor, or *wage rates*, determine the rewards for working in different jobs and professions. Many of the independent decisions made in a market economy involve the weighing of prices and costs, so it is not surprising that much of economic theory focuses on the factors that influence and determine prices. This is why microeconomic theory is often simply called *price theory*.

In sum:

In a free market system, the basic economic questions are answered without the help of a central government plan or directives. This is what the "free" in free market means—the system is left to operate on its own with no outside interference. Individuals pursuing their own self-interest will go into business and produce the products and services that people want. Other individuals will decide whether to acquire skills; whether to work; and whether to buy, sell, invest, or save the income that they earn. The basic coordinating mechanism is price.

Mixed Systems, Markets, and Governments

The differences between command economies and laissez-faire economies in their pure forms are enormous. In fact, these pure forms do not exist in the world; all real systems are in some sense "mixed." That is, individual enterprise exists and independent choice is exercised even in economies in which the government plays a major role.

Conversely, no market economies exist without government involvement and government regulation. The United States has basically a free market economy, but government purchases accounted for just over 20 percent of the country's total production in 2010. Governments in the United States (local, state, and federal) directly employ about 14 percent of all workers (15 percent including active duty military). They also redistribute income by means of taxation and social welfare expenditures, and they regulate many economic activities.

One of the major themes in this book, and indeed in economics, is the tension between the advantages of free, unregulated markets and the desire for government involvement. Advocates of free markets argue that such markets work best when left to themselves. They produce only what people want; without buyers, sellers go out of business. Competition forces firms to adopt efficient production techniques. Wage differentials lead people to acquire needed skills. Competition also leads to innovation in both production techniques and products. The result is quality and variety, but market systems have problems too. Even staunch defenders of the free enterprise system recognize that market systems are not perfect. First, they do not always produce what people want at the lowest cost—there are inefficiencies. Second, rewards (income) may be unfairly distributed and some groups may be left out. Third, periods of unemployment and inflation recur with some regularity.

Many people point to these problems as reasons for government involvement. Indeed, for some problems, government involvement may be the only solution. However, government decisions are made by people who presumably, like the rest of us, act in their own self-interest. While governments may be called on to improve the functioning of the economy, there is no guarantee that they will do so. Just as markets may fail to produce an allocation of resources that is perfectly efficient and fair, governments may fail to improve matters. We return to this debate many times throughout this text.

Looking Ahead

2.3 LEARNING OBJECTIVE

This chapter described the economic problem in broad terms. We outlined the questions that all economic systems must answer. We also discussed very broadly the two kinds of economic systems.

CHAPTER 3

Trade-offs, Comparative Advantage, and the Market System

Chapter Outline and Learning Objectives

Managers Making Choices at BMW

When you think of cars that combine fine engineering, high performance, and cutting-edge styling, you are likely to think of BMW. Founded in Germany in 1916, BMW today has 23 factories in 15 countries and worldwide sales of more than 1.5 million cars.

To compete in the automobile market, the managers of BMW must make many strategic decisions, such as whether to introduce new car models. BMW has begun selling a hydrogen-powered version of the 7-Series sedan and is also working on fuel cell–powered cars. Another strategic decision BMW's managers face is where to advertise. Although some of BMW's managers did not believe the company could sell cars in China, BMW decided to advertise heavily there. The advertising paid off: China has become the company's third-largest market, after Germany and the United States, with sales increasing by more than 85 percent in 2010 alone.

BMW's managers have also faced the strategic decision of whether to concentrate production in factories in Germany or to build new factories in overseas markets. Keeping production in Germany makes it easier for BMW's managers to supervise production and to employ German workers, who generally have high levels of technical training. By building factories in other countries, BMW can benefit from paying lower wages and can reduce political friction by producing vehicles in the same country in which it sells them. BMW opened a plant in Shenyang, in northeast China and a plant in Chennai in India. It also opened a U.S. factory in Spartanburg, South Carolina, which currently produces the X3, X5, and X6 models for sale both in the United States and worldwide.

Managers also face smaller-scale—or tactical—business decisions. For instance, in scheduling production at BMW's Spartanburg plant, managers must decide each month the quantity of X3, X5, and X6 models to produce. Like other decisions managers make, this one involves a trade-off: Producing more of one of these three models means producing fewer of the others.

Based on Christoph Rauwald, "BMW's Quarterly Profit Soars," *The Wall Street Journal*, May 4, 2011; and BMW, *Annual Report, 2010.*

Economics in Your Life

The Trade-offs When You Buy a Car

When you buy a car, you probably consider factors such as safety and fuel efficiency. To increase fuel efficiency, automobile manufacturers make cars small and light. Large cars absorb more of the impact of an accident than do small cars. As a result, people are usually safer driving large cars than small cars. What can we conclude from these facts about the relationship between safety and fuel efficiency? Under what circumstances would it be possible for automobile manufacturers to make cars safer and more fuel efficient? As you read the chapter, see if you can answer these questions. You can check your answers against those provided on **page 75** at the end of this chapter.

Scarcity A situation in which unlimited wants exceed the limited resources available to fulfill those wants.

In a market system, managers at most firms must make decisions like those made by BMW's managers. The decisions managers face reflect a key fact of economic life: *Scarcity requires trade-offs.* **Scarcity** exists because we have unlimited wants but only limited resources available to fulfill those wants. Goods and services are scarce. So, too, are the economic resources, or *factors of production*—workers, capital, natural resources, and entrepreneurial ability—used to make goods and services. Your time is scarce, which means you face trade-offs: If you spend an hour studying for an economics exam, you have one less hour to spend studying for a psychology exam or going to the movies. If your university decides to use some of its scarce budget to buy new computers for the computer labs, those funds will not be available to buy new books for the library or to resurface the student parking lot. If BMW decides to devote some of the scarce workers and machinery in its Spartanburg assembly plant to producing more X6 hybrid cars, those resources will not be available to produce more X5 SUVs.

Households and firms make many of their decisions in markets. Trade is a key activity that takes place in markets. Trade involves the decisions of millions of households and firms spread around the world. By engaging in trade, people can raise their standard of living. In this chapter, we provide an overview of how the market system coordinates the independent decisions of these millions of households and firms. We begin our analysis of the economic consequences of scarcity and the working of the market system by introducing an important economic model: the *production possibilities frontier.*

3.1 LEARNING OBJECTIVE

Use a production possibilities frontier to analyze opportunity costs and trade-offs.

Production Possibilities Frontiers and Opportunity Costs

As we saw in the chapter opener, BMW operates an automobile factory in Spartanburg, South Carolina, where it assembles several car models. Because the firm's resources—workers, machinery, materials, and entrepreneurial skills—are limited, BMW faces a trade-off: Resources devoted to producing one model are not available for producing other models. Chapter 1 explained that economic models can be useful in analyzing many questions. We can use a simple model called the *production possibilities frontier* to analyze the trade-offs BMW faces in its Spartanburg plant. A **production possibilities frontier (*PPF*)** is a curve showing the maximum attainable combinations of two products that may be produced with available resources and current technology. In BMW's case, we simplify by assuming that the company produces only X6 hybrids and X5 SUVs at the Spartanburg plant, using workers, materials, robots, and other machinery.

Production possibilities frontier (*PPF*) A curve showing the maximum attainable combinations of two products that may be produced with available resources and current technology.

Graphing the Production Possibilities Frontier

Figure 3.1 uses a production possibilities frontier to illustrate the trade-offs that BMW faces. The numbers from the table are plotted in the graph. The line in the graph is BMW's production possibilities frontier. If BMW uses all its resources to produce hybrids, it can produce 800 per day—point *A* at one end of the production possibilities frontier. If BMW uses all its resources to produce SUVs, it can produce 800 per day—point *E* at the other end of the production possibilities frontier. If BMW devotes resources to producing both vehicles, it could be at a point like *B*, where it produces 600 hybrids and 200 SUVs.

All the combinations either on the frontier—like *A*, *B*, *C*, *D*, and *E*—or inside the frontier—like point *F*—are *attainable* with the resources available. Combinations on the frontier are *efficient* because all available resources are being fully utilized, and the

BMW's Production Choices at Its Spartanburg Plant		
Choice	Quantity of Hybrids Produced	Quantity of SUVs Produced
A	800	0
B	600	200
C	400	400
D	200	600
E	0	800

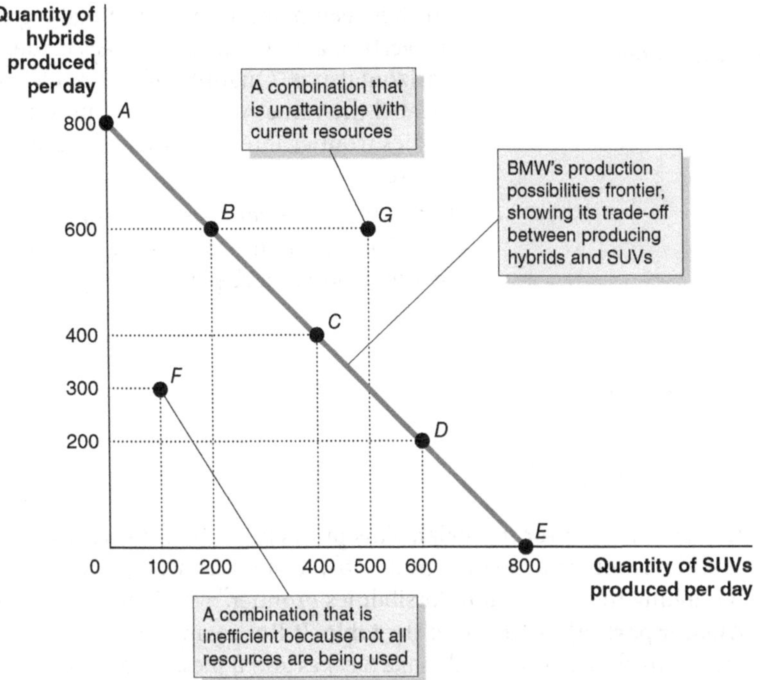

Figure 3.1

BMW's Production Possibilities Frontier

BMW faces a trade-off: To build one more hybrid, it must build one less SUV. The production possibilities frontier illustrates the trade-off BMW faces. Combinations on the production possibilities frontier—like points *A*, *B*, *C*, *D*, and *E*—are *technically efficient* because the maximum output is being obtained from the available resources. Combinations inside the frontier—like point *F*—are *inefficient* because some resources are not being used. Combinations outside the frontier—like point *G*—are *unattainable* with current resources.

fewest possible resources are being used to produce a given amount of output. Combinations inside the frontier—like point *F*—are *inefficient* because maximum output is not being obtained from the available resources—perhaps because the assembly line is not operating at capacity. BMW might like to be beyond the frontier—at a point like *G*, where it would be producing 600 hybrids and 500 SUVs—but points beyond the production possibilities frontier are *unattainable*, given the firm's current resources. To produce the combination at *G*, BMW would need more machines or more workers.

Notice that if BMW is producing efficiently and is on the production possibilities frontier, the only way to produce more of one vehicle is to produce fewer of the other vehicle. Recall from Chapter 1 that the **opportunity cost** of any activity is the highest-valued alternative that must be given up to engage in that activity. For BMW, the opportunity cost of producing one more SUV is the number of hybrids the company will not be able to produce because it has shifted those resources to producing SUVs. For example, in moving from point *B* to point *C*, the opportunity cost of producing 200 more SUVs per day is the 200 fewer hybrids that can be produced.

Opportunity cost The highest-valued alternative that must be given up to engage in an activity.

What point on the production possibilities frontier is best? We can't tell without further information. If consumer demand for SUVs is greater than the demand for hybrids, the company is likely to choose a point closer to *E*. If demand for hybrids is greater than demand for SUVs, the company is likely to choose a point closer to *A*.

Solved Problem 3.1

Drawing a Production Possibilities Frontier for Rosie's Boston Bakery

Rosie's Boston Bakery specializes in cakes and pies. Rosie has 5 hours per day to devote to baking. In 1 hour, Rosie can prepare 2 pies or 1 cake.

a. Use the information given to complete the following table:

	Hours Spent Making		Quantity Made	
Choice	Cakes	Pies	Cakes	Pies
A	5	0		
B	4	1		
C	3	2		
D	2	3		
E	1	4		
F	0	5		

b. Use the data in the table to draw a production possibilities frontier graph illustrating Rosie's trade-offs between making cakes and making pies. Label the vertical axis "Quantity of cakes made." Label the horizontal axis "Quantity of pies made." Make sure to label the values where Rosie's production possibilities frontier intersects the vertical and horizontal axes.

c. Label the points representing choice *D* and choice *E*. If Rosie is at choice *D*, what is her opportunity cost of making more pies?

Solving the Problem

Step 1: Review the chapter material. This problem is about using production possibilities frontiers to analyze trade-offs, so you may want to review the section "Graphing the Production Possibilities Frontier," which begins on page 56.

Step 2: Answer part (a) by filling in the table. If Rosie can produce 1 cake in 1 hour, then with choice *A*, she will make 5 cakes and 0 pies. Because she can produce 2 pies in 1 hour, with choice *B*, she will make 4 cakes and 2 pies. Using similar reasoning, you can fill in the remaining cells in the table as follows:

	Hours Spent Making		Quantity Made	
Choice	Cakes	Pies	Cakes	Pies
A	5	0	5	0
B	4	1	4	2
C	3	2	3	4
D	2	3	2	6
E	1	4	1	8
F	0	5	0	10

Step 3: Answer part (b) by drawing the production possibilities frontier graph. Using the data in the table in Step 2, you should draw a graph that looks like this:

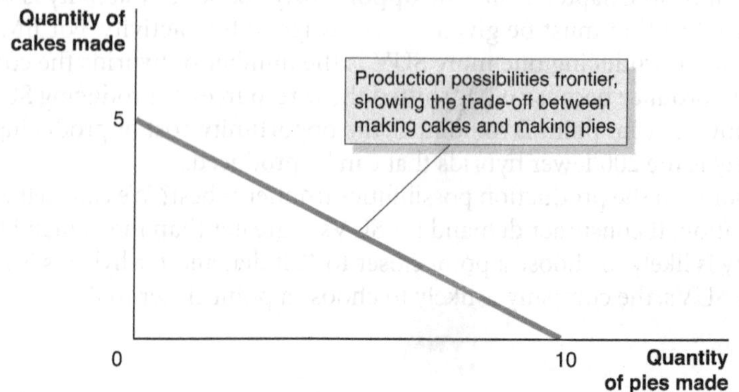

If Rosie devotes all 5 hours to making cakes, she will make 5 cakes. Therefore, her production possibilities frontier will intersect the vertical axis at 5 cakes made. If Rosie devotes all 5 hours to making pies, she will make 10 pies. Therefore, her production possibilities frontier will intersect the horizontal axis at 10 pies made.

Step 4: Answer part (c) by showing choices *D* and *E* on your graph. The points for choices *D* and *E* can be plotted using the information from the table:

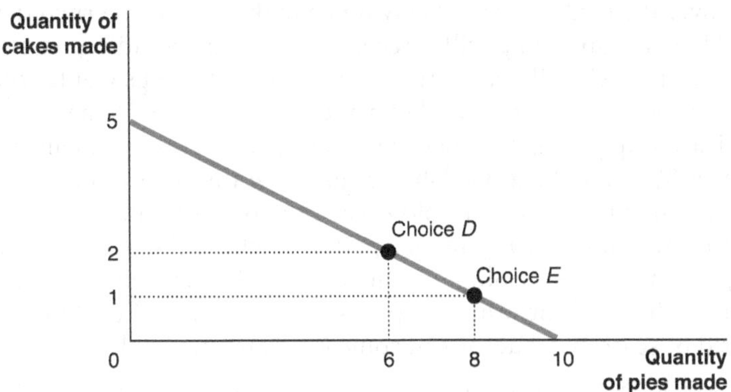

Moving from choice *D* to choice *E* increases Rosie's production of pies by 2 but lowers her production of cakes by 1. Therefore, her opportunity cost of making 2 more pies is making 1 less cake.

Making the Connection

Facing Trade-offs in Health Care Spending

Households have limited incomes. If the price of health care rises, households have to choose whether to buy less health care or spend less on other goods and services. The same is true of the federal government's spending on health care. The government provides health insurance to about 30 percent of the population through programs such as Medicare for people over age 65 and Medicaid for low-income people. If the price of health care rises, the government has to either cut back on the services provided through Medicare and Medicaid or cut spending in another part of the government's budget. (Of course, both households and the government can borrow to pay for some of their spending, but ultimately the funds they can borrow are also limited.)

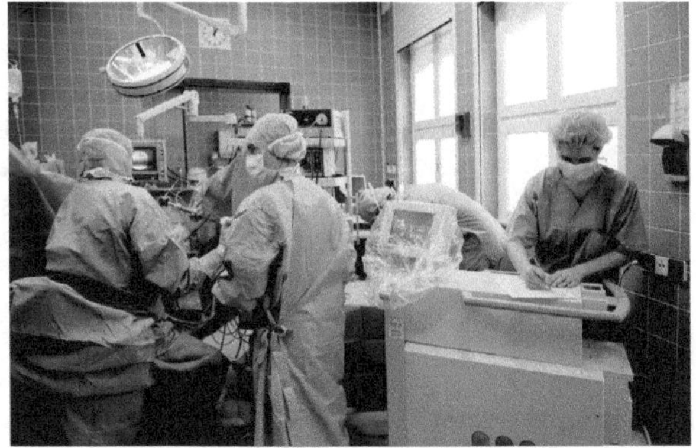

Spending more on health care means spending less on other goods and services for both households and governments.

About 54 percent of the population has private health insurance, often provided by an employer. When the fees doctors charge, the cost of prescription drugs, and the cost of hospital stays rise, the cost to employers of providing health insurance increases. As a result, employers will typically increase the amount they withhold from employees' paychecks to pay for the insurance. Some employers—particularly small firms—will even stop offering health insurance to their employees. In either case, the price employees pay for health care will rise. How do people respond to rising health care costs? Isn't health care a necessity that people continue to consume the same amount of, no matter how much its price increases? In fact, studies have shown that rising health care costs cause people to cut back their spending on medical services, just as people cut back their spending on other goods and services when their prices rise. One academic study indicates that for every 1 percent increase in the amount employers charge employees for insurance,

164,000 people become uninsured. Of course, people without health insurance can still visit the doctor and obtain prescriptions, but they have to pay higher prices than do people with insurance. Although the consequences of being uninsured can be severe, particularly if someone develops a serious illness, economists are not surprised that higher prices for health insurance lead to less health insurance being purchased: Faced with limited incomes, people have to make choices among the goods and services they buy.

The Congressional Budget Office estimates that as the U.S. population ages and medical costs continue to rise, federal government spending on Medicare will more than double over the next 10 years. Many policymakers are concerned that this rapid increase in Medicare spending will force a reduction in spending on other government programs. Daniel Callahan, a researcher at the Hastings Center for Bioethics, has argued that policymakers should consider taking some dramatic steps, such as having Medicare stop paying for open-heart surgery and other expensive treatments for people over 80 years of age. Callahan argues that the costs of open-heart surgery and similar treatments for the very old exceed the benefits, and the funds would be better spent on treatments for younger patients, where the benefits would exceed the costs. Spending less on prolonging the lives of the very old in order to save resources that can be used for other purposes is a very painful trade-off to consider. But in a world of scarcity, trade-offs of some kind are inevitable.

Based on Daniel Callahan, "The Economic Woes of Medicare," *The New York Times*, November 13, 2008; Ezekiel J. Emanuel, "The Cost-Coverage Trade-off," *Journal of the American Medical Association*, Vol. 299, No. 8, February 27, 2008, pp. 947–949; and Congressional Budget Office, *A Preliminary Analysis of the President's Budget and an Update of CBO's Budget and Economic Outlook*, March 2009.

Increasing Marginal Opportunity Costs

We can use the production possibilities frontier to explore issues concerning the economy as a whole. For example, suppose we divide all the goods and services produced in the economy into just two types: military goods and civilian goods. In Figure 3.2, we let tanks represent military goods and automobiles represent civilian goods. If all the country's resources are devoted to producing military goods, 400 tanks can be produced in one year. If all resources are devoted to producing civilian goods, 500 automobiles can be produced in one year. Devoting resources to producing both goods results in the economy being at other points along the production possibilities frontier.

Notice that this production possibilities frontier is bowed outward rather than being a straight line. Because the curve is bowed out, the opportunity cost of automobiles in terms of tanks depends on where the economy currently is on the production possibilities frontier. For example, to increase automobile production from 0 to 200—moving from point *A* to point *B*—the economy has to give up only 50 tanks. But to increase

Figure 3.2

Increasing Marginal Opportunity Costs

As the economy moves down the production possibilities frontier, it experiences *increasing marginal opportunity costs* because increasing automobile production by a given quantity requires larger and larger decreases in tank production. For example, to increase automobile production from 0 to 200—moving from point *A* to point *B*—the economy has to give up only 50 tanks. But to increase automobile production by another 200 vehicles—moving from point *B* to point *C*—the economy has to give up 150 tanks.

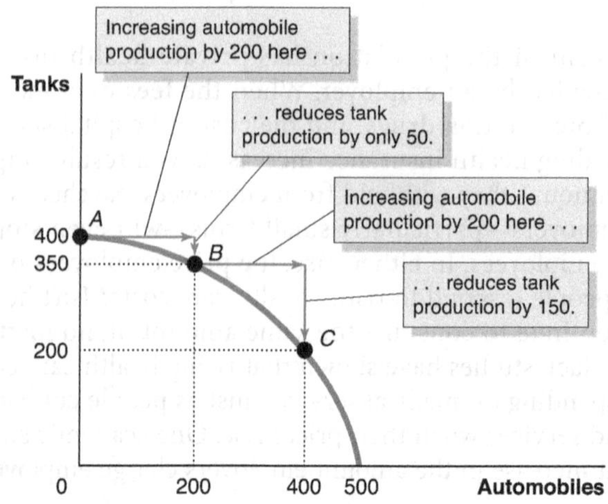

automobile production by another 200 vehicles—moving from point *B* to point *C*—the economy has to give up 150 tanks.

As the economy moves down the production possibilities frontier, it experiences *increasing marginal opportunity costs* because increasing automobile production by a given quantity requires larger and larger decreases in tank production. Increasing marginal opportunity costs occur because some workers, machines, and other resources are better suited to one use than to another. At point *A*, some resources that are well suited to producing automobiles are forced to produce tanks. Shifting these resources into producing automobiles by moving from point *A* to point *B* allows a substantial increase in automobile production, without much loss of tank production. But as the economy moves down the production possibilities frontier, more and more resources that are better suited to tank production are switched into automobile production. As a result, the increases in automobile production become increasingly smaller, while the decreases in tank production become increasingly larger. We would expect in most situations that production possibilities frontiers will be bowed outward rather than linear, as in the BMW example discussed earlier.

The idea of increasing marginal opportunity costs illustrates an important economic concept: *The more resources already devoted to an activity, the smaller the payoff to devoting additional resources to that activity.* For example, the more hours you have already spent studying economics, the smaller the increase in your test grade from each additional hour you spend—and the greater the opportunity cost of using the hour in that way. The more funds a firm has devoted to research and development during a given year, the smaller the amount of useful knowledge it receives from each additional dollar—and the greater the opportunity cost of using the funds in that way. The more funds the federal government spends cleaning up the environment during a given year, the smaller the reduction in pollution from each additional dollar—and, once again, the greater the opportunity cost of using the funds in that way.

Economic Growth

At any given time, the total resources available to any economy are fixed. Therefore, if the United States produces more automobiles, it must produce less of something else—tanks in our example. Over time, though, the resources available to an economy may increase. For example, both the labor force and the capital stock—the amount of physical capital available in the country—may increase. The increase in the available labor force and the capital stock shifts the production possibilities frontier outward for the U.S. economy and makes it possible to produce both more automobiles and more

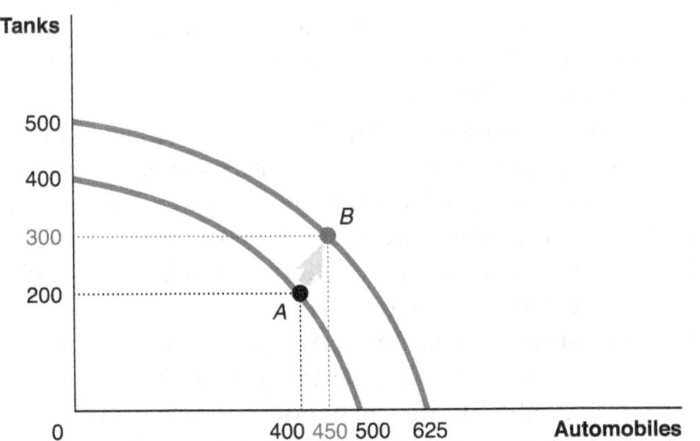

(a) Shifting out the production possibilities frontier

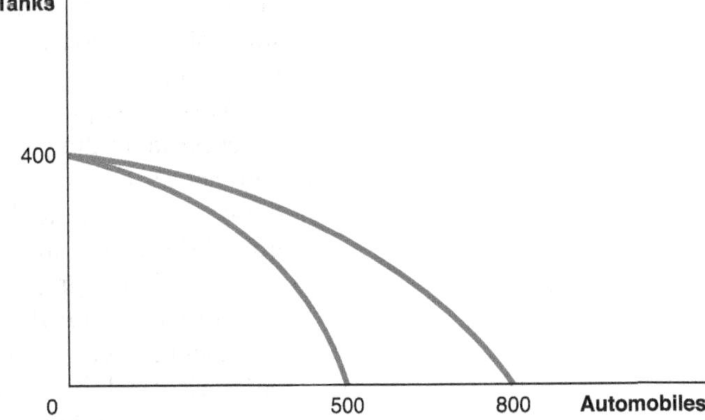

(b) Technological change in the automobile industry

Figure 3.3 Economic Growth

Panel (a) shows that as more economic resources become available and technological change occurs, the economy can move from point *A* to point *B*, producing more tanks and more automobiles. Panel (b) shows the results of technological change in the automobile industry that increases the quantity of vehicles workers can produce per year while leaving unchanged the maximum quantity of tanks that can be produced. Shifts in the production possibilities frontier represent *economic growth*.

tanks. Panel (a) of Figure 3.3 shows that the economy can move from point *A* to point *B*, producing more tanks and more automobiles.

Similarly, technological change makes it possible to produce more goods with the same number of workers and the same amount of machinery, which also shifts the production possibilities frontier outward. Technological change need not affect all sectors equally. Panel (b) of Figure 3.3 shows the results of technological change in the automobile industry that increases the quantity of automobiles workers can produce per year while leaving unchanged the quantity of tanks that can be produced.

Economic growth The ability of the economy to increase the production of goods and services.

Shifts in the production possibilities frontier represent **economic growth** because they allow the economy to increase the production of goods and services, which ultimately raises the standard of living. In the United States and other high-income countries, the market system has aided the process of economic growth, which over the past 200 years has greatly increased the well-being of the average person.

3.2 LEARNING OBJECTIVE

Understand comparative advantage and explain how it is the basis for trade.

Comparative Advantage and Trade

Trade The act of buying and selling.

We can use the ideas of production possibilities frontiers and opportunity costs to understand the basic economic activity of *trade*. Markets are fundamentally about **trade**, which is the act of buying and selling. Sometimes we trade directly, as when children trade one baseball card for another baseball card. But often we trade indirectly: We sell our labor services as, say, an accountant, a salesperson, or a nurse for money, and then we use the money to buy goods and services. Although in these cases, trade takes place indirectly, ultimately the accountant, salesperson, or nurse is trading his or her services for food, clothing, and other goods and services. One of the great benefits of trade is that it makes it possible for people to become better off by increasing both their production and their consumption.

Specialization and Gains from Trade

Consider the following situation: You and your neighbor both have fruit trees on your property. Initially, suppose you have only apple trees and your neighbor has only cherry trees. In this situation, if you both like apples and cherries, there is an obvious opportunity for both of you to gain from trade: You trade some of your apples for some of your neighbor's cherries, making you both better off. But what if there are apple and cherry trees growing on both of your properties? In that case, there can still be gains from trade. For example, your neighbor might be very good at picking apples, and you might be very good at picking cherries. It would make sense for your neighbor to concentrate on picking apples and for you to concentrate on picking cherries. You can then trade some of the cherries you pick for some of the apples your neighbor picks. But what if your neighbor is actually better at picking both apples and cherries than you are?

We can use production possibilities frontiers (*PPFs*) to show how your neighbor can benefit from trading with you *even though she is better than you are at picking both apples and cherries*. (For simplicity, and because it will not have any effect on the conclusions we draw, we will assume that the *PPFs* in this example are straight lines.) The table in Figure 3.4 shows how many apples and how many cherries you and your neighbor can pick in one week. The graph in the figure uses the data from the table to construct *PPFs*. Panel (a) shows your *PPF*. If you devote all your time to picking apples, you can pick 20 pounds of apples per week. If you devote all your time to picking cherries, you can pick 20 pounds per week. Panel (b) shows that if your neighbor devotes all her time to picking apples, she can pick 30 pounds. If she devotes all her time to picking cherries, she can pick 60 pounds.

The production possibilities frontiers in Figure 3.4 show how many apples and cherries you and your neighbor can consume, *without trade*. Suppose that when you don't trade with your neighbor, you pick and consume 8 pounds of apples and 12 pounds of cherries per week. This combination of apples and cherries is represented by point *A* in panel (a) of Figure 3.5. When your neighbor doesn't trade with you, she picks and consumes 9 pounds of apples and 42 pounds of cherries per week. This combination of apples and cherries is represented by point *C* in panel (b) of Figure 3.5.

	You		Your Neighbor	
	Apples	Cherries	Apples	Cherries
Devote all time to picking apples	20 pounds	0 pounds	30 pounds	0 pounds
Devote all time to picking cherries	0 pounds	20 pounds	0 pounds	60 pounds

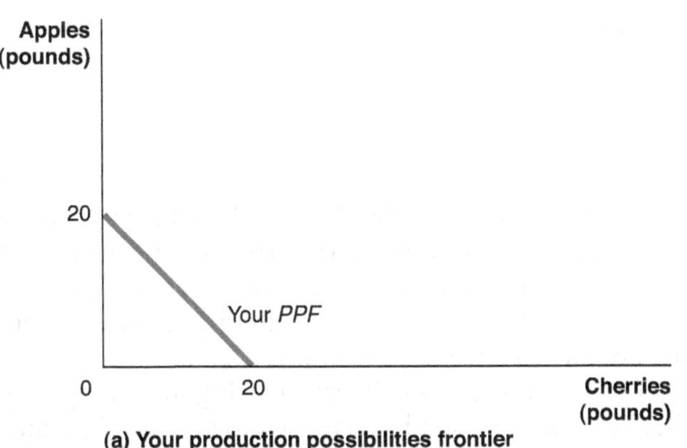

(a) Your production possibilities frontier

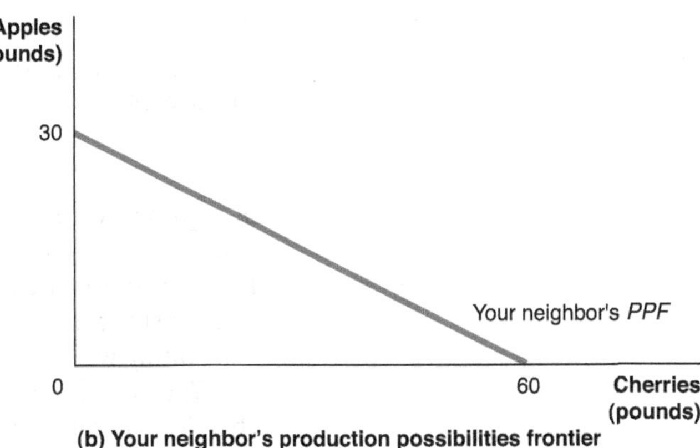

(b) Your neighbor's production possibilities frontier

Figure 3.4 Production Possibilities for You and Your Neighbor, without Trade

The table in this figure shows how many pounds of apples and how many pounds of cherries you and your neighbor can each pick in one week. The graphs in the figure use the data from the table to construct production possibilities frontiers (*PPF*s) for you and your neighbor. Panel (a) shows your *PPF*. If you devote all your time to picking apples and none of your time to picking cherries, you can pick 20 pounds. If you devote all your time to picking cherries, you can pick 20 pounds. Panel (b) shows that if your neighbor devotes all her time to picking apples, she can pick 30 pounds. If she devotes all her time to picking cherries, she can pick 60 pounds.

After years of picking and consuming your own apples and cherries, suppose your neighbor comes to you one day with the following proposal: She offers to trade you 15 pounds of her cherries for 10 pounds of your apples next week. Should you accept this offer? You should accept because you will end up with more apples and more cherries to consume. To take advantage of her proposal, you should specialize in picking only apples rather than splitting your time between picking apples and picking cherries. We know this will allow you to pick 20 pounds of apples. You can trade 10 pounds

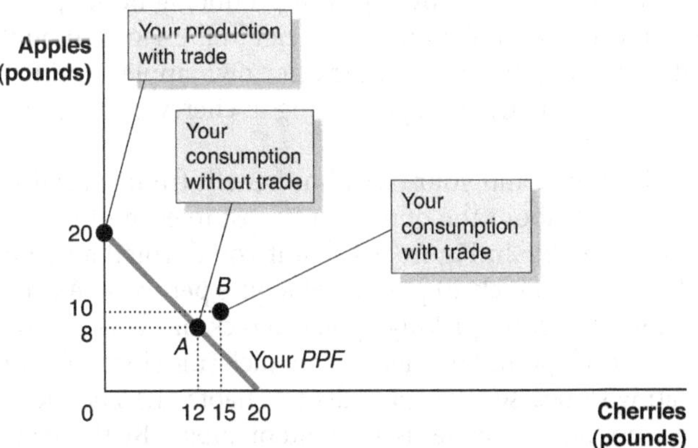

(a) Your production and consumption after trade

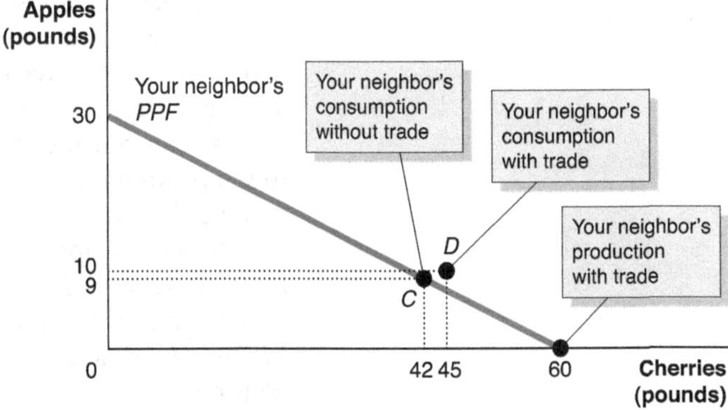

(b) Your neighbor's production and consumption with trade

Figure 3.5 Gains from Trade

When you don't trade with your neighbor, you pick and consume 8 pounds of apples and 12 pounds of cherries per week—point *A* in panel (a). When your neighbor doesn't trade with you, she picks and consumes 9 pounds of apples and 42 pounds of cherries per week—point *C* in panel (b). If you specialize in picking apples, you can pick 20 pounds. If your neighbor specializes in picking cherries, she can pick 60 pounds. If you trade 10 pounds of your apples for 15 pounds of your neighbor's cherries, you will be able to consume 10 pounds of apples and 15 pounds of cherries—point *B* in panel (a). Your neighbor can now consume 10 pounds of apples and 45 pounds of cherries—point *D* in panel (b). You and your neighbor are both better off as a result of the trade.

Table 3.1

A Summary of the Gains from Trade

	You		Your Neighbor	
	Apples (in pounds)	Cherries (in pounds)	Apples (in pounds)	Cherries (in pounds)
Production *and* consumption *without* trade	8	12	9	42
Production *with* trade	20	0	0	60
Consumption *with* trade	10	15	10	45
Gains from trade (increased consumption)	2	3	1	3

of apples to your neighbor for 15 pounds of her cherries. The result is that you will be able to consume 10 pounds of apples and 15 pounds of cherries (point *B* in panel (a) of Figure 3.5). You are clearly better off as a result of trading with your neighbor: You now can consume 2 more pounds of apples and 3 more pounds of cherries than you were consuming without trading. You have moved beyond your *PPF*!

Your neighbor has also benefited from the trade. By specializing in picking only cherries, she can pick 60 pounds. She trades 15 pounds of cherries to you for 10 pounds of apples. The result is that she can consume 10 pounds of apples and 45 pounds of cherries (point *D* in panel (b) of Figure 3.5). This is 1 more pound of apples and 3 more pounds of cherries than she was consuming before trading with you. She also has moved beyond her *PPF*. Table 3.1 summarizes the changes in production and consumption that result from your trade with your neighbor. (In this example, we chose one specific rate of trading cherries for apples—15 pounds of cherries for 10 pounds of apples. There are, however, many other rates of trading cherries for apples that would also make you and your neighbor better off.)

Absolute Advantage versus Comparative Advantage

Absolute advantage The ability of an individual, a firm, or a country to produce more of a good or service than competitors, using the same amount of resources.

Perhaps the most remarkable aspect of the preceding example is that your neighbor benefits from trading with you even though she is better than you at picking both apples and cherries. **Absolute advantage** is the ability of an individual, a firm, or a country to produce more of a good or service than competitors, using the same amount of resources. Your neighbor has an absolute advantage over you in producing both apples and cherries because she can pick more of each fruit than you can in the same amount of time. Although it seems that your neighbor should pick her own apples *and* her own cherries, we have just seen that she is better off specializing in cherry picking and leaving the apple picking to you.

We can consider further why both you and your neighbor benefit from specializing in picking only one fruit. First, think about the opportunity cost to each of you of picking the two fruits. We saw from the *PPF* in Figure 3.4 that if you devoted all your time to picking apples, you would be able to pick 20 pounds of apples per week. As you move down your *PPF* and shift time away from picking apples to picking cherries, you have to give up 1 pound of apples for each pound of cherries you pick (the slope of your *PPF* is −1. For a review of calculating slopes, see the appendix to Chapter 1.) Therefore, your opportunity cost of picking 1 pound of cherries is 1 pound of apples. By the same reasoning, your opportunity cost of picking 1 pound of apples is 1 pound of cherries. Your neighbor's *PPF* has a different slope, so she faces a different trade-off: As she shifts time from picking apples to picking cherries, she has to give up 0.5 pound of apples for every 1 pound of cherries she picks (the slope of your neighbor's *PPF* is −0.5). As she shifts time from picking cherries to picking apples, she gives up 2 pounds of cherries for every 1 pound of apples she picks. Therefore, her opportunity cost of picking 1 pound of apples is 2 pounds of cherries, and her opportunity cost of picking 1 pound of cherries is 0.5 pound of apples.

Table 3.2

Opportunity Costs of Picking Apples and Cherries

	Opportunity Cost of Picking 1 Pound of Apples	Opportunity Cost of Picking 1 Pound of Cherries
You	1 pound of cherries	1 pound of apples
Your Neighbor	2 pounds of cherries	0.5 pound of apples

Table 3.2 summarizes the opportunity costs for you and your neighbor of picking apples and cherries. Note that even though your neighbor can pick more apples in a week than you can, the *opportunity cost* of picking apples is higher for her than for you because when she picks apples, she gives up more cherries than you do. So, even though she has an absolute advantage over you in picking apples, it is more costly for her to pick apples than it is for you. The table also shows that her opportunity cost of picking cherries is lower than your opportunity cost of picking cherries. **Comparative advantage** is the ability of an individual, a firm, or a country to produce a good or service at a lower opportunity cost than competitors. In apple picking, your neighbor has an *absolute advantage* over you, but you have a *comparative advantage* over her. Your neighbor has both an absolute advantage and a comparative advantage over you in picking cherries. As we have seen, you are better off specializing in picking apples, and your neighbor is better off specializing in picking cherries.

Comparative advantage The ability of an individual, a firm, or a country to produce a good or service at a lower opportunity cost than competitors.

Comparative Advantage and the Gains from Trade

We have just derived an important economic principle: *The basis for trade is comparative advantage, not absolute advantage.* The fastest apple pickers do not necessarily do much apple picking. If the fastest apple pickers have a comparative advantage in some other activity—picking cherries, playing Major League Baseball, or being industrial engineers—they are better off specializing in that other activity. Individuals, firms, and countries are better off if they specialize in producing goods and services for which they have a comparative advantage and obtain the other goods and services they need by trading.

Don't Let This Happen to You

Don't Confuse Absolute Advantage and Comparative Advantage

First, make sure you know the definitions:

- **Absolute advantage.** The ability of an individual, a firm, or a country to produce more of a good or service than competitors, using the same amount of resources. In our example, your neighbor has an absolute advantage over you in both picking apples and picking cherries.
- **Comparative advantage.** The ability of an individual, a firm, or a country to produce a good or service at a lower opportunity cost than competitors. In our example, your neighbor has a comparative advantage in picking cherries, but you have a comparative advantage in picking apples.

Keep these two key points in mind:

1. It is possible to have an absolute advantage in producing a good or service without having a comparative advantage. This is the case with your neighbor picking apples.
2. It is possible to have a comparative advantage in producing a good or service without having an absolute advantage. This is the case with you picking apples.

Solved Problem 3.2

Comparative Advantage and the Gains from Trade

Suppose that Canada and the United States both produce maple syrup and honey, which sell for the same prices in both countries. These are the combinations of the two goods that each country can produce in one day using the same amounts of capital and labor:

Canada		United States	
Honey (in tons)	Maple Syrup (in tons)	Honey (in tons)	Maple Syrup (in tons)
0	60	0	50
10	45	10	40
20	30	20	30
30	15	30	20
40	0	40	10
		50	0

a. Who has a comparative advantage in producing maple syrup? Who has a comparative advantage in producing honey?

b. Suppose that Canada is currently producing 30 tons of honey and 15 tons of maple syrup, and the United States is currently producing 10 tons of honey and 40 tons of maple syrup. Demonstrate that Canada and the United States can both be better off if they specialize in producing only one good and engage in trade.

c. Illustrate your answer to question (b) by drawing a *PPF* for the United States and a *PPF* for Canada. Show on your *PPFs* the combinations of honey and maple syrup produced and consumed in each country before and after trade.

Solving the Problem

Step 1: Review the chapter material. This problem is about comparative advantage, so you may want to review the section "Absolute Advantage versus Comparative Advantage," which begins on page 64.

Step 2: Answer part (a) by calculating who has a comparative advantage in each activity. Remember that a country has a comparative advantage in producing a good if it can produce the good at the lowest opportunity cost. When Canada produces 1 more ton of honey, it produces 1.5 tons less of maple syrup. When the United States produces 1 more ton of honey, it produces 1 ton less of maple syrup. Therefore, the United States' opportunity cost of producing honey—1 ton of maple syrup—is lower than Canada's—1.5 tons of maple syrup. When Canada produces 1 more ton of maple syrup, it produces 0.67 ton less of honey. When the United States produces 1 more ton of maple syrup, it produces 1 ton less of honey. Therefore, Canada's opportunity cost of producing maple syrup—0.67 ton of honey—is lower than that of the United States—1 ton of honey. We can conclude that the United States has a comparative advantage in the production of honey and Canada has a comparative advantage in the production of maple syrup.

Step 3: Answer part (b) by showing that specialization makes Canada and the United States better off. We know that Canada should specialize where it has a comparative advantage, and the United States should specialize where it has a comparative advantage. If both countries specialize, Canada will produce 60 tons of maple syrup and 0 tons of honey, and the United States will produce 0 tons of maple syrup and 50 tons of honey. After both countries specialize, the United States could then trade 30 tons of honey to Canada in exchange for 40 tons of maple syrup. (Other mutually beneficial trades are possible as well.) We can summarize the results in a table:

	Before Trade		After Trade	
	Honey (in tons)	Maple Syrup (in tons)	Honey (in tons)	Maple Syrup (in tons)
Canada	30	15	30	20
United States	10	40	20	40

The United States is better off after trade because it can consume the same amount of maple syrup and 10 more tons of honey. Canada is better off after trade because it can consume the same amount of honey and 5 more tons of maple syrup.

Step 4: Answer part (c) by drawing the *PPFs*.

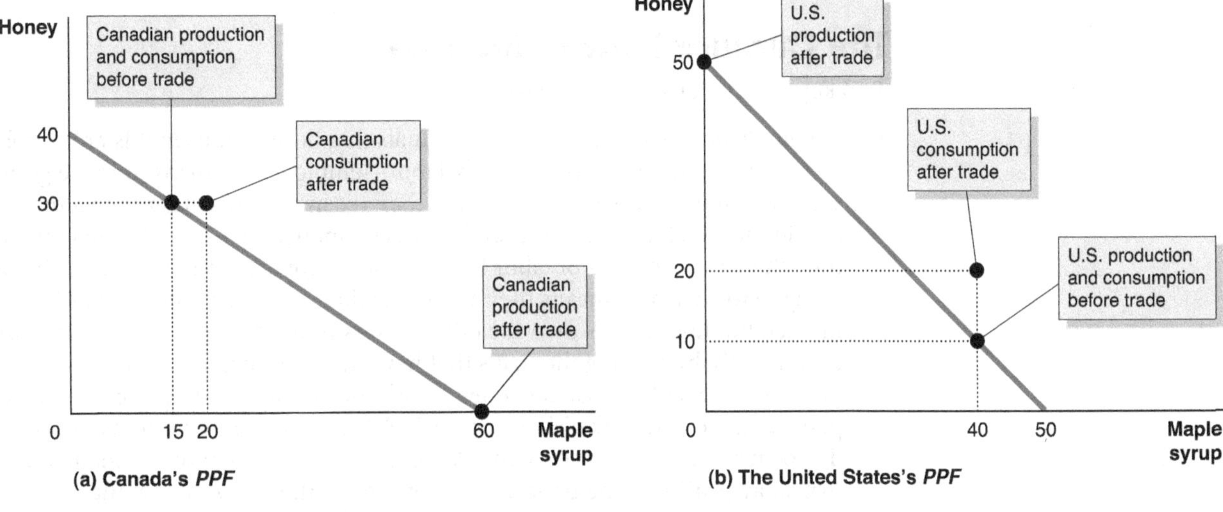

(a) Canada's *PPF*

(b) The United States's *PPF*

The Market System

3.3 LEARNING OBJECTIVE

Explain the basic idea of how a market system works.

We have seen that households, firms, and the government face trade-offs and incur opportunity costs because resources are scarce. We have also seen that trade allows people to specialize according to their comparative advantage. By engaging in trade, people can raise their standard of living. Of course, trade in the modern world is much more complex than the examples we have considered so far. Trade today involves the decisions of millions of people around the world. But how does an economy make trade possible, and how are the decisions of these millions of people coordinated? In the United States and most other countries, trade is carried out in markets. Markets also determine the answers to the three fundamental questions discussed in Chapter 1: What goods and services will be produced? How will the goods and services be produced? and Who will receive the goods and services produced?

Recall that the definition of **market** is a group of buyers and sellers of a good or service and the institution or arrangement by which they come together to trade. Markets take many forms: They can be physical places, such as a local pizza parlor or the New York Stock Exchange, or virtual places, such as eBay. In a market, the buyers are demanders of goods or services, and the sellers are suppliers of goods or services. Households and firms interact in two types of markets: *product markets* and *factor markets*. **Product markets** are markets for goods—such as computers—and services—such as medical treatment. In product markets, households are demanders and firms are suppliers. **Factor markets** are markets for the *factors of production*. **Factors of production** are the inputs used to make goods and services. Factors of production are divided into four broad categories:

Market A group of buyers and sellers of a good or service and the institution or arrangement by which they come together to trade.

Product market A market for goods—such as computers—or services—such as medical treatment.

Factor market A market for the factors of production, such as labor, capital, natural resources, and entrepreneurial ability.

Factors of production The inputs used to make goods and services.

- *Labor* includes all types of work, from the part-time labor of teenagers working at McDonald's to the work of senior managers in large corporations.
- *Capital* refers to physical capital, such as computers and machine tools, that is used to produce other goods.

- *Natural resources* include land, water, oil, iron ore, and other raw materials (or "gifts of nature") that are used in producing goods.
- An *entrepreneur* is someone who operates a business. *Entrepreneurial ability* is the ability to bring together the other factors of production to successfully produce and sell goods and services.

The Circular Flow of Income

Two key groups participate in markets:

- A *household* consists of all the individuals in a home. Households are suppliers of factors of production—particularly labor—employed by firms to make goods and services. Households use the income they receive from selling the factors of production to purchase the goods and services supplied by firms. We are familiar with households as suppliers of labor because most people earn most of their income by going to work, which means they are selling their labor services to firms in the labor market. But households own the other factors of production as well, either directly or indirectly, by owning the firms that have these resources. All firms are owned by households. Small firms, like a neighborhood restaurant, might be owned by one person. Large firms, like Microsoft or BMW, are owned by millions of households that own shares of stock in them. (We discuss the stock market in Chapter 8.) When firms pay profits to the people who own them, the firms are paying for using the capital and natural resources that are supplied to them by those owners. So, we can generalize by saying that in factor markets, households are suppliers and firms are demanders.
- *Firms* are suppliers of goods and services. Firms use the funds they receive from selling goods and services to buy the factors of production needed to make the goods and services.

Circular-flow diagram A model that illustrates how participants in markets are linked.

We can use a simple economic model called the **circular-flow diagram** to see how participants in markets are linked. Figure 3.6 shows that in factor markets, households supply labor and other factors of production in exchange for wages and other payments from firms. In product markets, households use the payments they earn in factor markets to purchase the goods and services supplied by firms. Firms produce these goods and services using the factors of production supplied by households. In the figure, the blue arrows show the flow of factors of production from households through factor markets to firms. The red arrows show the flow of goods and services from firms through product markets to households. The green arrows show the flow of funds from firms through factor markets to households and the flow of spending from households through product markets to firms.

Like all economic models, the circular-flow diagram is a simplified version of reality. For example, Figure 3.6 leaves out the important role of government in buying goods from firms and in making payments, such as Social Security or unemployment insurance payments, to households. The figure also leaves out the roles played by banks, the stock and bond markets, and other parts of the *financial system* in aiding the flow of funds from lenders to borrowers. Finally, the figure does not show that some goods and services purchased by domestic households are produced in foreign countries and some goods and services produced by domestic firms are sold to foreign households. (We explore the government, the financial system, and the international sector further in later chapters.) Despite these simplifications, the circular-flow diagram in Figure 3.6 is useful for seeing how product markets, factor markets, and their participants are linked together. One of the great wonders of the market system is that it manages to successfully coordinate the independent activities of so many households and firms.

Free market A market with few government restrictions on how a good or service can be produced or sold or on how a factor of production can be employed.

The Gains from Free Markets

A **free market** exists when the government places few restrictions on how goods and services can be produced or sold or on how factors of production can be employed.

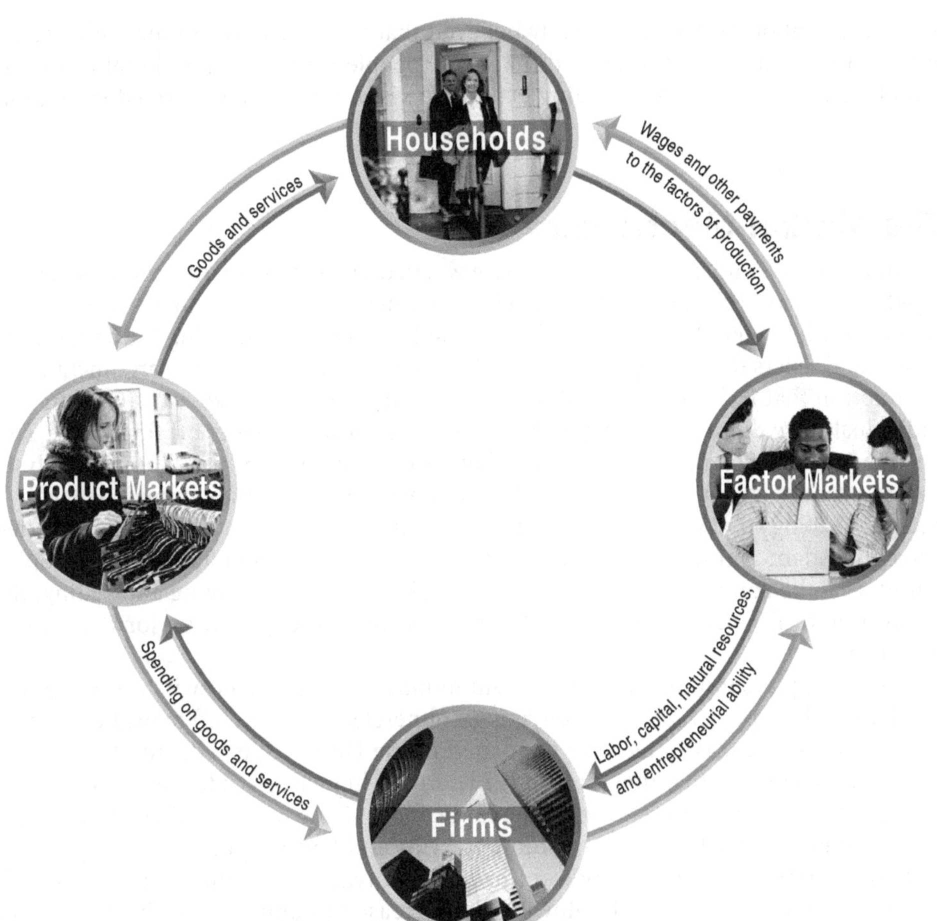

Figure 3.6

The Circular-Flow Diagram

Households and firms are linked together in a circular flow of production, income, and spending. The blue arrows show the flow of the factors of production. In factor markets, households supply labor, entrepreneurial ability, and other factors of production to firms. Firms use these factors of production to make goods and services that they supply to households in product markets. The red arrows show the flow of goods and services from firms to households. The green arrows show the flow of funds. In factor markets, households receive wages and other payments from firms in exchange for supplying the factors of production. Households use these wages and other payments to purchase goods and services from firms in product markets. Firms sell goods and services to households in product markets, and they use the funds to purchase the factors of production from households in factor markets.

Governments in all modern economies intervene more than is consistent with a fully free market. In that sense, we can think of the free market as being a benchmark against which we can judge actual economies. There are relatively few government restrictions on economic activity in the United States, Canada, the countries of Western Europe, Hong Kong, Singapore, and Estonia. So these countries come close to the free market benchmark. In countries such as Cuba and North Korea, the free market system has been rejected in favor of centrally planned economies with extensive government control over product and factor markets. Countries that come closest to the free market benchmark have been more successful than countries with centrally planned economies in providing their people with rising living standards.

The Scottish philosopher Adam Smith is considered the father of modern economics because his book *An Inquiry into the Nature and Causes of the Wealth of Nations*, published in 1776, was an early and very influential argument for the free market system. Smith was writing at a time when extensive government restrictions on markets were still common. In many parts of Europe, the *guild system* still prevailed. Under this system, governments would give guilds, or organizations of producers, the authority to control the production of a good. For example, the shoemakers' guild controlled who was allowed to produce shoes, how many shoes they could produce, and what price they could charge. In France, the cloth makers' guild even dictated the number of threads in the weave of the cloth.

Smith argued that such restrictions reduced the income, or wealth, of a country and its people by restricting the quantity of goods produced. Some people at the time supported the restrictions of the guild system because it was in their financial interest to do so. If you were a member of a guild, the restrictions served to reduce the competition you faced. But other people sincerely believed that the alternative to the guild system was economic chaos. Smith argued that these people were wrong and that a country could enjoy a smoothly functioning economic system if firms were freed from guild restrictions.

The Market Mechanism

In Smith's day, defenders of the guild system worried that if, for instance, the shoemakers' guild did not control shoe production, either too many or too few shoes would be produced. Smith argued that prices would do a better job of coordinating the activities of buyers and sellers than the guilds could. A key to understanding Smith's argument is the assumption that *individuals usually act in a rational, self-interested way*. In particular, individuals take those actions most likely to make themselves better off financially. This assumption of rational, self-interested behavior underlies nearly all economic analysis. In fact, economics can be distinguished from other fields that study human behavior—such as sociology and psychology—by its emphasis on the assumption of self-interested behavior. Adam Smith understood—as economists today understand—that people's motives can be complex. But in analyzing people in the act of buying and selling, the motivation of financial reward usually provides the best explanation for the actions people take.

For example, suppose that a significant number of consumers switch from buying regular gasoline-powered cars to buying gasoline/electric-powered hybrid cars, such as the Toyota Prius, as in fact has happened in the United States during the past 10 years. Firms will find that they can charge relatively higher prices for hybrid cars than they can for regular cars. The self-interest of these firms will lead them to respond to consumers' wishes by producing more hybrids and fewer regular cars. Or suppose that consumers decide that they want to eat less bread, pasta, and other foods high in carbohydrates, as many did following the increase in popularity of the Atkins and South Beach diets. Then the prices firms can charge for bread and pasta will fall. The self-interest of firms will lead them to produce less bread and pasta, which in fact is what happened.

Note that for the market mechanism to work in responding to changes in consumers' wants, *prices must be flexible*. Changes in *relative prices*—that is, the price of one good or service relative to other goods or services—provides information, or a signal, to both consumers and firms. For example, in 2010, consumers worldwide increased their demand for cattle and poultry. Because corn is fed to cattle and poultry, prices for corn soared relative to prices for other crops. Many farmers in the United States received this price signal and responded by increasing the amount of corn they planted and decreasing the amount of soybeans and wheat. One Kansas farmer was quoted as saying, "It seemed to me there was \$100 to \$150 per acre more money in the corn than there was in the beans. That's the kind of math that a lot of guys were using." Similarly, falling prices for DVDs or music CDs in the 2000s was a signal to movie studios and record companies to devote fewer resources to these products and more resources to making movies and music available online. In the United States today, governments at the federal, state, and local levels set or regulate the price of only about 10 to 20 percent of goods and services. The prices of other goods and services are free to change as consumer wants change and as costs of production change.

In the case where consumers want more of a product, and in the case where they want less of a product, the market system responds without a guild or the government giving orders about how much to produce or what price to charge. In a famous phrase, Smith said that firms would be led by the "invisible hand" of the market to provide consumers with what they want. Firms respond *individually* to changes in prices by making decisions that *collectively* end up satisfying the wants of consumers.

Making the Connection

A Story of the Market System in Action: How Do You Make an iPad?

The market coordinates the activities of the many people spread around the world who contribute to the making of an iPad.

Apple produces the iPad 2. Because Apple's headquarters is in Cupertino, California, it seems reasonable to assume that iPads are also manufactured in that state. In fact, although engineers at Apple designed the iPad, the company produces none of the components of the iPad, nor does it assemble the components into a finished product. Far from being produced entirely by one company in one place, the iPad requires the coordinated activities of thousands of workers and dozens of firms spread around the world.

Foxconn, which is based in Taiwan, assembles the iPad in factories in Shenzhen and Chengdu, China, and ships them to Apple for sale in the United States. Foxconn has announced plans to begin assembling some iPads in a new factory in Brazil by 2012. Although Foxconn does final assembly, it doesn't make any of the components and, in fact, charges Apple less than $15 for assembling each iPad.

The table below lists just some of the many suppliers of components for the iPad 2.

Firm	Location of the Firm	iPad Component the Firm Supplies
ARM	Great Britain	Processor design
Broadcom	United States (California)	Touchscreen controller
Infineon Technologies	Germany	Semiconductors
LG Electronics	South Korea	Screen
Samsung	South Korea	Flash memory and processor
Texas Instruments	United States (Texas)	Touchscreen controller

Each of these suppliers in turn relies on its own suppliers. For example, Broadcom designs the touchscreen controller for the iPad and supplies it to Apple, but it does not manufacture the components of the controller or assemble them. To manufacture the components, Broadcom relies on SilTerra, based in Malaysia; SMIC, based in mainland China; and Taiwan Semiconductor Manufacturing Corporation (TSMC) and UMC, based in Taiwan. TSMC's factories are for the most part not in Taiwan but in mainland China and Eastern Europe. To assemble the components, Broadcom uses several companies, including Amkor Technology, based in Chandler, Arizona, and STATS ChipPAC, based in Singapore.

All told, an iPad contains hundreds of parts that are designed, manufactured, and assembled by firms around the world. Many of these firms are not even aware of which other firms are also producing components for the iPad. Few of the managers of these firms have met managers of the other firms or shared knowledge of how their particular components are produced. In fact, no one person from Tim Cook, the chief executive officer of Apple, on down possesses the knowledge of how to produce all the components that are assembled into an iPad. Instead, the invisible hand of the market has led these firms to contribute their knowledge and resources to the process that ultimately results in an iPad available for sale in a store in the United States. Apple has so efficiently organized the process of producing the iPad that you can order a custom iPad with a personal engraving and have it delivered from an assembly plant in China to your doorstep in the United States in as little as three days.

Based on Andrew Rassweiler, "iPad 2 Carries Bill of Materials of $326.60, IHS iSuppli Teardown Analysis Shows," iSuppli.com, March 13, 2011; Arik Hesseldahl, "Apple iPad Components Cost At Least $259," *Bloomberg Businessweek*, April 7, 2010; and Chinmei Sung, "Foxconn Faces Limited Impact from Chengdu Fire, Analysts Say," *Bloomberg Businessweek*, May 22, 2011.

The Role of the Entrepreneur

Entrepreneur Someone who operates a business, bringing together the factors of production—labor, capital, and natural resources—to produce goods and services.

Entrepreneurs are central to the working of the market system. An **entrepreneur** is someone who operates a business. Entrepreneurs must first determine what goods and services they believe consumers want, and then they must decide how to produce those goods and services most profitably, using the available factors of production—labor, capital, and natural resources. Successful entrepreneurs are able to search out opportunities to provide new goods and services. Often these opportunities are created by new technology. Consumers and existing businesses typically do not at first realize that the new technology makes new products feasible. For example, even after the development of the internal combustion engine had made automobiles practicable, Henry Ford remarked, "If I had asked my customers what they wanted, they would have said a faster horse." Because consumers often cannot evaluate a new product before it exists, some of the most successful entrepreneurs, such as the late Steve Jobs of Apple, rarely use *focus groups*, or meetings with consumers in which the customers are asked what new products they would like to see. Instead, entrepreneurs think of products that consumers may not even realize they need, such as, in Jobs's case, an MP3 player—iPod—or a tablet computer—iPad.

Entrepreneurs are of great importance to the economy because they are often responsible for making new products widely available to consumers, as Henry Ford did with the automobile and Steve Jobs did with the iPod. Table 3.3 lists some of the

Table 3.3

Important Products Introduced by Entrepreneurs at Small Firms

Product	Inventor
Air conditioning	William Haviland Carrier
Airplane	Orville and Wilbur Wright
Biomagnetic imaging	Raymond Damadian
Biosynthetic insulin	Herbert Boyer
DNA fingerprinting	Alec Jeffries
FM radio	Edwin Howard Armstrong
Helicopter	Igor Sikorsky
High-resolution CAT scanner	Robert Ledley
Hydraulic brake	Malcolm Lockheed
Integrated circuit	Jack Kilby
Microprocessor	Ted Hoff
Optical scanner	Everett Franklin Lindquist
Oral contraceptives	Carl Djerassi
Overnight delivery service	Fred Smith
Personal computer	Steve Jobs and Steve Wozniak
Quick-frozen foods	Clarence Birdseye
Safety razor	King Gillette
Soft contact lens	Kevin Tuohy
Solid fuel rocket engine	Robert Goddard
Supercomputer	Seymour Cray
Vacuum tube	Philo Farnsworth
Zipper	Gideon Sundback

Based on William J. Baumol, *The Microtheory of Innovative Entrepreneurship*, (Princeton, NJ: Princeton University Press, 2010) and various sources. Note that the person who first commercially developed a particular product is sometimes disputed by historians.

important products entrepreneurs at small firms introduced during the twentieth century.

Entrepreneurs put their own funds at risk when they start businesses. If they are wrong about what consumers want or about the best way to produce goods and services, they can lose those funds. In fact, it is not unusual for entrepreneurs who eventually achieve great success to fail at first. For instance, early in their careers, both Henry Ford and Sakichi Toyoda, who eventually founded the Toyota Motor Corporation, started companies that quickly failed. Research by Richard Freeman of Harvard University has shown that the typical entrepreneur earns less than someone with the same education and other characteristics who is an employee at a large firm. Few entrepreneurs make the fortunes earned by Henry Ford, Steve Jobs, or Bill Gates.

Entrepreneurs make a vital contribution to economic growth through their roles in responding to consumer demand and in introducing new products. So, government policies that encourage entrepreneurship are also likely to increase economic growth and raise the standard of living. In the next section, we consider the legal framework required for a successful market in which entrepreneurs can succeed.

The Legal Basis of a Successful Market System

In a free market, government does not restrict how firms produce and sell goods and services or how they employ factors of production. But the absence of government intervention is not enough for the market system to work well. Government has to take active steps to provide a *legal environment* that will allow the market system to succeed.

Protection of Private Property For the market system to work well, individuals must be willing to take risks. Someone with $250,000 can be cautious and keep it safely in a bank—or even in cash, if the person doesn't trust banks. But the market system won't work unless a significant number of people are willing to risk their funds by investing them in businesses. Investing in businesses is risky in any country. Many businesses fail every year in the United States and other high-income countries. But in high-income countries, someone who starts a new business or invests in an existing business doesn't have to worry that the government, the military, or criminal gangs might decide to seize the business or demand payments for not destroying the business. Unfortunately, in many poor countries, owners of businesses are not well protected from having their businesses seized by the government or from having their profits taken by criminals. Where these problems exist, opening a business can be extremely risky. Cash can be concealed easily, but a business is difficult to conceal and difficult to move.

Property rights are the rights individuals or firms have to the exclusive use of their property, including the right to buy or sell it. Property can be tangible, physical property, such as a store or factory. Property can also be intangible, such as the right to an idea. Two amendments to the U.S. Constitution guarantee property rights: The 5th Amendment states that the federal government shall not deprive any person "of life, liberty, or property, without due process of law." The 14th Amendment extends this guarantee to the actions of state governments: "No state . . . shall deprive any person of life, liberty, or property, without due process of law." Similar guarantees exist in every high-income country. Unfortunately, in many developing countries, such guarantees do not exist or are poorly enforced.

Property rights The rights individuals or firms have to the exclusive use of their property, including the right to buy or sell it.

In any modern economy, *intellectual property rights* are very important. Intellectual property includes books, films, software, and ideas for new products or new ways of producing products. To protect intellectual property, the federal government grants a *patent* that gives an inventor—which is often a firm—the exclusive right to produce and sell a new product for a period of 20 years from the date the patent was filed. For instance, because Microsoft has a patent on the Windows operating system, other firms cannot sell their own versions of Windows. The government grants patents to encourage firms to spend money on the research and development necessary to create new products. If other companies could freely copy Windows, Microsoft would not have spent the funds necessary to develop it. Just as a new product or a new method of making a product receives patent protection, books, films, and software receive *copyright* protection. Under U.S. law, the creator of a book, film, or piece of music has the exclusive right to use the creation during the creator's lifetime. The creator's heirs retain this exclusive right for 50 years after the death of the creator.

Enforcement of Contracts and Property Rights Business activity often involves someone agreeing to carry out some action in the future. For example, you may borrow $20,000 to buy a car and promise the bank—by signing a loan contract—that you will pay back the money over the next five years. Or Microsoft may sign a licensing agreement with a small technology company, agreeing to use that company's technology for a period of several years in return for a fee. Usually these agreements take the form of legal contracts. For the market system to work, businesses and individuals have to rely on these contracts being carried out. If one party to a legal contract does not fulfill its obligations—perhaps the small company had promised Microsoft exclusive use of its technology but then began licensing it to other companies—the other party can go to court to have the agreement enforced. Similarly, if property owners in the United States believe that the federal or state government has violated their rights under the 5th or 14th Amendments, they can go to court to have their rights enforced.

But going to court to enforce a contract or private property rights will be successful only if the court system is independent and judges are able to make impartial decisions on the basis of the law. In the United States and other high-income countries, the court systems have enough independence from other parts of the government and enough protection from intimidation by outside forces—such as criminal gangs—that they are able to make their decisions based on the law. In many developing countries, the court systems lack this independence and will not provide a remedy if the government violates private property rights or if a person with powerful political connections decides to violate a business contract.

If property rights are not well enforced, fewer goods and services will be produced. This reduces economic efficiency, leaving the economy inside its production possibilities frontier.

Continued from page 55

Economics in Your Life

The Trade-offs When You Buy a Car

At the beginning of the chapter, we asked you to think about two questions: When buying a new car, what is the relationship between safety and fuel efficiency? and Under what circumstances would it be possible for automobile manufacturers to make cars safer and more fuel efficient? To answer the first question, you have to recognize that there is a trade-off between safety and fuel efficiency. With the technology available at any particular time, an automobile manufacturer can increase fuel efficiency by making a car smaller and lighter. But driving a lighter car increases your chances of being injured if you have an accident. The trade-off between safety and fuel efficiency would look much like the relationship in Figure 3.1 on page 57. To get more of both safety and gas mileage, automobile makers would have to discover new technologies that allow them to make cars lighter and safer at the same time. Such new technologies would make points like *G* in Figure 3.1 attainable.

CHAPTER 4

Where Prices Come From: The Interaction of Demand and Supply

Chapter Outline and Learning Objectives

The Tablet Computer Revolution

Bill Gates, who was then chairman of Microsoft, made a famous—but wrong!—prediction in 2001. At a computer industry trade show, he predicted that tablet computers would make up a majority of personal computer sales within five years. Microsoft had developed new software that made it possible to use a stylus to write on a laptop computer screen, and Gates hoped that consumers would respond to compact lightweight computers. But many consumers found them awkward to use and thought that the prices, at $2,000 or more, were too high. As a result, rather than making up a majority of computer sales in 2006, tablets were just 1 percent of the market.

Fast forward to 2010: After years of stating that his company would not enter the market for netbooks—or lightweight computers smaller than laptops—Apple CEO Steve Jobs introduced the iPad in April. The iPad was an immediate success, selling nearly 15 million units by the end of the year. The iPad 2, released in early 2011, experienced similarly rapid sales.

The iPad was very different from the tablet computers that had failed to win favor with consumers a few years earlier. The iPad was more awkward to use for word processing or working on spreadsheets, but it was lighter than earlier tablets, and its wireless connectivity and portability made it better for Web surfing, checking e-mail, texting, and watching videos.

Although initially Apple had the market for new-style tablets largely to itself, competitors appeared rapidly. Toshiba, Samsung, Dell, LG, Motorola, Lenovo, Amazon, and ZTE all introduced tablets running on Google's Android operating system. Research in Motion (RIM) introduced the BlackBerry Playbook, based on its operating system.

The intense competition among firms selling the new tablets is a striking example of how the market responds to changes in consumer tastes. As many consumers indicated that they would buy small tablets, firms scrambled to meet the demand for this new product. Although intense competition is not always good news for firms trying to sell products, it is a boon to consumers because it increases the available choice of products and lowers the prices consumers pay for those products.

Based on Matt Berger and James Niccolai, "Gates Unveils Portable Tablet PC," *PC World*, November 12, 2001; Wolfgang Gruener, "240 Million Tablets: The Gazillion-Dollar Forecast Game," www.fool.com, February 6, 2011; David Pogue, "Pretty Tablet, Though Late for the Ball," *New York Times*, June 29, 2011; and Stu Woo and Yukari Iwatani Kane, "Amazon to Battle Apple iPad with Tablet," *Wall Street Journal*, July 14, 2011.

Economics in Your Life

Will You Buy an Apple iPad or a Samsung Galaxy Tab?

Suppose you are considering buying a tablet computer and that you are choosing between an Apple iPad and a Samsung Galaxy Tab. Apple introduced the iPad in April 2010, and Samsung introduced the Galaxy Tab in November 2010; seven months is a long time in the world of high-tech gadgets. Apple products have become very fashionable, and if you buy an iPad, you will have access to many more applications—or "apps"—that can increase the enjoyability and productivity of your tablet. One strategy Samsung can use to overcome those advantages is to compete based on price and value. Would you choose to buy a Galaxy Tab if it had a lower price than an iPad? If your income increased, would it affect your decision about which tablet to buy? As you read the chapter, see if you can answer these questions. You can check your answers against those we provide **page 99** at the end of this chapter.

Recall from Chapter 1 that because economic models rely on assumptions, the models are simplifications of reality. In some cases, the assumptions of the model may not seem to describe exactly the economic situation being analyzed. For example, the model of demand and supply assumes that we are analyzing a *perfectly competitive market*. In a **perfectly competitive market**, there are many buyers and sellers, all the products sold are identical, and there are no barriers to new firms entering the market. These assumptions are very restrictive and apply exactly to only a few markets, such as the markets for wheat and other agricultural products. Experience has shown, however, that the model of demand and supply can be very useful in analyzing markets where competition among sellers is intense, even if there are relatively few sellers and the products being sold are not identical. In fact, in recent studies, the model of demand and supply has been successful in analyzing markets with as few as four buyers and four sellers. In the end, the usefulness of a model depends on how well it can predict outcomes in a market. As we will see in this chapter, this model is often very useful in predicting changes in quantities and prices in many markets.

Perfectly competitive market A market that meets the conditions of (1) many buyers and sellers, (2) all firms selling identical products, and (3) no barriers to new firms entering the market.

We begin considering the model of demand and supply by discussing consumers and the demand side of the market, before turning to firms and the supply side. Throughout the book we will apply this model to understand business, the economy, and economic policy.

4.1 LEARNING OBJECTIVE

Discuss the variables that influence demand.

The Demand Side of the Market

The most successful businesses are the ones that respond best to consumer demand. But what determines consumer demand for a product? Certainly, many factors influence the willingness of consumers to buy a particular product. For example, consumers who are considering buying a tablet computer, such as an Apple iPad or an Samsung Galaxy Tab, will make their decisions based on, among other factors, the income they have available to spend and the effectiveness of the advertising campaigns of the companies that sell tablets. The main factor in most consumer decisions, though, is the price of the product. So, it makes sense to begin with price when analyzing the decisions of consumers to buy a product. It is important to note that when we discuss demand, we are considering not what a consumer *wants* to buy but what the consumer is both willing and *able* to buy.

Demand Schedules and Demand Curves

Tables that show the relationship between the price of a product and the quantity of the product demanded are called **demand schedules**. The table in Figure 4.1 shows the number of tablet computers consumers would be willing to buy over the course of a day at five different prices. The amount of a good or a service that a consumer is willing and able to purchase at a given price is referred to as the **quantity demanded**. The graph in Figure 4.1 plots the numbers from the table as a **demand curve**, a curve that shows the relationship between the price of a product and the quantity of the product demanded. (Note that for convenience, we made the demand curve in Figure 4.1 a straight line, or linear. There is no reason that all demand curves need to be straight lines.) The demand curve in Figure 4.1 shows the **market demand**, or the demand by all the consumers of a given good or service. The market for a product, such as restaurant meals, that is purchased locally would include all the consumers in a city or a relatively small area. The market for a product that is sold internationally, such as tablet computers, would include all the consumers in the world.

Demand schedule A table that shows the relationship between the price of a product and the quantity of the product demanded.

Quantity demanded The amount of a good or service that a consumer is willing and able to purchase at a given price.

Demand curve A curve that shows the relationship between the price of a product and the quantity of the product demanded.

Market demand The demand by all the consumers of a given good or service.

The demand curve in Figure 4.1 slopes downward because consumers will buy more tablets as the price falls. When the price of a tablet is $700, consumers buy 3 million

Demand Schedule	
Price (dollars per tablet)	Quantity (millions of tablets per month)
$700	3
600	4
500	5
400	6
300	7

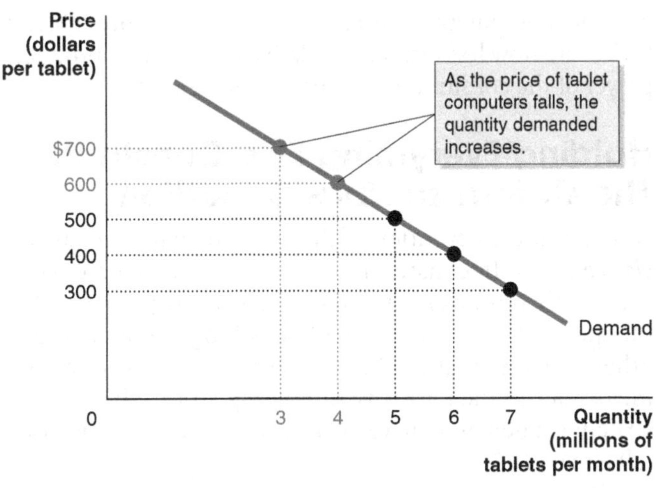

Figure 4.1

A Demand Schedule and Demand Curve

As the price changes, consumers change the quantity of tablet computers they are willing to buy. We can show this as a *demand schedule* in a table or as a *demand curve* on a graph. The table and graph both show that as the price of tablet computers falls, the quantity demanded increases. When the price of tablet computers is $700, consumers buy 3 million tablets per month. When the price drops to $600, consumers buy 4 million tablets. Therefore, the demand curve for tablet computers is downward sloping.

tablets per month. If the price of a tablet falls to $600, consumers buy 4 million tablets. Buyers demand a larger quantity of a product as the price falls because the product becomes less expensive relative to other products and because they can afford to buy more at a lower price.

The Law of Demand

The inverse relationship between the price of a product and the quantity of the product demanded is called the **law of demand**: Holding everything else constant, when the price of a product falls, the quantity demanded of the product will increase, and when the price of a product rises, the quantity demanded of the product will decrease. The law of demand holds for any market demand curve. Economists have found only a very few exceptions to this law.

Law of demand The rule that, holding everything else constant, when the price of a product falls, the quantity demanded of the product will increase, and when the price of a product rises, the quantity demanded of the product will decrease.

What Explains the Law of Demand?

It makes sense that consumers will buy more of a good when the price falls and less of a good when the price rises, but let's look more closely at why this is true. When the price of tablet computers falls, consumers buy a larger quantity because of the *substitution effect* and the *income effect.*

Substitution Effect The **substitution effect** refers to the change in the quantity demanded of a good that results from a change in price, making the good more or less expensive *relative* to other goods that are *substitutes.* When the price of tablet computers falls, consumers will substitute buying tablet computers for buying other goods, such as laptop computers, netbook computers, or even smartphones.

Substitution effect The change in the quantity demanded of a good that results from a change in price, making the good more or less expensive relative to other goods that are substitutes.

The Income Effect The **income effect** of a price change refers to the change in the quantity demanded of a good that results from the effect of a change in the good's price on consumers' purchasing power. Purchasing power is the quantity of goods a consumer can buy with a fixed amount of income. When the price of a good falls, the increased purchasing power of consumers' incomes will usually lead them to purchase a larger quantity of the good. When the price of a good rises, the decreased purchasing power of consumers' incomes will usually lead them to purchase a smaller quantity of the good.

Income effect The change in the quantity demanded of a good that results from the effect of a change in the good's price on consumers' purchasing power.

Note that although we can analyze them separately, the substitution effect and the income effect happen simultaneously whenever a price changes. So, a fall in the price of tablet computers leads consumers to buy more tablet computers, both because the tablets are now less expensive relative to substitute products and because the purchasing power of the consumers' incomes has increased.

Holding Everything Else Constant: The *Ceteris paribus* Condition

Notice that the definition of the law of demand contains the phrase *holding everything else constant.* In constructing the market demand curve for tablet computers, we focused only on the effect that changes in the price of tablet computers would have on the quantity consumers would be willing and able to buy. We were holding constant other variables that might affect the willingness of consumers to buy tablets. Economists refer to the necessity of holding all variables other than price constant in constructing a demand curve as the ***ceteris paribus* condition**; *ceteris paribus* is Latin for "all else equal."

***Ceteris paribus* ("all else equal") condition** The requirement that when analyzing the relationship between two variables—such as price and quantity demanded—other variables must be held constant.

What would happen if we allowed a change in a variable—other than price—that might affect the willingness of consumers to buy tablet computers? Consumers would then change the quantity they demanded at each price. We can illustrate this effect by shifting the market demand curve. A shift of a demand curve is *an increase or a decrease in demand.* A movement along a demand curve is *an increase or a decrease in the quantity demanded.* As Figure 4.2 shows, we shift the demand curve to the right if consumers decide to buy more of the good at each price, and we shift the demand curve to the left if consumers decide to buy less at each price.

Variables That Shift Market Demand

Many variables other than price can influence market demand. These five are the most important:

- Income
- Prices of related goods
- Tastes
- Population and demographics
- Expected future prices

We next discuss how changes in each of these variables affect the market demand curve.

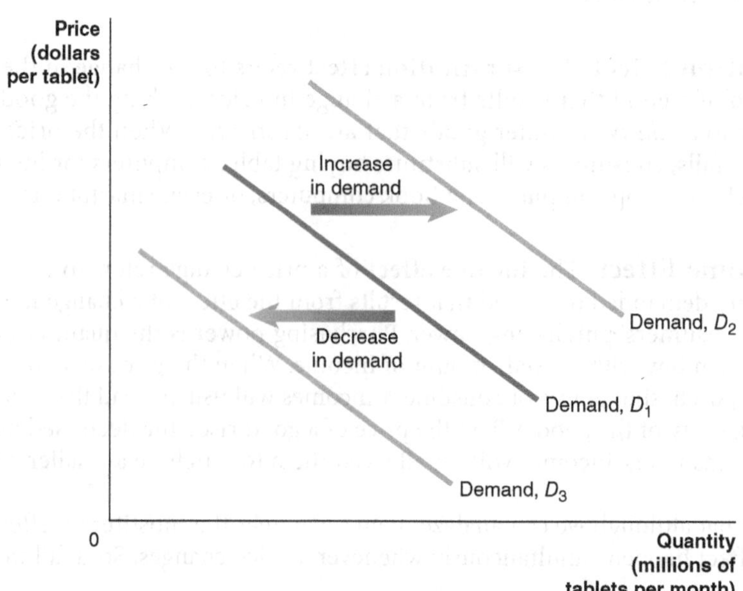

Figure 4.2

Shifting the Demand Curve

When consumers increase the quantity of a product they want to buy at a given price, the market demand curve shifts to the right, from D_1 to D_2. When consumers decrease the quantity of a product they want to buy at a given price, the demand curve shifts to the left, from D_1 to D_3.

Income The income that consumers have available to spend affects their willingness and ability to buy a good. Suppose that the market demand curve in Figure 4.1 on page 79 represents the willingness of consumers to buy tablet computers when average household income is $50,000. If household income rises to $52,000, the demand for tablets will increase, which we show by shifting the demand curve to the right. A good is a **normal good** when demand increases following a rise in income and decreases following a fall in income. Most goods are normal goods, but the demand for some goods falls when income rises and rises when income falls. For instance, as your income rises, you might buy less canned tuna or fewer hot dogs and buy more shrimp or prime rib. A good is an **inferior good** when demand decreases following a rise in income and increases following a fall in income. So, for you, canned tuna and hot dogs would be examples of inferior goods—not because they are of low quality but because you buy less of them as your income increases.

Normal good A good for which the demand increases as income rises and decreases as income falls.

Inferior good A good for which the demand increases as income falls and decreases as income rises.

Making the Connection: Are Quiznos Sandwiches Normal Goods and Subway Sandwiches Inferior Goods?

In recent years, as American families juggle busy schedules, they have increasingly relied on eating out rather than preparing meals at home. According to a survey by *Restaurants and Institutions* magazine, adults eat an average of nearly four meals per week outside the home. Nearly one-third of consumers frequently eat lunch away from home, and on weekdays more than 15 percent frequently eat dinner away from home, a proportion that rises to more than 35 percent on weekends.

Subway experienced increased sales during 2008 and 2009, while sales of Quiznos sandwiches fell.

Does this behavior change during a recession? We might expect that it would because recessions result in declining incomes, as some people lose their jobs and others are forced to work fewer hours or have their wages reduced. Dining out is more expensive than preparing meals at home, so one way to save during a recession is to cut back on restaurant meals. In fact, during the 2007–2009 recession, many restaurants had a difficult time. Particularly hard hit were "casual dining" restaurants that provide table service and serve moderately priced food. Among other restaurants, Ruby Tuesday, Olive Garden, Red Lobster, and LongHorn Steakhouse all experienced declining demand, while Bennigan's and Steak and Ale filed for bankruptcy.

However, the recession hurt some restaurants more than others. McDonald's restaurants experienced increased sales during 2008 and 2009. In the market for fast-food sandwiches, Subway reported increasing sales, while sales of Quiznos sandwiches, which are higher-priced, fell. So, Big Macs and Subway sandwiches seem to fit the economic definition of an inferior good because demand increases as income falls, while Quiznos sandwiches fit the definition of a normal good. But remember that inferior goods are not necessarily of low quality; they are just goods for which consumers increase their demand as their incomes fall.

Based on Julie Jargon and Mike Spector, "LBO, Recession Singe Quiznos," *Wall Street Journal*, July 21, 2011; Melodie Warner, "McDonald's Profit Rises 15%," *Wall Street Journal*, July 22, 2011; and "The New American Diner," *Restaurants and Institutions*, January 1, 2008.

Prices of Related Goods The prices of other goods can also affect consumers' demand for a product. Goods and services that can be used for the same purpose—such as tablet computers and laptop computers—are **substitutes**. When two goods are substitutes, the more you buy of one, the less you will buy of the other. A decrease in the price

Substitutes Goods and services that can be used for the same purpose.

of a substitute causes the demand curve for a good to shift to the left. An increase in the price of a substitute causes the demand curve for a good to shift to the right.

Suppose that the market demand curve in Figure 4.1 on page 79 represents the willingness and ability of consumers to buy laptop computers during a week when the average price of a laptop computer is $800. If the average price of laptops falls to $700, how will the market demand for tablets change? Consumers will demand fewer tablets at every price. We show this by shifting the demand curve for tablets to the left.

Complements Goods and services that are used together.

Goods and services that are used together—such as hot dogs and hot dog buns—are **complements**. When two goods are complements, the more consumers buy of one, the more they will buy of the other. A decrease in the price of a complement causes the demand curve for a good to shift to the right. An increase in the price of a complement causes the demand curve for a good to shift to the left.

Many people use applications, or "apps," on their tablet computers. So, tablets and apps are complements. Suppose the market demand curve in Figure 4.1 represents the willingness of consumers to buy tablets at a time when the average price of an app is $2.99. If the average price of apps drops to $0.99, consumers will buy more apps *and* more tablets: The demand curve for tablets will shift to the right.

Tastes Consumers can be influenced by an advertising campaign for a product. If Apple, Samsung, Amazon, and other firms making tablet computers begin to advertise heavily online, consumers are more likely to buy tablets at every price, and the demand curve will shift to the right. An economist would say that the advertising campaign has affected consumers' *taste* for tablet computers. Taste is a catchall category that refers to the many subjective elements that can enter into a consumer's decision to buy a product. A consumer's taste for a product can change for many reasons. Sometimes trends play a substantial role. For example, the popularity of low-carbohydrate diets caused a decline in demand for some goods, such as bread and donuts, and an increase in demand for beef. In general, when consumers' taste for a product increases, the demand curve will shift to the right, and when consumers' taste for a product decreases, the demand curve for the product will shift to the left.

Population and Demographics Population and demographic factors can affect the demand for a product. As the population of the United States increases, so will the number of consumers, and the demand for most products will increase. The **demographics** of a population refers to its characteristics, with respect to age, race, and gender. As the demographics of a country or region change, the demand for particular goods will increase or decrease because different categories of people tend to have different preferences for those goods. For instance, Hispanics are expected to increase from 16 percent of the U.S. population in 2010 to 29 percent in 2050. This increase will expand demand for Spanish-language books and cable television channels, among other goods and services.

Demographics The characteristics of a population with respect to age, race, and gender.

Making the Connection: The Aging of the Baby Boom Generation

The average age of the U.S. population is increasing. After World War II in 1945, the United States experienced a "baby boom," as birthrates rose and remained high through the early 1960s. Falling birthrates after 1965 mean that the baby boom generation is larger than the generation before it and the generations after it. The figure on the next page uses projections from the U.S. Census Bureau to show that as boomers age, they are increasing the fraction of the U.S. population that is older than 65.

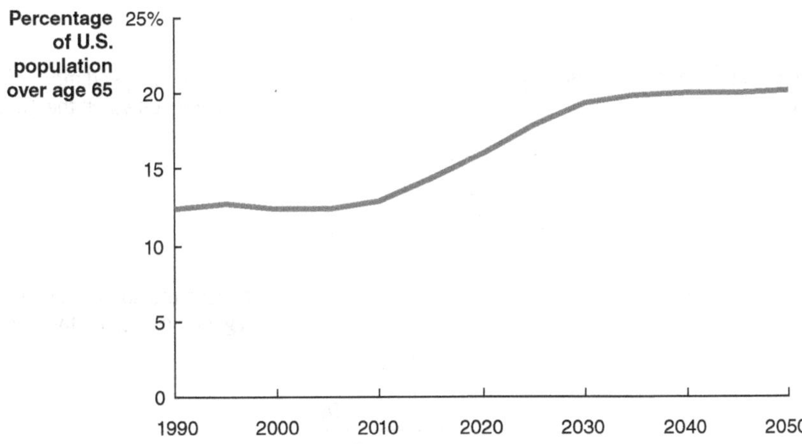

Data from U.S. Census Bureau.

What effects will the aging of the baby boom generation have on the economy? Older people have a greater demand for medical care than do younger people. So, in coming years, the demand for doctors, nurses, and hospital facilities should all increase. The increasing demand for health care is so strong that between the beginning of the 2007–2009 recession and June 2011, 1 million new jobs were created in health care—at the same time as total employment in the United States *declined* by 7 million jobs. As we mentioned in Chapter 3, the increased demand for medical care will also drive up the federal government's costs under the Medicare program, which pays part of the medical bills of people who are 65 and older.

Aging boomers will also have an effect on the housing market. Older people often "downsize" their housing by moving from large, single-family homes, whose maintenance can be difficult and expensive, to smaller homes, condominiums, or apartments. So, in coming years, the demand for large homes may decrease, while the demand for smaller homes and apartments may increase. Older people also tend to drive less often and for shorter distances than do younger drivers. So, their cars wear out more slowly and, therefore, need to be replaced less often, reducing the total demand for cars.

Based on U.S. Bureau of Labor Statistics, "Employment, Hours, and Earnings from the Current Employment Statistics Survey," July 2011; Liam Denning, "Car Makers Hit the Age Speed Bump," *Wall Street Journal*, September 18, 2010; Kendra Marr, "The Economy's Steady Pulse—Health-Care Sector Is Poised to Keep Expanding, but So Are Its Costs," *Washington Post*, June 13, 2008; and Peter Francese, "The Changing Face of the U.S. Consumer," *Advertising Age*, July 7, 2008.

Expected Future Prices Consumers choose not only which products to buy but also when to buy them. For instance, if enough consumers become convinced that houses will be selling for lower prices in three months, the demand for houses will decrease now, as some consumers postpone their purchases to wait for the expected price decrease. Alternatively, if enough consumers become convinced that the price of houses will be higher in three months, the demand for houses will increase now, as some consumers try to beat the expected price increase.

Table 4.1 on page 84 summarizes the most important variables that cause market demand curves to shift. Note that the table shows the shift in the demand curve that results from an *increase* in each of the variables. A *decrease* in these variables would cause the demand curve to shift in the opposite direction.

A Change in Demand versus a Change in Quantity Demanded

It is important to understand the difference between a *change in demand* and a *change in quantity demanded.* A change in demand refers to a shift of the demand curve. A shift occurs if there is a change in one of the variables, *other than the price of the product,* that

Table 4.1

Variables That Shift Market Demand Curves

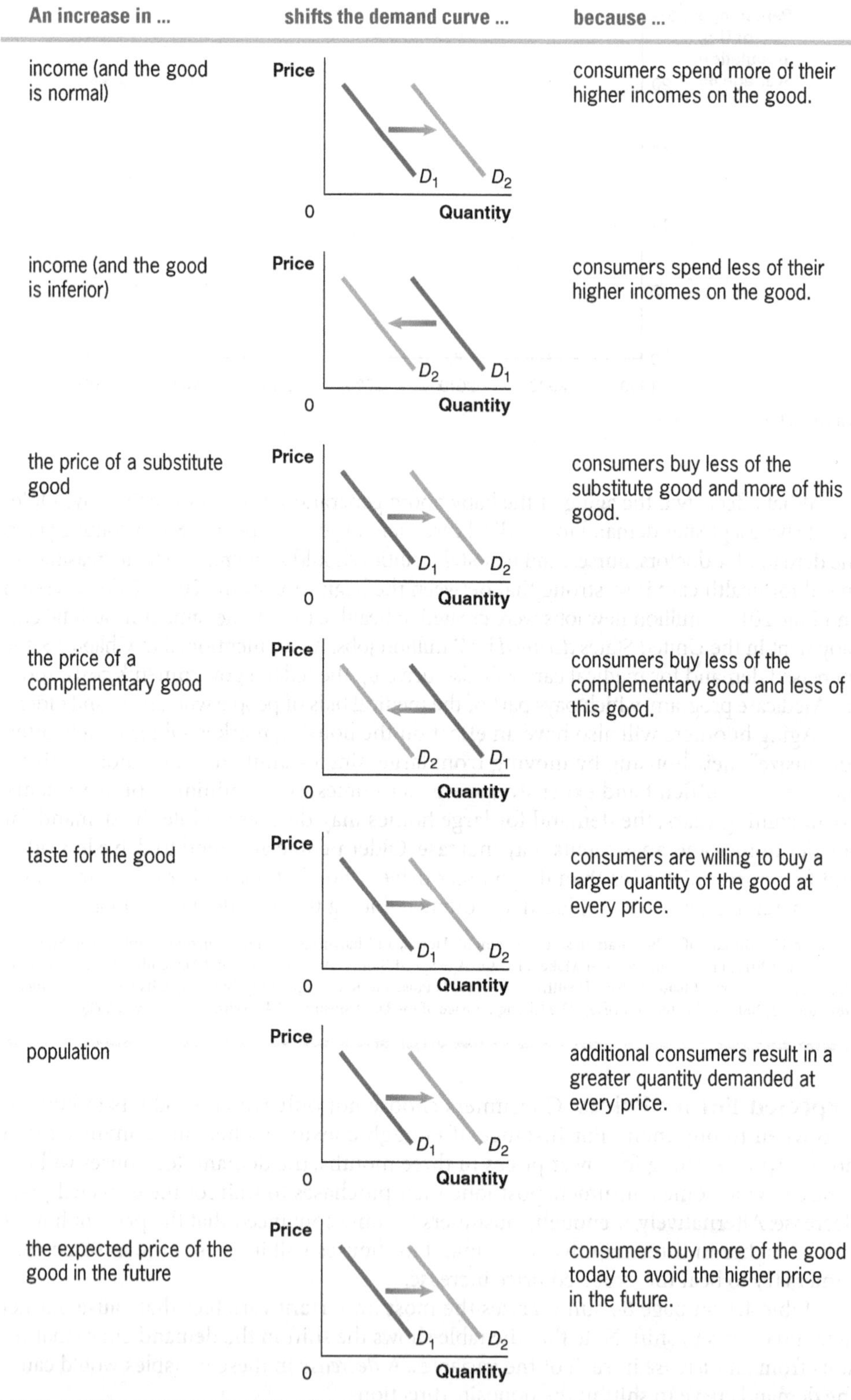

An increase in ...	shifts the demand curve ...	because ...
income (and the good is normal)	Price, D_1, D_2, 0, Quantity	consumers spend more of their higher incomes on the good.
income (and the good is inferior)	Price, D_2, D_1, 0, Quantity	consumers spend less of their higher incomes on the good.
the price of a substitute good	Price, D_1, D_2, 0, Quantity	consumers buy less of the substitute good and more of this good.
the price of a complementary good	Price, D_2, D_1, 0, Quantity	consumers buy less of the complementary good and less of this good.
taste for the good	Price, D_1, D_2, 0, Quantity	consumers are willing to buy a larger quantity of the good at every price.
population	Price, D_1, D_2, 0, Quantity	additional consumers result in a greater quantity demanded at every price.
the expected price of the good in the future	Price, D_1, D_2, 0, Quantity	consumers buy more of the good today to avoid the higher price in the future.

affects the willingness of consumers to buy the product. A change in quantity demanded refers to a movement along the demand curve as a result of a change in the product's price. Figure 4.3 illustrates this important distinction. If the price of tablet computers falls from $700 to $600 per tablet, the result will be a movement along the demand curve from point *A* to point *B*—an increase in quantity demanded from 3 million to 4 million. If consumers' incomes increase, or if another factor changes that makes consumers want more of the product at every price, the demand curve will shift to the right—an increase

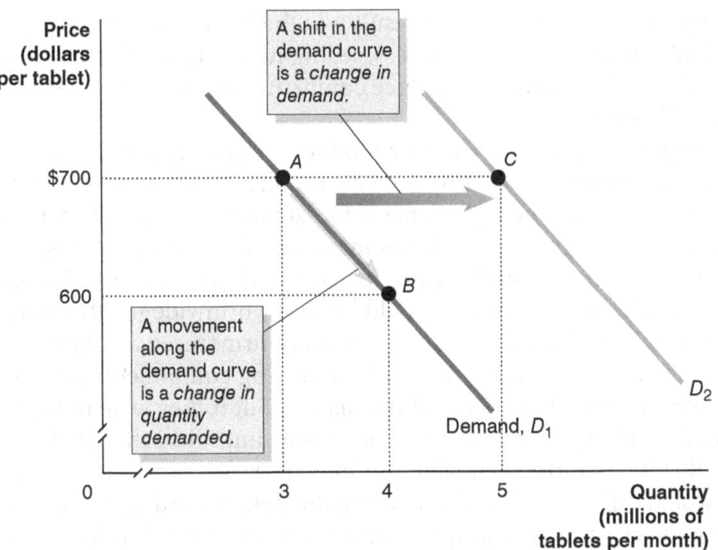

Figure 4.3

A Change in Demand versus a Change in Quantity Demanded

If the price of tablet computers falls from $700 to $600, the result will be a movement along the demand curve from point *A* to point *B*—an increase in quantity demanded from 3 million tablets to 4 million tablets. If consumers' incomes increase, or if another factor changes that makes consumers want more of the product at every price, the demand curve will shift to the right—an increase in demand. In this case, the increase in demand from D_1 to D_2 causes the quantity of tablet computers demanded at a price of $700 to increase from 3 million tablets at point *A* to 5 million tablets at point *C*.

in demand. In this case, the increase in demand from D_1 to D_2 causes the quantity of tablet computers demanded at a price of $700 to increase from 3 million at point *A* to 5 million at point *C*.

Making the Connection: Forecasting the Demand for iPads

One of the most important decisions that the managers of any large firm face is which new products to develop. A firm must devote people, time, and money to designing a new product, negotiating with suppliers, formulating a marketing campaign, and many other tasks. But any firm has only limited resources and so faces a trade-off: Resources used to develop one product will not be available to develop another product. Ultimately, the products a firm chooses to develop will be those that it believes will be the most profitable. So, to decide which products to develop, firms need to forecast the demand for those products.

Will the future demand for tablets such as the iPad continue to grow?

We saw at the beginning of the chapter that in 2001, Bill Gates predicted that within five years, a majority of computers sold would be tablets. If Gates had been correct about the way the computer market was changing, then any computer firm that didn't develop a tablet would have run the risk of being left behind. David Sobotta, who worked at Apple for 20 years and eventually became its national sales manager, has described discussions at Apple during 2002 about whether to develop a tablet. According to Sobotta, representatives of the federal government's National Institutes of Health urged Apple to develop a tablet computer, arguing that it would be particularly useful to doctors, nurses, and hospitals. Apple's managers decided not to develop a tablet, however, because they believed the technology available at that time was too complex for the average computer user and they also believed that the demand from doctors and nurses would be small. As we saw in the chapter opener, Apple's forecast was correct. Despite Bill Gates's prediction, in 2006, tablets made up only 1 percent of the computer market. According to Sobotta, "Apple executives had a theory that the route to success will not be through selling thousands of relatively expensive things, but millions of very inexpensive things like iPods."

Apple continued to work on tablets, though, developing the technology to eliminate keyboards in favor of touchscreen displays. Rather than proceed immediately to building a tablet, Steve Jobs, who was then Apple's CEO, realized he could use this technology in a different way: "I thought 'My God we can build a phone out of this.'" After the technology had been successfully embodied in the iPhone, Apple and Jobs turned back to developing a tablet computer. The result was the iPad, first offered for sale in April 2010. The iPad was an immediate success, selling nearly 15 million units by the end of 2010 and leading other firms to introduce competing products. But how rapidly would demand for tablets grow?

Forecasting the demand for any new product is challenging because it is difficult to gauge how many consumers will find the new product to be useful. For instance, would consumers see tablets as good replacements for laptop computers? If so, the demand for tablets might be very large. Or would consumers see tablets as being more like e-readers, such as the Amazon Kindle? In that case, demand was likely to be much smaller. In mid-2011, forecasts of how many tablets would be sold worldwide in 2012 ranged between 54.8 million and 120 million. Given this uncertainty, firms faced a difficult choice: If they were too cautious in expanding capacity or in buying components for a new product, other firms might seize a large share of the market. But if they were too optimistic, they ran the risk of spending on capacity to produce more units than they could actually sell—an outcome that might turn potential profits into losses. For example, in 2011, Apple forecast that it would sell 40 million iPads during the year. Accordingly, the company spent several billion dollars to buy large quantities of touchscreen panels from manufacturers, including Wintek, Sharp, and TPK. That would be money well spent . . . if the forecast demand turns out to be accurate. Time will tell whether the future demand for tablets will be as large as Apple and other firms were forecasting it would be during 2011.

Based on Wolfgang Gruener, "240 Million Tablets: The Gazillion-Dollar Forecast Game," www.fool.com, February 6, 2011; "Apple Conference Call on Q1 2011 Financial Results," www.apple.com, January 18, 2011; David Sobotta, "What Jobs Told Me on the iPhone," *The Guardian* (London), January 3, 2007, p. 1; "Jobs Says iPad Idea Came Before iPhone," *Associated Press*, January 2, 2010; and Laura June, "The Apple Tablet: A Complete History, Supposedly," endgadget.com, January 26, 2010.

4.2 LEARNING OBJECTIVE

Discuss the variables that influence supply.

The Supply Side of the Market

Quantity supplied The amount of a good or service that a firm is willing and able to supply at a given price.

Just as many variables influence the willingness and ability of consumers to buy a particular good or service, many variables also influence the willingness and ability of firms to sell a good or service. The most important of these variables is price. The amount of a good or service that a firm is willing and able to supply at a given price is the **quantity supplied**. Holding other variables constant, when the price of a good rises, producing the good is more profitable, and the quantity supplied will increase. When the price of a good falls, the good is less profitable, and the quantity supplied will decrease. In addition, as we saw in Chapter 3, devoting more and more resources to the production of a good results in increasing marginal costs. If, for example, Apple, Toshiba, Samsung, LG, and other firms increase production of tablet computers during a given time period, they are likely to find that the cost of producing additional tablets increases as their suppliers run existing factories for longer hours and pay higher prices for components and higher wages for workers. With higher marginal costs, firms will supply a larger quantity only if the price is higher.

Supply Schedules and Supply Curves

Supply schedule A table that shows the relationship between the price of a product and the quantity of the product supplied.

Supply curve A curve that shows the relationship between the price of a product and the quantity of the product supplied.

A **supply schedule** is a table that shows the relationship between the price of a product and the quantity of the product supplied. The table in Figure 4.4 is a supply schedule showing the quantity of tablet computers that firms would be willing to supply per month at different prices. The graph in Figure 4.4 plots the numbers from the supply schedule as a *supply curve*. A **supply curve** shows the relationship between the price of a product and the quantity of the product supplied. The supply schedule and supply curve both show that as the price of tablet computers rises, firms will increase the quantity they supply. At a price of $600 per tablet, firms will supply 6 million tablets per month. At the higher price of $700, firms will supply 7 million. (Once again, we are assuming for convenience that the supply curve is a straight line, even though not all supply curves are actually straight lines.)

Supply Schedule	
Price (dollars per tablet)	Quantity (millions of tablets per month)
$700	7
600	6
500	5
400	4
300	3

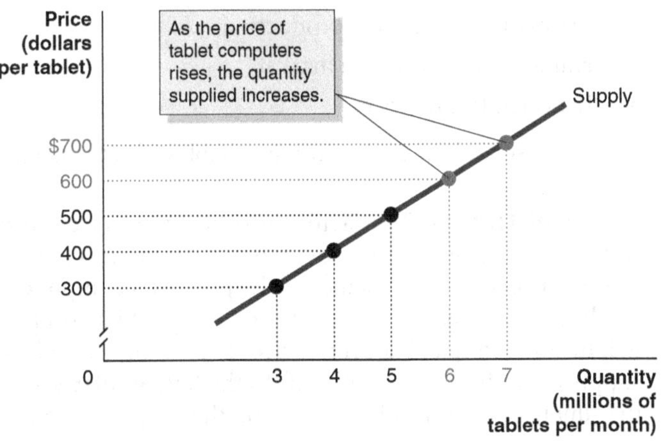

Figure 4.4

A Supply Schedule and Supply Curve

As the price changes, Apple, Toshiba, Samsung, LG, and other firms producing tablet computers change the quantity they are willing to supply. We can show this as a *supply schedule* in a table or as a *supply curve* on a graph. The supply schedule and supply curve both show that as the price of tablet computers rises, firms will increase the quantity they supply. At a price of $600 per tablet, firms will supply 6 million tablets. At a price of $700, firms will supply 7 million tablets.

The Law of Supply

The *market supply curve* in Figure 4.4 is upward sloping. We expect most supply curves to be upward sloping, according to the **law of supply**, which states that, holding everything else constant, increases in price cause increases in the quantity supplied, and decreases in price cause decreases in the quantity supplied. Notice that the definition of the law of supply—like the definition of the law of demand—contains the phrase *holding everything else constant.* If only the price of the product changes, there is a movement along the supply curve, which is *an increase or a decrease in the quantity supplied.* As Figure 4.5 shows, if any other variable that affects the willingness of firms to supply a good changes, the supply curve will shift, which is *an increase or a decrease in supply.* When firms increase the quantity of a product they want to sell at a given price, the supply curve shifts to the right. The shift from S_1 to S_3 represents *an increase in supply.* When firms decrease the quantity of a product they want to sell at a given price, the supply curve shifts to the left. The shift from S_1 to S_2 represents *a decrease in supply.*

Law of supply The rule that, holding everything else constant, increases in price cause increases in the quantity supplied, and decreases in price cause decreases in the quantity supplied.

Variables That Shift Market Supply

The following are the most important variables that shift market supply:

- Prices of inputs
- Technological change

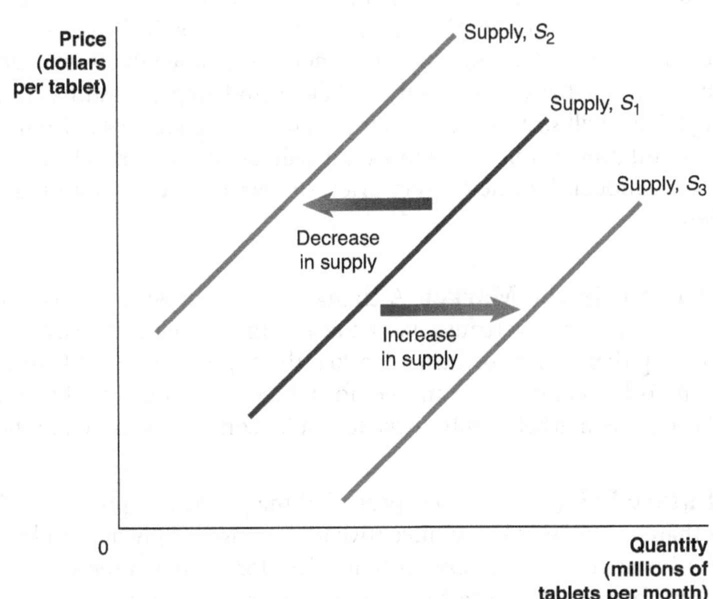

Figure 4.5

Shifting the Supply Curve

When firms increase the quantity of a product they want to sell at a given price, the supply curve shifts to the right. The shift from S_1 to S_3 represents an *increase in supply*. When firms decrease the quantity of a product they want to sell at a given price, the supply curve shifts to the left. The shift from S_1 to S_2 represents a *decrease in supply.*

- Prices of substitutes in production
- Number of firms in the market
- Expected future prices

We next discuss how each of these variables affects the market supply curve.

Prices of Inputs The factor most likely to cause the supply curve for a product to shift is a change in the price of an *input*. An input is anything used in the production of a good or service. For instance, if the price of a component of tablet computers, such as Flash memory, rises, the cost of producing tablet computers will increase, and tablets will be less profitable at every price. The supply of tablets will decline, and the market supply curve for tablets will shift to the left. Similarly, if the price of an input declines, the supply of tablets will increase, and the supply curve will shift to the right.

Technological change A positive or negative change in the ability of a firm to produce a given level of output with a given quantity of inputs.

Technological Change A second factor that causes a change in supply is *technological change*. **Technological change** is a positive or negative change in the ability of a firm to produce a given level of output with a given quantity of inputs. Positive technological change occurs whenever a firm is able to produce more output using the same amount of inputs. This shift will happen when the *productivity* of workers or machines increases. If a firm can produce more output with the same amount of inputs, its costs will be lower, and the good will be more profitable to produce at any given price. As a result, when positive technological change occurs, the firm will increase the quantity supplied at every price, and its supply curve will shift to the right. Normally, we expect technological change to have a positive effect on a firm's willingness to supply a product.

Negative technological change is relatively rare, although it could result from an earthquake or another natural disaster or from a war that reduces firms' ability to supply as much output with a given amount of inputs. Negative technological change will raise firms' costs, and the good will be less profitable to produce. Therefore, negative technological change will cause the market supply curve to shift to the left.

Prices of Substitutes in Production Firms often choose which good or service they will produce. Alternative products that a firm could produce are called *substitutes in production*. To this point, we have considered the market for all types of tablet computers. A key feature of tablet computers is whether they connect to the Internet just by Wi-Fi or by either Wi-Fi or a cellular network. Suppose we consider as separate markets tablet computers capable of only connecting to the Internet by Wi-Fi and tablet computers that can connect either by Wi-Fi or a cellular network. If the price of tablets that connect by either Wi-Fi or a cellular network increases, these tablets will become more profitable than tablets that connect only by Wi-Fi, and Apple, Toshiba, and the other firms making tablets will shift some of their productive capacity away from Wi-Fi–only models and toward models that also allow for a cellular connection. The firms will offer fewer Wi-Fi–only models for sale at every price, so the supply curve for these tablets will shift to the left.

Number of Firms in the Market A change in the number of firms in the market will change supply. When new firms *enter* a market, the supply curve shifts to the right, and when existing firms leave, or *exit*, a market, the supply curve shifts to the left. For instance, when Toshiba entered the market for tablet computers in July 2011 by introducing the Thrive, the market supply curve for tablet computers shifted to the right.

Expected Future Prices If a firm expects that the price of its product will be higher in the future than it is today, it has an incentive to decrease supply now and increase it in the future. For instance, if Apple believes that prices for tablet computers are temporarily low—perhaps because of a recession—it may store some of its production today to sell later on, when it expects prices to be higher.

Table 4.2

Variables That Shift Market Supply Curves

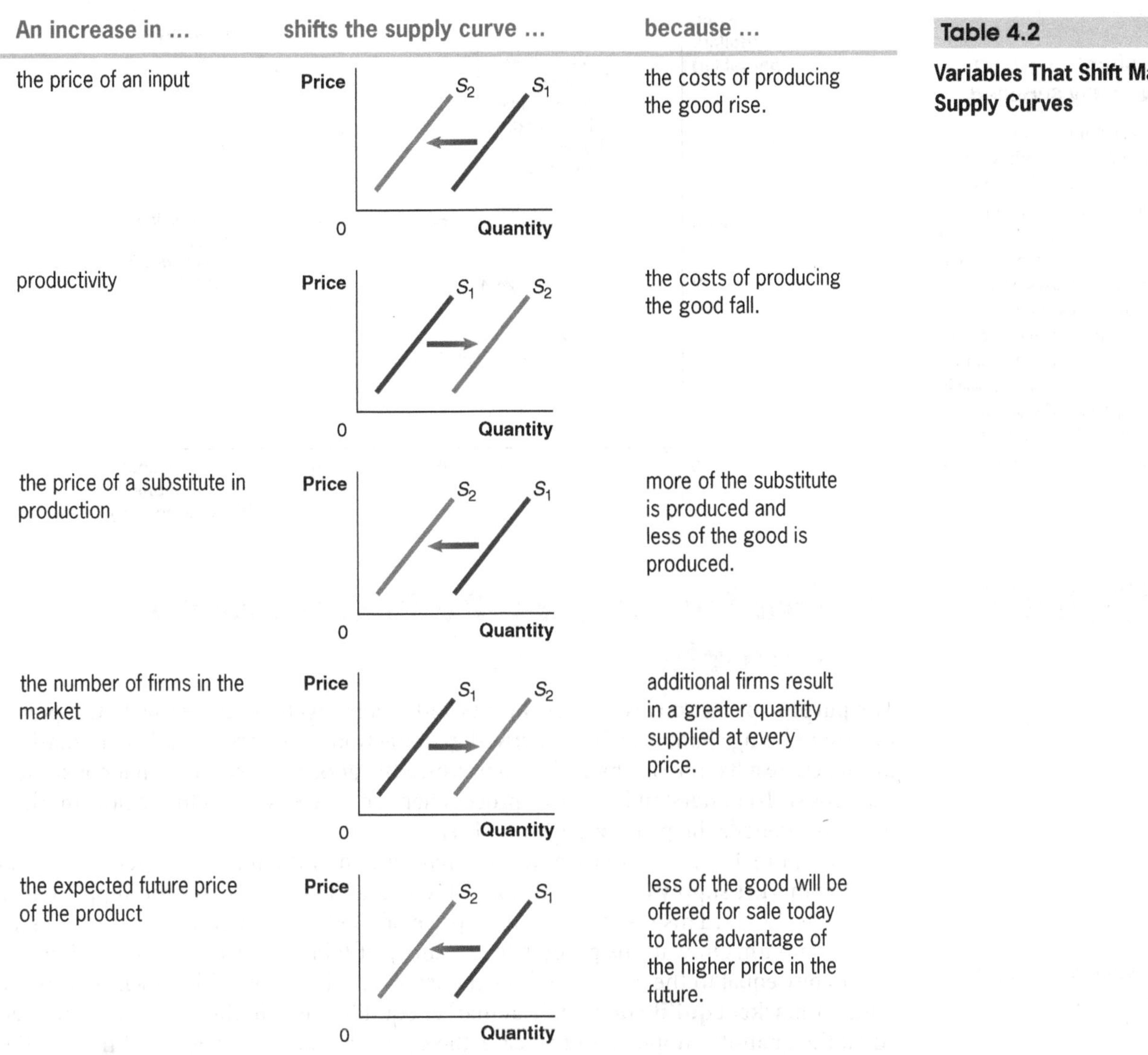

An increase in ...	shifts the supply curve ...	because ...
the price of an input	Price, S_2, S_1, 0, Quantity	the costs of producing the good rise.
productivity	Price, S_1, S_2, 0, Quantity	the costs of producing the good fall.
the price of a substitute in production	Price, S_2, S_1, 0, Quantity	more of the substitute is produced and less of the good is produced.
the number of firms in the market	Price, S_1, S_2, 0, Quantity	additional firms result in a greater quantity supplied at every price.
the expected future price of the product	Price, S_2, S_1, 0, Quantity	less of the good will be offered for sale today to take advantage of the higher price in the future.

Table 4.2 summarizes the most important variables that cause market supply curves to shift. Note that the table shows the shift in the supply curve that results from an *increase* in each of the variables. A *decrease* in these variables would cause the supply curve to shift in the opposite direction.

A Change in Supply versus a Change in Quantity Supplied

We noted earlier the important difference between a change in demand and a change in quantity demanded. There is a similar difference between a *change in supply* and a *change in quantity supplied*. A change in supply refers to a shift of the supply curve. The supply curve will shift when there is a change in one of the variables, *other than the price of the product*, that affects the willingness of suppliers to sell the product. A change in quantity supplied refers to a movement along the supply curve as a result of a change in the product's price. Figure 4.6 illustrates this important distinction. If the price of tablet computers rises from $500 to $600 per tablet, the result will be a movement up the supply curve from point *A* to point *B*—an increase in quantity supplied from 5 million tablets to 6 million tablets. If the price of an input decreases or another factor changes that causes sellers to supply more of the product at every price, the supply curve will shift to the right—an increase in supply. In this case, the increase in supply from S_1 to S_2 causes the quantity of tablet computers supplied at a price of $600 to increase from 6 million at point *B* to 8 million at point *C*.

Figure 4.6

A Change in Supply versus a Change in Quantity Supplied

If the price of tablet computers rises from \$500 to \$600 per tablet, the result will be a movement up the supply curve from point *A* to point *B*—an increase in quantity supplied by Apple, Toshiba, Samsung, and the other firms from 5 million to 6 million tablets. If the price of an input decreases or another factor changes that causes sellers to supply more of the product at every price, the supply curve will shift to the right—an increase in supply. In this case, the increase in supply from S_1 to S_2 causes the quantity of tablet computers supplied at a price of \$600 to increase from 6 million at point *B* to 8 million at point *C*.

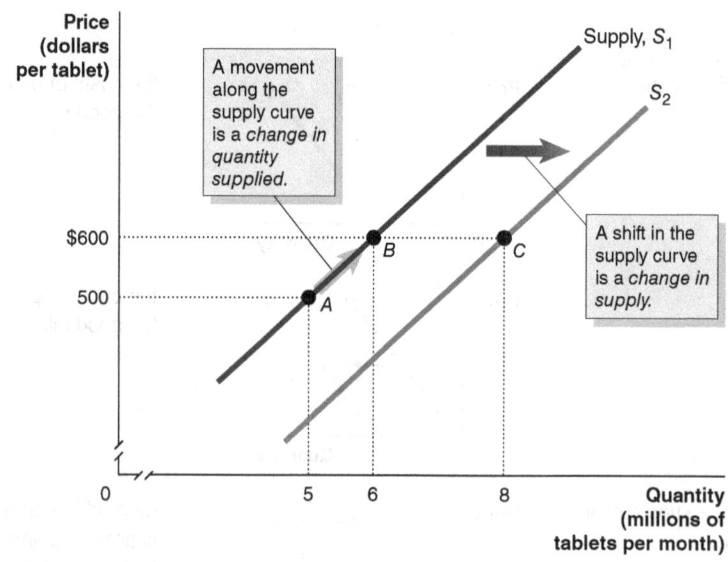

4.3 LEARNING OBJECTIVE

Use a graph to illustrate market equilibrium.

Market Equilibrium: Putting Demand and Supply Together

The purpose of markets is to bring buyers and sellers together. As we saw in Chapter 3, instead of being chaotic and disorderly, the interaction of buyers and sellers in markets ultimately results in firms being led to produce the goods and services that consumers want most. To understand how this process happens, we first need to see how markets work to reconcile the plans of buyers and sellers.

In Figure 4.7, we bring together the market demand curve for tablet computers and the market supply curve. Notice that the demand curve crosses the supply curve at only one point. This point represents a price of \$500 and a quantity of 5 million tablets per month. Only at this point is the quantity of tablets consumers are willing and able to buy equal to the quantity of tablets firms are willing and able to sell. This is the point of **market equilibrium**. Only at market equilibrium will the quantity demanded equal the quantity supplied. In this case, the *equilibrium price* is \$500, and the *equilibrium quantity* is 5 million. As we noted at the beginning of the chapter, markets that have many buyers and many sellers are competitive markets, and equilibrium in these markets is a **competitive market equilibrium**. In the market for tablet computers,

Market equilibrium A situation in which quantity demanded equals quantity supplied.

Competitive market equilibrium A market equilibrium with many buyers and many sellers.

Figure 4.7

Market Equilibrium

Where the demand curve crosses the supply curve determines market equilibrium. In this case, the demand curve for tablet computers crosses the supply curve at a price of \$500 and a quantity of 5 million tablets. Only at this point is the quantity of tablet computers consumers are willing to buy equal to the quantity that Apple, Amazon, Samsung, and the other firms are willing to sell: The quantity demanded is equal to the quantity supplied.

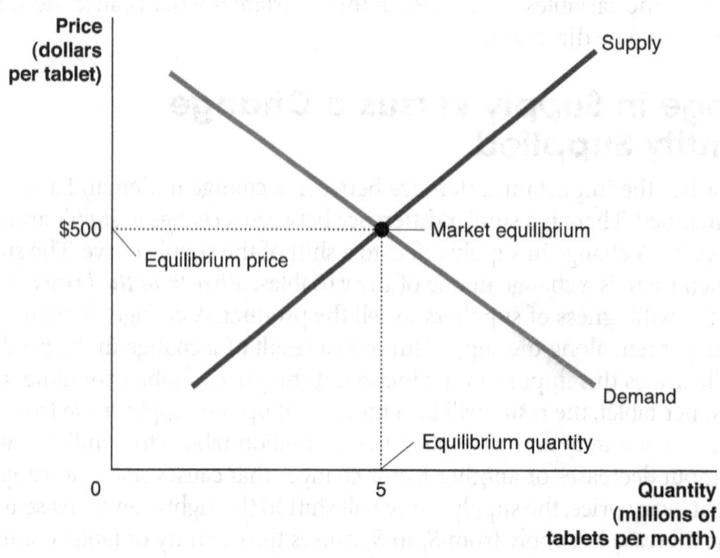

there are many buyers but only about 20 firms. Whether 20 firms is enough for our model of demand and supply to apply to this market is a matter of judgment. In this chapter, we are assuming that the market for tablet computers has enough sellers to be competitive.

How Markets Eliminate Surpluses and Shortages

A market that is not in equilibrium moves toward equilibrium. Once a market is in equilibrium, it remains in equilibrium. To see why, consider what happens if a market is not in equilibrium. For instance, suppose that the price in the market for tablet computers was \$600, rather than the equilibrium price of \$500. As Figure 4.8 shows, at a price of \$600, the quantity of tablets supplied would be 6 million, and the quantity of tablets demanded would be 4 million. When the quantity supplied is greater than the quantity demanded, there is a **surplus** in the market. In this case, the surplus is equal to 2 million tablets (6 million − 4 million = 2 million). When there is a surplus, firms have unsold goods piling up, which gives them an incentive to increase their sales by cutting the price. Cutting the price will simultaneously increase the quantity demanded and decrease the quantity supplied. This adjustment will reduce the surplus, but as long as the price is above \$500, there will be a surplus, and downward pressure on the price will continue. Only when the price has fallen to \$500 will the market be in equilibrium.

Surplus A situation in which the quantity supplied is greater than the quantity demanded.

If, however, the price were \$300, the quantity demanded would be 7 million, and the quantity supplied would be 3 million, as shown in Figure 4.8. When the quantity demanded is greater than the quantity supplied, there is a **shortage** in the market. In this case, the shortage is equal to 4 million tablets (7 million − 3 million = 4 million). When a shortage occurs, some consumers will be unable to buy tablet computers at the current price. In this situation, firms will realize that they can raise the price without losing sales. A higher price will simultaneously increase the quantity supplied and decrease the quantity demanded. This adjustment will reduce the shortage, but as long as the price is below \$500, there will be a shortage, and upward pressure on the price will continue. Only when the price has risen to \$500 will the market be in equilibrium.

Shortage A situation in which the quantity demanded is greater than the quantity supplied.

At a competitive market equilibrium, all consumers willing to pay the market price will be able to buy as much of the product as they want, and all firms willing to accept the market price will be able to sell as much of the product as they want. As a result, there will be no reason for the price to change unless either the demand curve or the supply curve shifts.

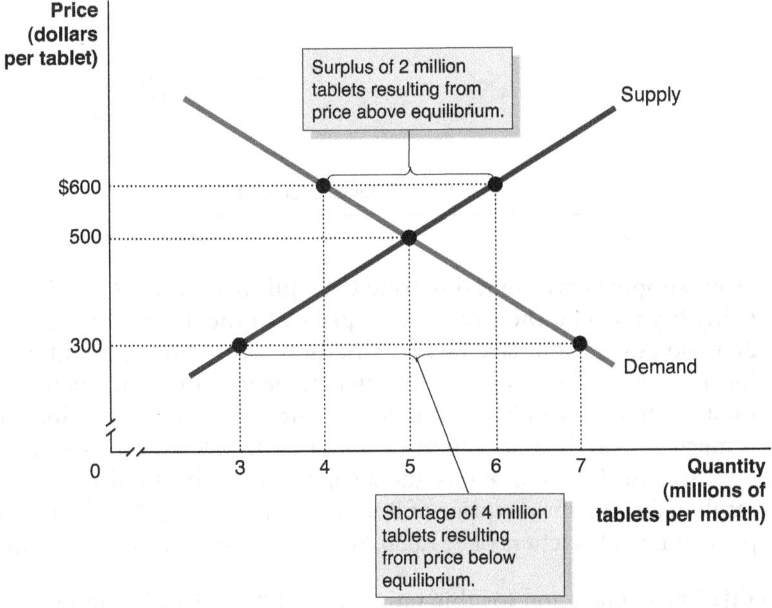

Figure 4.8

The Effect of Surpluses and Shortages on the Market Price

When the market price is above equilibrium, there will be a *surplus*. In the figure, a price of \$600 for tablet computers results in 6 million tablets being supplied but only 4 million tablets being demanded, or a surplus of 2 million. As Apple, Toshiba, Dell, and other firms cut the price to dispose of the surplus, the price will fall to the equilibrium of \$500. When the market price is below equilibrium, there will be a *shortage*. A price of \$300 results in 7 million tablets being demanded but only 3 million tablets being supplied, or a shortage of 4 million tablets. As firms find that consumers who are unable to find tablet computers available for sale are willing to pay higher prices to get them, the price will rise to the equilibrium of \$500.

Demand and Supply Both Count

Keep in mind that the interaction of demand and supply determines the equilibrium price. Neither consumers nor firms can dictate what the equilibrium price will be. No firm can sell anything at any price unless it can find a willing buyer, and no consumer can buy anything at any price without finding a willing seller.

Solved Problem 4.3

Demand and Supply Both Count: A Tale of Two Letters

Which letter is likely to be worth more: one written by Abraham Lincoln or one written by his assassin, John Wilkes Booth? Lincoln is one of the greatest presidents, and many people collect anything he wrote. The demand for letters written by Lincoln surely would seem to be much greater than the demand for letters written by Booth. Yet when R. M. Smythe and Co. auctioned off on the same day a letter written by Lincoln and a letter written by Booth, the Booth letter sold for $31,050, and the Lincoln letter sold for only $21,850. Use a demand and supply graph to explain how the Booth letter has a higher market price than the Lincoln letter, even though the demand for letters written by Lincoln is greater than the demand for letters written by Booth.

Solving the Problem

Step 1: **Review the chapter material.** This problem is about prices being determined at market equilibrium, so you may want to review the section "Market Equilibrium: Putting Demand and Supply Together," which begins on page 90.

Step 2: **Draw demand curves that illustrate the greater demand for Lincoln's letters.** Begin by drawing two demand curves. Label one "Demand for Lincoln's letters" and the other "Demand for Booth's letters." Make sure that the Lincoln demand curve is much farther to the right than the Booth demand curve.

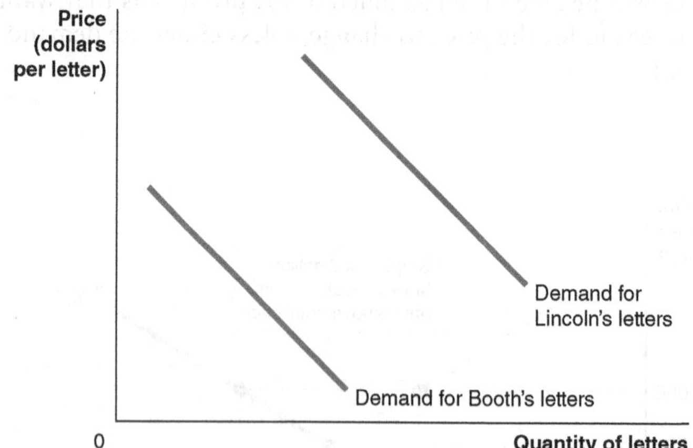

Step 3: **Draw supply curves that illustrate the equilibrium price of Booth's letters being higher than the equilibrium price of Lincoln's letters.** Based on the demand curves you have just drawn, think about how it might be possible for the market price of Lincoln's letters to be lower than the market price of Booth's letters. The only way this can be true is if the supply of Lincoln's letters is much greater than the supply of Booth's letters. Draw on your graph a supply curve for Lincoln's letters and a supply curve for Booth's letters that will result in an equilibrium price of Booth's letters of $31,050 and an equilibrium price of Lincoln's letters of $21,850. You have now solved the problem.

Extra Credit: The explanation for this puzzle is that both demand and supply count when determining market price. The demand for Lincoln's letters is much greater than the

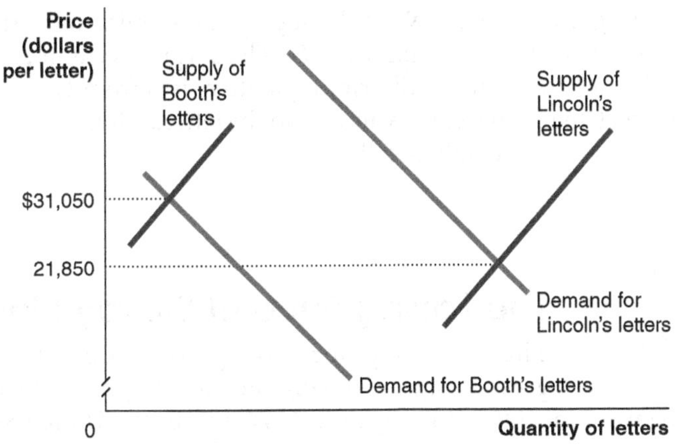

demand for Booth's letters, but the supply of Booth's letters is very small. Historians believe that only eight letters written by Booth exist today. (Note that the supply curves for letters written by Booth and by Lincoln are upward sloping, even though only a fixed number of each of these types of letters is available and, obviously, no more can be produced. The upward slope of the supply curves occurs because the higher the price, the larger the quantity of letters that will be offered for sale by people who currently own them.)

The Effect of Demand and Supply Shifts on Equilibrium

4.4 LEARNING OBJECTIVE

Use demand and supply graphs to predict changes in prices and quantities.

We have seen that the interaction of demand and supply in markets determines the quantity of a good that is produced and the price at which it sells. We have also seen that several variables cause demand curves to shift and other variables cause supply curves to shift. As a result, demand and supply curves in most markets are constantly shifting, and the prices and quantities that represent equilibrium are constantly changing. In this section, we look at how shifts in demand and supply curves affect equilibrium price and quantity.

The Effect of Shifts in Supply on Equilibrium

When Toshiba entered the market for tablet computers by introducing the Thrive, the market supply curve for tablet computers shifted to the right. Figure 4.9 shows the

Price (dollars per tablet)

S_1

S_2

1. As Toshiba enters the market for tablet computers, the supply curve shifts to the right ...

P_1

P_2

2. ... decreasing the equilibrium price ...

Demand

0

Q_1 Q_2

Quantity (millions of tablets per month)

3. ... and increasing the equilibrium quantity.

Figure 4.9

The Effect of an Increase in Supply on Equilibrium

If a firm enters a market, as Toshiba entered the market for tablet computers when it introduced the Thrive, the equilibrium price will fall, and the equilibrium quantity will rise:

1. As Toshiba enters the market for tablet computers, a larger quantity of tablets will be supplied at every price, so the market supply curve shifts to the right, from S_1 to S_2, which causes a surplus of tablets at the original price, P_1.
2. The equilibrium price falls from P_1 to P_2.
3. The equilibrium quantity rises from Q_1 to Q_2.

supply curve shifting from S_1 to S_2. When the supply curve shifts to the right, there will be a surplus at the original equilibrium price, P_1. The surplus is eliminated as the equilibrium price falls to P_2, and the equilibrium quantity rises from Q_1 to Q_2. If existing firms exit the market, the supply curve will shift to the left, causing the equilibrium price to rise and the equilibrium quantity to fall.

Making the Connection

The Falling Price of Blu-ray Players

The technology for playing prerecorded movies has progressed rapidly during the past 30 years. Video cassette recorders (VCRs) were introduced in Japan in 1976 and in the United States in 1977. As the first way of recording television programs or playing prerecorded movies, VHS players were immensely popular. In 1997, though, digital video disc (DVD) players became available in the United States. DVDs could store more information than could the VHS tapes played on VCRs and could produce a crisper picture. Within a few years, sales of DVD players were greater than sales of VCRs, and by 2006 the movie studios had stopped releasing films on VHS tapes. In 2006, Blu-ray players were introduced. Because Blu-ray discs can store 25 gigabytes of data, compared with fewer than 5 gigabytes on a typical DVD, Blu-ray players can reproduce high-definition images that DVD players cannot.

When firms first began selling VCRs, DVD players, and Blu-ray players, they initially charged high prices that declined rapidly within a few years. As the figure below shows, the average price of a Blu-ray player was about \$800 in May 2006, but it had declined to about \$120 in December 2010. Sales of Blu-ray players rose from about 425,000 in 2006 to 11.25 million in 2010. The figure shows that the decline in price and increase in quantity resulted from a large shift to the right of the supply curve. The supply curve in 2010 was much farther to the right than the supply curve in 2006 for two reasons: First, after Samsung introduced the first Blu-ray player—at a price of \$999—other firms entered the industry, increasing the quantity supplied at every price. Second, the prices of the parts used in manufacturing Blu-ray players, particularly the laser components, declined sharply. As the cost of manufacturing the players declined, the quantity supplied at every price increased.

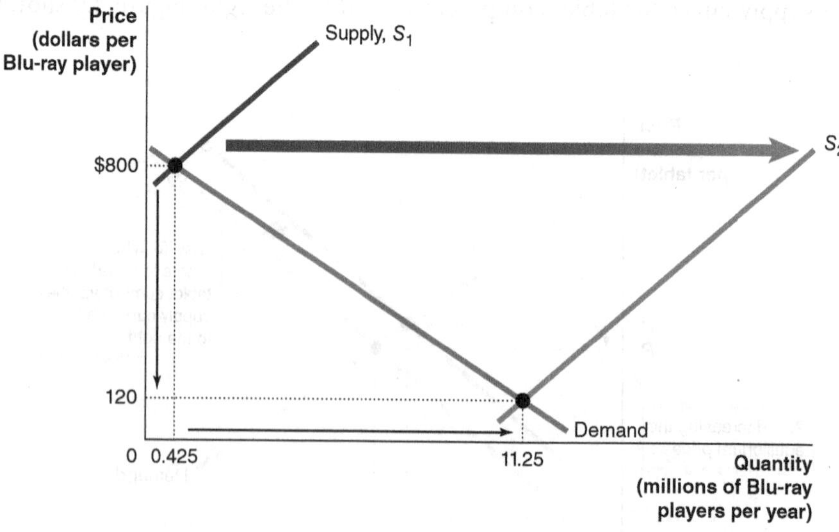

Based on Sarah McBride, "New DVD Players Resolve Battle of Formats," *Wall Street Journal*, January 4, 2007; Yukari Iwatani Kane and Miguel Bustillo, "Dreaming of a Blu Christmas," *Wall Street Journal*, December 23, 2009; and "DEG 2010 Year-End Home Entertainment Report," www.degonline.com.

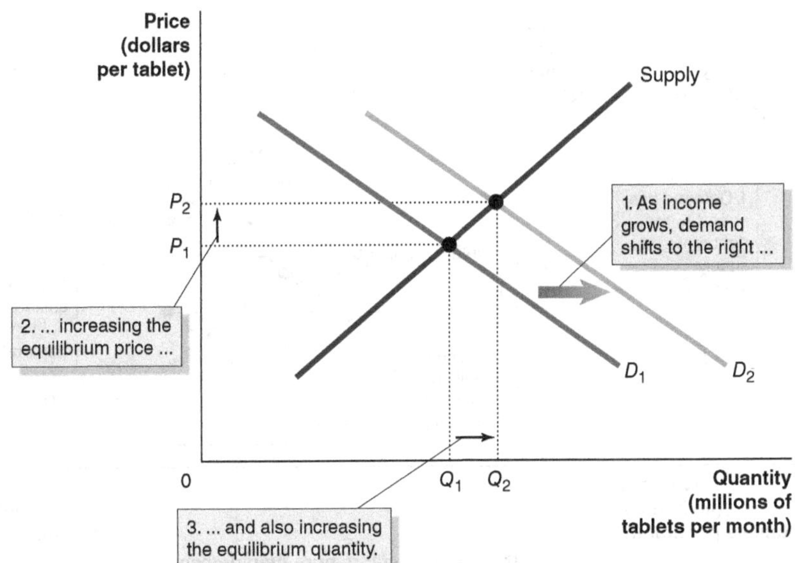

Figure 4.10

The Effect of an Increase in Demand on Equilibrium

Increases in income will cause the equilibrium price and quantity to rise:

1. Because tablet computers are a normal good, as income grows, the quantity demanded increases at every price, and the market demand curve shifts to the right, from D_1 to D_2, which causes a shortage of tablet computers at the original price, P_1.
2. The equilibrium price rises from P_1 to P_2.
3. The equilibrium quantity rises from Q_1 to Q_2.

The Effect of Shifts in Demand on Equilibrium

Because tablet computers are a normal good, when incomes increase, the market demand curve for tablet computers shifts to the right. Figure 4.10 shows the effect of a demand curve shifting to the right, from D_1 to D_2. This shift causes a shortage at the original equilibrium price, P_1. To eliminate the shortage, the equilibrium price rises to P_2, and the equilibrium quantity rises from Q_1 to Q_2. In contrast, if the price of a substitute good, such as laptop computers, were to fall, the demand for tablet computers would decrease, shifting the demand curve for tablets to the left. When the demand curve shifts to the left, the equilibrium price and quantity will both decrease.

The Effect of Shifts in Demand and Supply over Time

Whenever only demand or only supply shifts, we can easily predict the effect on equilibrium price and quantity. But what happens if *both* curves shift? For instance, in many markets, the demand curve shifts to the right over time as population and income grow. The supply curve also often shifts to the right as new firms enter the market and positive technological change occurs. Whether the equilibrium price in a market rises or falls over time depends on whether demand shifts to the right more than does supply. Panel (a) of Figure 4.11 shows that when demand shifts to the right more than supply, the equilibrium price rises. But, as panel (b) shows, when supply shifts to the right more than demand, the equilibrium price falls.

Table 4.3 summarizes all possible combinations of shifts in demand and supply over time and the effects of the shifts on equilibrium price (P) and quantity (Q). For example, the entry in red in the table shows that if the demand curve shifts to the right and the supply curve also shifts to the right, the equilibrium quantity will increase, while the equilibrium price may increase, decrease, or remain unchanged. To make sure you understand each entry in the table, draw demand and supply graphs to check whether you can reproduce the predicted changes in equilibrium price and quantity. If the entry in the table says the predicted change in equilibrium price or quantity can be either an increase or a decrease, draw two graphs similar to panels (a) and (b) of Figure 4.11, one showing the equilibrium price or quantity increasing and the other showing it decreasing. Note also that in the ambiguous cases where either price or quantity might increase or decrease, it is also possible that price or quantity might remain unchanged. Be sure you understand why this is true.

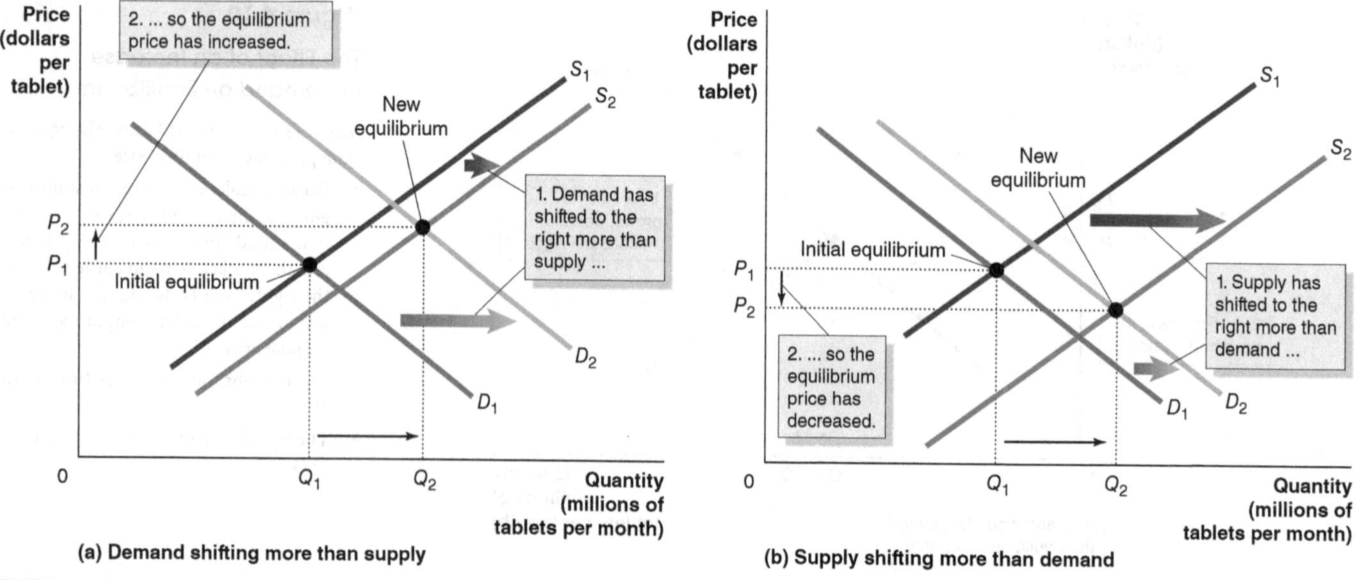

Figure 4.11 **Shifts in Demand and Supply over Time**

Whether the price of a product rises or falls over time depends on whether demand shifts to the right more than supply.

In panel (a), demand shifts to the right more than supply, and the equilibrium price rises:

1. Demand shifts to the right more than supply.
2. The equilibrium price rises from P_1 to P_2.

In panel (b), supply shifts to the right more than demand, and the equilibrium price falls:

1. Supply shifts to the right more than demand.
2. The equilibrium price falls from P_1 to P_2.

Table 4.3

How Shifts in Demand and Supply Affect Equilibrium Price (*P*) and Quantity (*Q*)

	Supply Curve Unchanged	Supply Curve Shifts to the Right	Supply Curve Shifts to the Left
Demand Curve Unchanged	*Q* unchanged *P* unchanged	*Q* increases *P* decreases	*Q* decreases *P* increases
Demand Curve Shifts to the Right	*Q* increases *P* increases	*Q* increases *P* increases or decreases	*Q* increases or decreases *P* increases
Demand Curve Shifts to the Left	*Q* decreases *P* decreases	*Q* increases or decreases *P* decreases	*Q* decreases *P* increases or decreases

Solved Problem 4.4

High Demand and Low Prices in the Lobster Market?

During a typical spring, when demand for lobster is relatively low, Maine lobstermen can typically sell their lobster catches for about $6.00 per pound. During the summer, when demand for lobster is much higher, Maine lobstermen can typically sell their lobster catches for only about $3.00 per pound. One recent July, a lobster-boat captain noted, "Per pound, it's less expensive than hot dogs right now." It may seem strange that the market price is higher when demand is low than when demand is high. Resolve this paradox, with the help of a demand and supply graph.

Solving the Problem

Step 1: Review the chapter material. This problem is about how shifts in demand and supply curves affect the equilibrium price, so you may want to review the section "The Effect of Shifts in Demand and Supply over Time," which begins on page 95.

Step 2: Draw the demand and supply graph. Draw a demand and supply graph, showing the market equilibrium in the spring. Label the equilibrium price $6.00. Label both the demand and supply curves "in spring."

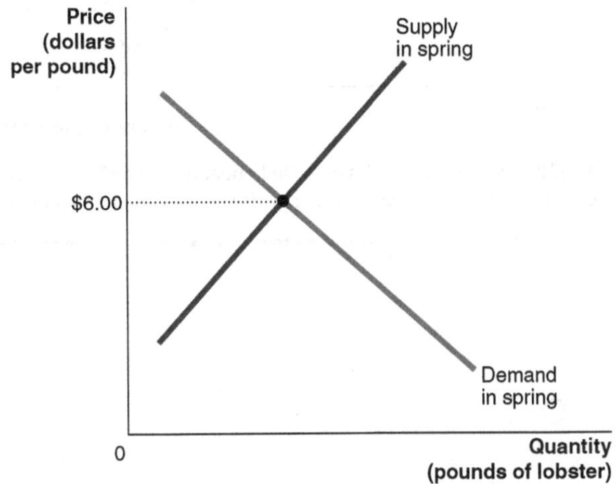

Step 3: Add to your graph a demand curve for summer.

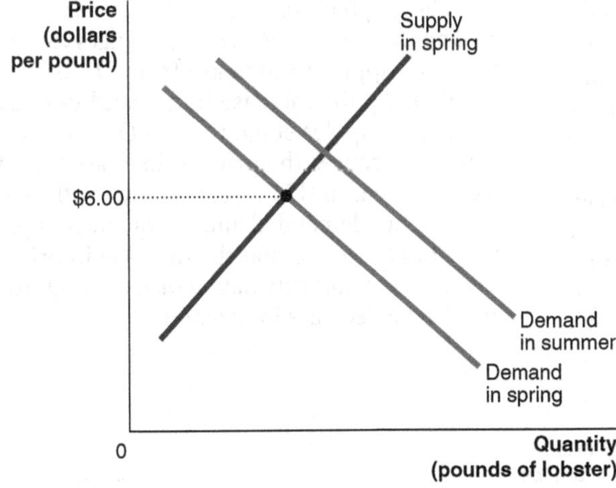

Step 4: Explain the graph. After studying the graph, it is possible to see how the equilibrium price can fall from $6.00 to $3.00, despite the increase in demand: The supply curve must have shifted to the right by enough to cause the equilibrium price to fall to $3.00. Draw the new supply curve, label it "in summer," and label the new equilibrium price $3.00. The demand for lobster does increase in summer compared with spring. But the increase in the supply of lobster between spring and summer is even greater. So, the equilibrium price falls.

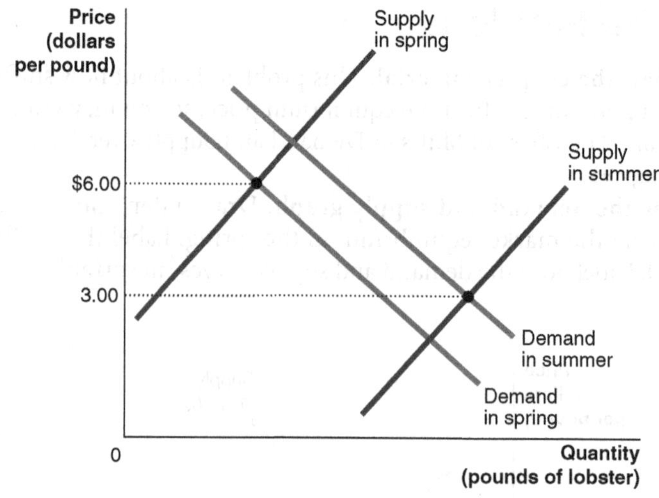

Based on Beth D'Addono, "With Prices Falling, Lobster Is No Longer a Splurge," *Philadelphia Daily News*, June 16, 2011; and Jon Birger, "Looking for a Bargain Dinner: Try Lobster," cnnmoney.com, July 18, 2009.

Don't Let This Happen to You

Remember: A Change in a Good's Price Does *Not* Cause the Demand or Supply Curve to Shift

Suppose a student is asked to draw a demand and supply graph to illustrate how an increase in the price of oranges would affect the market for apples, other variables being constant. He draws the graph on the left below and explains it as follows: "Because apples and oranges are substitutes, an increase in the price of oranges will cause an initial shift to the right in the demand curve for apples, from D_1 to D_2. However, because this initial shift in the demand curve for apples results in a higher price for apples, P_2, consumers will find apples less desirable, and the demand curve will shift to the left, from D_2 to D_3, resulting in a final equilibrium price of P_3." Do you agree or disagree with the student's analysis?

You should disagree. The student has correctly understood that an increase in the price of oranges will cause the demand curve for apples to shift to the right. But the second demand curve shift the student describes, from D_2 to D_3, will not take place. Changes in the price of a product do not result in shifts in the product's demand curve. Changes in the price of a product result only in movements along a demand curve.

The graph on the right below shows the correct analysis. The increase in the price of oranges causes the demand curve for apples to increase from D_1 to D_2. At the original price, P_1, the increase in demand initially results in a shortage of apples equal to $Q_3 - Q_1$. But, as we have seen, a shortage causes the price to increase until the shortage is eliminated. In this case, the price will rise to P_2, where the quantity demanded and the quantity supplied are both equal to Q_2. Notice that the increase in price causes a decrease in the *quantity demanded*, from Q_3 to Q_2, but does *not* cause a decrease in demand.

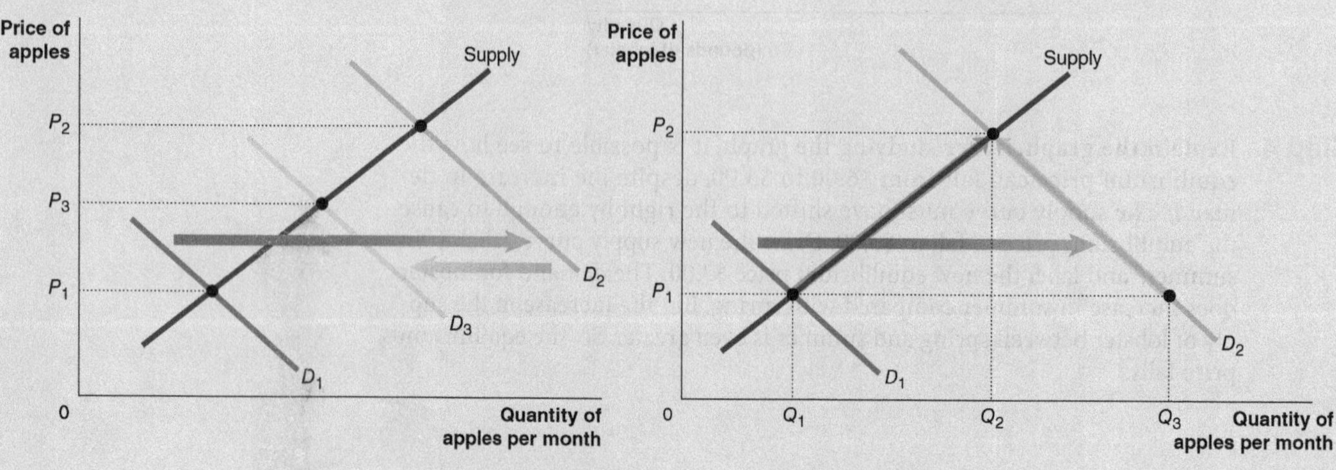

Shifts in a Curve versus Movements along a Curve

When analyzing markets using demand and supply curves, it is important to remember that *when a shift in a demand or supply curve causes a change in equilibrium price, the change in price does not cause a further shift in demand or supply.* For instance, suppose an increase in supply causes the price of a good to fall, while everything else that affects the willingness of consumers to buy the good is constant. The result will be an increase in the quantity demanded but not an increase in demand. For demand to increase, the whole curve must shift. The point is the same for supply: If the price of the good falls but everything else that affects the willingness of sellers to supply the good is constant, the quantity supplied decreases, but the supply does not. For supply to decrease, the whole curve must shift.

Continued from page 77

Economics in Your Life

Will You Buy an Apple iPad or a Samsung Galaxy Tab?

At the beginning of the chapter, we asked you to consider two questions: Would you choose to buy a Samsung Galaxy Tab tablet if it had a lower price than an Apple iPad? and Would your decision be affected if your income increased? To determine the answer to the first question, you have to recognize that the iPad and the Galaxy Tab are substitutes. If you consider the two tablets to be very close substitutes, then you are likely to buy the one with the lower price. In the market, if consumers generally believe that iPad and the Galaxy Tab are close substitutes, a fall in the price of the iPad will increase the quantity of iPads demanded and decrease the demand for Galaxy Tabs. Suppose that you are currently leaning toward buying the Galaxy Tab because its price is lower than the price of the iPad. If an increase in your income would cause you to change your decision and buy the iPad, then the Galaxy Tab is an inferior good for you.

Conclusion

The interaction of demand and supply determines market equilibrium. The model of demand and supply is a powerful tool for predicting how changes in the actions of consumers and firms will cause changes in equilibrium prices and quantities. As we have seen in this chapter, we can use the model to analyze markets that do not meet all the requirements for being perfectly competitive. As long as there is intense competition among sellers, the model of demand and supply can often successfully predict changes in prices and quantities. We will use this model to analyze economic efficiency and the results of government-imposed price floors and price ceilings.

CHAPTER 5

Measuring a Nation's Production and Income

Chapter Outline and Learning Objectives

Applying the Concepts

During the deep economic downturn in 2009 and 2010, economists, business writers, and politicians anxiously awaited the news from the government about the latest economic developments. They pored over the data to determine if the economy was beginning to recover from its doldrums and when more robust economic activity would resume.

At the same time, a distinguished group of economists, led by Nobel Laureates Joseph Stiglitz and Amartya Sen and French economist Jean-Paul Fitoussi, issued a report calling for major revision in the way we measure economic performance. They suggested that our government statisticians focus more on how much we consume and how much leisure we enjoy, and not solely on what we produce. They also suggested that we should be more concerned about whether our current activities are sustainable over the long run, perhaps recognizing environmental constraints.

But perhaps their most radical suggestion was that we switch our focus away from economic production to measuring people's economic well-being. This could include examining the diets and living conditions of the poorest people. For residents of developed countries, this might involve analyzing surveys of people's reported happiness with their own lives.

These changes, however, may be far in the future. Economists and businesses will still rely for some time on the traditional measures of economic activity that we study in this chapter.

This chapter begins your study of **macroeconomics**: the branch of economics that deals with a nation's economy as a whole. Macroeconomics focuses on the economic issues—unemployment, inflation, growth, trade, and the gross domestic product—that are most often discussed in newspapers, on the radio and television, and on the Internet.

Macroeconomics The study of the nation's economy as a whole; focuses on the issues of inflation, unemployment, and economic growth.

Macroeconomic issues lie at the heart of political debates. In fact, all presidential candidates learn a quick lesson in macroeconomics. Namely, their prospects for reelection will depend on how well the economy performs during their term in office. If voters believe the economy has performed well, the president will be reelected. Democrat Jimmy Carter as well as Republican George H. W. Bush failed in their bids for reelection in 1980 and 1992, respectively, partly because of voters' macroeconomic concerns. Both Republican Ronald Reagan in 1984 and Democrat Bill Clinton in 1996 won reelection easily because voters believed the economy was performing well in their first terms. Public opinion polling shows that presidential popularity rises and falls with the performance of the economy.

Macroeconomic events profoundly affect our everyday lives. For example, if the economy fails to create enough jobs, workers will become unemployed throughout the country, and millions of lives will be disrupted. Similarly, slow economic growth means that living standards will not increase rapidly. If prices for goods begin rising rapidly, some people will find it difficult to maintain their lifestyles.

This chapter and the next will introduce you to the concepts you need to understand what macroeconomics is all about. In this chapter, we'll focus on a nation's production and income. We'll learn how economists measure the income and production for an entire country and how they use these measures. In the next chapter, we'll look carefully at unemployment and inflation. Both chapters will explain the terms the media often uses when reporting economic information.

Macroeconomics focuses on two basic issues: long-run economic growth and economic fluctuations. We need to understand what happens during the long run to understand the factors behind the rise in living standards in modern economies. Today, living standards are much higher in the United States than they were for our grandparents. Living standards are also much higher than those of millions of people throughout the globe. Although living standards have improved over time, the economy has not always grown smoothly. Economic performance has fluctuated over time. During periods of slow economic growth, not enough jobs are created, and large numbers of workers become unemployed. Both the public and policy makers become concerned about the lack of jobs and the increase in unemployment.

At other times, unemployment may not be a problem, but we become concerned that the prices of everything that we buy seem to increase rapidly. Sustained increases in prices are called **inflation**. We'll explore inflation in the next chapter.

Inflation Sustained increases in the average prices of all goods and services.

5.1 LEARNING OBJECTIVE

The "Flip" Sides of Macroeconomic Activity: Production and Income

Before we can study growth and fluctuations, we need to have a basic vocabulary and understanding of some key concepts. We begin with the terms *production* and *income* because these are the "flip" sides of the macroeconomic "coin," so to speak. Every day, men and women go off to work, where they produce or sell merchandise or provide services. At the end of the week or month, they return home with their paychecks or "income." They spend some of that money on other products and services, which are produced by other people. In other words, production leads to income, and income leads to production.

But this chapter really isn't about production and income of individuals in markets. That's what a microeconomist studies. On the contrary, this chapter is about the production and income of the economy as a whole. From a "big picture" perspective, we will look at certain measures that will tell us how much the economy is producing and how well it is growing. We will also be able to measure the total income generated in the economy and how this income flows back to workers and investors. These two measures—a country's production and income—are critical to a nation's economic health. Macroeconomists collect and analyze production and income data to understand how many people will find jobs and whether their living standards are rising or falling. Government officials use the data and analysis to develop economic policies.

The Circular Flow of Production and Income

Let's begin with a simple diagram known as the *circular flow*, shown in Figure 5.1. We'll start with a very simple economy that does not have a government or a foreign sector. Households and firms make transactions in two markets known as *factor markets and product markets.* In factor, or input, markets, households supply labor to firms. Households are also the ultimate owners of firms, as well as of all the resources firms use in their production, which we call *capital.* Consequently, we can think of households as providing capital to firms—land, buildings, and equipment—to produce output. Product, or output, markets are markets in which firms sell goods and services to consumers.

The point of the circular flow diagram is simple and fundamental: Production generates income. In factor markets, when households supply labor and capital to firms they are compensated by the firms. They earn wages for their work, and they earn interest, dividends, and rents on the capital they supply to the firms. The households then use their income to purchase goods and services in the product markets.

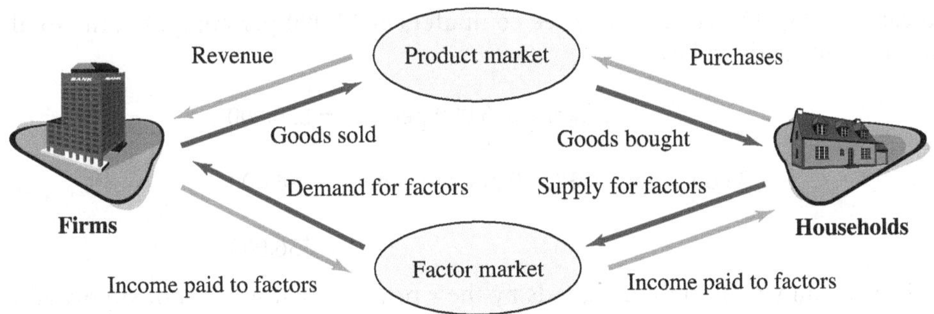

Figure 5.1

The Circular Flow of Production and Income

The circular flow shows how the production of goods and services generates income for households and how households purchase goods and services produced by firms.

The firm uses the revenues it receives from the sale of its products to pay for the factors of production (land, labor, and capital).

When goods and services are produced, income flows throughout the economy. For example, consider a manufacturer of computers. At the same time the computer manufacturer produces and sells new computers, it also generates income through its production. The computer manufacturer pays wages to workers, perhaps pays rent on offices and factory buildings, and pays interest on money it borrowed from a bank. Whatever is left over after paying for the cost of production is the firm's profit, which is income to the owners of the firm. Wages, rents, interest, and profits are all different forms of income.

In an example with a government, your taxes pay for a school district to hire principals, teachers, and other staff to provide educational services to the students in your community. These educational services are an important part of production in our modern economy that produces both goods and services. At the same time, the principals, teachers, and staff all earn income through their employment with the school district. The school district may also rent buildings where classes are held and pay interest on borrowed funds.

Our goal is to understand both sides of this macroeconomic "coin"—the production in the economy and the generation of income in the economy. In the United States, the national income and product accounts, published by the Department of Commerce, are the source for the key data on production and income in the economy. As we will see, we can measure the value of output produced in the economy by looking at either the production or income side of the economy. Let's begin by learning how to measure the production for the entire economy.

The Production Approach: Measuring a Nation's Macroeconomic Activity Using Gross Domestic Product

5.2 LEARNING OBJECTIVE

To measure the production of the entire economy, we need to combine an enormous array of goods and services—everything from new computers to NBA and WNBA basketball games. We can actually add computers to basketball games, as we could add apples and oranges if we were trying to determine the total monetary value of a fruit harvest. Our goal is to summarize the total production of an entire economy into a single number, which we call the **gross domestic product (GDP)**. Gross domestic product is the total market value of all the final goods and services produced within an economy in a given year. GDP is also the most common measure of an economy's total output. All the words in the GDP definition are important, so let's analyze them.

Gross domestic product (GDP) The total market value of final goods and services produced within an economy in a given year.

"Total market value" means we take the quantity of goods produced, multiply them by their respective prices, and then add up the totals. If an economy produced two cars at $25,000 per car and three computers at $2,000 per computer, the total value of these goods will be

$$\begin{aligned} 2 \text{ cars} \times \$25{,}000 \text{ per car} &= \$50{,}000 \\ + \\ 3 \text{ computers} \times \$2{,}000 \text{ per computer} &= \$6{,}000 \\ &= \$56{,}000 \end{aligned}$$

The reason we multiply the goods by their prices is that we cannot simply add together the number of cars and the number of computers. Using prices allows us to express the value of everything in a common unit of measurement—in this case, dollars. (In countries other than the United States, we express the value in terms of the local currency.) We add apples and oranges together by finding out the value of both the apples and the oranges, as measured by what you would pay for them, and adding them up in terms of their prices.

"Final goods and services" in the definition of GDP means those goods and services that are sold to ultimate, or final, purchasers. For example, the two cars that were produced would be final goods if they were sold to households or to a business. However, to produce the cars the automobile manufacturer bought steel that went into the body of the cars, and we do not count this steel as a final good or service in GDP. Steel is an example of an **intermediate good,** one that is used in the production process. An intermediate good is not considered a final good or service.

Intermediate goods Goods used in the production process that are not final goods and services.

The reason we do not count intermediate goods as final goods is to avoid double-counting. The price of the car already reflects the price of the steel contained in it. We do not want to count the steel twice. Similarly, the large volumes of paper a commercial printing firm uses also are intermediate goods, because the paper becomes part of the final product delivered by the printing firm to its clients.

The final words in our definition of GDP are "in a given year." GDP is expressed as a rate of production, that is, as "X" amount of dollars per year. In 2008, for example, GDP in the United States was $14,196 billion. Goods produced in prior years, such as cars or houses, are not included in GDP for a given year, even if one consumer sells a house or car to another in that year. Only *newly produced* products are included in GDP.

Because we measure GDP using the current prices for goods and services, GDP will increase if prices increase, even if the physical amount of goods that are produced remains the same. Suppose that next year the economy again produces two cars and three computers, but all the prices in the economy double: The price of cars is $50,000, and the price of computers is $4,000. GDP will also be twice as high, or $112,000, even though the quantity produced is the same as during the prior year:

$$\begin{aligned} 2 \text{ cars} \times \$50{,}000 \text{ per car} &= \$100{,}000 \\ + \\ 3 \text{ computers} \times \$4{,}000 \text{ per computer} &= \$12{,}000 \\ &= \$112{,}000 \end{aligned}$$

But to say that GDP has doubled would be misleading, because exactly the same goods were produced. To avoid this problem, let's apply the real-nominal principle, one of our five basic principles of economics.

Real-Nominal Principle

What matters to people is the real value of money or income—its purchasing power—not the face value of money or income.

What we need is another measure of total output that doesn't increase just because prices increase. For this reason, economists have developed the concept of **real GDP**, a measure that controls for changes in prices. Later in this chapter, we explain how real GDP is calculated. The basic idea is simple. When we use current prices to measure GDP, we are using **nominal GDP**. Nominal GDP can increase for one of two reasons: Either the production of goods and services has increased, or the prices of those goods and services have increased.

Real GDP A measure of GDP that controls for changes in prices.

Nominal GDP The value of GDP in current dollars.

To explain the concept of real GDP, we first need to look at a simple example. Suppose an economy produces a single good: computers. In year 1, 10 computers were produced, and each sold for \$2,000. In year 2, 12 computers were produced, and each sold for \$2,100. Nominal GDP is \$20,000 in year 1 and \$25,200 in year 2; it has increased by a factor of 1.26 or 26 percent. However, we can also measure real GDP by using year 1 prices as a measure of what was produced in year 1 and what was produced in year 2. In year 1, real GDP is

$$10 \text{ computers} \times \$2{,}000 \text{ per computer} = \$20{,}000$$

In year 2, real GDP (in year 1 terms) is

$$12 \text{ computers} \times \$2{,}000 \text{ per computer} = \$24{,}000$$

Real GDP in year 2 is still greater than real GDP in year 1, now by a factor of 1.2, or 20 percent. The key idea is that we construct a measure using the same prices for both years and thereby take price changes into account.

Figure 5.2 plots real GDP for the U.S. economy for the years 1930 through 2009. The graph shows that real GDP has grown substantially over this period. This is what economists call **economic growth**—sustained increases in the real GDP of an economy

Economic growth Sustained increases in the real GDP of an economy over a long period of time.

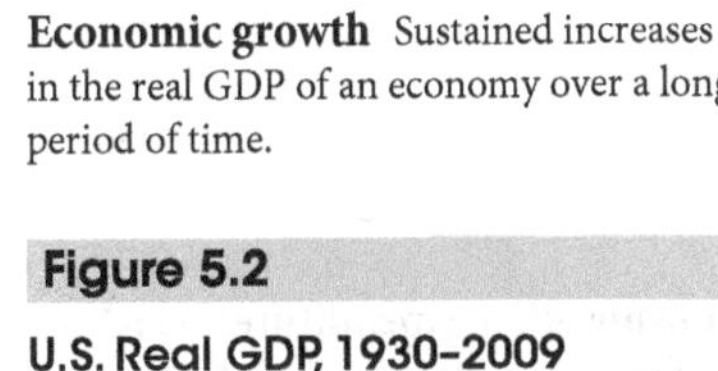

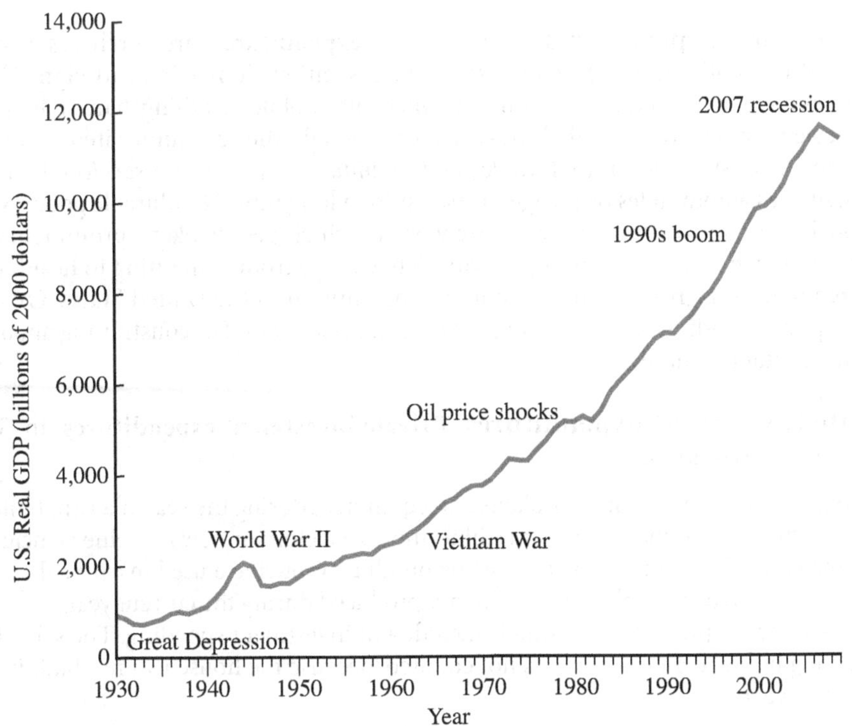

Figure 5.2

U.S. Real GDP, 1930–2009

During the Great Depression in the 1930s, GDP initially fell and then was relatively flat. The economy was not growing much. However, the economy began growing rapidly in the 1940s during Word War II and has grown substantially since then.

SOURCE: U.S. Department of Commerce.

Table 5.1

Composition of U.S. GDP, Fourth Quarter 2009 (Billions of Dollars Expressed at Annual Rates)

GDP	Consumption Expenditures	Private Investment Expenditures	Government Purchases	Net Exports
$14,461	$10,234	$1,716	$2,960	–$449

SOURCE: U.S. Department of Commerce.

over a long period of time. Later in this chapter, we'll look carefully at the behavior of real GDP over shorter periods, during which time it can rise and fall. Decreases in real GDP disrupt the economy greatly and lead to unemployment.

The Components of GDP

Economists divide GDP into four broad categories, each corresponding to different types of purchases represented in GDP:

1. *Consumption expenditures:* purchases by consumers
2. *Private investment expenditures:* purchases by firms
3. *Government purchases:* purchases by federal, state, and local governments
4. *Net exports:* net purchases by the foreign sector (domestic exports minus domestic imports)

Before discussing these categories, let's look at some data for the U.S. economy to get a sense of the size of each of these four components. Table 5.1 shows the figures for GDP for the fourth quarter of 2009. (A quarter is a three-month period; the first quarter runs from January through March, while the fourth quarter runs from October through December. Quarterly GDP expressed at annual rates is GDP for a year if the entire year were the same as the measured quarter.) In the fourth quarter of 2009, GDP was $14,461 billion, or approximately $14.4 trillion. To get a sense of the magnitude, consider that the U.S. population is approximately 300 million people, making GDP per person approximately $48,203. (This does not mean every man, woman, and child actually spends $48,203, but it is a useful indicator of the productive strength of the economy.)

Consumption expenditures Purchases of newly produced goods and services by households.

Consumption Expenditures **Consumption expenditures** are purchases by consumers of currently produced goods and services, either domestic or foreign. These purchases include flat-screen TVs, smart phones, automobiles, clothing, hair-styling services, jewelry, movie or basketball tickets, food, and all other consumer items. We can break down consumption into *durable goods, nondurable goods,* and *services.* Durable goods, such as automobiles or refrigerators, last for a long time. Nondurable goods, such as food, last for a short time. Services are work in which people play a prominent role in delivery (such as a dentist filling a cavity). They range from haircutting to health care and are the fastest-growing component of consumption in the United States. Overall, consumption spending is the most important component of GDP, constituting about 70 percent of total purchases.

Private investment expenditures Purchases of newly produced goods and services by firms.

Private Investment Expenditures **Private investment expenditures** in GDP consist of three components:

1. First, there is spending on new plants and equipment during the year. If a firm builds a new factory or purchases a new machine, the new factory or new machine is included in the year's GDP. Purchasing an existing building or buying a used machine does not count in GDP, because the goods were not produced during the current year.
2. Second, newly produced housing is included in investment spending. The sale of an existing home to a new owner is not counted, because the house was not built in the current year.

3. Finally, if firms add to their stock of inventories, the increase in inventories during the current year is included in GDP. If a hardware store had $1,000 worth of nuts and bolts on its shelves at the beginning of the year and $1,100 at the year's end, its inventory investment is $100 ($1,100 – $1,000). This $100 increase in inventory investment is included in GDP.

We call the total of new investment expenditures **gross investment**. During the year, some of the existing plant, equipment, and housing will deteriorate or wear out. This wear and tear is called **depreciation**, or sometimes a *capital consumption allowance*. If we subtract depreciation from gross investment, we obtain net investment. **Net investment** is the true addition to the stock of plant, equipment, and housing in a given year.

Gross investment Total new investment expenditures.

Depreciation Reduction in the value of capital goods over a one-year period due to physical wear and tear and also to obsolescence; also called *capital consumption allowance.*

Make sure you understand this distinction between gross investment and net investment. Consider the $1,716 billion in total investment spending for the fourth quarter of 2009, a period in which there was $1,525 billion in depreciation in the private sector. That means there was only $191 billion ($1,716 – $1,525) in net investment by firms in that year; 88 percent of gross investment went to make up for depreciation of existing capital.

Net investment Gross investment minus depreciation.

Warning: When we discuss measuring production in the GDP accounts, we use *investment* in a different way than that with which you may be accustomed. For an economist, investment in the GDP accounts means purchases of new final goods and services by firms. In everyday conversation, we may talk about investing in the stock market or investing in gold. Buying stock for $1,800 on the stock market is a purchase of an existing financial asset; it is not the purchase of new goods and services by firms. Therefore, that $1,800 does not appear anywhere in GDP. The same is true of purchasing a gold bar. In GDP accounting, *investment* denotes the purchase of new capital. Be careful not to confuse the common usage of *investment* with the definition of *investment* as we use it in the GDP accounts.

Government Purchases

Government purchases are the purchases of newly produced goods and services by federal, state, and local governments. They include any goods that the government purchases plus the wages and benefits of all government workers (paid when the government purchases their services as employees). Investment spending by government is also included. The majority of spending in this category comes from state and local governments: $1,790 billion of the total $2,960 billion in 2009. Government purchases affect our lives very directly. For example, all salaries of U.S. postal employees and federal airport security personnel are counted as government purchases.

Government purchases Purchases of newly produced goods and services by local, state, and federal governments.

This category does not include all spending by governments. It excludes **transfer payments**, payments to individuals that are not associated with the production of goods and services. For example, payments for Social Security, welfare, and interest on government debt are all considered transfer payments and thus are not included in government purchases in GDP. Nothing is being produced by the recipients in return for money being paid, or "transferred," to them. But wage payments to the police, postal workers, and the staff of the Internal Revenue Service are all included, because they do correspond to services these workers are currently producing.

Transfer payments Payments from governments to individuals that do not correspond to the production of goods and services.

Because transfer payments are excluded from GDP, a vast portion of the budget of the federal government is not part of GDP. In 2008, the federal government spent approximately $3,454 billion, of which only $1,170 billion (about 33 percent) was counted as federal government purchases. Transfer payments are important, however, because they affect both the income of individuals and their consumption and savings behavior. Transfer payments also affect the size of the federal budget deficit, which we will study in a later chapter. At this point, keep in mind the distinction between government purchases—which are included in GDP—and total government spending or expenditure—*which may not* be included.

Import A good or service produced in a foreign country and purchased by residents of the home country (for example, the United States).

Export A good or service produced in the home country (for example, the United States) and sold in another country.

Net exports Exports minus imports.

Net Exports To understand the role of the foreign sector, we first need to define three terms. **Imports** are goods and services we buy from other countries. **Exports** are goods and services made here and sold to other countries. **Net exports** are total exports minus total imports. In Table 5.1, we see that net exports in the first quarter of 2009 were –$449 billion. Net exports were negative because our imports exceeded our exports.

Consumption, investment, and government purchases include all purchases by consumers, firms, and the government, whether or not the goods were produced in the United States. However, GDP is supposed to measure the goods produced in the United States. Consequently, we subtract purchases of foreign goods by consumers, firms, or the government when we calculate GDP, because these goods were not produced in the United States. At the same time, we add to GDP any goods produced here and sold abroad, for example, airplanes made in the United States and sold in Europe. By including net exports as a component of GDP, we correctly measure U.S. production by adding exports and subtracting imports.

Suppose someone in the United States buys a $25,000 car made in Japan. If we look at final purchases, we will see that consumption spending rose by $25,000 because a consumer made a purchase of a consumption good. Net exports fell by $25,000, however, because we subtracted the value of the import (the car) from total exports. Notice that total GDP did not change with the purchase of the car. This is exactly what we want in this case, because the car wasn't produced in the United States.

Now suppose the United States sells a car for $22,000 to a resident of Spain. In this case, net exports increase by $22,000 because the car was a U.S. export. GDP will also be a corresponding $22,000 higher because this sale represents U.S. production.

Trade deficit The excess of imports over exports.

Trade surplus The excess of exports over imports.

Recall that for the United States in the fourth quarter of 2009 net exports were –$449 billion dollars. In other words, in that quarter the United States bought $449 billion more goods from abroad than it sold abroad. When we buy more goods from abroad than we sell, we have a **trade deficit.** A **trade surplus** occurs when our exports exceed our imports. Figure 5.3 shows the U.S. trade surplus as a share of GDP from 1960 to 2009. Although at times the United States has had a small trade surplus, it has generally run a trade deficit. In recent years, the trade deficit has increased and has fluctuated between 3 and 6 percent of GDP. In later chapters, we study how trade deficits can affect a country's GDP.

Figure 5.3

U.S. Trade Balance as a Share of GDP, 1960–2009

In the early 1980s, the United States ran a trade surplus (when the line on the graph is above zero, this indicates a surplus). However, in other years the United States has run a trade deficit. In 2004 through 2006, the trade deficit exceeded 5 percent of GDP, although it most recently is near 3 percent of GDP.

SOURCE: Department of Commerce.

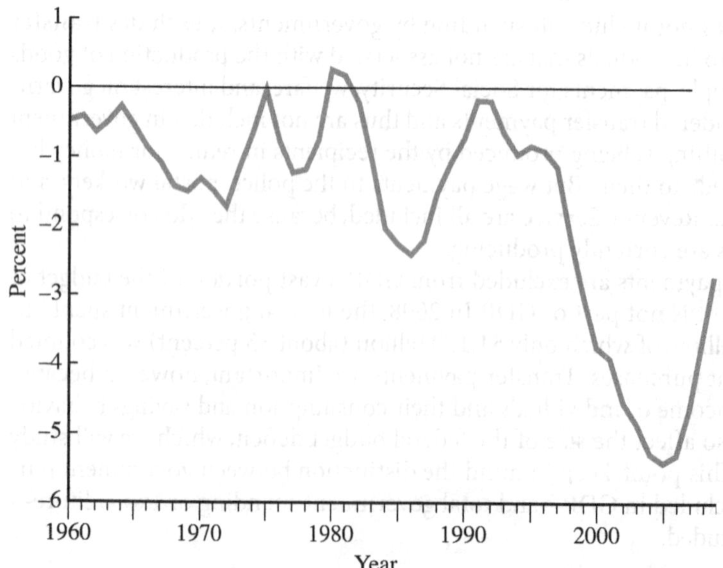

Putting It All Together: The GDP Equation

We can summarize our discussion of who purchases GDP with a simple equation that combines the four components of GDP:

$$Y = C + I + G + NX$$

where

$$\begin{aligned} Y &= \text{GDP} \\ C &= \text{Consumption} \\ I &= \text{Invest} \\ G &= \text{Government purchases} \\ NX &= \text{Net exports} \end{aligned}$$

In other words,

$$\text{GDP} = \text{consumption} + \text{investment} + \text{government purchases} + \text{net exports}$$

This equation is an *identity*, which means it is always true no matter what the values of the variables are. In any economy, GDP consists of the sum of its four components.

The Income Approach: Measuring A Nation's Macroeconomic Activity Using National Income

5.3 LEARNING OBJECTIVE

Recall from the circular flow that one person's production ends up being another person's income. Income is the flip side of our macroeconomic "coin." As a result, in addition to measuring a nation's activity by measuring production, we can also gauge it by measuring a nation's income. The total income earned by U.S. residents working in the United States and abroad is called **national income.**

National income The total income earned by a nation's residents both domestically and abroad in the production of goods and services.

Measuring National Income

To measure national income, economists first make two primary adjustments to GDP.

First, we add to GDP the net income earned by U.S. firms and residents abroad. To make this calculation, we add to GDP any income earned abroad by U.S. firms or residents and subtract any income earned in the United States by foreign firms or residents. For example, we add the profits earned by U.S. multinational corporations that are sent back to the United States but subtract the profits from multinational corporations operating in the United States that are sent back to their home countries. The profits Wal-Mart sends back to the United States from its stores in Mexico are added to GDP. The profits Toyota earns in the United States that it sends back to Japan are subtracted from GDP. The result of these adjustments is the total income earned worldwide by U.S. firms and residents. This is the **gross national product (GNP).**

Gross national product GDP plus net income earned abroad

The distinction between what they produce within their borders, GDP, and what their citizens earn, GNP, is not that important to most countries. For the United States, the difference between GDP and GNP is typically just 1 percent. In some countries, however, the differences are much larger. The country of Kuwait, for example, earned vast amounts of income from its oil riches, which it invested abroad in stocks, bonds, and other types of investments. These earnings comprised approximately 9 percent of Kuwait's 2006 GNP. Foreigners have traditionally made large investments in Australia. As they sent their profits back to their home countries, Australia's net income from abroad was negative in 2006, and Australian GDP in that year exceeded Australian GNP by 4.1 percent.

Table 5.2

From GDP to National Income, Fourth Quarter 2009 (Billions of Dollars)

Gross domestic product	$14,242
Gross national product	14,363
Net national product	12,513
National income	12,259

The second adjustment we make when calculating national income is to subtract depreciation from GNP. Recall that depreciation is the wear and tear on plant and equipment that occurred during the year. In a sense, our income is reduced because our buildings and machines are wearing out. When we subtract depreciation from GNP, we reach *net national product* (NNP), where *net* means "after depreciation."

After making these adjustments and taking into account statistical discrepancies, we reach *national income.* (Statistical discrepancies arise when government statisticians make their calculations using different sources of the same data.) Table 5.2 shows the effects of these adjustments for the fourth quarter of 2009.

In turn, national income is divided among six basic categories: compensation of employees (wages and benefits), corporate profits, rental income, proprietors' income (income of unincorporated business), net interest (interest payments received by households from business and from abroad), and other items. Approximately 65 percent of all national income goes to workers in the form of wages and benefits. For most of the countries in the world, wages and benefits are the largest part of national income.

Personal income Income, including transfer payments, received by households.

Personal disposable income Personal income that households retain after paying income taxes.

In addition to national income, which measures the income earned in a given year by the entire private sector, we are sometimes interested in determining the total payments that flow directly into households, a concept known as **personal income.** To calculate personal income, we begin with national income and subtract any corporate profits that are retained by the corporation and not paid out as dividends to households. We also subtract all taxes on production and imports and social insurance taxes, which are payments for Social Security and Medicare. We then add any personal interest income received from the government and consumers and all transfer payments. The result is the total income available to households, or personal income. The amount of personal income that households retain after paying income taxes is called **personal disposable income.**

Measuring National Income through Value Added

Value added The sum of all the income—wages, interest, profits, and rent—generated by an organization. For a firm, we can measure value added by the dollar value of the firm's sales minus the dollar value of the goods and services purchased from other firms.

Another way to measure national income is to look at the **value added** of each firm in the economy. For a firm, we can measure its value added by the dollar value of the firm's sales minus the dollar value of the goods and services purchased from other firms. What remains is the sum of all the income—wages, profits, rents, and interest—that the firm generates. By adding up the value added for all the firms in the economy (plus nonprofit and governmental organizations), we can calculate national income. Let's consider a simple example illustrated in Table 5.3.

Table 5.3

Calculating Value Added in a Simple Economy

	Automobile Firm	Steel Firm	Total Economy
Total sales	$16,000	$6,000	$22,000
Less purchases from other firms	6,000	0	6,000
Equals value added: the sum of all wages, interest, profits, and rents	10,000	6,000	16,000

Suppose an economy consists of two firms: an automobile firm that sells its cars to consumers and a steel firm that sells only to the automobile firm. If the automobile company sells a car for \$16,000 to consumers and purchases \$6,000 worth of steel from the steel firm, the auto firm has \$10,000 remaining—its value added—which it can then distribute as wages, rents, interest, and profits. If the steel firm sells \$6,000 worth of steel but does not purchase any inputs from other firms, its value added is \$6,000, which it pays out in the form of wages, rents, interest, and profits. Total value added in the economy from both firms is \$16,000 (\$10,000 + \$6,000), which is the sum of wages, rents, interest, and profits for the entire economy (consisting of these two firms).

As this example illustrates, we measure the value added for a typical firm by starting with the value of its total sales and subtracting the value of any inputs it purchases from other firms. The amount of income that remains is the firm's value added, which is then distributed as wages, rents, interest, and profits. In calculating national income, we need to include all the firms in the economy, even the firms that produce intermediate goods.

An Expanded Circular Flow

Now that we have examined both production and income, including both the government and the foreign sector, let's take another look at a slightly more realistic circular flow. Figure 5.4 depicts a circular flow that includes both the government and the foreign sector. Both households and firms pay taxes to the government. The government, in turn, supplies goods and services in the product market and also purchases inputs—labor and capital—in the factor markets, just like private-sector firms do. Net exports, which can be positive or negative, are shown entering or leaving the product market.

In summary, we can look at GDP from two sides: We can ask who buys the output that is produced, or we can ask how the income that is created through the production process is divided between workers and investors. From the spending side, we saw that nearly 70 percent of GDP consists of consumer expenditures. From the income side, we saw that nearly 65 percent of national income is paid in wages and benefits. Macroeconomists may use data based either on the production that occurs in the economy or on its flip side, the income that is generated, depending on whether they are more focused on current production or on current income.

Application 1

Using Value Added to Measure the True Size of Wal-Mart

Applying the Concepts #1: How can we use economic analysis to compare the size of a major corporation to the size of a country?

During 2008, Wal-Mart's sales were approximately \$374 billion, nearly 2.6 percent of U.S. GDP. Some social commentators might want to measure the impact of Wal-Mart just through its sales. But to produce those sales, Wal-Mart had to buy goods from many other companies. Wal-Mart's value added was substantially less than its total sales. Based on Wal-Mart's annual reports, its cost of sales was \$286 billion, leaving approximately \$88 billion in value added. This is a very large number, as might be expected from the world's largest retailer, but it is much smaller than its total sales. If we used Wal-Mart's sales to compare it to a country, it would have a GDP similar to that of Belgium, which is ranked 28th in the world. However, using the more appropriate measure of value added, Wal-Mart's size is closer to Bulgaria, ranked 56th in the world.

SOURCE: Based on Wal-Mart Annual Report, 2008, http://walmartstores.com/sites/AnnualReport/2008/docs/finrep_00.pdf (accessed July, 2008).

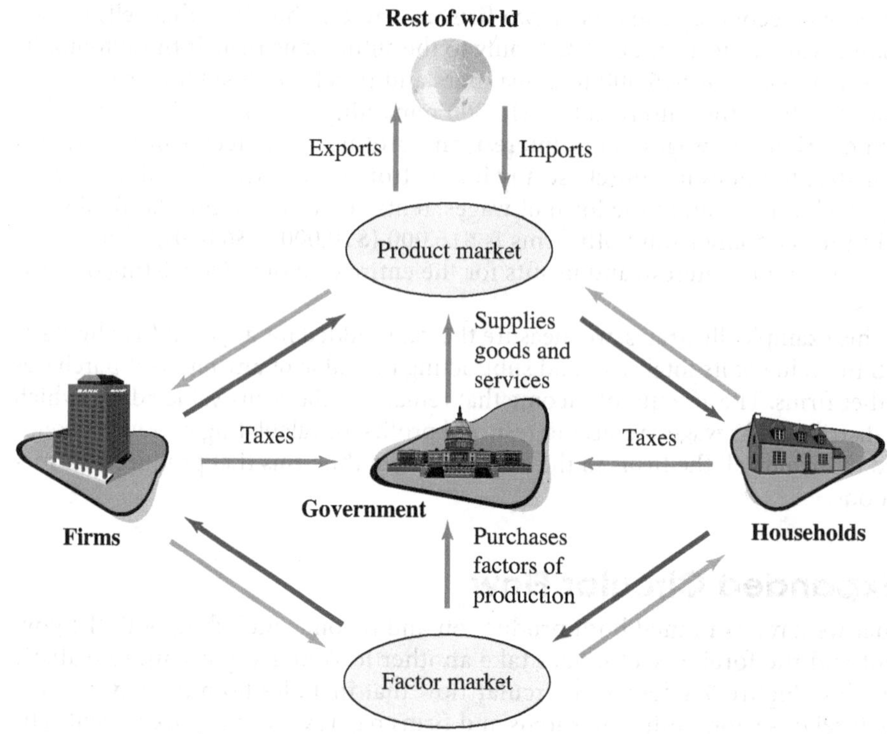

Figure 5.4

The Circular Flow with Government and the Foreign Sector

The new linkages (in blue) demonstrate the roles that the government and the foreign sector (imports and exports) play in the circular flow.

5.4 LEARNING OBJECTIVE

A Closer Examination of Nominal and Real GDP

We have discussed different ways to measure the production of an economy, looking at both who purchases goods and services and the income it generates. Of all the measures we have discussed, GDP is the one most commonly used both by the public and by economists. Let's take a closer look at it.

Measuring Real versus Nominal GDP

Output in the economy can increase from one year to the next. And prices can rise from one year to the next. Recall that we defined nominal GDP as GDP measured in current prices, and we defined real GDP as GDP adjusted for price changes.

Now we take a closer look at how real GDP is measured in modern economies. Let's start with a simple economy in which there are only two goods—cars and computers—produced in the years 2011 and 2012. The data for this economy—the prices and quantities produced for each year—are shown in Table 5.4. The production of cars and the production of computers increased, but the production of computers increased more rapidly. The price of cars rose, while the price of computers remained the same.

Table 5.4

GDP Data for a Simple Economy

	Quantity Produced		Price	
Year	Cars	Computers	Cars	Computers
2011	4	1	$10,000	$5,000
2012	5	3	12,000	5,000

Let's first calculate nominal GDP for this economy in each year. Nominal GDP is the total market value of goods and services produced in each year. Using the data in the table, we can see that nominal GDP for the year 2011 is

$$(4 \text{ cars} \times \$10{,}000) + (1 \text{ computer} \times \$5{,}000) = \$45{,}000$$

Similarly, nominal GDP for the year 2012 is

$$(5 \text{ cars} \times \$12{,}000) + (3 \text{ computers} \times \$5{,}000) = \$75{,}000$$

Now we'll find real GDP. To compute real GDP, we calculate GDP using constant prices. What prices should we use? For the moment, let's use the prices for the year 2011. Because we are using 2011 prices, real GDP and nominal GDP for 2011 are both equal to $45,000. But for 2012, they are different. In 2012, real GDP is

$$(5 \text{ cars} \times \$10{,}000) + (3 \text{ computers} \times \$5{,}000) = \$65{,}000$$

Note that real GDP for 2012, which is $65,000, is less than nominal GDP for 2012, which is $75,000. The reason real GDP is less than nominal GDP here is that prices of cars rose by $2,000 between 2011 and 2012, and we are measuring GDP using 2011 prices. We can measure real GDP for any other year simply by calculating GDP using constant prices.

We now calculate the growth in real GDP for this economy between 2011 and 2012. Because real GDP was $45,000 in 2011 and $65,000 in 2012, real GDP grew by $20,000. In percentage terms, this is a $20,000 increase from the initial level of $45,000 or

$$\text{Percentage growth in real GDP} = \frac{\$20{,}000}{\$45{,}000} = .444$$

which equals 44.4 percent. This percentage is an average of the growth rates for both goods—cars and computers.

Figure 5.5 depicts real and nominal GDP for the United States from 1950 to 2009. Real GDP is measured in 2000 dollars, so the curves cross in 2000. Before 2000, nominal GDP is less than real GDP because prices in earlier years were lower than they were in 2000. After 2000, nominal GDP exceeds real GDP because prices in later years were higher than they were in 2000.

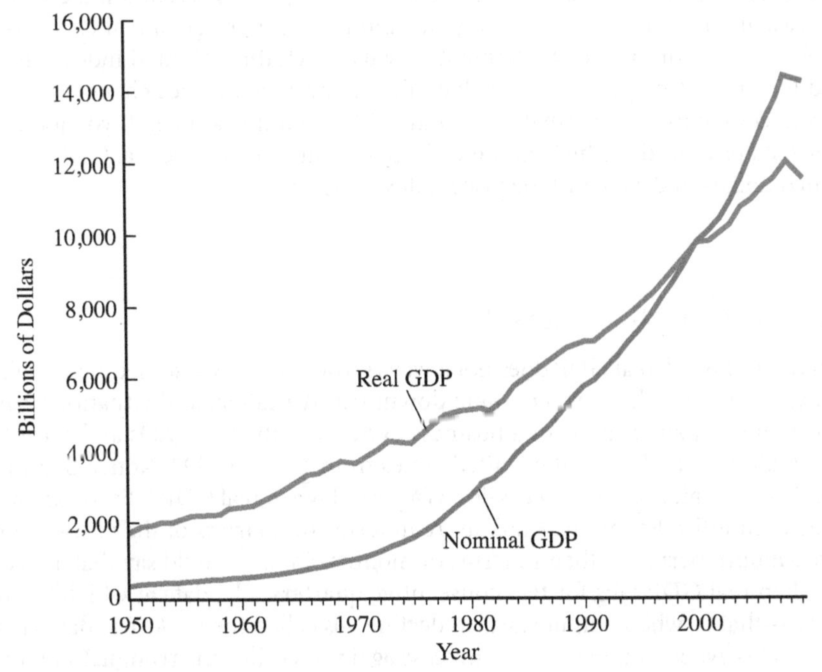

Figure 5.5

U.S. Nominal and Real GDP, 1950–2009

This figure plots both real and nominal GDP for the United States in billions of dollars. Real GDP is measured in 2000 dollars.

How to Use the GDP Deflator

We can also use the data in Table 5.4 to measure the changes in prices for this economy of cars and computers. The basic idea is that the differences between nominal GDP and real GDP for any year arise only because of changes in prices. So by comparing real GDP and nominal GDP, we can measure the changes in prices for the economy. In practice, we do this by creating an index, called the GDP deflator, that measures how prices of goods and services change over time. Because we are calculating real GDP using year 2011 prices, we will set the value of this index equal to 100 in the year 2011, which we call the base year. To find the value of the GDP deflator for the year 2012 (or other years), we use the following formula:

$$\text{GDP Deflator} = \frac{\text{Nominal GDP}}{\text{Real GDP}} \times 100$$

Using this formula, we find that the value of the GDP deflator for 2012 is

$$\frac{\$75{,}000}{\$65{,}000} \times 100 = 1.15 \times 100 = 115$$

Because the value of the GDP deflator is 115 in 2012 and was 100 in the base year of 2011, this means prices rose by 15 percent between the two years:

$$\frac{115 - 100}{100} = \frac{15}{100} = 0.15$$

Note that this 15 percent is a weighted average of the price changes for the two goods—cars and computers.

Until 1996, the Commerce Department, which produces the GDP figures, used these formulas to calculate real GDP and measure changes in prices. Economists at the department chose a base year and measured real GDP by using the prices in that base year. They also calculated the GDP deflator, just as we did, by taking the ratio of nominal GDP to real GDP. Today, the Commerce Department calculates real GDP and the price index for real GDP using a more complicated method. In our example, we measured real GDP using 2011 prices. But we could have also measured real GDP using prices from 2012. If we did, we would have come up with slightly different numbers both for the increase in prices between the two years and for the increase in real GDP. To avoid this problem, the Commerce Department now uses a **chain-weighted** index, which is a method for calculating price changes that takes an average of price changes using base years from consecutive years (that is, 2011 and 2012 in our example). If you look online or at the data produced by the Commerce Department, you will see real GDP measured in chained dollars and a chain-type price index for GDP.

Chain-weighted index A method for calculating changes in prices that uses an average of base years from neighboring years.

5.5 LEARNING OBJECTIVE

Fluctuations in GDP

As we have discussed, real GDP does not always grow smoothly—sometimes it collapses suddenly, and the result is an economic downturn. We call such fluctuations *business cycles*. Let's look at an example of a business cycle from the late 1980s and early 1990s. Figure 5.6 plots real GDP for the United States from 1988 to 1992. Notice that in mid-1990, real GDP begins to fall. A **recession** is a period when real GDP falls for six or more consecutive months. Economists talk more in terms of quarters of the year—consecutive three-month periods—than in terms of months. So they would say that a recession occurs when real GDP falls for two consecutive quarters. The date at which the recession starts—that is, when output starts to decline—is called the **peak**. The date at which it ends—that is, when output starts to increase again—is called the **trough**. In Figure 5.6,

Recession Commonly defined as six consecutive months of declining real GDP.

Peak The date at which a recession starts.

Trough The date at which output stops falling in a recession.

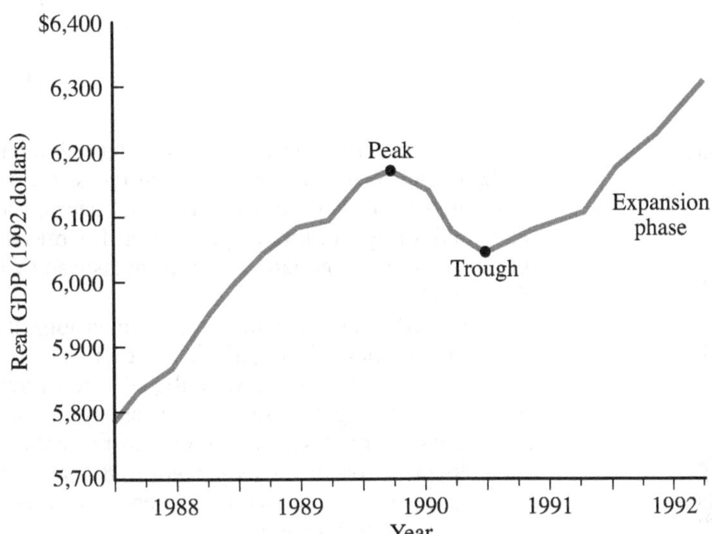

Figure 5.6

The 1990 Recession

Recessions can be illustrated by peaks, troughs, and an expansion phase. The date at which the recession starts and output begins to fall is called the peak. The date at which the recession ends and output begins to rise is called the trough. The expansion phase begins after the trough.

SOURCE: U.S. Department of Commerce.

we see the peak and trough of the recession. After a trough, the economy enters a recovery period, or period of **expansion.**

Expansion The period after a trough in the business cycle during which the economy recovers.

From World War II through 2010, the United States experienced 11 recessions. Table 5.5 contains the dates of the peaks and troughs of each recession, the percent decline in real GDP from each peak to each trough, and the length of the recessions in months. Complete information is not yet available for the most recent recession, which began in December 2007. Aside from the most recent recession, which was very severe, the sharpest decline in output occurred during the recession from 1973 to 1975, which started as a result of a sharp rise in world oil prices. This was also one of the longest recessions, although the most recent recession will most likely be the longest.

In the last three decades, there have been four recessions, three of them starting near the beginning of each of the decades: 1981, 1990, and 2001. In the 2001 recession, employment began to fall in March 2001, before the terrorist attack on the United States on September 11, 2001. The attack further disrupted economic activity and damaged producer and consumer confidence, and the economy tumbled through a recession. The recession that began in December 2007 followed a sharp decline in the housing sector

Table 5.5

Eleven Postwar Recessions

Peak	Trough	Percent Decline in Real GDP	Length of Recession (months)
November 1948	October 1949	−1.5	11
July 1953	May 1954	-3.2	10
August 1957	April 1958	-3.3	8
April 1960	February 1961	−1.2	10
December 1969	November 1970	−1.0	11
November 1973	March 1975	−4.1	16
January 1980	July 1980	-2.5	6
July 1981	November 1982	-3.0	16
July 1990	March 1991	-1.4	8
March 2001	November 2001	−0.6	8
December 2007	June 2009	−4.1	18

SOURCE: National Bureau of Economic Research, "Business Cycle Expansions and Contractions," http://wwwdev.nber.org/cycles/cyclesmain.html.

Application 2

Comparing the Severity of Recessions

Applying the Concepts #2: How severe was the most recent recession for the United States?

Was the most recent recession the most severe economic downturn since the Great Depression? With the data now in, it appears that the recession starting in December 2007 will rival the recession starting in November 1973, which was caused by a sharp and unexpected rise in oil prices. From Table 5.5, we see that the fall in output from peak to trough was 4.1 percent. A similar calculation based on available quarterly data for the recent recession from the fourth quarter of 2007 to the second quarter of 2009 reveals a fall of approximately 4.1%. On this measure, the 2007 recession was equally severe as measured by the decline in GDP.

However, along other important dimensions, the 2007 recession was more damaging to the economy. The 1973 recession lasted 16 months, while the 2007 recession lasted 18 months, the longest in the postwar era. Additionally, the toll on workers appears greater in the most recent recession. Unemployment rose from 4.9 percent to 8.5 percent in the earlier recession as compared to 4.6 percent to 10.0 percent in the most recent recession.

Of course, governments can offset some of these effects on individuals through social programs such as payments to those individuals who become unemployed or welfare payments. For a complete analysis, we would want to look at the incomes of those who lost their jobs as well as those who kept their jobs.

and the financial difficulties associated with this decline. It deepened during the financial crisis that hit in September and October of 2008. As credit became less available to both businesses and consumers, the effects of the financial crisis began to show up in reduced consumer spending for durable goods such as automobiles and reduced business investment.

Throughout the broader sweep of U.S. history, other downturns have occurred—20 of them from 1860 up to World War II. Not all were particularly severe, and in some unemployment hardly changed. However, some economic downturns, such as those in 1893 and 1929, were severe.

Although we used the common definition of a recession as a period when real GDP falls for six months, in practice, a committee of economists at the National Bureau of Economics Research (NBER), a private research group in Cambridge, Massachusetts, of primarily academic economists, officially proclaims the beginning and end of recessions in the United States using a broader set of criteria than just GDP. The NBER's formal definition is "a significant decline in economic activity, spread across the economy, lasting more than a few months, normally visible in production, employment, real income, and other indicators." As you can see, it uses a wide variety of indicators to determine whether a recession has occurred and its length.

Depression The common name for a severe recession.

Depression is the common term for a severe recession. In the United States, the Great Depression refers to the years 1929 through 1933, the period when real GDP fell by over 33 percent. This drop in GDP created the most severe disruptions to ordinary economic life in the United States during the twentieth century. Throughout the country and in much of the world, banks closed, businesses failed, and many people lost their jobs and their life savings. Unemployment rose sharply. In 1933, over 25 percent of people who were looking for work failed to find jobs.

Although the United States has not experienced a depression since that time, other countries have. In the last 20 years, several Asian countries (for example, Thailand) and Latin American countries (for example, Argentina) suffered severe economic disruptions that were true depressions.

GDP as a Measure of Welfare

5.6 LEARNING OBJECTIVE

GDP is our best measure of the value of output produced by an economy. As we have seen, we can use GDP and related indicators to measure economic growth within a country. In a later chapter, we will use GDP to compare the value of output across countries as well. Economists use GDP and related measures to determine if an economy has fallen into a recession or has entered into a depression. But while GDP is a very valuable measure of the health of an economy, it is not a perfect measure.

Shortcomings of GDP as a Measure of Welfare

There are several recognized flaws in the construction of GDP. We should thus be cautious in interpreting GDP as a measure of our economic well-being, because it does not take into account housework and childcare, leisure, the underground economy, or pollution.

Housework and Childcare First, GDP ignores transactions that do not take place in organized markets. The most important example is services, such as cleaning, cooking, and providing free childcare, that people do for themselves in their own homes. Because these services are not transferred through markets, GDP statisticians cannot

Application 3

The Links Between Self-Reported Happiness and GDP

Applying the Concepts #3: Do increases in gross domestic product necessarily translate into improvements in the welfare of citizens?

Two economists, David Blanchflower of Dartmouth College and Andrew Oswald of Warwick University in the United Kingdom, have systematically analyzed surveys over a nearly 30-year period that ask individuals to describe themselves as "happy, pretty happy, or not too happy." The results of their work are provocative. Over the last 30 years, reported levels of happiness have declined slightly in the United States and remained relatively flat in the United Kingdom despite very large increases in per capita income in both countries. Could it be the increased stress of everyday life has taken its toll on our happiness despite the increase in income?

At any point in time, however, money does appear to buy happiness. Holding other factors constant, individuals with higher incomes do report higher levels of personal satisfaction. But these "other factors" are quite important. Unemployment and divorce lead to sharply lower levels of satisfaction. Blanchflower and Oswald calculate that a stable marriage is worth $100,000 per year in terms of equivalent reported satisfaction.

Perhaps most interesting are their findings about trends in the relative happiness of different groups in our society. While whites report higher levels of happiness than African Americans, the gap has decreased over the last 30 years, as the happiness of African Americans has risen faster than that of whites. Men's happiness has risen relative to that of women over the last 30 years.

Finally, in recent work Blanchflower and Oswald looked at how happiness varies over the life cycle. Controlling for income, education, and other personal factors, they found that in the United States, happiness among men and women reaches a minimum at the ages of 49 and 45, respectively. Since these are also the years in which earnings are usually the highest, it does suggest that work takes its toll on happiness.

SOURCE: David Blanchflower and Andrew Oswald, "Well-Being Over Time in Britain and the USA," (working paper 7847, National Bureau of Economic Research, January 2000) and "Is Well-being U-Shaped over the Life Cycle," (working paper 12935, February 2007).

Table 5.6
The World Underground Economy, 2002–2003

Region of the World	Underground Economy as Percent of Reported GDP
Africa	41%
Central and South America	41
Asia	30
Transition Economies	38
Europe, United States, and Japan	17
Unweighted Average over 145 Countries	35

SOURCE: Based on estimates by Friedrich Schneider in "The Size of Shadow Economies in 145 Countries from 1999 to 2003," unpublished paper, 2005.

measure them. If we included household production in GDP, measured GDP would be considerably higher than currently reported.

Leisure Second, leisure time is not included in GDP because GDP is designed to be a measure of the production that occurs in the economy. To the extent that households value leisure, increases in leisure time will lead to higher social welfare, but not to higher GDP.

Underground Economy Third, GDP ignores the underground economy, where transactions are not reported to official authorities. These transactions can be legal, but people don't report the income they have generated because they want to avoid paying taxes on it. For example, wait staff may not report all their tips and owners of flea markets may make under-the-table cash transactions with their customers. Illegal transactions, such as profits from the illegal drug trade, also result in unreported income. In the United States in 2005, the Internal Revenue Service estimated (based on tax returns from 2001) that about $310 billion in federal income taxes from the underground economy was not collected each year. If the federal income tax rate that applies to income evaded from taxes was about 20 percent, approximately $1.5 trillion ($310 billion ÷ 0.20) in income from the underground economy escaped the GDP accountants that year, or about 15 percent of GDP at the time.

Economists have used a variety of methods to estimate the extent of the underground economy throughout the world. They typically find that the size of the underground economy is much larger in developing countries than in developed countries. For example, in the highly developed countries, estimates of the underground economy are between 15 and 20 percent of reported or official GDP. However, in developing countries, estimates are closer to 40 percent of reported GDP. Table 5.6 contains estimates of the underground economy as a percent of reported GDP for different regions of the world.

Pollution Fourth, GDP does not value changes in the environment that occur in the production of output. Suppose a factory produces $1,000 of output but pollutes a river and lowers its value by $2,000. Instead of recording a loss to society of $1,000, GDP will show a $1,000 increase. This is an important limitation of GDP accounting as a measure of our economic well-being, because changes in the environment affect our daily lives. Previous attempts by the Commerce Department to measure the effects of changes in environment by adding positive or subtracting negative changes to the environment from national income did not yield major results. But they were limited and looked only at a very select part of the environment. Has our environment improved or deteriorated as we experienced economic growth? Finding the answer to this question will pose a real challenge for the next generation of economic statisticians.

Most of us would prefer to live in a country with a high standard of living, and few of us would want to experience poverty up close. But does a higher level of GDP really lead to more satisfaction?

Summary

In this chapter, we learned how economists and government statisticians measure the income and production for an entire country and what these measures are used for. Developing meaningful statistics for an entire economy is difficult. As we have seen, statistics can convey useful information—if they are used with care. Here are some of the main points to remember in this chapter:

1 The circular flow diagram shows how the production of goods and services generates income for households and how households purchase goods and services by firms. The expanded circular flow diagram includes government and the foreign sector.

2 *Gross domestic product* (GDP) is the market value of all final goods and services produced in a given year.

3 GDP consists of four components: consumption, investment, government purchases, and net exports. The following equation combines these components:

$$Y = C + I + G + NX$$

The *GDP deflator* is an index that measures how the prices of goods and services included in GDP change over time. The following equation helps us find the GDP deflator:

$$\text{GDP Deflator} = \frac{\text{Nominal GDP}}{\text{Real GDP}} \times 100$$

4 *National income* is obtained from GDP by adding the net income U.S. individuals and firms earn from abroad, then subtracting depreciation.

5 *Real GDP* is calculated by using constant prices. The Commerce Department now uses methods that take an average using base years from neighboring years.

6 *A recession* is commonly defined as a six-month consecutive period of negative growth. However, in the United States, the National Bureau of Economic Research uses a broader definition.

7 GDP does not include nonmarket transactions, leisure time, the underground economy, or changes to the environment.

Key Terms

Chain-weighted index, p. 114
Consumption expenditures, p. 106
Depreciation, p. 107
Depression, p. 116
Economic growth, p. 105
Expansion, p. 115
Export, p. 108
Government purchases, p. 107
Gross domestic product (GDP), p. 103
Gross investment, p. 107
Gross national product (GNP), p. 109
Import, p. 108
Inflation, p. 102
Intermediate good, p. 104
Macroeconomics, p. 101
National income, p. 109
Net exports, p. 108
Net investment, p. 107
Nominal GDP, p. 105
Peak, p. 114
Personal disposable income, p. 110
Personal income, p. 110
Private investment expenditures, p. 106
Real GDP, p. 105
Recession, p. 114
Trade deficit, p. 108
Trade surplus, p. 108
Transfer payments, p. 107
Trough, p. 114
Value added, p. 110

CHAPTER 6

Unemployment and Inflation

Chapter Outline and Learning Objectives

Applying the Concepts

For February 2010, the Bureau of Labor Statistics (BLS) reported that the unemployment rate was 9.7 percent. The unemployed were those who did not have jobs, but were actively looking for work.

However, the official unemployment statistics did not include the following individuals:

- A steelworker in Ohio who was laid off two years ago. He stopped looking for work because there were no steel mills remaining in his town, and he believed no jobs were available.
- A young woman living in the far suburbs of a city. She wanted to work and had worked in the past, but she had no transportation to the places where jobs were available.
- A young computer programmer who was working 25 hours a week. He wanted to work 40 hours a week, but his employer did not have enough work for him, because most of the company's programming work had been contracted to India. Nor could he easily find another job.

The BLS publishes an alternative measure of unemployment that includes these cases. In February 2010 the unemployment rate by that measure was 16.8 percent. Which unemployment measure gives a more accurate picture of the labor market?

In this chapter, we look at unemployment and inflation, two key phenomena in macroeconomics. Losing a job is one of the most stressful experiences a person can suffer. For the elderly, the fear that the purchasing power of their wealth will evaporate with inflation is also a source of deep concern.

We will examine how economists define unemployment and inflation and the problems in measuring them. We also will explore the various costs that unemployment and inflation impose on society. Once we have a basic understanding of what unemployment and inflation are, we will be able to investigate their causes further.

Examining Unemployment

6.1 LEARNING OBJECTIVE

When an economy performs poorly, it imposes costs on individuals and society. Recall from Chapter 5 that one of the key issues for macroeconomics is understanding fluctuations—the ups and downs of the economy. During periods of poor economic performance and slow economic growth, unemployment rises sharply and becomes a cause of public concern. During times of good economic performance and rapid economic growth, unemployment falls, but does not disappear. Our first task is to understand how economists and government statisticians measure unemployment and then learn to interpret what they measure.

How is Unemployment Defined and Measured?

Let's begin with some definitions. The *unemployed* are those individuals who do not currently have a job but who are actively looking for work. The phrase *actively looking* is critical. Individuals who looked for work in the past but who are not looking currently are not counted as unemployed. The *employed* are individuals who currently have jobs. Together, the unemployed and employed comprise the **labor force**:

labor force = employed + unemployed

Labor force The total number of workers, both the employed and the unemployed.

Unemployment rate The percentage of the labor force that is unemployed.

The **unemployment rate** is the number of unemployed divided by the total labor force. This rate represents the percentage of the labor force unemployed and looking for work:

$$\text{unemployment rate} = \frac{\text{unemployed}}{\text{labor force}} \times 100$$

Labor force participation rate The percentage of the population over 16 years of age that is in the labor force.

Finally, we need to understand what is meant by the **labor force participation rate**, which is the labor force divided by the population 16 years of age and older. This rate represents the percentage of the population 16 years of age and older that is in the labor force:

$$\text{labor force participation rate} = \frac{\text{labor force}}{\text{population 16 years and older}} \times 100$$

To illustrate these concepts, suppose an economy consists of 200,000 individuals 16 years of age and older. Of all these people, 122,000 are employed and 8,000 are unemployed. This means that 130,000 (122,000 + 8,000) people are in the labor force. The labor force participation rate is 0.65, or 65 percent (130,000/200,000), and the unemployment rate is 0.0615, or 6.15 percent (8,000/130,000).

Figure 6.1 helps to put these measurements into perspective for the U.S. economy. The total civilian population 16 years of age and older in February 2010 was 236,998,000 individuals. We divide this population into two groups: those in the labor force (the employed plus the unemployed, totaling 153,512,000) and those outside the labor force 83,487,000. For this year, the labor force participation rate was 65 percent (153,512,000/236,998,000). As you can see, approximately two thirds of the U.S. population participates in the labor force. Within the labor force, 138,641,000 were employed and 14,871,000 were unemployed. The unemployment rate was 9.7 percent (14,871,000/153,512,000). Military personnel are excluded from these measures.

One of the most important trends in the last 50 years has been the increase in the participation of women in the labor force. But, as the next Application indicates, it appears that increase has come to an end.

Figure 6.2 contains international data on unemployment for 2010 for developed countries. Despite the fact these countries all have modern, industrial economies, notice the sharp differences in unemployment. For example, Belgium had a 12.1 percent unemployment rate, whereas Japan had an unemployment rate of 4.9 percent. These sharp differences reflect a number of factors, including how much government support is provided to unemployed workers. In countries in which support is the most generous, there is less incentive to work and unemployment will tend to be higher.

Figure 6.1

Unemployment Data, February 2010

Approximately 65 percent of the civilian population is in the labor force. The unemployment rate in February 2010 was 9.7 percent.

SOURCE: Bureau of Labor Statistics, U.S. Department of Labor, 2010.

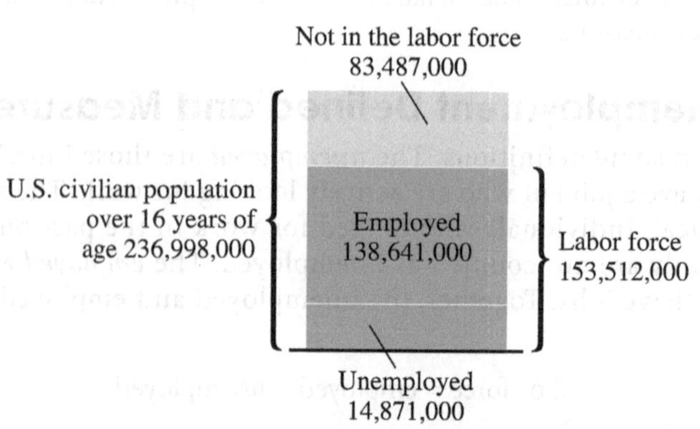

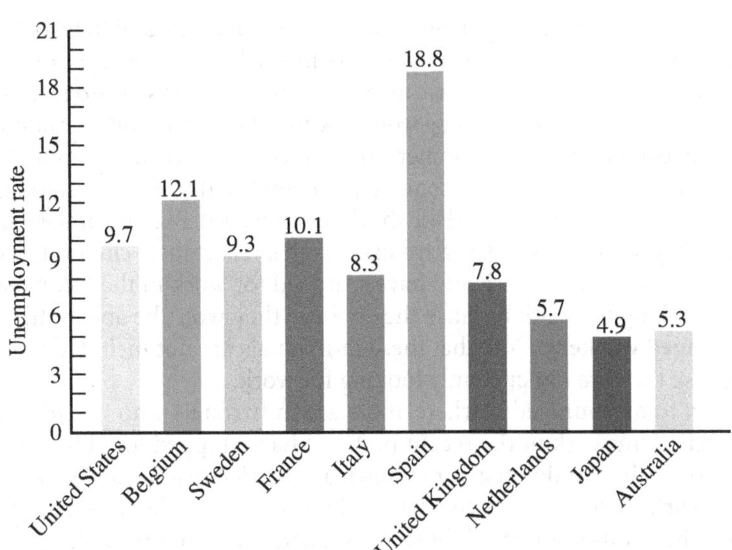

Figure 6.2

Unemployment Rates in Developed Countries

Among the developed countries, unemployment rates vary substantially.

SOURCE: The Economist, March 20–26, 2010.

Alternative Measures of Unemployment and Why They Are Important

We defined the unemployed as those people who are looking for work but who do not currently have jobs. With that in mind, let's take a closer look at our measures of unemployment.

It is relatively straightforward in principle to determine who is employed: Just count the people who are working. What is more difficult is to distinguish between those who are unemployed and those who are not in the labor force. How are these two groups distinguished? The BLS, which is part of the Department of Labor, interviews a large sample of households each month. The BLS asks about the employment situation of all household members 16 years of age and older. If someone in a household is not working, the interviewer asks whether the person is actively looking for work. If the answer is "yes," he or she is classified as unemployed. If the answer is "no"—he or she is not actively looking for work—that person is classified as not being in the labor force.

Application 1

After Growing Sharply, Women's Labor Force Participation has Leveled Off

Applying the Concepts #1: What do the recent data show about trends in the percentage of women who are working?

In 1948, the labor force participation rate for women 20 years and older was 32 percent. By 1970, it had grown to 43 percent, and by 1997 it had reached 60 percent. This trend reflected remarkable changes in our economy and society as women dramatically increased their presence in the workforce. But since 1997, the figure has remained virtually constant at 60 percent. It appears that women's labor force participation has reached a peak in the United States, somewhat short of the men's labor force participation rate of approximately 76 percent.

One explanation for this trend is that women may simply have run out of available time. From 1948 to the mid-1990s, women were able to increase their hours of work by cutting back on the time that they spent on housework and other home duties. With the advent of new technologies such as washing machines, dishwashers, and other labor-saving devices, women could increase their labor force participation yet still take primary care of their households. But even with new technology, housework and childcare do take time. Because women provide more household services than men, it is understandable why their labor force participation may have reached a peak.

SOURCE: Based on Bureau of Labor Statistics, 2010.

The BLS measure of unemployment, however, does not capture all the employment experiences individuals face. In the chapter opener, we highlighted the cases of three individuals who wanted full-time jobs but did not have them: a steelworker who stopped looking for work because he felt there were no jobs, a young woman who did not seek work because she had no transportation, and a computer programmer who worked only part-time but sought full-time employment. None of them would be counted as unemployed in the official statistics—the first two were not in the labor force and the third was employed. Because of these limitations, in 1994 the BLS began to publish alternative statistics that reflect these circumstances.

Discouraged workers Workers who left the labor force because they could not find jobs.

Individuals who want to work and have searched for work in the prior year, but are not currently looking for work because they believe they won't be able to find a job are called **discouraged workers**. Note that these individuals are not included in the official statistics because they are not currently looking for work.

In addition to discouraged workers, there are individuals who would like to work and have searched for work in the recent past, but have stopped looking for work for a variety of reasons. These individuals are known as *marginally attached workers*. Marginally attached workers consist of two groups: discouraged workers (who left the labor force because they could not find jobs) and workers who are not looking for jobs for other reasons, including lack of transportation or childcare.

Finally, there are those workers who would like to be employed full-time but hold part-time jobs. These individuals are counted as employed in the BLS statistics because they have a job. However, they would like to be working more hours. They are known as *individuals working part time for economic reasons*. We do not include in this category individuals who prefer part-time employment.

How important are these alternative measures? Figure 6.3 puts them into perspective. In February 2010, 14.87 million individuals were officially classified as unemployed. The number of discouraged workers was 1.20 million. Including the discouraged workers, there were 2.52 million marginally attached workers. If we add the marginally attached individuals to those who were involuntarily working part time, the total is 11.31 million. Thus, depending on the statistic you want to emphasize, there were anywhere between 14.87 million unemployed (the official number) and 26.18 million unemployed

Figure 6.3

Alternative Measures of Unemployment, February 2010

Including discouraged workers, marginally attached workers, and individuals working part time for economic reasons substantially increases measured unemployment in 2010 from 14.87 million to 26.18 million.

SOURCE: Bureau of Labor Statistics, U.S. Department of Labor, 2010.

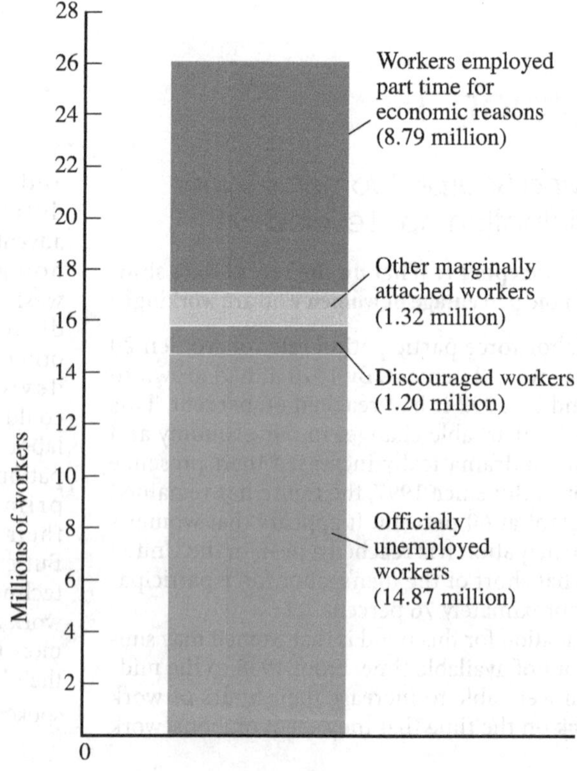

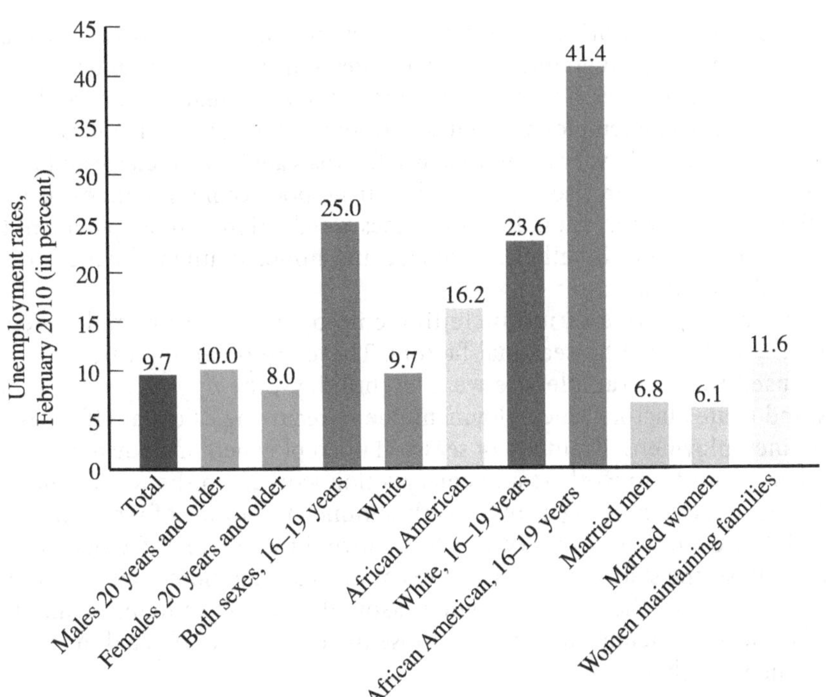

Figure 6.4

Selected U.S. Unemployment Statistics, Unemployment Rates for February 2010

The incidence of unemployment differs sharply among demographic groups.

SOURCE: Bureau of Labor Statistics, U.S. Department of Labor, 2010.

(the official number plus all those seeking full-time employment who did not have it). If we count those 26.18 million as unemployed, the unemployment rate in 2010 would be 16.8 percent—substantially higher than the official rate of 9.7 percent. As we have seen, the official statistics for unemployment do not include the full range of individuals who would like to participate fully in the labor market.

Who Are the Unemployed?

Another fact about unemployment is that different groups of people suffer more unemployment than others. Figure 6.4 contains some unemployment statistics for selected groups for February 2010. Adults have substantially lower unemployment

Application 2

More Disability, Less Unemployment?

Applying the Concepts #2: Does more liberal disability insurance decrease measured unemployment?

The federal Disability Insurance program provides income to nonelderly workers who are deemed unable to engage in substantial employment. It also provides health care to these individuals. After 1984, the guidelines were changed to make it easier for individuals to enter the program. From 1984 to 2001, the number of nonelderly adults receiving payments from this program rose by 60 percent to 5.3 million.

Economists David Autor and Mark Duggan studied the impact of this program on labor force participation. They found that the changes in the rules administering the program, the increased generosity of the benefits of the program for low-skilled workers, and the increase in the value of health-care services all contributed to an increase in participation in this program. They estimated that the combination of these factors led to a decrease in the labor force participation for high school dropouts and other low-skilled workers.

Since these workers, a portion of whom would have been unemployed, were no longer in the labor force, the economists estimated that the effect of the Disability Insurance program was to lower the measured unemployment rate by 0.5 percent, a very large effect.

SOURCE: Based on David H. Autor and Mark G. Duggan, "The Rise in Disability Rolls and the Decline in Unemployment," *Quarterly Journal of Economics* (February 2003): 157–206.

rates than teenagers. Minorities have higher unemployment rates. African-American teenagers have extremely high unemployment rates. On average, men and women have similar unemployment rates, but the unemployment rates for married men and married women are lower than unemployment rates of women who maintain families alone.

These differentials do vary somewhat as GDP rises and falls. Teenage and minority unemployment rates often rise very sharply during poor economic times, as was the case in the most recent recession. In better times, a reduction of unemployment for all groups typically occurs. Nonetheless, teenage and minority unemployment remains relatively high at all times.

Many economic time series, including employment and unemployment, are substantially influenced by seasonal factors. These are recurring calendar-related effects caused by, for example, the weather, holidays, the opening and closing of schools, and related factors. Unemployment due to recurring calendar effects is called **seasonal unemployment**. Examples of seasonal unemployment include higher rates of unemployment for farm workers and construction workers in the winter and higher unemployment rates for teenagers in the early summer as they look for summer jobs.

Seasonal unemployment The component of unemployment attributed to seasonal factors.

The BLS uses statistical procedures to remove these seasonal factors—that is, it seasonally adjusts the statistics—so that users of the data can more accurately interpret underlying trends in the economy. The seasonally adjusted unemployment rates control for these predictable patterns, so those patterns aren't reflected in the overall unemployment numbers.

6.2 LEARNING OBJECTIVE

Categories of Unemployment

To better understand the labor market, economists have found it very useful to break unemployment into a variety of categories. As we shall see, it is valuable to distinguish among the several different types of unemployment.

Types of Unemployment: Cyclical, Frictional, and Structural

After seasonally adjusting the unemployment statistics, we can divide unemployment into three other basic types: cyclical, frictional, and structural. By studying each type separately, we can gain insight into some of the causes of each type of unemployment.

The unemployment rate is closely tied to the overall fortunes of the economy. Unemployment rises sharply during periods when real GDP falls and decreases when real GDP grows rapidly. During periods of falling GDP, firms will not want to employ as many workers as they do in good times because they are not producing as many goods and services. Firms will lay off or fire some current workers and will be more reluctant to add new workers to their payrolls. The result will be fewer workers with jobs and rising unemployment. Economists call the unemployment that occurs during fluctuations in real GDP **cyclical unemployment**. Cyclical unemployment rises during periods when real GDP falls or grows at a slower-than-normal rate and decreases when the economy improves.

Cyclical unemployment Unemployment that occurs during fluctuations in real GDP.

However, unemployment still exists even when the economy is growing. For example, the unemployment rate in the United States has not fallen below 3.9 percent of the labor force since 1970. Unemployment that is not associated with economic fluctuations is either frictional unemployment or structural unemployment.

Frictional unemployment is the unemployment that occurs naturally during the normal workings of an economy. It occurs because it simply takes time for people to find the right jobs and for employers to find the right people to hire. This happens when people change jobs, move across the country, get laid off from their current jobs and search for new opportunities, or take their time after they enter the labor force to find an appropriate job. Suppose that when you graduate from college, you take six months to find a job you like. During the six months in which you are looking for a good job, you

Frictional unemployment Unemployment that occurs with the normal workings of the economy, such as workers taking time to search for suitable jobs and firms taking time to search for qualified employees.

are among those unemployed who make up frictional unemployment. Searching for a job, however, makes good sense. It would not be wise to take the first job you were offered if it had low wages, poor benefits, and no future. Likewise, employers are wise to interview multiple applicants for jobs to find the best employees, even if it takes some time.

Could we eliminate unemployment by posting all job vacancies on the Internet along with the résumés of job seekers and automatically match them up with one another? It's possible that such an automated system could shorten the duration of frictional unemployment, but it wouldn't eliminate it entirely. Some workers, for example, would prefer to continue searching for jobs in their own area rather than moving across the country to take the jobs they had been automatically matched with. Firms would also still want to scrutinize employees very carefully, because hiring and training a worker is costly.

Structural unemployment Unemployment that occurs when there is a mismatch of skills and jobs.

Structural unemployment occurs when the economy evolves. It occurs when different sectors give way to other sectors or certain jobs are eliminated while new types of jobs are created. For example, when the vinyl record industry gave way to the CD music industry in the 1980s, some workers found themselves structurally unemployed, which meant they had to take the time to train themselves for jobs in different industries. Structural unemployment is more of a "permanent condition" than frictional unemployment.

The line between frictional unemployment and structural unemployment is sometimes hard to draw. Suppose a highly skilled software engineer is laid off because his company shuts down its headquarters in his area and moves his job overseas. The worker would like to find a comparable job, but only lower-wage work is available in his immediate geographic location. Jobs are available, but not his kind of job, and this high-tech company will never return to the area. Is this person's unemployment frictional or structural? There really is no correct answer. You might think of the software engineer as experiencing either frictional or structural unemployment. For all practical purposes, however, it does not matter which it is. The former software engineer is still unemployed.

The Natural Rate of Unemployment

Natural rate of unemployment The level of unemployment at which there is no cyclical unemployment. It consists of only frictional and structural unemployment.

Full employment The level of unemployment that occurs when the unemployment rate is at the natural rate.

Total unemployment in an economy is composed of all three types of unemployment: cyclical, frictional, and structural. The level of unemployment at which there is no cyclical unemployment is called the **natural rate of unemployment**. The natural rate of unemployment consists of only frictional unemployment and structural unemployment. The natural rate of unemployment is the economist's notion of what the rate of unemployment should be when there is **full employment**. It may seem strange to think that workers can be unemployed when the economy is at full employment. However, the economy actually needs some frictional unemployment to operate efficiently: Frictional unemployment exists so that workers and firms find the right employment matches. An economy that lacks frictional unemployment will become stagnant.

In the United States today, economists estimate that the natural rate of unemployment is between 5.0 and 6.5 percent. The natural rate of unemployment varies over time and differs across countries. In Europe, for example, estimates of the natural rate of unemployment place it between 7 and 10 percent. In a later chapter, we explore why the natural rate of unemployment is higher in Europe than in the United States and why the natural rate of unemployment can vary over time in the same country.

The actual unemployment rate can be higher or lower than the natural rate of unemployment. During a period in which the real GDP fails to grow at its normal rate, there will be positive cyclical unemployment, and actual unemployment can far exceed the natural rate of unemployment. For example, in the United States in 2010 unemployment was about 10 percent of the labor force. As we pointed out in the previous chapter, a more extreme example occurred in 1933 during the Great Depression, when the unemployment rate reached 25 percent. When the economy grows very rapidly for a long period, actual unemployment can fall below the natural rate of unemployment. With sustained rapid economic growth, employers will be aggressive in hiring workers. During the late 1960s, unemployment rates fell below 4 percent, and the natural rate of unemployment was estimated to be over 5 percent. In this case, cyclical unemployment was negative.

Unemployment also fell to 4 percent in 2000. In this case, many economists believed that the natural rate of unemployment had fallen to close to 5 percent, so that cyclical unemployment in that year was negative.

Just as a car will overheat if the engine is overworked, so will the economy overheat if economic growth is too rapid. At low unemployment rates, firms will find it difficult to recruit workers, and competition among firms will lead to increases in wages. As wages increase, increases in prices soon follow. The sign of this overheating will be a general rise in prices for the entire economy, which we commonly call *inflation*. As we discuss in later chapters, when the actual unemployment rate falls below the natural rate of unemployment, inflation will increase.

6.3 LEARNING OBJECTIVE

The Costs of Unemployment

When there is excess unemployment—actual unemployment above the natural rate of unemployment—both society and individuals suffer economic loss. From a social point of view, excess unemployment means that the economy is no longer producing at its potential. The resulting loss of output can be very large. For example, in 1983, when the unemployment rate averaged 9.6 percent, typical estimates of the shortfall of GDP from potential were near 6 percent. Simply put, this meant that society was wasting 6 percent of the total resources at its disposal.

Unemployment insurance Payments unemployed people receive from the government.

To families with fixed obligations such as mortgage payments, the loss in income can bring immediate hardships. **Unemployment insurance**, payments received from the government upon becoming unemployed, can cushion the blow to some degree, but unemployment insurance is typically only temporary and does not replace a worker's full earnings.

The effects of unemployment can also linger into the future. Workers who suffer from a prolonged period of unemployment are likely to lose some of their skills. For example, an unemployed stockbroker might be unaware of the latest developments and trends in financial markets. This lack of knowledge will make it more difficult for that person to find a job in the future. Economists who have studied the high rates of unemployment among young people in Europe point to the loss of both skills and good work habits (such as coming to work on time) as key factors leading to long-term unemployment.

The costs of unemployment are not simply financial. In our society, a person's status and position are largely associated with the type of job the person holds. Losing a job can impose severe psychological costs. Some studies have found, for example, that increased crime, divorce, and suicide rates are associated with increased unemployment.

Not all unemployment lasts a long period of time for individuals. Some unemployment is very short term. Table 6.1 shows the percent of unemployed by the duration or length of unemployment. In February 2010, approximately 18.3 percent of unemployed workers had been out of work less than 5 weeks. At the other end, 40.9 percent were unemployed more than 27 weeks. During better economic times with lower overall

Table 6.1

The Duration of Unemployment, February 2010

SOURCE: Bureau of Labor Statistics, U.S. Department of Labor, 2010.

Weeks of Unemployment	Percent of the Unemployed
Fewer than 5 weeks	18.3
5 to 14 weeks	22.8
15 to 26 weeks	18.0
Greater than 27 weeks	40.9

Application 3

Social Norms, Unemployment, and Perceived Happiness

Applying the Concepts #3: Are you less upset from being unemployed if unemployment is common in your peer group?

We know that individuals do not like to become unemployed. But how do feelings about becoming unemployed depend on the experiences of those around one? Economist Andrew E. Clark carefully examined the perceptions and the behavior of the unemployed in Great Britain over a seven-year period. He looked at the responses to survey questions by those individuals who became unemployed and constructed an index of their general happiness or well-being.

He found, as expected, that people's perceived well-being declined as they became unemployed, and also that employed people become less happy if others around them became unemployed. But his interesting and somewhat surprising finding was that, for men, becoming unemployed caused *less* of a decrease in perceived well-being if those in their peer group—family, household, or region—were also unemployed. In other words, misery loved company. It was better (or less worse) to be unemployed if others in their peer group were also unemployed.

Why did this matter? Clark also found that the more unhappy an individual was, the more aggressive he or she would be to try to find a new job. So, if your peer group is also unemployed, you may not be as aggressive in searching for work. Unemployment, therefore, may last longer for individuals in these circumstances.

SOURCE: Based on Andrew E, Clark, "Unemployment as a Social Norm: Psychological Evidence from Panel Data," *Journal of Labor Economics* 21, no. 2 (2003): 323–351.

unemployment, the percentage of short-term spells of unemployment increases and percentage of long-term spells decrease. In the United States, unemployment is a mixture of both short- and long-term unemployment.

Although unemployment insurance can temporarily offset some of the financial costs of job loss, the presence of unemployment insurance also tends to increase the length of time that unemployed workers remain unemployed. The extra financial cushion that unemployment insurance provides allows workers to remain unemployed a bit longer before obtaining another job. In other words, unemployment insurance actually leads to additional time spent unemployed.

The Consumer Price Index and the Cost of Living

6.4 LEARNING OBJECTIVE

Suppose you were reading a book written in 1964 in which the main character received a starting salary of $5,000. Was that a high or low salary back then? To answer that, we need to know what $5,000 could purchase. Or, to put it another way, we need to know the *value* of the dollar—what a dollar would actually buy—in 1964. Only then could we begin to know whether this was a high or low salary.

Or take another example. In 1976, a new starting professor in economics received a salary of $15,000. In 2010, at the same university, a new starting professor received $90,000. Prices, of course, had risen in these 30 years along with salaries. Which starting professor had the better deal?

These examples are illustrations of one of our five principles of economics, the real-nominal principle.

Real-Nominal Principle | **What matters to people is the real value of money or income—its purchasing power—not the face value of money or income.**

Consumer Price Index A price index that measures the cost of a fixed basket of goods chosen to represent the consumption pattern of a typical consumer.

Economists have developed a number of different measures to track the cost of living over time. The best known of these measures is the **Consumer Price Index (CPI)**.

The CPI is widely used to measure changes in the prices consumers face. It measures changes in prices of a fixed *basket of goods*—a collection of items chosen to represent the purchasing pattern of a typical consumer. We first find out how much this basket of goods costs in a given year. This is called the *base year* (it serves a similar purpose as the base year we designated for the GDP deflator). We then ask how much it costs in other years and measure changes in the cost of living relative to this base year. The CPI index for a given year, say year *K*, is defined as

$$\text{CPI in year } K = \frac{\text{cost of basket in year } K}{\text{cost of basket in base year}} \times 100$$

Suppose a basket of goods costs $200 in 1992, which we'll define as the base year. In 2004, the same basket of goods is $250. First, the value for the CPI in 1992 (the base year) is

$$\text{CPI in 1992} = \frac{200}{200} \times 100 = 100$$

That is, the CPI for 1992 is 100. Note that the base year for the CPI will always equal 100. Now let's calculate the value of the CPI for 2004:

$$\text{CPI in 2004} = \frac{250}{200} \times 100 = 125$$

The CPI in 2004 is 125. The CPI rose from 100 in 1992 to 125 in 2004 in this example, a 25 percent increase in average prices over this 12-year period.

Here is how you would use this information. Suppose you had $300 in 1992. How much money would you need to be able to have the same standard of living in 2004? Find the answer by multiplying the $300 by the ratio of the CPI in 2004 to the CPI in 1992:

$$\$300 \times \frac{125}{100} = \$375$$

You need $375 in 2004 just to maintain what was your standard of living in 1992. This is the type of calculation that economists do to evaluate changes in living standards over time.

How do we actually calculate the CPI in practice? Each month, the BLS sends its employees out to sample prices for over 90,000 specific items around the entire country. This is how they construct their representative basket of goods. Figure 6.5 shows the broad categories the BLS uses in the CPI and the importance of each category in household budgets. Rent and food and beverages account for 44 percent of total spending by households.

The CPI versus the Chain Index for GDP

In Chapter 5, we discussed measuring nominal GDP and real GDP. We also mentioned that since 1996 the Commerce Department has used a chain-weighted index (replacing the GDP deflator) to measure changes in prices for goods and services included in GDP. The chain-weighted index for GDP and the CPI are both measures of average prices for the economy, yet they differ in several ways.

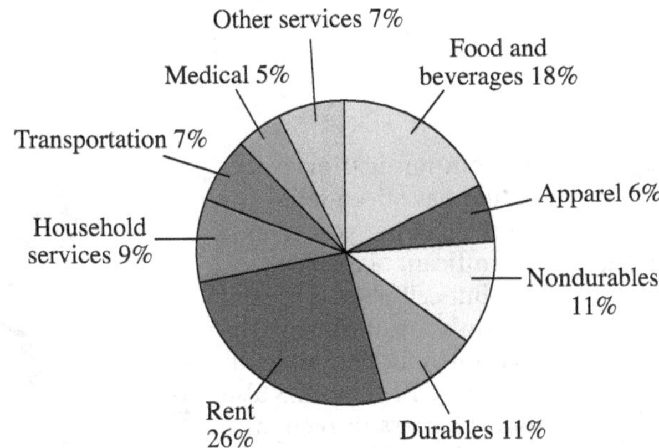

Figure 6.5

Components of the Consumer Price Index (CPI)

Rent and food and beverages make up 44 percent of the CPI basket. The remainder consists of other goods and services.

SOURCE: Bureau of Labor Statistics, U.S. Department of Labor, 2006.

First, the CPI measures the costs of a typical basket of goods for consumers. It includes goods produced in prior years (such as older cars) as well as imported goods. The chain-weighted price index for GDP does not measure price changes from either used goods or imports. The reason is that it is based on the calculation of GDP, which, as we've seen, measures only goods and services produced in the United States in the current year.

Second, unlike the chain-weighted price index for GDP, the CPI asks how much a *fixed* basket of goods costs in the current year compared to the cost of those same goods in a base year. Because consumers tend to buy less of goods whose prices rise, the CPI will tend to overstate true changes in the cost of living. For example, if the price of steak rises, consumers may switch to chicken and spend less on steak. But if the current basket of goods and services in the CPI includes steak, the CPI thinks the amount of higher-priced steak in the basket is the same as the amount of steak before its price increase. It does not allow the amount of steak in the index to decrease. Another measurement problem occurs when new products are introduced into the marketplace, again because the CPI measures a fixed basket of goods. The BLS will eventually adjust its "basket" to account for successful new products, but it takes some time.

Problems in Measuring Changes in Prices

Most economists believe that in reality all the indexes, including the chain-weighted index for GDP and the CPI, overstate actual changes in prices. In other words, the increase in prices is probably less than the reported indexes tell us. The principal reason for this overstatement is that we have a difficult time measuring quality improvements. Suppose the new computers sold to consumers become more powerful and more efficient each year. Suppose further that the dollar price of a new computer remains the same each year. Even though the price remains the same, the computers in later years are of much higher quality. If we looked simply at the price and did not take into account the change in quality, we would say there was no price change for computers. But in later years we are getting more computer power for the same price. If we failed to take the quality change into account, we would not see that the price of computer power has fallen.

Government statisticians do try to adjust for quality when they can. But quality changes are so common in our economy and products evolve so rapidly that it is impossible to keep up with all that is occurring. As a result, most economists believe we overestimate the inflation rate by between 0.5 and 1.5 percent each year. This overstatement has important consequences. Some government programs, such as Social Security, automatically increase payments when the CPI goes up. Some union contracts also have **cost-of-living adjustments (COLAs),** automatic wage changes based on the CPI. If the CPI overstates increases in the cost of living, the government and employers might be overpaying Social Security recipients and workers for changes in the cost of living.

Cost-of-living adjustments (COLAs) Automatic increases in wages or other payments that are tied to the CPI.

Application 4

The Introduction of Cell Phones and the Bias in the CPI

Applying the Concepts #4: How large is the bias in the CPI due to not immediately incorporating new goods?

Today, it is hard to imagine a world without cell phones. Every college student and most high school students carry them everywhere. But cell phones were not introduced to the public until 1983, and it took 15 years, until 1998, before the Bureau of Labor Statistics included them in calculating the CPI!

Economist Jerry Hausman of MIT estimated the bias in the CPI caused by the failure to include cell phones in a timely manner. He calculated that because of this delay, the telecommunication component of the price index was biased upwards by between 0.8 and 1.9 percent per year. In other words, instead of rising by 1.1 percent per year, telecommunication prices should have been falling by 0.8 percent per year. This is a significant bias.

But cell phones are not the only examples of the slow introduction of goods into the CPI. The BLS also took 15 years to recognize room air conditioners in the CPI. Since new products are constantly invented and introduced, the bias in the CPI can be large.

SOURCE: Based on Jerry Hausman, "Cellular Telephone, New Products, and the CPI," *Journal of Business & Economic Statistics* 17, no. 2 (1999): 186–194.

6.5 LEARNING OBJECTIVE

Inflation

Inflation rate The percentage rate of change in the price level.

We have now looked at two different price indexes: the chain-weighted price index used for calculating real GDP and the Consumer Price Index. Using either price index, we can calculate the percentage rate of change of the index. The percentage rate of change of a price index is the **inflation rate**:

$$\text{inflation rate} = \text{percentage rate of change of a price index}$$

Here is an example. Suppose a price index in a country was 200 in 1998 and 210 in 1999. Then the inflation rate between 1998 and 1999 was

$$\text{inflation rate} = \frac{210 - 200}{200} = 0.05 = 5\%$$

In other words, the country experienced a 5 percent inflation rate.

It is important to distinguish between the price level and the inflation rate. In everyday language, people sometimes confuse the level of prices with inflation. You might hear someone say inflation is high in San Francisco because rents for apartments are high, but this is not a correct use of the term *inflation*. Inflation refers not to the level of prices, whether they are high or low, but to their *percentage change*. If rents were high in San Francisco but remained constant over two years, there would be no inflation in rents there during that time.

Historical U.S. Inflation Rates

To gain some historical perspective, Figure 6.6 plots a price index for GDP from 1875 to 2009 for the United States. As you can see from the figure, from 1875 to the period just before World War I, there was virtually no change in the price level. The price level rose during World War I, fell after the war ended, and also fell sharply during the early 1930s. However, the most pronounced feature of the figure is the sustained rise in prices beginning around the 1940s. Unlike the earlier periods, in which the price level did not have a trend, after 1940 the price level increased sharply. By 2010, the price level had increased

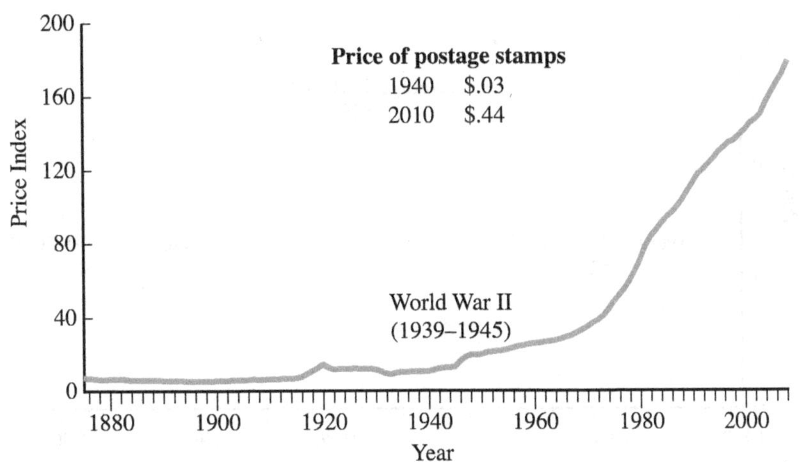

Figure 6.6

Price Index for U.S. GDP, 1875–2009

After remaining relatively flat for 60 years, the price level began to steadily increase after World War II. The price of a postage stamp in 1940 and 2009 illustrates the change in the overall price level that occurred.

SOURCES: R. J. Gordon, Macroeconomics (New York: Harper Collins, 1993) and U.S. Department of Commerce, 2010.

by a factor of 14 over its value in 1940. Table 6.2 contains the prices of a few selected goods from the 1940s and in 2010. Wouldn't you like to buy a postage stamp today for $0.03?

Taking a closer look at the period following World War II, Figure 6.7 plots the inflation rate, the percentage change in the price index, from 1950 to 2009. In the 1950s and 1960s, the inflation rate was frequently less than 2 percent a year. The inflation rate was a lot higher in the 1970s, reaching nearly 10 percent per year. In those years, the economy suffered from several increases in the world price of oil. In recent years, the inflation rate has subsided and has been between 2 and 3 percent.

The Perils of Deflation

Prices rarely fall today, but they have actually fallen at times in world history. You might think it would be great if prices fell and we had what economists term a **deflation**. It may surprise you, however, that we think you should hope deflation never occurs.

Deflation Negative inflation or falling prices of goods and services.

During the Great Depression, the United States underwent a severe deflation. Prices fell 33 percent on average, and wages fell along with prices. The biggest problem caused by a deflation is that people cannot repay their debts. Imagine you owe $40,000 for your

Table 6.2

Prices of Selected Goods, 1940s and 2010

Item	1940s Price	2010 Price
Gallon of gasoline	$0.18	$3.10
Loaf of bread	0.08	3.59
Gallon of milk	0.34	3.49
Postage stamp	0.03	0.44
House	6,550	350,000
Car	800	22,000
Haircut in New York City	0.50	50
Movie tickets in New York City	0.25	11.00
Men's tweed sports jacket in New York City	15	189
Snake tattoo on arm	0.25	60.00

SOURCES: Scott Derks, *The Value of a Dollar* 1860–1989 (Farmington Hills, MI: Gale Group, 1993) and author's research and estimates.

Figure 6.7

U.S. Inflation Rate, 1950–2009, Based on Chain-Weighted Price Index

Inflation reached its highest peaks in the postwar era during the decade of the 1970s when the economy was hit with several increases in oil prices. In recent years, the inflation rate has been relatively low.

SOURCE: U.S. Department of Commerce, 2010.

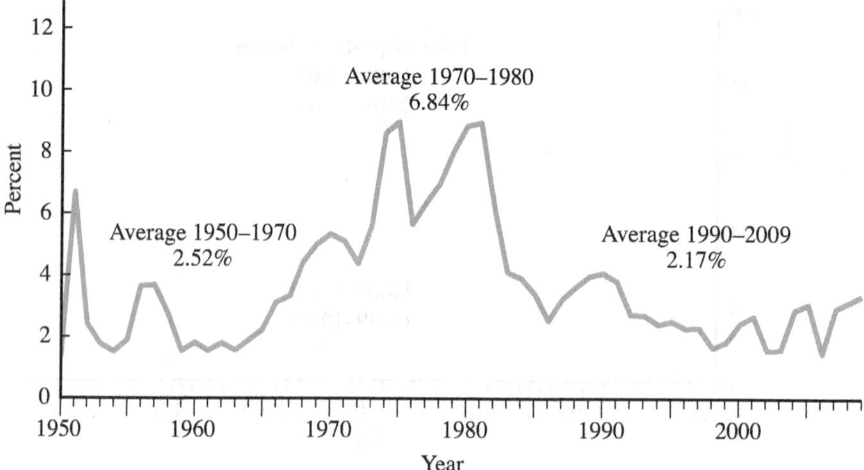

education and expect to be able to pay it off over several years if you earn $27,000 a year. If a massive deflation caused your wages to fall to $18,000, you might not be able to pay your $40,000 debt, which does not fall with deflation. You would be forced to default on your loan, as millions of people did during the Great Depression.

In the 1990s, Japan experienced a deflation, although much milder than the Great Depression in the United States—only about 1 percent per year. Nonetheless, banks in Japan faced rocky economic times as borrowers, including large corporations, defaulted on their loans. With its banks in difficult shape, Japan's economy has suffered. Its experience in the 1990s mirrored the experience of other countries throughout the world in the 1930s during the period of deflation.

6.6 LEARNING OBJECTIVE

The Costs of Inflation

Anticipated inflation Inflation that is expected.

Unanticipated inflation Inflation that is not expected.

Economists typically separate the costs of inflation into two categories. One includes costs associated with fully expected or **anticipated inflation**. The other includes the costs associated with unexpected or **unanticipated inflation**. Although inflation causes both types of costs, it is convenient to discuss each case separately.

Anticipated Inflation

Let's consider the costs of anticipated inflation first. Suppose the economy had been experiencing 5 percent annual inflation for many years and everyone was fully adjusted to it.

Menu costs The costs associated with changing prices and printing new price lists when there is inflation.

Even in this case, inflation still has some costs. First, there are the actual physical costs of changing prices, which economists call **menu costs**. Restaurant owners, catalog producers, and any other business that must post prices will have to incur costs to physically change their prices because of inflation. For example, they will need to pay to reprint their menus or billboards. Economists believe these costs are relatively small for the economy.

Second, inflation will erode the value of the cash people hold. They will respond by holding less cash at any one time. If they hold less cash, they must visit the bank or their ATM more frequently because they will run out of cash sooner. Economists use the term **shoe-leather costs** to refer to the additional costs people incur to hold less cash. Economists who have estimated these costs find that they can be large, as much as 1 percent of GDP.

Shoe-leather costs Costs of inflation that arise from trying to reduce holdings of cash.

In practice, our tax and financial systems do not fully adjust even to anticipated inflation. It is difficult for the government and businesses to change their normal rules of operation every time inflation changes. As an example, consider the tax system. Our tax system is typically based on nominal income, not real income. Suppose you own a stock in a corporation and its value increases by 5 percent during the year. If the inflation rate is also 5 percent a year, your stock did not increase in real terms—it just kept up with inflation. Nonetheless, if you sold your stock at the end of the year, you would be taxed on the full 5 percent gain, despite the fact that the real value of your stock did not increase. Inflation distorts the operation of our tax and financial system.

Unanticipated Inflation

What if inflation is unexpected? The cost of unexpected inflation is arbitrary redistributions of income. Suppose you expected the inflation rate would be 5 percent and you negotiated a salary based on that expectation. On the one hand, if you miscalculate and the inflation rate turns out to be higher, the purchasing power of your wages will be less than you anticipated. Your employer will have gained at your expense. On the other hand, if the inflation rate turned out to be less than 5 percent, the purchasing power of your wage would be higher than you had anticipated. In this case, you would gain at the expense of the company. As long as the inflation rate differs from what is expected, there will be winners and losers.

These redistributions eventually impose real costs on the economy. Consider an analogy. Suppose you live in a very safe neighborhood where no one locks the doors. If a rash of burglaries (transfers between you and crooks) starts to occur, people will invest in locks, alarms, and more police. You and your community will incur real costs to prevent these arbitrary redistributions.

The same is true for unanticipated inflation. If a society experiences unanticipated inflation, individuals and institutions will change their behavior. For example, potential homeowners will not be able to borrow from banks at fixed rates of interest, but will be required to accept loans whose rates can be adjusted as inflation rates change. Banks do not want to lend money at a fixed interest rate if there is a strong likelihood that inflation will erode the real value of the income stream they expected. However, if banks become reluctant to make loans with fixed interest rates, this imposes more risk on homeowners.

What about the loans made prior to the unanticipated inflation? In this case, debtors will gain at the expense of creditors. Creditors, on the one hand, will lose because inflation will erode the amount of money they planned to earn on the loans. But since the loans have already been made, there's nothing they can do about it. Debtors, on the other hand, will get a deal. It will be easier for them to repay their loans with inflated dollars.

If unanticipated inflation becomes extreme, individuals will spend more of their time trying to profit from inflation rather than working at productive jobs. As inflation became more volatile in the late 1970s in the United States, many people devoted their time to speculation in real estate and commodity markets to try to beat inflation, and the economy became less efficient. Latin American countries that have experienced high and variable inflation rates know all too well these costs from inflation. Indeed, when inflation rates exceed 50 percent per month, we have what is called **hyperinflation**. Think

Hyperinflation An inflation rate exceeding 50 percent per month.

about what an inflation rate of 50 percent a month means: If a can of soda costs $1.25 at the beginning of the year, it would cost $162.00 at the end of year! In a later chapter, we'll study the causes of hyperinflation, but you can readily see that inflation of this magnitude would seriously disrupt normal commerce.

Even in less extreme cases, the costs of inflation are compounded as inflation rises. At high inflation rates, these costs grow rapidly, and at some point policymakers are forced to take actions to reduce inflation. As we mentioned earlier, when unemployment falls below the natural rate, inflation increases. Similarly, in later chapters we'll see that stopping inflation may require unemployment to exceed its natural rate and even plunge an economy into a recession. Although unemployment and recessions are quite costly to society, they sometimes become necessary in the face of high inflation.

Summary

In this chapter, we continued our introduction to the basic concepts of macroeconomics and explored the nature of both unemployment and inflation. We also looked at the complex issues involved in measuring unemployment and inflation as well as the costs of both to society. Here are the key points to remember:

1. The unemployed are individuals who do not have jobs but who are actively seeking employment. The *labor force* comprises both the employed and the unemployed. The *unemployment rate* is the percentage of the labor force that is unemployed:

$$\text{unemployment rate} = \frac{\text{unemployed}}{\text{labor force}} \times 100$$

2. Economists distinguish among different types of unemployment. Seasonal patterns of economic activity lead to *seasonal unemployment*. There are three other types of unemployment. *Frictional unemployment* occurs through the normal dynamics of the economy as workers change jobs and industries expand and contract. *Structural unemployment* arises because of a mismatch of workers' skills with job opportunities. *Cyclical unemployment* occurs with the fluctuations in economic activity.
3. Unemployment rates vary across demographic groups. Alternative measures of unemployment take into account individuals who would like to work full time, but who are no longer in the labor force or are holding part-time jobs.
4. Economists measure changes in the cost of living through the *Consumer Price Index* (CPI), which is based on the cost of purchasing a standard basket of goods and services. The CPI is used to measure changes in average prices over different periods of time. The CPI index for a given year, say year K, is defined as

$$\text{CPI in year } K = \frac{\text{cost of basket in year K}}{\text{cost of basket in base year}} \times 100$$

5. We measure inflation as the percentage change in the price level.
6. Economists believe that most price indexes, including the CPI and the chain-weighted index for GDP, overstate true inflation because they fail to capture quality improvements in goods and services.
7. Unemployment imposes both financial and psychological costs on workers.
8. Both *anticipated* and *unanticipated* inflation impose costs on society.

Key Terms

Anticipated inflation, p. 134
Consumer Price Index (CPI), p. 130
Cost-of-living adjustments (COLAs), p. 131
Cyclical unemployment, p. 126
Deflation, p. 133
Discouraged workers, p. 124
Frictional unemployment, p. 126
Full employment, p. 127
Hyperinflation, p. 135
Inflation rate, p. 132
Labor force, p. 121
Labor force participation rate, p. 122
Menu costs, p. 134
Natural rate of unemployment, p. 127
Seasonal unemployment, p. 126
Shoe-leather costs, p. 135
Structural unemployment, p. 127
Unanticipated inflation, p. 134
Unemployment insurance, p. 128
Unemployment rate, p. 122

CHAPTER 7

Why Do Economies Grow?

Chapter Outline and Learning Objectives

Applying the Concepts

For many people, the thought of poverty conjures up poor, African children. Indeed, Africa is a poor continent, but as economists Xavier Sali-i-Martin and Maxim Pinkovskiy have recently shown, prospects are improving.

Since 1995, poverty rates in Africa have been falling steadily. Indeed, if this trend continues, the rate of poverty could meet ambitious goals set by the United Nations for poverty reduction by 2015. Economic growth in Africa has not come at the expense of the poor. The current income distribution in Africa is less unequal than it was in 1995, indicating that the growth of income has been shared across the population. The decline in poverty has been widespread across the continent. It has fallen in landlocked as well as coastal countries, mineral-rich and mineral-poor countries, and in countries with varying degrees of agriculture.

Their results even apply to countries that were particularly disadvantaged by slavery. The message of these economists is optimistic: Even countries hindered by geography or history can still reduce poverty through economic growth.[1]

Our living standards are dramatically different today because of the remarkable growth in GDP per person. Growth in GDP is perhaps the most critical aspect of a country's economic performance. Over long periods, it is the only way to raise the standard of living in an economy.

This chapter begins by looking at some data from both rich and poor countries over the last several decades. We will see how GDP per capita (meaning per person—every man, woman, and child) compares over this period. We'll then look at how growth occurs. Economists believe two basic mechanisms increase GDP per capita over the long term. One is **capital deepening**, or increases in an economy's stock of capital (such as buildings and equipment) relative to its workforce. **Technological progress** is the other; to economists this means an economy operates more efficiently, producing more output, but without using any more inputs such as capital or labor. We'll examine different theories of the origins of technological progress and discuss how to measure its overall importance for the economy. We'll also discuss in detail the role of education, experience, and investments in human beings, which are called **human capital**.

Capital deepening Increases in the stock of capital per worker.

Technological progress More efficient ways of organizing economic affairs that allow an economy to increase output without increasing inputs.

Human capital The knowledge and skills acquired by a worker through education and experience and used to produce goods and services.

The appendix to this chapter contains a simple model of capital deepening known as the Solow model. It shows how increases in capital per worker lead to economic growth. The model will also allow us to better understand the role of technological progress in sustaining economic growth.

Economic Growth Rates

7.1 LEARNING OBJECTIVE

Throughout the world there are vast differences in standards of living and in rates of economic growth. To understand these differences, we first need to look at the concepts and the tools economists use to study economic growth.

[1]Xavier Sala-i-Martin and Martin Pinkovskiy, "African Poverty is Falling: Much Faster Than You Think," NBER Working Paper Series, Working Paper No. 15775, February 2010.

Figure 7.1

What Is Economic Growth?

Economic growth means an expanded production possibilities curve (PPC).

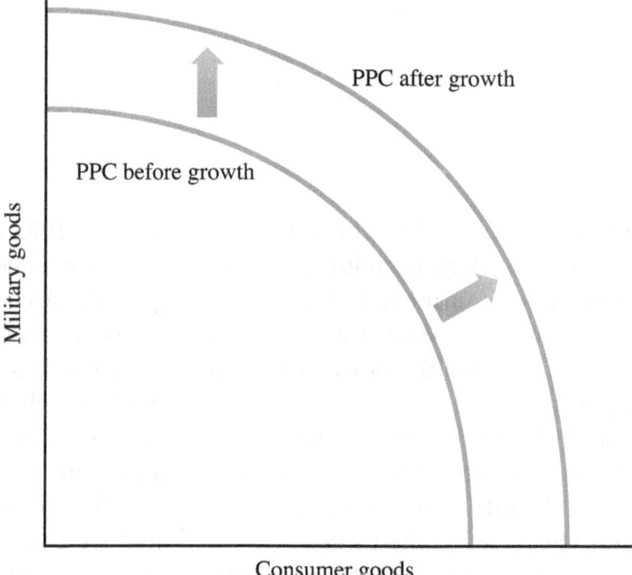

But before we learn how to measure growth, let's take a broad overview of what we mean by *economic growth*. We can understand economic growth by using one of the tools we developed in Chapter 2: the production possibilities curve. The production possibilities curve shows the set of feasible production options for an economy at a given point of time. In Figure 7.1 we show an economy's trade-off when it comes to producing consumer goods versus military goods. As the economy grows, the entire production possibilities curve shifts outward. This means the economy can produce more of both goods—that is what we mean by economic growth. Growth also expands the amount of goods available for people to consume. Just think about your own family. A typical family 40 years ago had only one car, whereas today many families have two or three. As our chapter-opening story highlights, the economic growth we take for granted is recent and does not apply evenly across all societies.

Measuring Economic Growth

From earlier chapters we know that real gross domestic product (GDP) measures in constant prices the total value of final goods and services in a country. Because countries differ in the size of their populations, we want to know a country's real GDP per person, or its **real GDP per capita**.

Real GDP per capita Gross domestic product per person adjusted for changes in prices. It is the usual measure of living standards across time and among countries.

Growth rate The percentage rate of change of a variable from one period to another.

Real GDP per capita typically grows over time. A convenient way to describe the changes in real GDP per capita is with growth rates. The **growth rate** of a variable is the percentage change in that variable from one period to another. For example, to calculate the growth rate of real GDP from year 1 to year 2, suppose real GDP was 100 in year 1 and 104 in year 2. In this case, the growth rate of real GDP is

$$\begin{aligned}\text{growth rate} &= \frac{(\text{GDP in year 2} - \text{GDP in year 1})}{(\text{GDP in year 1})} \\ &= \frac{(104 - 100)}{(100)} \\ &= \frac{4}{100} \\ &= 4\% \text{ per year}\end{aligned}$$

In other words, real GDP grew by 4 percent from year 1 to year 2. This also means that GDP in year 2 was (1 + 0.04) times GDP in the year 1.

Economies can grow at different rates from one year to the next. But it often is useful to consider what happens when an economy grows at a constant rate, say *g*, for a number of years. Let's start simply. Suppose real GDP for an economy was 100 and the economy grew at a rate *g* for two years. How large would the real GDP be two years later? After one year, GDP would be (1+g) 100. In the second year, it would grow by (1+g) again, or

$$\text{GDP [2 years later]} = (1 + g)^2(100)$$

We can generalize this to consider the case where the economy grows a constant rate *g* for *n* years. How large would GDP be after *n* years? A simple formula gives the answer:

$$\text{GDP [}n\text{ years later]} = (1 + g)^n(100)$$

Example: If the economy starts at 100 and grows at a rate of 4 percent a year for 10 years, output (after 10 years) will be

$$\text{GDP [10 years later]} = (1 + 0.04)^{10}(100) = (1.48)(100) = 148$$

which is nearly 50 percent higher than in the first year.

Here's a rule of thumb to help you understand the power of growth rates. Suppose you know the growth rate of real GDP, and it is constant, but you want to know how many years it will take until the level of real GDP doubles. The answer is given by the **rule of 70:**

Rule of 70 A rule of thumb that says output will double in 70/*x* years, where *x* is the percentage rate of growth.

$$\text{years to double} = \frac{70}{\text{(percentage growth rate)}}$$

Example: For an economy that grew at 5 percent a year, it would take

$$\frac{70}{5} = 14 \text{ years}$$

for real GDP to double. (In case you are curious, the rule of 70 is derived by using the mathematics of logarithms.)

Comparing the Growth Rates of Various Countries

Making comparisons of real GDP or GNP across countries is difficult. Not only do countries have their own currencies, but patterns of consumption and prices can differ sharply among countries. Two examples can illustrate this point. First, because land is scarce in Japan, people live in smaller spaces than do residents of the United States, so the price of housing is higher (relative to other goods) than in the United States. Second, developing countries (such as India or Pakistan) have very different price structures than developed countries. In particular, in developing countries goods that are not traded—such as household services or land—are relatively cheaper than goods that are traded in world markets. In other words, while all residents of the world may pay the same price for gold jewelry, hiring a cook or household helper is considerably less expensive in India or Pakistan than in the United States.

It is important to take these differences into account. Fortunately, a team of economists led by Robert Summers and Alan Heston of the University of Pennsylvania has devoted decades to developing methods for measuring real GNP across countries. The team's procedures are based on gathering extensive data on prices of comparable goods in each country and making adjustments for differences in relative prices and consumption patterns. These methods are now used by the World Bank and the International Monetary Fund, two prominent international organizations.

According to these methods, the country with the highest level of income in 2008 was Luxembourg; its real income per capita was $64,320. Norway, with its oil wealth, was at $58,500 while the United States was at $46,970.

Table 7.1

Gross National Income Per Capita and Economic Growth

SOURCE: *World Bank Development Indicators* (2010) and Alan Heston, Robert Summers, and Bettina Aten, Penn World Table Version 6.3, Center for International Comparisons at the University of Pennsylvania (CICUP), October 2010.

Country	Gross National Income Per Capita in 2008 Dollars	Per Capita Growth Rate 1960–2008
United States	$46,970	2.38%
United Kingdom	36,130	2.54
Japan	35,220	4.09
France	34,400	2.91
Italy	30,250	2.92
Mexico	14,270	2.95
Costa Rica	10,950	2.35
India	2,960	2.05
Pakistan	2,770	1.53
Nigeria	1,940	1.11
Zambia	1,230	–0.60

Table 7.1 lists real Gross National Income (GNI) per capita for 2004 and the average annual growth rate of GNI per capita between 1960 and 2008 for 11 countries. (Gross National Income is most commonly used in international comparisons, while 2008 is the most recent year for which fully consistent data back to 1960 is available.) The United Kingdom, with a GNI per capita of $36,130, follows the United States. Not far behind are Japan, France, and Italy. More representative of typical countries are Mexico and Costa Rica, with GNIs per capita in 2008 of $14,270 and $10,950, respectively. Costa Rica's GNI per capita is less than 25 percent of per capita GNI in the United States. Very poor countries have extremely low GNI per capita. Pakistan, for example, had a GNI per capita of $2,770—less than 6 percent of the GNI per capita of the United States.

In the third column of Table 7.1, notice the differences in growth rates. Consider Japan. In 1960, Japan had a GNI per capita that was only one-half that of France and one-fourth that of the United States. But notice from the third column that Japan's GNI per capita grew on average 4.09 percent per year during the period, compared to 2.38 percent for the United States and 2.91 percent for France. To place Japan's growth rate for this period into perspective, recall the rule of 70. If an economy grows at an average annual rate of x percent a year, it takes $70/x$ years for output to double. In Japan's case, per capita output was doubling every 70/4.09 years, or approximately every 17 years. At this rate, from the time someone was born to the time he or she reached the age of 34, living standards would have increased by a factor of four—an extraordinary rate of growth. The rule of 70 reinforces the importance of small differences in economic growth rates. A per capita GDP growth rate of 5 percent per year means that the living standard doubles in 14 years. With only 1 percent growth, doubling would take 70 years.

The differences in per capita incomes between the developed and developing countries are very large and are also reflected in many different aspects of society. Take, for example, child labor. In the developed world, we disapprove of child labor and wonder how we can work toward its elimination. The answer is relatively simple—more economic growth has been shown to lead to less child labor.

Are Poor Countries Catching Up?

Convergence The process by which poorer countries close the gap with richer countries in terms of real GDP per capita.

One question economists ask is whether poorer countries can close the gap between their level of GDP per capita and the GDP per capita of richer countries. Closing this gap is called **convergence**. To converge, poorer countries have to grow at more rapid rates than richer countries. Since 1960, Japan, Italy, and France all have grown more rapidly than the United States and have narrowed the gap in per capita incomes.

Let's look at some evidence provided by two distinguished international economists, Maurice Obstfeld of the University of California, Berkeley, and Kenneth Rogoff of Harvard University. Figure 7.2 plots the average growth rate for 16 currently developed countries from 1870 to 1979 against the level of per capita income in 1870. Each point

Application 1

Global Warming, Rich Countries, and Poor Countries

Applying the Concepts #1: How may global warming affect economic growth?

Many people believe that global warming will hurt economic development, but research shows that the effects are more complex. Recent research by economists Melissa Dell, Benjamin Jones, and Benjamin Olken provides some useful insights. First, the effects of increases in temperature seem to be confined to poor countries. Rich countries do not suffer from increases in temperature. In a study of municipalities within Latin and South America, the economists found that a one-degree Celsius rise in temperature was associated with between a 1.2 and 1.9 percentage decline in municipal per capita income. Over time, as economies adapt to higher temperatures approximately half of this effect disappears. Second, some of the adverse effects from higher temperatures seem to work through international trade. A one-degree Celsius increase in temperatures reduces poor countries' exports between 2.0 and 5.7 percentage points. The effect appears to be concentrated within the agricultural and light manufacturing goods sectors.

The fact that poor countries are affected but not rich countries suggests that the timing of global warming may matter. If global warming can be deferred sufficiently far into the future, poorer countries will have opportunities to develop and perhaps be less subject to global warming trends. However, if global warming occurs relatively soon, then poor countries are likely to be adversely affected.

SOURCE: Based on Melissa Dell, Benjamin Jones, and Benjamin Olken, "Temperature and Income: Reconciling Cross-Sectional and Panel Estimates," *American Economic Review Papers & Proceedings* (May 2009): 199–204 and Benjamin Jones and Benjamin Olken, "Climate Shocks and Exports," forthcoming *American Economic Review Papers & Proceedings* (May 2010).

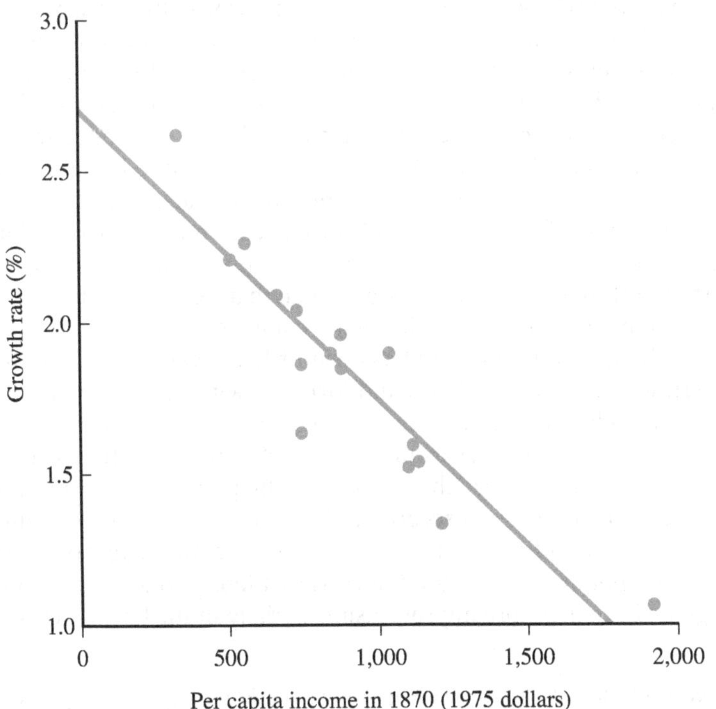

Figure 7.2

Growth Rates versus Per Capita Income, 1870–1979

Each point on the graph represents a different currently developed country. Notice that the countries with the lowest per capita incomes in 1870 (shown along the horizontal axis) are plotted higher on the graph. In other words, the tendency was for countries with lower levels of initial income to grow faster.

SOURCE: M. Obstfeld and K. Rogoff, Foundations of International Macroeconomics (Cambridge, MA: MIT Press, 1996), Table 7.1.

Application 2

Growth Need Not Cause Increased Inequality

Applying the Concepts #2: Does economic growth necessarily cause more inequality?

For many years, following the work of Nobel Laureate Simon Kuznets, economists believed that as a country developed, inequality within it followed an inverted "U" pattern—it initially increased and then narrowed over time. However, recent research by economists Emmanuel Saez of Harvard and Thomas Piketty, a French economist, challenges the assumption that this phenomenon is solely the result of growth.

Piketty and Saez looked carefully at data in the United States over the twentieth century. Inequality—as measured by the income share of the top 10 percent of families—increased from 40 percent at the beginning of the 1920s to 45 percent through the end of the Great Depression, consistent with Kuznets's theory. But things changed during World War II. During that time, the share fell to 32 percent by 1944 and remained at that level until the early 1970s, at which time inequality began to again increase.

Piketty and Saez suggest that wage and price controls during World War II reduced differentials in wages and salaries and thereby reduced inequality. Moreover, even after the war these patterns persisted until the 1970s, because society perceived them to be fair. After the 1970s, salaries at the top of the income distribution increased sharply. (Think of the vast sums paid to some major league baseball players or corporate executives.) These findings, as well as related results from other countries, suggest that inequality does not naturally accompany economic development. Social norms and other factors, such as perceived fairness of compensation and the nature of the tax system, also play a role in generating inequality. Moreover, the U.S. experience suggests these norms can change over time, even within the same country, regardless of growth rates.

SOURCE: Based on Thomas Piketty and Emmanuel Saez, "Income Inequality in the United States, 1913–1998," *Quarterly Journal of Economics* 118, no. 1 (2003): 1–39.

represents a different country. Notice that the countries with the lowest initial per capita incomes are plotted higher on the graph. That is, they had higher growth rates than the countries with more income per capita. The downward-sloping line plotted through the points indicates that the countries with higher levels of per capita income in 1870 grew more slowly than countries with lower levels. In other words, the tendency was for countries with lower levels of initial income to grow faster and catch up. The graph shows that among the currently developed countries—for example, the United States, France, and the United Kingdom—there was a tendency for convergence over the last century.

Now let's compare the countries that are currently less developed to the advanced industrial countries using the data in Table 7.1. Here, the picture is not so clear in recent times. While India grew at a faster rate than the United States, Pakistan grew only 1.53 percent per year and fell farther behind advanced economies. In Africa, Zambian GNI per capita grew less than 1 percent. In general, economists who have studied the process of economic growth in detail find weak evidence that poorer countries are currently closing the gap in per capita income with richer countries.

Indeed, in the last 20 years there has been little convergence. Economist Stanley Fischer, governor of the Bank of Israel and formerly with the IMF and the Massachusetts Institute of Technology, found that, on average, countries with higher GDP per capita in 1980 grew slightly faster from 1980 to 2000 than countries with lower GDP per capita.[2] African countries, which were among the poorest, grew most slowly. However, there were some important exceptions: The two most populous countries, China and India, grew very rapidly. Because these countries contain approximately 35 percent of the world's population, the good news is that living conditions for many people around the globe have therefore improved substantially in the last 20 years.

[2]Stanley Fischer, "Globalization and Its Challenges," *American Economic Review Papers and Proceedings* 93, no.2 (May 2003): 1–32.

Other commentators are less sanguine. Professor Brad DeLong at UC Berkeley wrote, "Those nations and economies that were relatively rich at the start of the twentieth century have by and large seen their material wealth and prosperity explode. Those nations and economies that were relatively poor have grown richer, but for the most part slowly. And the relative gulf between rich and poor economies has grown steadily. Today this relative gulf is larger than at any time in humanity's previous experience, or at least larger than at any time since there were some tribes that had discovered how to use fire and other tribes that had not."[3]

What about the distribution of income *within* countries as they develop? Many economists thought that as countries developed, inequality would increase among their populations. But recent research challenges this finding.

Capital Deepening

7.2 LEARNING OBJECTIVE

One of the most important mechanisms of economic growth economists have identified is increases in the amount of capital per worker due to capital deepening.

Figure 7.3 shows the effects on output and real wages. For simplicity, we assume the supply of labor is not affected by real wages and therefore draw a vertical line

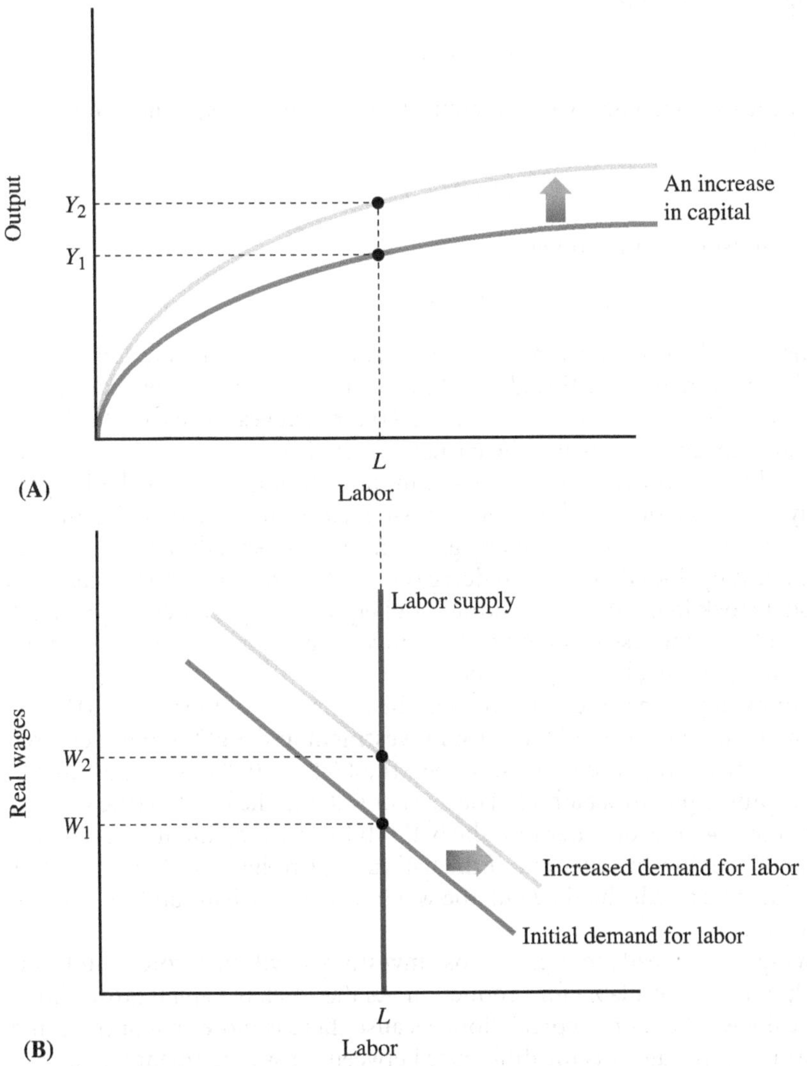

Figure 7.3

Increase in the Supply of Capital

An increase in the supply of capital will shift the production function upward, as shown in Panel A, and increase the demand for labor, as shown in Panel B. Real wages will increase from W_1 to W_2, and potential output will increase from Y_1 to Y_2.

[3]Bradford DeLong, "Slouching Toward Utopia," http://www.j-bradford-delong.net/TCEH/Slouch_divergence5.html (accessed June 27, 2008).

(see Panel B). In Panel A, an increase in capital shifts the production function upward because more output can be produced from the same amount of labor. In addition, firms increase their demand for labor because the marginal benefit from employing labor will increase. Panel B shows how the increase in capital raises the demand for labor and increases real wages. That is, as firms increase their demand and compete for a fixed supply of labor, they will bid up real wages in the economy.

An economy is better off with an increase in the stock of capital. With additions to the stock of capital, workers will enjoy higher wages, and total GDP in the economy will increase. Workers are more productive because each worker has more capital at his or her disposal. But how does an economy increase its stock of capital per worker? The answer is with saving and investment, which we'll discuss next.

Saving and Investment

Let's begin with the simplest case: an economy with a constant population, producing at full employment. This particular economy has no government or foreign sector. Its output can be purchased only by consumers or by firms. In other words, output consists solely of consumption (C) and investment (I). At the same time, output generates an amount of income equivalent to the amount of output. That is, output (Y) equals income. Any income that is not consumed we call **saving**.

Saving Income that is not consumed.

In this economy, saving must equal investment. Here's why: By definition, consumption plus saving equals income:

$$C + S = Y$$

but at the same time income—which is equivalent to output—also equals consumption plus investment:

$$C + I = Y$$

Thus, saving must equal investment:

$$S = I$$

This means that whatever consumers decide to save goes directly into investment. Here is a simple way to remember this idea: A farmer produces corn (Y) and can either consume it directly (C) or set it aside as "seed corn" (I) for next year. The part the farmer sets aside and does not consume is also the farmer's saving (S).

Next, we need to link the level of investment in the economy to the stock of capital in the economy. The stock of capital depends on two factors: investment and depreciation. The stock of capital increases with any gross investment spending but decreases with depreciation. Why does depreciation decrease the stock of capital? The answer is simple: As capital stock items such as buildings and equipment get older (depreciate), they wear out and become less productive. New investment is needed to replace the buildings and equipment that become obsolete.

Suppose, for example, the stock of capital at the beginning of the year is \$10,000. During the year, if there were \$1,000 in gross investment and \$400 in depreciation, the capital stock at the end of the year would be \$10,600 (= \$10,000 + \$1000 – \$400).

It may be helpful to picture a bathtub. The level of water in the bathtub (the stock of capital) depends on the flow of water into the bathtub through the input faucet (gross investment) minus the flow of water out of the bathtub down the drain (depreciation). As long as the flow in exceeds the flow out, the water level in the bathtub (the stock of capital) will increase.

Higher saving, which leads to higher gross investment, will therefore tend to increase the stock of capital available for production. As the stock of capital grows, however, there typically will be more depreciation, because there is more capital (building and equipment) to depreciate. It is the difference between gross investment and depreciation—*net investment*—that ultimately determines the change in the stock of capital for the economy, the level of real wages, and output. In our example, net investment is \$1,000 – \$400 = \$600.

How Do Population Growth, Government, and Trade Affect Capital Deepening?

So far, we've considered the simplest economy. Let's consider a more realistic economy that includes population growth, a government, and trade.

First, consider the effects of population growth: A larger labor force will allow the economy to produce more total output. However, with a fixed amount of capital and an increasing labor force, the amount of capital per worker will be less. With less capital per worker, output per worker will also be less, because each worker has fewer machines to use. This is an illustration of the principle of diminishing returns.

Principle of Diminishing Returns

Suppose that output is produced with two or more inputs and that we increase one input while holding the other inputs fixed. Beyond some point—called the *point of diminishing returns*—output will increase at a decreasing rate.

Consider India, the world's second most populous country, with over a billion people. Although India has a large labor force, its amount of capital per worker is low. With sharp diminishing returns to labor, per capita output in India is low, only $2,960 per person.

The government can affect the process of capital deepening in several ways through its policies of spending and taxation. Suppose the government taxed its citizens so that it could fight a war, pay its legislators higher salaries, or give foreign aid to needy countries—in other words, to engage in government consumption spending. The higher taxes will reduce total income. If consumers save a fixed fraction of their income, total private savings (savings from the nongovernmental sector) will fall. This taxation drains the private sector of savings that would have been used for capital deepening.

Now suppose the government took all the extra tax revenues and invested them in valuable infrastructure, such as roads, buildings, and airports. These infrastructure investments add to the capital stock. We illustrate this idea in Figure 7.4. If consumers were saving 20 percent of their incomes and the government collected $100 in taxes from each taxpayer, private saving and investment would fall by $20 per taxpayer, but government investment in the infrastructure would increase by a full $100 per taxpayer. In other words, the government "forces" consumers (by taxing them) to invest an additional $80 in infrastructure that they otherwise wouldn't invest. The net result is an increase in total social investment (private plus government) of $80 per taxpayer.

Finally, the foreign sector can affect capital deepening. The United States, Canada, and Australia built their vast railroad systems in the nineteenth century by running *trade deficits*—selling fewer goods and services to the rest of the world than they were

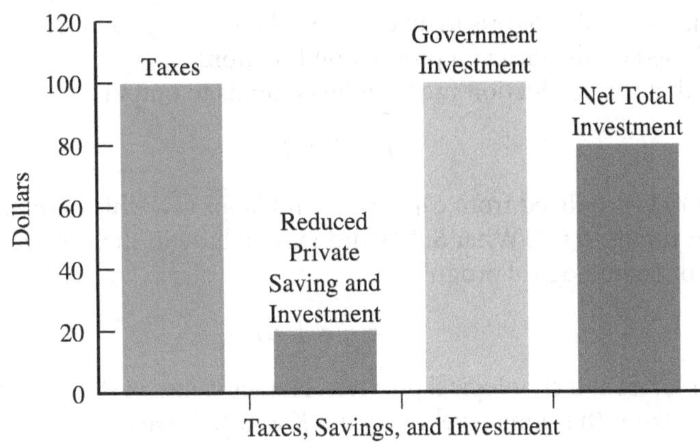

Figure 7.4

Taxes and Government Investment

If the government raises taxes by $100 and the people tend to save 20 percent of changes in income, then private savings and investment will fall by $20. However, if the government invests the funds, total investment—private and public—will increase by $80.

buying—and financing this gap by borrowing. This enabled them to purchase the large amount of capital needed to build their rail networks and grow at more rapid rates by deepening capital. Eventually, these economies had to pay back the funds they had borrowed from abroad by running *trade surpluses*—selling more goods and services to the rest of the world than they were buying from abroad. But because economic growth had increased their GDP and wealth, the three countries were able to afford to pay back the borrowed funds. Therefore, this approach to financing deepening capital was a reasonable strategy for them to pursue.

Not all trade deficits promote capital deepening, however. Suppose a country runs a trade deficit because it wants to buy more consumer goods. The country would be borrowing from abroad, but there would be no additional capital deepening—just additional consumption spending. When the country is forced to pay back the funds, there will be no additional GDP to help foot the bill. In order to fund current consumption, the country will be poorer in the future.

7.3 LEARNING OBJECTIVE

The Key Role of Technological Progress

The other mechanism affecting economic growth is technological progress. Economists use the term *technological progress* in a very specific way: It means an economy operates more efficiently by producing more output without using any more inputs.

In practice, technological progress can take many forms. The invention of the lightbulb made it possible to read and work indoors at night, the invention of the thermometer assisted doctors and nurses in their diagnoses, and the invention of disposable diapers made life easier at home. All these examples—and you could provide many more—enable society to produce more output without more labor or more capital. With higher output per person, we enjoy a higher standard of living.

We can think of technological progress as the birth of new ideas. These new ideas enable us to rearrange our economic affairs and become more productive. Not all technological innovations are necessarily major scientific breakthroughs; some are much more basic. An employee of a soft-drink company who discovers a new and popular flavor for a soft drink is engaged in technological progress, just like scientists and engineers. Even simple, commonsense ideas from workers or managers can help a business use its capital and labor more efficiently to deliver a better product to consumers at a lower price. For example, a store manager may decide that rearranging the layout of merchandise and location of cash registers helps customers find products and pay for them more quickly and easily. This change is also technological progress. As long as there are new ideas, inventions, and new ways of doing things, the economy can become more productive and per capita output can increase.

How Do We Measure Technological Progress?

If someone asked you how much of the increase in your standard of living was due to technological progress, how would you answer? Robert Solow, a Nobel Laureate in economics from the Massachusetts Institute of Technology, developed a method for measuring technological progress in an economy. Like most good ideas, his theory was simple. It was based on the idea of a production function.

You know that the production function links inputs to outputs:

$$Y = F(K,L)$$

where output (Y) is produced from capital (K) and labor (L), which are linked through the production function (F). What Solow did was include in the production function some measure of technological progress, A:

$$Y = F(K,L,A)$$

Increases in A represent technological progress. Higher values of A mean that more output is produced from the same level of inputs K and L. If we could find some way to measure A, we could estimate how much technological progress affects output.

Solow noted that over any period we can observe increases in capital, labor and output. Using these we can measure technological progress indirectly. We first ask how much of the change in output can be explained by contributions from increases in the amount of capital and labor used. Whatever growth we cannot explain in this way must therefore be caused by technological progress. The method Solow developed to measure the contributions to economic growth from capital, labor, and technological progress is called **growth accounting**.

Growth accounting A method to determine the contribution to economic growth from increased capital, labor, and technological progress.

Figure 7.5 illustrates the relative contributions of these growth sources for the U.S. economy from 1929 to 1982 using growth accounting, based on a classic study by the

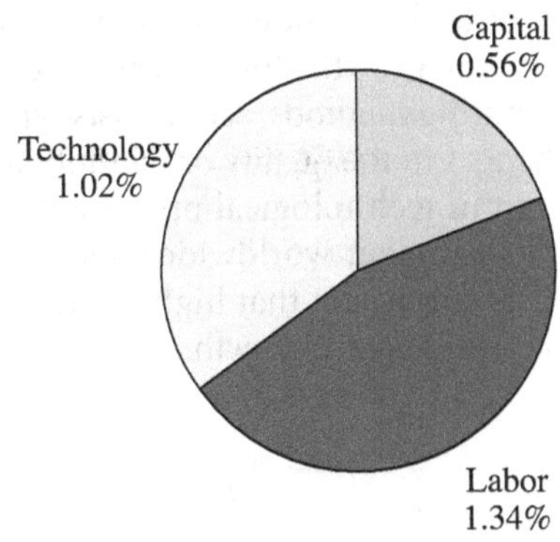

Figure 7.5

Contributions to Real GDP Growth, 1929–1982 (average annual percentage rates)

SOURCE: *Edward F. Denison,* Trends in American Economic Growth 1929–1982 *(Washington, D.C.: The Brookings Institution, 1985).*

Application 3

Sources of Growth in China and India

Applying the Concepts #3: How can we use economic analysis to understand the sources of growth in different countries?

China and India are the two most populous countries in the world and have also grown very rapidly in recent years. From 1978 to 2004, GDP in China grew at the astounding rate of 9.3 percent per year while India's GDP grew at a lower but still robust rate of 5.4 percent per year. What were the sources of this growth? Economists Barry Bosworth from the Brookings Institution and Susan Collins from the University of Michigan used growth accounting to answer this question.

Employment in China and India both grew at 2 percent per year over the period, so the remaining differences must be attributed to capital deepening and technological progress. Bosworth and Collins in turn broke capital deepening into two parts: increases in physical capital (buildings, machines, and equipment) and increases in human capital (the knowledge of workers, as measured by their educational attainment). Their analysis revealed that China's more rapid growth was primarily caused by more rapid accumulation of physical capital and more rapid technological progress. The contributions from human capital for each country were similar. Why did China grow faster than India over this 26-year period? Simply put, China invested much more than India in physical capital and was able to increase its technological progress at a more rapid rate.

Looking ahead, Bosworth and Collins find no evidence that growth in China and India is slowing. Capital formation and technological progress is still rapid in both countries and India has even improved its rate of technological advance in recent years. Despite this rapid growth and pockets of wealth in major cities, both countries are still poor: Chinese GNP per capita is only 15 percent and India's GDP is only 8 percent of U.S. GNP per capita. But at these growth rates, the gap will diminish in the coming decades.

SOURCE: Based on Barry Bosworth and Susan M. Collins, "Accounting for Growth: Comparing China and India," *Journal of Economic Perspectives* (Winter 2008): 45–66.

economist Edward Denison. During this period, total output grew at a rate of nearly 3 percent. Because capital and labor growth are measured at 0.56 and 1.34 percent per year, respectively, the remaining portion of output growth, 1.02 percent per year, must be due to technological progress. That means approximately 35 percent of output growth came directly from technological progress.

Other recent estimates give a similar picture of the contribution of technological progress to economic growth. For example, the Bureau of Labor Statistics estimates that between 1987 and 2007 technological progress accounted for 1.0 percentage points of economic growth in the private nonfarm business sector, very similar to Denison's estimates.

Using Growth Accounting

Growth accounting is a useful tool for understanding different aspects of economic growth. As an example, economic growth slowed throughout the entire world during the 1970s. Using growth accounting methods, economists typically found the slowdown could not be attributed to changes in the quality or quantity of labor inputs or to capital deepening. Either a slowdown in technological progress or other factors not directly included in the analysis, such as higher worldwide energy prices, must have been responsible. This led economists to suspect that higher energy prices were the primary explanation for the reduction in economic growth.

Labor productivity Output produced per hour of work.

Application 4

Growth Accounting and Information Technology

Applying the Concepts #4: How much did the information revolution contribute to U.S. productivity growth?

In analyses of the sources of economic growth, a common statistic reported about the U.S. economy is **labor productivity**. Defined as output per hour of work, labor productivity is a simple measure of how much a typical worker can produce given the amount of capital in the economy and the state of technological progress. From 1973 to 1993, the growth of labor productivity slowed in the United States. Figure 7.6 shows U.S. productivity growth for different periods since 1959.

The figure shows that productivity growth was extremely high during the 1960s. It slowed a bit in the late 1960s, and then slowed dramatically after the oil shocks in the 1970s. In recent years, productivity growth has increased, reaching 2.5 percent from 1994 to 2007.

As the figure shows, U.S. productivity growth did climb in the last half of the 1990s. Some observers believe the computer and Internet revolution are responsible for the increase in productivity growth. Skeptics wonder, however, whether this increase in productivity growth is truly permanent or just temporary. Higher investment in computer technology began in the mid-1980s, but until recently there was little sign of increased productivity growth. Had the investment in information technology finally paid off? And would it continue?

Robert J. Gordon of Northwestern University used growth accounting methods to shed light on this issue. After making adjustments for the low unemployment rate and high GDP growth rate in the late 1990s, he found there *had* been increases in technological progress. In earlier work, Gordon had found these increases were largely confined to the durable goods manufacturing industry, including the production of computers themselves. Because the increase in technological progress was confined to a relatively small portion of the economy, Gordon was originally skeptical that we were now operating in a "new

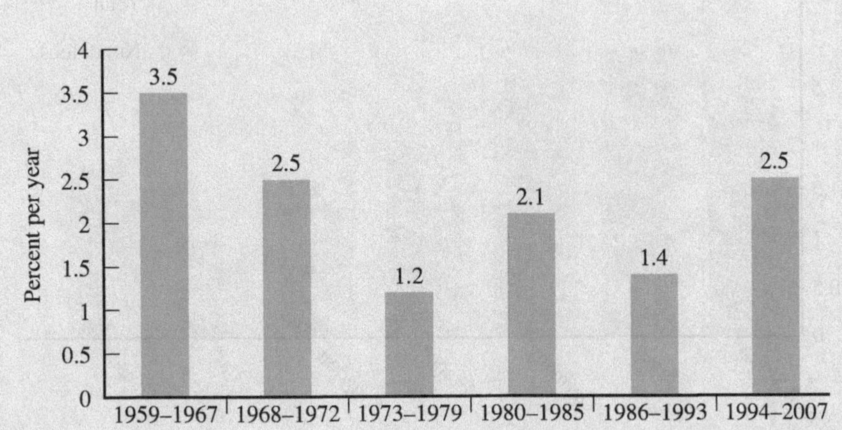

Figure 7.6

U.S. Annual Productivity Growth, 1959–2007

In recent years, there has been a resurgence of productivity growth in part caused by the information technology revolution.

economy" with permanently higher productivity growth. However, in subsequent studies he found that productivity growth had spread to other sectors of the economy, such as retail sales and financial institutions.

But will this contribution from information technology to labor productivity growth last? Professor Dale Jorgenson of Harvard University and his co-authors looked carefully at the contributions of information technology to labor productivity in recent years. They examined the effects of information technology on labor productivity growth, both through increased investment or capital deepening in that sector and also through its impact on technological progress. They found that from 2000 to 2006, labor productivity had continued to grow at rates like those in the late 1990s, but the contribution the information technology sector made to this growth had decreased. This naturally raises questions as to whether productivity growth will continue to be robust in future decades.

SOURCE: Based on Robert J. Gordon, "Exploding Productivity Growth: Contexts, Causes, Implications," *Brookings Papers on Economic Activity* 2 (2003): 207–298 and Dale W. Jorgenson et. al., "A Retrospective Look at the U.S. Productivity Growth Resurgence," *Journal of Economic Perspectives* (Winter 2008): 3–24.

Review the two other applications of how economists use growth accounting. The first compares growth in China and India, the second explores how the Internet and information technology have affected U.S. GDP.

What Causes Technological Progress?

7.4 LEARNING OBJECTIVE

Because technological progress is an important source of growth, we want to know how it occurs and what government policies can do to promote it. Economists have identified a variety of factors that may influence the pace of technological progress in an economy.

Research and Development Funding

One way for a country to induce more technological progress in its economy is to pay for it. If the government or large firms employ workers and scientists to advance the frontiers of knowledge in basic sciences, their work can lead to technological progress in the long run. Figure 7.7 presents data on the spending on research and development as a percent of GDP for seven major countries for 1999. The United States has the highest number of scientists and engineers in the world. However, although it spends the most money overall, as a percent of GDP the United States spends less than Japan. Moreover, a big part of U.S. spending on research and development is in defense-related areas, unlike in Japan. Some economists believe defense-related research and development is less likely to lead to long-run technological change than nondefense spending; however, many important technological developments, including the Internet, partly resulted from military-sponsored research and development.

Figure 7.7

Research and Development as a Percent of GDP, 1999

The United States spends more total money than any other country on research and development. However, when the spending is measured as a percentage of each nation's GDP, Japan spends more. A big part of U.S. spending on research and development is in defense-related areas.

SOURCE: National Science Foundation, National Patterns of R&D Resources, 2002, Washington D.C.

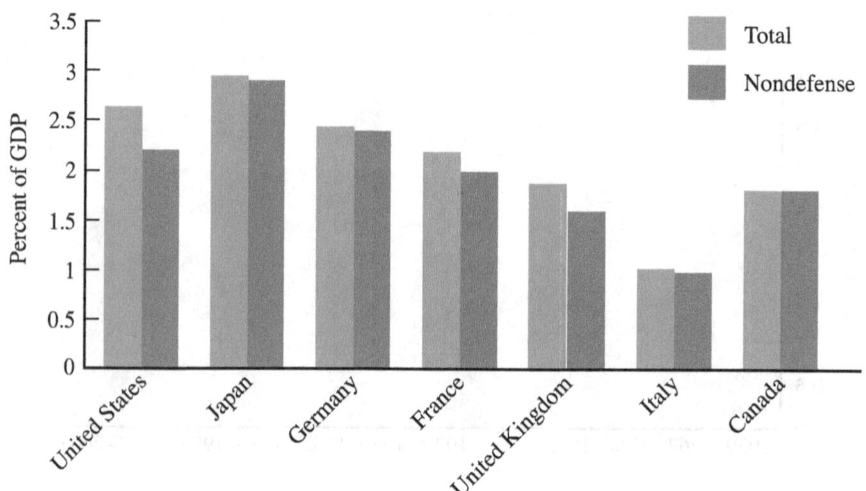

Monopolies That Spur Innovation

The radical notion that monopolies spur innovation was put forth by economist Joseph Schumpeter. In Schumpeter's view, a firm will try to innovate—that is, come up with new products and more efficient ways to produce existing products—only if it reaps a reward. The reward a firm seeks from its innovations is high profit, and it can obtain a high profit if it is the sole seller, or monopolist, for the product. Other firms will try to break the firm's monopoly through more innovation, a process Schumpeter called **creative destruction**. Schumpeter believed that by allowing firms to compete to become monopolies, society benefits from increased innovation.

Creative destruction The view that a firm will try to come up with new products and more efficient ways to produce products to earn monopoly profits.

Governments do allow temporary monopolies for new ideas by issuing patents. A *patent* allows the inventor of a product to have a monopoly until the term of the patent expires, which in the United States is now 20 years. With a patent, we tolerate some monopoly power (the power to raise prices that comes with limited competition) in the hope of spurring innovation.

An idea related to patents that is becoming increasingly important is the need to protect intellectual property rights. Information technology has made possible the free flow of products and ideas around the world. Publishers of both books and computer software face problems of unauthorized copying, particularly in some developing countries. While residents of those countries clearly benefit from inexpensively copied books or software, producers in the developed countries then face reduced incentives to enter the market. Even in the United States, pirated music and movies pose a threat to the viability of the entertainment industry. Large and profitable firms may continue to produce despite unauthorized copying, but other firms may be discouraged. The United States has put piracy and unauthorized reproduction among its top agenda items in recent trade talks with several countries.

The Scale of the Market

Adam Smith stressed that the size of a market was important for economic development. In larger markets, firms have more incentives to come up with new products and new methods of production. Just as Schumpeter suggested, the lure of profits guides the activities of firms, and larger markets provide firms the opportunity to make larger profits. This supplies another rationale for free trade. With free trade, markets are larger, and there is more incentive to engage in technological progress.

Induced Innovations

Some economists have emphasized that innovations come about through inventive activity designed specifically to reduce costs. This is known as *induced innovation*. For example, during the nineteenth century in the United States, the largest single cost in agriculture was wages. Ingenious farmers and inventors came up with many different machines and methods to cut back on the amount of labor required.

Education, Human Capital, and the Accumulation of Knowledge

Education can contribute to economic growth in two ways. First, the increased knowledge and skills of people complement our current investments in physical capital. Second, education can enable the workforce in an economy to use its skills to develop new ideas or to copy ideas or import them from abroad. Consider a developing country today. In principle, it has at its disposal the vast accumulated knowledge of the developed economies. But using this knowledge probably requires a skilled workforce—one reason why many developing countries send their best students to educational institutions in developed countries.

Increasing knowledge and skills are part of human capital—an investment in human beings. Human capital is as important, maybe even more important, than physical capital. Many economists, including Nobel Laureate Gary Becker of the University of Chicago, have studied human capital in detail.

A classic example of human capital is the investment a student makes to attend college. The costs of attending college consist of the direct out-of-pocket costs (tuition and fees) plus the opportunity costs of forgone earnings while at school. The benefits of attending college are the higher wages and more interesting jobs offered to college graduates compared to high-school graduates. Individuals decide to attend college when these benefits exceed the costs, and it is a rational economic decision. A similar calculation faces a newly graduated doctor who must decide whether to pursue a specialty. Will the

Application 5

The Role of Political Factors in Economic Growth

Applying the Concepts #5: How do varying political institutions affect economic growth?

Economist Daron Acemoglu of the Massachusetts Institute of Technology has written extensively about the role of political institutions and economic growth. Acemoglu distinguishes broadly between two types of political institutions: *authoritarian* institutions, such as monarchies, dictatorships, or tightly controlled oligarchies, and *participatory* institutions, such as constitutionally limited monarchies and democracies. History has witnessed growth under both types of regimes. At various points in time, China, Spain, Turkey and ancient Greece and Rome all exhibited technological innovation and economic growth.

But transformative economic growth, such as the world witnessed with the Industrial Revolution that began in western Europe in the late 1700s, typically requires more participatory institutions. The key reason is that sustained technological progress is disruptive and authoritarian regimes have difficulty coping with all the subsequent changes. Acemoglu highlights the fall in the old, authoritarian regimes in Europe and the rise of constitutional or limited monarchies that set the preconditions for the birth of the Industrial Revolution.

Acemoglu's theory does raise important questions for today. Can China, with its authoritarian political culture, continue to grow without eventual political transformation? If that does eventually come, can it be absorbed peacefully within the society?

SOURCE: Based on Daron Acemoglu, epilogue to *Introduction to Modern Economic Growth* (University Press, 2009).

Application 6

Culture, Evolution, and Economic Growth

Applying the Concepts #6: Did culture or evolution spark the Industrial Revolution?

In studying the economic history of England before the Industrial Revolution, Professor Gregory Clark discovered an interesting fact. Examining archival data on wills and estates, he found that children of the more affluent members of English society were more likely to survive than those of the less affluent. Coupled with the slow growth of population over several centuries, this differential survival of the wealthy had the effect of creating downward mobility for the rich, as their sons and daughters increasingly populated the society.

According to Professor Clark, this change had profound effects on English society. The cultural habits of the rich filtered through the entire society. Social virtues such as thrift, prudence, and hard work became more commonplace, while impulsive and violent behaviors were reduced. Eventually, these changes in culture became sufficiently pronounced that a qualitative change took place in society. Individuals now were able to take advantage of new developments in science and technology and embrace new technologies and social change.

Economists Oded Galor and Omer Moav suggest that development can be viewed in more traditional evolutionary terms. They argue that at some point during the human evolutionary process, families that had fewer children but invested more in them, gained a competitive advantage in the evolutionary cycle. The offspring of these families had more human capital and more easily adapted to technological progress and the other changes that were taking place in societies. Human genetic evolution, in their view, set the stage for the Industrial Revolution. Both views share some similarities. According to Clark, the evolution was primarily cultural, whereas for Galor and Moav it was genetic. In both cases, however, humans transformed themselves as the Industrial Revolution began.

SOURCE: Based on Gregory Clark, *A Farewell to Alms* (Princeton: Princeton University Press, 2007) and Oded Galor and Omer Moav, "Natural Selection and the Origin of Economic Growth," *Quarterly Journal of Economics* (November 2002): 1133–1191.

forgone earnings of a general physician (which are quite substantial) be worth the time spent learning a specialty that will eventually result in extra income? We can analyze investments in health and nutrition within the same framework. The benefits of regular exercise and watching your weight are a healthier lifestyle and higher energy level.

Human capital theory has two implications for understanding economic growth. First, not all labor is equal. When economists measure the labor input in a country, they must adjust for differing levels of education. These levels of education reflect past investments in education and skills; individuals with higher educational levels will, on average, be more productive. Second, health and fitness also affect productivity. In developing countries, economists have found a strong correlation between the height of individuals (reflecting their health) and the wages they can earn in the farming sector.

Human capital theory can also serve as a basis for important public policy decisions. Should a developing country invest in capital (either public or private) or in education? The poorest developing countries lack good sanitation systems, effective transportation, and capital investment for agriculture and industry. However, the best use of investment funds may not be for bridges, sewer systems, and roads, but for human capital and education. Studies demonstrate that the returns from investing in education are extremely high in developing countries. The gains from elementary and secondary education, in particular, often exceed the gains from more conventional investments. In developing countries, an extra year in school can often raise individuals' wages by 15 to 20 percent a year.

New Growth Theory

For many years, economists who studied technological progress typically did so independently of economists who studied models of economic growth. But starting in the mid-1980s, several economists, including Nobel Laureate Robert E. Lucas of the University of Chicago and Paul Romer of Stanford University, began to develop models of growth that contained technological progress as essential features. Their work helped to initiate what is known as **new growth theory**, which accounts for technological progress within a model of economic growth.

New growth theory Modern theories of growth that try to explain the origins of technological progress.

In this field, economists study, for example, how incentives for research and development, new product development, or international trade interact with the accumulation of physical capital. New growth theory enables economists to address policy issues, such as whether subsidies for research and development are socially justified and whether policies that place fewer taxes on income earned from investment will spur economic growth or increase economic welfare. Current research in economic growth now takes place within a broad framework that includes explanations of technological progress. As an example, new growth theory suggests that investment in comprehensive education in a developing country will lead to permanent increases in the rate of technological progress as the workforce will be better able to incorporate new ideas and technologies into the workplace.

Some researchers also suggest the type of education might also matter for technological innovation. Phillipe Aghion of Harvard University and Peter Howitt of Brown University make the case that when a country is far behind the world's technological frontier, it is best for that country to invest in relatively basic education so that the workforce can essentially copy the changes that are occurring in the more advanced economies. But once an economy reaches the world's technological frontier, investment in the most advanced higher education might be most advantageous.[4]

New growth theory suggests that any social factor influencing the willingness of individuals to pursue technological advancement will be a key to understanding economic growth. Can cultural factors also play a role? The historical sociologist Max Weber argued that changes in religious beliefs could help us understand growth, as he emphasized how the rise of Protestantism, with its emphasis on the individual, set the stage for the Industrial Revolution in Europe. This thesis has always been controversial because the links between changes in religious beliefs and changes in economic or other behaviors are not well understood. More recently, Professor Gregory Clark has emphasized how the growth of middle-class values in England could possibly explain why the Industrial Revolution began there.

A Key Governmental Role: Providing the Correct Incentives and Property Rights

7.5 LEARNING OBJECTIVE

Governments play a critical role in a market economy. They must enforce the rules of the market economy, using police powers to ensure that contracts are upheld, individual property rights are enforced, and firms can enter safely into economic transactions. Although we may take these features of our economy for granted, not all countries enjoy the benefits of clear enforcement of property rights.

What is the connection between property rights and economic growth? Without clear property rights, there are no proper incentives to invest in the future—the essence of economic growth. Suppose, for example, that you lived on land that needed costly improvements in order to be made valuable. You might be willing to make the investment in these improvements if you were sure you would gain the economic benefits from making them. But suppose there was a risk someone else would reap the benefits—in that case, you would not have incentive to invest.

[4]Phillipe Aghion and Peter Howitt, "Appropriate Growth Theory: A Unifying Framework," December 2005, http://www.economics.harvard.edu/faculty/aghion/papers.html (accessed February 2006).

Clear property rights are, unfortunately, lacking in many developing countries throughout the world. As many economists have argued, their absence has severely impeded the growth of these economies.

Governments also have a broader role in designing the institutions in which individuals and firms work, save, and invest. Economists have increasingly recognized the importance of these institutions in determining economic growth. For example, the residents of Hong Kong link their rapid economic growth to free and open institutions that provide the right incentives for technological innovations. They wanted to preserve these institutions after they officially became part of China in 1997 and have indeed been successful in maintaining an open society.

But for many countries, growth has been more elusive. For many years, international organizations such as the World Bank—a consortium of countries created to promote development—have tried a variety of diverse methods to assist developing countries. These have included increases in foreign aid, infusions of new machinery, promotion of universal education, and efforts to stem population growth. Despite these efforts, some areas of the world, such as sub-Saharan Africa, have failed to grow at all.

William Easterly, a former World Bank economist, believes the World Bank and other international organizations have failed to take into account one of the basic laws of economics: Individuals and firms respond to incentives. According to Easterly, governments in developing countries have failed to provide the proper economic environment that would motivate individuals and firms to take actions that promote economic development.[5] As an example, providing free schooling is not enough—individuals need to know their investments in education will pay off in the future in terms of higher incomes or better jobs. Without the prospect that it will lead to an improvement in their lives, individuals will not make the effort to obtain an education.

What else can go wrong? Governments in developing countries often adopt policies that effectively tax exports, pursue policies that lead to rampant inflation, and enforce laws that inhibit the growth of the banking and financial sectors. The results are predictable: fewer exports, an uncertain financial environment, and reduced saving and investment. All these outcomes can cripple an economy's growth prospects. Sometimes they are based on bad economic advice. Other times, racial or ethnic groups in polarized societies use the economic system to take advantage of their rivals.

What can be done? In Easterly's view, the World Bank and other international organizations need to stop searching for the magic bullet for development. Instead, they should hold governments responsible for creating the proper economic environment. With the right incentives, Easterly believes individuals and firms in developing countries will take actions that promote economic growth.

[5]William Easterly, The Elusive Quest for Growth: Economists' Adventures and Misadventures in the Tropics (Cambridge, MA: MIT Press, 2002).

Application 7

Lack of Property Rights Hinders Growth in Peru

Applying the Concepts #7: Why are clear property rights important for economic growth in developing countries?

On the hills surrounding Lima, Peru, and many other South American cities, large numbers of residents live in urban slums, many having taken over these lands through "urban invasions." Many families have resided in these dwellings for a long time, and most have basic water, sewage, and electricity. But what they don't have is clear titles to their properties.

Hernando DeSoto, a Peruvian economist and author of *The Mystery of Capital*, has studied the consequences of "informal ownership" in detail. He argues that throughout the developing world, property is often held without clear title. Without this evidence of ownership, people are not willing to make long-term investments to improve their lives. But there are other important consequences as well.

Economists recognize that strong credit systems—the ability to borrow and lend easily—are critical to the health of developing economies. But without clear title, people cannot use property as collateral (or security) for loans. As a consequence, the poor may in fact be living on very valuable land, but are unable to borrow against that land to start a new business. Also, the types of investments made will depend on the availability of credit. DeSoto observed that producing palm oil in Peru is very profitable, but it takes time and depends upon the ability to borrow funds. Production of coca paste—an ingredient of cocaine—does not take as much time and does not depend on finance. It is also a plague on the developed world. Switching farmers away from production of coca paste to palm oil requires improvements in finance, which are very difficult without clear property rights.

SOURCE: Based on Hernando DeSoto, *The Mystery of Capital: Why Capitalism Triumphs in the West and Fails Everywhere Else* (New York: Basic Books, 2000).

Summary

In this chapter, we explored the mechanisms of economic growth. Although economists do not have a complete understanding of what leads to growth, they regard increases in capital per worker, technological progress, human capital, and governmental institutions as key factors. Here are the main points to remember:

1 *Per capita GDP* varies greatly throughout the world. There is debate about whether poorer countries in the world are converging in per capita incomes to richer countries.

2 Economies grow through two basic mechanisms: *capital deepening and technological progress*. Capital deepening is an increase in capital per worker. Technological progress is an increase in output with no additional increases in inputs.

3 Ongoing technological progress will lead to sustained economic growth.

4 Various theories try to explain the origins of technological progress and determine how we can promote it. They include spending on research and development, *creative destruction*, the scale of the market, induced inventions, and education and the accumulation of knowledge, including investments in human capital.

5 Governments can play a key role in designing institutions that promote economic growth, including providing secure property rights.:

Key Terms

Capital deepening, p. 139
Convergence, p. 142
Creative destruction, p. 152
Growth accounting, p. 149
Growth rate, p. 140
Human capital, p. 139
Labor productivity, p. 150
New growth theory, p. 157
Real GDP per capita, p. 140
Rule of 70, p. 141
Saving, p. 146
Technological progress, p. 139

Appendix

LEARNING OBJECTIVE

A Model of Capital Deepening

Here's a simple model showing the links among saving, depreciation, and capital deepening. Developed by Nobel Laureate Robert Solow of the Massachusetts Institute of Technology, the Solow model will help us understand more fully the critical role technological progress must play in economic growth. We rely on one of our basic principles of economics to help explain the model as well as make a few simplifying assumptions. We assume constant population and no government or foreign sector. In the chapter, we discussed the qualitative effects of population growth, government, and the foreign sector on capital deepening. Here we focus solely on the relationships among saving, depreciation, and capital deepening.

Figure 7A.1 plots the relationship in the economy between output and the stock of capital, holding the labor force constant. Notice that output increases as the stock of capital increases, but at a decreasing rate. This is an illustration of the principle of diminishing returns.

Principle of Diminishing Returns

Suppose output is produced with two or more inputs and we increase one input while holding the other inputs fixed. Beyond some point—called the point of *diminishing* returns—output will increase at a decreasing rate.

Increasing the stock of capital while holding the labor force constant will increase output, but at a decreasing rate.

As Figure 7A.1 indicates, output increases with the stock of capital. But what causes the stock of capital to increase? The capital stock will increase as long as gross investment exceeds depreciation. Therefore, we need to determine the level of gross investment and the level of depreciation to see how the capital stock changes over time.

Recall that without government or a foreign sector, saving equals gross investment. Thus, to determine the level of investment, we need to specify how much of output is saved and how much is consumed. We will assume that a fraction s of total output (Y) is saved.

Figure 7A.1

Diminishing Returns to Capital

Holding labor constant, increases in the stock of capital increase output, but at a decreasing rate.

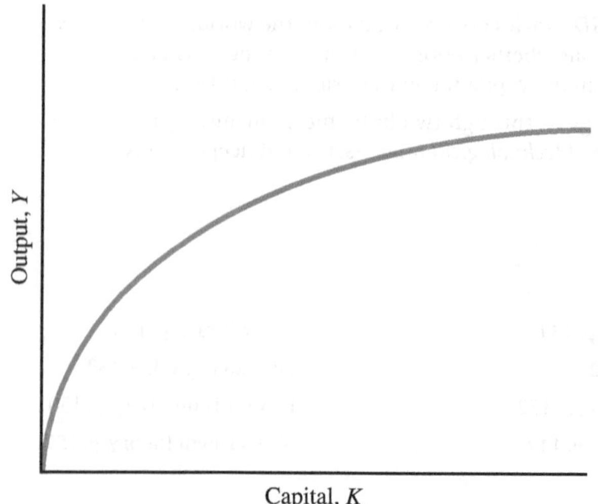

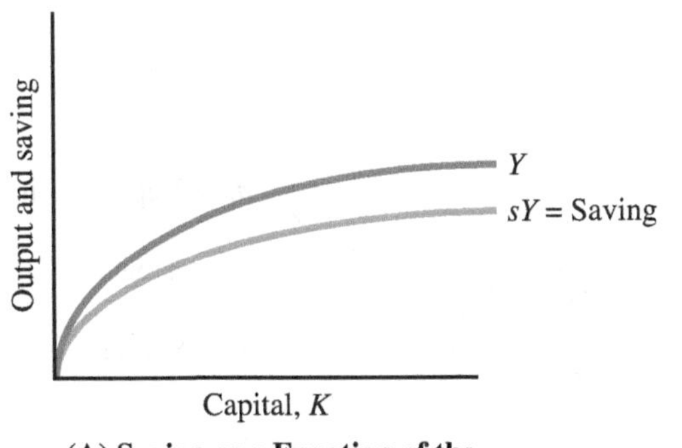

(A) Saving as a Function of the Stock of Capital

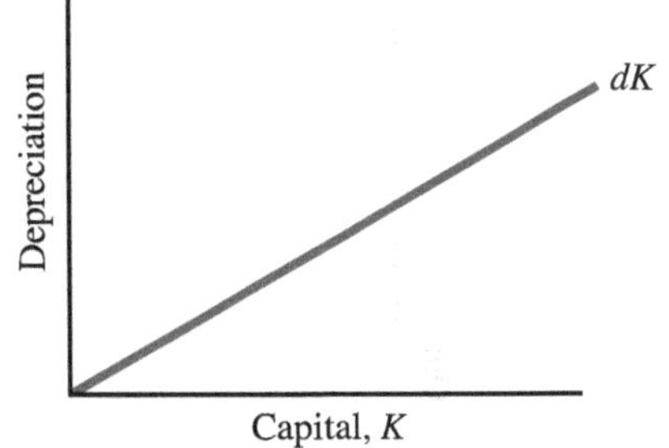

(B) Depreciation as a Function of the Stock of Capital

Figure 7A.2

Saving and Depreciation as Functions of the Stock of Capital

For example, if $s = 0.20$, then 20 percent of GDP would be saved and 80 percent would be consumed. Total saving will be sY, the product of the saving rate and total output.

In Panel A of Figure 7A.2, the top curve is total output as a function of the stock of capital. The curve below it represents saving as a function of the stock of capital. Because saving is a fixed fraction of total output, the saving curve is a constant fraction of the output curve. If the saving rate is 0.2, saving will always be 20 percent of output for any level of the capital stock. Total saving increases in the economy with the stock of capital, but at a decreasing rate.

To complete our model, we need to determine depreciation. Let's say the capital stock depreciates at a constant rate of d per year. If $d = 0.03$, the capital stock would depreciate at 3 percent per year. If the capital stock were 100 at the beginning of the year, depreciation would equal 3. Total depreciation can be written as dK, where K is the stock of capital.

Panel B of Figure 7A.2 plots total depreciation as a function of the stock of capital. The larger the stock of capital, the more total depreciation there will be. Because the depreciation rate is assumed to be constant, total depreciation as a function of the stock of capital will be a straight line through the origin. Then if there is no capital, there will be no depreciation, no matter what the depreciation rate.

If the depreciation rate is 3 percent and the stock of capital is 100, depreciation will be 3; if the stock of capital is 200, the depreciation rate will be 6. Plotting these points will give a straight line through the origin.

We are now ready to see how the stock of capital changes:

$$\text{change in the stock of capital} = \text{saving} - \text{depreciation} = sY - dK$$

The stock of capital will increase—the change will be positive—as long as total saving in the economy exceeds depreciation.

Figure 7A.3 shows how the Solow model works by plotting output, saving, and depreciation all on one graph. Suppose the economy starts with a capital stock K_0. Then total saving will be given by point a on the saving schedule. Depreciation at the capital stock K_0 is given by point b. Because a lies above b, total saving exceeds depreciation, and the capital stock will increase. As the capital stock increases, there will be economic growth through capital deepening. With more capital per worker in the economy, output is higher and real wages increase. The economy benefits from the additional stock of capital.

Using the graph, we can trace the future for this economy. As the stock of capital increases, we move to the right. When the economy reaches K_1, total saving is at point c and total depreciation is at point d. Because c is still higher than d, saving exceeds depreciation and the capital stock continues to increase. Economic growth continues. Eventually, after many years, the economy reaches capital stock K^*. The level of output in the economy now is Y^*, and the saving and depreciation schedules intersect at point e. Because total saving equals depreciation, the stock of capital no longer increases. The process of economic growth through capital deepening has stopped.

Figure 7A.3

Basic Growth Model

Starting at K_0, saving exceeds depreciation. The stock of capital increases. This process continues until the stock of capital reaches its long-run equilibrium at K^*.

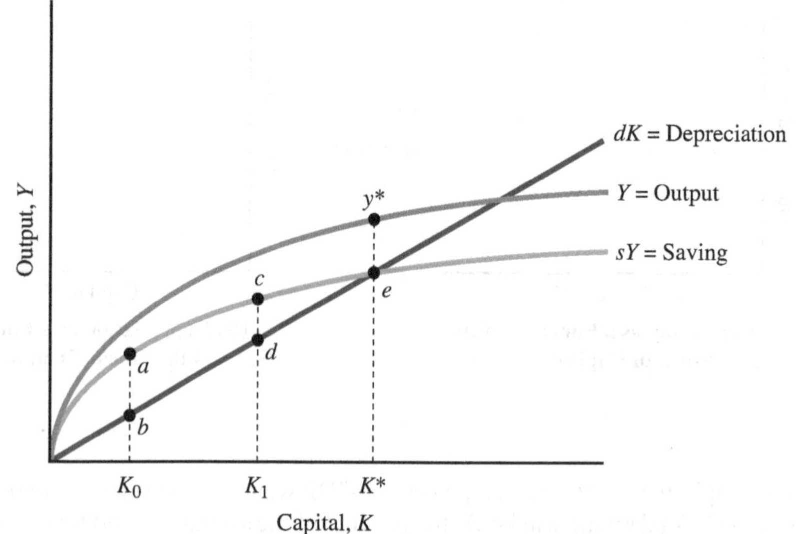

In this simple model, the process of capital deepening must eventually come to an end. As the stock of capital increases, output increases, but at a decreasing rate because of diminishing returns. Because saving is a fixed fraction of output, it will also increase but at a diminishing rate. On the other hand, total depreciation is proportional to the stock of capital. As the stock of capital increases, depreciation will always catch up with total saving in the economy. It may take decades for the process of capital deepening to come to an end. But as long as total saving exceeds depreciation, the process of economic growth through capital deepening will continue.

What would happen if a society saved a higher fraction of its output? Figure 7A.4 shows the consequences of a higher saving rate. Suppose the economy were originally saving at a rate s_1. Eventually, the economy would reach e_1, where saving and depreciation meet. If the economy had started to save at the higher rate s_2, saving would exceed depreciation at K_1, and the capital stock would increase until the economy reached K_2. At K_2, the saving line again crosses the line representing depreciation. Output is higher than it was initially, but the process of capital deepening stops at this higher level of output.

If there is ongoing technological progress, economic growth can continue. If technological progress raises GDP, saving will increase as well, because saving increases with GDP. This will lead to a higher stock of capital. In Figure 7A.5, technological progress is depicted as an upward shift of the saving function. The saving function shifts up because saving is a fixed fraction of output, and we have assumed that technological progress has raised the level of output.

With a higher level of saving, the stock of capital will increase. If the stock of capital were originally at K_0, the upward shift in the saving schedule will lead to increases in the

Figure 7A.4

Increase in the Saving Rate

A higher saving rate will lead to a higher stock of capital in the long run. Starting from an initial capital stock of K_1, the increase in the saving rate leads the economy to K_2..

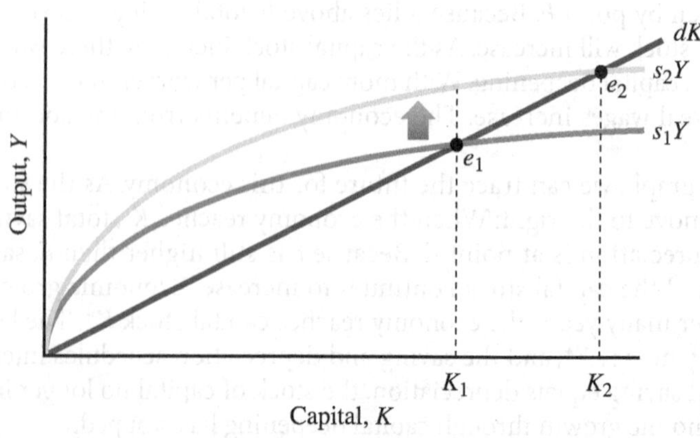

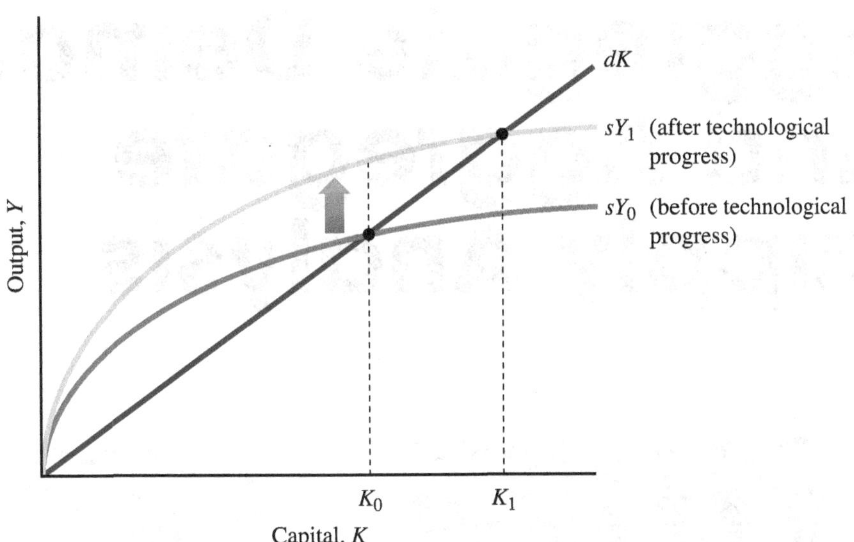

Figure 7A.5

Technological Progress and Growth

Technological progress shifts up the saving function and promotes capital deepening..

stock of capital to K_1. If there is further technological progress, capital deepening will continue.

Technological progress conveys a double benefit to a society. Not only does the increased efficiency directly raise per capita output, it also leads to additional capital deepening. Therefore, output increases for two reasons.

Let's summarize the basic points of the Solow model:

1. Capital deepening, an increase in the stock of capital per worker, will occur as long as total saving exceeds depreciation. As capital deepening occurs, there will be economic growth and increased real wages.
2. Eventually, the process of capital deepening will come to a halt as depreciation catches up with total saving.
3. A higher saving rate will promote capital deepening. If a country saves more, it will have a higher output. But eventually, the process of economic growth through capital deepening alone comes to an end, even though this may take decades to occur.
4. Technological progress not only directly raises output, but also it allows capital deepening to continue.

It is possible to relax our assumptions and allow for population growth, government taxes and spending, and the foreign sector. In more advanced courses, these issues are treated in detail, but the underlying message is the same. There is a natural limit to economic growth through capital deepening. Technological progress is required to ensure that per capita incomes grow over time.

EXERCISES

A.1 ___________ and ___________ are the two factors that determine how the stock of capital changes over time.

A.2 Which of the following causes capital deepening to come to an end?
   a. The marginal principle
   b. The principle of diminishing returns
   c. The principle of opportunity cost
   d. The reality principle

A.3 A higher saving rate leads to a permanently higher rate of growth. ___________ (True/False)

A.4 **Germany and Japan after World War II.** Much of the stock of capital in the economies of Japan and Germany was destroyed during World War II. Use the Solow model graph to show and explain why growth in these economies after the war was higher than that in the United States.

A.5 **Faster Depreciation.** Suppose a society switches to equipment that depreciates rapidly. Use the Solow model graph to show what will happen to the stock of capital and output if the rate of depreciation increases.

CHAPTER 8

Aggregate Demand and Aggregate Supply Analysis

Chapter Outline and Learning Objectives

The Fortunes of FedEx Follow the Business Cycle

FedEx plays a large role in moving packages around the United States and around the world. The value of packages handled by FedEx is about 4 percent of U.S. GDP and 1.5 percent of global GDP. Some Wall Street analysts use a "FedEx indicator" to guage the state of the economy because there is usually a close relationship between fluctuations in FedEx's business and fluctuations in GDP.

Fred Smith came up with the idea for the company in 1965, in an undergraduate term paper. He proposed an entirely new system of delivering packages: One firm would control shipping freight, from pickup to delivery. The firm would operate its own planes on a "hub-and-spoke" system: Packages would be collected and flown to a central hub, where they would be sorted and then flown to their destination for final delivery by truck.

Despite FedEx's tremendous success over the past 40 years, the business cycle has always affected the company's business. For example, as the U.S. entered a recession in December 2007, businesses and individuals cut back on shipping packages. In the first quarter of 2008, FedEx reported its first loss, after 11 straight years of profits. As the 2007–2009 recession dragged on, FedEx announced in March 2009 that it was laying off 1,000 employees and was imposing a 5 to 20 percent pay cut on its remaining employees. By September 2009, economic conditions had begun to improve, and FedEx announced that its profits for the three months ending on August 31 were 35 percent higher than its executives had expected. But as U.S. GDP growth slowed in 2011, so did FedEx's fortunes. Weak consumer demand and half-empty cargo planes led FedEx to announce in September that it was lowering its forecast for end-of-the-year profits. Fred Smith explained: "We expect sluggish economic growth will continue. . . . The consumer just doesn't have an appetite" for increased spending.

To understand how the business cycle affects FedEx and other firms, we need to explore the effects that recessions and expansions have on production, employment, and prices.

Based on Lynn Adler, "FedEx Pares 2012 Outlook, Shares Hit 2-Year Low," *Reuters*, September 22, 2011; Hal Weiztman, "FedEx to Cut Costs by $1 Bn," *Financial Times*, March 19, 2009; "FedEx Confirms 1,000 Layoffs, 500 in Memphis," *Memphis Business Journal*, April 3, 2009; Bob Sechler, "FedEx Boosts Outlook," *Wall Street Journal*, September 11, 2009; and David Gaffen, "The FedEx Indicator," *Wall Street Journal*, February 20, 2007.

Economics in Your Life

Is an Employer Likely to Cut Your Pay during a Recession?

Suppose that you have worked as a barista for a local coffeehouse for two years. From on-the-job training and experience, you have honed your coffee-making skills and mastered the perfect latte. Then the economy moves into a recession, and sales at the coffeehouse decline. Is the owner of the coffeehouse likely to cut the prices of lattes and other drinks? Suppose the owner asks to meet with you to discuss your wages for next year. Is the owner likely to cut your pay? As you read the chapter, see if you can answer these questions.

The U.S. economy has experienced a long-run upward trend in real GDP. This upward trend has resulted in the standard of living in the United States being much higher today than it was 50 years ago. In the short run, however, real GDP fluctuates around this long-run upward trend because of the business cycle. Fluctuations in GDP lead to fluctuations in employment. These fluctuations in real GDP and employment are the most visible and dramatic part of the business cycle. During recessions, we are more likely to see factories close, small businesses declare bankruptcy, and workers lose their jobs. During expansions, we are more likely to see new businesses open and new jobs created. In addition to these changes in output and employment, the business cycle causes changes in wages and prices. Some firms react to a decline in sales by cutting back on production, but they may also cut the prices they charge and the wages they pay. Other firms respond to a recession by raising prices and workers' wages by less than they otherwise would have.

In this chapter, we expand our story of the business cycle by developing the aggregate demand and aggregate supply model. This model will help us analyze the effects of recessions and expansions on production, employment, and prices.

8.1 LEARNING OBJECTIVE

Identify the determinants of aggregate demand and distinguish between a movement along the aggregate demand curve and a shift of the curve.

Aggregate Demand

To understand what happens during the business cycle, we need an explanation of why real GDP, the unemployment rate, and the inflation rate fluctuate. We have already seen that fluctuations in the unemployment rate are caused mainly by fluctuations in real GDP. In this chapter, we use the **aggregate demand and aggregate supply model** to explain short-run fluctuations in real GDP and the price level. As Figure 8.1 shows, real GDP and the price level in this model are determined in the short run by the intersection of the *aggregate demand curve* and the *aggregate supply curve*. Fluctuations in real GDP and the price level are caused by shifts in the aggregate demand curve or in the aggregate supply curve.

The **aggregate demand (*AD*) curve** shows the relationship between the price level and the quantity of real GDP demanded by households, firms, and the government. The **short-run aggregate supply (*SRAS*) curve** shows the relationship in the short run between the price level and the quantity of real GDP supplied by firms. The aggregate demand and short-run aggregate supply curves in Figure 8.1 look similar to the individual market demand and supply curves we studied in Chapter 4. However, because these curves apply to the whole economy, rather than to just a single market, the aggregate demand and aggregate supply model is very different from the model of demand and supply in individual markets. Because we are dealing with the economy as a whole, we need

Aggregate demand and aggregate supply model A model that explains short-run fluctuations in real GDP and the price level.

Aggregate demand (*AD*) curve A curve that shows the relationship between the price level and the quantity of real GDP demanded by households, firms, and the government.

Short-run aggregate supply (*SRAS*) curve A curve that shows the relationship in the short run between the price level and the quantity of real GDP supplied by firms.

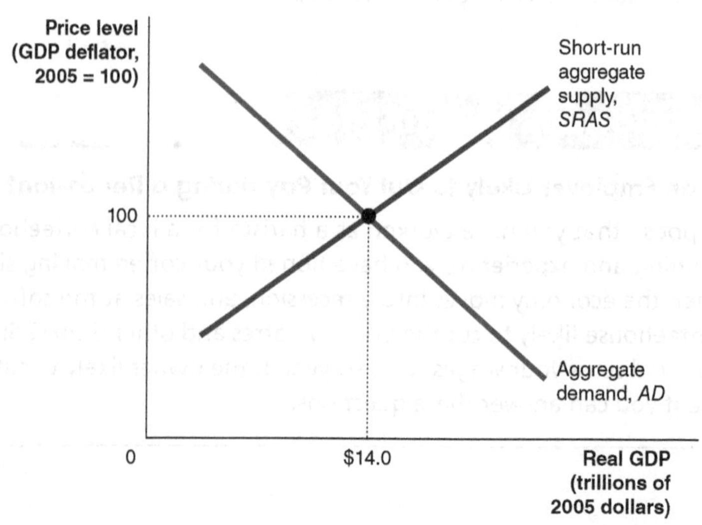

Figure 8.1

Aggregate Demand and Aggregate Supply

In the short run, real GDP and the price level are determined by the intersection of the aggregate demand curve and the short-run aggregate supply curve. In the figure, real GDP is measured on the horizontal axis, and the price level is measured on the vertical axis by the GDP deflator. In this example, the equilibrium real GDP is $14.0 trillion, and the equilibrium price level is 100.

macroeconomic explanations of why the aggregate demand curve is downward sloping, why the short-run aggregate supply curve is upward sloping, and why the curves shift. We begin by explaining why the aggregate demand curve is downward sloping.

Why Is the Aggregate Demand Curve Downward Sloping?

GDP has four components: consumption (C), investment (I), government purchases (G), and net exports (NX). If we let Y stand for GDP, we have the following relationship:

$$Y = G + I + G + NX.$$

The aggregate demand curve is downward sloping because a fall in the price level increases the quantity of real GDP demanded. To understand why this is true, we need to look at how changes in the price level affect each component of aggregate demand. We begin with the assumption that government purchases are determined by the policy decisions of lawmakers and are not affected by changes in the price level. We can then consider the effect of changes in the price level on the three other components: consumption, investment, and net exports.

The Wealth Effect: How a Change in the Price Level Affects Consumption Current income is the most important variable determining the consumption of households. As income rises, consumption will rise, and as income falls, consumption will fall. But consumption also depends on household wealth. A household's wealth is the difference between the value of its assets and the value of its debts. Consider two households, both with incomes of $80,000 per year. The first household has wealth of $5 million, and the second household has wealth of $50,000. The first household is likely to spend more of its income than the second household. So, as total household wealth rises, consumption will rise. Some household wealth is held in cash or other *nominal assets* that lose value as the price level rises and gain value as the price level falls. For instance, if you have $10,000 in cash, a 10 percent increase in the price level will reduce the purchasing power of that cash by 10 percent. When the price level rises, the *real value* of household wealth declines, and so will consumption, thereby reducing the demand for goods and services. When the price level falls, the real value of household wealth rises, and so will consumption and the demand for goods and services. This effect of the price level on consumption is called the *wealth effect*, and it is one reason the aggregate demand curve is downward sloping.

The Interest-Rate Effect: How a Change in the Price Level Affects Investment When prices rise, households and firms need more money to finance buying and selling. Therefore, when the price level rises, households and firms will try to increase the amount of money they hold by withdrawing funds from banks, borrowing from banks, or selling financial assets, such as bonds. These actions tend to drive up the interest rate charged on bank loans and the interest rate on bonds. (In Chapter 11, we analyze in more detail the relationship between money and interest rates.) A higher interest rate raises the cost of borrowing for firms and households. As a result, firms will borrow less to build new factories or to install new machinery and equipment, and households will borrow less to buy new houses. To a smaller extent, consumption will also fall as households borrow less to finance spending on automobiles, furniture, and other durable goods. So, because a higher price level increases the interest rate and reduces investment spending, it also reduces the quantity of goods and services demanded. A lower price level will decrease the interest rate and increase investment spending, thereby increasing the quantity of goods and services demanded. This effect of the price level on investment is known as the *interest-rate effect*, and it is a second reason the aggregate demand curve is downward sloping.

The International-Trade Effect: How a Change in the Price Level Affects Net Exports *Net exports* equal spending by foreign households and firms on goods and services produced in the United States minus spending by U.S. households and firms on goods and services produced in other countries. If the price level in the United States rises relative to the price levels in other countries, U.S. exports will become relatively more expensive, and foreign imports will become relatively less expensive. Some consumers in foreign countries will shift from buying U.S. products to buying domestic products, and some U.S. consumers will also shift from buying U.S. products to buying imported products. U.S. exports will fall, and U.S. imports will rise, causing net exports to fall, thereby reducing the quantity of goods and services demanded. A lower price level in the United States relative to other countries has the reverse effect, causing net exports to rise, increasing the quantity of goods and services demanded. This effect of the price level on net exports is known as the *international-trade effect*, and it is a third reason the aggregate demand curve is downward sloping.

Shifts of the Aggregate Demand Curve versus Movements along It

An important point to remember is that the aggregate demand curve tells us the relationship between the price level and the quantity of real GDP demanded, *holding everything else constant*. If the price level changes but other variables that affect the willingness of households, firms, and the government to spend are unchanged, the economy will move up or down a stationary aggregate demand curve. If any variable other than the price level changes, the aggregate demand curve will shift. For example, if government purchases increase and the price level remains unchanged, the aggregate demand curve will shift to the right at every price level. Or, if firms become pessimistic about the future profitability of investment and cut back spending on factories and machinery, the aggregate demand curve will shift to the left.

The Variables That Shift the Aggregate Demand Curve

The variables that cause the aggregate demand curve to shift fall into three categories:

- Changes in government policies
- Changes in the expectations of households and firms
- Changes in foreign variables

Monetary policy The actions the Federal Reserve takes to manage the money supply and interest rates to pursue macroeconomic policy objectives.

Fiscal policy Changes in federal taxes and purchases that are intended to achieve macroeconomic policy objectives.

Changes in Government Policies As we will discuss further in Chapters 11 and 9, the federal government uses monetary policy and fiscal policy to shift the aggregate demand curve. **Monetary policy** involves actions the Federal Reserve—the nation's central bank—takes to manage the money supply and interest rates and to ensure the flow of funds from lenders to borrowers. The Federal Reserve takes these actions to attain macroeconomic policy objectives, such as high employment, price stability, and high rates of economic growth. For example, by lowering interest rates, the Federal Reserve can lower the cost to firms and households of borrowing. Lowering borrowing costs increases consumption and investment spending, which shifts the aggregate demand curve to the right. Higher interest rates shift the aggregate demand curve to the left. **Fiscal policy** involves changes in federal taxes and purchases that are intended to achieve macroeconomic policy objectives. Because government purchases are one component of aggregate demand, an increase in government purchases shifts the aggregate demand curve to the right, and a decrease in government purchases shifts the aggregate demand curve to the left. An increase in personal income taxes reduces the amount of spendable income available to households. Higher personal income taxes reduce consumption spending and shift the aggregate demand curve to the left. Lower personal income taxes shift the aggregate demand curve to the right. Increases in business taxes reduce the profitability of investment spending and shift the aggregate demand curve to the left. Decreases in business taxes shift the aggregate demand curve to the right.

Changes in the Expectations of Households and Firms If households become more optimistic about their future incomes, they are likely to increase their current

Don't Let This Happen to You

Understand Why the Aggregate Demand Curve Is Downward Sloping

The aggregate demand curve and the demand curve for a single product are both downward sloping—but for different reasons. When we draw a demand curve for a single product, such as apples, we know that it will slope downward because as the price of apples rises, apples become more expensive relative to other products—such as oranges—and consumers will buy fewer apples and more of the other products. In other words, consumers substitute other products for apples. When the overall price level rises, the prices of all domestically produced goods and services are rising, so consumers have no other domestic products to which they can switch. The aggregate demand curve slopes downward for the reasons given on pages 165–166: A lower price level raises the real value of household wealth (which increases consumption), lowers interest rates (which increases investment and consumption), and makes U.S. exports less expensive and foreign imports more expensive (which increases net exports).

consumption. This increased consumption will shift the aggregate demand curve to the right. If households become more pessimistic about their future incomes, the aggregate demand curve will shift to the left. Similarly, if firms become more optimistic about the future profitability of investment spending, the aggregate demand curve will shift to the right. If firms become more pessimistic, the aggregate demand curve will shift to the left.

Changes in Foreign Variables If firms and households in other countries buy fewer U.S. goods or if firms and households in the United States buy more foreign goods, net exports will fall, and the aggregate demand curve will shift to the left. When real GDP increases, so does the income available for consumers to spend. If real GDP in the United States increases faster than real GDP in other countries, U.S. imports will increase faster than U.S. exports, and net exports will fall. Net exports will also fall if the *exchange rate* between the dollar and foreign currencies rises because the price in foreign currency of U.S. products sold in other countries will rise, and the dollar price of foreign products sold in the United States will fall. For example, if the current exchange rate between the dollar and the euro is $1 = €1 then a $500 iPad exported from the United States to France will cost €500 in France, and a €50 bottle of French wine will cost $50 in the United States. But if the exchange rate rises to $1 = €1.50, the iPad's price will rise to €750 in France, causing its sales to decline, and the price of the French wine will fall to $33.33 per bottle in the United States, causing its sales to increase. U.S. exports will fall, U.S. imports will rise, and the aggregate demand curve will shift to the left.

An increase in net exports at every price level will shift the aggregate demand curve to the right. Net exports will increase if real GDP grows more slowly in the United States than in other countries or if the value of the dollar falls against other currencies. A change in net exports that results from a change in the price level in the United States will result in a movement along the aggregate demand curve, *not* a shift of the aggregate demand curve.

Solved Problem 8.1

Movements along the Aggregate Demand Curve versus Shifts of the Aggregate Demand Curve

Suppose the current price level is 110, and the current level of real GDP is $14.2 trillion. Illustrate each of the following situations on a graph.

a. The price level rises to 115, while all other variables remain constant.

b. Firms become pessimistic and reduce their investment. Assume that the price level remains constant.

Solving the Problem

Step 1: Review the chapter material. This problem is about understanding the difference between movements along an aggregate demand curve and shifts of an aggregate demand curve, so you may want to review the section "Shifts of the Aggregate Demand Curve versus Movements along It," on page 166.

Step 2: To answer part a. draw a graph that shows a movement along the aggregate demand curve. Because there will be a movement along the aggregate demand curve but no shift of the aggregate demand curve, your graph should look like this:

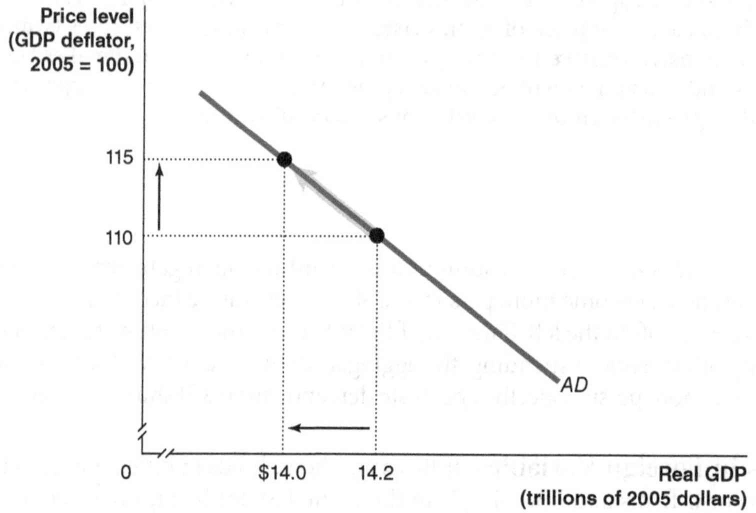

We don't have enough information to be certain what the new level of real GDP demanded will be. We only know that it will be less than the initial level of $14.2 trillion; the graph shows the value as $14.0 trillion.

Step 3: To answer part b. draw a graph that shows a shift of the aggregate demand curve. We know that the aggregate demand curve will shift to the left, but we don't have enough information to know how far to the left it will shift. Let's assume that the shift is $300 billion (or $0.3 trillion). In that case, your graph should look like this:

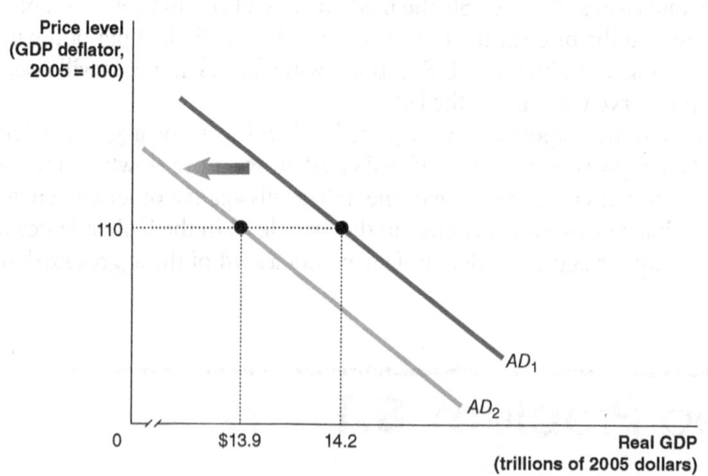

The graph shows a parallel shift in the aggregate demand curve so that at every price level, the quantity of real GDP demanded declines by $300 billion. For example, at a price level of 110, the quantity of real GDP demanded declines from $14.2 trillion to $13.9 trillion.

Table 8.1 summarizes the most important variables that cause the aggregate demand curve to shift. The table shows the shift in the aggregate demand curve that results from an increase in each of the variables. A *decrease* in these variables would cause the aggregate demand curve to shift in the opposite direction.

Table 8.1

Variables That Shift the Aggregate Demand Curve

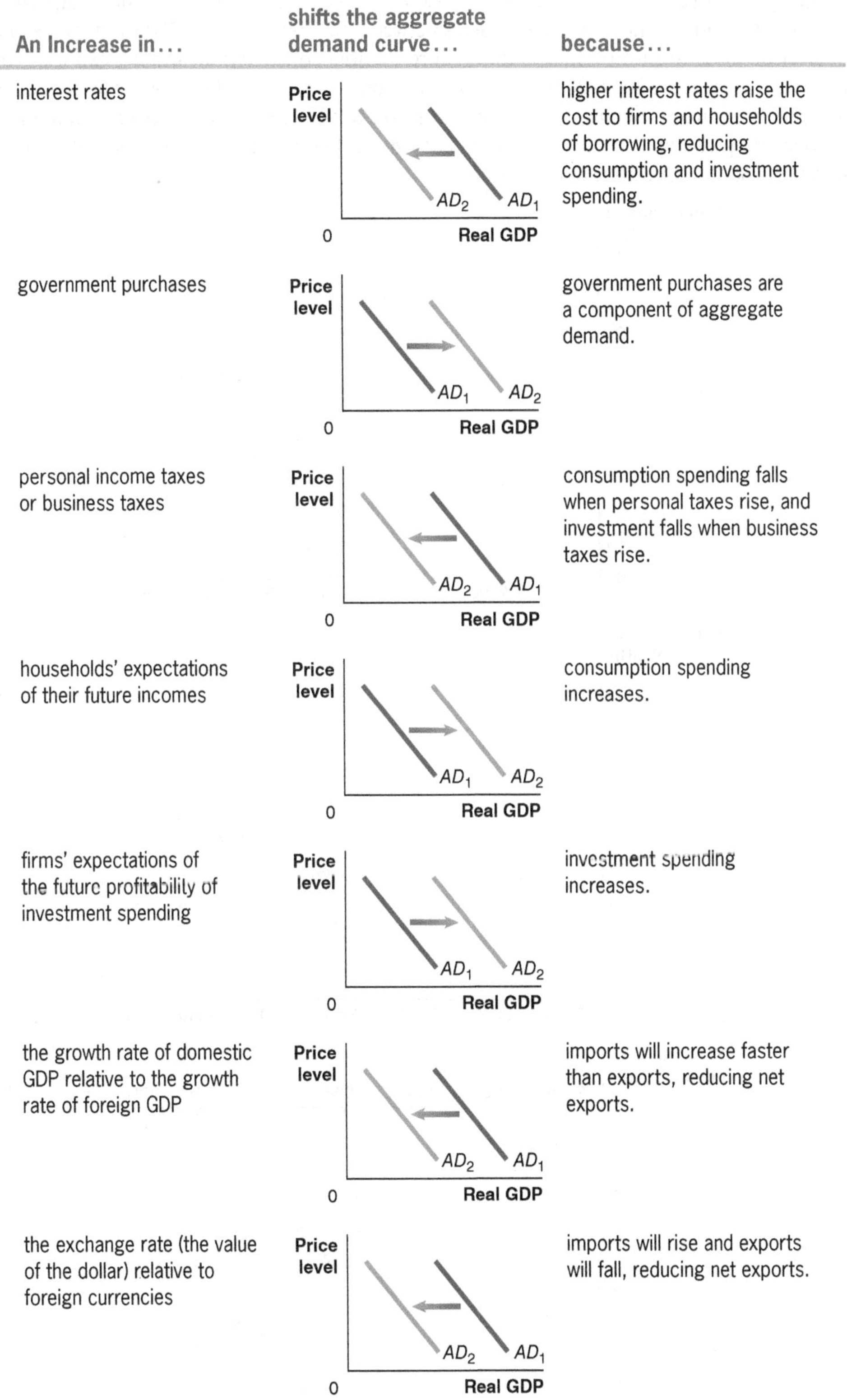

An Increase in...	shifts the aggregate demand curve...	because...
interest rates	Price level; AD_2 AD_1; 0 Real GDP	higher interest rates raise the cost to firms and households of borrowing, reducing consumption and investment spending.
government purchases	Price level; AD_1 AD_2; 0 Real GDP	government purchases are a component of aggregate demand.
personal income taxes or business taxes	Price level; AD_2 AD_1; 0 Real GDP	consumption spending falls when personal taxes rise, and investment falls when business taxes rise.
households' expectations of their future incomes	Price level; AD_1 AD_2; 0 Real GDP	consumption spending increases.
firms' expectations of the future profitability of investment spending	Price level; AD_1 AD_2; 0 Real GDP	investment spending increases.
the growth rate of domestic GDP relative to the growth rate of foreign GDP	Price level; AD_2 AD_1; 0 Real GDP	imports will increase faster than exports, reducing net exports.
the exchange rate (the value of the dollar) relative to foreign currencies	Price level; AD_2 AD_1; 0 Real GDP	imports will rise and exports will fall, reducing net exports.

Making the Connection — Which Components of Aggregate Demand Changed the Most during the 2007–2009 Recession?

The recession of 2007–2009 was the longest and most severe since the Great Depression of the 1930s. We can gain some insight into the reasons for the length and severity of the 2007–2009 recession by looking at changes over time in the components of aggregate demand. In the graphs below, we show changes in three components of aggregate demand that showed the largest movements between the first quarter of 2005 and the second quarter of 2011: consumption, spending on residential construction, and net exports. The red bars represent the 2007–2009 recession. We know that potential GDP, or the level of GDP when all firms are producing at capacity, grows over time. So, economists are often interested in measuring changes in the components of aggregate demand *relative to potential GDP*, which is what we have done in these graphs.

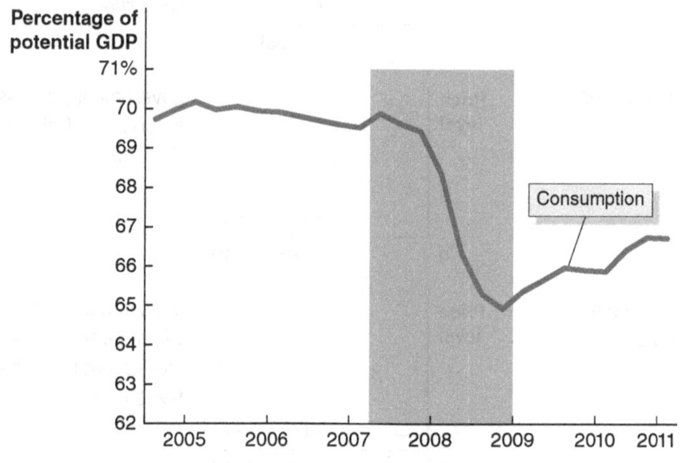

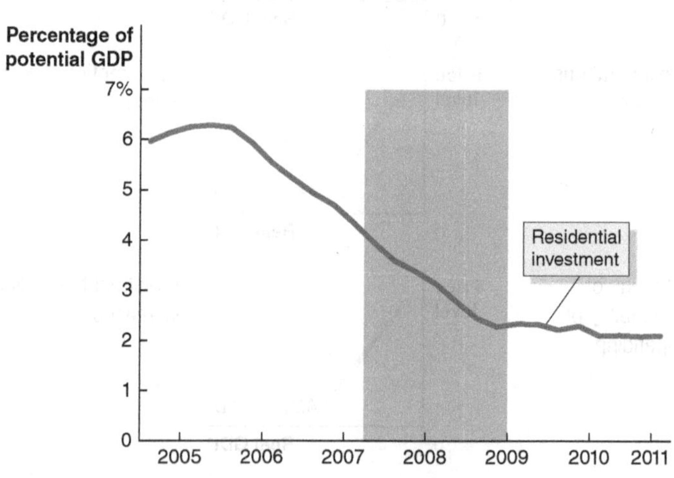

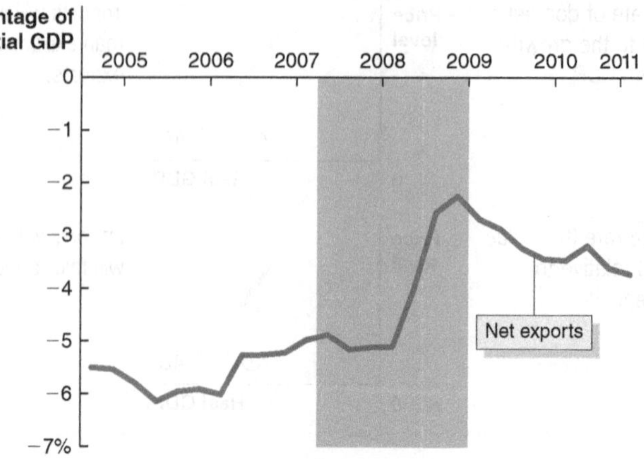

The figure allows us to note a number of facts about the 2007–2009 recession:

- In the two years before the beginning of the recession, spending on residential construction had already declined significantly relative to potential GDP.
- For more than two years following the end of the recession, spending on residential construction did not increase relative to potential GDP.
- Consumption, which usually remains relatively stable during a recession, declined significantly relative to potential GDP during the recession and remained low for more than two years after the recession had ended.
- Net exports increased just before, during, and after the recession. (Because net exports were negative throughout this period, it increased by becoming a smaller negative number.)

Although not shown in the graphs, business fixed investment and changes in business inventories—the nonresidential construction components of investment spending—actually rose relative to potential GDP during the recession. Government purchases remained fairly stable relative to potential GDP throughout the recession, before declining in late 2010 and the first half of 2011. Federal government purchases surged during the recession, but state and local governments reduced their spending as falling household incomes and falling business profits reduced state and local tax revenues.

We can briefly account for these facts. The housing sector underwent a boom from 2002 to 2005, with rapid increases in both housing prices and spending on new housing. The housing boom, though, turned into a housing bust beginning in 2006, which explains the sharp decline in spending on residential construction. The continued low levels of spending on residential construction helps explain why the recession was the longest since the Great Depression and why the economic expansion that began in June 2009 was relatively weak. As one newspaper article noted in late 2011: "Americans aren't spending because their home values are declining and employment prospects are dimming, and housing and employment is struggling because Americans won't spend."

High levels of unemployment reduced household incomes and led to declines in consumption spending. In addition, many households increased their saving and paid off debts, further reducing consumption spending. The continuing low levels of consumption spending also contributed to the severity of the recession and the weakness of the following expansion. Finally, efforts by the Federal Reserve to reduce interest rates helped to lower the value of the U.S. dollar, thereby reducing the prices of U.S. exports and increasing the prices of foreign imports. The result was an increase in net exports. (We will discuss further the effect of Federal Reserve policy on net exports in Chapters 11.)

Based on U.S. Bureau of Economic Analysis; Congressional Budget Office; and S. Mitra Kalita, "Housing's Job Engine Falters," *Wall Street Journal*, October 5, 2011.

Aggregate Supply

8.2 LEARNING OBJECTIVE

Identify the determinants of aggregate supply and distinguish between a movement along the short-run aggregate supply curve and a shift of the curve.

The aggregate demand curve is one component of the aggregate demand and aggregate supply model. Now we turn to aggregate supply, which shows the effect of changes in the price level on the quantity of goods and services that firms are willing and able to supply. Because the effect of changes in the price level on aggregate supply is very different in the short run from what it is in the long run, we use two aggregate supply curves: one for the short run and one for the long run. We start by considering the *long-run aggregate supply curve.*

The Long-Run Aggregate Supply Curve

In the long run, the level of real GDP is determined by the number of workers, the *capital stock*—including factories, office buildings, and machinery and equipment—and the available technology. Because changes in the price level do not affect the number of workers, the capital stock, or technology, *in the long run, changes in the price level do not affect the level of real GDP*. Remember that the level of real GDP

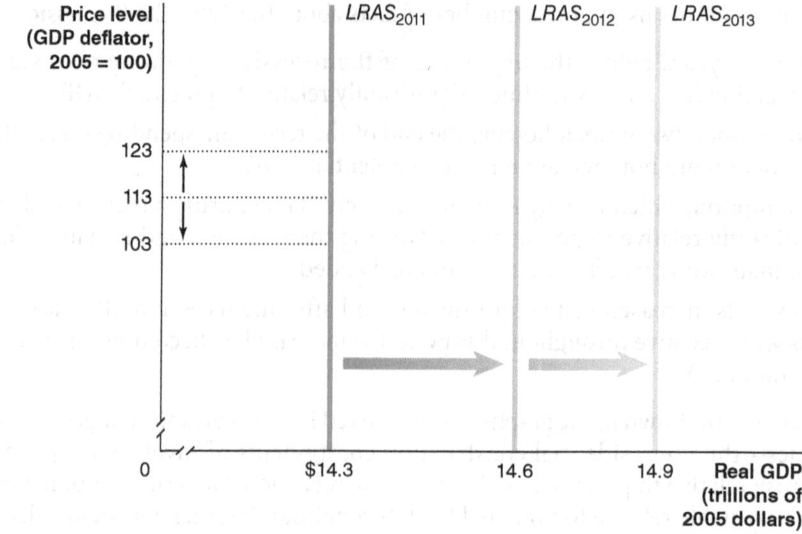

Figure 8.2

The Long-Run Aggregate Supply Curve

Changes in the price level do not affect the level of aggregate supply in the long run. Therefore, the long-run aggregate supply (*LRAS*) curve is a vertical line at the potential level of real GDP. For instance, the price level was 113 in 2011, and potential real GDP was $14.3 trillion. If the price level had been 123, or if it had been 103, long-run aggregate supply would still have been a constant $14.3 trillion. Each year, the long-run aggregate supply curve shifts to the right, as the number of workers in the economy increases, more machinery and equipment are accumulated, and technological change occurs.

in the long run is called *potential GDP*, or *full-employment GDP*. At potential GDP, firms will operate at their normal level of capacity, and everyone who wants a job will have one, except the structurally and frictionally unemployed. There is no reason for this normal level of capacity to change just because the price level has changed. The **long-run aggregate supply (*LRAS*) curve** shows the relationship in the long run between the price level and the quantity of real GDP supplied. As Figure 8.2 shows, in 2011, the price level was 113, and potential real GDP was $14.3 trillion. If the price level had been 123, or if it had been 103, long-run aggregate supply would still have been a constant $14.3 trillion. Therefore, the *LRAS* curve is a vertical line.

Long-run aggregate supply (*LRAS*) curve A curve that shows the relationship in the long run between the price level and the quantity of real GDP supplied.

Figure 8.2 also shows that the long-run aggregate supply curve shifts to the right each year. This shift occurs because potential real GDP increases each year, as the number of workers in the economy increases, the economy accumulates more machinery and equipment, and technological change occurs. Figure 8.2 shows potential real GDP increasing from $14.3 trillion in 2011 to $14.6 trillion in 2012 and to $14.9 trillion in 2013.

The Short-Run Aggregate Supply Curve

While the *LRAS* curve is vertical, the *SRAS* curve is upward sloping. The *SRAS* curve is upward sloping because, over the short run, as the price level increases, the quantity of goods and services firms are willing to supply will increase. The main reason firms behave this way is that, *as prices of final goods and services rise, prices of inputs—such as the wages of workers or the price of natural resources—rise more slowly.* Profits rise when the prices of the goods and services firms sell rise more rapidly than the prices they pay for inputs. Therefore, a higher price level leads to higher profits and increases the willingness of firms to supply more goods and services. A secondary reason the *SRAS* curve slopes upward is that, as the price level rises or falls, some firms are slow to adjust their prices. A firm that is slow to raise its prices when the price level is increasing may find its sales increasing and, therefore, will increase production. A firm that is slow to reduce its prices when the price level is decreasing may find its sales falling and, therefore, will decrease production.

Why do some firms adjust prices more slowly than others, and why might the wages of workers and the prices of other inputs change more slowly than the prices of final goods and services? Most economists believe the explanation is that *some firms and workers fail to accurately predict changes in the price level.* If firms and workers could predict the future price level exactly, the short-run aggregate supply curve would be the same as the long-run aggregate supply curve.

But how does the failure of workers and firms to predict the price level accurately result in an upward-sloping *SRAS* curve? Economists are not in complete agreement on this point, but we can briefly discuss the three most common explanations:

1. Contracts make some wages and prices "sticky."
2. Firms are often slow to adjust wages.
3. Menu costs make some prices sticky.

Contracts Make Some Wages and Prices "Sticky" Prices or wages are said to be "sticky" when they do not respond quickly to changes in demand or supply. Contracts can make wages or prices sticky. For example, suppose United Parcel Service (UPS) negotiates a three-year contract with the Independent Pilots Association, the union for the pilots who fly the company's cargo planes, during a time when the economy is in recession and the volume of packages being shipped is falling. Suppose that after the union signs the contract, the economy begins to expand rapidly, and the volume of packages shipped increases, so that UPS can raise the rates it charges. UPS will find that shipping more packages will be profitable because the prices it charges are rising, while the wages it pays its pilots are fixed by contract. Or a steel mill might have signed a multiyear contract to buy coal, which is used in making steel, at a time when the demand for steel was stagnant. If steel demand and steel prices begin to rise rapidly, producing additional steel will be profitable because coal prices will remain fixed by contract. In both of these cases, rising prices lead to higher output. If these examples are representative of enough firms in the economy, a rising price level should lead to a greater quantity of goods and services supplied. In other words, the short-run aggregate supply curve will be upward sloping.

Notice, though, that if the pilots at UPS or the managers of the coal companies had accurately predicted what would happen to prices, this prediction would have been reflected in the contracts, and UPS and the steel mill would not have earned greater profits when prices rose. In that case, rising prices would not have led to higher output.

Firms Are Often Slow to Adjust Wages We just noted that the wages of many union workers remain fixed by contract for several years. Many nonunion workers also have their wages or salaries adjusted only once a year. For instance, suppose you accept a job at a management consulting firm in June, at a salary of $45,000 per year. The firm probably will not adjust your salary until the following June, even if the prices it can charge for its services later in the year are higher or lower than the firm had expected them to be when they hired you. If firms are slow to adjust wages, a rise in the price level will increase the profitability of hiring more workers and producing more output. A fall in the price level will decrease the profitability of hiring more workers and producing more output. Once again, we have an explanation for why the short-run aggregate supply curve slopes upward.

It is worth noting that firms are often slower to *cut* wages than to increase them. Cutting wages can have a negative effect on the morale and productivity of workers and can also cause some of a firm's best workers to quit and look for jobs elsewhere.

Menu Costs Make Some Prices Sticky Firms base their prices today partly on what they expect future prices to be. For instance, before it prints menus, a restaurant has to decide the prices it will charge for meals. Many firms print catalogs that list the prices of their products. If demand for their products is higher or lower than the firms had expected, they may want to charge prices that are different from the ones printed in their menus or catalogs. Changing prices would be costly, however, because it would involve printing new menus or catalogs. The costs to firms of changing prices are called **menu costs**. To see why menu costs can lead to an upward-sloping short-run aggregate supply curve, consider the effect of an unexpected increase in the price level. In this case, firms will want to increase the prices they charge. Some firms, however, may not be willing to increase prices because of menu costs. Because of their relatively low prices, these firms will find their sales increasing, which will cause them to increase output. Once again, we have an explanation for a higher price level leading to a larger quantity of goods and services supplied.

Menu costs The costs to firms of changing prices.

Shifts of the Short-Run Aggregate Supply Curve versus Movements along It

It is important to remember the difference between a shift in a curve and a movement along a curve. The short-run aggregate supply curve tells us the short-run relationship between the price level and the quantity of goods and services firms are willing to supply, *holding constant all other variables that affect the willingness of firms to supply goods and services.* If the price level changes but other variables are unchanged, the economy will move up or down a stationary aggregate supply curve. If any variable other than the price level changes, the aggregate supply curve will shift.

Variables That Shift the Short-Run Aggregate Supply Curve

We now briefly discuss the five most important variables that cause the short-run aggregate supply curve to shift.

Increases in the Labor Force and in the Capital Stock A firm will supply more output at every price if it has more workers and more physical capital. The same is true of the economy as a whole. So, as the labor force and the capital stock grow, firms will supply more output at every price level, and the short-run aggregate supply curve will shift to the right. In Japan, the population is aging, and the labor force is decreasing. Holding other variables constant, this decrease in the labor force causes the short-run aggregate supply curve in Japan to shift to the left.

Technological Change As positive technological change takes place, the productivity of workers and machinery increases, which means firms can produce more goods and services with the same amount of labor and machinery. This increase in productivity reduces the firms' costs of production and, therefore, allows them to produce more output at every price level. As a result, the short-run aggregate supply curve shifts to the right.

Expected Changes in the Future Price Level If workers and firms believe that the price level is going to increase by 3 percent during the next year, they will try to adjust their wages and prices accordingly. For instance, if a labor union believes there will be 3 percent inflation next year, it knows that wages must rise 3 percent to preserve the purchasing power of those wages. Similar adjustments by other workers and firms will result in costs increasing throughout the economy by 3 percent. The result, shown in Figure 8.3, is that the short-run aggregate supply curve will shift to the left, so that any level of real

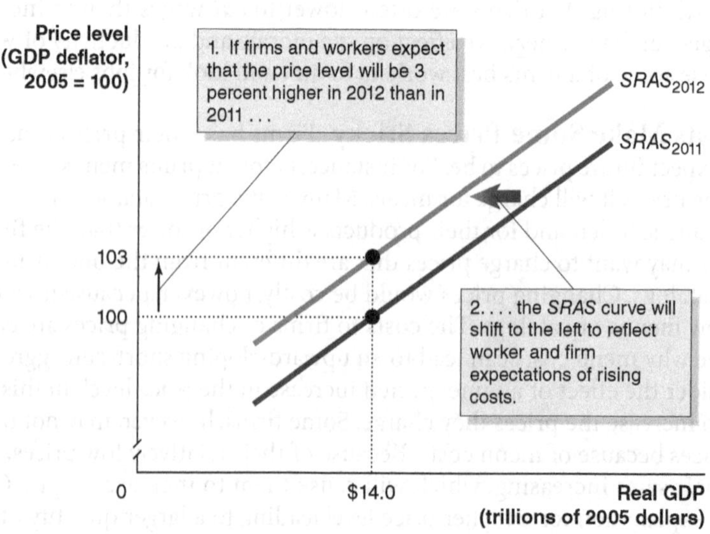

Figure 8.3

How Expectations of the Future Price Level Affect the Short-Run Aggregate Supply Curve

The *SRAS* curve shifts to reflect worker and firm expectations of future prices.

1. If workers and firms expect that the price level will rise by 3 percent, from 100 to 103, they will adjust their wages and prices by that amount.
2. Holding constant all other variables that affect aggregate supply, the short-run aggregate supply curve will shift to the left.

If workers and firms expect that the price level will be lower in the future, the short-run aggregate supply curve will shift to the right.

GDP is now associated with a price level that is 3 percent higher. In general, *if workers and firms expect the price level to increase by a certain percentage, the* SRAS *curve will shift by an equivalent amount*, holding constant all other variables that affect the *SRAS* curve.

Adjustments of Workers and Firms to Errors in Past Expectations about the Price Level Workers and firms sometimes make incorrect predictions about the price level. As time passes, they will attempt to compensate for these errors. Suppose, for example, that the Independent Pilots Association signs a contract with UPS that provides for only small wage increases because the company and the union both expect only small increases in the price level. If increases in the price level turn out to be unexpectedly large, the union will take this into account when negotiating the next contract. The higher wages UPS pilots receive under the new contract will increase UPS's costs and result in UPS needing to receive higher prices to produce the same level of output. If workers and firms across the economy are adjusting to the price level being higher than expected, the *SRAS* curve will shift to the left. If they are adjusting to the price level being lower than expected, the *SRAS* curve will shift to the right.

Unexpected Changes in the Price of an Important Natural Resource An unexpected event that causes the short-run aggregate supply curve to shift is known as a **supply shock**. Supply shocks are often caused by unexpected increases or decreases in the prices of important natural resources that can cause firms' costs to be different from what they had expected. Oil prices can be particularly volatile. Some firms use oil in the production process. Other firms use products, such as plastics, that are made from oil. If oil prices rise unexpectedly, the costs of production will rise for these firms. Some utilities also burn oil to generate electricity, so electricity prices will rise. Rising oil prices lead to rising gasoline prices, which raise transportation costs for many firms. Because firms face rising costs, they will supply the same level of output only if they receive higher prices, and the short-run aggregate supply curve will shift to the left.

Supply shock An unexpected event that causes the short-run aggregate supply curve to shift.

Because the U.S. economy has experienced at least some inflation every year since the 1930s, workers and firms always expect next year's price level to be higher than this year's price level. Holding everything else constant, expectations of a higher price level will cause the *SRAS* curve to shift to the left. But everything else is not constant because every year, the U.S. labor force and the U.S. capital stock expand, and changes in technology occur, which cause the *SRAS* curve to shift to the right. Whether in any particular year the *SRAS* curve shifts to the left or to the right depends on how large an impact these variables have during that year.

Table 8.2 summarizes the most important variables that cause the *SRAS* curve to shift. The table shows the shift in the *SRAS* curve that results from an *increase* in each of the variables. A *decrease* in these variables would cause the *SRAS* curve to shift in the opposite direction.

Macroeconomic Equilibrium in the Long Run and the Short Run

8.3 LEARNING OBJECTIVE

Use the aggregate demand and aggregate supply model to illustrate the difference between short-run and long-run macroeconomic equilibrium.

Now that we have discussed the components of the aggregate demand and aggregate supply model, we can use it to analyze changes in real GDP and the price level. In Figure 8.4, we bring the aggregate demand curve, the short-run aggregate supply curve, and the long-run aggregate supply curve together in one graph, to show the *long-run macroeconomic equilibrium* for the economy. In the figure, equilibrium occurs at real GDP of \$14.0 trillion and a price level of 100. Notice that in long-run equilibrium, the short-run aggregate supply curve and the aggregate demand curve intersect at a point on the long-run aggregate supply curve. Because equilibrium occurs at a point along the long-run aggregate supply curve, we know the economy is at potential real GDP: Firms will be operating at their normal level of capacity, and everyone who wants a job will have one, except the structurally and frictionally unemployed. We know, however, that the economy

Table 8.2

Variables That Shift the Short-Run Aggregate Supply Curve

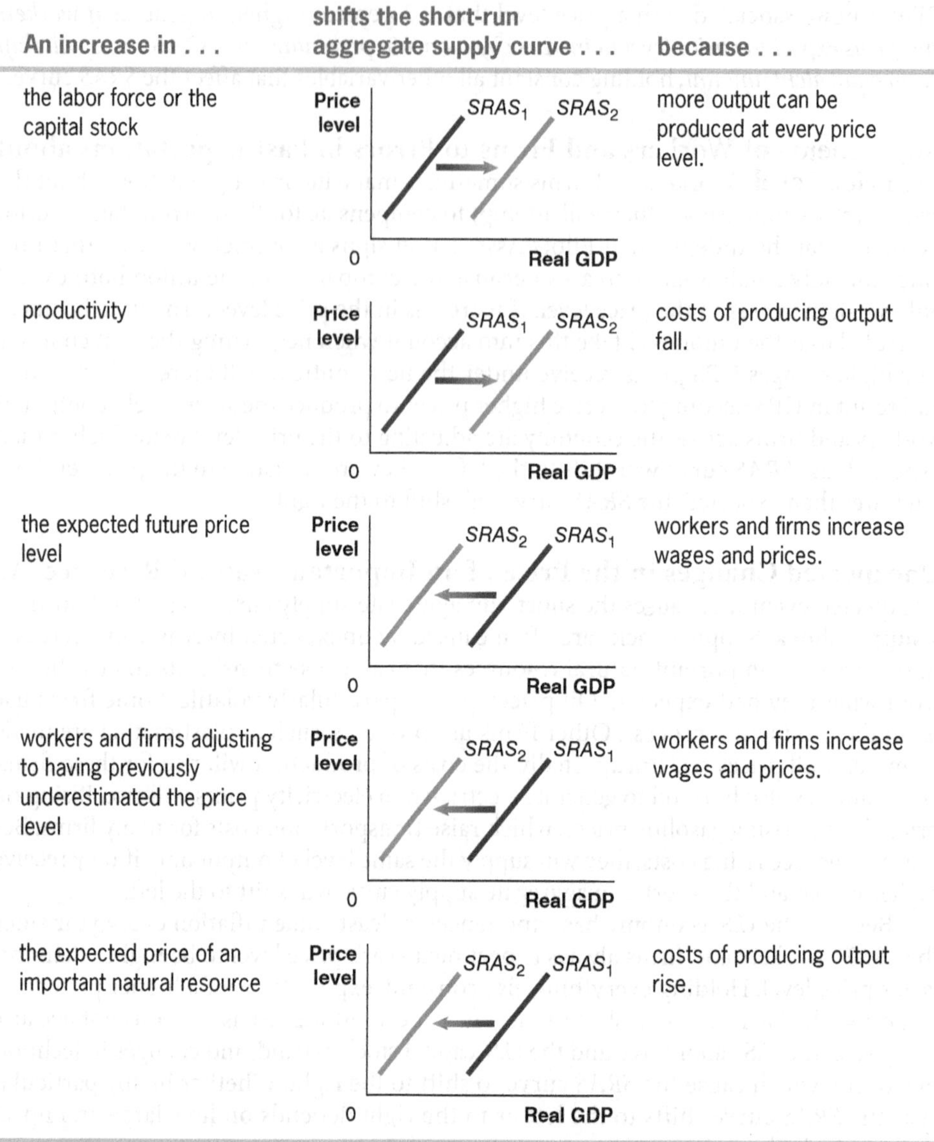

An increase in . . .	shifts the short-run aggregate supply curve . . .	because . . .
the labor force or the capital stock	Price level; $SRAS_1$ → $SRAS_2$ (shift right); 0; Real GDP	more output can be produced at every price level.
productivity	Price level; $SRAS_1$ → $SRAS_2$ (shift right); 0; Real GDP	costs of producing output fall.
the expected future price level	Price level; $SRAS_2$ ← $SRAS_1$ (shift left); 0; Real GDP	workers and firms increase wages and prices.
workers and firms adjusting to having previously underestimated the price level	Price level; $SRAS_2$ ← $SRAS_1$ (shift left); 0; Real GDP	workers and firms increase wages and prices.
the expected price of an important natural resource	Price level; $SRAS_2$ ← $SRAS_1$ (shift left); 0; Real GDP	costs of producing output rise.

Figure 8.4

Long-Run Macroeconomic Equilibrium

In long-run macroeconomic equilibrium, the *AD* and *SRAS* curves intersect at a point on the *LRAS* curve. In this case, equilibrium occurs at real GDP of $14.0 trillion and a price level of 100.

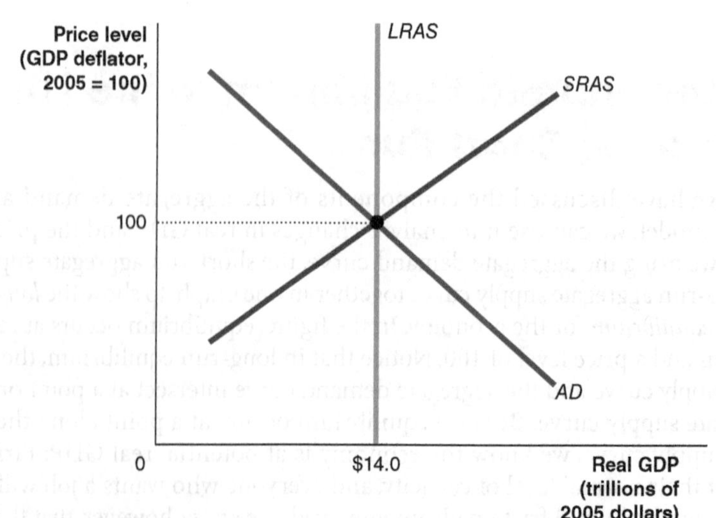

is often not in long-run macroeconomic equilibrium. In the following section, we discuss the economic forces that can push the economy away from long-run equilibrium.

Recessions, Expansions, and Supply Shocks

Because the full analysis of the aggregate demand and aggregate supply model can be complicated, we begin with a simplified case, using two assumptions:

1. The economy has not been experiencing any inflation. The price level is currently 100, and workers and firms expect it to remain at 100 in the future.
2. The economy is not experiencing any long-run growth. Potential real GDP is $14.0 trillion and will remain at that level in the future.

These assumptions are simplifications because in reality, the U.S. economy has experienced at least some inflation every year since the 1930s, and the potential real GDP also increases every year. However, the assumptions allow us to understand more easily the key ideas of the aggregate demand and aggregate supply model. In this section, we examine the short-run and long-run effects of recessions, expansions, and supply shocks.

Recession

The Short-Run Effect of a Decline in Aggregate Demand Suppose that rising interest rates cause firms to reduce spending on factories and equipment and cause households to reduce spending on new homes. The decline in investment that results will shift the aggregate demand curve to the left, from AD_1 to AD_2, as shown in Figure 8.5. The economy moves from point *A* to a new *short-run macroeconomic equilibrium*, where the AD_2 curve intersects the $SRAS_1$ curve at point *B*. In the new short-run equilibrium, real GDP has declined from $14.0 trillion to $13.8 trillion and is below its potential level. This lower level of GDP will result in declining profitability for many firms and layoffs for some workers: the economy will be in recession.

Adjustment Back to Potential GDP in the Long Run We know that a recession will eventually end because there are forces at work that push the economy back to potential GDP in the long run. Figure 8.5 shows how the economy moves from recession back to potential GDP. The shift from AD_1 to AD_2 initially leads to a short-run equilibrium, with the price level having fallen from 100 to 98 (point *B*). Workers and firms will

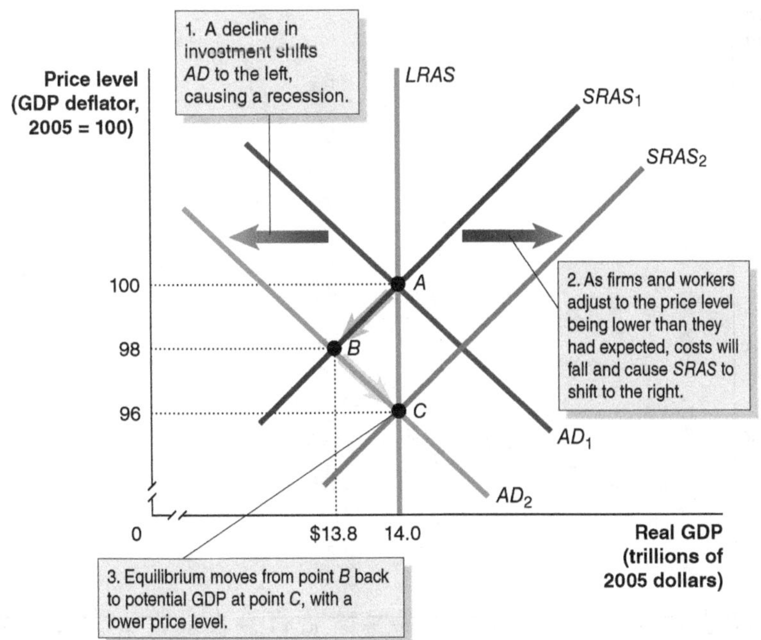

Figure 8.5

The Short-Run and Long-Run Effects of a Decrease in Aggregate Demand

In the short run, a decrease in aggregate demand causes a recession. In the long run, it causes only a decrease in the price level.

begin to adjust to the price level being lower than they had expected it to be. Workers will be willing to accept lower wages—because each dollar of wages is able to buy more goods and services—and firms will be willing to accept lower prices. In addition, the unemployment resulting from the recession will make workers more willing to accept lower wages, and the decline in demand will make firms more willing to accept lower prices. As a result, the *SRAS* curve will shift to the right, from $SRAS_1$ to $SRAS_2$. At this point, the economy will be back in long-run equilibrium (point *C*). The shift from $SRAS_1$ to $SRAS_2$ will not happen instantly. It may take the economy several years to return to potential GDP. The important conclusion is that a decline in aggregate demand causes a recession in the short run, but in the long run it causes only a decline in the price level.

Economists refer to the process of adjustment back to potential GDP just described as an *automatic mechanism* because it occurs without any actions by the government. An alternative to waiting for the automatic mechanism to end a recession is for the government to use monetary and fiscal policy to shift the *AD* curve to the right and restore potential GDP more quickly. We will discuss monetary and fiscal policy in Chapters 9 and 11. Economists debate whether it is better to wait for the automatic mechanism to end recessions or whether it is better to use monetary and fiscal policy.

Making the Connection

Does It Matter What Causes a Decline in Aggregate Demand?

The collapse in spending on housing added to the severity of the 2007–2009 recession.

We have seen that GDP has four components and that a decrease in any of the four components can cause the aggregate demand curve to shift to the left, bringing on a recession. In practice, though, most recessions in the United States since World War II have begun with a decline in residential construction. Edward Leamer of the University of California, Los Angeles has gone so far as to argue that "housing *is* the business cycle," meaning that declines in residential construction are the most important reason for the declines in aggregate demand that lead to recessions. The shaded periods in the graph below represent recessions. The graph shows that spending on residential construction has declined prior to every recession since 1955.

The figure shows again a fact that we noted earlier in the chapter: The decline in residential construction during the 2007–2009

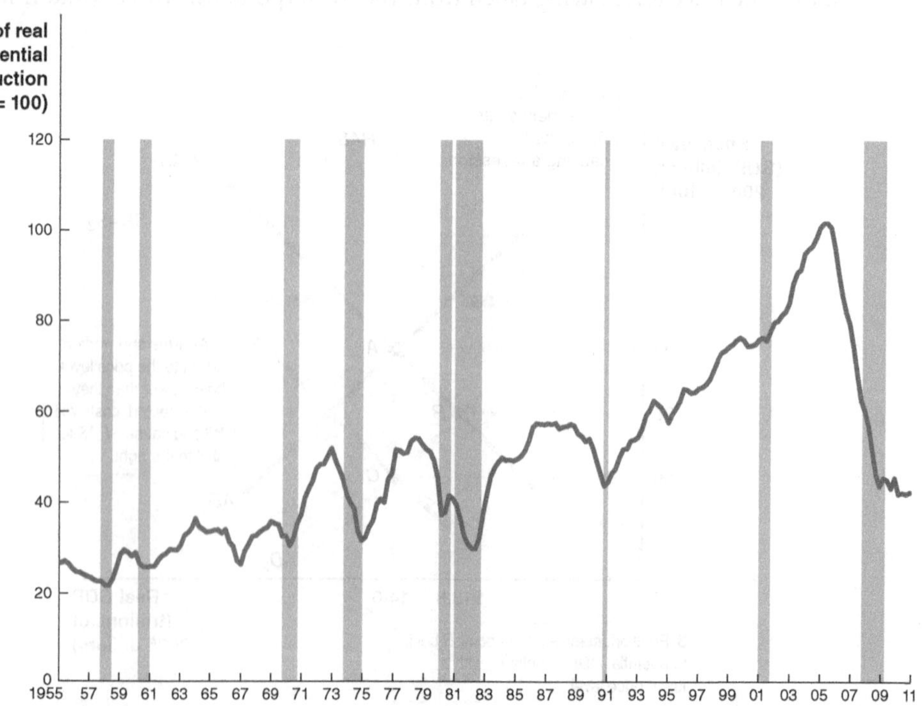

Data from U.S. Bureau of Economic Analysis.

recession was particularly severe. Spending on residential construction declined by almost 60 percent from the fourth quarter of 2005 to the second quarter of 2010. Largely because of these problems in the housing sector, the decline in real GDP during the recession of 2007–2009 was larger than during any other recession since the Great Depression of the 1930s.

What causes declines in spending on residential construction, and why was the decline that preceded the 2007–2009 recession so severe? Late in a business cycle expansion, the inflation rate and interest rates start to increase. As we will discuss in Chapter 11, higher interest rates often result from monetary policy actions as the Federal Reserve tries to slow down the economy and reduce the rate of inflation. Higher interest rates reduce consumer demand for new houses by increasing the cost of loans.

But the collapse in residential construction prior to and during the recession of 2007–2009 was due more to the deflating of the "housing bubble" of 2002–2005 and to the financial crisis that began in 2007 than to higher interest rates. We will discuss both the housing bubble and the financial crisis later in this chapter. At this point, we can note that research by Carmen M. Reinhart of the University of Maryland and Kenneth S. Rogoff of Harvard University shows that declines in aggregate demand that result from financial crises tend to be larger and more long lasting than declines due to other factors. So, the experience of 2007–2009 indicates that, in fact, the source of the decline in aggregate demand can be important in determining the severity of a recession.

Based on Edward E. Leamer, "Housing Is the Business Cycle," in *Housing, Housing Finance, and Monetay Policy*, Federal Reserve Bank of Kansas City, August 2007; and Carmen M. Reinhart and Kenneth S. Rogoff, "The Aftermath of Financial Crises," *American Economic Review*, Vol. 99, No. 2, May 2009, pp. 466–472.

Expansion

The Short-Run Effect of an Increase in Aggregate Demand Suppose that instead of becoming pessimistic, many firms become optimistic about the future profitability of new investment, as happened during the information technology and telecommunications booms of the late 1990s. The resulting increase in investment will shift the *AD* curve to the right, as shown in Figure 8.6. Equilibrium moves from point *A* to point *B*. Real GDP rises from \$14.0 trillion to \$14.3 trillion, and the price level rises from 100 to 103. The economy will be above potential real GDP: Firms are operating beyond their normal level of capacity, and some workers who would ordinarily be structurally or frictionally unemployed or who would not be in the labor force are employed.

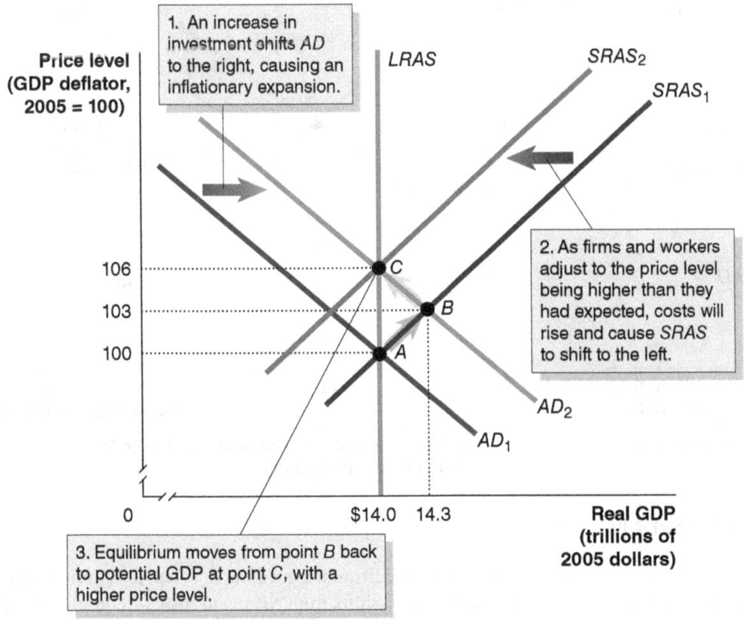

Figure 8.6

The Short-Run and Long-Run Effects of an Increase in Aggregate Demand

In the short run, an increase in aggregate demand causes an increase in real GDP. In the long run, it causes only an increase in the price level.

Adjustment Back to Potential GDP in the Long Run Just as an automatic mechanism brings the economy back to potential GDP from a recession, an automatic mechanism brings the economy back from a short-run equilibrium beyond potential GDP. Figure 8.6 illustrates this mechanism. The shift from AD_1 to AD_2 initially leads to a short-run equilibrium, with the price level rising from 100 to 103 (point *B*). Workers and firms will begin to adjust to the price level being higher than they had expected. Workers will push for higher wages—because each dollar of wages is able to buy fewer goods and services—and firms will charge higher prices. In addition, the low levels of unemployment resulting from the expansion will make it easier for workers to negotiate for higher wages, and the increase in demand will make it easier for firms to receive higher prices. As a result, the *SRAS* curve will shift to the left, from $SRAS_1$ to $SRAS_2$. At this point, the economy will be back in long-run equilibrium. Once again, the shift from $SRAS_1$ to $SRAS_2$ will not happen instantly. The process of returning to potential GDP may stretch out for more than a year.

Supply Shock

The Short-Run Effect of a Supply Shock Suppose oil prices increase substantially. This supply shock will increase many firms' costs and cause the *SRAS* curve to shift to the left, as shown in panel (a) of Figure 8.7. Notice that the price level is higher in the new short-run equilibrium (102 rather than 100), but real GDP is lower ($13.7 trillion rather than $14 trillion). This unpleasant combination of inflation and recession is called **stagflation**.

Stagflation A combination of inflation and recession, usually resulting from a supply shock.

Adjustment Back to Potential GDP in the Long Run The recession caused by a supply shock increases unemployment and reduces output. This eventually results in workers being willing to accept lower wages and firms being willing to accept lower prices. In panel (b) of Figure 8.7, the short-run aggregate supply curve shifts from $SRAS_2$ to $SRAS_1$, moving the economy from point *B* back to point *A*. The economy is back to potential GDP at the original price level. It may take several years for this process to be completed. An alternative would be to use monetary and fiscal policy to shift the aggregate demand to the right. Using policy in this way would bring the economy back to potential GDP more quickly but would result in a permanently higher price level.

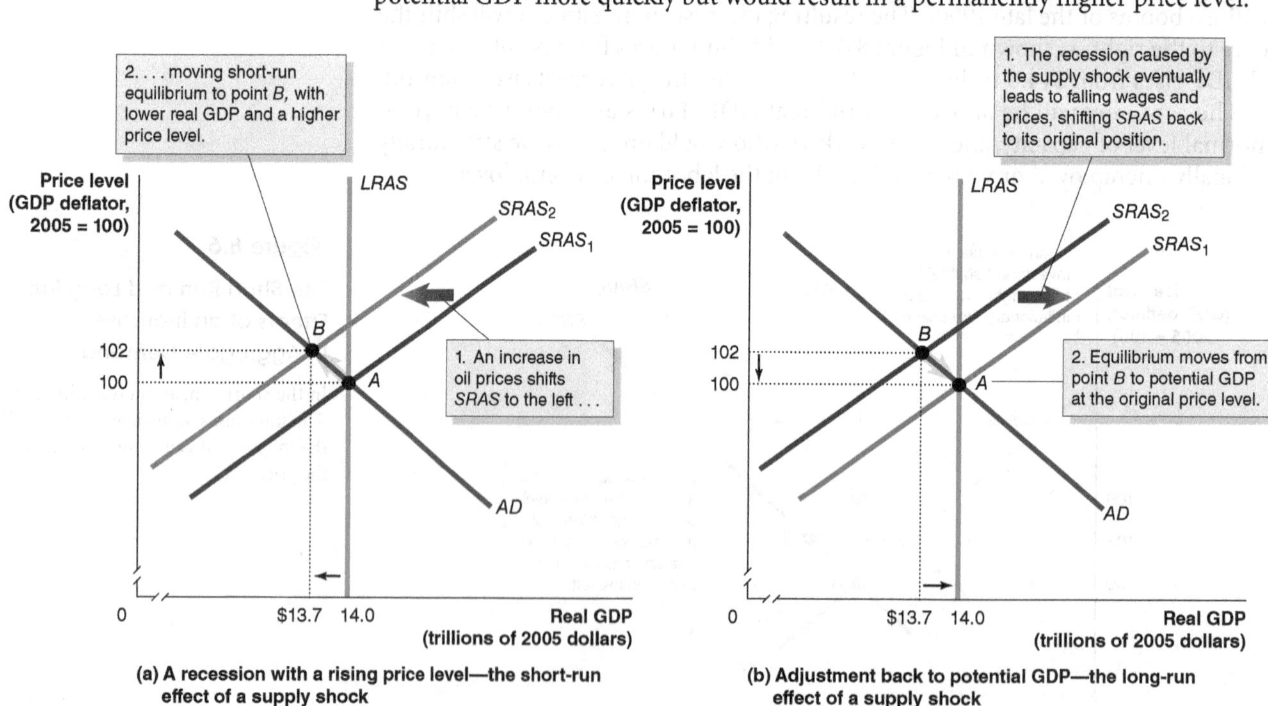

Figure 8.7 The Short-Run and Long-Run Effects of a Supply Shock

Panel (a) shows that a supply shock, such as a large increase in oil prices, will cause a recession and a higher price level in the short run. The recession caused by the supply shock increases unemployment and reduces output. In panel (b), rising unemployment and falling output result in workers being willing to accept lower wages and firms being willing to accept lower prices. The short-run aggregate supply curve shifts from $SRAS_2$ to $SRAS_1$. Equilibrium moves from point *B* back to potential GDP and the original price level at point *A*.

Making the Connection

How Long Does It Take to Return to Potential GDP? Economic Forecasts Following the Recession of 2007–2009

Alan Krueger, the chair of the Council of Economic Advisers in the Obama administration, provided an estimate of how long the economy would take to return to potential GDP.

Making accurate macroeconomic forecasts is difficult. As we have seen, many factors can cause aggregate demand or aggregate supply to shift. Because it is challenging to predict how much aggregate demand and aggregate supply will shift, economists often have difficulty predicting the beginning and end of a recession. The Federal Reserve, foreign central banks, other government agencies, large banks, forecasting firms, and academic economists use a variety of forecasting models to predict changes in GDP. Most forecasting models consist of equations that represent the macroeconomic relationships—such as the relationship between disposable income and consumption spending—that underlie the aggregate demand and aggregate supply model. After economists have statistically estimated the equations using economic data, they can use the models to forecast values for GDP and the price level.

Most economists agree that an automatic mechanism brings the economy back to potential GDP in the long run. But how long is the long run? When the recession of 2007–2009 ended in June 2009, the economy was far from potential GDP. Even two years later, in mid-2011, real GDP remained more than 7 percent below potential GDP. How long would it take for the economy to finally return to potential GDP? The figure below shows the Congressional Budget Office's estimates of potential GDP along with three forecasts of real GDP made in 2011 by the following:

- Economists on the president's staff at the White House
- Officials at the Federal Reserve
- Economists at the Congressional Budget Office (CBO)

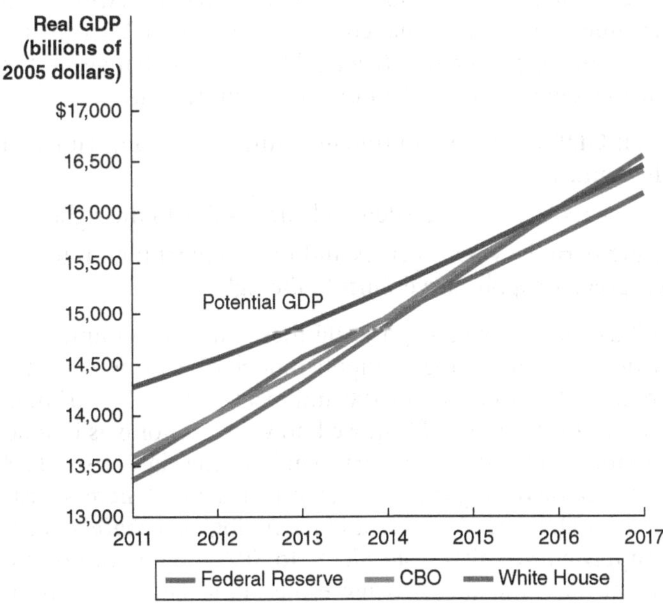

The forecasts of the White House and the CBO agreed that real GDP would not return to potential GDP until 2016. The projections of the Federal Reserve were even more pessimistic, with real GDP remaining below potential GDP in 2017. These forecasts indicate how severe the 2007–2009 recession was in that real GDP was not expected to return to potential GDP until nearly seven years after the end of the recession. Prior to the 2007–2009 recession, the recession of 1981–1982 had been the most severe since the Great Depression. Yet it took less than three years after the end of that recession for real GDP to return to potential GDP.

These macroeconomic forecasts played an important role in the policy debates of 2011 and 2012. As we will discuss in Chapters 9, economists and policymakers disagreed about why the U.S. economy would take so long to return to potential GDP and about what measures the federal government might take to shorten the time.

Note: The Federal Reserve's forecast uses averages of the forecasts of the individual members of the Federal Open Market Committee.

Based on Board of Governors of the Federal Reserve System, "Economic Projections of Federal Reserve Board Members and Federal Reserve Bank Presidents, April 2011," April 27, 2011; Congressional Budget Office, "Data Underlying Selected Economic Figures, Real Gross Domestic Product, 1980–2021," January 27, 2011; and Office of Management and Budget, "Budget of the U.S. Government, Fiscal Year 2012, Mid-Session Review," September 1, 2011.

8.4 LEARNING OBJECTIVE

Use the dynamic aggregate demand and aggregate supply model to analyze macroeconomic conditions.

A Dynamic Aggregate Demand and Aggregate Supply Model*

The basic aggregate demand and aggregate supply model used so far in this chapter provides important insights into how short-run macroeconomic equilibrium is determined. Unfortunately, the model also provides some misleading results. For instance, it incorrectly predicts that a recession caused by the aggregate demand curve shifting to the left will cause the price level to fall, which has not happened for an entire year since the 1930s. The difficulty with the basic model arises from the following two assumptions we made: (1) The economy does not experience continuing inflation, and (2) the economy does not experience long-run growth. We can develop a more useful aggregate demand and aggregate supply model by dropping these assumptions. The result will be a model that takes into account that the economy is not *static*, with an unchanging level of potential real GDP and no continuing inflation, but *dynamic*, with potential real GDP that grows over time and inflation that continues every year. We can create a *dynamic aggregate demand and aggregate supply model* by making changes to the basic model that incorporate the following important macroeconomic facts:

- Potential real GDP increases continually, shifting the long-run aggregate supply curve to the right.
- During most years, the aggregate demand curve shifts to the right.
- Except during periods when workers and firms expect high rates of inflation, the short-run aggregate supply curve shifts to the right.

Figure 8.8 illustrates how incorporating these macroeconomic facts changes the basic aggregate demand and aggregate supply model. We start with $SRAS_1$ and AD_1 intersecting at point *A*, at a price level of 100 and real GDP of \$14.0 trillion. Because this intersection occurs at a point on $LRAS_1$, we know the economy is in long-run equilibrium. The long-run aggregate supply curve shifts to the right, from $LRAS_1$ to $LRAS_2$. This shift occurs because during the year, potential real GDP increases as the U.S. labor force and the U.S. capital stock increase and technological progress occurs. The short-run aggregate supply curve shifts from $SRAS_1$ to $SRAS_2$. This shift occurs because the same variables that cause the long-run aggregate supply curve to shift to the right will also increase the quantity of goods and services that firms are willing to supply in the short run. Finally, the aggregate demand curve shifts to the right, from AD_1 to AD_2. The aggregate demand curve shifts for several reasons: As the population grows and incomes rise, consumption will increase over time. As the economy grows, firms will expand capacity, and new firms will be formed, increasing investment. An expanding population and an expanding economy require increased government services, such as more police officers and teachers, so government purchases will increase.

The new equilibrium in Figure 8.8 occurs at point *B*, where AD_2 intersects $SRAS_2$ on $LRAS_2$. In the new equilibrium, the price level remains at 100, while real GDP increases to \$14.3 trillion. Notice that there has been no inflation because the price level is unchanged, at 100. There has been no inflation because aggregate demand and aggregate

*This section may be omitted without loss of continuity.

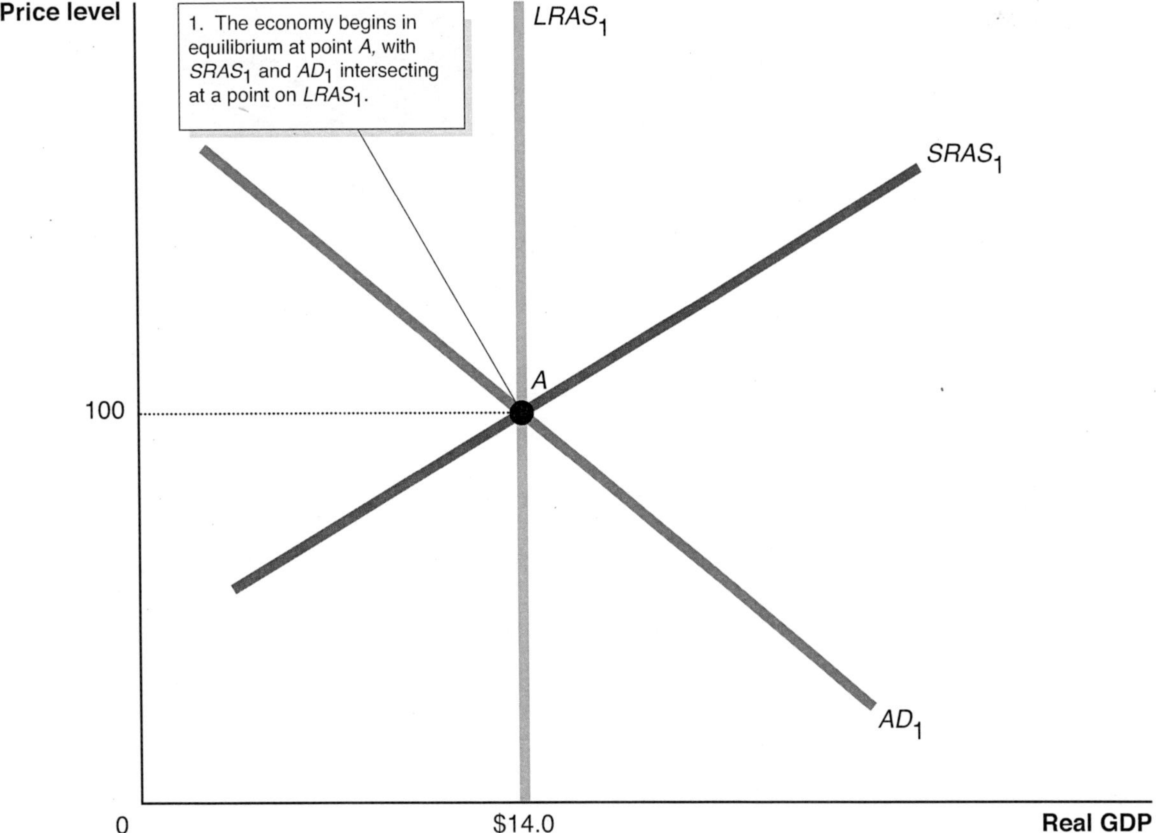

Figure 8.8 **A Dynamic Aggregate Demand and Aggregate Supply Model**

We start with the basic aggregate demand and aggregate supply model.

supply shifted to the right by exactly as much as long-run aggregate supply. We would not expect this to be the typical situation for two reasons. First, the *SRAS* curve is also affected by workers' and firms' expectations of future changes in the price level and by supply shocks. These variables can partially or completely offset the normal tendency of the *SRAS* curve to shift to the right over the course of a year. Second, we know that consumers, firms, and the government may cut back on expenditures. This reduced spending will result in the aggregate demand curve shifting to the right less than it normally would or, possibly, shifting to the left. In fact, as we will see shortly, *changes in the price level and in real GDP in the short run are determined by shifts in the* SRAS *and* AD *curves.*

What Is the Usual Cause of Inflation?

The dynamic aggregate demand and aggregate supply model provides a more accurate explanation than the basic model of the source of most inflation. If total spending in the economy grows faster than total production, prices rise. Figure 8.9 illustrates this point by showing that if the *AD* curve shifts to the right by more than the *LRAS* curve, inflation results because equilibrium occurs at a higher price level, point *B*. In the new equilibrium, the *SRAS* curve has shifted to the right by less than the *LRAS* curve because the anticipated increase in prices offsets some of the technological change and increases in the labor force and capital stock that occur during the year. Although inflation generally results from total spending growing faster than total production, a shift to the left of the short-run aggregate supply curve can also cause an increase in the price level, as we saw earlier, in the discussion of supply shocks.

As we saw in Figure 8.8, if aggregate demand increases by the same amount as short-run and long-run aggregate supply, the price level will not change. In this case, the economy experiences economic growth without inflation.

Figure 8.9

Using Dynamic Aggregate Demand and Aggregate Supply to Understand Inflation

The most common cause of inflation is total spending increasing faster than total production.

1. The economy begins at point A, with real GDP of \$14.0 trillion and a price level of 100. An increase in full-employment real GDP from \$14.0 trillion to \$14.3 trillion causes long-run aggregate supply to shift from $LRAS_1$ to $LRAS_2$. Aggregate demand shifts from AD_1 to AD_2.
2. Because AD shifts to the right by more than the $LRAS$ curve, the price level in the new equilibrium rises from 100 to 104.

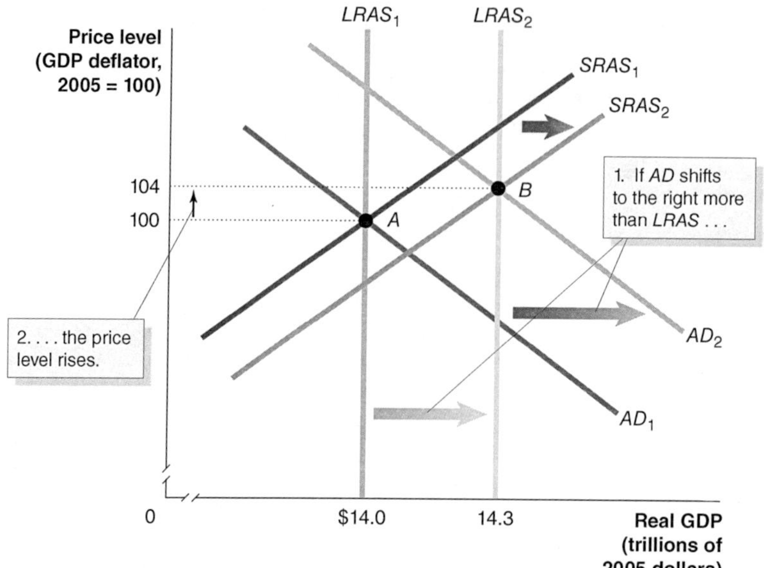

The Recession of 2007–2009

We can use the dynamic aggregate demand and aggregate supply model to analyze the recession of 2007–2009. The recession began in December 2007, with the end of the economic expansion that had begun in November 2001. Several factors combined to bring on the recession:

- ***The end of the housing bubble.*** The figure in the *Making the Connection* on page 178 shows that spending on residential construction increased rapidly from 2002 to 2005, before declining more than 60 percent between the end of 2005 and the beginning of 2010. The increase in spending on housing was partly the result of actions the Federal Reserve had taken to lower interest rates during and after the recession of 2001. As interest rates on mortgage loans declined, more consumers began to buy new homes. But by 2005, it was clear that a speculative bubble was partly responsible for the rapidly rising prices of both newly built and existing homes. A bubble occurs when people become less concerned with the underlying value of an asset—either a physical asset, such as a house, or a financial asset, such as a stock—and focus instead on expectations of the price of the asset increasing. In some areas of the country, such as California, Arizona, and Florida, many homes were purchased by investors who intended to resell them for higher prices than they paid for them and did not intend to live in them. Some popular television programs explored ways that people could "flip" houses by buying and quickly reselling them. Speculative bubbles eventually end, and the housing bubble started to deflate in 2006. Both new home sales and housing prices began to decline. The growth of aggregate demand slowed as spending on residential construction—a component of investment spending—fell. We will discuss the housing bubble further in Chapter 11.
- ***The financial crisis.*** Problems in the housing market were bad news for workers and firms involved with residential construction. In addition, falling housing prices led to an increased number of borrowers defaulting on their mortgage loans. These defaults caused banks and some other financial institutions to suffer heavy losses. Beginning in the spring of 2008, the U.S. Department of the Treasury and the Federal Reserve intervened to save several large financial institutions from bankruptcy. We will look at the details of the financial crisis in Chapters 10 and 11. For now we can note that the financial crisis led to a "credit crunch" that made it difficult for many households and firms to obtain the loans they needed to finance their spending. This drying up of credit contributed to declines in consumption spending and investment spending.
- ***The rapid increase in oil prices during 2008.*** Oil prices, which had been as low as \$34 per barrel in 2004, had risen to \$140 per barrel by mid-2008. The increase in the

price of oil appeared to be caused by increased demand in rapidly growing economies, particularly India and China, and by the difficulty in developing new supplies of oil in the short run. With the deepening of the recession, worldwide demand for oil declined, and oil prices fell to about $40 per barrel in early 2009. As we have seen in this chapter, rising oil prices can result in a *supply shock* that causes the short-run aggregate supply curve to shift to the left. Although rising oil prices contributed to the severity of the recession, they had less impact than some economists had predicted. The U.S. economy appears to have become less vulnerable to increases in oil prices. Increases in the price of oil during the 1970s and early 1980s led many firms to switch to less-oil-dependent production processes. For example, FedEx and other firms used more fuel-efficient jets and trucks. As a result, the U.S. economy was consuming almost 60 percent less oil per dollar of GDP than it had in the mid-1970s. During 2008, oil price increases did not shift the short-run aggregate supply curve as far to the left as similar increases had 30 years earlier.

Figure 8.10 illustrates the beginning of the recession by showing the economy's short-run macroeconomic equilibrium in 2007 and 2008. In the figure, short-run equilibrium for 2007 occurs where AD_{2007} intersects $SRAS_{2007}$ at real GDP of $13.21 trillion and a price level of 106.2. Real GDP in 2007 was slightly above potential real GDP of $13.20 trillion, shown by $LRAS_{2007}$. During 2008, aggregate demand shifted to the right, from AD_{2007} to AD_{2008}. Aggregate demand increased by less than potential GDP because of the negative effects of the bursting of the housing bubble and the financial crisis on consumption spending and investment spending. The supply shock from higher oil prices caused short-run aggregate supply to shift to the left, from $SRAS_{2007}$ to $SRAS_{2008}$. Short-run equilibrium for 2008 occurred at real GDP of $13.16 trillion and a price level of 108.6. A large gap opened between short-run equilibrium real GDP and potential GDP. Not surprisingly, unemployment rose from 4.6 percent in 2007 to 5.8 percent in 2008. The price level increased only from 106.2 to 108.6, so the inflation rate was a low 2.3 percent.

The recession persisted into 2009, as potential real GDP increased to $13.78 trillion, while real GDP fell to $12.70 trillion. This increased gap between real GDP and potential GDP caused the unemployment rate to soar to 9.3 percent—the highest unemployment rate since the recession of 1981–1982 and the second highest since the Great Depression of the 1930s. Although the recession ended in June 2009, real GDP grew only slowly during 2010 and 2011, leaving the unemployment rate above 9 percent.

The severity of the recession of 2007–2009 resulted in some of the most dramatic changes in government economic policy since the Great Depression. We will explore these new policies in Chapters 9 and 11.

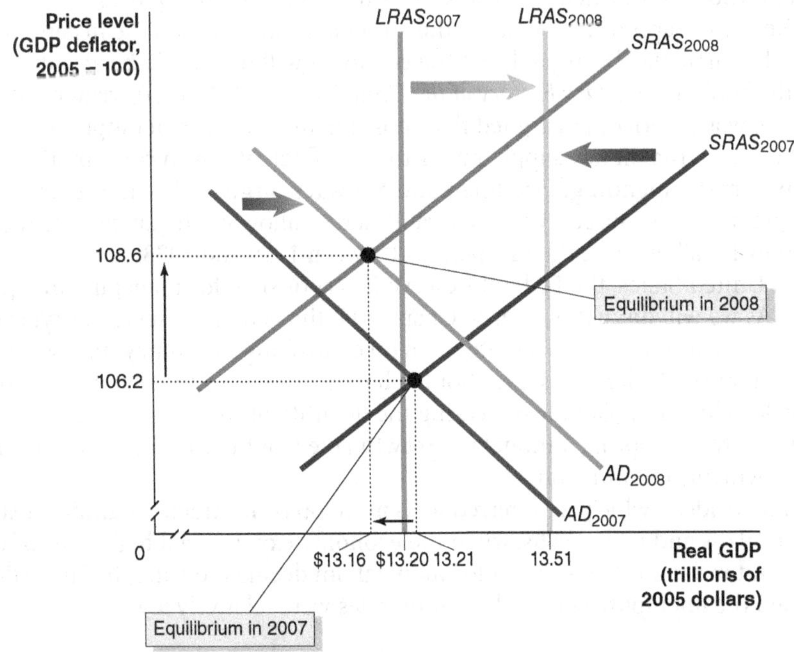

Figure 8.10

The Beginning of the Recession of 2007–2009

Between 2007 and 2008, the *AD* curve shifted to the right, but not by nearly enough to offset the shift to the right of the *LRAS* curve, which represented the increase in potential real GDP from $13.20 trillion to $13.51 trillion. Because of a sharp increase in oil prices, short-run aggregate supply shifted to the left, from $SRAS_{2007}$ to $SRAS_{2008}$. Real GDP decreased from $13.21 trillion in 2007 to $13.16 trillion in 2008, which was far below the potential real GDP, shown by $LRAS_{2008}$. As a result, the unemployment rate rose from 4.6 percent in 2007 to 5.8 percent in 2008. Because the increase in aggregate demand was small, the price level increased only from 106.2 in 2007 to 108.6 in 2008, so the inflation rate for 2008 was only 2.3 percent.

Appendix

LEARNING OBJECTIVE

Understand macroeconomic schools of thought.

Macro economic Schools of Thought

Macroeconomics became a separate field of economics in 1936, with the publication of John Maynard Keynes's book *The General Theory of Employment, Interest, and Money.* Keynes, an economist at the University of Cambridge in England, was attempting to explain the devastating Great Depression of the 1930s. Real GDP in the United States declined more than 25 percent between 1929 and 1933 and did not return to its potential level until the United States entered World War II in 1941. The unemployment rate soared to 25 percent by 1933 and did not return to its 1929 level until 1942. Keynes developed a version of the aggregate demand and aggregate supply model to explain these facts. The widespread acceptance during the 1930s and 1940s of Keynes's model became known as the **Keynesian revolution.**

Keynesian revolution The name given to the widespread acceptance during the 1930s and 1940s of John Maynard Keynes's macroeconomic model.

In fact, using the aggregate demand and aggregate supply model remains the most widely accepted approach to analyzing macroeconomic issues. Because the model has been modified significantly from Keynes's day, many economists who use the model today refer to themselves as *new Keynesians.* The new Keynesians emphasize the importance of the stickiness of wages and prices in explaining fluctuations in real GDP. A significant number of economists, however, dispute whether using the aggregate demand and aggregate supply model, as we have discussed it in this chapter, is the best way to analyze macroeconomic issues. These alternative *schools of thought* use models that differ significantly from the standard aggregate demand and aggregate supply model. We can briefly consider each of the three major alternative models:

1. The monetarist model
2. The new classical model
3. The real business cycle model

The Monetarist Model

The monetarist model—also known as the neo-Quantity Theory of Money model—was developed beginning in the 1940s by Milton Friedman, an economist at the University of Chicago who was awarded the Nobel Prize in Economics in 1976. Friedman argued that the Keynesian approach overstates the amount of macroeconomic instability in the economy. In particular, he argued that the economy will ordinarily be at potential real GDP. In the book *A Monetary History of the United States: 1867–1960,* written with Anna Jacobson Schwartz, Friedman argued that most fluctuations in real output were caused by fluctuations in the money supply rather than by fluctuations in consumption spending or investment spending. Friedman and Schwartz argued that the severity of the Great Depression was caused by the Federal Reserve's allowing the quantity of money in the economy to fall by more than 25 percent between 1929 and 1933.

In the United States, the Federal Reserve is responsible for managing the quantity of money. As we will discuss further in Chapter 11, the Federal Reserve has typically focused more on controlling interest rates than on controlling the money supply. Friedman has argued that the Federal Reserve should change its practices and adopt a **monetary growth rule**, which is a plan for increasing the quantity of money at a fixed rate. Friedman believed that adopting a monetary growth rule would reduce fluctuations in real GDP, employment, and inflation.

Monetary growth rule A plan for increasing the quantity of money at a fixed rate that does not respond to changes in economic conditions.

Monetarism The macroeconomic theories of Milton Friedman and his followers, particularly the idea that the quantity of money should be increased at a constant rate.

Friedman's ideas, which are referred to as **monetarism**, attracted significant support during the 1970s and early 1980s, when the economy experienced high rates of unemployment and inflation. The support for monetarism declined during the late 1980s and 1990s, when the unemployment and inflation rates were relatively low.

The New Classical Model

The new classical model was developed in the mid-1970s by a group of economists including Nobel Laureate Robert Lucas of the University of Chicago, Nobel Laureate Thomas Sargent of New York University, and Robert Barro of Harvard University. Some of the views held by the new classical macroeconomists are similar to those held by economists before the Great Depression. Keynes referred to the economists before the Great Depression as "classical economists." Like the classical economists, the new classical macroeconomists believe that the economy normally will be at potential real GDP. They also believe that wages and prices adjust quickly to changes in demand and supply. Put another way, they believe the stickiness in wages and prices emphasized by the new Keynesians is unimportant.

Lucas argues that workers and firms have *rational expectations*, meaning that they form their expectations of the future values of economic variables, such as the inflation rate, by making use of all available information, including information on variables—such as changes in the quantity of money—that might affect aggregate demand. If the actual inflation rate is lower than the expected inflation rate, the actual real wage will be higher than the expected real wage. These higher real wages will lead to a recession because they will cause firms to hire fewer workers and cut back on production. As workers and firms adjust their expectations to the lower inflation rate, the real wage will decline, and employment and production will expand, bringing the economy out of recession. The ideas of Lucas and his followers are referred to as the **new classical macroeconomics.** Supporters of the new classical model agree with supporters of the monetarist model that the Federal Reserve should adopt a monetary growth rule. They argue that a monetary growth rule will make it easier for workers and firms to accurately forecast the price level, thereby reducing fluctuations in real GDP.

New classical macroeconomics The macroeconomic theories of Robert Lucas and others, particularly the idea that workers and firms have rational expectations.

The Real Business Cycle Model

Beginning in the 1980s, some economists, including Nobel Laureates Finn Kydland of Carnegie Mellon University and Edward Prescott of Arizona State University, began to argue that Lucas was correct in assuming that workers and firms formed their expectations rationally and that wages and prices adjust quickly to supply and demand but was wrong about the source of fluctuations in real GDP. They argue that fluctuations in real GDP are caused by temporary shocks to productivity. These shocks can be negative, such as a decline in the availability of oil or other raw materials, or positive, such as technological change that makes it possible to produce more output with the same quantity of inputs.

According to this school of thought, shifts in the aggregate demand curve have no impact on real GDP because the short-run aggregate supply curve is vertical. Other schools of thought believe that the short-run aggregate supply curve is upward sloping and that only the *long-run* aggregate supply curve is vertical. Fluctuations in real GDP occur when a negative productivity shock causes the short-run aggregate supply curve to shift to the left—reducing real GDP—or a positive productivity shock causes the short-run aggregate supply curve to shift to the right—increasing real GDP. Because this model focuses on "real" factors—productivity shocks—rather than changes in the quantity of money to explain fluctuations in real GDP, it is known as the **real business cycle model.**

Real business cycle model A macroeconomic model that focuses on real, rather than monetary, causes of the business cycle.

Making the Connection

Karl Marx: Capitalism's Severest Critic

The schools of macroeconomic thought we have discussed in this appendix are considered part of mainstream economic theory because of their acceptance of the market system as the best means of raising living standards in the long run. One quite influential critic of mainstream economic theory was Karl Marx. Marx was born in Trier, Germany, in 1818. After graduating from the University of Berlin in 1841, he began a career as a political journalist and agitator. His political activities caused him to be expelled first from Germany and then from France and Belgium. In 1849, he moved to London, where he spent the remainder of his life.

CHAPTER 9

Fiscal Policy

Chapter Outline and Learning Objectives

Does Government Spending Create Jobs?

Tutor-Saliba was founded in Southern California in 1949 and is today one of the largest heavy construction firms in the United States. In the fall of 2011, workers employed by Tutor-Saliba were hard at work on the Caldecott Tunnel in Northern California. The project would expand the tunnel through the Berkeley Hills from six lanes to eight in order to ease congestion between the cities of Orinda and Oakland. Part of the funding for the project came from the American Recovery and Reinvestment Act (ARRA, often referred to as the "stimulus bill"), which President Barack Obama and Congress had enacted in early 2009, in an attempt to increase aggregate demand during the recession of 2007–2009. Without this funding, the state of California would not have gone ahead with the project. The ARRA is an example of *discretionary fiscal policy* aimed at increasing real GDP and employment. To carry out the Caldecott Tunnel project, Tutor-Saliba hired an additional 106 workers. A spokesperson for the state agency in charge of the project argued that the increased employment effects from the project were even larger: "There is a ripple effect. There's truckers and equipment builders, and the deli in Orinda has never been as busy before."

The project to expand the Caldecott Tunnel is an example of increased government spending leading to increased employment. Or is it? A majority of economists agree that increased government spending leads to increased employment. But some economists argue that government spending shifts employment from one group of workers to another but doesn't increase *total* employment. Casey Mulligan, an economist at the University of Chicago, compares the effect of increases in government spending on projects like the Caldecott Tunnel to the effect of the New York Yankees building a new Yankee Stadium on the north side of East 161st Street in New York, across the street from the old Yankee Stadium on the south side of East 161st Street: "Not surprisingly, . . . spending by consumers, news organizations and entertainment businesses, among others, on the north side of East 161st Street was a lot more than it had been in years past. . . . [But] much of what happened north of East 161st Street was just a displacement of activity from the south side, rather than a creation of new activity."

The debate over the effects of government spending were particularly important during 2011 because the economy was recovering slowly from the 2007–2009 recession, with the unemployment rate remaining above 9 percent. In this chapter, we will examine discretionary fiscal policy and the debate over its effects. **AN INSIDE LOOK AT POLICY** on **page 220** discusses whether government-sponsored infrastructure spending is an effective means to create jobs in a slow-growing U.S. economy.

Based on Zusha Elinson, "Caldecott Tunnel Edges Forward, Tribute to Stimulus Bill," *New York Times*, September 10, 2011; and Casey B. Mulligan, "Local and National Stimulus," *New York Times*, August 24, 2011.

Economics in Your Life

What Would You Do with $500?

Suppose that the federal government announces that it will immediately mail you, and everyone else in the economy, a $500 tax rebate. In addition, you expect that in future years, your taxes will also be $500 less than they would otherwise have been. How will you respond to this increase in your disposable income? What effect will this tax rebate likely have on equilibrium real GDP in the short run? As you read the chapter, see if you can answer these questions. You can check your answers against those we provide on **page 219** at the end of this chapter.

In Chapter 11, we discussed how the Federal Reserve uses monetary policy to pursue macroeconomic policy goals, including price stability and high employment. In this chapter, we will explore how the government uses *fiscal policy*, which involves changes in taxes and government purchases, to achieve similar policy goals. As we have seen, in the short run, the price level and the levels of real GDP and total employment in the economy depend on aggregate demand and short-run aggregate supply. The government can affect the levels of both aggregate demand and aggregate supply through fiscal policy. We will explore how Congress and the president decide which fiscal policy actions to take to achieve their goals. We will also discuss the debates among economists and policymakers over the effectiveness of fiscal policy.

9.1 LEARNING OBJECTIVE

Define fiscal policy.

What Is Fiscal Policy?

Since the end of World War II, the federal government has been committed under the Employment Act of 1946 to intervening in the economy "to promote maximum employment, production, and purchasing power." As we saw in Chapter 11, the Federal Reserve closely monitors the economy, and the Federal Open Market Committee meets eight times per year to decide whether to change monetary policy. Less frequently, Congress and the president also make changes in taxes and government purchases to achieve macroeconomic policy objectives, such as high employment, price stability, and high rates of economic growth. Changes in federal taxes and spending that are intended to achieve macroeconomic policy objectives are called **fiscal policy**.

Fiscal policy Changes in federal taxes and purchases that are intended to achieve macroeconomic policy objectives.

What Fiscal Policy Is and What It Isn't

In the United States, federal, state, and local governments all have responsibility for taxing and spending. Economists typically use the term *fiscal policy* to refer only to the actions of the federal government. State and local governments sometimes change their taxing and spending policies to aid their local economies, but these are not fiscal policy actions because they are not intended to affect the national economy. The federal government makes many decisions about taxes and spending, but not all of these decisions are fiscal policy actions because they are not intended to achieve macroeconomic policy goals. For example, a decision to cut the taxes of people who buy hybrid cars is an environmental policy action, not a fiscal policy action. Similarly, the spending increases to fund the war on terrorism and the wars in Iraq and Afghanistan were part of defense and homeland security policy, not fiscal policy.

Automatic Stabilizers versus Discretionary Fiscal Policy

There is an important distinction between *automatic stabilizers* and *discretionary fiscal policy*. Some types of government spending and taxes, which automatically increase and decrease along with the business cycle, are referred to as **automatic stabilizers**. The word *automatic* in this case refers to the fact that changes in these types of spending and taxes happen without actions by the government. For example, when the economy is expanding and employment is increasing, government spending on unemployment insurance payments to workers who have lost their jobs will automatically decrease. During a recession, as employment declines, this type of spending will automatically increase. Similarly, when the economy is expanding and incomes are rising, the amount the government collects in taxes will increase as people pay additional taxes on their higher incomes. When the economy is in recession, the amount the government collects in taxes will fall.

Automatic stabilizers Government spending and taxes that automatically increase or decrease along with the business cycle.

With discretionary fiscal policy, the government takes actions to change spending or taxes. The tax cuts Congress passed in 2008, 2009, and 2010 are examples of discretionary fiscal policy actions.

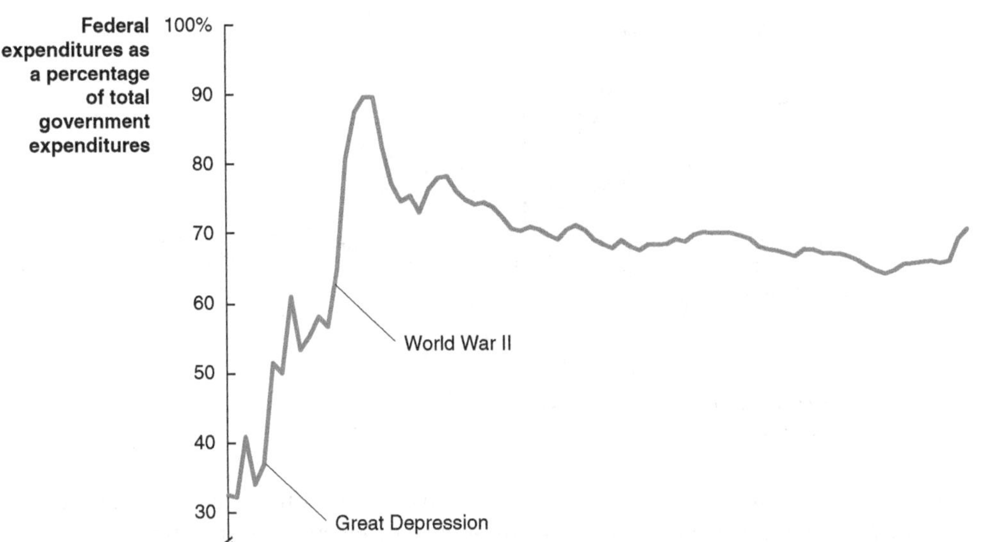

Figure 9.1

The Federal Government's Share of Total Government Expenditures, 1929–2010

Until the Great Depression of the 1930s, the majority of government spending in the United States occurred at the state and local levels. Since World War II, the federal government's share of total government expenditures has been between two-thirds and three-quarters.
Data from U.S. Bureau of Economic Analysis.

An Overview of Government Spending and Taxes

To provide a context for understanding fiscal policy, it is important to understand the big picture of government taxing and spending. Before the Great Depression of the 1930s, the majority of government spending took place at the state and local levels. As Figure 9.1 shows, the size of the federal government expanded significantly during the crisis of the Great Depression. Since World War II, the federal government's share of total government expenditures has been between two-thirds and three-quarters.

Economists often measure government spending relative to the size of the economy by calculating government spending as a percentage of GDP. Remember that there is a difference between federal government *purchases* and federal government *expenditures*. When the federal government purchases an aircraft carrier or the services of an FBI agent, it receives a good or service in return. Federal government expenditures include purchases plus all other federal government spending. As Figure 9.2 shows, federal government *purchases* as a percentage of GDP have actually been falling since the end of the Korean War in the early 1950s. Total federal *expenditures* as a percentage of GDP rose from 1950 to the early 1990s and then fell from 1992 to 2001, before rising again. The decline in expenditures between 1992 and 2001 was partly the result of the end of the Cold War between the Soviet Union and the United States, which allowed for a substantial reduction in defense spending. Real federal government spending on national defense declined by almost 25 percent between 1990 and 1998, before rising by more

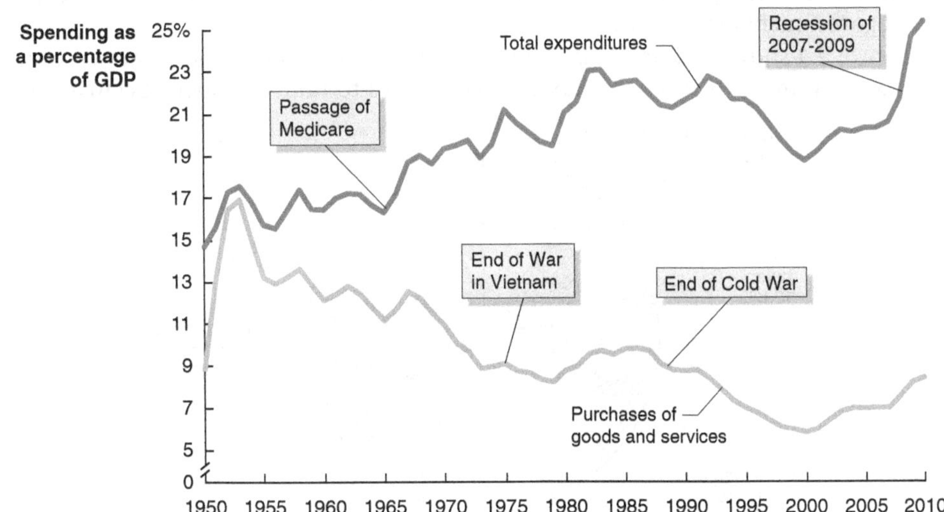

Figure 9.2

Federal Purchases and Federal Expenditures as a Percentage of GDP, 1950–2010

As a fraction of GDP, the federal government's *purchases* of goods and services have been declining since the Korean War in the early 1950s. Total *expenditures* by the federal government—including transfer payments—as a fraction of GDP slowly rose from 1950 through the early 1990s and fell from 1992 to 2001, before rising again. The recession of 2007–2009 and the slow recovery that followed led to a surge in federal government expenditures causing them to rise to their highest level as a percentage of GDP since World War II.
Data from U.S. Bureau of Economic Analysis.

Figure 9.3

Federal Government Expenditures, 2010

Federal government *purchases* can be divided into defense spending—which makes up 22.1 percent of the federal budget—and spending on everything else the federal government does—from paying the salaries of FBI agents, to operating the national parks, to supporting scientific research—which makes up 9.4 percent of the budget. In addition to purchases, there are three other categories of federal government *expenditures*: interest on the national debt, grants to state and local governments, and transfer payments. Transfer payments rose from about 25 percent of federal government expenditures in the 1960s to nearly 46.6 percent in 2010.
Data from U.S. Bureau of Economic Analysis.

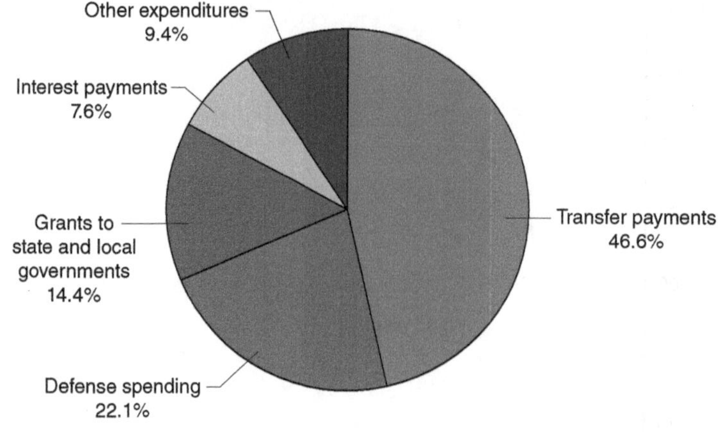

than 60 percent between 1998 and 2010 in response to the war on terrorism and the wars in Iraq and Afghanistan. The recession of 2007–2009 and the slow recovery that followed led to a surge in federal government expenditures causing them to rise to their highest level as a percentage of GDP since World War II.

In addition to purchases, there are three other categories of federal government expenditures: *interest on the national debt*, *grants to state and local governments*, and *transfer payments*. Interest on the national debt represents payments to holders of the bonds the federal government has issued to borrow money. Grants to state and local governments are payments made by the federal government to support government activity at the state and local levels. For example, to help reduce crime, Congress implemented a program of grants to local governments to hire more police officers. The largest and fastest-growing category of federal expenditures is transfer payments. Some of these programs, such as Social Security and unemployment insurance, began in the 1930s. Others, such as Medicare, which finances health care for the elderly, or the food stamps and Temporary Assistance for Needy Families programs, which are intended to aid the poor, began in the 1960s or later.

Figure 9.3 shows that in 2010, transfer payments were 46.6 percent of federal government expenditures. In the 1960s, transfer payments were only about 25 percent of federal government expenditures. As the U.S. population ages and medical costs continue to increase, federal government spending on the Social Security and Medicare programs will continue to increase, causing transfer payments to consume an increasing share of federal expenditures. Figure 9.3 shows that spending on most of the federal government's day-to-day activities—including running federal agencies such as the Environmental Protection Agency, the Federal Bureau of Investigation, the National Park Service, and the Immigration and Naturalization Service—makes up only 9.4 percent of federal government expenditures.

Figure 9.4 shows that in 2010, the federal government raised 36.9 percent of its revenue from individual income taxes. Payroll taxes to fund the Social Security and

Figure 9.4

Federal Government Revenue, 2010

In 2010, individual income taxes raised 36.9 percent of the federal government's revenues. Corporate income taxes raised 13.6 percent of revenue. Payroll taxes to fund the Social Security and Medicare programs rose from less than 10 percent of federal government revenues in 1950 to 40.0 percent in 2010. The remaining 9.6 percent of revenues were raised from excise taxes, tariffs on imports, and other sources.
Data from U.S. Bureau of Economic Analysis.

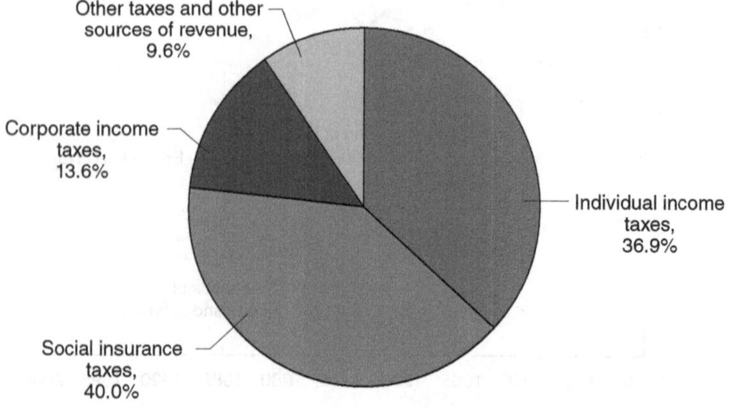

Medicare programs raised 40 percent of federal revenues. The tax on corporate profits raised 13.6 percent of federal revenues. The remaining 9.6 percent of federal revenues were raised from excise taxes on certain products, such as cigarettes and gasoline, from tariffs on goods imported from other countries, and from other sources, such as payments by companies that cut timber on federal lands.

Making the Connection

Is Spending on Social Security and Medicare a Fiscal Time Bomb?

Social Security, established in 1935 to provide payments to retired workers, began as a "pay-as-you-go" system, meaning that payments to current retirees were paid from taxes collected from current workers. In the early years of the program, many workers were paying into the system, and there were relatively few retirees. For example, in 1940, more than 35 million workers were paying into the system, and only 222,000 people were receiving benefits—a ratio of more than 150 workers to each beneficiary. In those early years, most retirees received far more in benefits than they had paid in taxes. For example, the first beneficiary was a legal secretary named Ida May Fuller. She worked for three years while the program was in place and paid total taxes of only $24.75. During her retirement, she collected $22,888.92 in benefits.

Will the federal government be able to keep the promises made by the Social Security and Medicare programs?

The Social Security and Medicare programs have been very successful in reducing poverty among elderly Americans, but in recent years, the ability of the federal government to finance current promises has been called into doubt. After World War II, the United States experienced a "baby boom," as birthrates rose and remained high through the early 1960s. Falling birthrates after 1965 have meant long-run problems for the Social Security system, as the number of workers per retiree has continually declined. Currently, there are only about three workers per retiree, and that ratio is expected to decline to two workers per retiree by 2035. Congress has attempted to deal with this problem by raising the age to receive full benefits from 65 to 67 and by increasing payroll taxes. In 1940, the combined payroll tax paid by workers and firms was 2 percent; in 2011, it was 15.3 percent (although a tax cut temporarily reduced it to 13.3 percent for that year).

Under the Medicare program, which was established in 1965, the federal government provides health care coverage to people age 65 and over. The long-term financial situation for Medicare is an even greater cause for concern than is Social Security. As Americans live longer and as new—and expensive—medical procedures are developed, the projected expenditures under the Medicare program will eventually far outstrip projected tax revenues. The federal government also faces increasing expenditures under the Medicaid program, which is administered by state governments and provides health care coverage to low-income people. In 2010, federal spending on Social Security, Medicare, and Medicaid equaled 10.4 percent of GDP. Spending on these three programs was less than 3 percent of GDP in 1962. The Congressional Budget Office (CBO) indicates that spending on these three programs will rise to 15.2 percent of GDP in 2030, 18.9 percent by 2050, and 25.8 percent by 2085. The graph on the next page illustrates these forecasts. Over the past 40 years, the federal government has spent an average of about 18.5 percent of GDP on *all programs* combined—from buying aircraft carriers to paying the salaries of FBI agents. So, if current trends continue, the federal government will eventually be spending, as a fraction of GDP, more on these three programs than it currently does on all programs combined. Over the coming decades, the gap between the benefits projected to be paid under the Social Security and Medicare programs and projected tax revenues is a staggering $72 *trillion*, or nearly five times the value of GDP in 2011. If current projections are accurate, policymakers are faced with the choice of significantly restraining spending on these programs, greatly increasing taxes on households and firms, or implementing some combination of spending restraints and tax increases. The alternatives will all clearly involve considerable pain. A report from the Congressional Budget Office concluded, "Even if taxation reached levels that were unprecedented in the United States, current spending policies could become financially unsustainable."

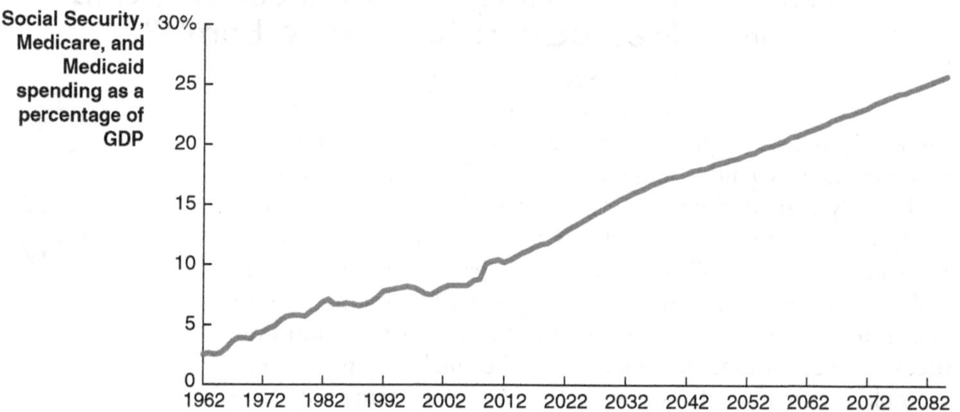

Note: The graph gives the Congressional Budget Office's "alternative fiscal scenario" of future spending.

A lively political debate has taken place over the future of the Social Security and Medicare programs. Some policymakers have proposed increasing taxes to fund future benefit payments. The tax increases needed, however, could be as much as 50 percent higher than current rates, and tax increases of that magnitude could discourage work effort, entrepreneurship, and investment, thereby slowing economic growth. There have also been proposals to slow the rate of growth of future benefits, while guaranteeing benefits to current recipients. While this strategy would avoid the need to raise taxes significantly, it would also require younger workers to save more for their retirement. Some economists and policymakers have argued for slower benefit growth for higher-income workers while leaving future benefits unchanged for lower-income workers. Whatever changes are ultimately made in the Medicare and Social Security programs, this policy debate is one of the most important for young people.

Based on Congressional Budget Office, The Long-Term Budget Outlook, June 2011; Congressional Budget Office, *Baseline Projections of Mandatory Outlays,* January 2009; 112th Congress, 1st Session, "The 2011 Annual Report of the Board of Trustees of the Federal Old-Age and Survivors Insurance and Disability Insurance Trust Funds," House Document 112–23, May 13, 2011; and the Social Security Administration Web site (www.ssa.gov).

9.2 LEARNING OBJECTIVE

Explain how fiscal policy affects aggregate demand and how the government can use fiscal policy to stabilize the economy.

The Effects of Fiscal Policy on Real GDP and the Price Level

The federal government uses macroeconomic policies to offset the effects of the business cycle on the economy. We saw in Chapter 11 that the Federal Reserve carries out monetary policy through changes in the money supply and interest rates. Congress and the president carry out fiscal policy through changes in government purchases and taxes. Because changes in government purchases and taxes lead to changes in aggregate demand, they can affect the level of real GDP, employment, and the price level. When the economy is in a recession, *increases* in government purchases or *decreases* in taxes will increase aggregate demand. As we saw in Chapter 8, the inflation rate may increase when real GDP is beyond potential GDP. Decreasing government purchases or raising taxes can slow the growth of aggregate demand and reduce the inflation rate.

Expansionary and Contractionary Fiscal Policy

Expansionary fiscal policy involves increasing government purchases or decreasing taxes. An increase in government purchases will increase aggregate demand directly because government purchases are a component of aggregate demand. A cut in taxes has an indirect effect on aggregate demand. The income that households have available to spend after they have paid their taxes is called *disposable income*. Cutting the individual income tax will increase household disposable income and consumption spending. Cutting taxes on business income can increase aggregate demand by increasing business investment.

Figure 9.5 shows the results of an expansionary fiscal policy, using the basic version of the aggregate demand and aggregate supply model. In this model, there is no economic growth, so the long-run aggregate supply (*LRAS*) curve does not shift. Notice that this figure is very similar to Figure 11.7 on page 269, which shows the effects of an expansionary monetary policy. The goal of both expansionary monetary policy and expansionary fiscal policy is to increase aggregate demand relative to what it would have been without the policy.

In panel (a) of Figure 9.5, we assume that the economy is in short-run equilibrium at point *A*, where the aggregate demand (AD_1) curve intersects the short-run aggregate supply (*SRAS*) curve. Real GDP is below potential real GDP, so the economy is in recession, with some firms operating below normal capacity and some workers having been laid off. To bring real GDP back to potential GDP, Congress and the president increase government purchases or cut taxes, which will shift the aggregate demand curve to the right, from AD_1 to AD_2. Real GDP increases from $14.2 trillion to potential GDP of $14.4 trillion, and the price level rises from 98 to 100 (point *B*). The policy has successfully returned real GDP to its potential level. Rising production will lead to increasing employment, reducing the unemployment rate.

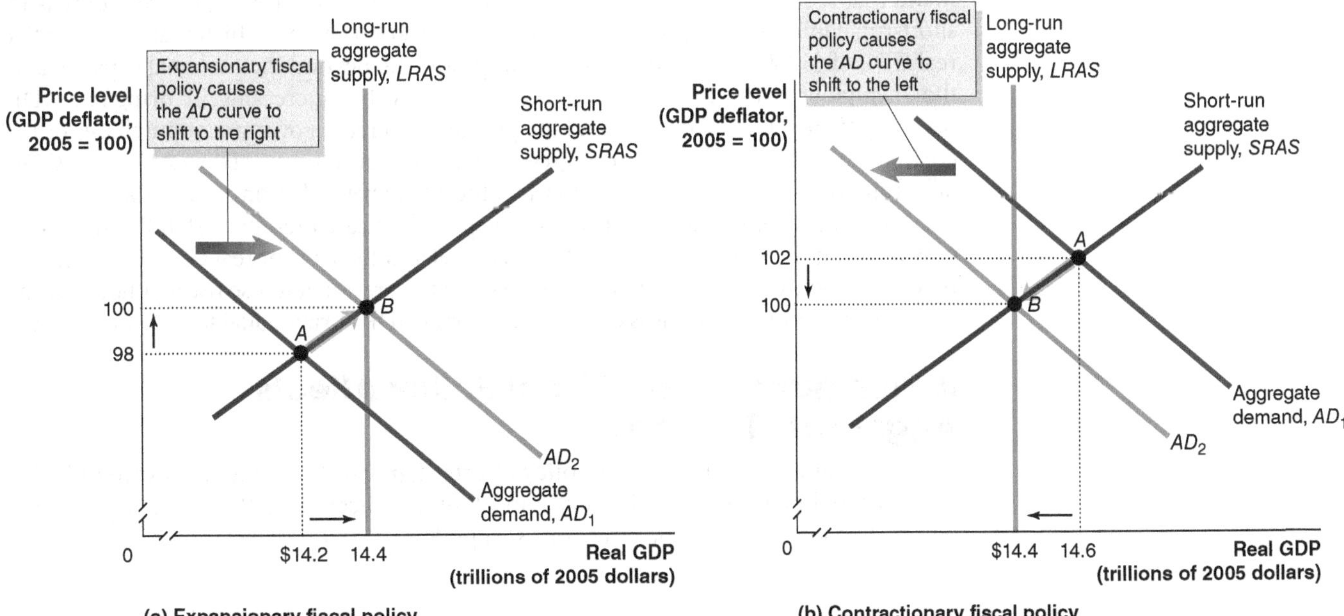

Figure 9.5 Fiscal Policy

In panel (a), the economy begins in recession at point *A*, with real GDP of $14.2 trillion and a price level of 98. An expansionary fiscal policy will cause aggregate demand to shift to the right, from AD_1 to AD_2, increasing real GDP from $14.2 trillion to $14.4 trillion and the price level from 98 to 100 (point *B*). In panel (b), the economy begins at point *A*, with real GDP at $14.6 trillion and the price level at 102. Because real GDP is greater than potential GDP, the economy will experience rising wages and prices. A contractionary fiscal policy will cause aggregate demand to shift to the left, from AD_1 to AD_2, decreasing real GDP from $14.6 trillion to $14.4 trillion and the price level from 102 to 100 (point *B*).

Don't Let This Happen to You

Don't Confuse Fiscal Policy and Monetary Policy

If you keep in mind the definitions of *money*, *income*, and *spending*, the difference between monetary policy and fiscal policy will be clearer. Students often make these two related mistakes: (1) They think of monetary policy as the Fed fighting recessions by increasing the money supply so people will have more money to spend; and (2) they think of fiscal policy as Congress and the president fighting recessions by spending more money. In this view, the only difference between fiscal policy and monetary policy is the source of the money.

To understand what's wrong with the descriptions of fiscal policy and monetary policy just given, first remember that the problem during a recession is not that there is too little *money*—currency plus checking account deposits—but too little *spending*. There may be too little spending for a number of reasons. For example, households may cut back on their spending on cars and houses because they are pessimistic about the future. Firms may cut back their spending because they have lowered their estimates of the future profitability of new machinery and factories. Or the major trading partners of the United States—such as Japan and Canada—may be suffering from recessions, which cause households and firms in those countries to cut back their spending on U.S. products.

The purpose of expansionary monetary policy is to lower interest rates, which in turn increases aggregate demand. When interest rates fall, households and firms are willing to borrow more to buy cars, houses, and factories. The purpose of expansionary fiscal policy is to increase aggregate demand either by having the government directly increase its own purchases or by cutting taxes to increase household disposable income and, therefore, consumption spending.

Just as increasing or decreasing the money supply does not have a direct effect on government spending or taxes, increasing or decreasing government spending or taxes does not have a direct effect on the money supply. Fiscal policy and monetary policy have the same goals, but they have different effects on the economy.

Contractionary fiscal policy involves decreasing government purchases or increasing taxes. Policymakers use contractionary fiscal policy to reduce increases in aggregate demand that seem likely to lead to inflation. In panel (b) of Figure 9.5, the economy is in short-run equilibrium at point *A*, with real GDP of \$14.6 trillion, which is above potential real GDP of \$14.4 trillion. With some firms producing beyond their normal capacity and the unemployment rate very low, wages and prices will be increasing. To bring real GDP back to potential GDP, Congress and the president decrease government purchases or increase taxes, which will shift the aggregate demand curve from AD_1 to AD_2. Real GDP falls from \$14.6 trillion to \$14.4 trillion, and the price level falls from 102 to 100 (point *B*).

We can conclude that Congress and the president can attempt to stabilize the economy by using fiscal policy to affect the price level and the level of real GDP. Of course, in practice it is extremely difficult for Congress and the president to use fiscal policy to eliminate the effects of the business cycle and keep real GDP always equal to potential GDP.

A Summary of How Fiscal Policy Affects Aggregate Demand

Table 9.1 summarizes how fiscal policy affects aggregate demand. Just as we did with monetary policy, we must add a very important qualification to this summary of fiscal policy: The table isolates the effect of fiscal policy *by holding constant monetary policy*

Table 9.1

Countercyclical Fiscal Policy

Problem	Type of Policy	Actions by Congress and the President	Result
Recession	Expansionary	Increase government spending or cut taxes	Real GDP and the price level rise.
Rising inflation	Contractionary	Decrease government spending or raise taxes	Real GDP and the price level fall.

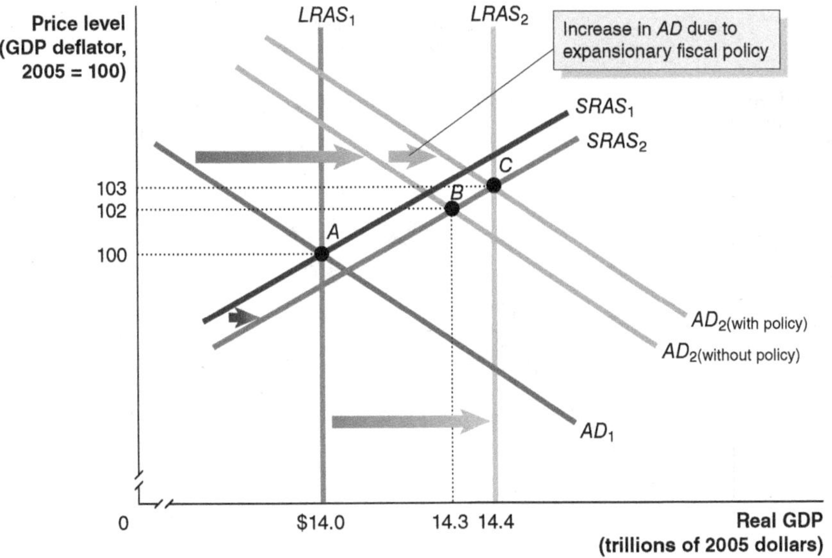

Figure 9.6

An Expansionary Fiscal Policy in the Dynamic Model

The economy begins in equilibrium at point *A*, at potential real GDP of $14.0 trillion and a price level of 100. Without an expansionary policy, aggregate demand will shift from AD_1 to $AD_{2(\text{without policy})}$, which is not enough to keep the economy at potential GDP because long-run aggregate supply has shifted from $LRAS_1$ to $LRAS_2$. The economy will be in short-run equilibrium at point *B*, with real GDP of $14.3 trillion and a price level of 102. Increasing government purchases or cutting taxes will shift aggregate demand to $AD_{2(\text{with policy})}$. The economy will be in equilibrium at point *C*, with real GDP of $14.4 trillion, which is its potential level, and a price level of 103. The price level is higher than it would have been without an expansionary fiscal policy.

and all other factors affecting the variables involved. In other words, we are again invoking the *ceteris paribus* condition we discussed in Chapter 4. This point is important because, for example, a contractionary fiscal policy does not cause the price level to fall. A contractionary fiscal policy causes the price level *to rise by less than it would have without the policy.*

Fiscal Policy in the Dynamic Aggregate Demand and Aggregate Supply Model*

9.3 LEARNING OBJECTIVE

Use the dynamic aggregate demand and aggregate supply model to analyze fiscal policy.

The overview of fiscal policy we just finished contains a key idea: Congress and the president can use fiscal policy to affect aggregate demand, thereby changing the price level and the level of real GDP. The discussion of expansionary and contractionary fiscal policy illustrated by Figure 9.5 on page 195 is simplified, however, because it ignores two important facts about the economy: (1) The economy experiences continuing inflation, with the price level rising every year, and (2) the economy experiences long-run growth, with the *LRAS* curve shifting to the right every year. In Chapter 8, we developed a *dynamic aggregate demand and aggregate supply model* that took these two facts into account. In this section, we use the dynamic model to gain a more complete understanding of fiscal policy.

To briefly review the dynamic model, recall that over time, potential real GDP increases, which we show by the long-run aggregate supply curve shifting to the right. The factors that cause the *LRAS* curve to shift also cause firms to supply more goods and services at any given price level in the short run, which we show by the short-run aggregate supply curve shifting to the right. Finally, during most years, the aggregate demand curve also shifts to the right, indicating that aggregate expenditure is higher at every price level.

Figure 9.6 shows the results of an expansionary fiscal policy using the dynamic aggregate demand and aggregate supply model. Notice that this figure is very similar to Figure 11.9 on page 275, which showed the effects of an expansionary monetary policy. The goal of both expansionary monetary policy and expansionary fiscal policy is to increase aggregate demand relative to what it would have been without the policy.

In the hypothetical situation shown in Figure 9.6, the economy begins in equilibrium at potential real GDP of $14.0 trillion and a price level of 100 (point *A*). In the second year, *LRAS* increases to $14.4 trillion, but *AD* increases only to $AD_{2(\text{without policy})}$,

*This section may be omitted without loss of continuity.

Figure 9.7

A Contractionary Fiscal Policy in the Dynamic Model

The economy begins in equilibrium at point A, with real GDP of \$14.0 trillion and a price level of 100. Without a contractionary policy, aggregate demand will shift from AD_1 to $AD_{2(\text{without policy})}$, which results in a short-run equilibrium beyond potential GDP at point B, with real GDP of \$14.5 trillion and a price level of 105. Decreasing government purchases or increasing taxes can shift aggregate demand to $AD_{2(\text{with policy})}$. The economy will be in equilibrium at point C, with real GDP of \$14.4 trillion, which is its potential level, and a price level of 103. The inflation rate will be 3 percent, as opposed to the 5 percent it would have been without the contractionary fiscal policy.

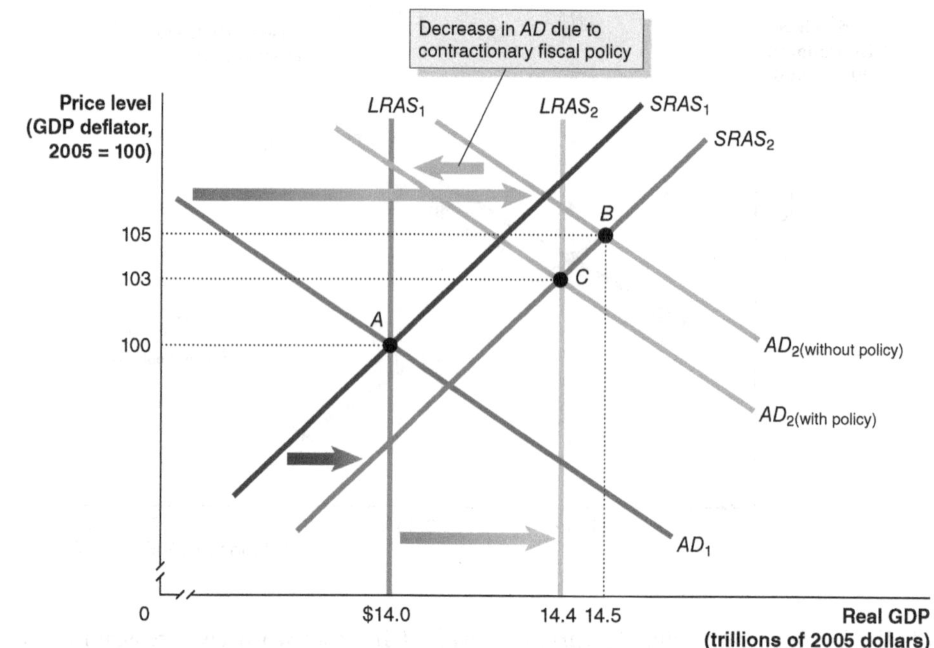

which is not enough to keep the economy in macroeconomic equilibrium at potential GDP. Let's assume that the Fed does not react to the situation with an expansionary monetary policy. In that case, without an expansionary fiscal policy of spending increases or tax reductions, the short-run equilibrium will occur at \$14.3 trillion (point B). The \$100 billion gap between this level of real GDP and the potential level means that some firms are operating at less than their full capacity. Incomes and profits will be falling, firms will begin to lay off workers, and the unemployment rate will rise.

Increasing government purchases or cutting taxes can shift aggregate demand to $AD_{2(\text{with policy})}$. The economy will be in equilibrium at point C, with real GDP of \$14.4 trillion, which is its potential level, and a price level of 103. The price level is higher than it would have been without an expansionary fiscal policy.

Contractionary fiscal policy involves decreasing government purchases or increasing taxes. Policymakers use contractionary fiscal policy to reduce increases in aggregate demand that seem likely to lead to inflation. In Figure 9.7, the economy again begins at potential real GDP of \$14.0 trillion and a price level of 100 (point A). Once again, *LRAS* increases to \$14.4 trillion in the second year. In this scenario, the shift in aggregate demand to $AD_{2(\text{without policy})}$ results in a short-run macroeconomic equilibrium beyond potential GDP (point B). If we assume that the Fed does not respond to the situation with a contractionary monetary policy, the economy will experience a rising inflation rate. Decreasing government purchases or increasing taxes can keep real GDP from moving beyond its potential level. The result, shown in Figure 9.7, is that in the new equilibrium at point C, the inflation rate is 3 percent rather than 5 percent.

9.4 LEARNING OBJECTIVE

Explain how the government purchases and tax multipliers work.

The Government Purchases and Tax Multipliers

We saw in the chapter opener that in 2009, Congress and the president authorized spending to widen the Caldecott Tunnel in Northern California, in an attempt to increase aggregate demand during the recession of 2007–2009. Suppose that Congress and the president decide to spend \$100 billion on expanding the Caldecott Tunnel and similar projects. (The total increase in federal spending under the ARRA was actually about \$500 billion, including the \$180 million spent to widen the Caldecott Tunnel.) How much will equilibrium real GDP increase as a result of this increase in government purchases? We might expect that the answer is greater than $100 billion because the initial increase in aggregate demand should lead to additional increases in income and spending. For example, to expand the Caldecott Tunnel, the California state government hired Tutor-Saliba, a private construction firm. Tutor-Saliba and the subcontractors it used hired workers to carry out the project. The firms that carried out the many other projects authorized under the ARRA also hired new workers. Newly hired workers are likely to increase their spending on cars, furniture, appliances, and other products. Sellers of these products will increase their production and hire more workers, and so on. At each step, real GDP and income will rise, thereby increasing consumption spending and aggregate demand. These additional waves of hiring are what the spokesperson for the state agency in charge of the Caldecott Tunnel project referred to in the chapter opener as a "ripple effect" from the project.

Economists refer to the initial increase in government purchases as *autonomous* because it is a result of a decision by the government and is not directly caused by changes in the level of real GDP. The increases in consumption spending that result from the initial autonomous increase in government purchases are *induced* because they are caused by the initial increase in autonomous spending. Economists refer to the series of induced increases in consumption spending that result from an initial increase in autonomous expenditures as the **multiplier effect**.

Multiplier effect The series of induced increases in consumption spending that results from an initial increase in autonomous expenditures.

Figure 9.8 illustrates how an increase in government purchases affects the aggregate demand curve. The initial increase in government purchases causes the aggregate demand curve to shift to the right because total spending in the economy is now higher at every price level. The shift to the right from AD_1 to the dashed AD curve represents the effect of the initial increase of $100 billion in government purchases. Because this initial increase in government purchases raises incomes and leads to further increases in consumption spending, the aggregate demand curve will ultimately shift from AD_1 all the way to AD_2.

To better understand the multiplier effect, let's start with a simplified analysis in which we assume that the price level is constant. In other words, initially we will ignore the effect of an upward-sloping *SRAS*. Figure 9.9 shows how spending and real GDP increase over a number of periods, beginning with the initial increase in government purchases in the first period. The initial spending in the first period raises real GDP and total income in the economy by $100 billion. How much additional consumption spending will result from $100 billion in additional income? We know that in addition to increasing their consumption spending on domestically produced goods, households will save some of the increase in income, use some to pay income taxes, and use some to purchase imported goods, which will have no direct effect on spending and production in the U.S. economy. In Figure 9.9, we assume that in the second period, households increase their consumption

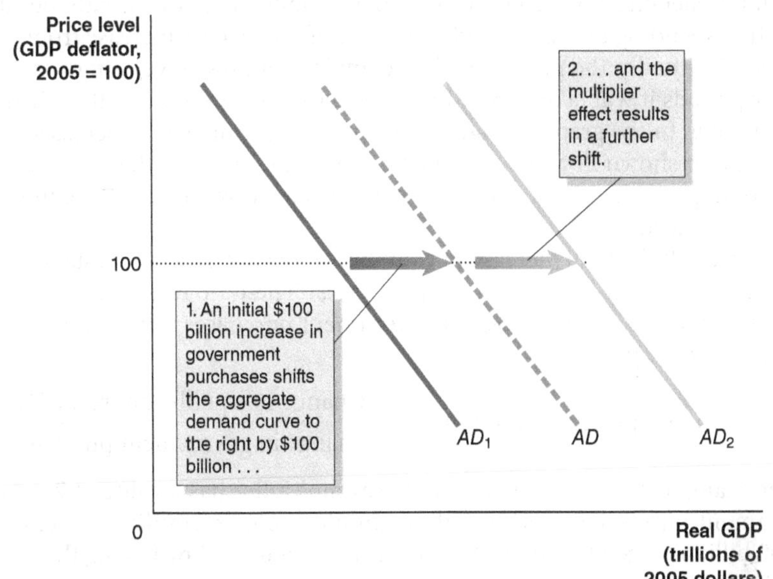

Figure 9.8

The Multiplier Effect and Aggregate Demand

An initial increase in government purchases of $100 billion causes the aggregate demand curve to shift to the right, from AD_1 to the dashed AD curve, and represents the effect of the initial increase of $100 billion in government purchases. Because this initial increase raises incomes and leads to further increases in consumption spending, the aggregate demand curve will ultimately shift further to the right, to AD_2.

Period	Additional Spending This Period	Cumulative Increase in Spending and Real GDP
1	$100 billion in government purchases	$100 billion
2	$50 billion in consumption spending	$150 billion
3	$25 billion in consumption spending	$175 billion
4	$12.5 billion in consumption spending	$187.5 billion
5	$6.25 billion in consumption spending	$193.75 billion
6	$3.125 billion in consumption spending	$196.875 billion
⋮	⋮	⋮
n	0	$200 billion

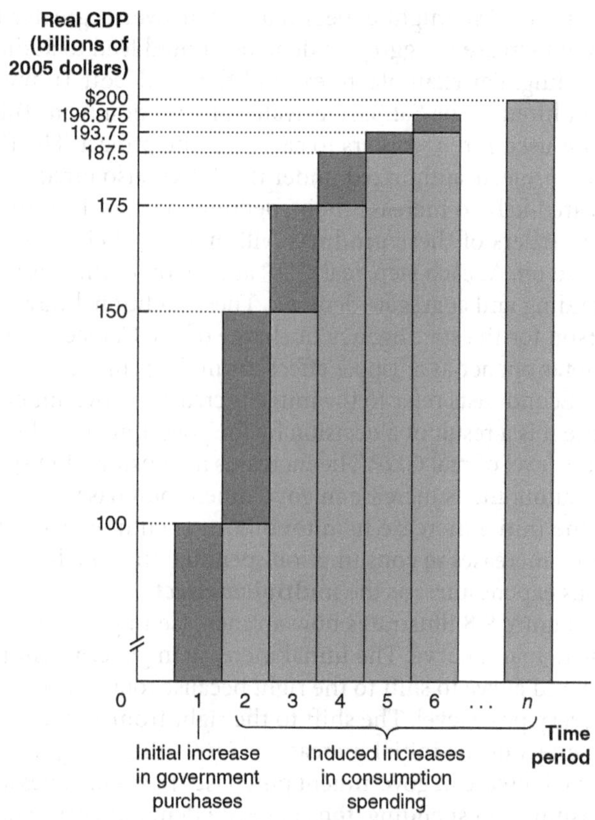

Figure 9.9 The Multiplier Effect of an Increase in Government Purchases

Following an initial increase in government purchases, spending and real GDP increase over a number of periods due to the multiplier effect. The new spending and increased real GDP in each period is shown in green, and the level of spending from the previous period is shown in orange. The sum of the orange and green areas represents the cumulative increase in spending and real GDP. In total, equilibrium real GDP will increase by $200 billion as a result of an initial increase of $100 billion in government purchases.

spending by one-half of the increase in income from the first period—or by $50 billion. This spending in the second period will, in turn, increase real GDP and income by an additional $50 billion. In the third period, consumption spending will increase by $25 billion, or one-half of the $50 billion increase in income from the second period.

The multiplier effect will continue through a number of periods, with the additional consumption spending in each period being half of the income increase from the previous period. Eventually, the process will be complete, although we cannot say precisely how many periods it will take, so we simply label the final period *n* rather than give it a specific number. In the graph in Figure 9.9, the new spending and increased real GDP in each period is shown in green, and the level of spending from the previous period is shown in orange. The sum of the orange and green areas represents the cumulative increase in spending and real GDP.

How large will the total increase in equilibrium real GDP be as a result of the initial increase of $100 billion in government purchases? The ratio of the change in equilibrium real GDP to the initial change in government purchases is known as the *government purchases multiplier*:

$$\text{Government purchases multiplier} = \frac{\text{Change in equilibrium real GDP}}{\text{Change in government purchases}}.$$

If, for example, the government purchases multiplier has a value of 2, an increase in government purchases of $100 billion should increase equilibrium real GDP by 2 × $100 billion = $200 billion. We show this in Figure 9.9 by having the cumulative increase in real GDP equal $200 billion.

Tax cuts also have a multiplier effect. Cutting taxes increases the disposable income of households. When household disposable income rises, so will consumption spending. These increases in consumption spending will set off further increases in real GDP and income, just as increases in government purchases do. Suppose we consider a change in taxes of a specific amount—say, a tax cut of $100 billion—with the tax *rate* remaining unchanged. The expression for this tax multiplier is

$$\text{Tax multiplier} = \frac{\text{Change in equilibrium real GDP}}{\text{Change in taxes}}.$$

The tax multiplier is a negative number because changes in taxes and changes in real GDP move in opposite directions: An increase in taxes reduces disposable income, consumption, and real GDP, and a decrease in taxes raises disposable income, consumption, and real GDP. For example, if the tax multiplier is −1.6, a $100 billion *cut* in taxes will increase real GDP by $-1.6 \times -\$100$ billion $=$ $160 billion. We would expect the tax multiplier to be smaller in absolute value than the government purchases multiplier. To see why, think about the difference between a $100 billion increase in government purchases and a $100 billion decrease in taxes. The whole of the $100 billion in government purchases results in an increase in aggregate demand. But households will save rather than spend some portion of a $100 billion decrease in taxes, and they will spend some portion on imported goods. The fraction of the tax cut that households save or spend on imports will not increase aggregate demand. Therefore, the first period of the multiplier process will see a smaller increase in aggregate demand than occurs when there is an increase in government purchases, and the total increase in equilibrium real GDP will be smaller.

The Effect of Changes in Tax Rates

A change in tax *rates* has a more complicated effect on equilibrium real GDP than does a tax cut of a fixed amount. To begin with, the value of the tax rate affects the size of the multiplier effect. The higher the tax rate, the smaller the multiplier effect. To see why, think about the size of the additional spending increases that take place in each period following an increase in government purchases. The higher the tax rate, the smaller the amount of any increase in income that households have available to spend, which reduces the size of the multiplier effect. So, a cut in tax rates affects equilibrium real GDP through two channels: (1) A cut in tax rates increases the disposable income of households, which leads them to increase their consumption spending, and (2) a cut in tax rates increases the size of the multiplier effect.

Taking into Account the Effects of Aggregate Supply

To this point, as we discussed the multiplier effect, we assumed that the price level was constant. We know, though, that because the *SRAS* curve is upward sloping, when the *AD* curve shifts to the right, the price level will rise. As a result of the rise in the price level, equilibrium real GDP will not increase by the full amount that the multiplier effect indicates. Figure 9.10 illustrates how an upward-sloping *SRAS* curve affects the size of the multiplier. To keep the graph relatively simple, we assume that the *SRAS* and *LRAS* curves do not shift. The economy starts at point *A*, with real GDP below its potential level. An increase in government purchases shifts the aggregate demand curve from AD_1 to the dashed *AD* curve. Just as in Figure 9.8, the multiplier effect causes a further shift in aggregate demand to AD_2. If the price level remained constant, real GDP would increase from $13.0 trillion at point *A* to $14.2 trillion at point *B*. However, because the *SRAS* curve is upward sloping, the price level rises from 100 to 103, reducing the total quantity of goods and services demanded in the economy. The new equilibrium occurs at point *C*, with real GDP having risen to $14.0 trillion, or by $200 billion less than if the price level had remained unchanged. We can conclude that the actual change in real GDP resulting from an increase in government purchases or a cut in taxes will be less than indicated by the simple multiplier effect with a constant price level.

Figure 9.10

The Multiplier Effect and Aggregate Supply

The economy is initially at point *A*. An increase in government purchases causes the aggregate demand curve to shift to the right, from AD_1 to the dashed *AD* curve. The multiplier effect results in the aggregate demand curve shifting further to the right, to AD_2 (point *B*). Because of the upward-sloping supply curve, the shift in aggregate demand results in a higher price level. In the new equilibrium at point *C*, both real GDP and the price level have increased. The increase in real GDP is less than indicated by the multiplier effect with a constant price level.

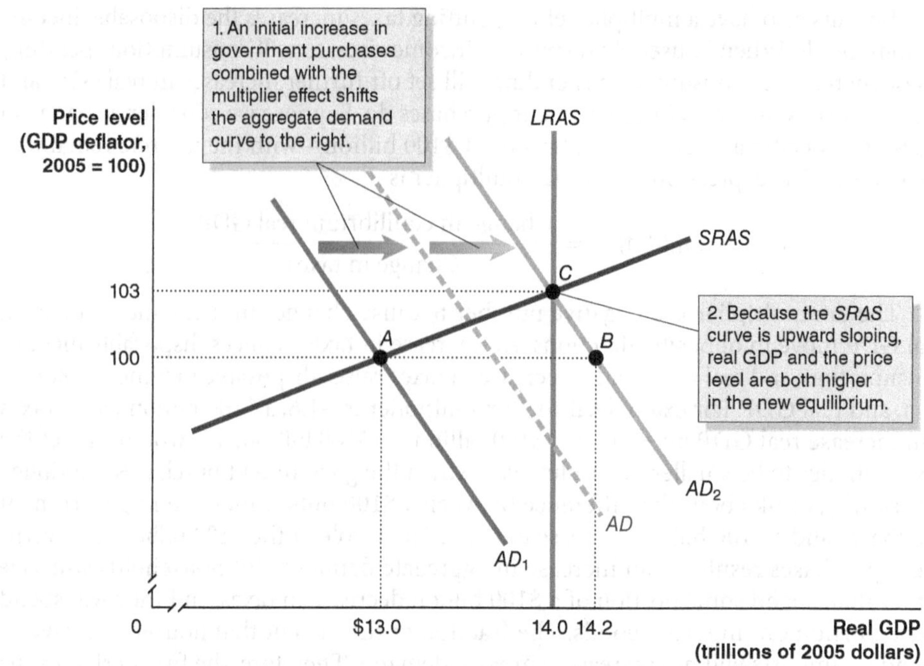

The Multipliers Work in Both Directions

Increases in government purchases and cuts in taxes have a positive multiplier effect on equilibrium real GDP. Decreases in government purchases and increases in taxes also have a multiplier effect on equilibrium real GDP, but in this case, the effect is negative. For example, an increase in taxes will reduce household disposable income and consumption spending. As households buy fewer cars, furniture, refrigerators, and other products, the firms that sell these products will cut back on production and begin laying off workers. Falling incomes will lead to further reductions in consumption spending. A reduction in government spending on defense would set off a similar process of decreases in real GDP and income. The cutback would be felt first by defense contractors selling directly to the government, and then it would spread to other firms.

We look more closely at the government purchases multiplier and the tax multiplier in the appendix to this chapter.

Solved Problem 9.4

Fiscal Policy Multipliers

Briefly explain whether you agree with the following statement: "Real GDP is currently $14.2 trillion, and potential real GDP is $14.4 trillion. If Congress and the president would increase government purchases by $200 billion or cut taxes by $200 billion, the economy could be brought to equilibrium at potential GDP."

Solving the Problem

Step 1: Review the chapter material. This problem is about the multiplier process, so you may want to review the section "The Government Purchases and Tax Multipliers," which begins on page 200.

Step 2: Explain how the necessary increase in purchases or cut in taxes is less than $200 billion because of the multiplier effect. The statement is incorrect because it does not consider the multiplier effect. Because of the multiplier effect, an increase in government purchases or a decrease in taxes of less than $200 billion is necessary to increase equilibrium real GDP by $200 billion. For instance, assume that the government purchases multiplier is 2 and the tax multiplier is −1.6. We can then calculate the necessary increase in government purchases as follows:

$$\text{Government purchases multiplier} = \frac{\text{Change in equilibrium real GDP}}{\text{Change in government purchases}}$$

$$2 = \frac{\$200 \text{ billion}}{\text{Change in government purchases}}$$

$$\text{Change in government purchases} = \frac{\$200 \text{ billion}}{2} = \$100 \text{ billion.}$$

And the necessary change in taxes:

$$\text{Tax multiplier} = \frac{\text{Change in equilibrium real GDP}}{\text{Change in taxes}}$$

$$-1.6 = \frac{\$200 \text{ billion}}{\text{Change in taxes}}$$

$$\text{Change in taxes} = \frac{\$200 \text{ billion}}{-1.6} = -\$125 \text{ billion.}$$

The Limits of Using Fiscal Policy to Stabilize the Economy

9.5 LEARNING OBJECTIVE

Discuss the difficulties that can arise in implementing fiscal policy.

Poorly timed fiscal policy, like poorly timed monetary policy, can do more harm than good. As we discussed in Chapter 11, it takes time for policymakers to collect statistics and identify changes in the economy. If the government decides to increase spending or cut taxes to fight a recession that is about to end, the effect may be to increase the inflation rate. Similarly, cutting spending or raising taxes to slow down an economy that has actually already moved into recession can increase the length and depth of the recession.

Getting the timing right can be more difficult with fiscal policy than with monetary policy for two main reasons. Control over monetary policy is concentrated in the hands of the Federal Open Market Committee, which can change monetary policy at any of its meetings. By contrast, the president and a majority of the 535 members of Congress have to agree on changes in fiscal policy. The delays caused by the legislative process can be very long. For example, in 1962, President John F. Kennedy concluded that the U.S. economy was operating below potential GDP and proposed a tax cut to stimulate aggregate demand. Congress eventually agreed to the tax cut—but not until 1964. The events of 2001 and 2009 show, though, that it is sometimes possible to authorize changes in fiscal policy relatively quickly. When George W. Bush came into office in January 2001, the economy was on the verge of recession, and he immediately proposed a tax cut. Congress passed the tax cut, and the president signed it into law in early June 2001. Similarly, Barack Obama proposed a stimulus package as soon as he came into office in January 2009, and Congress had passed the proposal by February.

Even after a change in fiscal policy has been approved, it takes time to implement the policy. Suppose Congress and the president agree to increase aggregate demand by spending $30 billion more on constructing subway systems in several cities. It will probably take at least several months to prepare detailed plans for the construction. Local governments will then ask for bids from private construction companies. Once the winning bidders have been selected, they will usually need several months to begin the project. Only then will significant amounts of spending actually take place. This delay may push the spending beyond the end of the recession that the spending was intended to fight. Delays of this type are less of a concern during long and severe recessions, such as that of 2007–2009.

Does Government Spending Reduce Private Spending?

In addition to the timing problem, using increases in government purchases to increase aggregate demand presents another potential problem. We have been assuming that when the federal government increases its purchases by $30 billion, the multiplier effect will cause the increase in aggregate demand to be greater than $30 billion. However, the size of the multiplier effect may be limited if the increase in government purchases causes one of the nongovernment, or private, components of aggregate expenditures—consumption, investment, or net exports—to fall. A decline in private expenditures as a result of an increase in government purchases is called **crowding out.**

Crowding out A decline in private expenditures as a result of an increase in government purchases.

Crowding Out in the Short Run

Consider the case of a temporary increase in government purchases. Suppose the federal government decides to fight a recession by spending $30 billion more this year on subway construction. When the $30 billion has been spent, the program will end, and government spending will drop back to its previous level. As the spending takes place, income and real GDP will increase. These increases in income and real GDP will cause households and firms to increase their demand for currency and checking account balances to accommodate the increased buying and selling. Figure 9.11 shows the result, using the money market graph introduced in Chapter 11.

At higher levels of real GDP and income, households and firms demand more money at every interest rate. When the demand for money increases, the equilibrium interest rate will rise. Higher interest rates will result in a decline in each component of private expenditures. Consumption spending and investment spending will decline because households will borrow less to buy houses, cars, furniture, and appliances, and firms will borrow less to buy factories, computers, and machine tools. Net exports will

Figure 9.11

An Expansionary Fiscal Policy Increases Interest Rates

If the federal government increases spending, the demand for money will increase from Money demand$_1$ to Money demand$_2$ as real GDP and income rise. With the supply of money constant, at $950 billion, the result is an increase in the equilibrium interest rate from 3 percent to 5 percent, which crowds out some consumption, investment, and net exports.

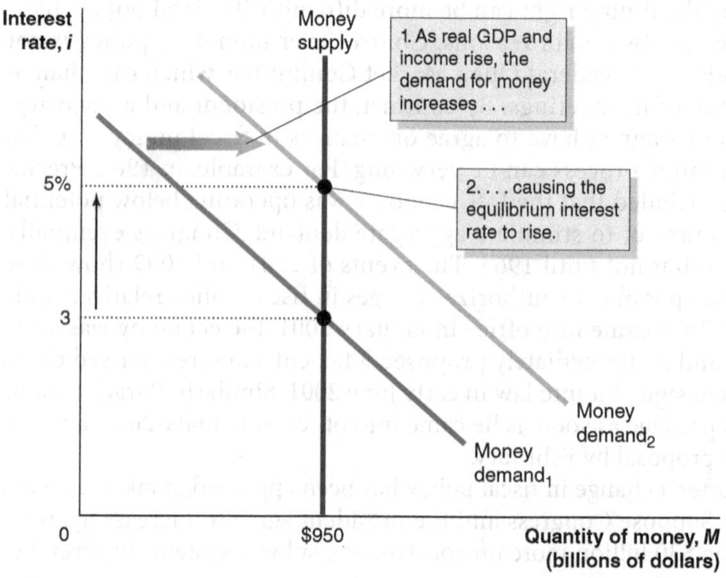

also decline because higher interest rates in the United States will attract foreign investors. German, Japanese, and Canadian investors will want to exchange the currencies of their countries for U.S. dollars to invest in U.S. Treasury bills and other U.S. financial assets. This increased demand for U.S. dollars will cause an increase in the exchange rate between the dollar and other currencies. When the dollar increases in value, the prices of U.S. products in foreign countries rise—causing a reduction in U.S. exports—and the prices of foreign products in the United States fall—causing an increase in U.S. imports. Falling exports and rising imports mean that net exports are falling.

The greater the sensitivity of consumption, investment, and net exports to changes in interest rates, the more crowding out will occur. In a deep recession, many firms may be so pessimistic about the future and have so much excess capacity that investment spending will fall to very low levels and will be unlikely to fall much further, even if interest rates rise. In this case, crowding out is unlikely to be a problem. If the economy is close to potential GDP, however, and firms are optimistic about the future, an increase in interest rates may result in a significant decline in investment spending.

Figure 9.12 shows that crowding out may reduce the effectiveness of an expansionary fiscal policy. The economy begins in short-run equilibrium at point *A*, with real GDP at $14.2 trillion. Real GDP is below potential GDP, so the economy is in recession. Suppose that Congress and the president decide to increase government purchases to bring the economy back to potential GDP. In the absence of crowding out, the increase in government purchases will shift aggregate demand to $AD_{2(\text{no crowding out})}$ and bring the economy to equilibrium at real GDP of $14.4 trillion, which is the potential level of GDP (point *B*). But the higher interest rate resulting from the increased government purchases will reduce consumption, investment, and net exports, causing aggregate demand to shift back to $AD_{2(\text{crowding out})}$. The result is a new short-run equilibrium at point *C*, with real GDP of $14.3 trillion, which is $100 billion short of potential GDP.

Crowding Out in the Long Run

Most economists agree that in the short run, an increase in government spending results in partial, but not complete, crowding out. What is the long-run effect of a *permanent* increase in government spending? In this case, most economists agree that the result is complete crowding out. In the long run, the decline in investment, consumption, and net exports exactly offsets the increase in government purchases, and aggregate demand remains unchanged. To understand crowding out in the long run, recall from Chapter 8 that *in the long run, the economy returns to potential GDP*. Suppose that the economy is currently at potential GDP and that government purchases are 35 percent of GDP. In

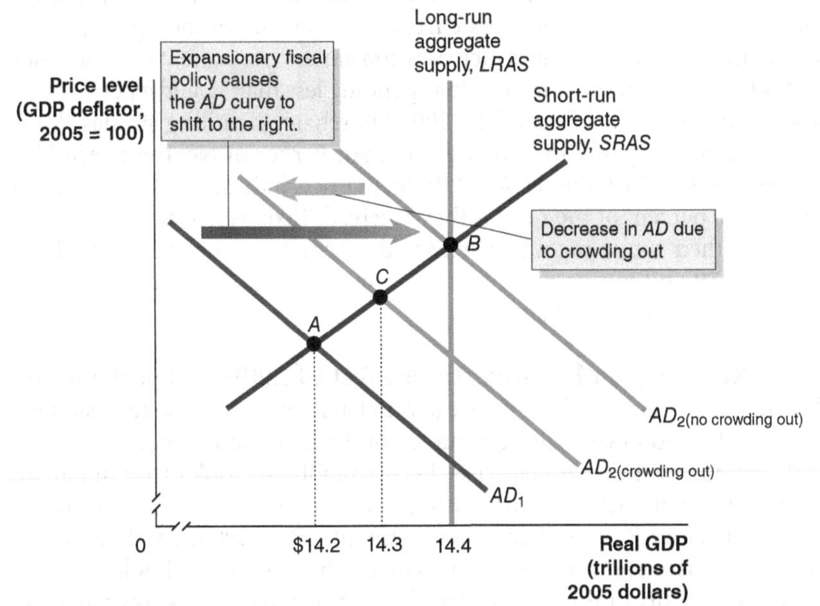

Figure 9.12

The Effect of Crowding Out in the Short Run

The economy begins in a recession, with real GDP of $14.2 trillion (point *A*). In the absence of crowding out, an increase in government purchases will shift aggregate demand to $AD_{2(\text{no crowding out})}$ and bring the economy to equilibrium at potential real GDP of $14.4 trillion (point *B*). But the higher interest rate resulting from the increased government purchases will reduce consumption, investment, and net exports, causing aggregate demand to shift to $AD_{2(\text{crowding out})}$. The result is a new short-run equilibrium at point *C*, with real GDP of $14.3 trillion, which is $100 billion short of potential real GDP.

that case, private expenditures—the sum of consumption, investment, and net exports—will make up the other 65 percent of GDP. If government purchases are increased permanently to 37 percent of GDP, in the long run, private expenditures must fall to 63 percent of GDP. There has been complete crowding out: Private expenditures have fallen by the same amount that government purchases have increased. If government spending is taking a larger share of GDP, then private spending must take a smaller share.

An expansionary fiscal policy does not have to cause complete crowding out in the short run. If the economy is below potential real GDP, it is possible for both government purchases and private expenditures to increase. But in the long run, any permanent increase in government purchases must come at the expense of private expenditures. Keep in mind, however, that it may take several—possibly many—years to arrive at this long-run outcome.

Fiscal Policy in Action: Did the Stimulus Package of 2009 Work?

As we have seen, Congress and the president can increase government purchases and cut taxes to increase aggregate demand either to avoid a recession or to shorten the length or severity of a recession that is already under way. The recession of 2007–2009 occurred during the end of the presidency of George W. Bush and the beginning of the presidency of Barack Obama. Both presidents used fiscal policy to fight the recession.

In early 2008, economists advising President Bush believed that the housing crisis, the resulting credit crunch, and rising oil prices were pushing the economy into a recession. (As we now know, a recession had actually already begun in December 2007.) These economists proposed cutting taxes to increase household disposable income, which would increase consumption spending and aggregate demand. Congress enacted a tax cut that took the form of *rebates* of taxes already paid. Rebate checks totaling $95 billion were sent to taxpayers between April and July 2008.

How effective were the rebates in increasing consumption spending? While economists are still studying the issue, economic analysis can give us some insight. Many economists believe that consumers base their spending on their *permanent income* rather than just on their *current income*. A consumer's permanent income reflects the consumer's expected future income. By basing spending on permanent income, a consumer can smooth out consumption over a period of years. For example, a medical student may have very low current income but a high expected future income. The student may borrow against this high expected future income rather than having to consume at a very low level in the present. Some people, however, have difficulty borrowing against their future income because banks or other lenders may not be convinced that a borrower's future income really will be significantly higher than his or her current income. One-time tax rebates, such as the one in 2008, increase consumers' current income but not their permanent income. Only a permanent decrease in taxes increases consumers' permanent income. Therefore, a tax rebate is likely to increase consumption spending less than would a permanent tax cut.

Some estimates of the effect of the 2008 tax rebate, including studies by Christian Broda of the University of Chicago and Jonathan Parker of Northwestern University, and by economists at the Congressional Budget Office, indicate that taxpayers spent between 33 and 40 percent of the rebates they received. Taxpayers who have difficulty borrowing against their future income increased their consumption the most. The 2008 tax rebates totaled $95 billion, so consumers may have increased their spending by about $35 billion as a result of the rebate.

American Recovery and Reinvestment Act of 2009 Although the tax rebates helped to increase aggregate demand, we saw in Chapter 11 that the recession worsened in September 2008, following the bankruptcy of the Lehman Brothers investment bank and the deepening of the financial crisis. President Obama took office in January 2009, pledging to pursue an expansionary fiscal policy. Congress responded in February by passing the American Recovery and Reinvestment Act of 2009, a $825 billion package of spending increases and tax cuts that was by far the largest fiscal policy action in U.S. history. The complexity of the "stimulus package," as it came to be known, makes its provisions difficult to summarize, but Figure 9.13 provides some highlights.

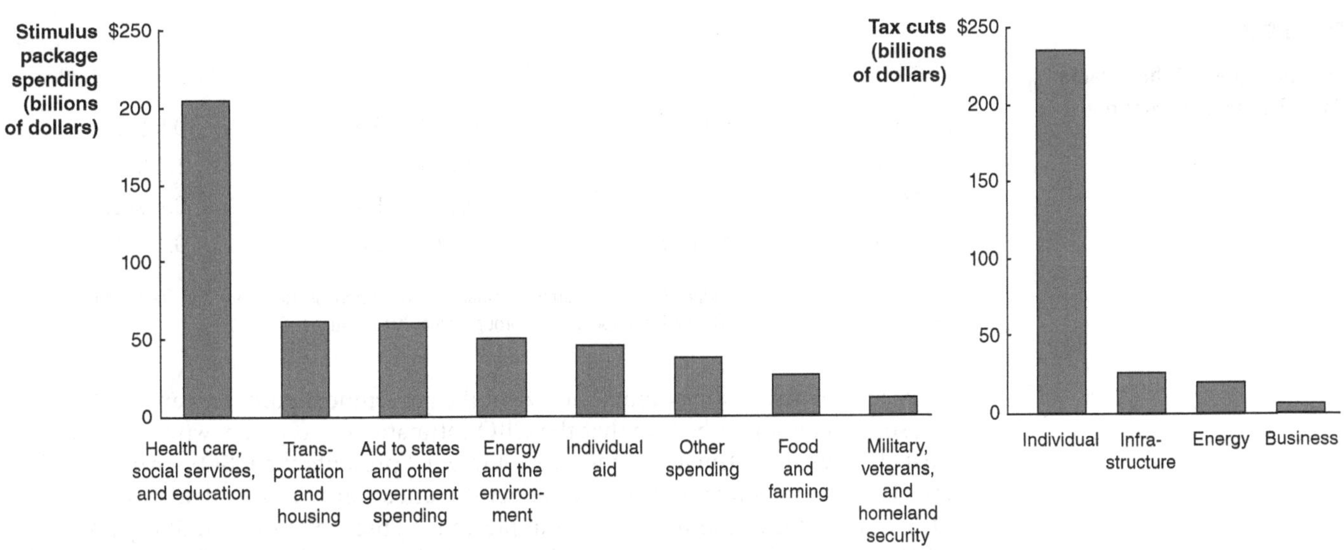

Figure 9.13 The 2009 Stimulus Package

Congress and President Obama intended the spending increases and tax cuts in the stimulus package to increase aggregate demand and help pull the economy out of the 2007–2009 recession. Panel (a) shows how the increases in spending were distributed, and panel (b) shows how the tax cuts were distributed.
Data from Congressional Budget Office.

About two-thirds of the stimulus package took the form of increases in government expenditures, and one-third took the form of tax cuts. Panel (a) shows the major categories of spending increases. The largest category—health care, social services, and education—included funds for biomedical research and grants to state governments to help fund Medicare spending, as well as funds for many other programs. The energy category included funding for research into alternative energy sources as well as modernization of the electric grid. Transportation and housing included substantial spending on infrastructure projects, such as repairing and expanding highways, bridges, and airports. Individual aid included spending on extended unemployment insurance payments. Panel (b) shows the major categories of tax cuts. The largest category was individual tax cuts, which included a $400 reduction in payroll taxes for workers earning up to $75,000 per year and a tax credit of up to $2,500 for tuition and other college expenses.

How Can We Measure the Effectiveness of the Stimulus Package? How effective was the Obama administration's stimulus package? At the time the package was passed, economists working for the administration estimated that the increase in aggregate demand resulting from the package would increase real GDP by 3.5 percent by the end of 2010 and increase employment by 3.5 million. In fact, between the beginning of 2009 and the end of 2010, real GDP increased by 4.4 percent, while employment declined by 3.3 million. Do these results indicate that the stimulus package was successful in increasing GDP, but not employment? We have to be careful in drawing that conclusion. To judge the effectiveness of the stimulus package, we have to measure its effects on real GDP and employment, *holding constant all other factors affecting real GDP and employment*. In other words, the actual movements in real GDP and employment are a mixture of the effects of the stimulus package and the effects of other factors, such as the Federal Reserve's monetary policy, other fiscal policy actions, and the typical changes in real GDP and employment during a business cycle that occur independently of government policy. Isolating the effects of the stimulus package from the effects of these other factors is very difficult and explains why economists differ in their views about how effective the stimulus package was.

Economists at the Congressional Budget Office (CBO) have provided estimates of the effectiveness of the stimulus package. The CBO is a nonpartisan organization, and many economists believe its estimates are reasonable. But because the estimates depend

Table 9.2

CBO Estimates of the Effects of the Stimulus Package

Year	Change in Real GDP	Change in the Unemployment Rate	Change in Employment (millions of people)
2009	0.9% to 1.9%	−0.3% to −0.5%	0.5 to 0.9
2010	1.5% to 4.2%	−0.7% to −1.8%	1.3 to 3.3
2011	0.8% to 2.3%	−0.5% to −1.4%	0.9 to 2.7
2012	0.3% to 0.8%	−0.2% to −0.6%	0.4 to 1.1

Data from Congressional Budget Office, "Estimated Impact of the American Recovery and Reinvestment Act on Employment and Economic Output from April 2011 Through June 2011," August 2011.

on particular assumptions about the size of the government purchases and tax multipliers, some economists believe that the CBO estimates are too high, while other economists believe the estimates are too low. Table 9.2 presents the CBO's estimates of the effects of the stimulus package. To reflect the uncertainty in its calculation, the CBO provides a range of estimates. For example, in the absence of the stimulus package, the CBO estimates that employment in 2010 would have been between 1.3 million and 3.3 million less than it actually was and the unemployment rate would have been between 0.7 percent and 1.8 percent higher than it actually was.

If the CBO's estimates of the effects of the stimulus package are accurate, then this fiscal policy action significantly reduced the severity of the recession of 2007–2009 and its aftermath. However, relative to the severity of the recession, the effect of the package was comparatively small. For example, in 2010, the unemployment rate was 9.6 percent, which was far above the unemployment rate of 4.6 percent in 2007. According to the CBO, without the stimulus package, the unemployment rate would have been somewhere between 10.3 percent and 11.4 percent. So, the stimulus package reduced the increase in the unemployment rate that might otherwise have occurred, but did not come close to bringing the economy back to full employment.

Making the Connection

Why Was the Recession of 2007–2009 So Severe?

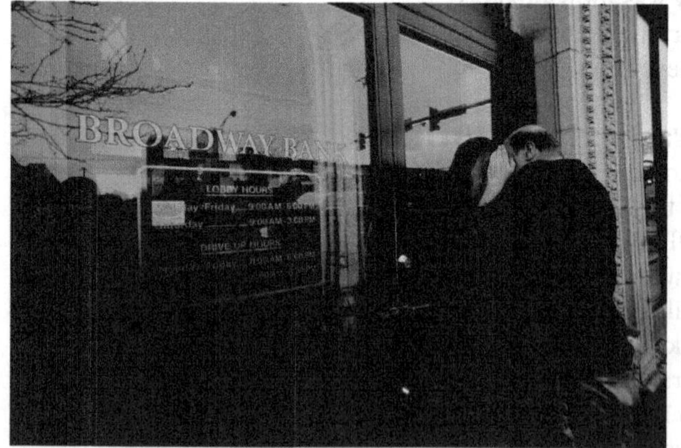

The financial crisis made the recession of 2007–2009 more severe and long-lasting than many other recessions.

The CBO estimates of the effects of the stimulus package indicate that even $825 billion in increased government spending and tax cuts left the economy with real GDP far from potential GDP and the unemployment rate above 9 percent. Why was the recession of 2007–2009 so severe? As we saw in Chapters 10 and 11, the recession was accompanied by a financial crisis. The U.S. economy had not experienced a significant financial crisis since the Great Depression of the 1930s. Both the Great Depression and the recession of 2007–2009 were severe. Was their severity the result of the accompanying financial crises? More generally, do recessions accompanied by financial crises tend to be more severe than recessions that do not involve bank crises?

Carmen Reinhart of the University of Maryland and Kenneth Rogoff of Harvard have gathered data on recessions and financial crises in a number of countries, in an attempt to answer this question. The table on the next page shows the average change in key economic variables during the period following a financial crisis for a number of countries, including the United States during the Great Depression and European and Asian countries in the post–World War II era. The table shows that for these countries, on average, the recessions following financial crises were quite severe. Unemployment rates increased by 7 percentage points—for example, from 5 percent to 12 percent—and continued increasing for nearly five years after a crisis had begun. Real GDP per capita also declined sharply, and the average length of a recession following a financial crisis has been nearly two years. Adjusted for inflation, stock prices dropped by more than half, and housing prices dropped by more than one-third. Government debt soared by 86 percent. The increased government debt was partly the result of increased government spending, including spending to bail out failed financial institutions. But most of the increased debt was the result of government budget deficits resulting from sharp declines in tax revenues as incomes and profits fell as a result of the recession. (We discuss government budget deficits and government debt in the next section.)

Economic Variable	Average Change	Average Duration of Change	Number of Countries
Unemployment rate	+7 percentage points	4.8 years	14
Real GDP per capita	−9.3%	1.9 years	14
Real stock prices	−55.9%	3.4 years	22
Real house prices	−35.5%	6 years	21
Real government debt	+86%	3 years	13

The table above does not include data for the United States during the 2007–2009 recession because that recession was still under way when Reinhart and Rogoff were compiling their data. The table below shows some key indicators for the 2007–2009 U.S. recession compared with other U.S. recessions of the post–World War II period:

	Duration	Decline in Real GDP	Peak Unemployment Rate
Average for postwar recessions	10.4 months	−1.7%	7.6%
Recession of 2007–2009	18 months	−4.1%	10.1%

Consistent with Reinhart and Rogoff's findings that recessions following financial panics tend to be unusually severe, the 2007–2009 recession was the worst in the United States since the Great Depression of the 1930s. The recession lasted nearly twice as long as the average of earlier postwar recessions, GDP declined by more than twice the average, and the peak unemployment rate was about one-third higher than the average.

Because most people did not see the financial crisis coming, they also failed to anticipate the severity of the 2007–2009 recession.

Note: In the second table, the duration of recessions is based on National Bureau of Economic Research business cycle dates, the decline in real GDP is measured as the simple percentage change from the quarter of the cyclical peak to the quarter of the cyclical trough, and the peak unemployment rate is the highest unemployment rate in any month following the cyclical peak.

Data from Carmen M. Reinhart and Kenneth S. Rogoff, *This Time Is Different: Eight Centuries of Financial Folly*, (Princeton, NJ: Princeton University Press, 2009), Figures 14.1–14.5; and the U.S. Bureau of Economic Analysis and National Bureau of Economic Research.

The Size of the Multiplier: A Key to Estimating the Effects of Fiscal Policy

In preparing the values shown in Table 9.2, the CBO relied on estimates of the government purchases and tax multipliers. Economists have been debating the size of these multipliers for many years. When British economist John Maynard Keynes and his followers first developed the idea of spending and tax multipliers in the 1930s, they argued that the government purchases multiplier might be as large as 10. In that case, a $1 billion increase in government purchases would increase real GDP by $10 billion. Later research by economists indicated that the government purchases multiplier was much smaller, perhaps less than 2.

Estimating an exact number for the multiplier is difficult because over time, several factors can cause the aggregate demand and short-run aggregate supply curves to shift, leading to a change in equilibrium real GDP. It can be challenging to isolate the effect of an increase in government purchases on equilibrium GDP. In preparing their estimates of the effect of the stimulus package on GDP, Obama administration economists used an average of multiplier estimates from the Federal Reserve and from a private macroeconomic forecasting firm. Their estimate of a government purchases multiplier of 1.57 indicates that a $1 billion increase in government purchases would increase equilibrium real GDP by $1.57 billion.

Because of the difficulty of estimating the size of the multiplier, some economists argue that the value used by the Obama administration's economists was too high, while others argued that it was too low. Robert Barro of Harvard University argues that increases in government spending during wartime are so large relative to other changes in aggregate demand that data from periods of war are best suited to estimating the size of the multiplier. Using such data, Barro estimated that the government purchases multiplier is only 0.8. Lawrence Christiano, Martin Eichenbaum, and Sergio Rebelo of Northwestern University argued, on the other hand, that the multiplier is likely to be larger when, as during 2009, short-term interest rates are near zero. They estimated that for these periods, the government purchases multiplier could be as large as 3.7.

As Table 9.3 shows, estimates of the size of the multiplier vary widely. The uncertainty about the size of the multiplier indicates the difficulty that economists have in arriving at a firm estimate of the effects of fiscal policy.

Table 9.3 Estimates of the Size of the Multiplier

Economist	Type of Multiplier	Size of Multiplier
Congressional Budget Office	Government purchases	1.0–2.5
Lawrence Christiano, Martin Eichenbaum, and Sergio Rebelo	Government purchases	1.05 (when short-term interest rates are not zero); 3.7 (when short-term interest rates are expected to be zero for at least five quarters)
Tommaso Monacelli, Roberto Perotti, and Antonella Trigari, Universita Bocconi	Government purchases	1.2 (after one year) and 1.5 (after two years)
Ethan Ilzetzki, London School of Economics, Enrique G. Mendoza, and Carlos A. Vegh, University of Maryland	Government purchases	0.8
Valerie Ramey, University of California, San Diego	Military expenditure	0.6–1.1
Robert J. Barro, Harvard University, and Charles J. Redlick, Bain Capital, LLC	Military expenditure	0.4–0.5 (after one year) and 0.6–0.7 (after two years)
John Cogan and John Taylor, Stanford University, and Tobias Cwik and Volker Wieland, Gothe University	A permanent increase in government expenditures	0.4
Christina Romer, University of California, Berkeley, and Jared Bernstein, chief economist and economic policy adviser to Vice President Joseph Biden	A permanent increase in government expenditures	1.6
Christina Romer (prior to serving as chair of the Council of Economic Advisers) and David Romer, University of California, Berkeley	Tax	2–3
Congressional Budget Office	Tax	0.6–1.5 (two-year tax cut for lower- and middle-income people) and 0.2–0.6 (one-year tax cut for higher-income people)
Robert J. Barro, Harvard University, and Charles J. Redlick, Bain Capital, LLC	Tax	1.1

Based on Tommaso Monacelli, Roberto Perotti, and Antonella Trigari, "Unemployment Fiscal Multipliers," *Journal of Monetary Economics*, Vol. 57, No. 5, July 2010, pp. 531–553; Ethan Ilzetzki, Enrique G. Mendoza, and Carlos A. Vegh, "How Big (Small?) Are Fiscal Multipliers?" National Bureau of Economic Research Working Paper No. 16479, December 2010; Robert J. Barro and Charles J. Redlick, "Macroeconomic Effects from Government Purchases and Taxes," National Bureau of Economic Research Working Paper 15369, September 2009; Lawrence Christiano, Martin Eichenbaum, and Sergio Rebelo, "When Is the Government Spending Multiplier Large?" *Journal of Political Economy*, Vol. 119, No. 1, February 2011, pp. 78–121; Jared Bernstein and Christina Romer, "The Job Impact of the American Reinvestment and Recovery Plan," January 9, 2009; John Cogan, Tobias Cwik, John Taylor, and Volker Wieland, "New Keynesian Versus Old Keynesian Government Spending Multipliers," *Journal of Economic Dynamics and Control*, Vol. 34, No. 3, March 2010, pp. 281–295; Valerie Ramey, "Identifying Government Spending Shocks: It's All in the Timing," *Quarterly Journal of Economics*, Vol. 126, No. 1, February 2011, pp. 1–50; Christina Romer and David Romer, "The Macroeconomic Effects of Tax Changes: Estimates Based on a New Measure of Fiscal Shocks," *American Economic Review*, Vol. 100, No. 3, June 2010, pp. 763–801; and U.S. Congressional Budget Office, "Estimated Impact of the American Recovery and Reinvestment Act on Employment and Economic Output from April 2011 through June 2011," August 2011.

Deficits, Surpluses, and Federal Government Debt

9.6 LEARNING OBJECTIVE

Define federal budget deficit and federal government debt and explain how the federal budget can serve as an automatic stabilizer.

The federal government's budget shows the relationship between its expenditures and its tax revenue. If the federal government's expenditures are greater than its tax revenue, a **budget deficit** results. If the federal government's expenditures are less than its tax revenue, a **budget surplus** results. As with many other macroeconomic variables, it is useful to consider the size of the surplus or deficit relative to the size of the overall economy. Figure 9.14 shows that, as a percentage of GDP, the largest deficits of the twentieth century came during World Wars I and II. During major wars, higher taxes only partially offset massive increases in government expenditures, leaving large budget deficits. Figure 9.14 also shows that during recessions government spending increases and tax revenues fall, increasing the budget deficit. In 1970, the federal government entered a long period of continuous budget deficits. From 1970 through 1997, the federal government's budget was in deficit every year. From 1998 through 2001, there were four years of budget surpluses. The recessions of 2001 and 2007–2009, tax cuts, and increased government spending on homeland security and the wars in Iraq and Afghanistan helped keep the budget in deficit in the years after 2001.

Budget deficit The situation in which the government's expenditures are greater than its tax revenue.

Budget surplus The situation in which the government's expenditures are less than its tax revenue.

Figure 9.14 also shows the effects on the federal budget deficit of the Obama administration's $825 billion stimulus package and the severity of the 2007–2009 recession. From 2009 through 2011, the federal budget deficit was greater than 8 percent of GDP, which was the first time the deficit had been this large except during major wars in the history of the country.

How the Federal Budget Can Serve as an Automatic Stabilizer

Discretionary fiscal policy can increase the federal budget deficit during recessions by increasing spending or cutting taxes to increase aggregate demand. For example, as we have just seen, the Obama administration's spending increases and tax cuts caused the federal budget deficit to soar during 2009. In many milder recessions, though, no significant fiscal policy actions are taken. In fact, most of the increase in the federal budget deficit during a typical recession takes place without Congress and the president taking

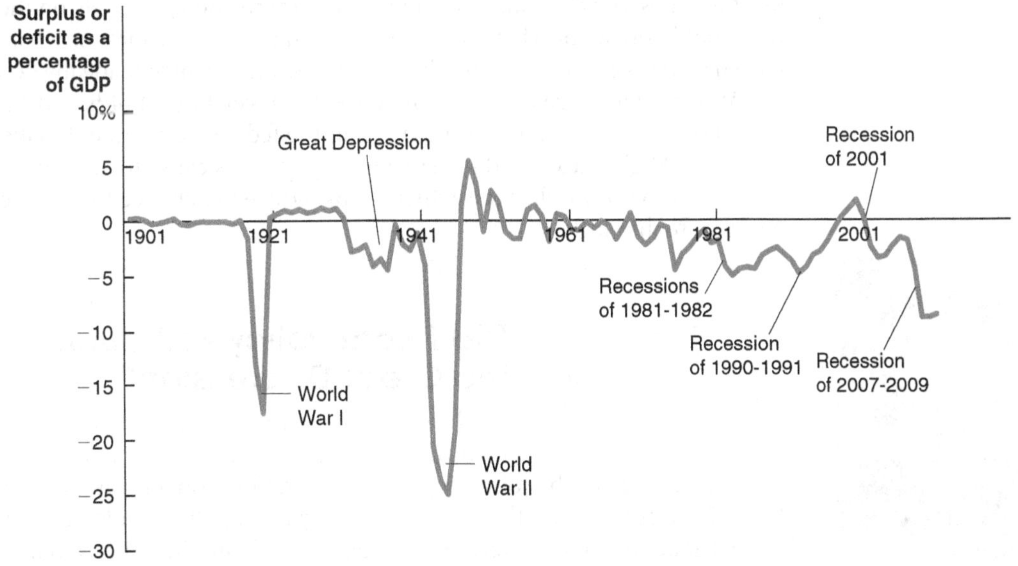

Figure 9.14 The Federal Budget Deficit, 1901–2011

During wars, government spending increases far more than tax revenues, increasing the budget deficit. The budget deficit also increases during recessions, as government spending increases and tax revenues fall.

Note: The value for 2011 is an estimate prepared by the Congressional Budget Office in June 2011.

Data from *Budget of the United States Government, Fiscal Year 2003, Historical Tables,* Washington, DC: U.S. Government Printing Office, 2002; U.S. Bureau of Economic Analysis; and Congressional Budget Office.

any action, but is instead due to the effects of the *automatic stabilizers* we mentioned earlier in this chapter.

Deficits occur automatically during recessions for two reasons: First, during a recession, wages and profits fall, causing government tax revenues to fall. Second, the government automatically increases its spending on transfer payments when the economy moves into recession. The government's contribution to the unemployment insurance program will increase as unemployment rises. Spending will also increase on programs to aid low-income people, such as the food stamps, Temporary Assistance for Needy Families, and Medicaid programs. These spending increases take place without Congress and the president taking any action. Existing laws already specify who is eligible for unemployment insurance and these other programs. As the number of eligible persons increases during a recession, so does government spending on these programs.

Because budget deficits automatically increase during recessions and decrease during expansions, economists often look at the *cyclically adjusted budget deficit or surplus*, which can provide a more accurate measure of the effects on the economy of the government's spending and tax policies than can the actual budget deficit or surplus. The **cyclically adjusted budget deficit or surplus** measures what the deficit or surplus would be if the economy were at potential GDP. In late 2011, the CBO projected that the deficit for 2012 would be about 6.2 percent of GDP. The CBO estimated that if real GDP were at its potential level, the deficit would be about 4.0 percent of GDP. The difference represented the effects of expansionary fiscal policy. If the federal government were to run a contractionary fiscal policy, the result would be a cyclically adjusted budget surplus.

Cyclically adjusted budget deficit or surplus The deficit or surplus in the federal government's budget if the economy were at potential GDP.

Automatic budget surpluses and deficits can help to stabilize the economy. When the economy moves into a recession, wages and profits fall, which reduces the taxes that households and firms owe the government. In effect, households and firms have received an automatic tax cut, which keeps their spending higher than it otherwise would have been. In a recession, workers who have been laid off receive unemployment insurance payments, and households whose incomes have dropped below a certain level become eligible for food stamps and other government transfer programs. By receiving this extra income, households are able to spend more than they otherwise would have spent. This extra spending helps reduce the length and severity of the recession. Many economists argue that the lack of an unemployment insurance system and other government transfer programs contributed to the severity of the Great Depression. During the Great Depression, workers who lost their jobs saw their wage incomes drop to zero and had to rely on their savings, what they could borrow, or what they received from private charities. As a result, many unemployed workers cut back drastically on their spending, which made the downturn worse.

When GDP increases above its potential level, households and firms have to pay more taxes to the federal government, and the federal government makes fewer transfer payments. Higher taxes and lower transfer payments cause total spending to rise by less than it otherwise would have, which helps reduce the chance that the economy will experience higher inflation.

Although government spending increased during the Great Depression, the cyclically adjusted budget was in surplus most years.

Making the Connection: Did Fiscal Policy Fail during the Great Depression?

Modern macroeconomic analysis began during the 1930s, with the publication of *The General Theory of Employment, Interest, and Money* by John Maynard Keynes. One conclusion many economists drew from Keynes's book was that an expansionary fiscal policy would be necessary to pull the United States out of the Great Depression. When Franklin D. Roosevelt became president in 1933, federal government expenditures increased as part of his New Deal program, and there was a federal budget deficit during each remaining year of the decade, except for 1937. The U.S. economy recovered very slowly, however, and did not reach potential GDP again until the outbreak of World War II in 1941.

Some economists and policymakers at the time argued that because the economy recovered slowly despite increases in government spending, fiscal policy had been ineffective. During the debate over President Obama's stimulus package, the argument that fiscal policy had failed during the New Deal was raised again. Economic historians have argued, however, that despite the increases in government spending, Congress and the president had not, in fact, implemented an expansionary fiscal policy during the 1930s. In separate studies, economists E. Cary Brown of MIT and Larry Peppers of Washington and Lee University argued that there was a cyclically adjusted budget deficit during only one year of the 1930s, and that one deficit was small. The following table provides data supporting their arguments. (All variables in the table are nominal rather than real.) The second column shows federal government expenditures increasing from 1933 to 1936, falling in 1937, and then increasing in 1938 and 1939. The third column shows a similar pattern, with the federal budget being in deficit each year after 1933 except for 1937. The fourth column, however, shows that in each year after 1933, the federal government ran a cyclically adjusted budget *surplus*. Because the level of income was so low and the unemployment rate was so high during these years, tax collections were far below what they would have been if the economy had been at potential GDP. As the fifth column shows, in 1933 and again in 1937 to 1939, the cyclically adjusted surpluses were large relative to GDP.

Year	Federal Government Expenditures (billions of dollars)	Actual Federal Budget Deficit or Surplus (billions of dollars)	Cyclically Adjusted Budget Deficit or Surplus (billions of dollars)	Cyclically Adjusted Budget Deficit or Surplus as a Percentage of GDP
1929	$2.6	$1.0	$1.24	1.20%
1930	2.7	0.2	0.81	0.89
1931	4.0	-2.1	-0.41	-0.54
1932	3.0	-1.3	0.50	0.85
1933	3.4	-0.9	1.06	1.88
1934	5.5	-2.2	0.09	0.14
1935	5.6	-1.9	0.54	0.74
1936	7.8	-3.2	0.47	0.56
1937	6.4	0.2	2.55	2.77
1938	7.3	-1.3	2.47	2.87
1939	8.4	-2.1	2.00	2.17

Although President Roosevelt proposed many new government spending programs, he had also promised during the 1932 presidential election campaign to balance the federal budget. He achieved a balanced budget only in 1937, but his reluctance to allow the actual budget deficit to grow too large helps explain why the cyclically adjusted budget remained in surplus. Many economists today would agree with E. Cary Brown's conclusion: "Fiscal policy, then, seems to have been an unsuccessful recovery device in the 'thirties—not because it did not work, but because it was not tried."

Based on E. Cary Brown, "Fiscal Policy in the "Thirties: A Reappraisal," *American Economic Review*, Vol. 46, No. 5, December 1956, pp. 857–879; Larry Peppers, "Full Employment Surplus Analysis and Structural Changes," *Explorations in Economic History*, Vol. 10, Winter 1973, pp. 197–210; and U.S. Bureau of Economic Analysis.

Solved Problem 9.6

The Effect of Economic Fluctuations on the Budget Deficit

The federal government's budget deficit was $207.8 billion in 1983 and $185.4 billion in 1984. A student comments, "The government must have acted during 1984 to raise taxes or cut spending or both." Do you agree? Briefly explain.

Solving the Problem

Step 1: Review the chapter material. This problem is about the federal budget as an automatic stabilizer, so you may want to review the section "How the Federal Budget Can Serve as an Automatic Stabilizer," which begins on page 213.

Step 2: Explain how changes in the budget deficit can occur without Congress and the president acting. If Congress and the president take action to raise taxes or cut spending, the federal budget deficit will decline. But the deficit will also decline automatically when GDP increases, even if the government takes no action. When GDP increases, rising household incomes and firm profits result in higher tax revenues. Increasing GDP also usually means falling unemployment, which reduces government spending on unemployment insurance and other transfer payments. So, you should disagree with the comment. A falling deficit does not mean that the government *must* have acted to raise taxes or cut spending.

Extra Credit: Although you don't have to know it to answer the question, GDP did increase from $3.5 trillion in 1983 to $3.9 trillion in 1984.

Should the Federal Budget Always Be Balanced?

Although many economists believe that it is a good idea for the federal government to have a balanced budget when the economy is at potential GDP, few economists believe that the federal government should attempt to balance its budget every year. To see why economists take this view, consider what the government would have to do to keep the budget balanced during a recession, when the federal budget automatically moves into deficit. To bring the budget back into balance, the government would have to raise taxes or cut spending, but these actions would reduce aggregate demand, thereby making the recession worse. Similarly, when GDP increases above its potential level, the budget automatically moves into surplus. To eliminate this surplus, the government would have to cut taxes or increase government spending. But these actions would increase aggregate demand, thereby pushing GDP further beyond potential GDP and increasing the risk of higher inflation. To balance the budget every year, the government might have to take actions that would destabilize the economy.

Some economists argue that the federal government should normally run a deficit, even at potential GDP. When the federal budget is in deficit, the U.S. Treasury sells bonds to investors to raise the funds necessary to pay the government's bills. Borrowing to pay the bills is a bad policy for a household, a firm, or the government when the bills are for current expenses, but it is not a bad policy if the bills are for long-lived capital goods. For instance, most families pay for a new home by taking out a 15- to 30-year mortgage. Because houses last many years, it makes sense to pay for a house out of the income the family makes over a long period of time rather than out of the income received in the year the house is bought. Businesses often borrow the funds to buy machinery, equipment, and factories by selling 30-year corporate bonds. Because these capital goods generate profits for the businesses over many years, it makes sense to pay for them over a period of years as well. By similar reasoning, when the federal government contributes to the building of a new highway, bridge, or subway, it may want to borrow funds by selling Treasury bonds. The alternative is to pay for these long-lived capital goods out of the tax revenues received in the year the goods were purchased. But that means that the taxpayers in that year have to bear the whole burden of paying for the projects, even though taxpayers for many years in the future will be enjoying the benefits.

The Federal Government Debt

Every time the federal government runs a budget deficit, the Treasury must borrow funds from investors by selling Treasury securities. For simplicity, we will refer to all Treasury securities as "bonds." When the federal government runs a budget surplus, the Treasury pays off some existing bonds. Figure 9.14 on page 211 shows that there are many more years of federal budget deficits than years of federal budget surpluses. As a result, the total number of Treasury bonds outstanding has grown over the years. The total value of U.S. Treasury bonds outstanding is referred to as the *federal government debt* or, sometimes, as the *national debt*. Each year the federal budget is in deficit, the federal government debt grows. Each year the federal budget is in surplus, the debt shrinks.

Figure 9.15 shows federal government debt as a percentage of GDP in the years since 1901. The ratio of debt to GDP increased during World Wars I and II and the Great Depression, reflecting the large government budget deficits of those years. After the end of World War II, GDP grew faster than the debt until the early 1980s, which caused the ratio of debt to GDP to fall. The large budget deficits of the 1980s and early 1990s sent the debt-to-GDP ratio climbing. The budget surpluses of 1998 to 2001 caused the debt-to-GDP ratio to fall, but it rose again with the return of deficits beginning in 2002. The large deficits beginning in 2008 caused the ratio to spike up to its highest level since 1947.

Is Government Debt a Problem?

Debt can be a problem for a government for the same reasons that debt can be a problem for a household or a business. If a family has difficulty making the monthly mortgage payment, it will have to cut back spending on other goods and services. If the family is unable to make the payments, it will have to *default* on the loan and will probably lose its house. The federal government is not in danger of defaulting on its debt. Ultimately, the government can raise the funds it needs through taxes to make the interest payments on the debt. If the debt becomes very large relative to the economy, however, the government may have to raise taxes to high levels or cut back on other types of spending to make the interest payments on the debt. Interest payments are currently about 10 percent of total federal expenditures. At this level, tax increases or significant cutbacks in other types of federal spending are not required.

In the long run, a debt that increases in size relative to GDP, as was happening after 2008, can pose a problem. As we discussed previously, crowding out of investment spending may occur if an increasing debt drives up interest rates. Lower investment spending means a lower capital stock in the long run and a reduced capacity of the economy to produce goods and services. This effect is somewhat offset if some of the government debt was incurred to finance improvements in *infrastructure*, such as

Figure 9.15

The Federal Government Debt, 1901–2011

The federal government debt increases whenever the federal government runs a budget deficit. The large deficits incurred during World Wars I and II, the Great Depression, and the 1980s and early 1990s increased the ratio of debt to GDP. The large deficits of 2009 to 2011 caused the ratio to spike up to its highest level since 1947.

Data from U.S. Bureau of the Census, *Historical Statistics of the United States, Colonial Times to 1970*, Washington, DC: U.S. Government Printing Office, 1975; Budget of the United States Government, Fiscal Year 2003, Historical Printing Office, 2002; Federal Reserve Bank of St. Louis, *National Economic Trends*, October 2011; and Congressional Budget Office.

bridges, highways, and ports; to finance education; or to finance research and development. Improvements in infrastructure, a better-educated labor force, and additional research and development can add to the productive capacity of the economy.

9.7 LEARNING OBJECTIVE

Discuss the effects of fiscal policy in the long run.

The Effects of Fiscal Policy in the Long Run

Some fiscal policy actions are intended to meet the short-run goal of stabilizing the economy. Other fiscal policy actions are intended to have long-run effects by expanding the productive capacity of the economy and increasing the rate of economic growth. Because these policy actions primarily affect aggregate supply rather than aggregate demand, they are sometimes referred to as *supply-side economics*. Most fiscal policy actions that attempt to increase aggregate supply do so by changing taxes to increase the incentives to work, save, invest, and start a business.

The Long-Run Effects of Tax Policy

Tax wedge The difference between the pretax and posttax return to an economic activity.

The difference between the pretax and posttax return to an economic activity is known as the **tax wedge**. The tax wedge applies to the *marginal tax rate*, which is the fraction of each additional dollar of income that must be paid in taxes. For example, the U.S. federal income tax has several tax brackets, which are the income ranges within which a tax rate applies. In 2011, for a single taxpayer, the tax rate was 10 percent on the first $8,500 earned during a year. The tax rate rose for higher income brackets, until it reached 35 percent on income earned above $379,150. Suppose you are paid a wage of $20 per hour. If your marginal income tax rate is 25 percent, then your after-tax wage is $15, and the tax wedge is $5. When discussing the model of demand and supply in Chapter 4, we saw that increasing the price of a good or service increases the quantity supplied. So, we would expect that reducing the tax wedge by cutting the marginal tax rate on income would result in a larger quantity of labor supplied because the after-tax wage would be higher. In general, economists believe that the smaller the tax wedge for any economic activity—such as working, saving, investing, or starting a business—the more of that economic activity that will occur. When workers, savers, investors, or entrepreneurs change their behavior as a result of a tax change, economists say that there has been a *behavioral response* to the tax change.

We can look briefly at the effects on aggregate supply of cutting each of the following taxes:

- ***Individual income tax.*** As we have seen, reducing the marginal tax rates on individual income will reduce the tax wedge faced by workers, thereby increasing the quantity of labor supplied. Many small businesses are *sole proprietorships*, whose profits are taxed at the individual income tax rates. Therefore, cutting the individual income tax rates also raises the return to entrepreneurship, encouraging the opening of new businesses. Most households are also taxed on their returns from saving at the individual income tax rates. Reducing marginal income tax rates, therefore, also increases the return to saving.

- ***Corporate income tax.*** The federal government taxes the profits earned by corporations under the corporate income tax. In 2011, most corporations faced a marginal corporate tax rate of 35 percent. Cutting the marginal corporate income tax rate would encourage investment spending by increasing the return corporations receive from new investments in equipment, factories, and office buildings. Because innovations are often embodied in new investment goods, cutting the corporate income tax can potentially increase the pace of technological change.

- ***Taxes on dividends and capital gains.*** Corporations distribute some of their profits to shareholders in the form of payments known as *dividends*. Shareholders also may benefit from higher corporate profits by receiving *capital gains*. A capital gain is the increase in the price of an asset, such as a share of stock. Rising profits usually result in rising stock prices and capital gains to shareholders. Individuals pay taxes on both dividends and capital gains (although the tax on capital gains can be postponed if the stock is not sold). As a result, the same earnings are, in effect, taxed twice: once when a corporation pays the corporate income tax on its profits and a second time when the profits are received by individual investors in the form of dividends or capital gains. Economists debate the costs and benefits of a separate tax on corporate profits. With the corporate income tax remaining in place, one way to reduce the "double taxation" problem is to reduce the taxes on dividends and capital gains. These taxes were, in fact, reduced in 2003, and in 2011, the marginal tax rates on dividends and capital gains were still well below the top marginal tax rate on individual income. Lowering the tax rates on dividends and capital gains increases the supply of loanable funds from households to firms, increasing saving and investment and lowering the equilibrium real interest rate.

Tax Simplification

In addition to the potential gains from cutting individual taxes, there are also gains from tax simplification. The complexity of the tax code has created a whole industry of tax preparation services, such as H&R Block. At almost 3,000 pages long, the tax code is extremely complex. The Internal Revenue Service estimates that taxpayers spend more than 6.4 billion hours each year filling out their tax forms, or about 45 hours per tax return. Households and firms have to deal with more than 480 tax forms to file their federal taxes. It is not surprising that there are more H&R Block offices around the country than Starbucks coffeehouses.

If the tax code were greatly simplified, the economic resources currently used by the tax preparation industry would be available to produce other goods and services. In addition to wasting resources, the complexity of the tax code may also distort the decisions made by households and firms. For example, the tax rate on dividends has clearly affected whether corporations pay dividends. When Congress passed a reduction in the tax on dividends in 2003, many firms—including Microsoft—began paying dividends for the first time. A simplified tax code would increase economic efficiency by reducing the number of decisions households and firms make solely to reduce their tax payments.

The Economic Effect of Tax Reform

We can analyze the economic effects of tax reduction and simplification by using the aggregate demand and aggregate supply model. Figure 9.16 shows that without tax changes, the long-run aggregate supply curve will shift from $LRAS_1$ to $LRAS_2$. This shift represents the increases in the labor force and the capital stock and the technological change that would occur even without tax reduction and simplification. To focus on the effect of tax changes on aggregate supply, we will ignore any shifts in the short-run aggregate supply curve, and we will assume that the aggregate demand curve remains unchanged, at AD_1. In this case, equilibrium moves from point *A* to point *B*, with real GDP increasing from Y_1 to Y_2 and the price level decreasing from P_1 to P_2.

If tax reduction and simplification are effective, the economy will experience increases in labor supply, saving, investment, and the formation of new firms. Economic efficiency will also be improved. Together these factors will result in an increase in the quantity of real GDP supplied at every price level. We show the effects of the tax changes in Figure 9.16 by a shift in the long-run aggregate supply curve to $LRAS_3$. With aggregate demand remaining unchanged, the equilibrium in the economy moves from point *A* to point *C* (rather than to point *B*, which is the equilibrium without tax changes), with real GDP increasing from Y_1 to Y_3 and the price level decreasing from P_1 to P_3. Notice that compared with the equilibrium without tax changes (point *B*), the equilibrium with tax changes (point *C*) occurs at a lower price level and a higher level of real GDP. We can conclude that the tax changes have benefited the economy by increasing output and employment while at the same time reducing the price level.

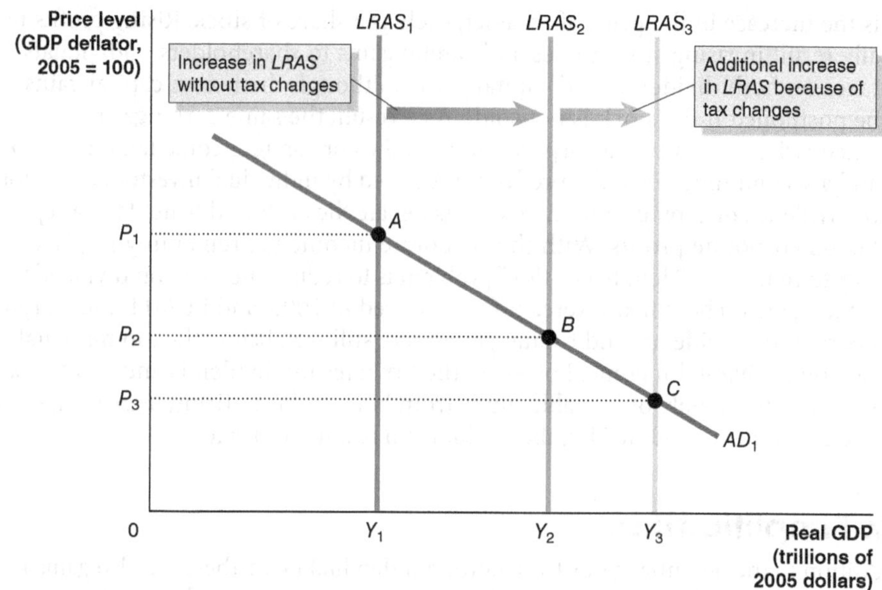

Figure 9.16

The Supply-Side Effects of a Tax Change

The economy's initial equilibrium is at point A. With no tax change, the long-run aggregate supply curve shifts to the right, from $LRAS_1$ to $LRAS_2$. Equilibrium moves to point B, with the price level falling from P_1 to P_2 and real GDP increasing from Y_1 to Y_2. With tax reductions and simplifications, the long-run aggregate supply curve shifts further to the right, to $LRAS_3$, and equilibrium moves to point C, with the price level falling to P_3 and real GDP increasing to Y_3.

Clearly, our analysis is unrealistic because we have ignored the changes in aggregate demand and short-run aggregate supply that will occur. How would a more realistic analysis differ from the simplified one in Figure 9.16? The change in real GDP would be the same because in the long run, real GDP is equal to its potential level, which is represented by the long-run aggregate supply curve. The results for the price level would be different, however, because we would expect both aggregate demand and short-run aggregate supply to shift to the right. The likeliest case is that the price level would end up higher in the new equilibrium than in the original equilibrium. However, because the position of the long-run aggregate supply curve is further to the right as a result of the tax changes, the increase in the price level will be smaller; that is, the price level at point C is likely to be lower than P_2, even if it is higher than P_3, although—as we will discuss in the next section—not all economists would agree. We can conclude that a successful policy of tax reductions and simplifications will benefit the economy by increasing output and employment and, at the same time, may result in smaller increases in the price level.

How Large Are Supply-Side Effects?

Most economists would agree that there are supply-side effects to reducing taxes: Decreasing marginal income tax rates will increase the quantity of labor supplied, cutting the corporate income tax will increase investment spending, and so on. The magnitude of the effects is the subject of considerable debate, however. For example, some economists argue that the increase in the quantity of labor supplied following a tax cut will be limited because many people work a number of hours set by their employers and lack the opportunity to work additional hours. Similarly, some economists believe that tax changes have only a small effect on saving and investment. In this view, saving and investment are affected much more by changes in income or changes in expectations of the future profitability of new investment due to technological change or improving macroeconomic conditions than they are by tax changes.

Economists who are skeptical of the magnitude of supply-side effects believe that tax cuts have their greatest effect on aggregate demand rather than on aggregate supply. In their view, focusing on the effect of tax cuts on aggregate demand, while ignoring any effect on aggregate supply, yields accurate forecasts of future movements in real GDP and the price level, which indicates that the supply-side effects must be small. If tax changes have only small effects on aggregate supply, it is unlikely that they will reduce the size of price increases to the extent shown in the analysis in Figure 9.16.

Ultimately, the debate over the size of the supply-side effects of tax policy can be resolved only through careful study of the effects of differences in tax rates on labor supply and on saving and investment decisions. Some recent studies have arrived at conflicting conclusions, however. For example, a study by Nobel Laureate Edward Prescott of Arizona State University concludes that the differences between the United States and Europe with respect to the average number of hours worked per week and the average number of weeks worked per year are due to differences in taxes. The lower marginal tax rates in the United States compared with Europe increase the return to working for U.S. workers and result in a larger quantity of labor supplied. But another study by Alberto Alesina and Edward Glaeser of Harvard University and Bruce Sacerdote of Dartmouth College argues that the more restrictive labor market regulations in Europe explain the shorter work weeks and longer vacations of European workers and that differences in taxes have only a small effect.

As in other areas of economics, differences among economists in their estimates of the supply-side effects of tax changes may narrow over time as they conduct more studies.

Continued from page 189

Economics in Your Life

What Would You Do with $500?

At the beginning of the chapter, we asked how you would respond to a $500 tax rebate and what effect this tax rebate would likely have on equilibrium real GDP in the short run. This chapter has shown that tax cuts increase disposable income and that when there is a permanent increase in disposable income, consumption spending increases. So, you will likely respond to a permanent $500 increase in your disposable income by increasing your spending. How much your spending increases depends in part on your overall financial situation. As mentioned in the chapter, people who are able to borrow usually try to smooth out their spending over time and don't increase spending much in response to a one-time increase in their income. But if you are a student struggling to get by on a low income and you are unable to borrow against the higher income you expect to earn in the future, you may well spend most of the rebate. This chapter has also shown that tax cuts have a multiplier effect on the economy. That is, an increase in consumption spending sets off further increases in real GDP and income. So, if the economy is not already at potential GDP, this tax rebate will likely increase equilibrium real GDP in the short run.

Conclusion

In this chapter, we have seen how the federal government uses changes in government purchases and taxes to achieve its economic policy goals. We have seen that economists debate the effectiveness of discretionary fiscal policy actions intended to stabilize the economy. Congress and the president share responsibility for economic policy with the Federal Reserve.

Read *An Inside Look at Policy* on the next page for a discussion of the arguments for and against using infrastructure spending to increase employment.

AN
INSIDE
LOOK
AT POLICY

Obama Proposes Additional Spending to Stimulate the Economy

U.S. NEWS & WORLD REPORT

Are Infrastructure Projects the Answer to America's Jobs Problem?

Infrastructure spending is expected to be one of the chief components of the jobs plan that President Obama will unveil in September. The idea of spending on public works projects like road-building as economic stimulus has been a mainstay of jobs proposals from both congressional Democrats and the White House in recent years. But opponents question its efficiency at creating jobs—and its cost.

a According to data from Moody's Analytics, which performs economic analysis and forecasting, infrastructure spending is more effective, dollar for dollar, than many forms of tax cuts at boosting jobs growth. But after passing legislation, going through the appropriations process, identifying projects, planning, and hiring workers, the time it takes the federal government bureaucracy to get that money out the door can mean delayed or even diminished economic impact. Add to that a particularly slow-moving Congress with a propensity for partisan divides that slow or halt much legislation—and the current climate of budget-cutting—and a potentially promising policy move could be greatly undercut or never enacted.

Many Republican lawmakers have in the past decried spending on infrastructure. When President Obama introduced the idea of a national infrastructure bank in September 2010, Representative Eric Cantor called it "yet another government stimulus effort" and House Speaker John Boehner called it "more of the same failed 'stimulus' spending," alluding to the 2009 American Recovery and Reinvestment Act that the president introduced to counteract the Great Recession. That $787-billion stimulus package created far fewer jobs than the White House had initially predicted, a point that stimulus critics often make. But not all Republicans are opposed to infrastructure spending; Texas Senator Kay Bailey Hutchison, for example, co-sponsored a bill with Massachusetts Democrat John Kerry in March, proposing an infrastructure bank.

b The theory behind infrastructure spending is the multiplier effect: the idea that every dollar in government expenditures can increase GDP by more than one dollar by starting economic chain reactions: the government pays firms for goods and services and those firms then pay employees who then spend their paychecks.

Moody's Analytics estimates that the multiplier effect for increases in government spending is generally larger than the multiplier for tax cuts. Any additional dollar spent on permanent tax cuts adds to GDP by significantly less than a dollar. Making the Bush tax cuts permanent, for example, would add to GDP by $0.29 for every dollar of revenue reduction, according to calculations from Moody's. Infrastructure spending would add by $1.59 for every dollar spent, while extending unemployment insurance and temporarily increasing food stamps would add even more.

c The mitigating factor, then, is the speed (or lack thereof) with which infrastructure spending works. In past recessions, infrastructure projects have taken so long to get off the ground that their effects were only felt after recovery had begun, says Alan Viard, resident scholar at the American Enterprise Institute, a conservative think tank. "Dollar for dollar, [tax cuts and direct government payments] may not stimulate the economy as much as infrastructure spending, but they can be timed effectively. . . . If we expect [economic weakness] to last long enough for new infrastructure spending to come online, we've really got pretty serious problems. . . ."

It is difficult to dispute that tax cuts and direct government payments could provide rapid stimulus, but like any policy, those also have their downsides. "It's true that if you want an instant stimulus, you'd send people checks. . . . And a certain amount of that would be lost. Some would go to savings and paying back debt, and a fair amount would go to buying things that are not made in the U.S.," says Ross Eisenbrey, vice president of the liberal Economic Policy Institute. . . .

Source: "Are Infrastructure Projects the Answer to America's Jobs Problem? Disappointing stimulus package gives ammunition to the policy's opponents," by Danielle Kurtzleban from *U.S. News & World Report*, August 22, 2011.

Key Points in the Article

Proponents of spending on infrastructure as a means of stimulating the economy argue that for each dollar spent, infrastructure spending is more effective than tax cuts at creating jobs. They also estimate that the multiplier effect for increases in government spending is larger than the multiplier effect for tax cuts. Those opposed to using infrastructure spending as a way to increase employment argue that the 2009 American Recovery and Reinvestment Act created considerably fewer jobs than had been predicted. An important factor in determining job creation through infrastructure spending is the time needed for the spending to occur and to have its full effect on the economy. Although infrastructure spending may stimulate the economy more than tax cuts, it may also take a long time for Congress to approve spending programs and for the programs actually to take effect.

Analyzing the News

a As you read in this chapter, expansionary fiscal policy involves increasing government purchases or decreasing taxes to increase aggregate demand. The Obama administration introduced the American Recovery and Reinvestment Act in 2009, a stimulus package designed to combat the recession that began in December 2007. A portion of this stimulus package was designated for infrastructure spending, and the administration believed that it would have a greater economic effect than the less-than-successful tax rebate program implemented by the Bush administration in 2008. According to Moody's Analytics, an economic analysis and forecasting company, each dollar of infrastructure spending has a greater effect on job growth than does each dollar in tax cuts, but infrastructure spending is subject to potentially significant time delays because Congress needs to approve the spending, infrastructure projects need to be identified and planned, and workers need to be hired. The amount of time it takes to actually implement these projects can delay or even weaken their economic effect.

b An increase in infrastructure spending is subject to the multiplier effect, where every dollar spent will increase GDP by more than one dollar. The figure below shows aggregate demand increasing from AD_1 to AD when infrastructure spending is first increased. The amount of the increase is equal to the initial increase in government spending. Due to the multiplier effect, aggregate demand continues to increase, from AD to AD_2. The increase in spending therefore results in a larger increase in real GDP. Moody's Analytics estimates that the multiplier for infrastructure spending is 1.59, so for every $1 increase in spending, real GDP will increase by $1.59.

c The length of time it takes for infrastructure spending to affect the economy can make a large difference in the overall effectiveness of the spending. If the spending begins only after a relatively long period of time, the economy may have already begun to recover by the time the additional spending can have an effect. In this case, the expansionary fiscal policy could expand aggregate demand by too great an amount, leading to an eventual increase in inflation.

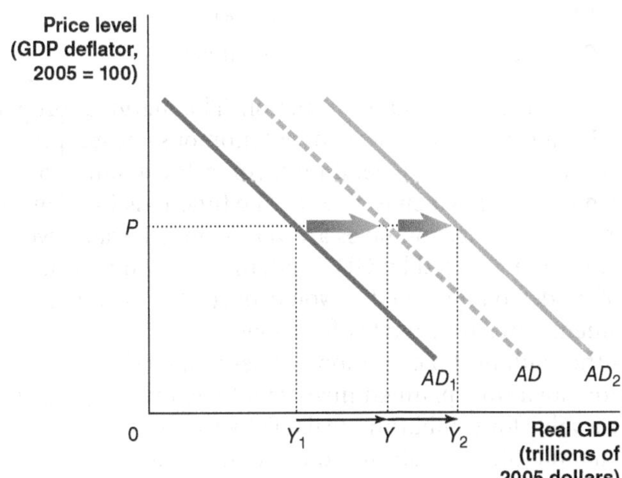

The effect on aggregate demand of infrastructure spending.

Thinking Critically About Policy

1. President Obama's economic team calculated the effects of its economic stimulus package using estimates of the government spending multiplier. Some economists, though, argue that administration economists have overestimated the sizes of the government purchases and tax multipliers. Other economists have argued that the sizes of these multipliers were underestimated. Why do economists have difficulty in reaching agreement on the sizes of these multipliers?
2. The Obama administration's stimulus spending resulted in a large increase in the federal budget deficit. Administration economists, however, were relatively unconcerned that crowding out would reduce the effect of the stimulus spending on real GDP. Briefly explain what crowding out is and why the administration was relatively unconcerned about it as it implemented the stimulus package.

Appendix

LEARNING OBJECTIVE

Apply the multiplier formula.

A Closer Look at the Multiplier

In this chapter, we saw that changes in government purchases and changes in taxes have a multiplied effect on equilibrium real GDP. In this appendix, we will build a simple economic model of the multiplier effect. When economists forecast the effect of a change in spending or taxes, they often rely on *econometric models.*

An Expression for Equilibrium Real GDP

We can write a set of equations that includes the key macroeconomic relationships we have studied in this and previous chapters. It is important to note that in this model, we will be assuming that the price level is constant. We know that this is unrealistic because an upward-sloping *SRAS* curve means that when the aggregate demand curve shifts, the price level will change. Nevertheless, our model will be approximately correct when changes in the price level are small. It also serves as an introduction to more complicated models that take into account changes in the price level. For simplicity, we also start out by assuming that taxes, T, do not depend on the level of real GDP, Y. We also assume that there are no government transfer payments to households. Finally, we assume that we have a closed economy, with no imports or exports. The numbers (with the exception of the *MPC*) represent billions of dollars:

(1) $C = 1{,}000 + 0.75(Y - T)$	Consumption function
(2) $I = 1{,}500$	Planned investment function
(3) $G = 1{,}500$	Government purchases function
(4) $T = 1{,}000$	Tax function
(5) $Y = C + I + G$	Equilibrium condition

The first equation is the consumption function. The marginal propensity to consume, or *MPC*, is 0.75, and 1,000 is the level of autonomous consumption, which is the level of consumption that does not depend on income. We assume that consumption depends on disposable income, which is $Y - T$. The functions for planned investment spending, government spending, and taxes are very simple because we have assumed that these variables are not affected by GDP and, therefore, are constant. Economists who use this type of model to forecast GDP would, of course, use more realistic planned investment, government purchases, and tax functions.

Equation (5)—the equilibrium condition—states that equilibrium GDP equals the sum of consumption spending, planned investment spending, and government purchases. To calculate a value for equilibrium real GDP, we need to substitute equations (1) through (4) into equation (5). This substitution gives us the following:

$$\begin{aligned} Y &= 1{,}000 + 0.75(Y - 1{,}000) + 1{,}500 + 1{,}500 \\ &= 1{,}000 + 0.75Y - 750 + 1{,}500 + 1{,}500. \end{aligned}$$

We need to solve this equation for Y to find equilibrium GDP. The first step is to subtract $0.75Y$ from both sides of the equation:

$$Y - 0.75Y = 1{,}000 - 750 + 1{,}500 + 1{,}500.$$

Then, we solve for Y:

$$0.25Y = 3{,}250$$

or

$$Y = \frac{3{,}250}{0.25} = 13{,}000.$$

To make this result more general, we can replace particular values with general values represented by letters:

$C = C + MPC(Y - T)$	Consumption function
$I = \bar{I}$	Planned investment function
$G = G$	Government purchases function
$T = \bar{T}$	Tax function
$Y = C + I + G$	Equilibrium condition

The letters with bars above them represent fixed, or *autonomous*, values that do not depend on the values of other variables. So, $\bar{C}$ represents autonomous consumption, which had a value of 1,000 in our original example. Now, solving for equilibrium, we get:

$$Y = \bar{C} + MPC(Y - \bar{T}) + \bar{I} + \bar{G}$$

or

$$Y - MPC(Y) = \bar{C} - (MPC \times \bar{T}) + \bar{I} + \bar{G}$$

or

$$Y(1 - MPC) = \bar{C} - (MPC \times \bar{T}) + \bar{I} + \bar{G}$$

or

$$Y = \frac{\bar{C} - (MPC \times \bar{T}) + \bar{I} + \bar{G}}{1 - MPC}.$$

A Formula for the Government Purchases Multiplier

To find a formula for the government purchases multiplier, we need to rewrite the last equation for changes in each variable rather than levels. Letting Δ stand for the change in a variable, we have

$$\Delta Y = \frac{\Delta\bar{C} - (MPC \times \Delta\bar{T}) + \Delta\bar{I} + \Delta\bar{G}}{1 - MPC}.$$

If we hold constant changes in autonomous consumption spending, planned investment spending, and taxes, we can find a formula for the government purchases multiplier, which is the ratio of the change in equilibrium real GDP to the change in government purchases:

$$\Delta Y = \frac{\Delta G}{1 - MPC}$$

or

$$\text{Government purchases multiplier} = \frac{\Delta Y}{\Delta G} = \frac{1}{1 - MPC}.$$

For an *MPC* of 0.75, the government purchases multiplier will be

$$\frac{1}{1 - 0.75} = 4.$$

A government purchases multiplier of 4 means that an increase in government spending of \$10 billion will increase equilibrium real GDP by $4 \times \$10$ billion $=$ \$40 billion.

A Formula for the Tax Multiplier

We can also find a formula for the tax multiplier. We start again with this equation:

$$\Delta Y = \frac{\Delta \bar{C} - (MPC \times \Delta \bar{T}) + \Delta \bar{I} + \Delta \bar{G}}{1 - MPC}.$$

Now we hold constant the values of autonomous consumption spending, planned investment spending, and government purchases, but we allow the value of taxes to change:

$$\Delta Y = \frac{- MPC \times \Delta T}{1 - MPC}.$$

Or:

$$\text{The tax multiplier} = \frac{\Delta Y}{\Delta T} = \frac{-MPC}{1 - MPC}.$$

For an *MPC* of 0.75, the tax multiplier will be:

$$\frac{-0.75}{1 - 0.75} = -3.$$

The tax multiplier is a negative number because an increase in taxes causes a decrease in equilibrium real GDP, and a decrease in taxes causes an increase in equilibrium real GDP. A tax multiplier of -3 means that a decrease in taxes of \$10 billion will increase equilibrium real GDP by $-3 \times -\$10$ billion $=$ \$30 billion. In this chapter, we discussed the economic reasons for the tax multiplier being smaller than the government spending multiplier.

The "Balanced Budget" Multiplier

What will be the effect of equal increases (or decreases) in government purchases and taxes on equilibrium real GDP? At first, it might appear that the tax increase would exactly offset the government purchases increase, leaving real GDP unchanged. But we have just seen that the government purchases multiplier is larger (in absolute value) than the tax multiplier. We can use our formulas for the government purchases multiplier and the tax multiplier to calculate the net effect of increasing government purchases by \$10 billion at the same time that taxes are increased by \$10 billion:

$$\text{Increase in real GDP from the increase in government purchases} = \$10 \text{ billion} \times \frac{1}{1 - MPC}$$

$$\text{Decrease in real GDP from the increase in taxes} = \$10 \text{ billion} \times \frac{-MPC}{1 - MPC}$$

So, the combined effect equals

$$\$10 \text{ billion} \times \left[\left(\frac{1}{1 - MPC}\right) + \left(\frac{- MPC}{1 - MPC}\right)\right]$$

or

$$\$10 \text{ billion} \times \left(\frac{1 - MPC}{1 - MPC}\right) = \$10 \text{ billion}.$$

The balanced budget multiplier is, therefore, equal to $(1 - MPC)/(1 - MPC)$, or 1. Equal dollar increases and decreases in government purchases and in taxes lead to the same dollar increase in real GDP in the short run.

The Effects of Changes in Tax Rates on the Multiplier

We now consider the effect of a change in the tax *rate*, as opposed to a change in a fixed amount of taxes. Changing the tax rate actually changes the value of the multiplier. To see this, suppose that the tax rate is 20 percent, or 0.2. In that case, an increase in household income of \$10 billion will increase *disposable income* by only \$8 billion [or 10 billion $\times (1 - 0.2)$]. In general, an increase in income can be multiplied by $(1 - t)$ to find the increase in disposable income, where t is the tax rate. So, we can rewrite the consumption function as:

$$C = \overline{C} + MPC(1 - t)Y.$$

We can use this expression for the consumption function to find an expression for the government purchases multiplier, using the same method we used previously:

$$\text{Government purchases multiplier} = \frac{\Delta Y}{\Delta G} = \frac{1}{1 - MPC(1 - t)}.$$

We can see the effect of changing the tax rate on the size of the multiplier by trying some values. First, assume that $MPC = 0.75$ and $t = 0.2$. Then:

$$\text{Government purchases multiplier} = \frac{\Delta Y}{\Delta G} = \frac{1}{1 - 0.75(1 - 0.2)} = \frac{1}{1 - 0.6} = 2.5.$$

This value is smaller than the multiplier of 4 that we calculated by assuming that there was only a fixed amount of taxes (which is the same as assuming that the marginal tax *rate* was zero). This multiplier is smaller because spending in each period is now reduced by the amount of taxes households must pay on any additional income they earn. We can calculate the multiplier for an *MPC* of 0.75 and a lower tax rate of 0.1:

$$\text{Government purchases multiplier} = \frac{\Delta Y}{\Delta G} = \frac{1}{1 - 0.75(1 - 0.1)} = \frac{1}{1 - 0.675} = 3.1.$$

Cutting the tax rate from 20 percent to 10 percent increased the value of the multiplier from 2.5 to 3.1.

The Multiplier in an Open Economy

Up to now, we have assumed that the economy is closed, with no imports or exports. We can consider the case of an open economy by including net exports in our analysis. Recall that net exports equal exports minus imports. Exports are determined primarily by factors—such as the exchange value of the dollar and the levels of real GDP in other countries—that we do not include in our model. So, we will assume that exports are fixed, or autonomous:

$$\text{Exports} = \overline{\textit{Exports}}$$

Imports will increase as real GDP increases because households will spend some portion of an increase in income on imports. We can define the *marginal propensity to import (MPI)* as the fraction of an increase in income that is spent on imports. So, our expression for imports is

$$\text{Imports} = MPI \times Y.$$

We can substitute our expressions for exports and imports into the expression we derived earlier for equilibrium real GDP:

$$Y = \overline{C} + MPC(1 - t)Y + \overline{I} + \overline{G} + [\overline{Exports} - (MPI \times Y)],$$

where the expression $[\overline{Exports} - (MPI \times Y)]$ represents net exports. We can now find an expression for the government purchases multiplier by using the same method we used previously:

$$\text{Government purchases multiplier} = \frac{\Delta Y}{\Delta G} = \frac{1}{1 - [MPC(1 - t) - MPI]}.$$

We can see the effect of changing the value of the marginal propensity to import on the size of the multiplier by trying some values of key variables. First, assume that $MPC = 0.75$, $t = 0.2$, and $MPI = 0.1$. Then:

$$\text{Government purchases multiplier} = \frac{\Delta Y}{\Delta G} = \frac{1}{1 - (0.75(1 - 0.2) - 0.1)} = \frac{1}{1 - 0.5} = 2.$$

This value is smaller than the multiplier of 2.5 that we calculated by assuming that there were no exports or imports (which is the same as assuming that the marginal propensity to import was zero). This multiplier is smaller because spending in each period is now reduced by the amount of imports households buy with any additional income they earn. We can calculate the multiplier with $MPC = 0.75$, $t = 0.2$, and a higher MPI of 0.2:

$$\text{Government purchases multiplier} = \frac{\Delta Y}{\Delta G} = \frac{1}{1 - (0.75(1 - 0.2) - 0.2)} = \frac{1}{1 - 0.4} = 1.7.$$

Increasing the marginal propensity to import from 0.1 to 0.2 decreases the value of the multiplier from 2 to 1.7. We can conclude that countries with a higher marginal propensity to import will have smaller multipliers than countries with a lower marginal propensity to import.

Bear in mind that the multiplier is a short-run effect which assumes that the economy is below the level of potential real GDP. In the long run, the economy is at potential real GDP, so an increase in government purchases causes a decline in the nongovernment components of real GDP but leaves the level of real GDP unchanged.

The analysis in this appendix is simplified compared to what would be carried out by an economist forecasting the effects of changes in government purchases or changes in taxes on equilibrium real GDP in the short run. In particular, our assumption that the price level is constant is unrealistic. However, looking more closely at the determinants of the multiplier has helped us see more clearly some important macroeconomic relationships.

A Closer Look at the Multiplier, pages 222-225

LEARNING OBJECTIVE: Apply the multiplier formula.

Problem and Applications

9A.1 Assuming a fixed amount of taxes and a closed economy, calculate the value of the government purchases multiplier, the tax multiplier, and the balanced budget multiplier if the marginal propensity to consume equals 0.6.

9A.2 Calculate the value of the government purchases multiplier if the marginal propensity to consume equals 0.8, the tax rate equals 0.25, and the marginal propensity to import equals 0.2.

9A.3 Use a graph to show the change in the aggregate demand curve resulting from an increase in government purchases if the government purchases multiplier equals 2. Now, on the same graph, show the change in the aggregate demand curve resulting from an increase in government purchases if the government purchases multiplier equals 4.

9A.4 Using your understanding of multipliers, explain why an increase in the tax rate would decrease the size of the government purchases multiplier. Similarly, explain why a decrease in the marginal propensity to import would increase the size of the government purchases multiplier.

CHAPTER 10

Money, Banks, and the Federal Reserve System

Chapter Outline and Learning Objectives

Coca-Cola Dries Up as Money Floods Zimbabwe

People in Africa buy 36 billion bottles of Coca-Cola a year. In 2008, Zimbabwe, a country in southern Africa, ran out of locally produced Coke for the first time in at least 40 years. Because they could not obtain U.S. dollars, local Coke bottlers were not able to import from the United States the concentrated syrup used to make the soft drink. A meager amount of Coke was imported from South Africa, but a single bottle sold for around 15 billion Zimbabwean dollars! Zimbabwe was suffering the effects of an inflation rate so high that it is called a *hyperinflation*. Zimbabwe's hyperinflation was of epic proportions, perhaps the worst in world history. When it was first introduced in 1980, 1 Zimbabwean dollar was worth 1.47 U.S. dollars. By the end of 2008, the exchange rate was 1 U.S. dollar to 2 *billion* Zimbabwean dollars, and prices for some large transactions in Zimbabwe were calculated in quadrillions (15 zeros) and quintillions (18 zeros).

In addition to the Coke shortage, Zimbabweans were suffering shortages of fuel, food, and other basic goods. As the value of the Zimbabwean currency fell against other currencies, it was difficult for local businesses such as the Coke bottlers to find anyone willing to exchange U.S. dollars for Zimbabwean dollars. What made Zimbabwe's currency almost worthless? The government of Zimbabwe had decided to pay for all of its expenses by printing more and more money. The faster the government printed money, the faster prices rose. Eventually, both foreigners and local residents refused to accept the Zimbabwean dollar in exchange for goods and services, and the country's economy plunged into a devastating recession, with real GDP falling more than 12 percent during 2008. In early 2009, the government issued 100 trillion dollar bills, not enough for a bus ticket in Harare, Zimbabwe's capital city. Eventually, in 2009, a new Zimbabwean government took the drastic step of abandoning its own currency and making the U.S. dollar the country's official currency.

AN INSIDE LOOK AT POLICY on **page 256** discusses how banks in 2011 increased their loans to both consumers and businesses and how that affected the recovery from the recession of 2007–2009.

Based on Angus Shaw, "Coca Cola Dries Up in Zimbabwe," newzimbabwe.com, December 1, 2008; Patrick McGroarty and Farai Mutsaka, "How to Turn 100 Trillion Dollars into Five and Feel Good About It," *Wall Street Journal*, May 11, 2011; Marcus Walker and Andrew Higgins, "Zimbabwe Can't Paper Over Its Million-Percent Inflation Anymore," *Wall Street Journal*, July 2, 2008; and "Wait and See," *Economist*, February 5, 2009.

Economics in Your Life

What if Money Became Increasingly Valuable?

Most people are used to the fact that as prices rise each year, the purchasing power of money falls. You will be able to buy fewer goods and services with $1,000 one year from now than you can buy today, and you will be able to buy even fewer goods and services the year after that. In fact, with an inflation rate of just 3 percent, in 25 years, $1,000 will buy only what $475 can buy today. Suppose, though, that you could live in an economy where the purchasing power of money rose each year? What would be the advantages and disadvantages of living in such an economy? As you read the chapter, see if you can answer these questions. You can check your answers against those we provide on **page 254** at the end of this chapter.

In this chapter, we will explore the role of money in the economy. We will see how the banking system creates money and what policy tools the Federal Reserve uses to manage the quantity of money. We will also look at the crisis in the banking system during the past few years. At the end of the chapter, we will explore the link between changes in the quantity of money and changes in the price level. What you learn in this chapter will serve as an important foundation for understanding monetary policy and fiscal policy, which we study in the next two chapters.

10.1 LEARNING OBJECTIVE

Define money and discuss the four functions of money.

What Is Money, and Why Do We Need It?

Could an economy function without money? We know the answer to this question is "yes" because there are many historical examples of economies in which people traded goods for other goods rather than using money. For example, a farmer on the American frontier during colonial times might have traded a cow for a plow. Most economies, though, use money. What is money? The economic definition of **money** is any asset that people are generally willing to accept in exchange for goods and services or for payment of debts. An **asset** is anything of value owned by a person or a firm. There are many possible kinds of money: In West Africa, at one time, cowrie shells served as money. During World War II, prisoners of war used cigarettes as money.

Money Assets that people are generally willing to accept in exchange for goods and services or for payment of debts.

Asset Anything of value owned by a person or a firm.

Barter and the Invention of Money

To understand the importance of money, let's consider further the situation in economies that do not use money. These economies, where goods and services are traded directly for other goods and services, are called *barter economies*. Barter economies have a major shortcoming. To illustrate this shortcoming, consider a farmer on the American frontier in colonial days. Suppose the farmer needed another cow and proposed trading a spare plow to a neighbor for one of the neighbor's cows. If the neighbor did not want the plow, the trade would not happen. For a barter trade to take place between two people, each person must want what the other one has. Economists refer to this requirement as a *double coincidence of wants*. The farmer who wants the cow might eventually be able to obtain one if he first trades with some other neighbor for something the neighbor with the cow wants. However, it may take several trades before the farmer is ultimately able to trade for what the neighbor with the cow wants. Locating several trading partners and making several intermediate trades can take considerable time and energy.

The problems with barter give societies an incentive to identify a product that most people will accept in exchange for what they have to trade. For example, in colonial times, animal skins were very useful in making clothing. The first governor of Tennessee actually received a salary of 1,000 deerskins per year, and the secretary of the Treasury received 450 otter skins per year. A good used as money that also has value independent of its use as money is called a **commodity money**. Historically, once a good became widely accepted as money, people who did not have an immediate use for it would be willing to accept it. A colonial farmer—or the governor of Tennessee—might not want a deerskin, but as long as he knew he could use the deerskin to buy other goods and services, he would be willing to accept it in exchange for what he had to sell.

Commodity money A good used as money that also has value independent of its use as money.

Trading goods and services is much easier when money becomes available. People only need to sell what they have for money and then use the money to buy what they want. If the colonial family could find someone to buy their plow, they could use the money to buy the cow they wanted. The family with the cow would accept the money because they knew they could use it to buy what they wanted. When money is available, families are less likely to produce everything or nearly everything they need themselves and more likely to specialize.

Most people in modern economies are highly specialized. They do only one thing—work as a nurse, an accountant, or an engineer—and use the money they earn to buy everything else they need. As we discussed in Chapter 3, people become much more productive by specializing because they can pursue their *comparative advantage*. The high income levels in modern economies are based on the specialization that money makes possible. We can now answer the question, "Why do we need money?" *By making exchange easier, money allows people to specialize and become more productive.*

The Functions of Money

Anything used as money—whether a deerskin, a cowrie seashell, cigarettes, or a dollar bill—should fulfill the following four functions:

- Medium of exchange
- Unit of account
- Store of value
- Standard of deferred payment

Medium of Exchange Money serves as a medium of exchange when sellers are willing to accept it in exchange for goods or services. When the local supermarket accepts your $5 bill in exchange for bread and milk, the $5 bill is serving as a medium of exchange. With a medium of exchange, people can sell goods and services for money and use the money to buy what they want. An economy is more efficient when a single good is recognized as a medium of exchange.

Unit of Account In a barter system, each good has many prices. A cow may be worth two plows, 20 bushels of wheat, or six axes. Once a single good is used as money, each good has a single price rather than many prices. This function of money gives buyers and sellers a *unit of account*, a way of measuring value in the economy in terms of money. Because the U.S. economy uses dollars as money, each good has a price in terms of dollars.

Store of Value Money allows value to be stored easily: If you do not use all your dollars to buy goods and services today, you can hold the rest to use in the future. Money is not the only store of value, however. Any asset—shares of Coca-Cola stock, Treasury bonds, real estate, or Renoir paintings, for example—represents a store of value. Financial assets, such as stocks and bonds, offer an important benefit relative to holding money because they pay a higher rate of interest or may increase in value in the future. Other assets also have advantages relative to money because they provide services. A house, for example, offers you a place to sleep.

Why, then, do people hold any money? The answer has to do with *liquidity*, or the ease with which an asset can be converted into the medium of exchange. Because money is the medium of exchange, it is the most liquid asset. If you want to buy something and you need to sell an asset to do so, you are likely to incur a cost. For example, if you want to buy a car and need to sell bonds or stocks in order to do so, you will need to pay a commission to your broker. To avoid such costs, people are willing to hold some of their wealth in the form of money, even though other assets offer a greater return as a store of value.

Standard of Deferred Payment Money is useful because it can serve as a standard of deferred payment in borrowing and lending. Money can facilitate exchange at a *given point in time* by providing a medium of exchange and unit of account. Money can facilitate exchange *over time* by providing a store of value and a standard of deferred payment. For example, a computer manufacturer may buy hard drives from another firm in exchange for the promise of making payment in 60 days.

How important is it that money be a reliable store of value and standard of deferred payment? People care about how much food, clothing, and other goods and services their dollars will buy. The value of money depends on its purchasing power, which refers to its ability to buy goods and services. Inflation causes a decline in purchasing power because with rising prices, a given amount of money can purchase fewer goods and services. When inflation reaches the levels seen in Zimbabwe, money is no longer a reliable store of value or standard of deferred payment.

What Can Serve as Money?

Having a medium of exchange helps to make transactions easier, allowing the economy to work more efficiently. The next logical question is this: What can serve as money? That is, which assets should be used as the medium of exchange? We saw earlier that an asset must, at a minimum, be generally accepted as payment to serve as money. In practical terms, however, it must be even more.

Five criteria make a good suitable for use as a medium of exchange:

1. The good must be *acceptable* to (that is, usable by) most people.
2. It should be of *standardized quality* so that any two units are identical.
3. It should be *durable* so that value is not lost by spoilage.
4. It should be *valuable* relative to its weight so that amounts large enough to be useful in trade can be easily transported.
5. The medium of exchange should be *divisible* because different goods are valued differently.

Dollar bills meet all these criteria. What determines the acceptability of dollar bills as a medium of exchange? Basically, it is through self-fulfilling expectations: You value something as money only if you believe that others will accept it from you as payment. A society's willingness to use paper dollars as money makes dollars an acceptable medium of exchange.

Commodity Money Commodity money has value independent of its use as money. Gold, for example, was a common form of money in the nineteenth century because it was a medium of exchange, a unit of account, a store of value, and a standard of deferred payment. But commodity money has a significant problem: Its value depends on its purity. Therefore, someone who wanted to cheat could mix impure metals with a precious metal. Another problem with using gold as money was that the money supply was difficult to control because it depended partly on unpredictable discoveries of new gold fields.

Fiat Money It can be inefficient for an economy to rely on only gold or other precious metals for its money supply. What if you had to transport bars of gold to settle your transactions? Not only would doing so be difficult and costly, but you would run the risk of being robbed. To get around this problem, private institutions or governments began to store gold and issue paper certificates that could be redeemed for gold. In modern economies, paper currency is generally issued by a *central bank*, which is an agency of the government that regulates the money supply. The **Federal Reserve** is the central bank of the United States. Today, no government in the world issues paper currency that can be redeemed for gold. Paper currency has no value unless it is used as money, and it is therefore not a commodity money. Instead, paper currency is a **fiat money**, which has no value except as money. If paper currency has no value except as money, why do consumers and firms use it?

Federal Reserve The central bank of the United States.

Fiat money Money, such as paper currency, that is authorized by a central bank or governmental body and that does not have to be exchanged by the central bank for gold or some other commodity money.

If you look at the top of a U.S. dollar bill, you will see that it is actually a *Federal Reserve Note*, issued by the Federal Reserve. Because U.S. dollars are fiat money, the Federal Reserve is not required to give you gold or silver for your dollar bills. Federal Reserve currency is *legal tender* in the United States, which means the federal government requires that it be accepted in payment of debts and requires that cash or checks denominated in dollars be used in payment of taxes. Despite being legal tender, dollar bills would not be a good medium of exchange and could not serve as money if they weren't widely accepted by people. The key to this acceptance is that *households and firms have confidence that if they accept paper dollars in exchange for goods and services, the dollars will not lose much value during the time they hold them*. Without this confidence, dollar bills would not serve as a medium of exchange.

Making the Connection

Apple Didn't Want My Cash!

If Federal Reserve Notes are legal tender, doesn't that mean that everyone in the United States, including every business, has to accept paper money? The answer to this question is "no," as a woman in California found out when she went to an Apple store in Palo Alto and tried to buy an iPad using $600 in currency. At that point, the iPad had just been released, and Apple did not want to sell large numbers to people who were buying them to resell on eBay, Craigslist, or elsewhere. So, a customer wanting to buy an iPad had to pay either with a credit card or a debit card, which would make it easier for Apple to keep track of anyone attempting to buy more than the limit of two per customer.

The law doesn't require Apple to accept paper money from these customers.

Because Federal Reserve Notes are legal tender, creditors must accept them in payment of debts, and the government will accept them in payment of taxes. However, as this incident makes clear, firms do not have to accept cash as payment for goods and services. As the U.S. Treasury Department explains on its Web site:

> There is . . . no Federal statute mandating that a private business, a person or an organization must accept currency or coins as payment for goods and/or services. . . . For example, a bus line may prohibit payment of fares in pennies or dollar bills. In addition, movie theaters, convenience stores and gas stations may refuse to accept large denomination currency (usually notes above $20) as a matter of policy.

The woman who tried to buy an iPad for cash was disabled and on a limited income, so the incident led to bad publicity for Apple. As a result, Apple decided to lift its ban on paying for iPads with cash, provided that the customer was willing to set up an Apple account at the time of purchase. In addition, Apple presented a free iPad to the customer who was originally turned down when she tried to pay with cash.

Based on Michael Winter, "Apple Ends No-Cash Policy and California Woman Gets Free iPad," www.usatoday.com, May 20, 2010; and U.S. Treasury, "FAQs: Currency," http://www.treasury.gov/resource-center/faqs/Currency/Pages/edu_faq_currency_index2.aspx.

How Is Money Measured in the United States Today?

10.2 LEARNING OBJECTIVE

Discuss the definitions of the money supply used in the United States today.

A narrow definition of money would include only those assets that obviously function as a medium of exchange: currency, checking account deposits, and traveler's checks. These assets can easily be used to buy goods and services and thus act as a medium of exchange. This strict interpretation is too narrow, however, as a measure of the money supply in the real world. Many other assets can fill the role of a medium of exchange, although they are not as liquid as checking account deposits or cash. For example, you can convert your savings account at a bank to cash.

In the United States, the Federal Reserve has conducted several studies of the appropriate definition of *money*. The job of defining the money supply has become more difficult during the past two decades, as innovation in financial markets and institutions has created new substitutes for traditional checking accounts. Outside the United States, other central banks use similar measures. Next, we will look more closely at the Fed's definitions of the money supply.

M1: The Narrowest Definition of the Money Supply

M1 The narrowest definition of the money supply: The sum of currency in circulation, checking account deposits in banks, and holdings of traveler's checks.

Figure 10.1 illustrates the definitions of the money supply. The narrowest definition is called **M1**. It includes:

1. *Currency*, which is all the paper money and coins that are in circulation, where "in circulation" means not held by banks or the government
2. The value of all checking account deposits at banks
3. The value of traveler's checks (Because this last category is so small—about $4.4 billion in August 2011—relative to the other two categories, we will ignore it in our discussion of the money supply.)

Although currency has a larger value than checking account deposits, checking account deposits are used much more often than currency to make payments. More than 80 percent of all expenditures on goods and services are made with checks rather than with currency. In fact, the total amount of currency in circulation—$977 billion in August 2011—is a misleading number. This amount is more than $2,800 per person—adult or child—in the United States. If this sounds like an unrealistically large amount of currency to be held per person, it is. Economists estimate that more than 60 percent of U.S. currency is actually outside the borders of the United States.

Who holds these dollars outside the United States? Foreign banks and foreign governments hold some dollars, but most are held by households and firms in countries where there is not much confidence in the local currency. When inflation rates are very high, many households and firms do not want to hold their domestic currency because it is losing its value too rapidly. The value of the U.S. dollar will be much more stable than their domestic currency. If enough people are willing to accept dollars as well as—or instead of—domestic currency, dollars become a second currency for the country. As we saw in the chapter opener, when inflation soared in Zimbabwe, the government was led to adopt the U.S. dollar as the country's official currency.

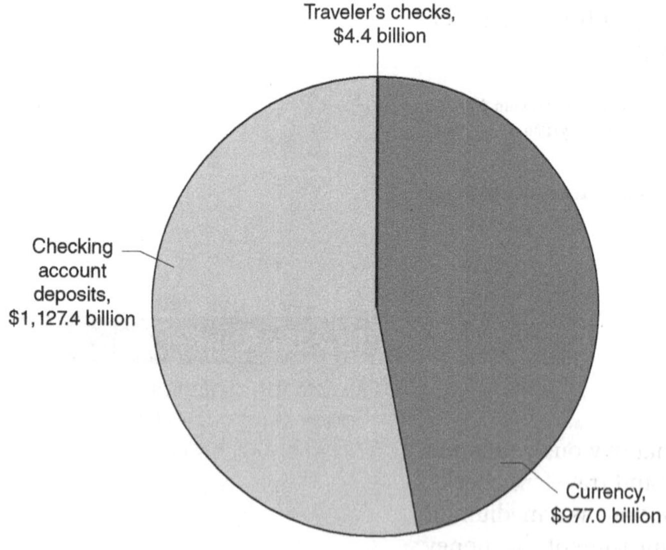

(a) M1 = $2,108.8 billion

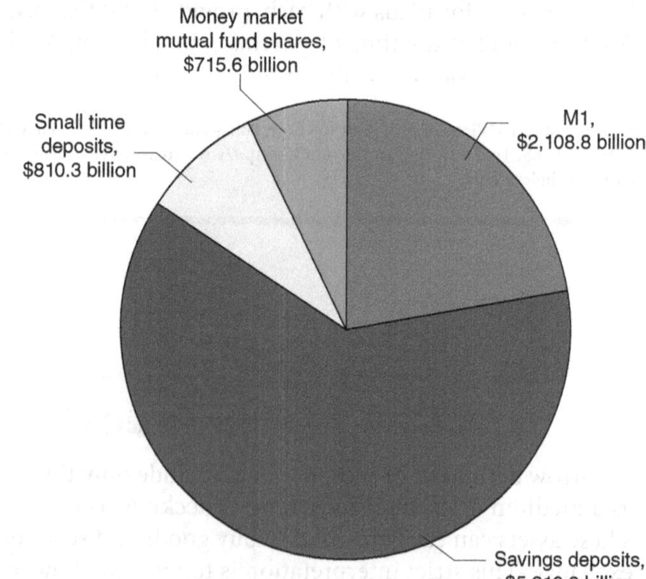

(b) M2 = $9,544.9 billion

Figure 10.1 Measuring the Money Supply, August 2011

The Federal Reserve uses two different measures of the money supply: M1 and M2. M2 includes all the assets in M1, as well as the additional assets shown in panel (b).

Data from Board of Governors of the Federal Reserve System, "Federal Reserve Statistical Release, H6," September 29, 2011.

Making the Connection

Do We Still Need the Penny?

We have seen that fiat money has no value except as money. Governments actually make a profit from issuing fiat money because fiat money is usually produced using paper or low-value metals that cost far less than the face value of the money. For example, it costs only about 4 cents for the federal Bureau of Engraving and Printing to manufacture a $20 bill. The government's profit from issuing fiat money—which is equal to the difference between the face value of the money and its production cost—is called *seigniorage*.

With small-denomination coins—like pennies or nickels—there is a possibility that the coins will cost more to produce than their face value. This was true in the early 1980s, when the rising price of copper meant the federal government was spending more than 1 cent to produce a penny. That led the government to switch from making pennies from copper to making them from zinc. Unfortunately, by 2007, the rising price of zinc meant that once again, the penny cost more than 1 cent to produce. Although the price of zinc later declined, many economists began to ask whether the penny should simply be abolished. Not only does it sometimes cost more to produce than it is worth, but inflation has eroded its purchasing power to such an extent that some people just find the penny to be a nuisance. Many people will not bother to pick up a penny from the sidewalk. In fact, several other countries, including Great Britain, Australia, and the European countries that use the euro, have eliminated their lowest-denomination coins; Canada is also considering doing so.

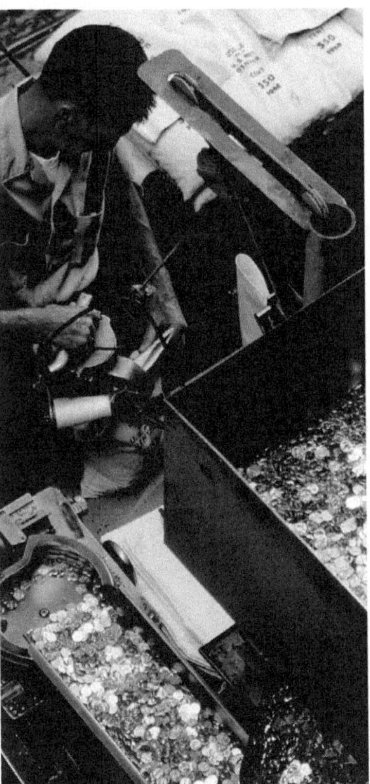

Unfortunately, these cost the government more than a penny to produce.

Some economists, though, have argued that eliminating the penny would subject consumers to a "rounding tax." For example, a good that had been priced at $2.99 will cost $3.00 if the penny is eliminated. Some estimates have put the cost to consumers of the rounding tax as high as $600 million. But Robert Whaples, an economist at Wake Forest University, after analyzing almost 200,000 transactions from a convenience store chain, concludes that "the 'rounding tax' is a myth. In reality, the number of times consumers' bills would be rounded upward is almost exactly equal to the number of times they would be rounded downward."

François Velde, an economist at the Federal Reserve Bank of Chicago, has come up with perhaps the most ingenious solution to the problem of the penny: The federal government would simply declare that Lincoln pennies are now worth 5 cents. There would then be two 5-cent coins in circulation—the current Jefferson nickels and the current Lincoln pennies—and no 1-cent coins. In the future, only the Lincoln coins—now worth 5 cents—would be minted. This would solve the problem of consumers and retail stores having to deal with pennies, it would make the face value of the Lincoln 5-cent coin greater than its cost of production, and it would also deal with the problem that the current Jefferson nickel frequently costs more than 5 cents to produce. But will Lincoln pennies actually be accepted as being worth 5 cents simply because the government says so? The answer is "yes" because as long as the government is willing to exchange 20 Lincoln coins for a paper dollar, everyone else will be willing to do so as well. Of course, if this plan were adopted, anyone with a hoard of pennies would find that their money would be worth five times as much overnight!

Whether or not pennies get turned into nickels, it seems very likely that one way or another, the penny will eventually disappear from the U.S. money supply.

Based on Robert Whaples, "Why Keeping the Penny No Longer Makes Sense," *USA Today*, July 12, 2006; Austan Goolsbee, "Now That a Penny Isn't Worth Much, It's Time to Make It Worth 5 Cents," *New York Times*, February 1, 2007; François Velde, "What's a Penny (or a Nickel) Really Worth?" Federal Reserve Bank of Chicago, Chicago Fed Letter, No. 235a, February 2007; and Nicholas Kohler, "A Penny Dropped," macleans.ca, January 14, 2011.

M2: A Broader Definition of Money

Before 1980, U.S. law prohibited banks from paying interest on checking account deposits. Households and firms held checking account deposits primarily to buy goods and services. M1 was, therefore, very close to the function of money as a medium of exchange. Almost all currency, checking account deposits, and traveler's checks were held with the intention of buying and selling, not with the intention of storing value. In 1980, the law was changed to allow banks to pay interest on certain types of checking accounts. This change reduced the difference between checking accounts and savings accounts, although people are still not allowed to write checks against their savings account balances.

M2 A broader definition of the money supply: It includes M1 plus savings account balances, small-denomination time deposits, balances in money market deposit accounts in banks, and noninstitutional money market fund shares.

After 1980, economists began to pay closer attention to a broader definition of the money supply, **M2**. As panel (b) of Figure 10.1 shows, M2 includes everything that is in M1, plus savings account deposits, small-denomination time deposits—such as certificates of deposit (CDs)—balances in money market deposit accounts in banks, and noninstitutional money market fund shares. Small-denomination time deposits are similar to savings accounts, but the deposits are for a fixed period of time—usually from six months to several years—and withdrawals before that time are subject to a penalty. Mutual fund companies sell shares to investors and use the funds raised to buy financial assets such as stocks and bonds. Some of these mutual funds, such as Vanguard's Treasury Money Market Fund or Fidelity's Cash Reserves Fund, are called *money market mutual funds* because they invest in very short-term bonds, such as U.S. Treasury bills. The balances in these funds are included in M2. Each week, the Federal Reserve publishes statistics on M1 and M2. In the discussion that follows, we will use the M1 definition of the money supply because it corresponds most closely to money as a medium of exchange.

There are two key points to keep in mind about the money supply:

1. The money supply consists of *both* currency and checking account deposits.
2. Because balances in checking account deposits are included in the money supply, banks play an important role in the way the money supply increases and decreases. We will discuss this second point further in the next section.

Don't Let This Happen to You

Don't Confuse Money with Income or Wealth

According to *Forbes* magazine, Bill Gates's wealth of $56 billion makes him the second-richest person in the world. He also has a very large income, but how much money does he have? Your *wealth* is equal to the value of your assets minus the value of any debts you have. Your *income* is equal to your earnings during the year. Bill Gates's earnings as chairman of Microsoft and from his investments are very large. But his *money* is just equal to what he has in currency and in checking accounts. Only a small proportion of Gates's $56 billion in wealth is likely to be in currency or checking accounts. Most of his wealth is invested in stocks and bonds and other financial assets that are not included in the definition of money.

In everyday conversation, we often describe someone who is wealthy or who has a high income as "having a lot of money." But when economists use the word *money*, they are usually referring to currency plus checking account deposits. It is important to keep straight the differences between wealth, income, and money.

Just as money and income are not the same for a person, they are not the same for the whole economy. National income in the United States was equal to $12.8 trillion in 2010. The money supply in 2010 was $1.8 trillion (using the M1 measure). There is no reason national income in a country should be equal to the country's money supply, nor will an increase in a country's money supply necessarily increase the country's national income.

Based on "The World's Billionaires," *Forbes*, March 19, 2011.

Solved Problem 10.2

The Definitions of M1 and M2

Suppose you decide to withdraw $2,000 from your checking account and use the money to buy a bank certificate of deposit (CD). Briefly explain how this will affect M1 and M2.

Solving the Problem

Step 1: **Review the chapter material.** This problem is about the definitions of the money supply, so you may want to review the section "How Is Money Measured in the United States Today?" which begins on page 235.

Step 2: **Use the definitions of M1 and M2 to answer the problem.** Funds in checking accounts are included in both M1 and M2. Funds in CDs are included only in M2. It is tempting to answer this problem by saying that shifting $2,000 from a checking account to a CD reduces M1 by $2,000 and increases M2 by $2,000, but the $2,000 in your checking account was already counted in M2. So, the correct answer is that your action reduces M1 by $2,000 but leaves M2 unchanged.

What about Credit Cards and Debit Cards?

Many people buy goods and services with credit cards, yet credit cards are not included in definitions of the money supply. The reason is that when you buy something with a credit card, you are in effect taking out a loan from the bank that issued the credit card. Only when you pay your credit card bill at the end of the month—often with a check or an electronic transfer from your checking account—is the transaction complete. In contrast, with a debit card, the funds to make the purchase are taken directly from your checking account. In either case, the cards themselves do not represent money.

How Do Banks Create Money?

10.3 LEARNING OBJECTIVE

Explain how banks create money.

We have seen that the most important component of the money supply is checking accounts in banks. To understand the role money plays in the economy, we need to look more closely at how banks operate. Banks are profit-making private businesses, just like bookstores and supermarkets. Some banks are quite small, with just a few branches, and they do business in a limited area. Others are among the largest corporations in the United States, with hundreds of branches spread across many states. The key role that banks play in the economy is to accept deposits and make loans. By doing this, they create checking account deposits.

Bank Balance Sheets

To understand how banks create money, we need to briefly examine a typical bank balance sheet. On a balance sheet, a firm's assets are listed on the left, and its liabilities and stockholders' equity are listed on the right. Assets are the value of anything owned by the firm, liabilities are the value of anything the firm owes, and stockholders' equity is the difference between the total value of assets and the total value of liabilities. Stockholders' equity represents the value of the firm if it had to be closed, all its assets were sold, and all its liabilities were paid off. A corporation's stockholders' equity is also referred to as its *net worth*.

Figure 10.2 shows the actual balance sheet of a large bank. The key assets on a bank's balance sheet are its *reserves*, loans, and holdings of securities, such as U.S. Treasury bills.

Figure 10.2

Balance Sheet for a Large Bank, December 31, 2010

The items on a bank's balance sheet of greatest economic importance are its reserves, loans, and deposits. Notice that the difference between the value of this bank's total assets and its total liabilities is equal to its stockholders' equity. As a consequence, the left side of the balance sheet always equals the right side. *Note:* Some entries have been combined to simplify the balance sheet.

Assets (in millions)		Liabilities and Stockholders' Equity (in millions)	
Reserves	$108,427	Deposits	$1,010,430
Loans	898,555	Short-term borrowing	394,572
Securities	896,097	Long-term debt	359,180
Buildings and equipment	14,306	Other liabilities	272,479
Other assets	347,524	Total liabilities	$2,036,661
		Stockholders' equity	228,248
Total assets	$2,264,909	Total liabilities and stockholders' equity	$2,264,909

Reserves Deposits that a bank keeps as cash in its vault or on deposit with the Federal Reserve.

Required reserves Reserves that a bank is legally required to hold, based on its checking account deposits.

Required reserve ratio The minimum fraction of deposits banks are required by law to keep as reserves.

Excess reserves Reserves that banks hold over and above the legal requirement.

Reserves are deposits that a bank has retained rather than loaned out or invested. Banks keep reserves either physically within the bank, as *vault cash*, or on deposit with the Federal Reserve. Banks are required by law to keep as reserves 10 percent of their checking account deposits above a threshold level, which in 2011 was $58.8 million. These reserves are called **required reserves**. The minimum fraction of deposits that banks are required to keep as reserves is called the **required reserve ratio**. We can abbreviate the required reserve ratio as *RR*. Any reserves that banks hold over and above the legal requirement are called **excess reserves**. The balance sheet in Figure 10.2 shows that loans are this bank's largest asset, which is true of most banks.

Banks make *consumer loans* to households and *commercial loans* to businesses. A loan is an asset to a bank because it represents a promise by the person taking out the loan to make certain specified payments to the bank. A bank's reserves and its holdings of securities are also assets because they are things of value owned by the bank.

As with most banks, this bank's largest liability is its deposits. Deposits include checking accounts, savings accounts, and certificates of deposit. Deposits are liabilities to banks because they are owed to the households or firms that have deposited the funds. If you deposit $100 in your checking account, the bank owes you the $100, and you can ask for it back at any time. So, your checking account is an asset to you, and it is a liability to the bank.

Using T-Accounts to Show How a Bank Can Create Money

It is easier to show how banks create money by using a T-account than by using a balance sheet. A T-account is a stripped-down version of a balance sheet that shows only how a transaction *changes* a bank's balance sheet. For example, suppose you deposit $1,000 in currency into an account at Bank of America. This transaction raises the total deposits at Bank of America by $1,000 and also raises its reserves by $1,000. We show this on the following T-account:

Assets		Liabilities	
Reserves	+$1,000	Deposits	+$1,000

Your deposit of $1,000 into your checking account increases Bank of America's assets and liabilities by the same amount.

Remember that because the total value of all the entries on the right side of a balance sheet must always be equal to the total value of all the entries on the left side of a balance sheet, any transaction that increases (or decreases) one side of the balance sheet must also increase (or decrease) the other side of the balance sheet. In this case, the T-account shows that we increased both sides of the balance sheet by $1,000.

Initially, this transaction does not increase the money supply. The currency component of the money supply declines by $1,000 because the $1,000 you deposited is no longer in circulation and, therefore, is not counted in the money supply. But the decrease in currency is offset by a $1,000 increase in the checking account deposit component of the money supply.

This initial change is not the end of the story, however. Banks are required to keep 10 percent of deposits as reserves. Because the Federal Reserve pays banks only a low rate of interest on their reserves, banks have an incentive to loan out or buy securities with the other 90 percent. In this case, Bank of America can keep $100 as required reserves and loan out the other $900, which represents excess reserves. Suppose Bank of America loans out the $900 to someone to buy a very inexpensive used car. Bank of America could give the $900 to the borrower in currency, but usually banks make loans by increasing the borrower's checking account. We can show this with another T-account:

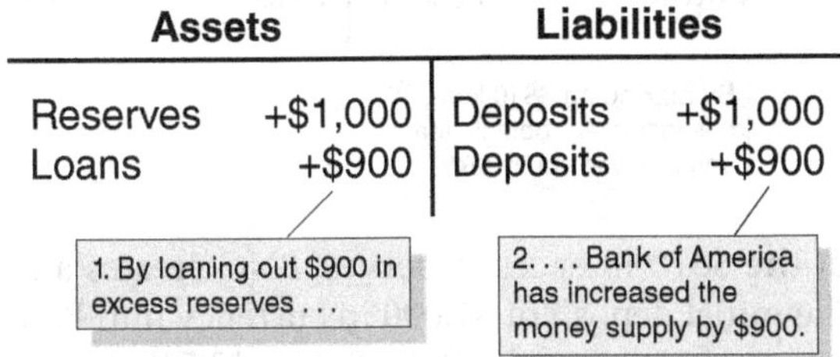

A key point to recognize is that *by making this $900 loan, Bank of America has increased the money supply by $900*. The initial $1,000 in currency you deposited into your checking account has been turned into $1,900 in checking account deposits—a net increase in the money supply of $900.

But the story does not end here. The person who took out the $900 loan did so to buy a used car. To keep things simple, let's suppose he buys the car for exactly $900 and pays by writing a check on his account at Bank of America. The seller of the used car will now deposit the check in her bank. That bank may also be a branch of Bank of America, but in most cities, there are many banks, so let's assume that the seller of the car has her account at a branch of PNC Bank. Once she deposits the check, PNC Bank will send it to Bank of America to *clear* the check and collect the $900. We show the result in the following T-accounts:

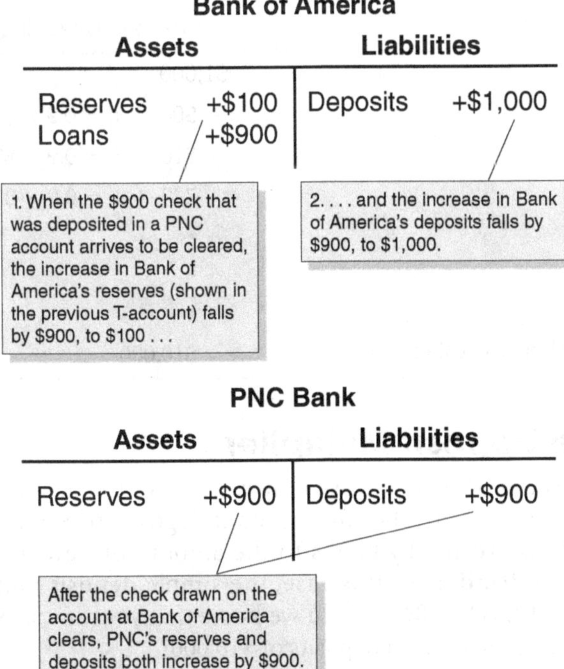

After the car buyer's check clears, Bank of America has lost $900 in deposits—the amount loaned to the car buyer—and $900 in reserves—the amount it had to pay PNC when PNC sent Bank of America the car buyer's check. PNC has an increase in checking account deposits of $900—the deposit of the car seller—and an increase in reserves of $900—the amount it received from Bank of America.

PNC has 100 percent reserves against this new $900 deposit, when it needs only 10 percent reserves. The bank has an incentive to keep $90 as reserves and to loan out the other $810, which are excess reserves. If PNC does this, we can show the change in its balance sheet by using another T-account:

PNC Bank

Assets		Liabilities	
Reserves	+$900	Deposits	+$900
Loans	+$810	Deposits	+$810

By making an $810 loan, PNC has increased both its loans and its deposits by $810.

In loaning out the $810 in excess reserves, PNC creates a new checking account deposit of $810. The initial deposit of $1,000 in currency into Bank of America has now resulted in the creation of $1,000 + $900 + $810 = $2,710 in checking account deposits. The money supply has increased by $2,710 − $1,000 = $1,710.

The process is still not finished. The person who borrows the $810 will spend it by writing a check against his account. Whoever receives the $810 will deposit it in her bank, which could be a Bank of America branch or a PNC branch or a branch of some other bank. That new bank—if it's not PNC—will send the check to PNC and will receive $810 in new reserves. That new bank will have an incentive to loan out 90 percent of these reserves—keeping 10 percent to meet the legal requirement—and the process will go on. At each stage, the additional loans being made and the additional deposits being created are shrinking by 10 percent, as each bank has to withhold that amount as required reserves. We can use a table to show the total increase in checking account deposits set off by your initial deposit of $1,000. The dots in the table represent additional rounds in the money creation process:

Bank	Increase in Checking Account Deposits	
Bank of America	$1,000	
PNC	+ 900	(= 0.9 × $1,000)
Third Bank	+ 810	(= 0.9 × $900)
Fourth Bank	+ 729	(= 0.9 × $810)
•	+ •	
•	+ •	
•	+ •	
Total change in checking account deposits	= $10,000	

The Simple Deposit Multiplier

Simple deposit multiplier The ratio of the amount of deposits created by banks to the amount of new reserves.

Your initial deposit of $1,000 increased the reserves of the banking system by $1,000 and led to a total increase in checking account deposits of $10,000. The ratio of the amount of deposits created by banks to the amount of new reserves is called the **simple deposit multiplier**. In this case, the simple deposit multiplier is equal to $10,000/$1,000 = 10. Why 10? How do we know that your initial $1,000 deposit ultimately leads to a total increase in deposits of $10,000?

There are two ways to answer this question. First, each bank in the process is keeping reserves equal to 10 percent of its deposits. For the banking system as a whole, the total increase in reserves is $1,000—the amount of your original currency deposit. Therefore, the system as a whole will end up with $10,000 in deposits because $1,000 is 10 percent of $10,000.

A second way to answer the question is by deriving an expression for the simple deposit multiplier. The total increase in deposits equals:

$$\$1{,}000 + [0.9 \times \$1{,}000] + [(0.9 \times 0.9) \times \$1{,}000] + [(0.9 \times 0.9 \times 0.9) \times \$1{,}000] + \ldots$$

or

$$\$1{,}000 + [0.9 \times \$1{,}000] + [0.9^2 \times \$1{,}000] + [0.9^3 \times \$1{,}000] + \ldots$$

or

$$\$1{,}000 + (1 + 0.9 + 0.9^2 + 0.9^3 + \ldots).$$

The rules of algebra tell us that an expression like the one in the parentheses sums to:

$$\frac{1}{1 - 0.9}.$$

Simplifying further, we have

$$\frac{1}{0.10} = 10.$$

So

$$\text{Total increase in deposit} = \$1{,}000 \times 10 = \$10{,}000.$$

Note that 10 is equal to 1 divided by the required reserve ratio, *RR*, which in this case is 10 percent, or 0.10. This gives us another way of expressing the simple deposit multiplier:

$$\text{Simple deposit multiplier} = \frac{1}{RR}.$$

This formula makes it clear that the higher the required reserve ratio, the smaller the simple deposit multiplier. With a required reserve ratio of 10 percent, the simple deposit multiplier is 10. If the required reserve ratio were 20 percent, the simple deposit multiplier would fall to 1/0.20, or 5. We can use this formula to calculate the total increase in checking account deposits from an increase in bank reserves due to, for instance, currency being deposited in a bank:

$$\text{Change in checking account deposits} = \text{Change in bank reserves} \times \frac{1}{RR}.$$

For example, if \$100,000 in currency is deposited in a bank and the required reserve ratio is 10 percent, then

$$\text{Change in checking account deposits} = \$100{,}000 \times \frac{1}{0.10}$$
$$= \$100{,}000 \times 10 = \$1{,}000{,}000.$$

Don't Let This Happen to You

Don't Confuse Assets and Liabilities

Consider the following reasoning: "How can checking account deposits be a liability to a bank? After all, they are something of value that is in the bank. Therefore, checking account deposits should be counted as a bank *asset* rather than as a bank liability."

This statement is incorrect. The balance in a checking account represents something the bank *owes* to the owner of the account. Therefore, it is a liability to the bank, although it is an asset to the owner of the account. Similarly, your car loan is a liability to you—because it is a debt you owe to the bank—but it is an asset to the bank.

Solved Problem 10.3

Showing How Banks Create Money

Suppose you deposit $5,000 in currency into your checking account at a branch of PNC Bank, which we will assume has no excess reserves at the time you make your deposit. Also assume that the required reserve ratio is 0.10.

a. Use a T-account to show the initial effect of this transaction on PNC's balance sheet.

b. Suppose that PNC makes the maximum loan it can from the funds you deposited. Use a T-account to show the initial effect on PNC's balance sheet from granting the loan. Also include in this T-account the transaction from question a.

c. Now suppose that whoever took out the loan in question b. writes a check for this amount and that the person receiving the check deposits it in Bank of America. Show the effect of these transactions on the balance sheets of PNC Bank and Bank of America *after the check has cleared.* On the T-account for PNC Bank, include the transactions from questions a. and b.

d. What is the maximum increase in checking account deposits that can result from your $5,000 deposit? What is the maximum increase in the money supply that can result from your deposit? Explain.

Solving the Problem

Step 1: Review the chapter material. This problem is about how banks create checking account deposits, so you may want to review the section "Using T-Accounts to Show How a Bank Can Create Money," which begins on page 240.

Step 2: Answer part a. by using a T-account to show the effect of the deposit. Keeping in mind that T-accounts show only the changes in a balance sheet that result from the relevant transaction and that assets are on the left side of the account and liabilities are on the right side, we have:

PNC Bank

Assets		Liabilities	
Reserves	+$5,000	Deposits	+$5,000

Because the bank now has your $5,000 in currency in its vault, its reserves (and, therefore, its assets) have risen by $5,000. But this transaction also increases your checking account balance by $5,000. Because the bank owes you this money, the bank's liabilities have also risen by $5,000.

Step 3: Answer part b. by using a T-account to show the effect of the loan. The problem tells you to assume that PNC Bank currently has no excess reserves and that the required reserve ratio is 10 percent. This requirement means that if the bank's checking account deposits go up by $5,000, the bank must keep $500 as reserves and can loan out the remaining $4,500. Remembering that new loans usually take the form of setting up, or increasing, a checking account for the borrower, we have:

PNC Bank

Assets		Liabilities	
Reserves	+$5,000	Deposits	+$5,000
Loans	+$4,500	Deposits	+$4,500

The first line of the T-account shows the transaction from question a. The second line shows that PNC has loaned out $4,500 by increasing the checking account of the borrower by $4,500. The loan is an asset to PNC because it represents a promise by the borrower to make certain payments spelled out in the loan agreement.

Step 4: **Answer part c. by using T-accounts for PNC and Bank of America to show the effect of the check clearing.** We now show the effect of the borrower having spent the $4,500 he received as a loan from PNC. The person who received the $4,500 check deposits it in her account at Bank of America. We need two T-accounts to show this activity:

PNC Bank

Assets		Liabilities	
Reserves	+$500	Deposits	+$5,000
Loans	+$4,500		

Bank of America

Assets		Liabilities	
Reserves	+$4,500	Deposits	+$4,500

Look first at the T-account for PNC. Once Bank of America sends the check written by the borrower to PNC, PNC loses $4,500 in reserves, and Bank of America gains $4,500 in reserves. The $4,500 is also deducted from the account of the borrower. PNC is now satisfied with the result. It received a $5,000 deposit in currency from you. When that money was sitting in the bank vault, it wasn't earning any interest for PNC. Now $4,500 of the $5,000 has been loaned out and is earning interest. These interest payments allow PNC to cover its costs and earn a profit, which it has to do to remain in business.

Bank of America now has an increase in deposits of $4,500, resulting from the check being deposited, and an increase in reserves of $4,500. Bank of America is in the same situation as PNC was in question a: It has excess reserves as a result of this transaction and a strong incentive to lend them out.

Step 5: **Answer part d. by using the simple deposit multiplier formula to calculate the maximum increase in checking account deposits and the maximum increase in the money supply.** The simple deposit multiplier expression is (remember that *RR* is the required reserve ratio)

$$\text{Change in checking account deposits} = \text{Change in bank reserves} \times \frac{1}{RR}.$$

In this case, bank reserves rose by $5,000 as a result of your initial deposit, and the required reserve ratio is 0.10, so:

$$\begin{aligned}\text{Change in checking account deposits} &= \$5{,}000 \times \frac{1}{0.10}\\ &= \$5{,}000 \times 10 = \$50{,}000.\end{aligned}$$

Because checking account deposits are part of the money supply, it is tempting to say that the money supply has also increased by $50,000. Remember, though, that your $5,000 in currency was counted as part of the money supply while you had it, but it is not included when it is sitting in a bank vault. Therefore:

Increase in checking account deposits − Decline in currency in circulation = Change in the money supply

or

$$\$50,000 - \$5,000 = \$45,000.$$

The Simple Deposit Multiplier versus the Real-World Deposit Multiplier

The story we have told about the way an increase in reserves in the banking system leads to the creation of new deposits and, therefore, an increase in the money supply has been simplified in two ways. First, we assumed that banks do not keep any excess reserves. That is, we assumed that when you deposited $1,000 in currency into your checking account at Bank of America, it loaned out $900, keeping only the $100 in required reserves. In fact, banks often keep some excess reserves to guard against the possibility that many depositors may simultaneously make withdrawals from their accounts. During the financial crisis that began in 2007, banks kept substantial excess reserves. The more excess reserves banks keep, the smaller the deposit multiplier. Imagine an extreme case in which Bank of America keeps your entire $1,000 as reserves. If Bank of America does not loan out any of your deposit, the process described earlier—loans leading to the creation of new deposits, leading to the making of additional loans, and so on—will not take place. The $1,000 increase in reserves will lead to a total increase of $1,000 in deposits, and the deposit multiplier will be only 1, not 10.

Second, we assumed that the whole amount of every check is deposited in a bank; no one takes any of it out as currency. In reality, households and firms keep roughly constant the amount of currency they hold relative to the value of their checking account balances. So, we would expect to see people increasing the amount of currency they hold as the balances in their checking accounts rise. Once again, think of the extreme case. Suppose that when Bank of America makes the initial $900 loan to the borrower who wants to buy a used car, the seller of the car cashes the check instead of depositing it. In that case, PNC does not receive any new reserves and does not make any new loans. Once again, the $1,000 increase in your checking account at Bank of America is the only increase in deposits, and the deposit multiplier is 1.

The effect of these two factors is to reduce the real-world deposit multiplier to about 2.5 during normal times. This means that a $1 increase in the reserves of the banking system results in about a $2.50 increase in deposits. During the financial crisis of 2007–2009, the surge in bank holdings of excess reserves reduced the multiplier to about 1.

Although the story of the deposit multiplier can be complicated, the key point to bear in mind is that the most important part of the money supply is the checking account balance component. When banks make loans, they increase checking account balances, and the money supply expands. Banks make new loans whenever they gain reserves. The whole process can also work in reverse: If banks lose reserves, they reduce their outstanding loans and deposits, and the money supply contracts.

We can summarize these important conclusions:

1. When banks gain reserves, they make new loans, and the money supply expands.
2. When banks lose reserves, they reduce their loans, and the money supply contracts.

The Federal Reserve System

10.4 LEARNING OBJECTIVE

Discuss the three policy tools the Federal Reserve uses to manage the money supply.

Many people are surprised to learn that banks do not keep locked away in their vaults all the funds that are deposited in checking accounts. The United States, like nearly all other countries, has a **fractional reserve banking system**, which means that banks keep less than 100 percent of deposits as reserves. When people deposit money in a bank, the bank loans most of the money to someone else. What happens, though, if depositors want their money back? This would seem to be a problem because banks have loaned out most of the money and can't easily get it back.

Fractional reserve banking system A banking system in which banks keep less than 100 percent of deposits as reserves.

In practice, though, withdrawals are usually not a problem for banks. On a typical day, about as much money is deposited as is withdrawn. If a small amount more is withdrawn than deposited, banks can cover the difference from their excess reserves or by borrowing from other banks. Sometimes depositors lose confidence in a bank when they question the value of the bank's underlying assets, particularly its loans. Often, the reason for a loss of confidence is bad news, whether true or false. When many depositors simultaneously decide to withdraw their money from a bank, there is a **bank run**. If many banks experience runs at the same time, the result is a **bank panic**. It is possible for one bank to handle a run by borrowing from other banks, but if many banks simultaneously experience runs, the banking system may be in trouble.

Bank run A situation in which many depositors simultaneously decide to withdraw money from a bank.

Bank panic A situation in which many banks experience runs at the same time.

A *central bank*, like the Federal Reserve in the United States, can help stop a bank panic by acting as a *lender of last resort*. In acting as a lender of last resort, a central bank makes loans to banks that cannot borrow funds elsewhere. The banks can use these loans to pay off depositors. When the panic ends and the depositors put their money back in their accounts, the banks can repay the loans to the central bank.

The Establishment of the Federal Reserve System

Bank panics lead to severe disruptions in business activity because households and firms have trouble gaining access to their accounts and may be unable to borrow money. Not surprisingly, in the United States, each bank panic in the late nineteenth and early twentieth centuries was accompanied by a recession. With the intention of putting an end to bank panics, in 1913, Congress passed the Federal Reserve Act, setting up the Federal Reserve System—often referred to as "the Fed." The system began operation in 1914, with the authority to make loans to banks. The loans the Fed makes to banks are called **discount loans**, and the interest rate it charges on the loans is called the **discount rate**. When a bank receives a loan from the Fed, its reserves increase by the amount of the loan.

Discount loans Loans the Federal Reserve makes to banks.

Discount rate The interest rate the Federal Reserve charges on discount loans.

The Fed's first test as a lender of last resort came in the early years of the Great Depression of the 1930s, when many banks were hit by bank runs as depositors pulled funds out of checking and savings accounts. Although the Fed had been established to act as a lender of last resort, Fed officials declined to make loans to many banks because the officials were worried that banks experiencing runs had made bad loans and other investments. The Fed believed that making loans to banks that were in financial trouble because of bad investments might reduce the incentive bank managers had to be careful in their investment decisions. Partly due to the Fed's unwillingness to act as a lender of last resort, more than 5,000 banks failed during the early 1930s. Today, many economists are critical of the Fed's decisions in the early 1930s because they believe these decisions increased the severity of the Great Depression. In 1934, Congress established the Federal Deposit Insurance Corporation (FDIC) to insure deposits in most banks up to a limit, which is currently $250,000 per deposit. Deposit insurance has greatly reduced bank runs because it has reassured all but the largest depositors that their deposits are safe, even if their bank goes out of business. During the financial crisis of 2007–2009, some banks experienced runs when depositors with funds exceeding the deposit insurance limit feared that they would suffer losses if their banks failed.

To aid the Fed in carrying out its responsibilities, in 1913 Congress divided the country into 12 Federal Reserve districts, as shown in Figure 10.3. Each district has its

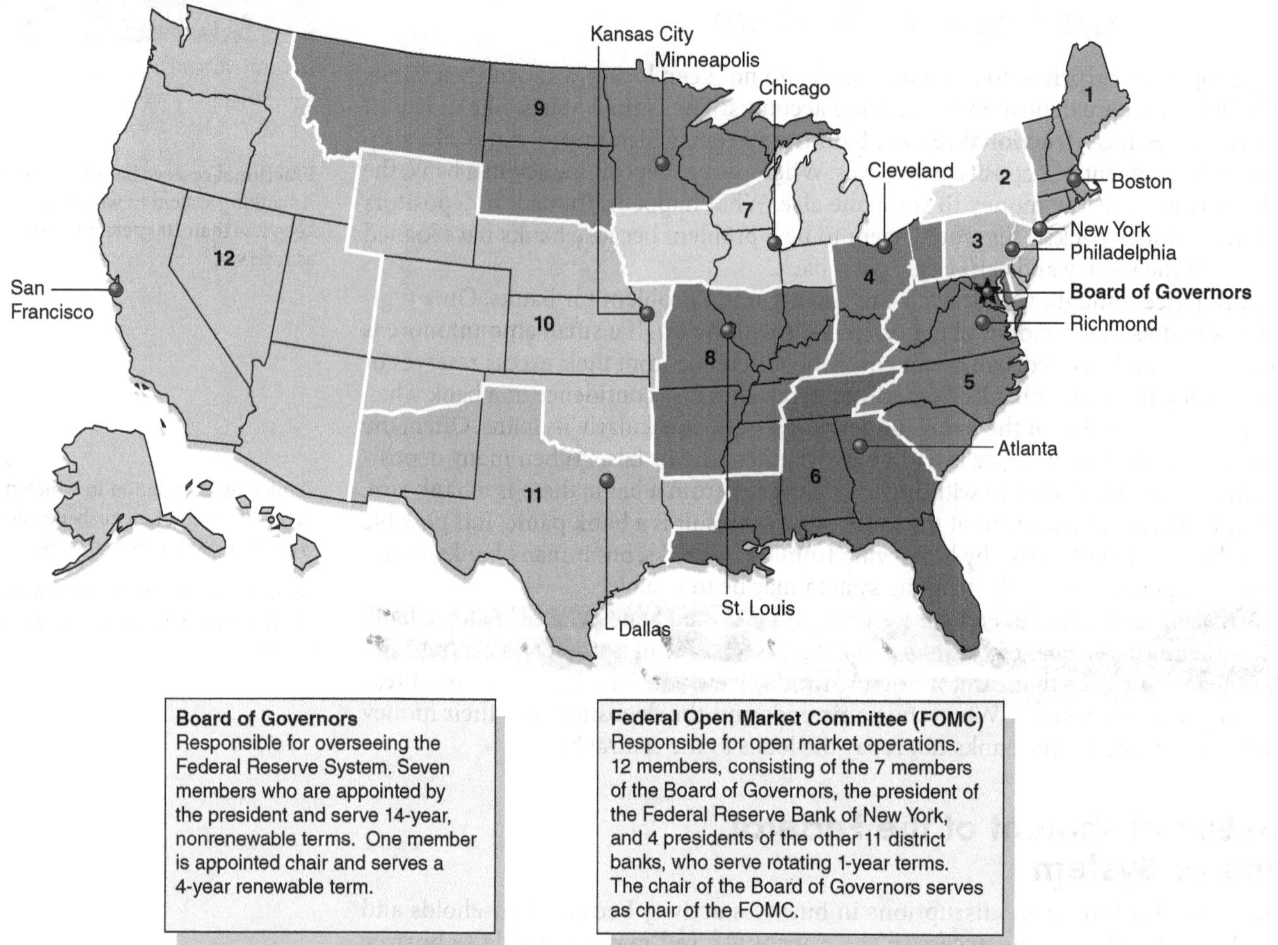

Figure 10.3 The Federal Reserve System

The United States is divided into 12 Federal Reserve districts, each of which has a Federal Reserve bank. The real power within the Federal Reserve System, however, lies in Washington, DC, with the Board of Governors, which consists of 7 members appointed by the president. Monetary policy is carried out by the 14-member Federal Open Market Committee.

Data from Board of Governors of the Federal Reserve System.

own Federal Reserve bank, which provides services to banks in that district. The real power of the Fed, however, lies in Washington, DC, with the Board of Governors. The seven members of the Board of Governors are appointed by the president of the United States to 14-year, nonrenewable terms. One member of the Board of Governors is chosen to be chair and serves a 4-year, renewable term. In 2012, the chair of the Board of Governors was Ben Bernanke. In addition to acting as a lender of last resort to banks, the Fed acts as a bankers' bank, providing services such as check clearing to banks, and also has the responsibility of managing the nation's money supply.

How the Federal Reserve Manages the Money Supply

Although Congress established the Fed primarily to stop bank panics by acting as a lender of last resort, today the Fed is also responsible for managing the money supply. As we will discuss in more detail in Chapter 11, managing the money supply is part of **monetary policy**, which the Fed undertakes to pursue macroeconomic objectives. To manage the money supply, the Fed uses three *monetary policy tools*:

Monetary policy The actions the Federal Reserve takes to manage the money supply and interest rates to pursue macroeconomic policy objectives.

1. Open market operations
2. Discount policy
3. Reserve requirements

Remember that the most important component of the money supply is checking account deposits. Not surprisingly, all three of the Fed's policy tools are aimed at affecting the reserves of banks as a means of changing the volume of checking account deposits.

Open Market Operations Eight times per year, the **Federal Open Market Committee (FOMC)** meets in Washington, DC, to discuss monetary policy. The committee has 12 voting members: the 7 members of the Federal Reserve's Board of Governors, the president of the Federal Reserve Bank of New York, and 4 presidents from the other 11 Federal Reserve banks. These 4 presidents serve one-year rotating terms on the FOMC. The chair of the Board of Governors also serves as the chair of the FOMC.

Federal Open Market Committee (FOMC) The Federal Reserve committee responsible for open market operations and managing the money supply in the United States.

The U.S. Treasury borrows money by selling bills, notes, and bonds. Remember that the *maturity* of a financial asset is the period of time until the purchaser receives payment of the face value or principal. Usually, bonds have face values of $1,000. Treasury bills have maturities of 1 year or less, Treasury notes have maturities of 2 years to 10 years, and Treasury bonds have maturities of 30 years. To increase the money supply, the FOMC directs the *trading desk*, located at the Federal Reserve Bank of New York, to *buy* U.S. Treasury securities—most frequently bills, but sometimes notes or bonds—from the public. When the sellers of the Treasury securities deposit the funds in their banks, the reserves of banks rise. This increase in reserves starts the process of increasing loans and checking account deposits that increases the money supply. To decrease the money supply, the FOMC directs the trading desk to *sell* Treasury securities. When the buyers of the Treasury securities pay for them with checks, the reserves of their banks fall. This decrease in reserves starts a contraction of loans and checking account deposits that reduces the money supply. The buying and selling of Treasury securities is called **open market operations.**

Open market operations The buying and selling of Treasury securities by the Federal Reserve in order to control the money supply.

There are three reasons the Fed conducts monetary policy principally through open market operations. First, because the Fed initiates open market operations, it completely controls their volume. Second, the Fed can make both large and small open market operations. Third, the Fed can implement its open market operations quickly, with no administrative delay or required changes in regulations. Many other central banks, including the European Central Bank and the Bank of Japan, also use open market operations to conduct monetary policy.

The Federal Reserve is responsible for putting the paper currency of the United States into circulation. Recall that if you look at the top of a dollar bill, you see the words "Federal Reserve Note." When the Fed takes actions to increase the money supply, commentators sometimes say that it is "printing more money." The main way the Fed increases the money supply, however, is not by printing more currency but by buying Treasury securities. Similarly, to reduce the money supply, the Fed does not set fire to stacks of paper currency. Instead, it sells Treasury securities. We will spend more time discussing how and why the Fed manages the money supply in Chapter 11, when we discuss monetary policy.

Discount Policy As we have seen, when a bank borrows money from the Fed by taking out a discount loan, the interest rate the bank pays is known as the discount rate. By lowering the discount rate, the Fed can encourage banks to take additional loans and thereby increase their reserves. With more reserves, banks will make more loans to households and firms, which will increase checking account deposits and the money supply. Raising the discount rate will have the reverse effect.

Reserve Requirements When the Fed reduces the required reserve ratio, it converts required reserves into excess reserves. For example, suppose a bank has $100 million in checking account deposits, and the required reserve ratio is 10 percent. The bank will be required to hold $10 million as reserves. If the Fed reduces the required reserve ratio to 8 percent, the bank will need to hold only $8 million as reserves. The Fed can thereby convert $2 million worth of reserves from required reserves to excess reserves. This $2 million is then available for the bank to lend out. If the Fed *raises* the required reserve ratio from 10 percent to 12 percent, it will have the reverse effect.

The Fed changes reserve requirements much more rarely than it conducts open market operations or changes the discount rate. Because changes in reserve requirements require significant alterations in banks' holdings of loans and securities, frequent changes would be disruptive. Also, because the Fed pays banks only a low interest rate on reserves, the use of reserve requirements to manage the money supply effectively places a tax on banks' deposit-taking and lending activities, which can be costly for the economy.

The "Shadow Banking System" and the Financial Crisis of 2007–2009

The banks we have been discussing in this chapter are *commercial banks*, whose most important economic role is to accept funds from depositors and lend those funds to borrowers. Large firms can sell stocks and bonds on financial markets but investors are typically unwilling to buy stocks and bonds from small and medium-sized firms because they lack sufficient information on the financial health of smaller firms. So, smaller firms—and households—have traditionally relied on bank loans for their credit needs. In the past 20 years, however, two important developments have occurred in the financial system: (1) Banks have begun to resell many of their loans rather than keep them until they are paid off, and (2) financial firms other than commercial banks have become sources of credit to businesses.

Security A financial asset—such as a stock or a bond—that can be bought and sold in a financial market.

Securitization The process of transforming loans or other financial assets into securities.

Securitization Comes to Banking Traditionally, when a bank made a *residential mortgage loan* to a household to buy a home or made a commercial loan to a business, the bank would keep the loan and collect the payments until the loan was paid off. A financial asset—such as a loan or a stock or a bond—is considered a **security** if it can be bought and sold in a *financial market* as, for instance, shares of stock issued by the Coca-Cola Company can be bought and sold on the New York Stock Exchange. When a financial asset is first sold, the sale takes place in the *primary market*. Subsequent sales take place in the *secondary market*. Prior to 1970, most loans were not securities because they could not be resold—there was no secondary market for them. First, residential mortgages and then other loans, including car loans and commercial loans, began to be *securitized*. The process of **securitization** involves creating a secondary market in which loans that have been bundled together can be bought and sold in financial markets, just as corporate or government bonds are. Figure 10.4 outlines the securitization process.

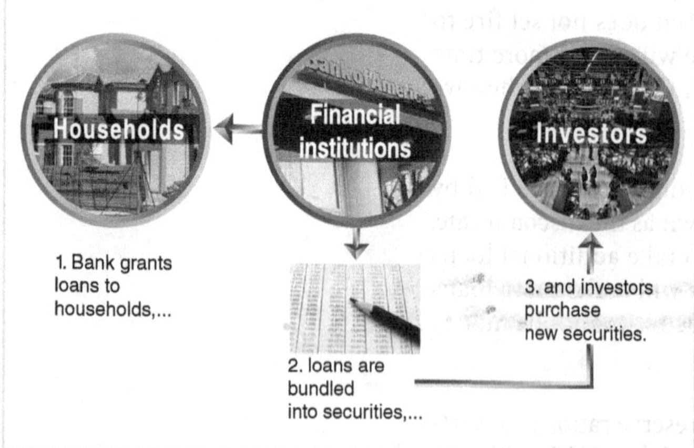

(a) Securitizing a loan

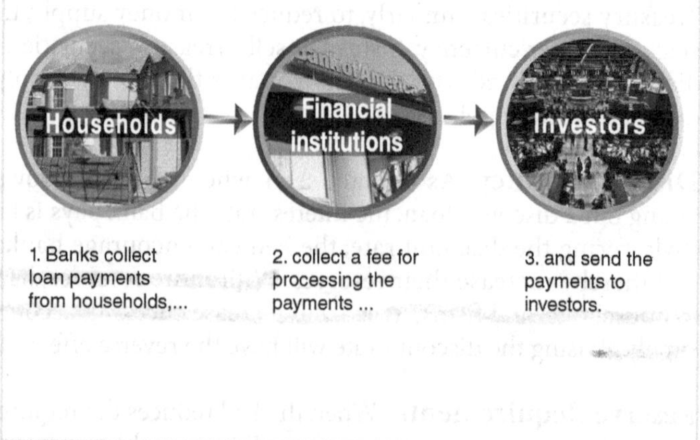

(b) The flow of payments on a securitized loan

Figure 10.4 The Process of Securitization

Panel (a) shows how in the securitization process banks grant loans to households and bundle the loans into securities that are then sold to investors. Panel (b) shows that banks collect payments on the original loans and, after taking a fee, send the payments to the investors who bought the securities.

We will discuss the process of securitization further in Chapter 11, when we discuss monetary policy.

The Shadow Banking System In addition to the changes resulting from securitization, the financial system was transformed in the 1990s and 2000s by the increasing importance of nonbank financial firms. Investment banks, such as Goldman Sachs and Morgan Stanley, differ from commercial banks in that they do not accept deposits, and they rarely lend directly to households. Instead, investment banks traditionally concentrated on providing advice to firms issuing stocks and bonds or considering mergers with other firms. In the late 1990s, investment banks expanded their buying of mortgages, bundling large numbers of them together as bonds known as *mortgage-backed securities*, and reselling them to investors. Mortgage-backed securities proved very popular with investors because they often paid higher interest rates than other securities with comparable default risk.

Money market mutual funds have also increased their importance in the financial system over time. These funds sell shares to investors and use the money to buy short-term securities such as Treasury bills and commercial paper issued by corporations. Commercial paper represents short-term borrowing corporations use to fund their day-to-day operations. Many corporations that previously met such needs by borrowing from banks began instead to sell commercial paper to money market mutual funds.

Hedge funds raise money from wealthy investors and use sophisticated investment strategies that often involve significant risk. By 2005, hedge funds had become an important source of demand for securitized loans and an important source of loans to other financial firms.

In 2008, Timothy Geithner, who became Treasury secretary in the Obama administration, referred to investment banks, money market mutual funds, hedge funds, and other financial firms engaged in similar activities as the "shadow banking system." By raising money from individual investors and providing it directly or indirectly to firms and households, these firms were carrying out a function that at one time was almost exclusively the domain of commercial banks.

The Financial Crisis of 2007–2009 The firms in the shadow banking system differed from commercial banks in two important ways: First, the government agencies—including the Federal Reserve—that regulated the commercial banking system did not regulate these firms. Second, these firms were more highly *leveraged*—that is, they relied more heavily on borrowed money to finance their operations—than were commercial banks. If a firm uses a small amount of its own money and a lot of borrowed money to make an investment, both the firm's potential profits and its potential losses are increased. For example, suppose a firm invests $100 of its own money. If the investment earns a return of $3, the firm has earned 3 percent ($3/$100) on its funds. But if the firm's investment consists of $10 of its own money and $90 it has borrowed, a return of $3 becomes a return of 30 percent ($3/$10) on the firm's $10 investment. If the investment loses $2, however, the firm's return is −20 percent (−$2/$10). Leveraged investments have a potential for both large gains and large losses.

As mentioned earlier, commercial banks have rarely experienced runs since Congress established federal deposit insurance in the 1930s. However, beginning in 2007, firms in the shadow banking system were quite vulnerable to runs. As we will discuss further in Chapter 11, the underlying cause of the financial crisis of 2007–2009 was problems in the U.S. housing market. As housing prices began to fall, a significant number of borrowers began to default on their mortgages, which caused mortgage-backed securities to lose value. Financial firms, including both commercial banks and many firms in the shadow banking system, that had invested in these securities suffered heavy losses. The more leveraged the firm, the larger the losses. Although deposit insurance helped commercial banks avoid runs, investment banks and other financial firms that had borrowed short term and invested the funds long term were in trouble. As lenders refused to renew their short-term loans, many of these firms had to sell their holdings of securities in an attempt to raise cash. But as the prices of these securities continued to fall, the losses to these firms increased.

In the spring of 2008, the investment bank Bear Stearns was saved from bankruptcy only when the Federal Reserve arranged for it to be acquired by JPMorgan Chase. In the fall of 2008, the Federal Reserve and the U.S. Treasury decided not to take action to save the investment bank Lehman Brothers, which failed. The failure of Lehman Brothers reverberated throughout the financial system, setting off a panic. The process of securitization—apart from government-guaranteed residential mortgages—ground to a halt. The well-publicized difficulties of a money market mutual fund that had suffered losses on loans to Lehman Brothers led to a wave of withdrawals from these funds. In turn, the funds were no longer able to fulfill their role as buyers of corporate commercial paper. As banks and other financial firms sold assets and cut back on lending to shore up their financial positions, the flow of funds from savers to borrowers was disrupted. The resulting credit crunch significantly worsened the recession that had begun in December 2007.

The Fed's Response The Fed, in combination with the U.S. Treasury, took vigorous action to deal with the financial panic. We will discuss the Fed's actions further in Chapter 11, but for now, we can mention several particularly important policy actions. First, in the fall of 2008, under the Troubled Asset Relief Program (TARP), the Fed and Treasury began attempting to stabilize the commercial banking system by providing funds to banks in exchange for stock. Taking partial ownership of private commercial banks was an unprecedented move by the federal government. The Fed also modified its discount policy by setting up several new "lending facilities." These lending facilities made it possible for the Fed to grant discount loans to financial firms—such as investment banks—that had not previously been eligible. In addition, the Fed addressed problems in the commercial paper market by directly buying commercial paper for the first time since the 1930s.

Although the recession continued into 2009, the extraordinary actions of the Treasury and Fed appeared to have stabilized the financial system. Still, even by late 2011, the flow of funds from savers to borrowers had not yet returned to normal levels, and economists and policymakers were debating the wisdom of some of the Fed's actions. We will return to the Fed's response to the recession of 2007–2009 in Chapter 10.

10.5 LEARNING OBJECTIVE

Explain the quantity theory of money and use it to explain how high rates of inflation occur.

The Quantity Theory of Money

People have been aware of the connection between increases in the money supply and inflation for centuries. In the sixteenth century, the Spanish conquered Mexico and Peru and shipped large quantities of gold and silver from those countries back to Spain. The gold and silver were minted into coins and spent across Europe to further the political ambitions of the Spanish kings. Prices in Europe rose steadily during these years, and many observers discussed the relationship between this inflation and the flow of gold and silver into Europe from the Americas.

Connecting Money and Prices: The Quantity Equation

In the early twentieth century, Irving Fisher, an economist at Yale, formalized the connection between money and prices by using the *quantity equation*:

$$M \times V = P \times Y.$$

The quantity equation states that the money supply (M) multiplied by the *velocity of money* (V) equals the price level (P) multiplied by real output (Y). Fisher defined the

velocity of money, often referred to simply as "velocity," as the average number of times each dollar of the money supply is used to purchase goods and services included in GDP. Rewriting the original equation by dividing both sides by M, we have the equation for velocity:

Velocity of money The average number of times each dollar in the money supply is used to purchase goods and services included in GDP.

$$V = \frac{P \times Y}{M}.$$

If we use M1 to measure the money supply, the GDP price deflator to measure the price level, and real GDP to measure real output, the value for velocity for 2010 was

$$V = \frac{1.11 \times \$13{,}088 \text{ billion}}{\$1{,}832 \text{ billion}} = 7.9.$$

This result tells us that, on average during 2010, each dollar of M1 was spent about eight times on goods or services included in GDP.

Because velocity is defined to be equal to $(P \times Y)/M$, we know that the quantity equation must always hold true: The left side *must* be equal to the right side. A theory is a statement about the world that might possibly be false. Therefore, the quantity equation is not a theory. Irving Fisher turned the quantity equation into the **quantity theory of money** by asserting that velocity was constant. He argued that the average number of times a dollar is spent depends on how often people get paid, how often they do their grocery shopping, how often businesses mail bills, and other factors that do not change very often. Because this assertion may be true or false, the quantity theory of money is, in fact, a theory.

Quantity theory of money A theory about the connection between money and prices that assumes that the velocity of money is constant.

The Quantity Theory Explanation of Inflation

The quantity equation gives us a way of showing the relationship between changes in the money supply and changes in the price level, or inflation. To see this relationship more clearly, we can use a handy mathematical rule that states that an equation where variables are multiplied together is equal to an equation where the *growth rates* of these variables are *added* together. So, we can transform the quantity equation from

$$M \times V = P \times Y$$

to

Growth rate of the money supply + Growth rate of velocity =
Growth rate of the price level (or inflation rate) + Growth rate of real output.

This way of writing the quantity equation is more useful for investigating the effect of changes in the money supply on the inflation rate. Remember that the growth rate for any variable is the percentage change in the variable from one year to the next. The growth rate of the price level is the inflation rate, so we can rewrite the quantity equation to help understand the factors that determine inflation:

Inflation rate = Growth rate of the money supply +
Growth rate of velocity − Growth rate of real output.

If Irving Fisher was correct that velocity is constant, then the growth rate of velocity will be zero. That is, if velocity is, say, always eight, then its percentage change from one year to the next will always be zero. This assumption allows us to rewrite the equation one last time:

Inflation rate = Growth rate of the money supply − Growth rate of real output.

This equation leads to the following predictions:

1. If the money supply grows at a faster rate than real GDP, there will be inflation.
2. If the money supply grows at a slower rate than real GDP, there will be deflation. (Recall that *deflation* is a decline in the price level.)
3. If the money supply grows at the same rate as real GDP, the price level will be stable, and there will be neither inflation nor deflation.

It turns out that Irving Fisher was wrong in asserting that the velocity of money is constant. From year to year, there can be significant fluctuations in velocity. As a result, the predictions of the quantity theory of money do not hold every year, but most economists agree that the quantity theory provides useful insight into the long-run relationship between the money supply and inflation: *In the long run, inflation results from the money supply growing at a faster rate than real GDP.*

How Accurate Are Estimates of Inflation Based on the Quantity Theory?

Note that the accuracy of the quantity theory depends on whether the key assumption that velocity is constant is correct. If velocity is not constant, then there may not be a tight link between increases in the money supply and increases in the price level. For example, an increase in the quantity of money might be offset by a decline in velocity, leaving the price level unaffected. Because velocity can move erratically in the short run, we would not expect the quantity equation to provide good forecasts of inflation in the short run. Over the long run, however, there is a strong link between changes in the money supply and inflation. Panel (a) of Figure 10.5 shows the relationship between the growth of the M2 measure of the money supply and the inflation rate by decade in the United States. (We use M2 here because data on M2 are available for a longer period of time than for M1.) Because of variations in the rate of growth of real GDP and in velocity, there is not an exact relationship between the growth rate of M2 and the inflation rate. But there is a clear pattern that decades with higher growth rates in the money supply were also decades with higher inflation rates. In other words, most of the variation in inflation rates across decades can be explained by variation in the rates of growth of the money supply.

Panel (b) provides further evidence consistent with the quantity theory by looking at rates of growth of the money supply and rates of inflation across countries for the decade from 1999 to 2008. Although there is not an exact relationship between rates

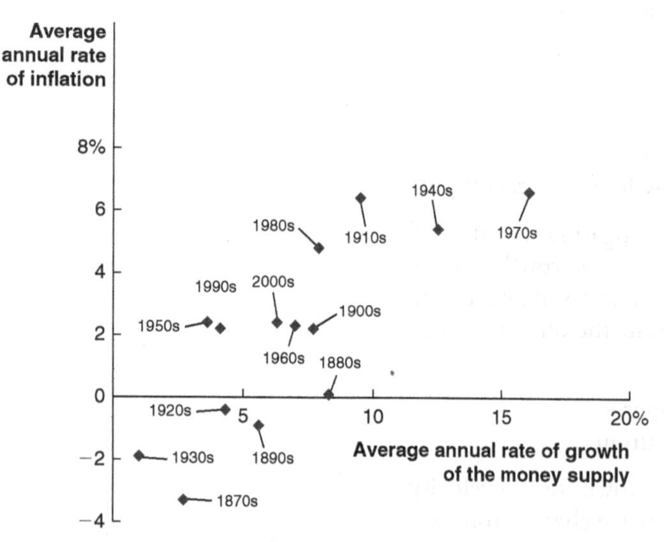

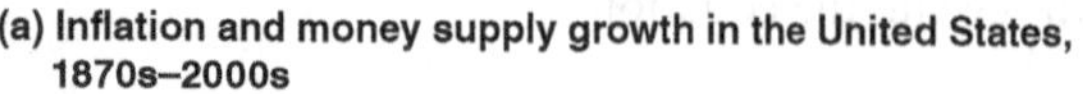
(a) Inflation and money supply growth in the United States, 1870s–2000s

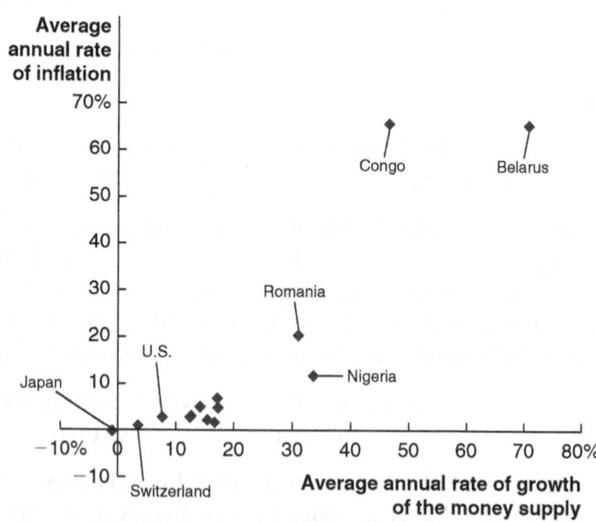

(b) Inflation and money supply growth in 14 countries, 1999–2008

Figure 10.5 The Relationship between Money Growth and Inflation over Time and around the World

Panel (a) shows that, by and large, in the United States, the rate of inflation has been highest during the decades in which the money supply has increased most rapidly, and the rate of inflation has been lowest during the decades in which the money supply has increased least rapidly. Panel (b) shows that for the decade from 1999 to 2008, there is not an exact relationship between money supply growth and inflation, but in countries such as the United States, Japan, and Switzerland, both the growth rate of the money supply and the rate of inflation were low, while countries such as Belarus, the Congo, and Romania had both high rates of growth of the money supply and high rates of inflation.

Data from: Panel (a): for 1870s to 1960s, Milton Friedman and Anna J. Schwartz, *Monetary Trends in the United States and United Kingdom: Their Relation to Income, Prices, and Interest Rates, 1867–1975*, (Chicago: University of Chicago Press, 1982), Table 4.8; and for the 1970s to 2000s: Federal Reserve Board of Governors and U.S. Bureau of Economic Analysis; Panel (b): World Bank.

of growth of the money supply and rates of inflation across countries, panel (b) shows that countries where the money supply grew rapidly tended to have high inflation rates, while countries where the money supply grew more slowly tended to have much lower inflation rates. Not included in panel (b) are data for the African country of Zimbabwe, which we mentioned at the beginning of the chapter. Over this decade, the money supply in Zimbabwe grew by more than 7,500 percent per year. The result was an accelerating rate of inflation that eventually reached 15 billion percent during 2008. Zimbabwe was suffering from hyperinflation—that is, a rate of inflation that exceeds 100 percent per year.

High Rates of Inflation

Why do governments allow high rates of inflation? The quantity theory can help us to understand the reasons for high rates of inflation, such as that experienced by Zimbabwe. Very high rates of inflation—in excess of 100 percent per year—are known as *hyperinflation*. Hyperinflation is caused by central banks increasing the money supply at a rate far in excess of the growth rate of real GDP. A high rate of inflation causes money to lose its value so rapidly that households and firms avoid holding it. If, as happened in Zimbabwe, the inflation becomes severe enough, people stop using paper currency, so it no longer serves the important functions of money discussed earlier in this chapter. Economies suffering from high inflation usually also suffer from very slow growth, if not severe recession.

Given the dire consequences that follow from high inflation, why do governments cause it by expanding the money supply so rapidly? The main reason is that governments often want to spend more than they are able to raise through taxes. Developed countries, such as the United States, can usually bridge gaps between spending and taxes by borrowing through selling bonds to the public. Developing countries, such as Zimbabwe, often have difficulty selling bonds because investors are skeptical of their ability to pay back the money. If they are unable to sell bonds to the public, governments in developing countries will force their central banks to purchase them. As we discussed previously, when a central bank buys bonds, the money supply will increase.

Making the Connection

The German Hyperinflation of the Early 1920s

When Germany lost World War I, a revolution broke out that overthrew Kaiser Wilhelm II and installed a new government known as the Weimar Republic. In the peace treaty of 1919, the Allies—the United States, Great Britain, France, and Italy—imposed payments called *reparations* on the new German government. The reparations were meant as compensation to the Allies for the damage Germany had caused during the war. It was very difficult for the German government to use tax revenue to cover both its normal spending and the reparations.

During the hyperinflation of the 1920s, people in Germany used paper currency to light their stoves.

The German government decided to pay for the difference between its spending and its tax revenues by selling bonds to the central bank, the Reichsbank. After a few years, the German government fell far behind in its reparations payments. In January 1923, the French government sent troops into the German industrial area known as the Ruhr to try to collect the payments directly. German workers in the Ruhr went on strike, and the German government decided to support them by paying their salaries. Raising the funds to do so was financed by an inflationary monetary policy: The German government sold bonds to the Reichsbank, thereby increasing the money supply.

The inflationary increase in the money supply was very large: The total number of marks—the German currency—in circulation rose from 115 million in January 1922 to 1.3 billion in January 1923 and then to 497 billion *billion*, or 497,000,000,000,000,000,000, in December 1923. Just as the quantity theory predicts, the result was a staggeringly high rate of inflation. The German price index that stood at 100 in 1914 and 1,440 in January 1922 had risen to 126,160,000,000,000 in December 1923. The German mark became worthless. The German government ended the hyperinflation by (1) negotiating a new agreement with the Allies that reduced its reparations payments, (2) reducing other government expenditures and raising taxes to balance its budget, and (3) replacing the existing mark with a new mark. Each new mark was worth 1 trillion old marks. The German central bank was also limited to issuing a total of 3.2 billion new marks.

These steps were enough to bring the hyperinflation to an end—but not before the savings of anyone holding the old marks had been wiped out. Most middle-income Germans were extremely resentful of this outcome. Many historians believe that the hyperinflation greatly reduced the allegiance of many Germans to the Weimar Republic and may have helped pave the way for Adolph Hitler and the Nazis to seize power 10 years later.

Based on Thomas Sargent, "The End of Four Big Hyperinflations," *Rational Expectations and Inflation*, (New York: Harper & Row, 1986).

Continued from page 229

Economics in Your Life

What if Money Became Increasingly Valuable?

At the beginning of the chapter, we asked you to consider whether you would like to live in an economy in which the purchasing power of money rises every year. The first thing to consider when thinking about the advantages and disadvantages of this situation is that the only way for the purchasing power of money to increase is for the price level to fall; in other words, *deflation* must occur. Because the price level in the United States hasn't fallen for an entire year since the 1930s, most people alive today have experienced only rising price levels—and declining purchasing power of money. Would replacing rising prices with falling prices necessarily be a good thing? It might be tempting to say "yes," because if you have a job, your salary will buy more goods and services each year. But, in fact, just as a rising price level results in most wages and salaries rising each year, a falling price level is likely to mean falling wages and salaries each year. So, it is likely that, on average, people would not see the purchasing power of their incomes increase, even if the purchasing power of any currency they hold would increase. There can also be a significant downside to deflation, particularly if the transition from inflation to deflation happens suddenly. We defined the real interest rate as being equal to the nominal interest rate minus the inflation rate. If an economy experiences deflation, then the real interest rate will be greater than the nominal interest rate. A rising real interest rate can be bad news for anyone who has borrowed, including homeowners who may have substantial mortgage loans. So, you are probably better off living in an economy experiencing mild inflation than one experiencing deflation.

Conclusion

Money plays a key role in the functioning of an economy by facilitating trade in goods and services and by making specialization possible. Without specialization, no advanced economy can prosper. Households and firms, banks, and the central bank (the Federal Reserve in the United States) are participants in the process of creating the money supply. In Chapter 11, we will explore how the Federal Reserve uses monetary policy to promote its economic objectives.

An Inside Look at Policy on the next page discusses how an increase in bank lending to consumers and businesses is a positive signal for the economy.

AN **INSIDE** LOOK AT POLICY

Increased Lending Boosts Money Supply Growth

FISCAL TIMES

Bank Lending Signals a Strengthening Economy

The financial crisis of 2008 rocked the foundation of the U.S. banking sector. The shock left banks short of capital and hesitant to lend, even as the recession cut deeply into loan demand. The Federal Reserve has pumped in an ocean of lendable funds, trying to prime the process of bringing banks and borrowers together. But many still wonder when, if ever, bank lending will return to normal.

We're not there yet, but recent signs have been encouraging. Despite the sluggish economy, loan growth is finally beginning to pick up in key areas, reflecting both greater willingness to lend and increased desire to borrow. Loan volume of U.S. commercial banks rose at a one percent annual rate in June as expansion in business loans and non-mortgage consumer lending more than offset the ongoing contraction in real estate financing. It was the third consecutive monthly increase after steady declines for more than two years....

a Lending to businesses is leading the credit upswing. The volume of commercial and industrial (C&I) loans in the second quarter rose at a 9.6 percent annual rate, the largest increase in 2½ years. Banks have progressively eased lending standards for C&I loans to large and medium-sized companies for the past six quarters. Small companies have seen easier terms and conditions in each of the past four quarters. Economists expect to see signs that this loosening in standards is continuing when the Fed issues it third-quarter report from bank senior loan officers in mid-August.

More credit is starting to flow to small businesses, as well. That's important, because small firms account for about half of U.S. job creation, and depend greatly on banks for credit, unlike large corporations that have the option to raise funds in the capital markets by issuing bonds. In the second quarter, the balance of banks reporting stronger vs. weaker demand for commercial and industrial (C&I) loans by small businesses was positive for the first time in five years, according to the latest Fed survey. Another positive sign is the gradual rise in C&I loans made by small banks, whose customers tend to be small local companies. Small-bank C&I loan volume has been rising gradually in 2011 after hitting bottom late last year.

Despite increased attention by policymakers over the past year to the dearth of small business lending, the problem has been not so much banks' unwillingness to lend but simply a lack of loan demand, reflecting weak sales. Although the percentage of small companies saying credit is harder to get is still somewhat higher than before the recession, it has fallen steadily over the past two years, from a peak of 16 percent, to 9 percent in June, according to the National Federation of Independent Business.

b Banks are also warming to consumer loans. Despite sluggish job markets, households have made great progress in getting their financial obligations under control, allowing qualified borrowers to take on more debt. So far this year, monthly financial obligations of households have fallen to only 16.4 percent of household income, the lowest since 1994. In the second quarter, the percentage of banks reporting increased demand for auto loans was the highest since 2003.

Banks began easing lending standards for auto loans, credit cards, and other borrowing this time last year. In the 2011 second quarter the percentage of loan officers saying they were more willing to make consumer loans rose to the highest level in 17 years....

c The ebb and flow of bank lending during recessions and recoveries exerts a powerful force on any business cycle. Aside from this cycle's problems in mortgage lending, banks are finally beginning to behave as they usually do in a recovery. Barring some new shock, especially from the debt troubles in Washington or Europe, evidence that loan growth is beginning to expand in response to easier lending standards and stronger loan demand is a key sign that the recovery has staying power.

Source: "Bank Lending Signals a Strengthening Economy" by James C. Cooper, from *Fiscal Times* website, August 1st, 2011.

Key Points in the Article

The financial crisis of 2007–2009 resulted in decreases in both the supply of funds available to lend and in the demand for those funds. Despite the Federal Reserve's infusion of large amounts of funds into the economy, bank lending continued to decline for more than two years. In April 2011, loan volumes finally began to increase. The largest increase occurred in business lending, with the volume of commercial and industrial (C&I) loans rising at an annual rate of 9.6 percent for the second quarter of 2011, which was the largest increase in over two years. The increase in small business lending was particularly encouraging, with banks in the second quarter reporting increased demand for small business loans for the first time in five years. The market for consumer loans was improving as well. As consumer debt as a percentage of income fell to its lowest level since 1994, banks became more willing to make consumer loans. The expansion of loan growth was a positive sign for the economy during what had been a sluggish recovery from the recession.

Analyzing the News

(a) Banks help channel funds from savers to borrowers by making loans to individuals and businesses. Rising defaults on home loans after the housing bubble burst led to the collapse of a number of financial intermediaries in 2008, and loan volume declined for more than two years. Growth in the market for loans reemerged in the second quarter of 2011, with business loans leading the upswing. Commercial and industrial loans rose at an annual rate of 9.6 percent as banks continued to loosen lending requirements for small, medium, and large companies. As Figure 1 below shows, the percentage change in commercial and industrial bank loans turned positive toward the end of 2010, and it accelerated for much of the second quarter of 2011.

(b) Loans to consumers began to increase in mid-2011. Following the collapse of financial markets in 2008, banks were much less willing to make consumer loans, increasing their lending standards as households' financial obligations grew. The decrease in the supply of funds available to households was met with a decrease in the demand for these funds as households worked to reduce their debts. As household debts became more manageable, banks became increasingly willing to make consumer loans, as shown in Figure 2 below.

(c) As you read in this chapter, banks create money by loaning out excess reserves. Because of the money multiplier process, a given amount of new reserves results in a multiple increase in bank deposits. In an attempt to bring lenders and borrowers together following the financial crisis of 2008, the Federal Reserve made a large amount of new funds available to financial markets. These extra funds had the potential to affect the economy as banks, responding to an increase in demand, finally began to see an increase in loans in 2011. The increases in excess reserves, bank deposits, and loan volume are indications that the economy was in the expansion phase of the business cycle and were positive signs for continued economic recovery.

Thinking Critically About Policy

1. During the financial crisis of 2007–2009, the Fed attempted to stimulate the economy by taking actions to increase the money supply. How effective would these actions be if banks remained reluctant to make consumer loans while households remained reluctant to obtain loans? Briefly explain.
2. The quantity theory of money predicts that a large increase in the money supply will result in inflation. Why, then, even though the money supply increased rapidly was inflation relatively low during the recession of 2007–2009 and its immediate aftermath?

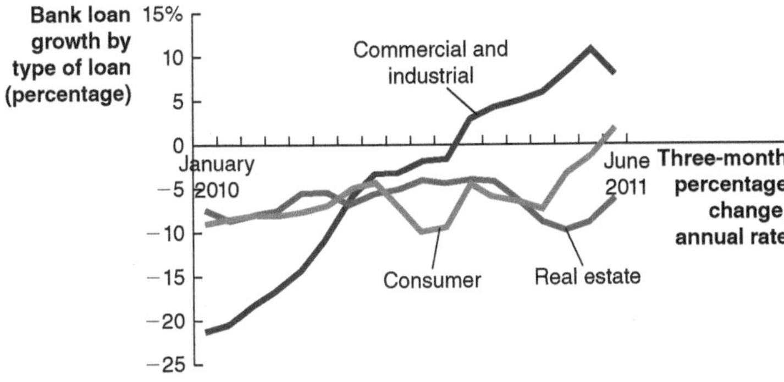

Figure 1

Loans to businesses and consumers are growing, but real estate loans keep falling.

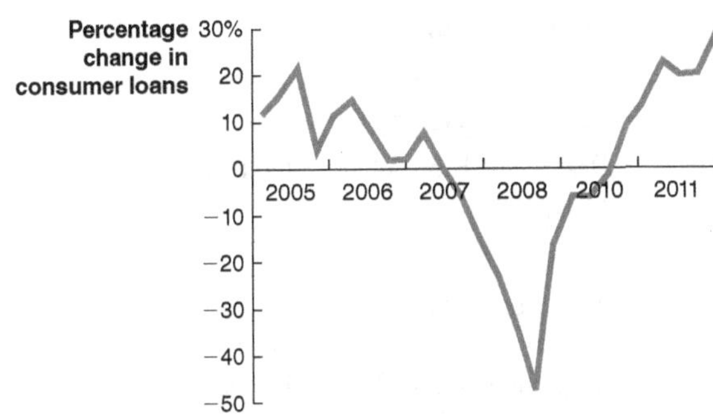

Figure 2

More banks say they are willing to make consumer loans.

CHAPTER 11

Monetary Policy

Chapter Outline and Learning Objectives

Monetary Policy, Toll Brothers, and the Housing Market

If you lose your job or are afraid that you might, you are not likely to buy a new house. It's not surprising, then, that residential construction tends to fall during a recession. In addition, recessions often begin after the Federal Reserve increases interest rates to slow the growth in aggregate demand in order to reduce the inflation rate. Higher interest rates increase the cost of buying houses, further reducing demand for them. Not surprisingly, firms that build homes usually don't do well during recessions. For example, during the recessions of 1974–1975 and 1981–1982, residential construction declined by more than 30 percent.

The recession of 2001 was different, however. In early 2001, the members of the Federal Reserve's Federal Open Market Committee (FOMC) concluded that a recession was about to begin and took action to drive down interest rates. This action succeeded in heading off what some economists had predicted would be a prolonged and severe recession. In fact, the Fed's strategy resulted in spending on residential construction actually rising by 5 percent during the 2001 recession.

Toll Brothers is a homebuilder headquartered in Huntingdon Valley, Pennsylvania. Toll Brothers' profit actually increased during 2001. However, the recession of 2007–2009 was a different story. Toll Brothers suffered a record loss of more than $750 million—and it wasn't alone. Nearly all homebuilders suffered severe declines in sales, and many went bankrupt. The key problem was that by 2005, the housing market boom had turned into a "bubble." In a bubble, prices soar to levels that are not sustainable. When the housing bubble finally burst in 2006, sales of new homes and prices of existing homes began a sharp decline. By 2007, the economy had entered a recession. This time, unfortunately, the Fed found that cutting interest rates was not enough to revive the housing market or the general economy. Beginning in 2008, the Fed was forced to turn to new policies to try to pull the economy out of recession.

In this chapter, we will study how monetary policy affects economic activity.

Based on Toll Brothers, *Annual Report*, 2010.

Economics in Your Life

Should You Buy a House during a Recession?

If you are like most college students, buying a house is one of the farthest things from your mind. But suppose you think forward a few years to when you might be married and maybe even (gasp!) have children. Leaving behind years of renting apartments, you are considering buying a house. But, suppose that according to an article in the *Wall Street Journal*, a majority of economists are predicting that a recession is likely to begin soon. What should you do? Would this be a good time or a bad time to buy a house? As you read the chapter, see if you can answer these questions. You can check your answers against those we provide on **page 287** at the end of this chapter.

In Chapter 10, we saw that banks play an important role in providing credit to households and firms, and in creating the money supply. We also saw that Congress established the Federal Reserve to stabilize the financial system and that the Fed is responsible for managing the money supply. In this chapter, we will discuss the Fed's four main policy goals: (1) price stability, (2) high employment, (3) stability of financial markets and institutions, and (4) economic growth. We will explore how the Federal Reserve decides which *monetary policy* actions to take to achieve its goals.

11.1 LEARNING OBJECTIVE

Define monetary policy and describe the Federal Reserve's monetary policy goals.

What Is Monetary Policy?

In 1913, Congress passed the Federal Reserve Act, creating the Federal Reserve System ("the Fed"). The main responsibility of the Fed was to make discount loans to banks to prevent the bank panics we discussed in Chapter 10. As a result of the Great Depression of the 1930s, Congress amended the Federal Reserve Act to give the Federal Reserve's Board of Governors broader responsibility to act "so as to promote effectively the goals of maximum employment, stable prices, and moderate long-term interest rates."

Since World War II, the Federal Reserve has carried out an active *monetary policy*. **Monetary policy** refers to the actions the Fed takes to manage the money supply and interest rates to pursue its macroeconomic policy goals.

Monetary policy The actions the Federal Reserve takes to manage the money supply and interest rates to pursue macroeconomic policy goals.

The Goals of Monetary Policy

The Fed has four main *monetary policy goals* that are intended to promote a well-functioning economy:

1. Price stability
2. High employment
3. Stability of financial markets and institutions
4. Economic growth

We briefly consider each of these goals.

Price Stability As we have seen in previous chapters, rising prices erode the value of money as a medium of exchange and a store of value. Especially after inflation rose dramatically and unexpectedly during the 1970s, policymakers in most industrial countries have had price stability as a policy goal. Figure 11.1 shows that from the early 1950s until 1968, the inflation rate remained below 4 percent per year. Inflation was above

Figure 11.1

The Inflation Rate, January 1952–August 2011

For most of the 1950s and 1960s, the inflation rate in the United States was 4 percent or less. During the 1970s, the inflation rate increased, peaking during 1979–1981, when it averaged more than 10 percent. After 1992, the inflation rate was usually less than 4 percent, until increases in oil prices pushed it above 5 percent during summer 2008. The effects of the recession caused several months of deflation—a falling price level—during early 2009.

Note: The inflation rate is measured as the percentage change in the consumer price index (CPI) from the same month in the previous year.

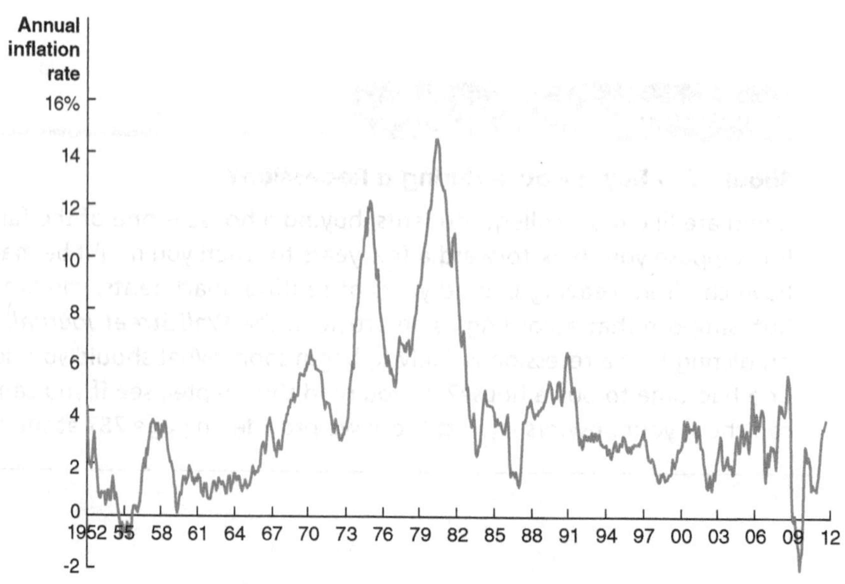

4 percent for most of the 1970s. In early 1979, the inflation rate increased to more than 10 percent, where it remained until late 1981, when it began to rapidly fall back to the 4 percent range. After 1992, the inflation rate was usually below 4 percent, until rapid increases in gasoline prices helped push it above 5 percent in summer 2008. The effects of the recession caused several months of deflation—a falling price level—during early 2009.

The inflation rates during the years 1979–1981 were the highest the United States has ever experienced during peacetime. When Paul Volcker became chairman of the Federal Reserve's Board of Governors in August 1979, he made fighting inflation his top policy goal. Alan Greenspan, who succeeded Volcker in August 1987, and Ben Bernanke, who succeeded Greenspan in January 2006, continued to focus on inflation. Volcker, Greenspan, and Bernanke argued that if inflation is low over the long run, the Fed will have the flexibility it needs to lessen the impact of recessions. Although the severity of the 2007–2009 recession led the Fed to adopt extraordinary policy measures that we will discuss later in this chapter, price stability remains a key policy goal of the Fed.

High Employment In addition to price stability, high employment, or a low rate of unemployment, is an important monetary policy goal. Unemployed workers and underused factories and office buildings reduce GDP below its potential level. Unemployment causes financial distress and decreases the self-esteem of workers who lack jobs. The goal of high employment extends beyond the Fed to other branches of the federal government. At the end of World War II, Congress passed the Employment Act of 1946, which stated that it was the "responsibility of the Federal Government ... to foster and promote ... conditions under which there will be afforded useful employment, for those able, willing, and seeking to work, and to promote maximum employment, production, and purchasing power." Because price stability and high employment are explicitly mentioned in the Employment Act, it is sometimes said that the Fed has a *dual mandate* to attain these two goals.

Stability of Financial Markets and Institutions Resources are lost when financial markets and institutions are not efficient in matching savers and borrowers. Firms with the potential to produce goods and services that consumers value cannot obtain the financing they need to design, develop, and market those products. Savers waste resources looking for satisfactory investments. The Fed promotes the stability of financial markets and institutions so that an efficient flow of funds from savers to borrowers will occur. As we saw in Chapter 10, the financial crisis of 2007–2009 brought the issue of stability in financial markets to the forefront.

The financial crisis of 2007–2009 was similar to the banking crises that led Congress to create the Federal Reserve System in 1913. A key difference is that while earlier banking crises affected commercial banks, the events of 2007–2009 also affected investment banks. Investment banks can be subject to *liquidity problems* because they often borrow short term—sometimes as short as overnight—and invest the funds in longer-term investments. Commercial banks borrow from households and firms in the form of checking and savings deposits, while investment banks borrow primarily from other financial firms, such as other investment banks, mutual funds, or hedge funds, which are similar to mutual funds but typically engage in more complex—and risky—investment strategies. Just as commercial banks can experience crises if depositors begin to withdraw funds, investment banks can experience crises if other financial firms stop offering them short-term loans. In 2008, the Fed decided to ease the liquidity problems facing investment banks by temporarily allowing them to receive discount loans, which had previously been available only to commercial banks. Later in this chapter, we will discuss in more detail the new policies the Fed enacted to help deal with the financial crisis.

Economic Growth Policymakers aim to encourage *stable* economic growth because it allows households and firms to plan accurately and encourages the long-run investment that is needed to sustain growth. Policy can spur economic growth by providing incentives for saving to ensure a large pool of investment funds, as well as by providing direct incentives for business investment. Congress and the president, however, may be better able to increase saving and investment than is the Fed. For example, Congress and the president can change the tax laws to increase the return to saving and investing. In fact, some economists question whether the Fed can play a role in promoting economic growth beyond attempting to meet its goals of price stability, high employment, and financial stability.

In the next section, we will look at how the Fed attempts to attain its monetary policy goals. Although the Fed has multiple monetary policy goals, during most periods, its most important goals have been price stability and high employment. But the turmoil in financial markets that began in 2007 led the Fed to put new emphasis on the goal of financial market stability.

11.2 LEARNING OBJECTIVE

Describe the Federal Reserve's monetary policy targets and explain how expansionary and contractionary monetary policies affect the interest rate.

The Money Market and the Fed's Choice of Monetary Policy Targets

The Fed aims to use its policy tools to achieve its monetary policy goals. Recall from Chapter 10 that the Fed's policy tools are open market operations, discount policy, and reserve requirements. At times, the Fed encounters conflicts between its policy goals. For example, as we will discuss later in this chapter, the Fed can raise interest rates to reduce the inflation rate. But, as we saw in Chapter 8, higher interest rates typically reduce household and firm spending, which may result in slower growth and higher unemployment. So, a policy that is intended to achieve one monetary policy goal, such as reducing inflation, may have an adverse effect on another policy goal, such as high employment.

Monetary Policy Targets

The Fed tries to keep both the unemployment and inflation rates low, but it can't affect either of these economic variables directly. The Fed cannot tell firms how many people to employ or what prices to charge for their products. Instead, the Fed uses variables, called *monetary policy targets*, that it can affect directly and that, in turn, affect variables, such as real GDP, employment, and the price level, that are closely related to the Fed's policy goals. The two main monetary policy targets are the money supply and the interest rate. As we will see, the Fed typically uses the interest rate as its policy target.

It's important to bear in mind that while the Fed has typically used the money supply and the interest rate as its targets, these targets were not central to the Fed's policy decisions during the recession of 2007–2009. As we will discuss later in this chapter, because U.S. financial markets suffered a degree of disruption not seen since the Great Depression of the 1930s, the Fed was forced to develop new policy tools. However, it is still important to have a good grasp of how the Fed carries out policy during normal times.

The Demand for Money

The Fed's two monetary policy targets are related in an important way. To see this relationship, we first need to examine the demand and supply for money. Figure 11.2 shows the demand curve for money. The interest rate is on the vertical axis, and the quantity of money is on the horizontal axis. Here we are using the M1 definition of money, which equals currency in circulation plus checking account deposits. Notice that the demand curve for money is downward sloping.

To understand why the demand curve for money is downward sloping, consider that households and firms have a choice between holding money and holding other financial assets, such as U.S. Treasury bills. Money has one particularly desirable characteristic: You can use it to buy goods, services, or financial assets. Money also has one undesirable characteristic: It earns either no interest or a very low rate of interest. The currency in your wallet earns no interest, and the money in your checking account earns

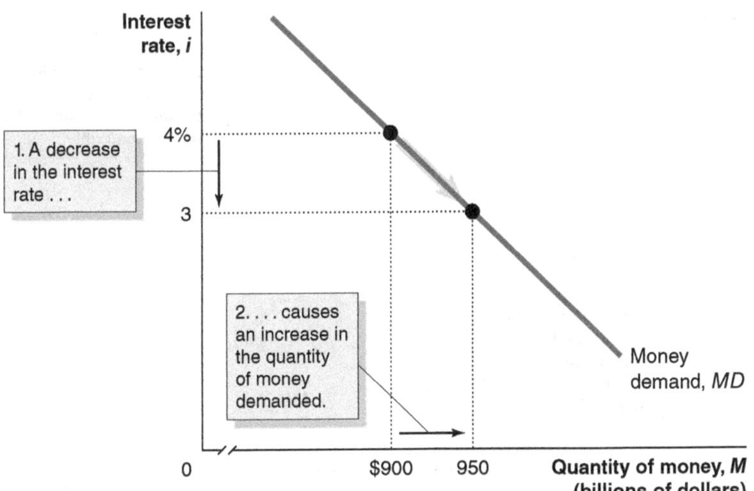

Figure 11.2

The Demand for Money

The money demand curve slopes downward because lower interest rates cause households and firms to switch from financial assets such as U.S. Treasury bills to money. All other things being equal, a fall in the interest rate from 4 percent to 3 percent will increase the quantity of money demanded from $900 billion to $950 billion. An increase in the interest rate will decrease the quantity of money demanded.

either no interest or very little interest. Alternatives to money, such as U.S. Treasury bills, pay interest but have to be sold if you want to use the funds to buy something. When interest rates rise on financial assets such as U.S. Treasury bills, the amount of interest that households and firms lose by holding money increases. When interest rates fall, the amount of interest households and firms lose by holding money decreases. Remember that *opportunity cost* is what you have to forgo to engage in an activity. The interest rate is the opportunity cost of holding money.

We now have an explanation of why the demand curve for money slopes downward: When interest rates on Treasury bills and other financial assets are low, the opportunity cost of holding money is low, so the quantity of money demanded by households and firms will be high; when interest rates are high, the opportunity cost of holding money will be high, so the quantity of money demanded will be low. In Figure 11.2, a decrease in interest rates from 4 percent to 3 percent causes the quantity of money demanded by households and firms to rise from $900 billion to $950 billion.

Shifts in the Money Demand Curve

We saw in Chapter 4 that the demand curve for a good is drawn holding constant all variables, other than the price, that affect the willingness of consumers to buy the good. Changes in variables other than the price cause the demand curve to shift. Similarly, the demand curve for money is drawn holding constant all variables, other than the interest rate, that affect the willingness of households and firms to hold money. Changes in variables other than the interest rate cause the demand curve to shift. The two most important variables that cause the money demand curve to shift are real GDP and the price level.

An increase in real GDP means that the amount of buying and selling of goods and services will increase. This additional buying and selling increases the demand for money as a medium of exchange, so the quantity of money households and firms want to hold increases at each interest rate, shifting the money demand curve to the right. A decrease in real GDP decreases the quantity of money demanded at each interest rate, shifting the money demand curve to the left. A higher price level increases the quantity of money required for a given amount of buying and selling. Eighty years ago, for example, when the price level was much lower and someone could purchase a new car for $500 and a salary of $30 per week put you in the middle class, the quantity of money demanded by households and firms was much lower than today, even adjusting for the effect of the lower real GDP and smaller population of those years. An increase in the price level increases the quantity of money demanded at each interest rate, shifting the money demand curve to the right. A decrease in the price level decreases the quantity of money demanded at each interest rate, shifting the money demand curve to the left. Figure 11.3 illustrates shifts in the money demand curve.

Figure 11.3

Shifts in the Money Demand Curve

Changes in real GDP or the price level cause the money demand curve to shift. An increase in real GDP or an increase in the price level will cause the money demand curve to shift from MD_1 to MD_2. A decrease in real GDP or a decrease in the price level will cause the money demand curve to shift from MD_1 to MD_3.

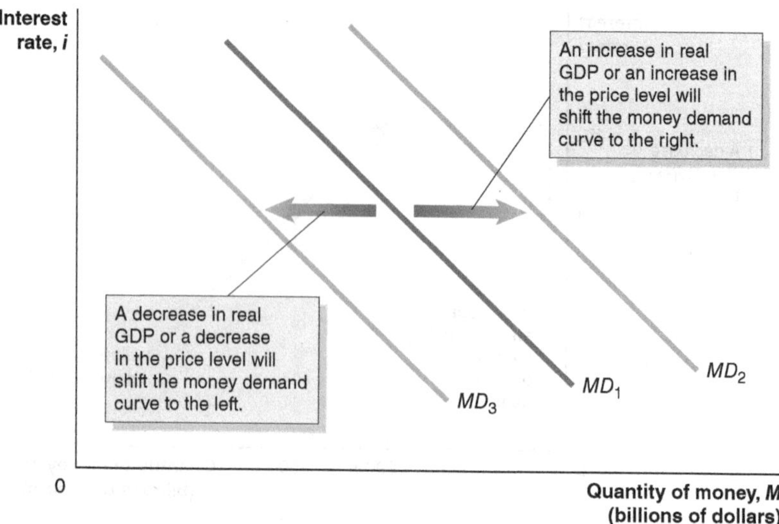

How the Fed Manages the Money Supply: A Quick Review

Having discussed money demand, we now turn to money supply. In Chapter 10, we saw how the Federal Reserve manages the money supply. Eight times per year, the Federal Open Market Committee (FOMC) meets in Washington, DC. If the FOMC decides to increase the money supply, it orders the trading desk at the Federal Reserve Bank of New York to purchase U.S. Treasury securities. The sellers of these Treasury securities deposit the funds they receive from the Fed in banks, which increases the banks' reserves. Typically, the banks loan out most of these reserves, which creates new checking account deposits and expands the money supply. If the FOMC decides to decrease the money supply, it orders the trading desk to sell Treasury securities, which decreases banks' reserves and contracts the money supply.

Equilibrium in the Money Market

In Figure 11.4, we include both the money demand and money supply curves. We can use this figure to see how the Fed affects both the money supply and the interest rate. For simplicity, we assume that the Federal Reserve is able to completely control the money supply. Therefore, the money supply curve is a vertical line, and changes

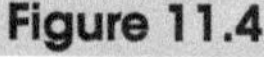

Figure 11.4

The Effect on the Interest Rate When the Fed Increases the Money Supply

When the Fed increases the money supply, households and firms will initially hold more money than they want, relative to other financial assets. Households and firms use the money they don't want to hold to buy Treasury bills and make deposits in interest-paying bank accounts. This increase in demand allows banks and sellers of Treasury bills and similar securities to offer lower interest rates. Eventually, interest rates will fall enough that households and firms will be willing to hold the additional money the Fed has created. In the figure, an increase in the money supply from \$900 billion to \$950 billion causes the money supply curve to shift to the right, from MS_1 to MS_2, and causes the equilibrium interest rate to fall from 4 percent to 3 percent.

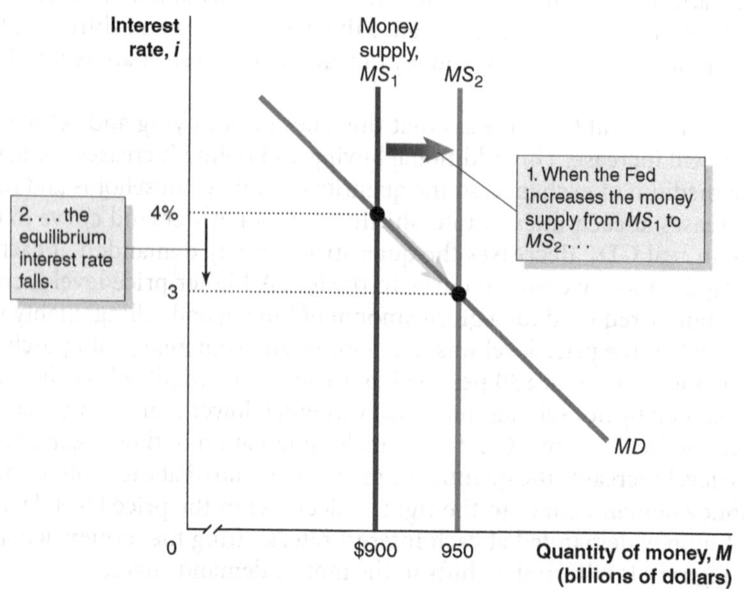

in the interest rate have no effect on the quantity of money supplied. Just as with other markets, equilibrium in the *money market* occurs where the money demand curve crosses the money supply curve. If the Fed increases the money supply, the money supply curve will shift to the right, and the equilibrium interest rate will fall. In Figure 11.4, when the Fed increases the money supply from \$900 billion to \$950 billion, the money supply curve shifts from MS_1 to MS_2, and the equilibrium interest rate falls from 4 percent to 3 percent.

In the money market, the adjustment from one equilibrium to another equilibrium is a little different from the adjustment in the market for a good. In Figure 11.4, the money market is initially in equilibrium, with an interest rate of 4 percent and a money supply of \$900 billion. When the Fed increases the money supply by \$50 billion, households and firms have more money than they want to hold at an interest rate of 4 percent. What do households and firms do with the extra \$50 billion? They are most likely to use the money to buy short-term financial assets, such as Treasury bills, or to deposit the money in interest-paying bank accounts, such as certificates of deposit. This increase in demand for interest-paying bank accounts and short-term financial assets allows banks to offer lower interest rates on certificates of deposit, and it allows sellers of Treasury bills and similar assets to also offer lower interest rates. As the interest rates on certificates of deposit, Treasury bills, and other short-term assets fall, the opportunity cost of holding money also falls. Households and firms move down the money demand curve. Eventually the interest rate will have fallen enough that households and firms are willing to hold the additional \$50 billion worth of money the Fed has created, and the money market will be back in equilibrium. To summarize: *When the Fed increases the money supply, the short-term interest rate must fall until it reaches a level at which households and firms are willing to hold the additional money.*

Figure 11.5 shows what happens when the Fed decreases the money supply. The money market is initially in equilibrium, at an interest rate of 4 percent and a money supply of \$900 billion. If the Fed decreases the money supply to \$850 billion, households and firms will be holding less money than they would like, relative to other financial assets, at an interest rate of 4 percent. To increase their money holdings, they will sell Treasury bills and other short-term financial assets and withdraw funds from certificates of deposit and other interest-paying bank accounts. Banks will have to offer higher interest rates in order to retain depositors, and sellers of Treasury bills and similar securities will have to offer higher interest rates in order to find buyers. Rising short-term interest rates increase the opportunity cost of holding money, causing households and firms to move up the money demand curve. Equilibrium is finally restored at an interest rate of 5 percent.

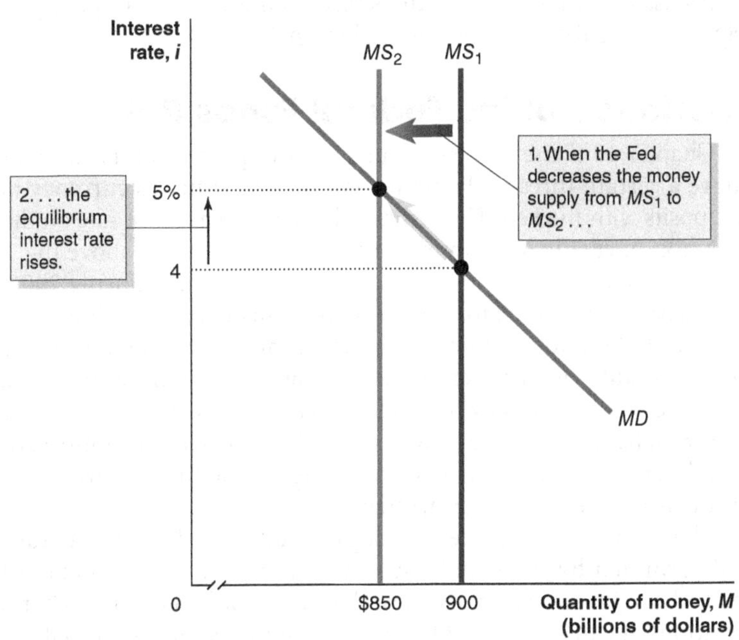

Figure 11.5

The Effect on Interest Rates When the Fed Decreases the Money Supply

When the Fed decreases the money supply, households and firms will initially hold less money than they want, relative to other financial assets. Households and firms will sell Treasury bills and other financial assets and withdraw money from interest-paying bank accounts. These actions will increase interest rates. Eventually, interest rates will rise to the point at which households and firms will be willing to hold the smaller amount of money that results from the Fed's actions. In the figure, a reduction in the money supply from \$900 billion to \$850 billion causes the money supply curve to shift to the left, from MS_1 to MS_2, and causes the equilibrium interest rate to rise from 4 percent to 5 percent.

A Tale of Two Interest Rates

In the loanable model, the equilibrium interest rate is determined by the demand and supply for loanable funds. Why do we need two models of the interest rate? The answer is that the loanable funds model is concerned with the *long-term real rate of interest*, and the money market model is concerned with the *short-term nominal rate of interest*. The long-term real rate of interest is the interest rate that is most relevant when savers consider purchasing a long-term financial investment such as a corporate bond. It is also the rate of interest that is most relevant to firms that are borrowing to finance long-term investment projects such as new factories or office buildings, or to households that are taking out mortgage loans to buy new homes.

When conducting monetary policy, however, the short-term nominal interest rate is the most relevant interest rate because it is the interest rate most affected by increases and decreases in the money supply. Often—but not always—there is a close connection between movements in the short-term nominal interest rate and movements in the long-term real interest rate. So, when the Fed takes actions to increase the short-term nominal interest rate, usually the long-term real interest rate also increases. In other words, as we will discuss in the next section, when the interest rate on Treasury bills rises, the real interest rate on mortgage loans usually also rises, although sometimes only after a delay.

Choosing a Monetary Policy Target

As we have seen, the Fed uses monetary policy targets to affect economic variables such as real GDP or the price level, that are closely related to the Fed's policy goals. The Fed can use either the money supply or the interest rate as its monetary policy target. As Figure 11.5 shows, the Fed is capable of affecting both. The Fed has generally focused more on the interest rate than on the money supply. Since 1980, deregulation and financial innovations, including paying interest on checking accounts and the introduction of money market mutual funds, have made M1 less relevant as a measure of the medium of exchange. For a time, these developments led the Fed to rely on M2, a broader measure of the money supply that had a more stable historical relationship to economic growth. Even this relationship broke down in the early 1990s. In July 1993, then Fed Chairman Alan Greenspan informed the U.S. Congress that the Fed would cease using M1 or M2 targets to guide the conduct of monetary policy. The Fed has correspondingly increased its reliance on interest rate targets.

There are many different interest rates in the economy. For purposes of monetary policy, the Fed has targeted the interest rate known as the *federal funds rate*. In the next section, we discuss the federal funds rate before examining how targeting the interest rate can help the Fed achieve its monetary policy goals.

The Importance of the Federal Funds Rate

Recall from Chapter 10 that every bank must keep 10 percent of its checking account deposits above a certain threshold amount as reserves, either as currency held in the bank or as deposits with the Fed. The Fed pays banks a low interest rate on their reserve deposits, so banks normally have an incentive to invest reserves above the 10 percent minimum. As the financial crisis that began in 2007 deepened during 2008, bank reserves soared as banks attempted to meet an increase in deposit withdrawals and as they became reluctant to lend to any borrowers except those with the most flawless credit histories. These conditions were very unusual, however. In normal times, banks keep few excess reserves, and when they need additional reserves, they borrow in the *federal funds market* from banks that have reserves available. The **federal funds rate** is the interest rate banks charge each other on loans in the federal funds market. The loans in that market are usually very short term, often just overnight.

Federal funds rate The interest rate banks charge each other for overnight loans.

Despite the name, the Fed does not legally set the federal funds rate. Instead, the rate is determined by the supply of reserves relative to the demand for them. Because the Fed can increase and decrease the supply of bank reserves through open market operations, it can set a *target* for the federal funds rate and usually come very close to hitting it. The FOMC announces a target for the federal funds rate after each

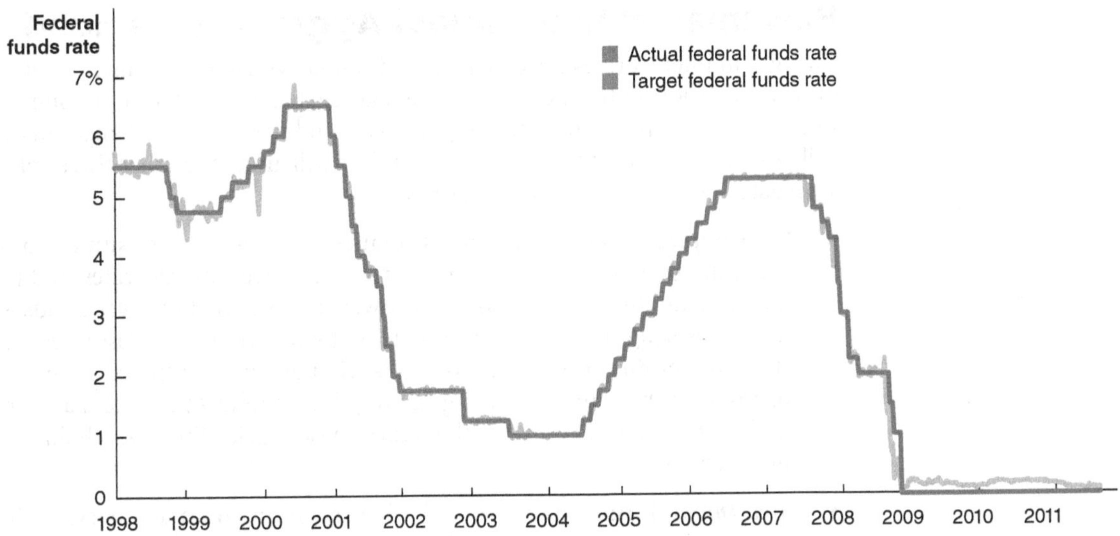

Figure 11.6 Federal Funds Rate Targeting, January 1998–September 2011

The Fed does not set the federal funds rate, but its ability to increase or decrease bank reserves quickly through open market operations keeps the actual federal funds rate close to the Fed's target rate. The line is the Fed's target for the federal funds rate, and the jagged line represents the actual value for the federal funds rate on a weekly basis.

Note: The federal funds target for the period after December 2008 was 0 to 0.25 percent.
Data from Board of Governers of the Federal Reserve System.

meeting. In Figure 11.6, the line shows the Fed's targets for the federal funds rate since 1998. The jagged line represents the actual federal funds rate on a weekly basis. The figure shows the rapid declines in the target for the federal funds rate beginning in September 2007, as the Fed responded to the start of the financial crisis. In December 2008, the Fed announced a range of 0 to 0.25 percent as its target. The actual federal funds rate fluctuated between 0.06 and 0.23 percent. These very low federal funds rates reflect the severity of the financial crisis.

The federal funds rate is not directly relevant for households and firms. Only banks can borrow or lend in the federal funds market. However, changes in the federal funds rate usually result in changes in interest rates on other short-term financial assets, such as Treasury bills, and changes in interest rates on long-term financial assets, such as corporate bonds and mortgages. A change in the federal funds rate has a greater effect on short-term interest rates than on long-term interest rates, and its effect on long-term interest rates may occur only after a lag in time. Although a majority of economists support the Fed's choice of the interest rate as its monetary policy target, some economists believe the Fed should concentrate on the money supply instead. We will discuss the views of these economists later in this chapter.

Monetary Policy and Economic Activity

11.3 LEARNING OBJECTIVE

Use aggregate demand and aggregate supply graphs to show the effects of monetary policy on real GDP and the price level.

Remember that the Fed uses the federal funds rate as a monetary policy target because it has good control of the federal funds rate through open market operations and because it believes that changes in the federal funds rate will ultimately affect economic variables that are related to its monetary policy goals. It is important to consider again the distinction between the nominal interest rate and the real interest rate. Recall that we calculate the real interest rate by subtracting the inflation rate from the nominal interest rate. Ultimately, the ability of the Fed to use monetary policy to affect economic variables such as real GDP depends on its ability to affect real interest rates, such as the real interest rates on mortgages and corporate bonds. Because the federal funds rate is a short-term nominal interest rate, the Fed sometimes has difficulty affecting long-term real interest rates. Nevertheless, for purposes of the following discussion, we will assume that the Fed is able to use open market operations to affect long-term real interest rates.

How Interest Rates Affect Aggregate Demand

Changes in interest rates affect *aggregate demand*, which is the total level of spending in the economy. Recall from Chapter 8 that aggregate demand has four components: consumption, investment, government purchases, and net exports. Changes in interest rates will not affect government purchases, but they will affect the other three components of aggregate demand in the following ways:

- ***Consumption.*** Many households finance purchases of consumer durables, such as automobiles and furniture, by borrowing. Lower interest rates lead to increased spending on durables because they lower the total cost of these goods to consumers by lowering the interest payments on loans. Higher interest rates raise the cost of consumer durables, and households will buy fewer of them. Lower interest rates also reduce the return to saving, leading households to save less and spend more. Higher interest rates increase the return to saving, leading households to save more and spend less.
- ***Investment.*** Firms finance most of their spending on machinery, equipment, and factories out of their profits or by borrowing. Firms borrow either from the financial markets by issuing corporate bonds or from banks. Higher interest rates on corporate bonds or on bank loans make it more expensive for firms to borrow, so they will undertake fewer investment projects. Lower interest rates make it less expensive for firms to borrow, so they will undertake more investment projects. Lower interest rates can also increase investment through their effect on stock prices. As interest rates decline, stocks become a more attractive investment relative to bonds. The increase in demand for stocks raises their price. An increase in stock prices sends a signal to firms that the future profitability of investment projects has increased. By issuing additional shares of stocks, firms can acquire the funds they need to buy new factories and equipment, thereby increasing investment.

  Finally, spending by households on new homes is also part of investment. When interest rates on mortgage loans rise, the cost of buying new homes rises, and fewer new homes will be purchased. When interest rates on mortgage loans fall, more new homes will be purchased.
- ***Net exports.*** Recall that net exports are equal to spending by foreign households and firms on goods and services produced in the United States minus spending by U.S. households and firms on goods and services produced in other countries. The value of net exports depends partly on the exchange rate between the dollar and foreign currencies. When the value of the dollar rises, households and firms in other countries will pay more for goods and services produced in the United States, but U.S. households and firms will pay less for goods and services produced in other countries. As a result, the United States will export less and import more, so net exports fall. When the value of the dollar falls, net exports will rise. If interest rates in the United States rise relative to interest rates in other countries, investing in U.S. financial assets will become more desirable, causing foreign investors to increase their demand for dollars, which will increase the value of the dollar. As the value of the dollar increases, net exports will fall. If interest rates in the United States decline relative to interest rates in other countries, the value of the dollar will fall, and net exports will rise.

The Effects of Monetary Policy on Real GDP and the Price Level

In Chapter 8, we developed the *aggregate demand and aggregate supply model* to explain fluctuations in real GDP and the price level. In the basic version of the model, we assume that there is no economic growth, so the long-run aggregate supply curve does not shift. In panel (a) of Figure 11.7, we assume that the economy is in short-run equilibrium at point *A*, where the aggregate demand (AD_1) curve intersects the short-run

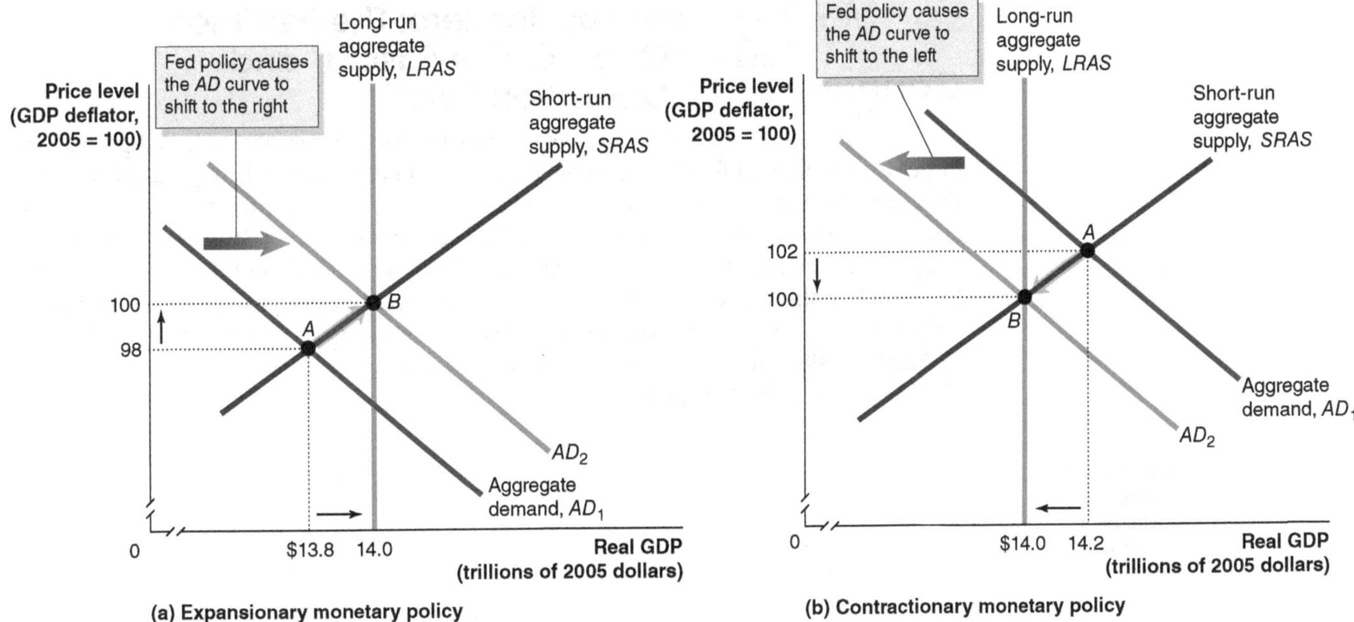

Figure 11.7 Monetary Policy

In panel (a), the economy begins in a recession at point *A*, with real GDP of \$13.8 trillion and a price level of 98. An expansionary monetary policy causes aggregate demand to shift to the right, from AD_1 to AD_2, increasing real GDP from \$13.8 trillion to \$14.0 trillion and the price level from 98 to 100 (point *B*). With real GDP back at its potential level, the Fed can meet its goal of high employment.

In panel (b), the economy begins at point *A*, with real GDP at \$14.2 trillion and the price level at 102. Because real GDP is greater than potential GDP, the economy experiences rising wages and prices. A contractionary monetary policy causes aggregate demand to shift to the left, from AD_1 to AD_2, decreasing real GDP from \$14.2 trillion to \$14.0 trillion and the price level from 102 to 100 (point *B*). With real GDP back at its potential level, the Fed can meet its goal of price stability.

aggregate supply (*SRAS*) curve. Real GDP is below potential real GDP, as shown by the *LRAS* curve, so the economy is in a recession, with some firms operating below normal capacity and some workers having been laid off. To reach its goal of high employment, the Fed needs to carry out an **expansionary monetary policy** by increasing the money supply and decreasing interest rates. Lower interest rates cause an increase in consumption, investment, and net exports, which shifts the aggregate demand curve to the right, from AD_1 to AD_2. Real GDP increases from \$13.8 trillion to potential GDP of \$14.0 trillion, and the price level rises from 98 to 100 (point *B*). The policy successfully returns real GDP to its potential level. Rising production leads to increasing employment, allowing the Fed to achieve its goal of high employment.

Expansionary monetary policy The Federal Reserve's decreasing interest rates to increase real GDP.

In panel (b) of Figure 11.7, the economy is in short-run equilibrium at point *A*, with real GDP of \$14.2 trillion, which is above potential real GDP of \$14.0 trillion. With some firms producing beyond their normal capacity and the unemployment rate very low, wages and prices are increasing. To reach its goal of price stability, the Fed needs to carry out a **contractionary monetary policy** by decreasing the money supply and increasing interest rates. Higher interest rates cause a decrease in consumption, investment, and net exports, which shifts the aggregate demand curve from AD_1 to AD_2. Real GDP decreases from \$14.2 trillion to \$14.0 trillion, and the price level falls from 102 to 100 (point *B*). Why would the Fed want to intentionally cause real GDP to decline? Because in the long run, real GDP cannot continue to remain above potential GDP. Attempting to keep real GDP above potential GDP would result in rising inflation. As aggregate demand declines and real GDP returns to its potential level, upward pressure on wages and prices will be reduced, allowing the Fed to achieve its goal of price stability.

Contractionary monetary policy The Federal Reserve's increasing interest rates to reduce inflation.

We can conclude that the Fed can use monetary policy to affect the price level and, in the short run, the level of real GDP, allowing it to attain its policy goals of high employment and price stability.

Making the Connection

Too Low for Zero: The Fed Tries "Quantitative Easing" and "Operation Twist"

Figure 11.6 shows that in December 2008, the Fed pushed the target for the federal funds rate to nearly zero and kept it there through 2011. Because the 2007–2009 recession was so severe, even this very low rate did little to stimulate the economy. To lower the federal funds rate, the Fed buys Treasury bills through open market purchases, which increases bank reserves. Banks then lend out these reserves. As the figure below shows, however, in late 2008, many banks began piling up excess reserves rather than lending the funds out. Total bank reserves had been less than $50 billion in August 2008, but with the deepening of the financial crisis, they had soared to more than $900 billion by May 2009.

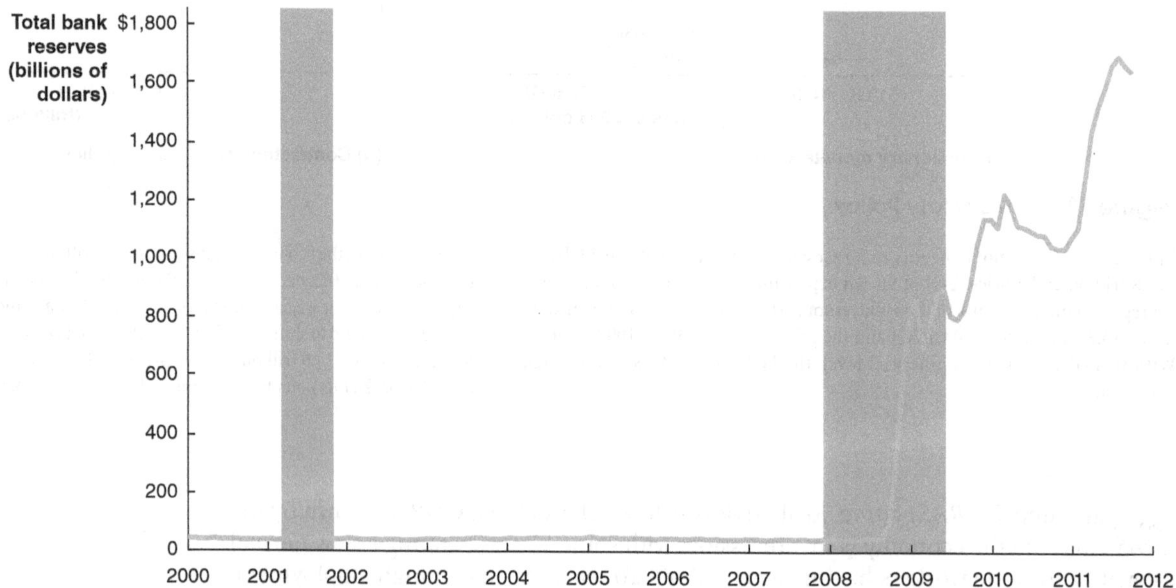

Data from The Federal Reserve Bank of St. Louis.

The increase in bank reserves was partly due to the Fed's decision in October 2008 to start paying interest of 0.25 percent on bank reserves held as deposits at the Fed. Primarily, though, the increase in reserves occurred because banks were reluctant to make loans at low interest rates to households and firms whose financial positions had been damaged by the recession. Some economists believed the Fed was facing a situation known as a *liquidity trap*, in which short-term interest rates are pushed to zero, leaving the central bank unable to lower them further. Some economists believe that liquidity traps occurred in the United States during the 1930s and in Japan during the 1990s.

Not being able to push the target for the federal funds rate below zero was a problem for the Fed. Glenn Rudebusch, an economist at the Federal Reserve Bank of San Francisco, calculated that given how high the unemployment rate was, the appropriate target for the federal funds rate was –5 percent. Because the federal funds rate cannot be negative, the Fed turned to other policies. In particular, the Fed decided to embark on a policy of *quantitative easing*, which involves buying securities beyond the short-term Treasury securities that are usually involved in open market operations. The Fed began purchasing 10-year Treasury notes to keep their interest rates from rising. Interest rates on home mortgage loans typically move closely with interest rates on 10-year Treasury notes. The Fed also purchased certain *mortgage-backed securities*. The Fed's objective was to keep interest rates on mortgages low and to keep funds flowing into the mortgage market in order to help stimulate demand for housing.

The Fed's first round of quantitative easing began in November 2008 and ended in June 2010. With the economy recovering only slowly, in November 2010, the Fed announced a second round of quantitative easing (dubbed QE2). With QE2, the Fed bought an additional $600 billion in long-term Treasury securities through June 2011. In September 2011, with the economic recovery remaining weak, the Fed announced a new program under which it would purchase $400 billion in long-term Treasury securities while selling an equal amount of shorter-term Treasury securities. This program, which some people in financial markets called "Operation Twist," had the same objective as quantitative easing: to reduce interest rates on long-term Treasury securities in order to increase aggregate demand.

Later in this chapter, we will consider other new programs the Fed put in place to deal with the recession of 2007–2009 and the slow recovery that followed, as its traditional focus on lowering the federal funds rate to stimulate the economy proved ineffective.

Based on Glenn Rudebusch, "The Fed's Monetary Policy Response to the Current Crisis," FRBSF Economic Letter, May 22, 2009.

The Fed pushed interest rates to very low levels during 2008 and 2009.

Can the Fed Eliminate Recessions?

Panel (a) of Figure 11.7 on page 267 shows an expansionary monetary policy that performs perfectly by shifting the *AD* curve to bring the economy back to potential GDP. In fact, however, this ideal is very difficult for the Fed to achieve, as the length and severity of the 2007–2009 recession indicates. In practice, the best the Fed can do is keep recessions shorter and milder than they would otherwise be.

If the Fed is to be successful in offsetting the effects of the business cycle, it needs to quickly recognize the need for a change in monetary policy. If the Fed is late in recognizing that a recession has begun or that the inflation rate is increasing, it may not be able to implement a new policy soon enough to do much good. In fact, implementing a policy too late may actually destabilize the economy. To see how this can happen, consider Figure 11.8. The straight line represents the long-run growth trend in real GDP in the United States. On average, real GDP grows about 3.3 percent per year. The actual path of real GDP differs from the underlying trend because of the business cycle, which is shown by the red curved line. The actual business cycle is more irregular than the styl ized cycle shown here.

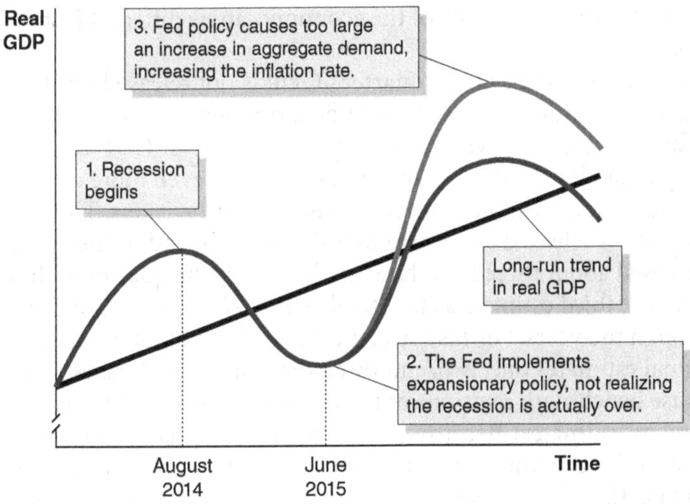

Figure 11.8

The Effect of a Poorly Timed Monetary Policy on the Economy

The upward-sloping straight line represents the long-run growth trend in real GDP. The curved red line represents the path real GDP takes because of the business cycle. If the Fed is too late in implementing a change in monetary policy, real GDP will follow the curved blue line. The Fed's expansionary monetary policy results in too great an increase in aggregate demand during the next expansion, which causes an increase in the inflation rate.

Suppose that a recession begins in August 2014. Because it takes months for economic statistics to be gathered by the Commerce Department, the Census Bureau, the Bureau of Labor Statistics, and the Fed itself, there is a *lag*, or delay, before the Fed recognizes that a recession has begun. Then it takes time for the Fed's economists to analyze the data. Finally, in June 2015, the FOMC concludes that the economy is in recession and begins an expansionary monetary policy. As it turns out, June 2015 is actually the trough of the recession, meaning that the recession has already ended, and an expansion has begun. In these circumstances, the Fed's expansionary policy is not needed to end the recession. The increase in aggregate demand caused by the Fed's lowering interest rates is likely to push the economy beyond potential real GDP and cause a significant acceleration in inflation. Real GDP ends up following the path indicated by the blue curved line. The Fed has inadvertently engaged in a *procyclical policy*, which increases the severity of the business cycle, as opposed to a *countercyclical policy*, which is meant to reduce the severity of the business cycle, and which is what the Fed intends to use. The typical recession since 1950 has lasted less than one year, which increases the likelihood that the Fed may accidentally engage in a procyclical policy. Making this mistake is, of course, less likely in a long and severe recession such as the recession of 2007–2009.

It is not unusual for employment or manufacturing production to decline for a month or two in the middle of an expansion. Distinguishing these minor ups and downs from the beginning of a recession is difficult. The National Bureau of Economic Research (NBER) announces dates for the beginning and end of recessions that most economists generally accept. An indication of how difficult it is to determine when recessions begin and end is that the NBER generally makes its announcements only after a considerable delay. The NBER did not announce that a recession had begun in March 2001 until November 2001, which is the same month it later determined that the recession had ended. The NBER did not announce that a recession had begun in December 2007 until December 2008. Failing to react until well after a recession has begun (or ended) can be a serious problem for the Fed. In the case of the 2007–2009 recession, however, the Fed did promptly cut the federal funds rate in September 2007, in response to the beginning of the financial crisis, even though the recession did not actually begin until two months later.

Making the Connection

Trying to Hit a Moving Target: Making Policy with "Real-Time Data"

The Fed relies on macroeconomic data to formulate monetary policy. One key piece of economic data is GDP, which is calculated quarterly by the Bureau of Economic Analysis (BEA). Unfortunately for Fed policymakers, the GDP data the BEA provides are frequently revised, and the revisions can be large enough that the actual state of the economy can be different from what it at first appeared to be.

The BEA's *advance estimate* of a quarter's GDP is not released until about a month after the quarter has ended. This delay can be a problem for policymakers because it means that, for instance, they will not receive an estimate of GDP for the period from January through March until the end of April. Presenting even more difficulty is the fact that the advance estimate will be subject to a number of revisions. The second estimate of a quarter's GDP is released about two months after the end of the quarter. The third estimate is released about three months after the end of the quarter. Although the BEA used to refer to the third estimate as the "final estimate," in fact, it continues to revise its estimates through the years. For instance, the BEA releases first annual, second annual, and third annual estimates one, two, and three years after the third estimate. Nor is that the end, because benchmark revisions of the estimates will occur in later years.

Why so many estimates? Because GDP is such a comprehensive measure of output in the economy, it is very time-consuming to collect the necessary data. To provide the advance estimate, the BEA relies on surveys conducted by the Commerce Department of retail sales and manufacturing shipments, as well as data from trade organizations, estimates of government spending, and so on. As time passes, these organizations gather additional data, and the BEA is able to refine its estimates.

Do these revisions to the GDP estimates matter? Sometimes they do, as the following example indicates. At the beginning of 2001, there were some indications that the U.S. economy might be headed for recession. The dot-com stock market bubble had burst the previous spring, wiping out trillions of dollars in stockholder wealth. Overbuilding of fiber-optic cable networks and other information technology also weighed on the economy. The advance estimate of the first quarter's GDP, though, showed a reasonably healthy increase in real GDP of 2.0% at an annual rate. It seemed as if there was nothing for government policymakers to be worried about. But, as the graph below shows, that estimate of 2.0% was revised a number of times over the years, mostly downward. Currently, BEA data indicate that real GDP actually declined by 1.3% at an annual rate during the first quarter of 2001. This swing of more than 3 percentage points is a large difference—a difference that changes the picture of what happened during the first quarter of 2001 from one of an economy experiencing moderate growth to one of an economy suffering a significant decline. The National Bureau of Economic Research dates the recession of 2001 as having begun in March, but some economists believe it actually began at the end of 2000. The current BEA estimates of GDP provide some support for this view.

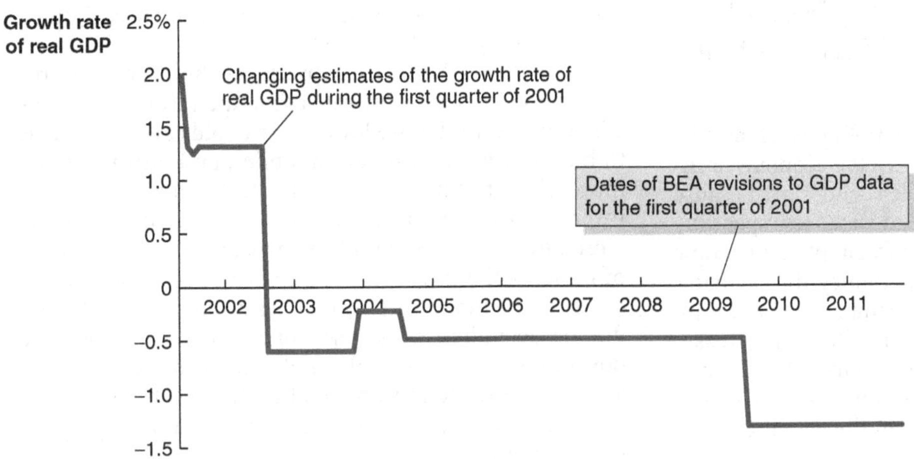

This example shows that in addition to the other problems the Federal Reserve encounters in successfully conducting monetary policy, it must make decisions using data that may be subject to substantial revisions.

Based on Federal Reserve Bank of Philadelphia, "Historical Data Files for the Real-Time Data Set," August 24, 2010; and Bruce T. Grimm and Teresa Weadock, "Gross Domestic Product: Revisions and Source Data," *Survey of Current Business*, Vol. 86, No. 2, February 2006, pp. 11–15.

A Summary of How Monetary Policy Works

Table 11.1 compares the steps involved in expansionary and contractionary monetary policies. We need to note an important qualification to this summary. At every point, we should add the phrase "relative to what would have happened without the policy." Table 11.1 isolates the impact of monetary policy, *holding constant all other factors affecting the variables involved*. In other words, we are invoking the *ceteris paribus* condition, discussed in Chapter 4. This point is important because, for example, a contractionary monetary policy does not cause the price level to fall; rather, a contractionary monetary policy causes the price level *to rise by less than it would have risen without the policy*. One final note on terminology: An expansionary monetary policy is sometimes referred to as a *loose* policy, or an *easy* policy. A contractionary monetary policy is sometimes referred to as a *tight* policy.

Table 11.1 Expansionary and Contractionary Monetary Policies

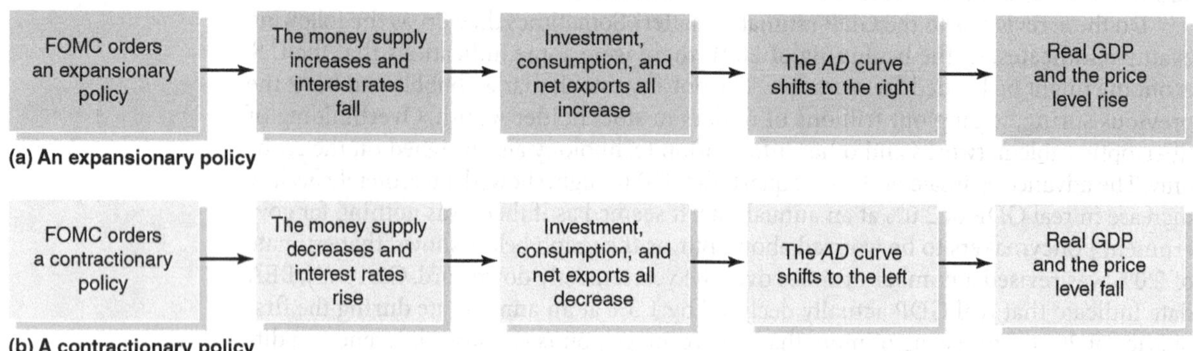

Don't Let This Happen to You

Remember That with Monetary Policy, It's the Interest Rates—Not the Money—That Counts

It is tempting to think of monetary policy working like this: If the Fed wants more spending in the economy, it increases the money supply, and people spend more because they now have more money. If the Fed wants less spending in the economy, it decreases the money supply, and people spend less because they now have less money. In fact, that is *not* how monetary policy works. Remember the important difference between money and income: The Fed increases the money supply by buying Treasury bills. The sellers of the Treasury bills have just exchanged one asset—Treasury bills—for another asset—a check from the Fed; the sellers have *not* increased their income. Even though the money supply is now larger, no one's income has increased, so no one's spending should be affected.

It is only when this increase in the money supply results in lower interest rates that spending is affected. When interest rates are lower, households are more likely to buy new homes and automobiles, and businesses are more likely to buy new factories and computers. Lower interest rates also lead to a lower value of the dollar, which lowers the prices of exports and raises the prices of imports, thereby increasing net exports. It isn't the increase in the money supply that has brought about this additional spending; *it's the lower interest rates.* To understand how monetary policy works, and to interpret news reports about the Fed's actions, remember that it is the change in interest rates, not the change in the money supply, that is most important.

11.4 LEARNING OBJECTIVE

Use the dynamic aggregate demand and aggregate supply model to analyze monetary policy.

Monetary Policy in the Dynamic Aggregate Demand and Aggregate Supply Model*

The overview of monetary policy we just finished contains a key idea: The Fed can use monetary policy to affect aggregate demand, thereby changing the price level and the level of real GDP. The discussion of monetary policy illustrated by Figure 11.7 on page 267 is simplified, however, because it ignores two important facts about the economy: (1) The economy experiences continuing inflation, with the price level rising every year, and (2) the economy experiences long-run growth, with the *LRAS* curve shifting to the right every year. In Chapter 8, we developed a *dynamic aggregate demand and aggregate supply model* that takes into account these two facts. In this section, we use the dynamic model to gain a more complete understanding of monetary policy. Let's briefly review the dynamic model. Recall from Chapter 8 that over time, the U.S. labor force and U.S. capital stock will increase. Technological change will also occur. The result will be an increase in potential real GDP, which we show by the long-run aggregate supply

*This section may be omitted without loss of continuity.

curve shifting to the right. These factors will also result in firms supplying more goods and services at any given price level in the short run, which we show by the short-run aggregate supply curve shifting to the right. During most years, the aggregate demand curve will also shift to the right, indicating that aggregate expenditure will be higher at every price level. There are several reasons aggregate expenditure usually increases: As population grows and incomes rise, consumption will increase over time. Also, as the economy grows, firms expand capacity, and new firms are established, increasing investment spending. Finally, an expanding population and an expanding economy require increased government services, such as more police officers and teachers, so government purchases will expand.

The Effects of Monetary Policy on Real GDP and the Price Level: A More Complete Account

During certain periods, *AD* does not increase enough during the year to keep the economy at potential GDP. This slow growth in aggregate demand may be due to households and firms becoming pessimistic about the future state of the economy, leading them to cut back their spending on consumer durables, houses, and factories. As we have seen, the collapse of the housing bubble and the resulting financial crisis had a negative effect on aggregate demand during the 2007–2009 recession. Other possibilities exist as well: The federal government might decide to balance the budget by cutting back its purchases, or recessions in other countries might cause a decline in U.S. exports. In the hypothetical situation shown in Figure 11.9, in the first year, the economy is in equilibrium, at potential real GDP of \$14.0 trillion and a price level of 100 (point *A*). In the second year, *LRAS* increases to \$14.4 trillion, but *AD* increases only to $AD_{2(\text{without policy})}$, which is not enough to keep the economy in macroeconomic equilibrium at potential GDP. If the Fed does not intervene, the short-run equilibrium will occur at \$14.3 trillion (point *B*). The \$100 billion gap between this level of real GDP and potential real GDP at $LRAS_2$ means that some firms are operating at less than their normal capacity. Incomes and profits will fall, firms will begin to lay off workers, and the unemployment rate will rise.

Economists at the Federal Reserve closely monitor the economy and continually update forecasts of future levels of real GDP and prices. When these economists anticipate that aggregate demand is not growing fast enough to allow the economy to remain at full employment, they present their findings to the FOMC, which decides

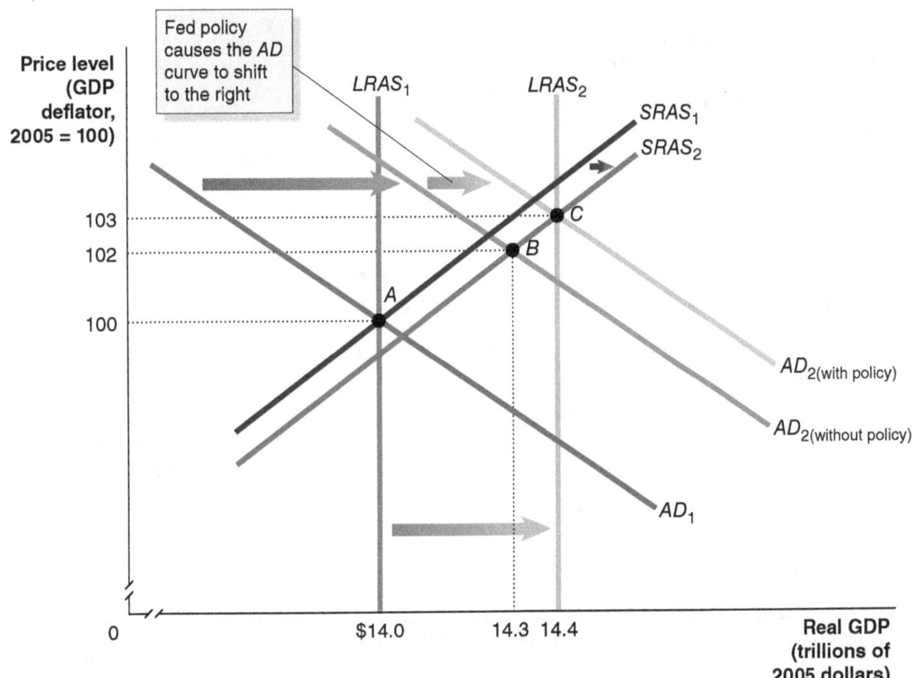

Figure 11.9

An Expansionary Monetary Policy

The economy begins in equilibrium at point *A*, with real GDP of \$14.0 trillion and a price level of 100. Without monetary policy, aggregate demand will shift from AD_1 to $AD_{2(\text{without policy})}$, which is not enough to keep the economy at full employment because long-run aggregate supply has shifted from $LRAS_1$ to $LRAS_2$. The economy will be in short-run equilibrium at point *B*, with real GDP of \$14.3 trillion and a price level of 102. By lowering interest rates, the Fed increases investment, consumption, and net exports sufficiently to shift aggregate demand to $AD_{2(\text{with policy})}$. The economy will be in equilibrium at point *C*, with real GDP of \$14.4 trillion, which is its full employment level, and a price level of 103. The price level is higher than it would have been if the Fed had not acted to increase spending in the economy.

whether circumstances require a change in monetary policy. For example, suppose that the FOMC meets and considers a forecast from the staff indicating that during the following year, a gap of $100 billion will open between equilibrium real GDP and potential real GDP. In other words, the macroeconomic equilibrium illustrated by point *B* in Figure 11.9 will occur. The FOMC may then decide to carry out an expansionary monetary policy to lower interest rates to stimulate aggregate demand. The figure shows the results of a successful attempt to do this: *AD* has shifted to the right, and equilibrium occurs at potential GDP (point *C*). The Fed will have successfully headed off the falling incomes and rising unemployment that otherwise would have occurred. Bear in mind that we are illustrating a perfectly executed monetary policy that keeps the economy at potential GDP, which is difficult to achieve in practice for reasons already discussed.

Notice in Figure 11.9 that the expansionary monetary policy caused the inflation rate to be higher than it would have been. Without the expansionary policy, the price level would have risen from 100 to 102, so the inflation rate for the year would have been 2 percent. By shifting the aggregate demand curve, the expansionary policy caused the price level to increase from 102 to 103, raising the inflation rate from 2 percent to 3 percent.

Using Monetary Policy to Fight Inflation

In addition to using an expansionary monetary policy to reduce the severity of recessions, the Fed can also use a contractionary monetary policy to keep aggregate demand from expanding so rapidly that the inflation rate begins to increase. Figure 11.10 shows the situation during 2005 and 2006, when the Fed faced this possibility. During 2005, the economy was at equilibrium at potential GDP, but Fed Chair Alan Greenspan and other members of the FOMC were concerned that the continuing boom in the housing market might lead aggregate demand to increase so rapidly that the inflation rate would begin to accelerate. The Fed had been gradually increasing the target for the federal funds rate since mid-2004.

When Ben Bernanke assumed office as Fed chair in early 2006, he advocated continued increases in the target for the federal funds rate to slow the growth in aggregate demand. By June 2006, the target for the federal funds rate had been raised to

Figure 11.10

A Contractionary Monetary Policy in 2006

The economy began 2005 in equilibrium at point *A*, with real GDP equal to potential GDP of $12.6 trillion and a price level of 100.0. From 2005 to 2006, potential GDP increased from $12.6 trillion to $12.9 trillion, as long-run aggregate supply increased from $LRAS_{2005}$ to $LRAS_{2006}$. The Fed raised interest rates because it believed the housing boom was causing aggregate demand to increase too rapidly. Without the increase in interest rates, aggregate demand would have shifted from AD_{2005} to $AD_{2006(\text{without policy})}$, and the new short-run equilibrium would have occurred at point *B*. Real GDP would have been $13.2 trillion—$300 billion greater than potential GDP—and the price level would have been 104.5. The increase in interest rates resulted in aggregate demand increasing only to $AD_{2006(\text{with policy})}$. Equilibrium occurred at point *C*, with real GDP of $13.0 trillion being only $100 billion greater than potential GDP and the price level rising only to 103.2.

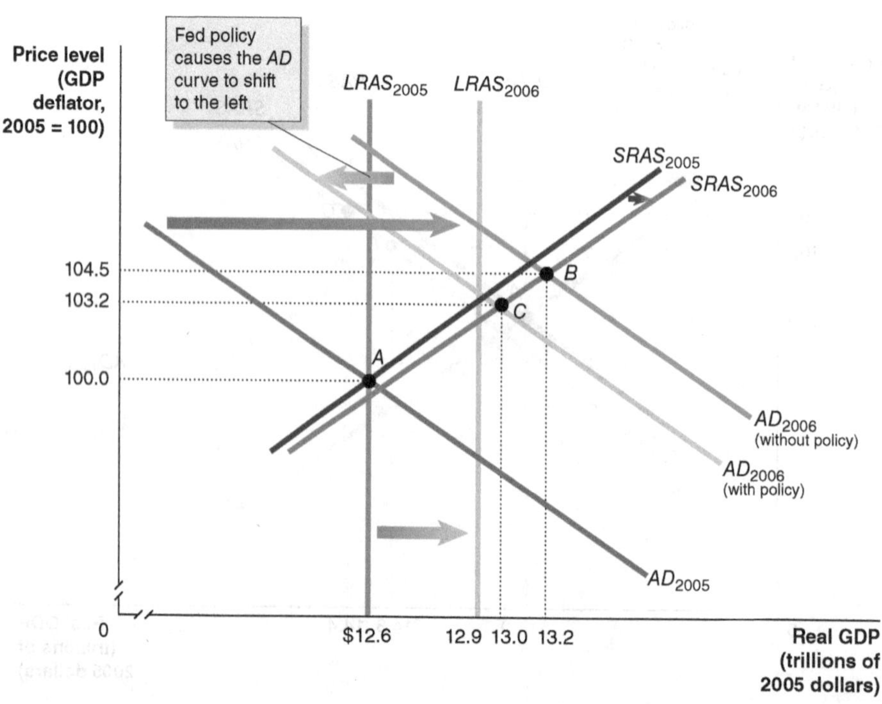

5.25 percent, from the low rate of 1 percent that had prevailed from June 2003 to May 2004. The FOMC issues a statement after each meeting that summarizes the committee's views on the current state of the economy and gives some indication of how monetary policy might change in the near future. After its meeting on June 29, 2006, the FOMC included the following remarks in its statement:

> The Federal Open Market Committee decided today to raise its target for the federal funds rate ... to 5-1/4 percent. Recent indicators suggest that economic growth is moderating from its quite strong pace earlier this year, partly reflecting a gradual cooling of the housing market and the lagged effects of increases in ... interest rates.... Although the moderation in the growth of aggregate demand should help to limit inflation pressures over time, the Committee judges that some inflation risks remain.

The committee kept the target for the federal funds rate constant at 5.25 percent until September 2007, when concern about difficulties in financial markets led it to cut the target to 4.75 percent. Although it is impossible to know exactly what would have happened during 2006 without the Fed's policy change, Figure 11.10 presents a plausible scenario. The figure shows that without the Fed's actions to increase interest rates, aggregate demand would have shifted farther to the right, and equilibrium would have occurred at a level of real GDP that was beyond the potential level. The price level would have risen from 100.0 in 2005 to 104.5 in 2006, meaning that the inflation rate would have been 4.5 percent. Because the Fed kept aggregate demand from increasing as much as it otherwise would have, equilibrium occurred at potential real GDP, and the price level in 2006 rose to only 103.2, keeping the inflation rate at 3.2 percent.

Solved Problem 11.4

The Effects of Monetary Policy

The hypothetical information in the following table shows what the values for real GDP and the price level will be in 2015 if the Fed does *not* use monetary policy:

Year	Potential GDP	Real GDP	Price Level
2014	$15.2 trillion	$15.2 trillion	114
2015	15.6 trillion	15.4 trillion	116

a. If the Fed wants to keep real GDP at its potential level in 2015, should it use an expansionary policy or a contractionary policy? Should the trading desk buy Treasury bills or sell them?

b. Suppose the Fed's policy is successful in keeping real GDP at its potential level in 2015. State whether each of the following will be higher or lower than if the Fed had taken no action:
   i Real GDP
   ii Potential real GDP
   iii The inflation rate
   iv The unemployment rate

c. Draw an aggregate demand and aggregate supply graph to illustrate your answer. Be sure that your graph contains *LRAS* curves for 2014 and 2015; *SRAS* curves for 2014 and 2015; *AD* curve for 2014 and 2015, with and without monetary policy action; and equilibrium real GDP and the price level in 2015, with and without policy.

Solving the Problem

Step 1: Review the chapter material. This problem is about the effects of monetary policy on real GDP and the price level, so you may want to review the section "The Effects of Monetary Policy on Real GDP and the Price Level: A More Complete Account," which begins on page 275.

Step 2: Answer the questions in part a. by explaining how the Fed can keep real GDP at its potential level. The information in the table tells us that without monetary policy, the economy will be below potential real GDP in 2015.

To keep real GDP at its potential level, the Fed must undertake an expansionary policy. To carry out an expansionary policy, the trading desk needs to buy Treasury bills. Buying Treasury bills will increase reserves in the banking system. Banks will increase their loans, which will increase the money supply and lower the interest rate.

Step 3: Answer part b. by explaining the effect of the Fed's policy. If the Fed's policy is successful, real GDP in 2015 will increase from $15.4 trillion, as given in the table, to its potential level of $15.6 trillion. Potential real GDP is not affected by monetary policy, so its value will not change. Because the level of real GDP will be higher, the unemployment rate will be lower than it would have been without policy. The expansionary monetary policy shifts the *AD* curve to the right, so short-run equilibrium will move up the short-run aggregate supply (*SRAS*) curve, and the price level will be higher.

Step 4: Answer part c. by drawing the graph. Your graph should look similar to Figure 11.9.

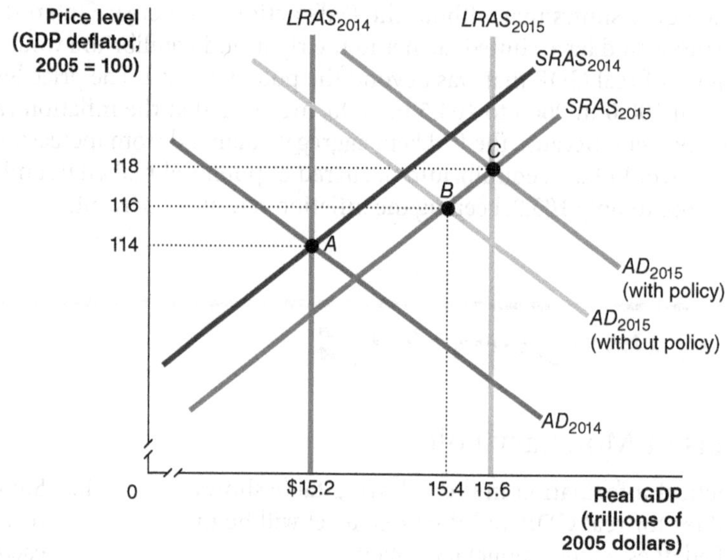

The economy starts in equilibrium in 2014 at point *A*, with the *AD* and *SRAS* curves intersecting along the *LRAS* curve. Real GDP is at its potential level of $15.2 trillion, and the price level is 114. Without monetary policy, the *AD* curve shifts to $AD_{2015\,(\text{without policy})}$, and the economy is in short-run equilibrium at point *B*. Because potential real GDP has increased from $15.2 trillion to $15.6 trillion, short-run equilibrium real GDP of $15.4 trillion is below the potential level. The price level has increased from 114 to 116. With policy, the *AD* curve shifts to $AD_{2015\,(\text{with policy})}$, and the economy is in equilibrium at point *C*. Real GDP is at its potential level of $15.6 trillion. We don't have enough information to be sure of the new equilibrium price level. We do know that it will be higher than 116. The graph shows the price level rising to 118. Therefore, without the Fed's expansionary policy, the inflation rate in 2015 would have been about 1.8 percent. With policy, it will be about 3.5 percent.

Extra Credit: Bear in mind that in reality, the Fed is unable to use monetary policy to keep real GDP exactly at its potential level, as this problem suggests.

A Closer Look at the Fed's Setting of Monetary Policy Targets

11.5 LEARNING OBJECTIVE

Discuss the Fed's setting of monetary policy targets.

We have seen that in carrying out monetary policy, the Fed changes its target for the federal funds rate, depending on the state of the economy. During times when the economy is not experiencing a financial crisis, is using the federal funds rate as a target the best way to conduct monetary policy? If the Fed targets the federal funds rate, how should it decide what the target level should be? In this section, we consider some important issues concerning the Fed's targeting policy.

Should the Fed Target the Money Supply?

Some economists have argued that rather than use an interest rate as its monetary policy target, the Fed should use the money supply. Many of the economists who make this argument belong to a school of thought known as *monetarism*. The leader of the monetarist school was Nobel Laureate Milton Friedman, who was skeptical that the Fed would be able to correctly time changes in monetary policy.

Friedman and his followers favored replacing *monetary policy* with a *monetary growth rule*. Ordinarily, we expect monetary policy to respond to changing economic conditions: When the economy is in recession, the Fed reduces interest rates, and when inflation is increasing, the Fed raises interest rates. A monetary growth rule, in contrast, is a plan for increasing the money supply at a constant rate that does not change in response to economic conditions. Friedman and his followers proposed a monetary growth rule of increasing the money supply every year at a rate equal to the long-run growth rate of real GDP, which is about 3.3 percent. If the Fed adopted this monetary growth rule, it would stick to it through changing economic conditions.

But what happens under a monetary growth rule if the economy moves into recession? Shouldn't the Fed abandon the rule to drive down interest rates? Friedman argued that the Fed should stick to the rule even during recessions because, he believed, active monetary policy destabilizes the economy, increasing the number of recessions and their severity. By keeping the money supply growing at a constant rate, Friedman argued, the Fed would greatly increase economic stability.

Although during the 1970s some economists and politicians pressured the Federal Reserve to adopt a monetary growth rule, most of that pressure has disappeared in recent years. A key reason is that the fairly close relationship between movements in the money supply and movements in real GDP and the price level that existed before 1980 has become much weaker. Since 1980, the growth rate of M1 has been unstable. In some years, M1 has grown more than 10 percent, while in other years, it has actually fallen. Yet despite these wide fluctuations in the growth of M1, growth in real GDP has been fairly stable, and inflation has remained low during most years.

Why Doesn't the Fed Target Both the Money Supply and the Interest Rate?

Most economists believe that an interest rate is the best monetary policy target, but, as we have just seen, other economists believe the Fed should target the money supply. Why doesn't the Fed satisfy both groups by targeting both the money supply and an interest rate? The simple answer to this question is that the Fed can't target both at the same time. To see why, look at Figure 11.11, which shows the money market.

Remember that the Fed controls the money supply, but it does not control money demand. Money demand is determined by decisions of households and firms as they weigh the trade-off between the convenience of money and its low interest rate

Figure 11.11

The Fed Can't Target Both the Money Supply and the Interest Rate

The Fed is forced to choose between using either an interest rate or the money supply as its monetary policy target. In this figure, the Fed can set a target of $900 billion for the money supply or a target of 5 percent for the interest rate, but the Fed can't hit both targets because it can achieve only combinations of the interest rate and the money supply that represent equilibrium in the money market.

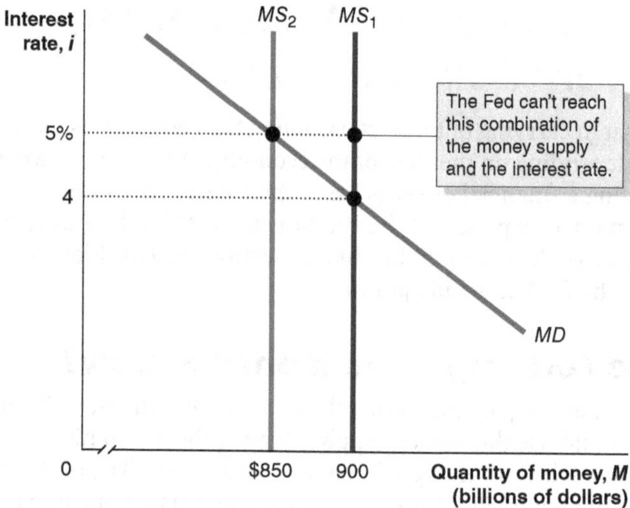

compared with other financial assets. Suppose the Fed is targeting the interest rate and decides, given conditions in the economy, that the interest rate should be 5 percent. Or, suppose the Fed is targeting the money supply and decides that the money supply should be $900 billion. Figure 11.11 shows that the Fed can bring about an interest rate of 5 percent or a money supply of $900 billion, but it can't bring about both. The point representing an interest rate of 5 percent and a money supply of $900 billion is not on the money demand curve, so it can't represent an equilibrium in the money market. Only combinations of the interest rate and the money supply that represent equilibrium in the money market are possible.

The Fed has to choose between targeting an interest rate and targeting the money supply. For most of the period since World War II, the Fed has chosen an interest rate target.

The Taylor Rule

Taylor rule A rule developed by John Taylor that links the Fed's target for the federal funds rate to economic variables.

How does the Fed choose a target for the federal funds rate? The discussions at the meetings of the FOMC can be complex, and they take into account many economic variables. John Taylor of Stanford University has analyzed the factors involved in Fed decision making and developed the **Taylor rule** to explain federal funds rate targeting. The Taylor rule begins with an estimate of the value of the equilibrium real federal funds rate, which is the federal funds rate—adjusted for inflation—that would be consistent with real GDP being equal to potential real GDP in the long run. According to the Taylor rule, the Fed should set the target for the federal funds rate so that it is equal to the sum of the inflation rate, the equilibrium real federal funds rate, and two additional terms. The first of these additional terms is the *inflation gap*—the difference between current inflation and a target rate; the second is the *output gap*—the percentage difference between real GDP and potential real GDP. The inflation gap and output gap are each given "weights" that reflect their influence on the federal funds target rate. With weights of 1/2 for both gaps, we have the following Taylor rule:

Federal funds target rate = Current inflation rate + Real equilibrium federal funds rate + ((1/2) × Inflation gap) + ((1/2) × Output gap).

The Taylor rule includes expressions for the inflation gap and the output gap because the Fed is concerned about both inflation and fluctuations in real GDP. Taylor demonstrated that if the equilibrium real federal funds rate is 2 percent and the target rate of inflation is 2 percent, the preceding expression does a good job of explaining changes in the Fed's target for the federal funds rate during most years. Consider an example in which the current inflation rate is 1 percent, and real GDP is 1 percent below potential real GDP. In that case, the inflation gap is 1 percent -2 percent $= -1$ percent and the output gap is also -1 percent. Inserting these values in the Taylor rule, we can calculate the predicted value for the federal funds target rate:

$$\text{Federal funds target rate} = 1\% + 2\% + ((1/2) \times -1\%) + ((1/2) \times -1\%) = 2\%.$$

The Taylor rule accurately predicted changes in the federal funds target during the period of Alan Greenspan's leadership of the Federal Reserve. For the period of the late 1970s and early 1980s, when Paul Volcker was chairman of the Federal Reserve, the Taylor rule predicts a federal funds rate target *lower* than the actual target the Fed used. This indicates that Chairman Volcker kept the federal funds rate at an unusually high level to bring down the very high inflation rates plaguing the economy in the late 1970s and early 1980s. In contrast, using data from the chairmanship of Arthur Burns from 1970 to 1978, the Taylor rule predicts a federal funds rate target *higher* than the actual target. This indicates that Chairman Burns kept the federal funds rate at an unusually low level during these years, which helps to explain why the inflation rate grew worse. During the mid-2000s the actual federal funds rate was also lower than the predicted federal funds rate. Some economists, including Taylor, argue that these low targets for the federal funds rate contributed to the excessive increase in spending on housing that we will discuss in the next section.

Although the Taylor rule does not account for changes in the target inflation rate or the equilibrium interest rate, many economists view the rule as a convenient tool for analyzing the federal funds target.

Should the Fed Target Inflation?

Over the past decade, many economists and central bankers, including the current Fed chair, Ben Bernanke, have proposed using *inflation targeting* as a framework for conducting monetary policy. With **inflation targeting**, the central bank commits to achieving a publicly announced inflation target of, for example, 2 percent. Inflation targeting does not impose an inflexible rule on the central bank. The central bank would still be free, for example, to take action in case of a severe recession. Nevertheless, monetary policy goals and operations would focus on inflation and inflation forecasts. Inflation targeting has been adopted by the central banks of New Zealand (1989), Canada (1991), the United Kingdom (1992), Finland (1993), Sweden (1993), and Spain (1994), and by the European Central Bank. Inflation targeting has also been used in some newly industrializing countries, such as Chile, South Korea, Mexico, and South Africa, as well as in some transition economies in Eastern Europe, such as the Czech Republic, Hungary, and Poland. Experience with inflation targeting has varied, but typically the move to inflation targeting has been accompanied by lower inflation (sometimes at the cost of temporarily higher unemployment).

Inflation targeting Conducting monetary policy so as to commit the central bank to achieving a publicly announced level of inflation.

Should the Fed adopt an inflation target? Arguments in favor of inflation targeting focus on four points. First, as we have already discussed, in the long run, real GDP returns to its potential level, and potential real GDP is not affected by monetary policy. Therefore, in the long run, the Fed can affect inflation but not real GDP. Having an explicit inflation target would draw the public's attention to this fact. Second, by announcing an inflation target, the Fed would make it easier for households and firms to form accurate expectations of future inflation, improving their planning and the efficiency of the economy. Third, an announced inflation target would help institutionalize good U.S. monetary policy. An inflation target would reduce the chances of abrupt changes in policy occurring as members join and leave the FOMC. Finally, an inflation target would promote accountability for the Fed by providing a yardstick against which Congress and the public could measure the Fed's performance.

Inflation targeting also has opponents, who typically raise three points. First, having a numeric target for inflation reduces the flexibility of monetary policy to address other policy goals. Second, inflation targeting assumes that the Fed can accurately forecast future inflation rates, which is not always the case. Finally, holding the Fed accountable only for an inflation goal may make it less likely that the Fed will achieve other important policy goals.

Although Ben Bernanke becoming chair of the Fed in January 2006 appeared to increase the chances that the Fed would adopt a policy of inflation targeting, the necessity of dealing with the recession of 2007–2009 at least temporarily pushed the issue off the Fed's agenda.

The Fed excludes food and energy prices from its main measure of inflation.

Making the Connection

How Does the Fed Measure Inflation?

To attain its goal of price stability, the Fed has to consider carefully the best way to measure the inflation rate. The consumer price index (CPI) is the most widely used measure of inflation. But we also saw that the CPI suffers from biases that cause it to overstate the true underlying rate of inflation. An alternative measure of changes in consumer prices can be constructed from the data gathered to calculate GDP. The GDP deflator is a broad measure of the price level that includes the price of every good or service that is in GDP. Changes in the GDP deflator are not a good measure of inflation experienced by the typical consumer, worker, or firm, however, because the deflator includes prices of goods, such as industrial equipment, that are not widely purchased. The *personal consumption expenditures price index (PCE)* is a measure of the price level that is similar to the GDP deflator, except it includes only the prices of goods from the consumption category of GDP.

In 2000, the Fed announced that it would rely more on the PCE than on the CPI in tracking inflation. The Fed noted three advantages that the PCE has over the CPI:

1. The PCE is a so-called chain-type price index, as opposed to the market-basket approach used in constructing the CPI. Because consumers shift the mix of products they buy each year, the market-basket approach causes the CPI to overstate actual inflation. A chain-type price index allows the mix of products to change each year.
2. The PCE includes the prices of more goods and services than the CPI, so it is a broader measure of inflation.
3. Past values of the PCE can be recalculated as better ways of computing price indexes are developed and as new data become available. This allows the Fed to better track historical trends in the inflation rate.

In 2004, the Fed announced that it would begin to rely on a subcategory of the PCE: the so-called core PCE, which excludes food and energy prices. Prices of food and energy tend to fluctuate up and down for reasons that may not be related to the causes of general inflation and that cannot easily be controlled by monetary policy. Oil prices, in particular, have moved dramatically up and down in recent years. Therefore, a price index that includes food and energy prices may not give a clear view of underlying trends in inflation. The following graph shows movements in the CPI, the PCE, and the core PCE from January 1999 through September 2011. Although the three measures of inflation move roughly together, the core PCE has been more stable than the others. Note in particular that in early 2009, when the CPI and the PCE were indicating that the economy was experiencing deflation, the core PCE was still showing moderate inflation rates of about 1.5 percent.

If you want to know what the Fed thinks the current inflation rate is, the best idea is to look at data on the core PCE. These data are published monthly by the Bureau of Economic Analysis.

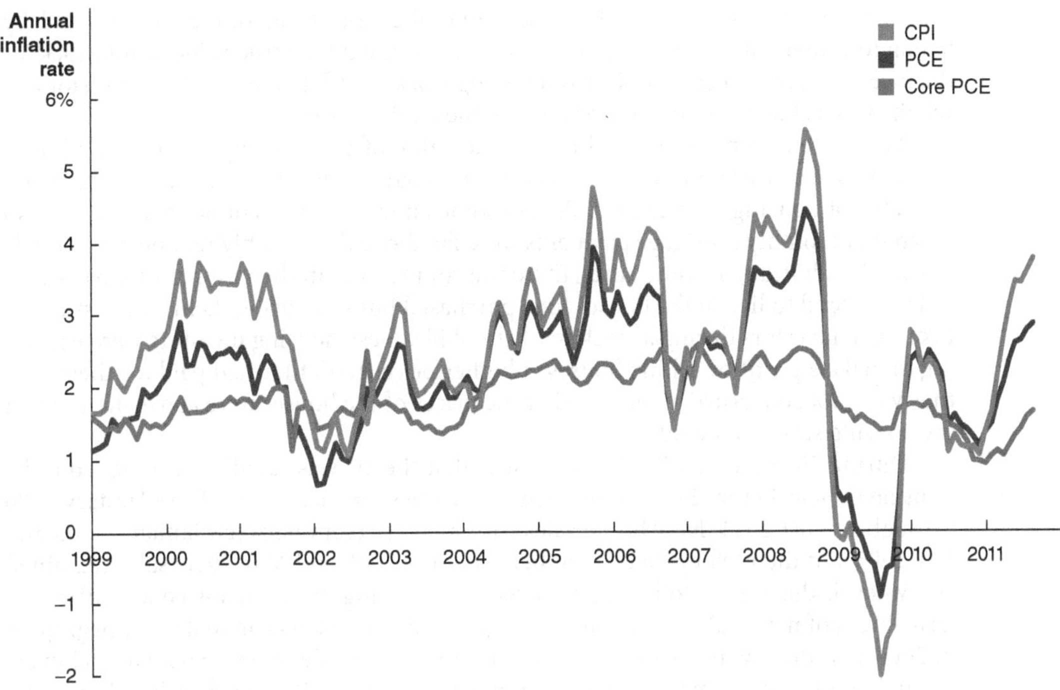

Data from U.S. Bureau of Economic Analysis; and U.S. Bureau of Labor Statistics.

Fed Policies during the 2007–2009 Recession

11.6 LEARNING OBJECTIVE

Discuss the policies the Federal Reserve used during the 2007–2009 recession.

As we have seen, the Fed's traditional response to a recession is to lower the target for the federal funds rate. The severity of the recession of 2007–2009, particularly the problems in financial markets during those years, complicated the Fed's job. By December 2008, the Fed had effectively lowered the target for the federal funds rate to zero, but the zero interest rate alone did not achieve the Fed's desired expansionary effect on the economy. In this section, we will discuss some of the additional policy measures the Fed took during the 2007–2009 recession. Some of these measures were used for the first time in the Fed's history.

The Inflation and Deflation of the Housing Market Bubble

To understand the 2007–2009 recession and the difficulties in financial markets that occurred during it, we need to start by considering the housing market. As we mentioned in the chapter opener, the Fed lowered the target for the federal funds rate during the 2001 recession to stimulate demand for housing. The policy was successful, and most builders, such as Toll Brothers, experienced several years of high demand. By 2005, however, many economists argued that a "bubble" had formed in the housing market. The price of any asset reflects the returns the owner of the asset expects to receive. For example, the price of a share of stock reflects the profitability of the firm issuing the stock because the owner of a share of stock has a claim on the firm's profits and assets. Many economists believe, however, that sometimes a *stock market bubble* can form when the prices of stocks rise above levels that can be justified by the profitability of the firms issuing the stock. Stock market bubbles end when enough investors decide stocks are overvalued and begin to sell. Why would an investor be willing to pay more for a share of stock than would be justified by its underlying value? There are two main explanations: The investor may be caught up in the enthusiasm of the moment and, by failing to gather sufficient information, may overestimate the true value of the stock; or the investor may expect to profit from buying stock at inflated prices if the investor can sell the stock at an even higher price before the bubble bursts.

The price of a house should reflect the value of the housing services the house provides. We can use the rents charged for comparable houses in an area to measure the value of housing services. By 2005, in some cities, the prices of houses had risen so much that monthly mortgage payments were far above the monthly rent on comparable houses. In addition, in some cities, there was an increase in the number of buyers who did not intend to live in the houses they purchased but were using them as investments. Like stock investors during a stock market bubble, these housing investors were expecting to make a profit by selling houses at higher prices than they had paid for them, and they were not concerned about whether the prices of the houses were above the value of the housing services provided.

During 2006 and 2007, it became clear that the air was rapidly escaping from the housing bubble. Figure 11.12 shows new home sales for each month from January 2000 through August 2011. New home sales rose by 60 percent between January 2000 and July 2005 and then fell by 80 percent between July 2005 and May 2010; sales remained at low levels during the following year. Sales of existing homes followed a similar pattern. Prices of new and existing homes in most markets also began to decline beginning in 2006, and the inventory of unsold homes offered for sale soared. Some homebuyers began having trouble making their loan payments. When lenders foreclosed on some of these loans, the lenders sold the homes, causing housing prices to decline further. *Subprime loans* are loans granted to borrowers with flawed credit histories. Some mortgage lenders that had concentrated on making subprime loans suffered heavy losses and went out of business, and most banks and other lenders tightened the requirements for borrowers. This *credit crunch* made it more difficult for potential homebuyers to obtain mortgages, further depressing the market.

Figure 11.12 The Housing Bubble

Sales of new homes in the United States went on a roller-coaster ride, rising by 60 percent between January 2000 and July 2005, before falling by 80 percent between July 2005 and May 2010.

Note: The data are seasonally adjusted at an annual rate.
Data from U.S. Bureau of the Census.

The decline in the housing market affected other markets as well. For example, with home prices falling, consumption spending on furniture, appliances, and home improvements declined as many households found it more difficult to borrow against the value of their homes.

Was the housing bubble the result of overly optimistic expectations by homebuyers and builders who believed that new residential construction and housing prices would continue to rise at rapid rates indefinitely? While overly optimistic expectations may have played some role in the housing bubble, many economists believe that changes in the market for mortgages may have played a bigger role.

The Changing Mortgage Market

Until the 1970s, the commercial banks and savings and loans that granted mortgages kept the loans until the borrowers paid them off. As we saw in Chapter 10, a financial asset such as a mortgage is a security only if it can be resold in a secondary market. Many members of Congress believed that home ownership could be increased by creating a secondary market in mortgages. If banks and savings and loans could resell mortgages, then, in effect, individual investors would be able to provide funds for mortgages. The process would work like this: If a bank or savings and loan granted a mortgage and then resold the mortgage to an investor, the bank could use the funds received from the investor to grant another mortgage. In this way, banks and savings and loans could grant more mortgage loans because they would no longer depend only on deposits for the funds needed to make the loans. One barrier to creating a secondary market in mortgages was that most investors were unwilling to buy mortgages because they were afraid of losing money if the borrower stopped making payments, or *defaulted*, on the loan.

To reassure investors, Congress used two *government-sponsored enterprises (GSEs)*: the Federal National Mortgage Association ("Fannie Mae") and the Federal Home Loan Mortgage Corporation ("Freddie Mac"). These two institutions stand between investors and banks that grant mortgages. Fannie Mae and Freddie Mac sell bonds to investors and use the funds to purchase mortgages from banks. By the 1990s, a large secondary market existed in mortgages, with funds flowing from investors through Fannie Mae and Freddie Mac to banks and, ultimately, to individuals and families borrowing money to buy houses.

The Role of Investment Banks

By the 2000s, further changes had taken place in the mortgage market. First, investment banks became significant participants in the secondary market for mortgages. As we have seen, investment banks, such as Goldman Sachs and Morgan Stanley, differ from commercial banks in that they do not take in deposits and rarely lend directly to households. Instead, investment banks concentrate on providing advice to firms issuing stocks and bonds or considering mergers with other firms. Investment banks began buying mortgages, bundling large numbers of them together as bonds known as *mortgage-backed securities*, and reselling them to investors. Mortgage-backed securities proved very popular with investors because they often paid higher interest rates than other securities with comparable default risk.

Second, by the height of the housing bubble in 2005 and early 2006, lenders had greatly loosened the standards for obtaining a mortgage loan. Traditionally, only borrowers with good credit histories and who were willing to make a down payment equal to at least 20 percent of the value of the house they were buying would be able to receive a mortgage. By 2005, however, lenders were issuing many mortgages to subprime borrowers with flawed credit histories. In addition, "Alt-A" borrowers who stated—but did not document—their incomes and borrowers who made very small down payments found it easier to take out loans. Lenders also created new types of *adjustable-rate mortgages* that allowed borrowers to pay a very low interest rate for the first few years of the mortgage and then pay a higher rate in later years. The chance that the borrowers using these nontraditional mortgages would default was higher than for borrowers using traditional mortgages. Why would borrowers take out mortgages if they doubted that they could make the payments, and why would lenders grant these mortgages? The answer seems to be that both borrowers and lenders were anticipating that housing prices would continue to rise, which would reduce the chance that borrowers would default on the mortgages and would also make it easier for borrowers to convert to more traditional mortgages in the future.

Unfortunately, the decline in housing prices led to rising defaults among subprime and Alt-A borrowers, borrowers with adjustable-rate mortgages, and borrowers who had made only small down payments. When borrowers began defaulting on mortgages, the value of many mortgage-backed securities declined sharply. Investors feared that if they purchased these securities, they would not receive the promised payments because the payments on the securities depended on borrowers making their mortgage payments, which an increasing number were failing to do. Many commercial and investment banks owned these mortgage-backed securities, so the decline in the value of the securities caused these banks to suffer heavy losses. By mid-2007, the decline in the value of mortgage-backed securities and the large losses suffered by commercial and investment banks began to cause turmoil in the financial system. Many investors refused to buy mortgage-backed securities, and some investors would buy only bonds issued by the U.S. Treasury.

Making the Connection

The Wonderful World of Leverage

Traditionally, most people taking out a mortgage make a down payment equal to 20 percent of the price of the house and borrow the remaining 80 percent. During the housing boom, however, many people purchased houses with down payments of 5 percent or less. In this sense, borrowers were highly *leveraged*, which means that their investment in their house was made mostly with borrowed money.

Making a very small down payment on a home mortgage leaves a buyer vulnerable to falling house prices.

To see how leverage works in the housing market, consider the following example: Suppose you buy a $200,000 house on January 1, 2014. On January 1, 2015, the price of the house—if you decide to sell it—has risen to $220,000. What return have you earned on your investment in the house? The answer depends on how much you invested when you bought the house. For example, if you paid $200,000 in cash for the house, your return on that $200,000 investment is the $20,000 increase in the price of the house divided by your $200,000 investment, or 10 percent. Suppose that rather than paying cash, you made a down payment of 20 percent, or $40,000, and borrowed the rest by taking out a mortgage loan of $160,000. Now the return on your investment in the house is the $20,000 increase in the price of the house divided by your $40,000 investment, or 50 percent. If the down payment is less than 20 percent, your return on investment will be higher. The second column in the table below shows how the return on your investment increases as your down payment decreases:

	Return on your investment from . . .	
Down Payment	A 10 Percent Increase in the Price of Your House	A 10 Percent Decrease in the Price of Your House
100%	10%	-10%
20	50	-50
10	100	-100
5	200	-200

An investment financed at least partly by borrowing is called a *leveraged investment*. As this example shows, the larger the fraction of an investment financed by borrowing, the greater the degree of leverage in the investment, and the greater the potential return. But as the third column in the table shows, the reverse is also true: The greater the leverage, the greater the potential loss. To see why, consider once again that you buy a house for $200,000, except that in this case, after one year the price of the house falls to $180,000. If you paid $200,000 in cash for the house—so your leverage was zero—the $20,000 decline in the price of the house represents a loss of 10 percent of your investment. But if you made a down payment of only $10,000 and borrowed the remaining $190,000, then the $20,000 decline in the price of the house represents a loss of 200 percent of your investment. In fact, the house is now worth $10,000 less than the amount of your mortgage loan. The *equity* in your house is the difference between the market price of the house and the amount you owe on a loan. If the amount you owe is greater than the price of the house, you have *negative equity*. A home owner who has negative equity is also said to be "upside down" on his or her mortgage.

When the housing bubble burst and housing prices started to fall, many people found that they had negative equity. In that situation, some people defaulted on their loans, sometimes by simply moving out and abandoning their homes. Leverage had contributed to the housing boom and bust and the severity of the 2007–2009 recession.

The Fed and the Treasury Department Respond

Because the problems in financial markets resulting from the bursting of the housing bubble were so profound, the Fed entered into an unusual partnership with the U.S. Treasury Department to develop suitable policies. Fed Chairman Ben Bernanke and U.S. Treasury Secretaries Henry Paulson (in the Bush administration) and Timothy Geithner (in the Obama administration) responded to the crisis by intervening in financial markets in unprecedented ways.

Initial Fed and Treasury Actions The financial crisis significantly worsened following the bankruptcy of the investment bank Lehman Brothers on September 15, 2008. So it is useful to look at the actions taken by the Fed and Treasury before and after that date. First, although the Fed traditionally made loans only to commercial banks, in March 2008, it announced it would temporarily make discount loans to *primary dealers*—firms that participate in regular open market transactions with the Fed. This change was intended to provide short-term funds to these dealers, some of which are investment banks. Second, also in March, the Fed announced that it would loan up to $200 billion of Treasury securities in exchange for mortgage-backed securities. This temporary program made it possible for primary dealers that owned mortgage-backed securities that were difficult or impossible to sell, to have access to Treasury securities that they could use as collateral for short-term loans. Third, once again in March, the Fed and the Treasury helped JPMorgan Chase acquire the investment bank Bear Stearns, which was on the edge of failing. The Fed agreed that if JPMorgan Chase would acquire Bear Stearns, the Fed would guarantee any losses JPMorgan Chase suffered on Bear Stearns's holdings of mortgage-backed securities, up to a limit of $29 billion. The Fed and Treasury were convinced that the failure of Bear Stearns had the potential of causing a financial panic, as many investors and financial firms would have stopped making short-term loans to other investment banks. Finally, in early September, the Treasury moved to have the federal government take control of Fannie Mae and Freddie Mac. Although Fannie Mae and Freddie Mac had been sponsored by the federal government, they were actually private businesses whose stock was bought and sold on the New York

Stock Exchange. Under the Treasury's plan, Fannie Mae and Freddie Mac were each provided with up to $100 billion in exchange for 80 percent ownership of the firms. The firms were placed under the supervision of the Federal Housing Finance Agency. The Treasury believed that the bankruptcy of Fannie Mae and Freddie Mac would have caused a collapse in confidence in mortgage-backed securities, further devastating this already weak housing market.

Responses to the Failure of Lehman Brothers Some economists and policymakers criticized the decision by the Fed and the Treasury to help arrange the sale of Bear Stearns to JPMorgan Chase. Their main concern was with what is known as the *moral hazard problem*, which is the possibility that managers of financial firms such as Bear Stearns might make riskier investments if they believe that the federal government will save them from bankruptcy. The Treasury and Fed acted to save Bear Stearns because they believed that the failure of a large financial firm could have wider economic repercussions. As we discussed in Chapter 10, when a financial firm sells off its holdings of bonds and other assets, it causes their prices to fall, which in turn can undermine the financial position of other firms that also own these assets. In September 2008, when the investment bank Lehman Brothers was near bankruptcy, the Fed and the Treasury had to weigh the moral hazard problem against the possibility that the failure of Lehman Brothers would lead to further declines in asset prices and endanger the financial positions of other firms.

The Fed and the Treasury decided to allow Lehman Brothers to go bankrupt, which it did on September 11. The adverse reaction in financial markets was stronger than the Fed and Treasury had expected, which led them to reverse course two days later, when the Fed agreed to provide an $85 billion loan to the American International Group (AIG)—the largest insurance company in the United States—in exchange for an 80 percent ownership stake, effectively giving the federal government control of the company. One important result of the failure of Lehman Brothers was the heavy losses suffered by Reserve Primary Fund, a money market mutual fund that had invested in loans to Lehman Brothers. The problems at Reserve led many investors to withdraw their funds from it and other money market funds. These withdrawals reduced the ability of the money market funds to purchase commercial paper from corporations. Because in recent years corporations had become dependent on selling commercial paper to finance their operations, the Treasury and the Fed moved to stabilize this market and ensure that the flow of funds from investors to corporations continued. The Treasury announced a plan to provide insurance for deposits in money market mutual funds, similar to the existing insurance on bank deposits. The Fed announced that for a limited time it would lend directly to corporations by purchasing three-month commercial paper issued by non-financial corporations.

Finally, in October 2008, Congress passed the *Troubled Asset Relief Program (TARP)*, under which the Treasury attempted to stabilize the commercial banking system by providing funds to banks in exchange for stock. Taking partial ownership positions in private commercial banks was an unprecedented action for the federal government.

Clearly, the recession of 2007–2009 and the accompanying financial crisis had led the Fed and the Treasury to implement new approaches to policy. Many of these new approaches were controversial because they involved partial government ownership of financial firms, implicit guarantees to large financial firms that they would not be allowed to go bankrupt, and unprecedented intervention in financial markets. Although the approaches were new, they were intended to achieve the traditional macroeconomic policy goals of high employment, price stability, and stability of financial markets. What remains to be seen is whether these new approaches represent a permanent increase in federal government involvement in U.S. financial markets or whether the end of the recession will see policy return to more traditional approaches.

Continued from page 257

Economics in Your Life

Should You Buy a House during a Recession?

At the beginning of this chapter, we asked whether buying a house during a recession is a good idea. Clearly, there are many considerations to keep in mind when buying a house, which is the largest purchase you are likely to make in your lifetime. Included among these considerations are the price of the house relative to other comparable houses in the neighborhood, whether house prices in the neighborhood have been rising or falling, and the location of the house relative to stores, work, and good schools. Also important is the interest rate you will have to pay on the mortgage loan you would need in order to buy the house. As we have seen in this chapter, during a recession the Fed often takes actions to lower interest rates. So, mortgage rates are typically lower during a recession than at other times. You may want to take advantage of low interest rates to buy a house during a recession. But, recessions are also times of rising unemployment, and you would not want to make a commitment to borrow a lot of money for 15 or more years if you were in significant danger of losing your job. We can conclude, then, that if your job seems secure, buying a house during a recession may be a good idea.

Conclusion

Monetary policy is one way governments pursue goals for inflation, employment, and financial stability. Many journalists and politicians refer to the chairman of the Federal Reserve as second only to the president of the United States in his ability to affect the U.S. economy. Congress and the president, however, also use their power over spending and taxes to try to stabilize the economy. In Chapter 9 We discuss how *fiscal policy*—changes in government spending and taxes—affect the economy.

CHAPTER 12

The World of International Finance

Chapter Outline and Learning Objectives

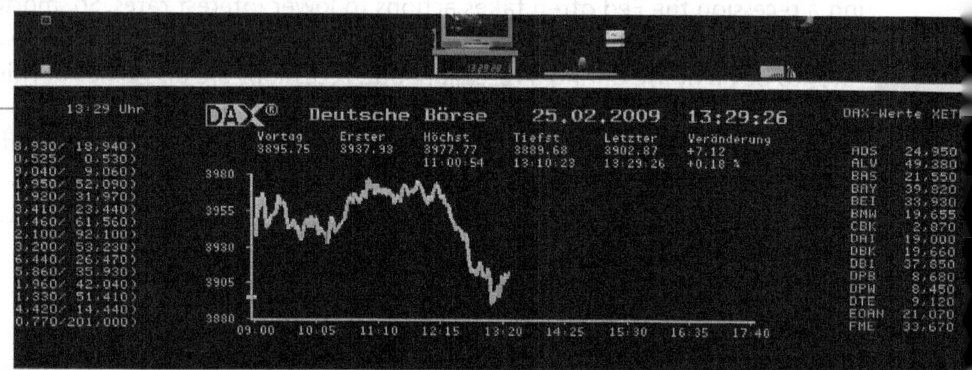

Applying the Concepts

Today, the world currency markets are always open. When foreign-exchange traders in New York City are sound asleep at 3:00 A.M., their counterparts in London are already on their phones and computers at 8:00 A.M. In Tokyo, it's 6:00 P.M., and the day is just ending. By the time Tokyo traders return home after their long commutes, the New York traders are back at work. The currency markets keep working even when the labor market rests.

On any given day, trillions of dollars of value are exchanged in currency markets. The fortunes of industries, and sometimes countries, are determined by the ups and downs of currencies. Controversies have always swirled around exchange markets. Are they dominated by large speculators, or are they driven by the necessities of doing business around the world? Most importantly, do these markets work efficiently and effectively?

All currencies are traded 24 hours a day. The value of every currency depends on news and late-breaking developments throughout the world. Rising gas prices, a new terrorist attack, or a change in the leadership of a foreign government can easily affect the price at which currencies trade with one another. If the U.S. secretary of the Treasury utters a casual remark about the dollar or the value of the Chinese currency, it reverberates instantly throughout the world. Modern communications—e-mail, instant messaging, smart phones, videoconferencing, and satellite transmissions—accelerate the process.

How do changes in the value of currencies affect the U.S. economy? We explored the role of monetary policy in an open economy and its effects on exchange rates. In this chapter, we take a more comprehensive and in-depth look at exchange rates as well as other aspects of the international financial system. Understanding our inter-national financial system will help you to interpret the often complex financial news from abroad. For example, if the value of the dollar starts to fall against the Japanese yen, what does it mean? Is this good news or bad news?

How Exchange Rates are Determined

12.1 **LEARNING** OBJECTIVE

In this section, we examine how the value of a currency is determined in world markets. We then look at the factors that can change the value of a currency.

What Are Exchange Rates?

To conduct international transactions between countries with different currencies, it is necessary to exchange one currency for another. The **exchange rate** is defined as the price at which we can exchange one currency for another.

Exchange rate The price at which currencies trade for one another in the market.

Suppose a U.S. songwriter sells the rights of a hit song to a Japanese producer. The U.S. songwriter agrees to accept $50,000. If the exchange rate between the U.S. dollar and Japanese yen is 100 yen per dollar, it will cost the Japanese producer 5,000,000 yen to purchase the rights to the song. Because international trade occurs between nations with different currencies, the exchange rate—the price at which one currency trades for another currency—is a crucial determinant of trade. Fluctuations in the exchange rate can have a huge impact on what goods countries import or export and the overall trade balance.

Euro The common currency in Europe.

Throughout this chapter, we will measure the exchange rate in units of foreign currency per U.S. dollar, that is, as 100 Japanese yen per dollar or 0.8 euro per dollar. The **euro** is the common currency in Europe. With these exchange rates, you would receive 100 yen for each dollar, but only 0.8 euro for each dollar.

We can think of the exchange rate as the price of dollars in terms of foreign currency. An increase in the value of a currency relative to the currency of another nation is called an *appreciation of a currency*. If the exchange rate between the dollar and the yen increases from 100 yen per dollar to 110 yen per dollar, one dollar will purchase more yen. Say, for instance, you've taken a trip to Japan for spring break. Because the dollar has appreciated, your dollar will exchange for more yen. You will now have more yen to spend on Japanese goods—say, MP3 players, DVD players, or entertainment—than you had before the dollar appreciated. The dollar has become more expensive in terms of yen. Its price has risen, in other words. Because the dollar has increased in value, we say the dollar has appreciated against the yen.

A *depreciation of a currency* is a decrease in the value of a currency relative to the currency of another nation. If the exchange rate falls from 100 to 90 yen per dollar, you'll get fewer yen for each dollar you exchange. Japanese goods—whose prices remain the same in Japanese yen—will become more expensive to U.S. residents. You'll have to use more dollars to obtain the yen to purchase the same MP3 and DVD players. The price of dollars in terms of yen has fallen, in other words, so we say the dollar has depreciated against the yen.

Be sure you understand that if one currency appreciates, the other must depreciate. If the dollar appreciates against the yen, for example, the yen must depreciate against the dollar. You'll get more yen in exchange for the dollar, but now when you trade your yen back, you'll get fewer dollars. For example, if the dollar appreciates from 100 to 110 yen per dollar, when you trade 100 yen back into U.S. currency, no longer will you get \$1.00—you'll get just \$0.91. Conversely, if the dollar depreciates against the yen, the yen must appreciate against the dollar. If the dollar depreciates from 100 yen to 90 yen per dollar, when you trade back 100 yen, you'll get \$1.11, rather than just \$1.00.

The exchange rate enables us to convert prices in one country to values in another country. A simple example illustrates how an exchange rate works. If you want to buy a watch from France, you need to know what it would cost. You e-mail the store in France and are told the watch sells for 240 euros. The store owners live in France and want to be paid in euros. To figure out what it will cost you in dollars, you need to know the exchange rate between euros and dollars. If the exchange rate is 0.8 euro per dollar, the watch will cost you \$300:

$$\frac{240 \text{ euros}}{0.8 \text{ euro per dollar}} = \$300$$

If the exchange rate is one euro per dollar, the watch will cost only \$240. As you can see, changes in the exchange rate will affect the prices of goods purchased on world markets and partly determine the pattern of imports and exports throughout the world.

How Demand and Supply Determine Exchange Rates

How are exchange rates determined? The exchange rate between U.S. dollars and euros is determined in the foreign-exchange market, the market in which dollars trade for euros. To understand this market, we can use demand and supply. In Figure 12.1, we plot the demand and supply curves for dollars in exchange for euros.

The supply curve is the quantity supplied of dollars in exchange for euros. Individuals or firms that want to buy European goods or assets will need to exchange dollars for euros. The supply curve is drawn under the assumption that as euros become cheaper, total spending on European goods and assets will increase. Therefore, the supply curve slopes upward: As the value of the dollar increases, more dollars will be supplied to the currency market in exchange for euros.

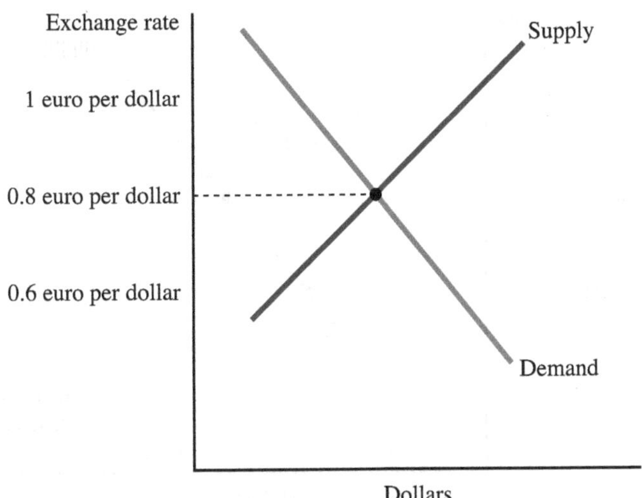

Figure 12.1

The Demand for and Supply of U.S. Dollars

Market equilibrium occurs where the demand for U.S. dollars equals the supply.

The demand curve represents the quantity demanded of dollars in exchange for euros. Individuals or firms in Europe that want to buy U.S. goods or assets must trade euros for dollars. For example, to visit Disney World in Florida, a German or French family must exchange euros for dollars. As the exchange rate for the U.S. dollar falls, dollars become cheaper in terms of euros. This makes U.S. goods and assets less expensive for European residents, because each euro buys more U.S. dollars. As U.S. goods and assets become cheaper, we assume more European residents will want to trade euros for dollars. Therefore, the demand curve for dollars in exchange for euros slopes downward: Total demand for dollars will increase as the price of the dollar falls, or depreciates, against the euro.

Equilibrium in the market for foreign exchange occurs where the demand curve intersects the supply curve. In Figure 12.1, equilibrium occurs at an exchange rate of 0.8 euro per dollar. At this price, the willingness to trade dollars for euros just matches the willingness to trade euros for dollars. The foreign exchange market is in balance, and the price of euros in terms of a dollar is $1.25.

Price of euros per dollar in equilibrium:

$$0.8 \text{ euro per dollar} = \frac{1 \text{ dollar}}{0.8 \text{ euro}} = 1.25 \text{ dollars per euro, or } \$1.25 \text{ per euro}$$

Now, however, suppose the demand and supply forces between dollars and euros change. If the exchange rate, *e*, increases, the dollar buys *more* euros—the price of dollars in terms of euros increases, in other words. For example, if *e* increases from 0.8 euro per dollar to 1 euro per dollar, the dollar has become more valuable—meaning it has appreciated against the euro. Be sure you see both sides of the same exchange coin: If the dollar appreciates against the euro, then the euro must depreciate against the dollar. So, if the exchange rate increases from 0.8 to 1 euro per dollar, what will the price of a single euro be now?

When the dollar appreciates, each euro is worth less. In this case, the price of the euro will fall from $1.25 per euro to $1.00 per euro.

Dollar appreciates:

$$1.0 \text{ euro per dollar} = \frac{1 \text{ dollar}}{1 \text{ euro}} = 1.0 \text{ dollars per euro, or } \$1.00 \text{ per euro}$$

If the exchange rate falls from 0.8 euro to 0.6 euro per dollar, the dollar has depreciated in value against the euro—the price of dollars in terms of euros has decreased, in

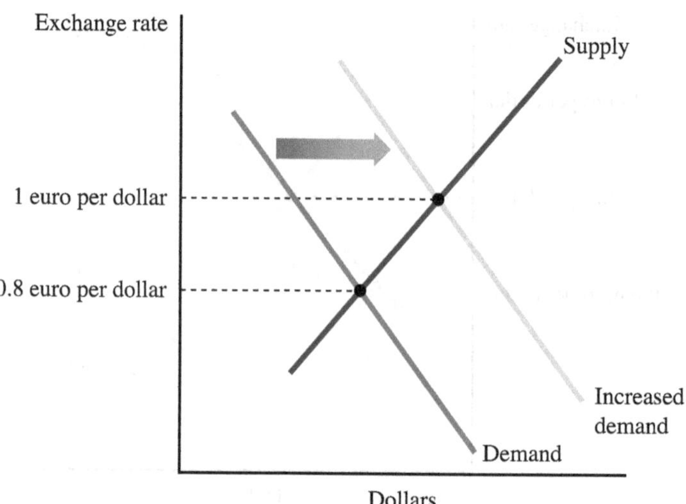

Figure 12.2

Shifts in the Demand for U.S. Dollars

An increase in the demand for dollars will increase (appreciate) the dollar's exchange rate. Higher U.S. interest rates or lower U.S. prices will increase the demand for dollars.

other words. When the dollar depreciates, each euro is worth more. In this case, the price of the euro will rise from $1.25 to $1.67.

Dollar depreciates:

$$0.6 \text{ euro per dollar} = \frac{1 \text{ dollar}}{0.6 \text{ euro}} = 1.67 \text{ dollars per euro, or } \$1.67 \text{ per euro}$$

Changes in Demand or Supply

Changes in demand or changes in supply will change equilibrium exchange rates. In Figure 12.2, we show how an increase in demand, a shift of the demand curve to the right, will increase, or appreciate, the exchange rate. U.S. dollars will become more expensive relative to euros as the price of U.S. dollars in terms of euros increases.

Two factors are the main causes of shifts of the demand curve for dollars: First, higher U.S. interest rates will lead to an increased demand for dollars. With higher returns in U.S. markets, investors throughout the world will want to buy dollars to invest in U.S. assets. The other factor, lower U.S. prices, will also lead to an increased demand for dollars. For example, if prices at Disney World fell, there would be an overall increase in the demand for dollars, because more tourists would want to visit Disney World.

Figure 12.3 shows the effects of an increase in the supply of dollars, a shift in the supply curve to the right. An increase in the supply of dollars will lead to a fall,

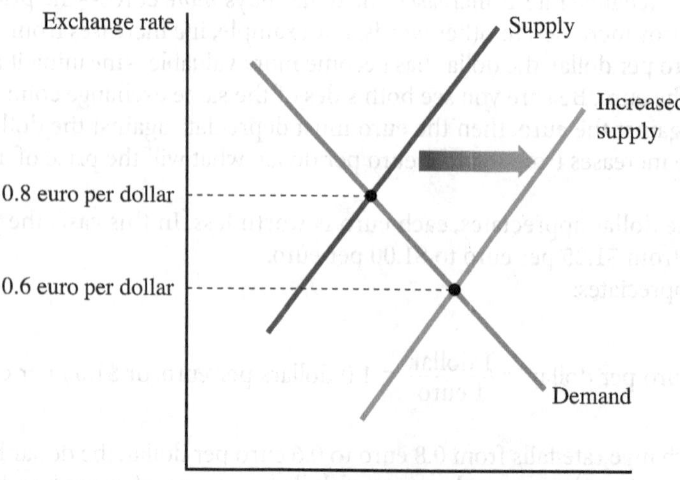

Figure 12.3

Shifts in the Supply of U.S. Dollars

An increase in the supply of dollars will decrease (depreciate) the dollar exchange rate. Higher European interest rates or lower European prices will increase the supply of dollars.

or depreciation, of the value of the dollar against the euro. What are the main causes of and increase in the supply of dollars? Again, the same two factors: interest rates and prices. Higher European interest rates will lead U.S. investors to purchase European bonds or other interest-paying assets. Purchasing European bonds will require U.S. investors to supply dollars for euros, which will drive down the exchange rate for dollars. Lower European prices will also lead to an increase in the supply of dollars for euros.

Let's summarize the key facts about the foreign exchange market, using euros as our example:

1. The demand curve for dollars represents the demand for dollars in exchange for euros. The curve slopes downward. As the dollar depreciates, there will be an increase in the quantity of dollars demanded in exchange for euros.
2. The supply curve for dollars is the supply of dollars in exchange for euros. The curve slopes upward. As the dollar appreciates, there will be an increase in the quantity of dollars supplied in exchange for euros.
3. Increases in U.S. interest rates and decreases in U.S. prices will increase the demand for dollars, leading to an appreciation of the dollar.
4. Increases in European interest rates and decreases in European prices will increase the supply of dollars in exchange for euros, leading to a depreciation of the dollar.

Real Exchange Rates and Purchasing Power Parity

12.2 LEARNING OBJECTIVE

As our examples of Disney World and watches from France indicate, changes in market exchange rates can affect the demand for a country's goods and services. However, we have been assuming that the prices of watches and trips to Disney World do not change. In general, prices do change over time, so we need to adjust the exchange rate determined in the foreign exchange market to take into account changes in prices. This adjustment is an application of the real-nominal principle.

Real-Nominal Principle | **What matters to people is the real value of money or income—its purchasing power—not the face value of money or income.**

Economists have developed a concept called the *real exchange rate* that adjusts the market exchange rates for changes in prices. The **real exchange rate** is defined as the price of U.S. goods and services relative to foreign goods and services, expressed in a common currency. We measure it by expressing U.S. prices for goods and services in foreign currency and comparing them to foreign prices. Here is the formula for the real exchange rate:

Real exchange rate The price of U.S. goods and services relative to foreign goods and services, expressed in a common currency.

$$\text{real exchange rate} = \frac{\text{exchange rate} \times \text{U.S. price index}}{\text{foreign price index}}$$

We can use this formula to help us understand the factors that change the real exchange rate. First, an increase in U.S. prices will raise the real exchange rate. When foreign prices and the exchange rate are held constant, an increase in U.S. prices will raise the relative price of U.S. goods. Second, an appreciation of the dollar when prices are held constant will also increase the price of U.S. goods relative to foreign goods. And if foreign prices fall, U.S. goods will become relatively more expensive as well.

Notice that the real exchange rate takes into account changes in a country's prices over time because of inflation. Suppose Country A had an inflation rate of 20 percent, and Country B had no inflation. Suppose, too, the exchange rate of Country A's currency

Figure 12.4

Real Exchange Rate and Net Exports as Percent of GDP, 1980–2009

The figure shows the real exchange rate for the United States compared to its net exports as a share of GDP. Notice that, in general, when the real (multilateral) exchange rate increased, U.S. net exports fell.

SOURCE: U.S. Department of Commerce and the Federal Reserve.

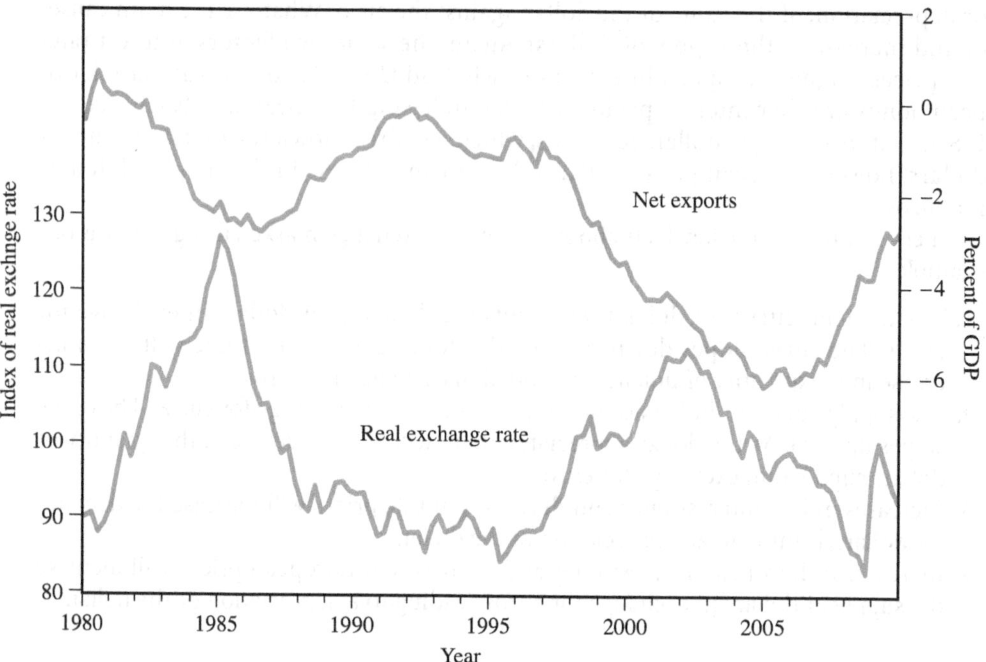

depreciated 20 percent against the currency of Country B. In this case, there would be no change in the real exchange rate between the two countries. Although prices in Country A would have increased by 20 percent, its currency would be 20 percent cheaper. From the point of view of residents of Country B, nothing has changed at all—they pay the same price in their currency to buy goods in Country A.

Economists have found that a country's net exports (exports minus its imports) will fall when its real exchange rate increases. For example, if the U.S. real exchange rate increases, the prices of U.S. goods will increase relative to foreign goods. This will reduce U.S. exports because our goods will have become more expensive; it will also increase imports to the United States because foreign goods will have become cheaper. As a result of the decrease in U.S. exports and the increase in U.S. imports, net exports will decline.

Figure 12.4 plots an index of the real exchange rate for the United States against net exports as a share of GDP from 1980 to 2009, a period in which there were large changes in the real exchange rate and net exports. The index, called a *multilateral real exchange rate*, is based on an average of real exchange rates with all U.S. trading partners. Notice that when the multilateral real exchange rate increased, U.S. net exports fell. As you can see in the figure, starting in both 1983 and 1996 the real exchange rate increased sharply. Subsequently, net exports as a share of GDP fell. A decrease in the real exchange rate increases net exports. For example, in 1986 and 2005, the real exchange rate began to decrease and net exports subsequently increased. The relationship between the real exchange rate and net exports is not perfect, however—other factors, such as the growth of GDP, also affect net exports.

Real exchange rates vary over time, as shown in Figure 12.4. But for goods traded easily across countries (such as gold bars), we would expect the price to be the same when expressed in a common currency. For example, the price of gold bars sold in France should be nearly identical to the price of gold bars sold in New York. If the price were higher in France, demand would shift to New York, raising the price in New York and lowering the price in France until the prices were equal. The tendency for easily tradable goods to sell at the same price when expressed in a common currency is known as the **law of one price**. Metals, agricultural commodities, computer chips, and other tradable goods follow the law of one price.

Law of one price The theory that goods easily tradable across countries should sell at the same price expressed in a common currency.

If all goods were easily tradable and the law of one price held exactly, exchange rates would reflect no more than the differences in the way the price levels are

Application 1

The Chinese Yuan and Big Macs

Applying the Concepts #1: How can the price of a Big Mac in China shed light on the U.S.-Chinese currency tensions?

In recent years, the U.S. and Chinese governments have been at odds about the appropriate value of the exchange rate between the Chinese yuan and the U.S. dollar. The United States believes that the Chinese government is holding the yuan below its true value. Can the price of a Big Mac in China shed light on this controversy?

For a number of years, the magazine the *Economist* measured the price of a Big Mac throughout the world and used these prices to explore whether currency values were too high or too low compared to the law of one price. Table 12.1 contains the results for selected countries, including China.

Big Macs sell for widely different prices around the globe, as measured in dollars compared to the $3.58 price in the United States in March 2010. They are a bargain in China at $1.83, but very expensive in Switzerland at $6.16. Table 12.1 also contains the market-exchange rate predicted by the theory of purchasing power parity. To obtain this exchange rate, divide the price of Big Macs in the foreign country by the dollar price. For example, for China the purchasing power exchange rate is

$$\frac{12.50 \text{ Chinese yuan (the price of a Big Mac in China)}}{\$3.58 \text{ (the price of a Big Mac in the United States)}} = 3.49 \text{ Chinese yuan per U.S. dollar}$$

Table 12.1

Big Mac Pricing Around the World Versus Actual Exchange Rates

Country	Price of a Big Mac in Local Currency	Price of a Big Mac in Dollars	Predicted Purchasing Power Exchange Rate Based on Big Mac Pricing (Foreign Currency per U.S. Dollar)	Actual Exchange Rate (Foreign Currency per U.S. Dollar)
United States	3.58 dollars	$ 3.58	—	—
United Kingdom	2.30 pounds	3.48	0.64	0.66
China	12.50 yuan	1.83	3.49	6.83
Switzerland	6.52 Swiss francs	6.16	1.82	1.06
Mexico	32.05 pesos	2.56	8.95	12.52
Euro Area	3.37 euros	4.62	0.94	0.73

At this "Big Mac" exchange rate—3.49 Chinese yuan to every U.S. dollar—the Big Mac in China would cost the same as in the United States. However, the actual exchange rate for the Chinese yuan in March 2010 when these prices were computed was 6.83 Chinese yuan per U.S. dollar, so the Big Mac was actually cheaper in China. Relative to the exchange rate implied by the law of one price, the Chinese yuan was 95 percent undervalued. This is a very large difference and cannot easily be attributed to measurement issues. This calculation gives a hint as to the Chinese-U.S. exchange rate controversy.

SOURCE: Based on the data on Big Mac prices from the *Economist* for March, 16, 2010 and market exchange rates.

expressed in the two countries. For example, if a basket of goods in Europe costs 3,000 euros and the identical basket costs $3,750 in the United States, an exchange rate of 0.8 euros to one dollar would make the costs the same in either currency ($\$3,750 \times 0.8$ euros/dollar $= 3,000$ euros).

According to one theory of how market exchange rates are determined, they simply reflect differences in the overall price levels between countries. According to the theory of **purchasing power parity**, a unit of any given currency should be able to buy the same quantity of goods in all countries. In our European-U.S. example, the theory of purchasing power parity predicts a market exchange rate of 0.8 euro per dollar. At that exchange rate, European and U.S. goods would sell for the same price if their products were expressed in a common currency. Research has shown that purchasing power parity does not hold precisely.

Purchasing power parity A theory of exchange rates whereby a unit of any given currency should be able to buy the same quantity of goods in all countries.

Many systematic studies have confirmed that purchasing power parity does not give fully accurate predictions for exchange rates. The reason is that many goods, such as housing and services like haircuts, are not traded across countries. The law of one price does not hold for notraded goods, which make up approximately 50 percent of the value of production in an economy. There is some truth to purchasing power parity, because exchange rates do reflect differences in the price level between countries. But, as the example with the Big Mac shows, purchasing power parity can provide a clue to exchange rates in some circumstances.

12.3 LEARNING OBJECTIVE

The Current Account, the Financial Account, and the Capital Account

Balance of payments A system of accounts that measures transactions of goods, services, income, and financial assets between domestic households, businesses, and governments and residents of the rest of the world during a specific time period.

Current account The sum of net exports (exports minus imports) plus net income received from abroad plus net transfers from abroad.

Financial account The value of a country's net sales (sales minus purchases) of assets.

Capital account The value of capital transfer and transaction in nonproduced, nonfinancial assets in the international accounts.

In this section, we examine international transactions in more detail. A useful framework for understanding international transactions is the **balance of payments**, a system of accounts that measures transactions of goods, services, income, and financial assets between domestic households, businesses, and governments and residents of the rest of the world during a specific time period.

Economists find it useful to divide international transactions in the balance of payments into three types: the current account, the financial account, and the capital account. These measures provide the most comprehensive picture of a country's balance of trade with the rest of the world and the consequences of that trade for a country's ownership of assets, such as stocks, bonds, and real estate. A country's **current account** is the sum of its

- net exports (exports minus imports),
- net income received from investments abroad, and
- net transfer payments from abroad (such as foreign aid).

If a country has a positive current account, we say that its current account is in surplus. If a country has a negative current account, we say that its current account is in deficit. If the income from investments abroad and net transfer payments is negligible, the current account becomes equivalent to a country's net exports.

A country's **financial account** transactions include all the purchases and sales of existing financial and produced assets (stocks, bonds, real estate) by the private sector and the government. The financial account is defined as the value of the country's net sales (sales minus purchases) of assets. If the United States sold $100 billion net in assets, its financial account would be $100 billion. If the value on the financial account is positive, we say the country has a surplus on the financial account. Similarly, if the value on the financial account is negative, we say it has a deficit on the financial account.

A country's **capital account** transactions consist of two components. First, they include the purchase or sale of nonproduced, nonfinancial assets, such as patents, copyrights, trademarks, and leases. Second, they also include transfers of capital, such as debt forgiveness or migrants' transfers (goods or financial assets accompanying migrants as they leave or enter the country). Capital account transactions are much smaller in magnitude than transactions on the current or financial account.

Rules for Calculating the Current, Financial, and Capital Accounts

Here is a simple rule for understanding transactions on the current, financial, and capital accounts: Any action that gives rise to a demand for foreign currency is a deficit item. Any action that gives rise to a supply of foreign currency is a surplus item.

Let's apply this rule to the current account and the financial account, taking the point of view of the United States (a similar logic applies to the capital account):

1. *Current account.* Items imported into the United States show up as a deficit (negative) on the current account because we have to trade U.S. currency for foreign currency to buy them. Items exported from the United States show up as a surplus (positive) in the current account because foreigners have to trade their currency for U.S. dollars to buy those products. Income from investments abroad and net transfers received are treated like exports because they result in a supply of foreign currency for dollars. Summarizing, we have

   U.S. current account surplus = U.S. exports − U.S. imports
   + net income from foreign investments + net transfers from abroad

2. *Financial account.* The purchase of a foreign asset by a U.S. resident leads to a deficit (negative) item on the financial account because it requires a demand for foreign currency. (You can think of the purchase of a foreign asset as just another import.) A purchase of a U.S. asset by a foreign resident leads to a supply of foreign currency and a surplus (positive) item on the financial account. (Think of this as an export.) Summarizing, we have

   U.S. financial account surplus = foreign purchases of U.S. assets
   − U.S. purchases of foreign assets

The current, financial, and capital accounts of a country are linked by a very important relationship:

current account + financial account + capital account = 0

The current account plus the financial account, plus the capital account must sum to zero. Why?

To keep things simple, let's ignore the relatively minor capital account transactions. In that case, the current plus financial accounts must sum to zero, because any excess demand for foreign currency that arises from transactions in goods and services—that means we're looking at the current account—must be met by an excess supply of foreign currency arising from asset transactions—the financial account. Suppose the United States has a current account deficit of $50 billion, which means it is importing more than it is exporting. This excess demand of foreign currency by people in the United States can be met only by an excess supply of foreign currency that arises from the financial account—where foreign residents are purchasing $50 billion more in U.S. assets than U.S. residents are purchasing of foreign assets. In other words, the current account deficit is offset by the financial account surplus.

Let's look at this from a slightly different angle. Consider again the case in which the United States is running a current account deficit because imports from abroad exceed exports. (For simplicity, transfers and income earned from investments abroad are both zero.) The current account deficit means that, on net, foreign residents and their governments are the recipients of dollars because they have sold more goods to the United States than they have purchased.

What do foreign residents do with these dollars? They can either hold the dollars or use them to purchase U.S. assets. In either case, foreign residents and their governments have acquired U.S. assets, either dollars or other U.S. assets, such as U.S. Treasury bills. The value of these assets is the U.S. current account deficit. Because a sale of a U.S. asset to a foreign resident is a surplus item on the U.S. financial account, the value of the financial account will be equal to the negative of the value of the current account. So, from this perspective also, the current account and the financial account must sum to zero.

Table 12.2

U.S. Balance of Payments: Current, Financial, and Capital Accounts, 2008 (Billions)

Current Account		Financial Account	
Goods	−840	Increases in U.S. holdings abroad	−1
Services	144	Increases in foreign holding in United States	534
Net Transfers	−128	Total on Financial Account (including other minor items)	507
Net Investment Income	118	**Capital Account**	1
Total on Current Account	−706	**Statistical Discrepancy**	−200
		Sum of Current, Financial, Capital Accounts and Statistical Discrepancy	0

SOURCE: Economic Report of the President (Washington, D.C.: U.S. Government Printing Office, 2010).

If a country runs a current account surplus—it is exporting more than importing, in other words—the country acquires foreign exchange. The country can either keep the foreign exchange or use it to buy foreign assets. In either case, its purchases of net foreign assets will equal its current account surplus. Because the financial account is the negative of the purchases of net foreign assets, the current account and financial account will again sum to zero.

Table 12.2 shows the balance of payments for the United States for 2008: the current account, the financial account, and the capital account. The current account is made up of the balance in goods, services, net investment income, and net transfers. In 2008, the United States had a negative balance on the goods account and net transfer, but a positive balance on the services and net income category. However, the large negative balance on the goods account made the overall current account balance negative. The financial account includes net increases in U.S. holdings abroad (negative entries in the financial account) and foreign holdings of U.S. assets (positive entries in the financial account). Because the government collects the current account, financial account, and capital account data from separate sources, a statistical discrepancy occurs. (In 2008, this was exceptionally large because of the difficulty of understanding all the transactions involved with the financial crisis.) Once we include this statistical discrepancy, the current account, the financial account, and the capital account sum to zero.

Since 1982, the United States has run a current account deficit every year. This means the United States has run a financial plus capital account surplus of equal value for these years as well. Because a financial account surplus means foreign nations acquire a country's assets, the United States has reduced its net holding of foreign assets. In 1986, the U.S. Department of Commerce estimated the United States had a **net international investment position** of $136 billion, meaning U.S. holdings of foreign assets exceeded foreign holdings of U.S. assets by $136 billion.

Net international investment position Domestic holding of foreign assets minus foreign holdings of domestic assets.

Because of its current account deficits, the U.S. net international investment position fell every year. By 2008 the U.S. net international investment position was negative $3.5 trillion, meaning foreign residents owned $3.5 trillion more U.S. assets than U.S. residents owned foreign assets. You may have heard the United States referred to as a *net debtor*. This is just another way of saying the U.S. net international investment position is negative. As a consequence of the United States being a net debtor, earnings from international assets flow out of the United States to foreign countries. In the future, part of the incomes earned in the United States will be paid to foreigners abroad. This is a natural consequence of the United States being a net debtor.

What are the consequences of the large U.S. trade deficits?

When the United States runs a trade deficit, U.S. residents are spending more on goods and services than they are currently producing. Although the United States does sell many goods and services abroad (such as supercomputers, movies, DVDs, and accounting services), it buys even more goods and services from abroad (such as clothes, electronics, and machine tools).

Application 2

World Savings and U.S. Current Account Deficits

Applying the Concepts #2: What factors may allow the United States to continue running large trade deficits with the rest of the world?

The 2006 *Economic Report of the President* directly addressed whether the United States can continue to run large current account deficits and, of course, financial account surpluses. In the report, the government recognized that the current account deficits would eventually be reduced. However, it also highlighted a number of factors suggesting the deficits could continue for a long period of time.

The report explains that the U.S. current account deficit needs to be placed in a global context. For the United States to continue to run a current account deficit, other countries in the world need to continue to purchase U.S. assets. In essence, they must have total savings in excess of their own investment desires. As long as there are countries in this situation, the United States could continue to run a trade deficit.

In recent years, four major countries experienced circumstances that encouraged them to save by purchasing assets from abroad. Both Japan and Germany had high savings rates, but low rates of domestic investment. Slow economic growth in both countries led firms to be very cautious about making domestic investment. With limited domestic investment opportunities, savers in Japan and Germany thus placed their funds abroad. Russia has large reserves of oil and gas, and increasing energy prices in the last several years provided Russians with substantial new revenue. They decided to use this revenue to invest abroad. Finally, China had high investment rates but even higher savings rates. As a result, China as a whole invested abroad. For the United States to continue to run trade deficits in the future, these or other countries must want to continue to save more than they want to invest domestically.

SOURCE: Based on *Economic Report of the President* (Washington, D.C.: United States Government Printing Office, 2006), chap. 6.

A trade deficit forces the United States to sell some of its assets to individuals or governments in foreign countries. Here is how it works: When U.S. residents buy more goods abroad than they sell, they give up more dollars for imports than they receive in dollars from the sale of exports. These dollars given up to purchase imports end up in the hands of foreigners, who can then use them to purchase U.S. assets such as stocks, government bonds, or even real estate. In recent years, Asian investors, including foreign governments, have bought a variety of assets in the United States, including U.S. Treasury bonds and even stakes in investment banking firms. Foreign governments have accumulated considerable assets and invested them in private markets abroad through **sovereign investment funds**. Current estimates place the value of assets in these funds at $3.8 trillion.

Sovereign investment fund Assets accumulated by foreign governments that are invested abroad.

The purchase of U.S. assets by foreign investors should not be surprising, because we have been running large trade deficits with many Asian economies, especially China. These countries were willing to sell us more goods than we were selling to them, and therefore they accumulated U.S. dollars with which they could purchase U.S. assets. There is considerable debate about whether the very large U.S. current account deficits can continue.

Fixed and Flexible Exchange Rates

12.4 LEARNING OBJECTIVE

To set the stage for understanding exchange rate systems, let's recall what happens when a country's exchange rate appreciates—increases in value. There are two distinct effects:

1. The increased value of the exchange rate makes imports less expensive for the residents of the country where the exchange rate appreciated. For example, if the

U.S. dollar appreciates against the euro, European watches will become less expensive for U.S. consumers. U.S. consumers would like an appreciated dollar, because it would lower their cost of living.

2. The increased value of the exchange rate makes U.S. goods more expensive on world markets. A U.S. exchange appreciation will increase imports, such as European watches, but decrease exports, such as California wine.

Because exports fall and imports rise, net exports (exports minus imports) will decrease. Similarly, when a country's exchange rate depreciates, there are two distinct effects:

1. For example, if the U.S. dollar depreciates against the Japanese yen, Japanese imports will become more expensive in the United States, thereby raising the cost of living in the United States.
2. At the same time, U.S. goods will become cheaper in world markets. U.S. exports will rise and imports will fall, so net U.S. exports will increase.

Fixing the Exchange Rate

Sometimes countries do not want their exchange rate to change. They may want to avoid sharp rises in the cost of living for their citizens when their currency depreciates, or they may want to keep net exports from falling when their currency appreciates. To prevent the value of the currency from changing, governments can enter the foreign exchange market to try to influence the price of foreign exchange. Economists call these efforts to influence the exchange rate **foreign exchange market intervention.**

Foreign exchange market intervention The purchase or sale of currencies by the government to influence the market exchange rate.

In the United States, the Treasury Department has the official responsibility for foreign exchange intervention, though it operates in conjunction with the Federal Reserve. In other countries, governments also intervene in the foreign exchange market. To influence the price at which one currency trades for another, governments have to affect the demand or supply for their currency. To increase the value of its currency, a government must increase the currency's demand. To decrease the value of its currency, the government must increase its supply.

In Figure 12.5, we show how governments can fix, or *peg*, the price of a currency. Suppose the U.S. and European governments want the exchange rate to be 0.8 euro per dollar. The price at which demand and supply are currently equal, however, is only 0.6 euro per dollar. To increase the price of the U.S. dollar, the governments will need to increase the dollar's demand. To do this, either government—the United States or European central banks—or both, can sell euros for dollars in the foreign exchange market.

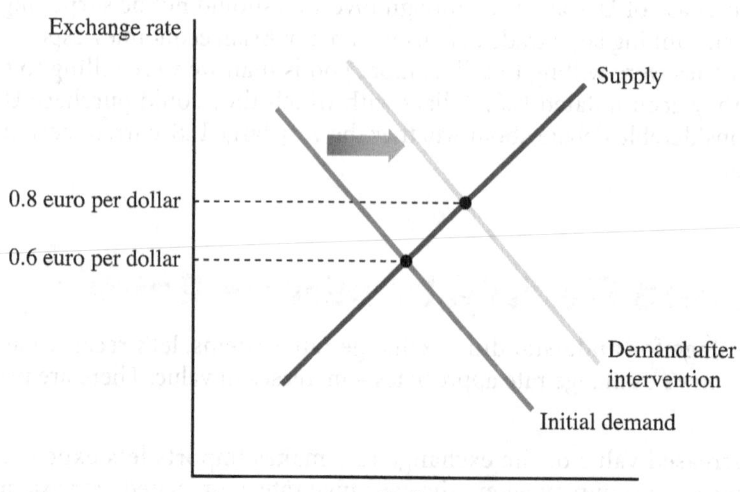

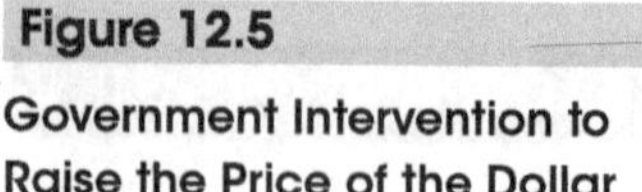
Figure 12.5

Government Intervention to Raise the Price of the Dollar

To increase the price of dollars, the U.S. government sells euros in exchange for dollars. This shifts the demand curve for dollars to the right.

This will shift the demand curve for dollars to the right until the price of dollars rises to 0.8 euro per dollar.

Conversely, if the governments want to lower the price of the dollar relative to euros, they will buy euros in exchange for dollars. By selling dollars for euros, they increase the supply of dollars. The price of the dollar therefore falls while the price of the euro increases. Note that to affect the price of the euro against the dollar, the U.S. government must exchange euros for dollars. The government will acquire and accumulate euros any time it tries to raise their price. To raise the price of the dollar, which lowers the value of the euro, the U.S. government must sell some of the euros it has accumulated. But what would happen if the United States had no euros to sell? The United States could borrow euros from European governments or persuade them to sell euros for dollars.

Fixed versus Flexible Exchange Rates

Next, we discuss two different types of exchange rate systems. Then we take a brief look at historical U.S exchange rate policy and developments in exchange rates in the world today.

Flexible Exchange Rate System If exchange rates are determined in free markets, we have a **flexible exchange rate system.** Under a pure flexible exchange rate system, the price of a currency will rise if the demand increases more than supply and will fall if supply increases more than demand. As we have seen, a variety of factors can determine exchange rates, including foreign and domestic interest rates as well as foreign and domestic prices. Other factors, including market psychology, can also affect the value of a nation's currency. Whatever its source, an increase in the demand for currency will raise its price. We have also seen that governments may intervene to prevent currency from changing its value. In the most extreme case, there would be no change in the value of a currency.

Flexible exchange rate system
A currency system in which exchange rates are determined by free markets.

Fixed Exchange Rates Whether you are in California, New York, or Indiana, all prices are quoted in dollars. No one asks whether your dollar came from San Francisco or Miami. Within the United States, a dollar is a dollar. Suppose, though, that every state had its own currency. There might be a California dollar (with a picture of the Golden Gate Bridge), an Oregon dollar (showing pictures of tall trees), and a Florida dollar (showing Disney World, of course). In principle, these dollars might trade at different rates, depending on the demand and supply of one state's dollar relative to the supply and demand for another state's dollar. For example, the Texas dollar might be worth more than the Michigan dollar, trading for 1.2 Michigan dollars.

Think how much more complicated it would be to do business. To buy goods from a mail-order company in Maine, you would have to find out the exchange rate between your state's dollar and the Maine dollar. Any large business operating in all 50 states would be overwhelmed trying to keep track of all the exchange rate movements across the states. The economy would become less efficient because individuals and businesses would have to focus a lot of their attention on exchange rates.

These same ideas apply across nations. Wouldn't it be nice if all countries either used the same currency or fixed their exchange rates against one another so that no one would have to worry about exchange rate movements? Currency systems in which governments try to keep constant the values of their currencies against one another are called **fixed exchange rate systems.** After World War II, the countries of the world operated under a fixed exchange system known as Bretton Woods. The Bretton Woods system was named after the town in New Hampshire where representatives of each nation met in 1944 and agreed to adopt this system. The system centered on the United States: All countries fixed or pegged their currencies against the U.S. dollar.

Fixed exchange rate system
A system in which governments peg exchange rates to prevent their currencies from fluctuating.

In a typical fixed exchange rate system, every country that pegs its rate to a central country's exchange rate must intervene in the foreign exchange market when necessary to keep its exchange rate constant. For example, a government would have to intervene if, at the fixed exchange rate, the private demand and supply for its currency were unequal.

Balance of Payments Deficits and Surpluses Suppose the supply of a country's currency exceeds the demand at the fixed exchange rate. An excess supply of a country's currency at the fixed exchange rate is known as a balance of payments deficit. A **balance of payments deficit** will occur whenever there is a deficit on the current account that is not matched by net sales of assets to foreigners by the private sector. For example, a current account deficit of $100 billion with net sales of assets to foreigners of only $80 billion would mean that there is an excess supply of $20 billion. With an excess supply of a country's currency in the currency market, that currency would fall in value without any intervention. To prevent the currency from depreciating in value and to maintain the fixed exchange rate, the government would have to sell foreign currency and buy its own currency. As you saw from our foreign exchange intervention discussion, if a country sells foreign exchange, its holdings of foreign exchange will fall. So you can see that when a country runs a balance of payments deficit, it has decreased its holdings of foreign exchange.

Balance of payments deficit Under a fixed exchange rate system, a situation in which the supply of a country's currency exceeds the demand for the currency at the current exchange rate.

It's also very possible that the demand for a country's currency will exceed its supply at the fixed exchange rate. An excess demand for a country's currency at the fixed exchange rate is known as a **balance of payments surplus.** A balance of payments surplus arises when there is a current account surplus that is not matched by net purchases of foreign assets by the private sector. With an excess demand for a country's currency, it will rise in value without any intervention. To prevent its currency from appreciating—to maintain the fixed exchange rate, in other words—the government will have to buy foreign currency and sell its own. Because it is buying foreign exchange, its holdings of foreign exchange will increase. From this discussion, you should be able to see that when a country runs a balance of payments surplus, it has increased its holding of foreign exchange.

Balance of payments surplus Under a fixed exchange rate system, a situation in which the demand of a country's currency exceeds the supply for the currency at the current exchange rate.

Under a fixed exchange rate system, countries that run persistent balance of payments deficits or balance of payments surpluses must take corrective actions. If domestic policy actions, such as changing taxes, government spending, or the money supply, do not cure the problem, a country will eventually have to change the level at which the exchange rate is fixed. A country that faces a balance of payments deficit can lower the value at which the currency is pegged to increase its net exports, a process called **devaluation.** Conversely, a country that faces a balance of payments surplus can increase the value at which its currency is pegged and reduce its net exports, a process called **revaluation.**

Devaluation A decrease in the exchange rate to which a currency is pegged under a fixed exchange rate system.

Revaluation An increase in the exchange rate to which a currency is pegged under a fixed exchange rate system.

The U.S. Experience with Fixed and Flexible Exchange Rates

As we discussed earlier, after World War II the countries of the world adopted the Bretton Woods fixed exchange rate system. In the 1970s, the Bretton Woods system was replaced by the current system—a flexible exchange rate system—in which supply and demand primarily determine exchange rates.

If a fixed exchange rate system makes it easier to trade, why did it break down in the early 1970s? Fixed exchange rate systems provide benefits, but they require countries to maintain similar economic policies—especially to maintain similar inflation rates and interest rates. To understand this, suppose the exchange rate between the United States and Germany were fixed, but the United States has an annual inflation rate of 6 percent compared to 0 percent in Germany. Because prices in the United States would be rising by 6 percent per year, the U.S. real exchange rate against Germany would also be increasing at 6 percent per year. This difference in their real exchange rates over time would cause a trade deficit to emerge in the United States as U.S. goods became more expensive on world markets—including in Germany. As long as the differences in inflation continued and the exchange rate remained fixed, the U.S. real exchange rate would continue to appreciate, and the U.S. trade deficit would grow even worse. Clearly, this course of events would have to be halted under an agreed-upon fixed exchange rate system.

In the late 1960s, inflation in the United States began to exceed inflation in other countries, and a U.S. balance of payments deficit emerged—just as in our example. In 1971, President Nixon surprised the world and devalued the U.S. dollar against the currencies of all the other countries. This was a sharp departure from the rules underlying Bretton Woods. Nixon hoped that a one-time devaluation of the dollar would alleviate the U.S. balance of payments deficit and maintain the underlying system of fixed exchange rates.

However, the U.S. devaluation did not stop the U.S. balance of payments deficit. Germany tried to maintain the mark's fixed exchange rate with the U.S. dollar by purchasing U.S. dollars in the foreign exchange market. What Germany was doing was importing inflation from the United States. With the U.S. balance of payments deficit continuing, Germany was required to buy U.S. dollars to keep the mark from appreciating. Germany bought U.S. dollars with German marks. Those German marks were then put into circulation. The German supply of marks in Germany therefore increased, and this increase in marks raised the inflation rate in Germany.

Private-sector investors knew that Germany did not wish to run persistent trade surpluses and import U.S. inflation. They bet that Germany would revalue the mark against the dollar—that is, raise the value of the mark against the dollar. They bought massive amounts of German assets, trading their dollars for marks to purchase them because they thought the mark's value would eventually sharply increase. Their actions forced the German government to buy even *more* dollars to force the price of the mark upward and keep it pegged to the dollar. The resulting flow of financial capital into Germany was so massive that the German government eventually gave up all attempts to keep its exchange rate fixed to the dollar. Instead, it let the exchange rate be determined in the free market. This was the end of the Bretton Woods system.

Exchange Rate Systems Today

The flexible exchange rate system has worked well enough since the breakdown of Bretton Woods. World trade has grown at a rapid rate. Moreover, the flexible exchange rate system has seamlessly managed many diverse situations, including two major oil shocks in the 1970s, large U.S. budget deficits in the 1980s, and large Japanese and Chinese current account surpluses in the last two decades.

During the Bretton Woods period, many countries placed restrictions on the flows of financial capital by, for example, not allowing their residents to purchase foreign assets or by limiting foreigners' purchases of domestic assets. By the 1970s, these restrictions began to be eliminated, and private-sector transactions in assets grew rapidly. With massive amounts of funds being traded in financial markets, it becomes very difficult to fix, or peg, an exchange rate.

Nonetheless, countries whose economies are closely tied together might want the advantages of fixed exchange rates. One way to avoid some of the difficulties of fixing exchange rates between countries is to abolish individual currencies and establish a single currency. This is precisely what a group of European countries decided to do. They adopted a single currency, the euro, throughout Europe and a single central bank to control the supply of the currency. With a single currency, European countries hope to capture the benefits of serving a large market like the United States does with its single currency.

The United Kingdom, Denmark, and Sweden decided to remain outside this European single currency system. Their currencies, like the U.S. dollar and the Japanese yen, now float against each of the other currencies and the euro. Many other countries have tied their exchange rate to either the dollar or the yen. Some economists believe that the world will eventually settle into three large currency blocs: the euro, the dollar, and the yen.

Application 3

A Downside to the Euro

Applying the Concepts #3: How did the 2008 financial crisis lead to problems for some countries in the Euro-zone?

When the euro was launched, countries with typically weaker currencies or fiscal discipline benefited from the discipline of one currency and a strong, single central bank. No longer would investors fear, for example, that Greece or Spain would pursue inflationary monetary polices, as monetary policy was decided by the European Central Bank. As a consequence, the stability created by the euro with the strong influence of Germany—recognized for its monetary and fiscal prudence—benefited the traditionally weaker countries.

As investment picked up worldwide in 2003, funds poured into a wide range of countries in the Euro-zone, fueling real estate and construction booms in Ireland and Spain, and financing a wide range of projects in Italy and Greece. As their economies boomed, prices and wages were driven up substantially. But when the investment boom came to a crashing end, these countries needed to make adjustments as their wage and price structure was out of line. But their options were limited because, as members of the Euro-zone, they could not depreciate their currencies. As a result, they were faced with the prospect of either making major budgetary adjustments, cutting spending or raising taxes, or a prolonged period of unemployment to reduce wages and prices. In 2010 Greece faced a major financial crisis as its budgetary imbalance was particularly severe and investors demanded major readjustments. A currency depreciation would have been a much easier solution for Greece in this situation, but this was no longer possible. This is a downside to a single currency for a collection of countries whose economies and political cultures differ sharply.

12.5 LEARNING OBJECTIVE

Managing Financial Crises

Hardly a year goes by without some international financial crisis. In 1994 Mexico experienced a severe financial crisis. In 1997 the Asian economic crisis began. The Argentinean economy collapsed in 2002. How do these crises originate? What policies can be followed to prevent or alleviate them?

Let's first consider the Mexican case. During the late 1980s and early 1990s, Mexico decided to fix, or peg, its exchange to the U.S. dollar. Mexico's goal was to signal to investors throughout the world that it was serious about controlling inflation and would take the steps needed to keep its inflation rates in line with that of the United States. Mexico also opened up its markets to let in foreign investors. The country seemed to be on a solid path to development.

However, in some sense, the policies proved to be too successful in encouraging foreign investment. As funds poured into the country, the demand for goods increased, and prices started to rise. This rise in prices caused an increase in Mexico's real exchange rate, and the rise in the real exchange rate caused a large trade deficit to emerge.

Initially, the trade deficit did not cause any difficulties for the Mexican government. Because foreign investors were willingly trading foreign currencies for Mexican pesos to buy Mexican securities, the government in Mexico did not have any problem maintaining its pegged exchange rate with the United States. Although the Mexicans were importing more than they were exporting, at this point they could still obtain the dollars they needed to finance the trade imbalance from foreign investors who were purchasing Mexican securities. The government did not have to intervene in the foreign exchange market to keep the price of the peso constant against the dollar. In other words, Mexico did not have a balance of payments deficit.

But then internal political difficulties ensued. Following an assassination of a political candidate and a rural uprising, foreign investors started to pull their funds out of Mexico. At this point, the Mexican government made a crucial mistake. Instead of trying to reduce its trade deficit by taking steps to reduce prices, it allowed

Application 4

The Argentine Financial Crisis

Applying the Concepts #4: What are the causes of financial collapses that occur throughout the globe?

During the late 1980s, Argentina suffered from hyperinflation. As part of its financial reforms, it pegged its currency to the U.S. dollar, making pesos "convertible" into dollars. To issue pesos, the central bank had to have an equal amount of dollars, or its equivalent in other hard currencies, on hand. Some economists believed this reform would bring stability to the financial system. Unfortunately, they were proved wrong.

The financial and other institutional reforms worked well in the early 1990s, but then several problems developed. As the dollar appreciated sharply on world markets after 1995, Argentina began to suffer from a large trade deficit because its currency was pegged to the dollar. Essentially, the United States' rising currency became Argentina's problem. Wage increases also pushed up the real exchange rate, exacerbating the trade deficit. The Argentinean government—including its provincial governments—found it difficult to control spending and had to borrow extensively from abroad in dollar-denominated loans. Then in 1999, Brazil devalued its currency, putting additional pressure on neighboring Argentina. As investors saw the persistent trade and government deficits that were occurring in Argentina, they became doubtful that the country could repay its debts and feared its currency would be devaluated. Local citizens also became fearful of a devaluation and tried to convert their pesos into dollars, further deepening the problem.

Eventually, Argentina was forced to default on its international debt in 2002 and freeze bank accounts. Middle-class Argentineans who still had funds in their banks suffered a sharp decrease in their wealth. A severe economic downturn ensued. The hopes of the reforms in the early 1990s had become a bitter memory. However, the Argentinean economy proved resilient and began a recovery over the next several years.

the trade deficit to continue. Moreover, both the government and the private sector began to find that they had to borrow in dollars because foreign investors thought Mexico might be forced to devalue the peso. If a devaluation were to occur, any lender of pesos would suffer a loss because the debt would be repaid at a lower exchange rate. Consequently, Mexican borrowers were forced to borrow in loans denominated in dollars.

Eventually, more political turmoil caused investors to pull out their funds, selling pesos for dollars. The Mexican central bank spent nearly $50 billion buying these pesos in an effort to keep the exchange rate constant. The $50 billion was not enough. Mexico ran out of dollars. Because it could no longer buy pesos to maintain the exchange rate, Mexico had to devalue, putting the peso more in line with its market value. The devaluation created even more turmoil because the government and the private sector had borrowed billions in dollars. When the peso was devalued against the dollar, the burden of these debts measured in pesos increased sharply, so more pesos were needed to pay the dollar-denominated debts. Mexico faced the prospect of massive bankruptcies and the potential collapse of its economy.

To prevent a financial collapse that could easily have spread to many other developing countries, the U.S. government (along with other international financial institutions) arranged for Mexico to borrow dollars with an extended period for repayment. This allowed Mexican banks and corporations to avoid bankruptcies and prevented a major disaster. In 1996, the Mexican government was able to pay off nearly three-fourths of the loan from the United States.

The Asian crisis had a similar flavor. Economic growth had been remarkable in Asia for over 20 years, improving to a great extent the standard of living of millions of people. In the early 1990s, several Asian countries began to open up their capital markets to foreign investors and borrow extensively from abroad. Billions of dollars poured into Asia. In many cases, there was little financial supervision, and many of the investments proved to be unwise. Companies in both Thailand and South Korea began to lose money. Domestic investors and world investors suddenly became pessimistic and pulled their funds out of South Korea and Thailand, among other Asian countries. The withdrawal of funds forced currencies throughout Asia to be devalued. Because many businesses had borrowed in dollars, the devaluations raised the burden of the debt and further deepened the crisis, taking its toll on other countries, including Indonesia, Malaysia, and Hong Kong. The International Monetary Fund attempted to help restore the health of these economies' financial systems, but in many cases, its policies were ineffective. Some economists, such as Nobel Laureate Joseph Stiglitz, believe the entire Asian crisis was an example of market overreaction and could have been avoided by bolder action from world organizations and developed countries.

Even when a country takes strong, institutional steps to peg its currency, a collapse is still possible.

These examples highlight some of the many factors that can bring about financial crises. In vast global capital markets, funds can move quickly from country to country, and economic policies sometimes do not keep pace with changing political and economic developments. It can be extremely difficult to maintain a fixed exchange rate in this environment. The flow of funds, moreover, is often so large that financial failures can rock trade and commerce.

The countries of the world are searching for a reliable set of rules and institutional mechanisms that can avoid and limit the spread of financial crises. Historically, the International Monetary Fund has played a key role in assisting countries that run into financial difficulties. However, in Mexico, the sums were so large that the United States was forced to take the lead in resolving the situation. In Asia, the International Monetary Fund did not have backing from the United States, so the efforts to alleviate the crisis were less successful. In Argentina, rigid adherence to a fixed exchange rate and a government that could not control spending both contributed to a collapse. As world capital markets continue to grow, governments throughout the world will almost surely be tested by new and often unpredictable financial crises, such as they experienced in 2008. They will need to anticipate and react to rapid changes in the economic and political environment to maintain a stable financial environment for world trade.

Summary

In this chapter, we examined the world of international finance. You saw how exchange rates are determined in markets and how governments can influence these markets. You also learned how the real exchange rate affects the trade deficit. Behind the complex world of international financial transactions are these few simple ideas:

1. *Exchange rates* are generally determined in *foreign exchange markets* by supply and demand.
2. *The real exchange rate* is the price of U.S. goods and services relative to foreign goods and services, expressed in a common currency. The equation for the real exchange rate is

$$\text{real exchange rate} = \frac{\text{exchange rate} \times \text{U.S. price index}}{\text{foreign price index}}$$

3. The *balance of payments* consists of three types of international transactions:
   - The *current account* is equal to net exports plus net income from existing investments abroad and net transfers from abroad.
   - The *financial account* is the value of a country's sales less purchases of assets.
   - The *capital account* is the net value of a country's capital transfers and the purchase and sale of nonproduced, nonfinancial assets.

   The sum of the current account, plus the financial account, plus the capital account is zero.
4. Governments can attempt to change the value of currencies by buying or selling currencies in the foreign exchange market. Purchasing a currency will raise its value; selling a currency will decrease its value.
5. A system of fixed exchange rates can provide a better environment for business but requires that countries keep their inflation rates and interest rates within narrow limits.

Key Terms

balance of payments, p. 298
balance of payments deficit, p. 304
balance of payments surplus, p. 304
capital account, p. 298
current account, p. 298
devaluation, p. 304
euro, p. 292
exchange rate, p. 291
financial account, p. 298
fixed exchange rate system, p. 303
flexible exchange rate system, p. 303
foreign exchange market intervention, p. 302
law of one price, p. 296
net international investment position, p. 300
purchasing power parity, p. 297
real exchange rate, p. 295
revaluation, p. 304
sovereign investment funds, p. 301

CHAPTER 13

Macroeconomic Policy Debates

Chapter Outline and **Learning Objectives**

Applying the Concepts

Economists are often cautious and try to warn policymakers that carrying out effective economic policy is difficult. But politicians must ultimately make decisions. President Harry S. Truman made the following observation about his cautious economists: "All my economists say, 'On the one hand, . . . ; On the other hand, . . .' Give me a one-handed economist!"

Decisions about government spending, taxes, deficits, interest rates, and exchange rates may seem very abstract, but they directly affect our lives. Poor economic policies can lead to the virtual collapse of countries. Policymaking therefore requires prudence. Of course, it is always very easy to criticize politicians in power when something goes wrong. In another famous quote, Truman recognized that decision making is not easy. Before air conditioning was commonplace, he was known to have remarked, "If you can't stand the heat, get out of the kitchen."

As a student and citizen, you are inevitably drawn into economic debates. In most cases, the debates are complex because they involve a mixture of facts, theories, and opinions. Value judgments play a large role in economic debates. Your views on the proper role of tax policy, for example, will depend on whether you believe low-income earners should receive a higher share of national income. Your views on the size of government will depend on whether you believe individuals or the government should play a larger role in economic affairs.

In previous chapters, you learned the basic vocabulary of economics and studied different theories of the economy. Now you are ready to examine some of the key policy issues in macroeconomics. In this chapter, we will focus on three macroeconomics issues that are the subject of much debate:

- Should we balance the federal budget?
- Should the Fed target inflation or pursue other objectives?
- Should we tax consumption rather than income?

Should We Balance the Federal Budget?

13.1 LEARNING OBJECTIVE

Before we begin to consider answers to the question "Should we balance the federal budget?" let's review some terms: *Government expenditures* include goods and services purchased by the government and transfer payments, such as Social Security and welfare, made to citizens. A *surplus* occurs when the government's revenues exceed its expenditures in a given year. The government runs a *deficit* when it spends more than it receives in revenues from either taxes or fees in a given year.

The *government debt* is the *total* of all its yearly deficits. For example, if a government initially had a debt of $100 billion and then ran deficits of $20 billion the next year, $30 billion the year after that, and $50 billion during the third year, its total debt at the end of the third year would be $200 billion: the initial $100 billion debt plus the successive yearly deficits of $20 billion, $30 billion, and $50 billion. If a government ran a surplus, it would decrease its total debt. For example, suppose the debt were $100 billion and the government ran a surplus of $10 billion. With the surplus, the government would buy back $10 billion of debt from the private sector, thereby reducing the remaining debt to $90 billion.

In this chapter, we focus on the government debt held by the public, not the total federal debt, which includes debt held by other governmental agencies. Sometimes popular accounts in the press or on the Web highlight the total federal debt. However, the debt held by the public is the best measure to assess the burden the federal debt can have on the economy.

The Budget in Recent Decades

The fiscal picture for the United States has changed substantially over the last 30 years. Beginning in the 1980s and through most of the 1990s, the federal budget ran large deficits—"deficits as far as the eye can see," as David Stockman, the director of the Office of Management and Budget in President Reagan's administration, put it. What Stockman could not see at that point, however, was what would occur in the late 1990s. In fiscal year 1998, during President Clinton's administration, the federal government ran a budget surplus of $69 billion—its first surplus in 30 years. It continued to run surpluses for the next 3 fiscal years as well.

The surplus emerged for two key reasons. First, economic growth was very rapid and tax revenues—including tax revenues from the sales of stocks and bonds—grew more quickly than anticipated. Second, federal budget rules were in place that limited total spending.

When President George W. Bush took office in January 2001, the large surplus led him to propose substantial tax cuts. Bush and Congress then passed a 10-year tax cut amounting to $1.35 trillion over the course of the decade. Although the tax cuts were large, the Congressional Budget Office (CBO) estimated at that time that the federal government would nonetheless continue to run surpluses through 2010.

The CBO noted that, as a result of these federal government surpluses, the outstanding stock of federal debt held by the public would be reduced. Because GDP would be growing over this period, the stock of debt relative to GDP, which is the standard way to measure the effect of debt in an economy, would also decline. The CBO estimated that in 2011, the ratio of debt to GDP would fall despite Bush's tax cuts, in part because the tax cuts were set to expire in 2010. Figure 13.1 depicts the debt/GDP ratio from 1791 to 2009. As you can see, except for a period in the 1980s typically the ratio rises sharply during wars and the Great Depression and falls during peacetime. With neither a war nor a recession looming on the horizon in early 2001, the CBO predicted that the debt/GDP ratio would be relatively low by the end of the decade.

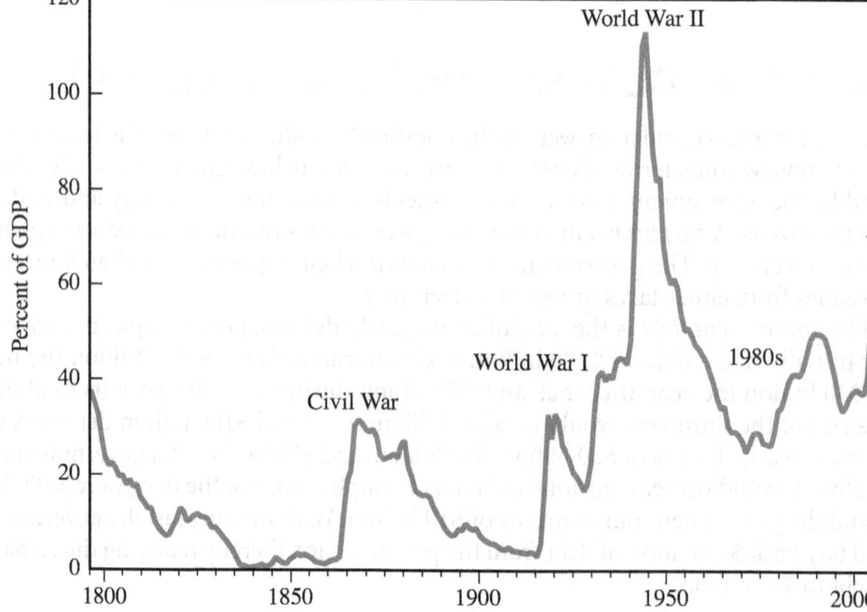

FIGURE 13.1

Debt as a Percent of GDP, 1791–2009

The nation's debt/GDP ratio tends to rise sharply during wars because more spending is needed to finance them. However, the ratio also can rise during peacetime, as it did during the Reagan presidency in the 1980s.

SOURCES: Congressional Budget Office, "The Long-Term Budget Outlook," December 2003, and yearly updates.

Unfortunately, a series of events intervened to bring deficits back into the picture and prevent the debt/GDP ratio from falling. The fight against terrorism led to higher spending on homeland security and military spending as wars were launched in Afghanistan and Iraq. The Bush tax cuts, the collapse of the stock market twice during the decade, the recessions that began in 2001 and 2007, and the housing bust mid-decade all sharply reduced tax revenues. President Obama's stimulus package in 2009 added new tax cuts and additional spending, which fueled the deficit. The federal government ran a budget deficit of approximately $1.3 trillion in fiscal year 2010, a far cry from the surpluses in the late 1990s. You can see from the last few years of Figure 13.1 that the debt-to-GDP ratio has recently risen. Current projections by the CBO suggest that the debt-to-GDP ratio will increase even when the economy resumes a normal level of economic growth.

Five Debates about Deficits

As we have seen, federal budgets are affected by a wide range of factors, including wars, demographic pressures, recessions, and the choices our politicians make on spending and taxes. But what principles should guide policymakers? Should they cut spending and raise taxes to reduce the national debt over time? Or does the level of the national debt really matter? Let's take a look at the debates over the national debt.

Debate 1: Do Deficits Lead to Inflation? If a government is spending $2,000 but collecting only $1,600 in taxes, where does it get the $400 needed to fill the gap? One option is to borrow $400 from the public in return for government bonds, which are, in effect, IOUs. In the future the government would have to pay back the $400 plus any interest on the bonds. Another way to cover the gap is simply to create $400 worth of new money. In principle, governments could use a mix of borrowing money and creating money, as long as the total covers its deficits:

government deficit = new borrowing from the public + new money created

In the United States, the Treasury Department issues government bonds to finance the deficit. The Federal Reserve has the option of buying existing government bonds, including those newly issued by the Treasury Department. If the Federal Reserve does purchase the government's bonds, the purchase creates money by taking debt out of the hands of the public in exchange for money. Economists call the purchase by a central bank of newly issued government debt **monetizing the deficit**. If governments finance deficits by creating new money, the result will be inflation. In the United States, we normally finance only a very small portion of our deficits by creating money. For example, between 2005 and 2006 the Federal Reserve purchased only $34 billion in government bonds of approximately $330 billion issued by the Treasury during that period. The Fed sold the remainder to the public. However, during the financial crisis, the Fed engaged in massive purchases in securities, adding over a trillion dollars to its balance sheet. However, by paying interest on reserves, it induced banks to hold matching excess reserves and thus prevented the money supply held by the public from increasing. This prevented inflation from emerging.

Monetizing the deficit Purchases by a central bank of newly issued government bonds.

If a country has no options other than creating money to finance its deficits—in other words, if the public is unwilling to buy its bonds, as was the case in Hungary following World War II—those deficits will inevitably cause inflation. Hyperinflations occur when economies run large deficits and monetize them. Germany and Russia after World War I, Bolivia and Argentina in the 1980s, Russia in the 1990s, and most recently Zimbabwe are just some of the countries that, in addition to Hungary, have endured massive inflations because they monetized their deficits. However, large, stable countries like the United Kingdom, the United States, and Japan don't monetize much of their debt because they are able to borrow from the public. In these countries, deficits do not lead inevitably to inflation.

Debate 2: Is Government Debt a Burden on Future Generations? The national debt, another commonly used term for total government debt, can impose two different burdens on society, both of which fall on the shoulders of future generations. First, a large debt can reduce the amount of capital in the economy and thereby reduce future income and real wages for its citizens. Here's how.

The savings of individuals and institutions flow into capital formation and increase an economy's capital stock. For example, when savers purchase new stocks and bonds, the companies issuing them use the proceeds to invest in plants and equipment.

When the government runs a deficit and increases its national debt, it also finances its spending by selling bonds to these same savers, who might hold both types of assets in, say, their retirement portfolios. Further, let's say that the total amount that the public can save is fixed at $1,000. If the government needs to finance a $200 deficit and does so by selling new bonds, then only $800 in savings is available to invest in private companies. The selling of $200 in government bonds to finance the deficit therefore "crowds out" $200 that could have been raised by private companies.

The result of government deficits is that less savings are available to firms for investment. This illustrates one of our basic principles in economics.

Principle of Opportunity Cost | **The opportunity cost of something is what you sacrifice to get it.** 

As we discussed in earlier chapters, reduced saving and investment will ultimately reduce the stock of private capital, the building of new factories, and the purchasing of equipment to expand production and raise GDP. As a result, there will be less capital deepening. With lower capital per worker, real incomes and real wages will be lower than they otherwise might have been. The government deficit (caused by increased spending or decreased taxes) comes at a cost in the future.

Governments can spend the proceeds of borrowing on investments, such as productive infrastructure—in this case, future real wages and incomes will not be adversely affected. With productive investment, government deficits will not be a burden on society.

Second, a large national debt will mean that higher taxes will be imposed on future generations to pay the interest that accumulates on the debt. Just like your college loans, the bill eventually comes due—even for the national debt.

Sometimes you hear that these interest payments are not a real burden because "we owe the national debt to ourselves." This is a misleading argument for several reasons. First, we don't owe the interest payments only to ourselves. In 2009, approximately 52 percent of U.S. public debt was held by foreigners. Second, a high proportion of the debt is held by older, wealthy individuals or by institutions, but the taxes levied to service it will be paid by everyone in the United States.

Ricardian equivalence The proposition that it does not matter whether government expenditure is financed by taxes or debt.

Some economists do not believe that government deficits, resulting in government debt, impose a burden on a society. These economists believe in **Ricardian equivalence**, the proposition that it does not matter whether government expenditure is financed by taxes or financed by issuing debt. This idea is named after David Ricardo, a nineteenth-century classical economist. To understand the case for Ricardian equivalence, consider the following example. A government initially has a balanced budget. It then cuts taxes and issues new debt to finance the deficit left by the reduction in taxes. Everyone understands the government will have to raise taxes in the future to service the debt, so everyone increases savings to pay for the taxes that will be increased in the future. If saving rises sufficiently, the public—everyone—will be able to purchase the new debt without reducing the funds they invest in the private sector. Because net investment doesn't decline, there will be no debt burden.

As you can see, Ricardian equivalence requires that savings by the private sector increase when the deficit increases. Do savers behave this way? It is actually difficult to provide a definite answer, because we must take many other factors into account in any empirical studies of savings. It appears, however, that during the early 1980s, savings decreased somewhat when government deficits increased. This is precisely the opposite of what Ricardian equivalence predicts. As long as Ricardian equivalence does not fully

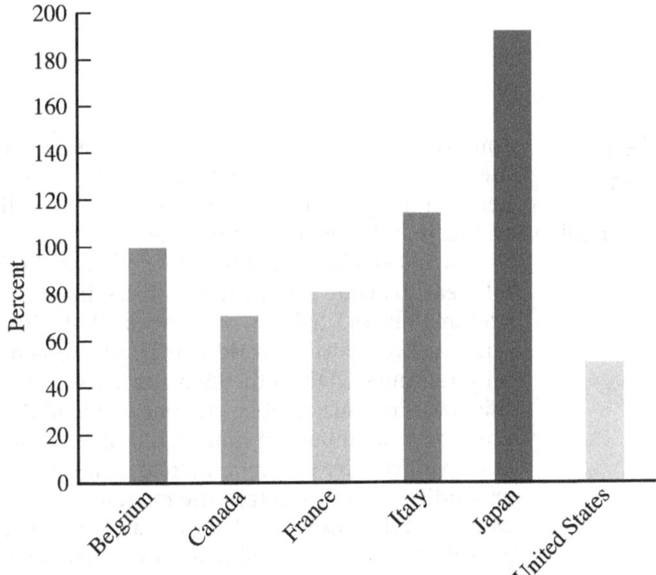

FIGURE 13.2

International Comparisons of Government Debt as Percentage of GDP, 2009

Among developed countries, the United States has a relatively small percentage of debt to GDP. Japan has the highest percentage of debt of the countries depicted.

SOURCE: Central Intelligence Agency, The World Factbook, https://www.cia.gov/library/publications/the-world-factbook/rankorder/2186rank.html (accessed April 26, 2010).

hold true, it's reasonable to assume the government debt imposes a burden on society. Nonetheless, many economists believe using the deficit as the sole measure of a society's future burdens doesn't tell the whole story. These economists believe we should look at broader measures that take into account long run promises of the federal government.

From an international perspective, the United States does not have the largest government debt measured relative to GDP. Figure 13.2 depicts the percentage of debt to GDP for several developed countries. By this measure, Japan has the most serious public debt problem.

Debate 3: How Do Deficits Affect the Size of Government? Nobel Laureate James Buchanan has argued that people are less aware of government deficits than of the taxes they're forced to pay. Therefore, financing government expenditures through deficits, rather than through higher taxes, will inevitably lead to higher government spending and bigger government. Although this argument may seem plausible, it presents two problems. First, in recent U.S. history, spending by state and local governments has grown much faster than federal spending. However, state and local governments face many more restrictions when it comes to borrowing money than the federal government faces. For example, many states require legislators to run a balanced budget. Deficit spending isn't allowed. Second, if politicians trying to get reelected really prefer higher government spending and deficits to higher taxes and surpluses, why did the federal government run surpluses in the late 1990s?

Some research suggests politicians can use deficits strategically to actually reduce the growth of government. During the 1980s, for example, the government ran large deficits caused by a combination of a deep recession and major tax cuts. The deficits subsequently made it difficult for other politicians to propose new spending programs. Proponents of smaller government, therefore, may wish to cut taxes to reduce surpluses or increase deficits in order to make it more difficult for other politicians to increase government spending. These deficit proponents want to create deficits to prevent Congress from having too much money to be able to spend. Some congressmen supported President Bush's tax cut in 2001, which reduced the surplus over a 10-year period, precisely for this reason.

Debate 4: Can Deficits Be Good for an Economy? Recall from the fiscal policy chapter that during a downturn, running a deficit helps stimulate private-sector spending. Consequently, the government may deliberately run a deficit to pull the economy out of a recession. The deficit the government creates puts additional income into the hands of the public. With more money, people don't have to drastically cut their

Application 1

New Methods to Measure the Long-Term Fiscal Imbalances for the United States

Applying the Concepts #1: What are the long-term fiscal imbalances for the United States?

Even though federal budget-deficit projections have increased sharply in recent years, they still don't accurately portray the long-run fiscal problems facing the United States. As the population ages, life expectancies increase, and health-care costs continue to grow, expenditures on Social Security and Medicare are expected to increase significantly, too. Although payroll taxes today exceed expenditures, in the not-too-distant future these taxes will fall far short of anticipated expenditures. Over time, there will be an escalating gap between revenues and expenditures, which will have to be met by outright borrowing.

How can we measure the size of the gap? Economists Jagadeesh Gokhale of the Cato Institute and Kent Smetters of the University of Pennsylvania have developed a more comprehensive measure of a nation's indebtedness. The method includes estimating the present value of the gap between the government's revenues and expenditures and adding it to the current national debt.

In 2005 Gokhale and Smetters calculated this new total measure, which they call the "fiscal imbalance," as approximately $63 trillion, or 5 times GDP. This is a huge number. Even during World War II, government debt was only 1.2 times GDP. In the long run, a fiscal imbalance of this size is not sustainable—no one will lend the U.S. government that amount of money. Eliminating these imbalances will require dramatic increases in taxes or reduced expenditures. To maintain the current level of benefits, workers and firms would have to pay nearly 30 percent in payroll taxes—about double what they pay today—or income taxes would have to nearly double. Alternatively, benefits programs could be scaled back.

Gokhale and Smetters estimate that about 80 percent of the fiscal imbalance will stem from Medicare—which pays the rising health-care costs for the elderly. What these numbers suggest is that our current health-care system for retirees will need to undergo fundamental reform to make it more sustainable. Otherwise, the United States will need to radically increase taxes to meet the shortfall.

SOURCE: Based on Jagadeesh Gokhale and Kent Smetters, "Fiscal and Generational Imbalances: An Update," August 2005, http://www.philadelphiafed.org/research-and-data/events/2005/fed-policy-forum/papers/Smetters-Assessing_the_Federal_Government.pdf (accessed April 27, 2010).

consumption spending. Because total spending in the economy does not fall as much, the severity of the recession is lessened.

Deficits automatically emerge during recessions, which also stabilize the economy. Recall how automatic stabilizers work. As incomes fall during a recession, so do tax payments. Moreover, transfer payments such as welfare and food stamps rise. Because government spending increases while tax revenues fall, the deficit must, of course, rise. However, a rising deficit may be what it takes to steer the economy back to full employment. Automatic stabilizers were clearly in evidence in the recession that began in late 2007, as tax revenues fell sharply for the next several years.

The existence of automatic stabilizers and the use of expansionary fiscal policy during recessions suggest that we should not worry about short-run government deficits. Over short time periods, deficits can help the economy to cope with shocks, such as oil price increases or a collapse in the stock market. They give the government some room to maneuver out of a recession. Most economists believe automatic stabilizers reduced economic fluctuations during the twentieth century.

Deficits can also play a role in tax smoothing. Suppose there is a large, temporary increase in government spending, as might occur during a war. The government could either finance the war by running a deficit and issuing debt or by increasing tax rates to keep the budget in balance. Professor Robert Barro of Harvard University has argued that it is more efficient to keep tax rates relatively constant than to raise them sharply and then lower them later. Temporarily raising tax rates to very high levels could cause distortions in economic behavior that we would like to avoid. Thus, by running deficits and only gradually raising taxes later to service the debt, we avoid creating excess distortions in the economy.

Debate 5: Would a Balanced-Budget Amendment Really Work? For many years, there were strong efforts to enact a Constitutional amendment to balance the federal budget. As recently as 1995, Congress came very close to passing a balanced-budget amendment, sending it back to the states for ratification. The amendment passed in the House of Representatives but failed by a single vote in the Senate. How would a balanced-budget amendment actually work?

Many different budgetary constitutional amendments have been proposed. They all require that, after a phase-in period, Congress propose in each fiscal year a budget in which total revenues (excluding borrowing) cover total expenditures. The amendments also have various escape clauses—for example, to allow borrowing during wartime. Some amendments also allow Congress to suspend the requirement to balance the budget for other reasons, such as during a recession when deficits naturally emerge. Finally, some versions would limit the rate of spending increases to the rate at which GDP is growing.

Proponents of the balanced-budget amendment say it will finally exert discipline on the federal government, preventing large deficits in peacetime, such as those that occurred in the 1980s. With a balanced budget we could be sure to avoid the negative effects of deficits: reduced capital formation and tax burdens that are shifted onto future generations.

Critics of a balanced-budget amendment point to many different problems, such as the following:

- A balanced budget may not allow enough flexibility, or room, for the government to effectively deal with recessions. Under some versions of the amendment, unless three-fifths of Congress votes to suspend requirements, the government would have to cut expenditures or raise taxes during a recession. This would make the recession worse and limit the ability of the government to use fiscal policy to stabilize the economy.
- The Constitution is not the right mechanism to try to enforce complicated budget rules. As various interested parties challenge the actions of Congress, the courts would become heavily engaged in federal budget matters.
- Congress could devise special budgets to get around the requirement, for example, by taking some types of spending "off budget," which means simply not counting them as part of the official budget.
- Congress could also find nonbudgetary ways to carry out the policies that it desires. For example, it could issue more regulations or impose mandates or requirements on businesses or other governments to carry out its will. These regulations or mandates could be even more costly to the economy than added deficits.

Should the Fed Target Inflation or Pursue Other Objectives?

13.2 LEARNING OBJECTIVE

In previous chapters we looked at the various roles that the Federal Reserve can play. Monetary policy can be used to stabilize the real economy, preventing unemployment from exceeding the natural rate or falling too far below the natural rate. The Fed also plays a critical role as a lender of last resort and a unique resource to combat financial crises.

On the other hand, we also learned that, in the long run, money was neutral and monetary policy cannot affect the real level of output or unemployment. We also saw that the natural rate can shift over time, making it difficult to target the appropriate unemployment rate. In these circumstances, what should the Fed do? Should it just focus on inflation or try to follow some other rule or procedure to balance concerns of inflation and unemployment?

In the early years of the first decade of the twenty-first century, the rate of inflation had fallen to between 1 and 2 percent. Some economists thought the time was right for the Fed to concentrate on simply keeping the inflation rate low and stable. In other words, they thought the Fed should use monetary policy to "target" an appropriate inflation rate and make its primary objective keeping inflation in check. Following the expansion of the Fed's activities during the financial crisis of 2008 and its aftermath, there is continuing concern about long-run inflation.

In recent years, various inflation-targeting methods have been adopted in a number of developed countries, including Canada, the United Kingdom, New Zealand, Sweden, Australia, and Spain. In addition, many developing countries have found that inflation targeting increased the autonomy of their central banks, helping them fight inflation.

Two Debates about Inflation Targeting

Inflation targeting has had many strong proponents. Let's take a close look at two key debates about this topic.

Debate 1: Should the Fed Focus on Only Inflation? We have learned that in the long run monetary policy can influence only the level of prices, not the level of employment. Proponents of inflation targeting argue that the Fed should have only one primary goal: controlling inflation. Having it worry about other factors—unemployment or the exchange rate—will, they say, distract it from its mission and lead to long-run inflationary pressures building in the economy. Moreover, if the Fed were committed to the single goal of controlling inflation, its credibility would be enhanced. As we have seen, if the Fed is credible, the private sector will become more responsive to changes in monetary policy. For example, long-term interest rates will become more responsive to changes in short-term rates if the public understands what the Fed's motives are and what it is doing. And credible policies may actually decrease the need for active monetary policies. Having a single goal would also help to keep the Fed free of political pressures.

Application 2

Would a Policy Rule Have Prevented the Housing Boom?

Applying the Concepts #2: Did the Federal Reserve cause the housing boom through excessively loose monetary policy?

John Taylor from Stanford University has argued that the Fed's "easy money" policy from mid-2001 through 2004 was largely responsible for the housing boom in the decade that ultimately caused so much financial damage. Taylor used his own model of monetary policy—the "Taylor rule"—to analyze the Fed's behavior. In his prior work, he demonstrated that the Fed's behavior could be closely described by a model that allowed for some monetary policy tightening and easing in response to output movements. Applying this model to the decade of 2000, however, Taylor found that, compared to past experience, the Fed was much too aggressive in lowering interest rates. Interest rates fell from 2 percent in mid-2001 to 1 percent by 2004. Past experience, however, would have suggested that the Fed would have raised interest rates to 4 percent by 2004—a very significant deviation.

Taylor then showed that housing starts—which are very sensitive to interest rates—would have been much lower if the Fed had not followed its easy money policy. The boom and bust would have been avoided. Finally, as an additional piece of evidence, Taylor looked at the experiences of European countries. There the same phenomenon occurred. Countries that deviated most from the Taylor rule—for example, Spain—experienced the worst boom and bust cycles for housing.

SOURCE: Based on John B. Taylor, "The Financial Crisis and Policy Responses: An Empirical Analysis of What Went Wrong," http://www.stanford.edu/~johntayl/FCPR.pdf (accessed April 27, 2010).

Such political pressures might include attempts by one political party or the other to stimulate the economy or give financial markets a temporary boost before an election.

Other proponents of inflation targeting hold a somewhat less rigid view. Although they believe fighting inflation should be the primary objective of the Fed, or of a central bank, they believe an inflation-targeting regimen could be designed to give the central bank some flexibility. For example, the central bank could be required to target a broader range of inflation—say, between 1 and 3 percent—and meet the target several years in the future. Under either of these alternatives, central banks would have some room to meet employment or other policy objectives besides just inflation. In practice, many countries do allow some "wiggle room" in their inflation targeting regimens by using broad inflation bands or distant targets. Before he took over as chairman of the Federal Reserve in 2006, Ben Bernanke was an advocate for inflation targeting. While he was a member of the Board of Governors in 2003, Bernanke gave a speech outlining his own views on the merits of inflation targeting. For Bernanke, inflation targeting increased the effectiveness of monetary policy because it provided a long-term anchor for inflation expectations. As long as the private sector—individuals and firms—understood the Fed was holding firm to long-run inflation targets, it would have added flexibility to use aggressive monetary policy in the short run to offset adverse shocks to the economy—without upsetting long-run inflation expectations. Bernanke called inflation targeting a policy of *constrained discretion*. Under inflation targeting, the Fed could take actions to offset shocks to real output or to the financial system, but it had to keep its long-run inflation targets in clear view. After the financial crisis of 2008, Bernanke stopped speaking about inflation targeting and devoted his speeches to explaining the Fed's actions during the crisis and designing an "exit strategy" for the Fed's massive interventions.

Even prior to the recent recession, many economists disagreed with the idea of inflation targeting because they strongly objected to the Fed concentrating solely on controlling inflation. In the United States, Congress and the president are frequently incapable of quickly agreeing on a fiscal policy to stave off or end a recession. Of course, automatic fiscal stabilizers exist, but they are often not sufficient to cushion the economy when a shock hits. Practically speaking, only monetary policy is available to stabilize output and prevent deep recessions from emerging. If monetary policy is geared solely toward controlling inflation, as inflation-targeting proponents would like, and if fiscal policies are difficult for Congress and the president to pass, that leaves the government no other tools to fight a recession.

Economists also debate the level for an inflation target. Suppose there were general agreement that the ultimate goal should be total price stability—that is, zero inflation. There would still be legitimate questions about what constitutes "stable" prices. It is very difficult to measure changes in prices accurately when there is a great deal of technological change occurring in the economy, because technological improvements change the quality of goods so rapidly that government statisticians can't easily catch up with them. If, as many economists believe, our price indexes overstate the true inflation rate, annual inflation of 2 percent may in reality be true price stability. Indeed, many proponents of inflation targeting agree with this point and recommend a 2 percent inflation rate as "price stability."

Critics of stabilization policy, of course, believe that not using monetary policy to try to stabilize the economy would actually improve our economic performance. In their view, attempts to stabilize the economy have done more harm than good over the years by making fluctuations worse. In previous chapters, we discussed the difficulties in conducting stabilization policy. These include lags, uncertainties about the strength and timing of policies, and difficulties in estimating the natural rate of unemployment. If you believe these difficulties are insurmountable, you will likely think the Fed should target just inflation. If you think they can be overcome, you will likely believe the Fed should be allowed to stabilize output and employment, too.

Some economists like the idea of the Fed having to meet targets, but they have suggested alternatives to inflation targeting. One approach that has wide appeal was developed by economist John Taylor of Stanford University. Taylor suggested that the Fed follow a rule that keeps a long-run inflation target but allows the Fed to raise or lower interest rates depending on whether output is above or below potential. His own analysis suggests that the performance of the Fed would be superior if it followed a rule of this type, rather than making ad hoc decisions. The advantage of a rule of this nature is that it allows the Fed to offset shocks to the economy, but requires the Fed to meet long run inflation targets.

Debate 2: If There Were an Inflation Target, Who Would Set It? Even if the United States decided to adopt inflation targeting as a policy, several important questions would remain. Perhaps the most important is "Who would set the target?"

In the United Kingdom, which adopted targeting in 1992, the elected government decides on the inflation target for the central bank. These elected officials typically specify a range for the inflation rate that the bank must meet. The central bank participates in the discussions and has an opportunity to present its views to the public through its publications and published minutes of its meetings. But ultimately it is the elected government that makes the final decision.

In other countries, the central bank has even more influence in setting the inflation target. In New Zealand, for example, the central bank has the responsibility of "achieving and maintaining stability in the general level of prices" without any competing goals, such as stabilizing employment or output. The law also requires the head of the central bank and the finance minister to negotiate inflation goals and make them public.

What would be an appropriate arrangement for the United States? Under current law, the Fed chairman reports regularly to Congress, but the Fed has considerable power to use monetary policy to stabilize output as well as to fight inflation as it pleases. Would our Congress and president be willing to cede power to the Fed and allow it to focus only on fighting inflation? And, if they did, would Congress or the president want to determine the target range for inflation and instruct the Fed how quickly to meet these targets?

As you can see, changing our current system would require major decisions about who has authority and control over our economic system. Currently, the Fed has considerable power and autonomy. Although inflation targeting might make the Fed more independent, another phenomenon could occur, too: Congress and the president might end up with more power over monetary policy. And that might lead to more inflation, not less.

13.3 LEARNING OBJECTIVE

Should We Tax Consumption Rather than Income?

As we discussed in earlier chapters, the United States is a country with a low saving rate. This hurts our long-run growth prospects because our investment spending is determined by our own savings and savings from abroad. Many factors—not purely economic ones—contribute to our low saving rate. For example, colleges generally give less financial aid to students whose families have saved for their education. Many of our welfare programs cut the benefits of families who have saved in the past and still have some funds left in their accounts. The U.S. tax system also discourages savings. Here's how.

In the United States, you must pay taxes on both the wages you earn and the earnings you make on your savings. Suppose you earn $100 at your job and you have a tax rate of 20 percent. That means you keep $80 after taxes. Now suppose you save $50 of that money and invest it at 10 percent. At the end of one year, you will have earned an additional $5 on the $50 you saved (10% 3 $50), but you will get to keep only $4 of it because the government will take $1 in taxes (20% 3 $5). So, you will have to pay the government $21 in total: $20 on the $100 you earned in wages, plus $1 on the $5 you earned on your savings. If you did not save at all, you would pay only $20 in taxes, not $21.

Consumption taxes Taxes based on the consumption, not the income, of individuals.

Not all tax systems work this way. Tax systems based on consumption do not penalize individuals who save. Sales taxes in the United States and value-added taxes abroad are familiar examples of **consumption taxes.** It is also possible to create a consumption tax from an income tax by not taxing the earnings on savings—just as we do with tax-exempt bonds issued by state and municipal governments. Or, as an alternative, the government could allow savings to be deducted from gross income before the calculation for total taxes owed is made. The key feature of consumption taxation is that you do not face any additional taxes if you decide to save more of your income.

There are, however, ways in the United States to save money and still limit your taxes. In addition to buying tax-exempt bonds, you can invest in an IRA (individual retirement account) or 401(k), 403(b), and Keogh plans, which are also types of retirement accounts. The money in pension funds is treated similarly. It isn't taxed until the person who contributed it retires and withdraws it. During retirement, most people earn less money than when they were working, so the tax rate they pay on the money they withdraw from these accounts is lower than when they saved it. Also, the money accumulates more quickly because it grows tax-free while it's in these accounts. In practice, the U.S. tax system is a hybrid system, part way between an income tax and a consumption tax.

Two Debates about Consumption Taxation

Proponents claim that taxes based on consumption will increase total savings and may even be more equitable. Let's explore these claims.

Debate 1: Will Consumption Taxes Lead to More Savings? There is no question that taxing consumption instead of savings creates an incentive to save. However, there's no guarantee the incentive will actually result in more money saved in the economy. Suppose the tax burden is shifted to consumption by reducing the tax rate on savings. People will want to take advantage of this incentive and reduce their consumption and increase their saving. On the other hand, people will also want to spend more because, with the tax cut, they are wealthier.

Although there has been much research done on how a consumption tax would affect savings, the results are far from conclusive. It is true that individuals will allocate their savings to tax-favored investments over investments that are not favored. For example, they will put money into their IRAs. What is not clear is whether the funds they will put there are literally new savings—meaning reduced consumption—or merely transfers from other accounts, such as conventional savings accounts, which do not have the same tax advantages. Untangling these effects is a difficult issue, and it remains an active area of ongoing research.

The tax system imposed on corporations in the United States also creates disincentives to save and invest. Suppose you purchase a share of stock in a corporation. When the corporation earns a profit, it pays taxes on the profit at the corporate tax rate. When the corporation pays you a dividend on the stock out of the profits it earns, you must pay taxes on the dividend income that you receive. Corporate income is taxed twice, in other words—first when it is earned by the corporation and again when it is paid out to shareholders.

Some economists have argued that the corporate taxes lead to less-efficient investment because they result in capital flowing into other sectors of the economy (into real estate, for example) that do not suffer from double taxation. For this reason, in 2003 Congress passed a bill introduced by President Bush that lowered—but did not eliminate—taxes on corporate dividends.

Debate 2: Are Consumption Taxes Fair? The basic idea behind a consumption tax seems fair. Individuals should be taxed on what they take away from the economy's total production—that is, what they consume—not on what they actually produce. If an individual produces a lot but does not consume the proceeds from what was produced and instead plows it back into the economy for investment, that individual is contributing to the growth of total output and should be rewarded, not punished. Individual A earns \$50 and consumes it all; individual B earns \$100 but consumes only \$40. Who should pay more?

In practice, moving to a consumption-tax system could have a major impact on the distribution of income in the economy. Suppose we simply exempted the returns from savings from the income tax. This exception would clearly favor wealthy and high-income individuals who save the most and earn a lot of income in interest, dividends,

Table 13.1

Distribution of Capital Gains and Dividends By Income Class, 2009

Cash Income Level	Share of Capital Gains and Dividends
Less than $40,000	0%
$40,000 to $50,000	0.1
$50,000 to $75,000	0.9
$75,000 to $100,000	1.4
$100,000 to $200,000	8.2
$200,000 to $500,000	19.5
$500,000 to $1,000,000	13.8
Greater than $1,000,000	55.9

SOURCE: Estimates from the Urban-Brookings Tax Policy Center Microsimulation Model, http://www.taxpolicycenter.org/index.cfm (Accessed April 27, 2010).

Capital gains Profits investors earn when they sell stocks, bonds, real estate, or other assets.

rents, and capital gains. Table 13.1 shows estimates based on the capital gains received by different income classes for the year 2009 and dividends paid by corporations. **Capital gains** are the profits investors earn when they sell stocks, bonds, real estate, or other assets. As you can see, taxpayers with annual incomes exceeding $1,000,000 earned over half of the economy's capital gains over this period. Obviously, capital assets are highly concentrated among the wealthy.

If capital gains and other types of capital income were not taxed, total tax revenue would fall, and the government would have to raise tax rates on everyone to maintain the same level of spending. Excluding capital income from taxation does have its costs.

Some economists believe it is important that high-income individuals continue to pay a significant share of total taxes. In the last several decades, the distribution of income has become more unequal, as superstar athletes, famous actors and musicians, CEOs, and successful entrepreneurs and investors have all earned large fortunes. The tax system is one way we have to at least partially reduce inequalities in income. Critics of consumption taxes worry that moving our tax system in that direction will take away this important tool for social equality. However, other economists believe that high-income individuals already shoulder a very high share of the total tax burden and that we need to focus on designing an efficient system to promote economic growth.

Application 3

Is a Vat in Our Future?

Applying the Concepts #3: Can the United States adopt a European-style value-added tax?

Virtually all developed countries and many developing countries have a value-added tax, commonly known as a VAT. The United States is a prominent exception. The VAT is essentially a sales tax that is levied on each stage of production. Firms pay the VAT on their sales and then receive a credit for VAT paid on their purchases. Unlike a sales tax, the VAT is embedded in the price of goods. It is rebated when goods are exported but imports are required to pay the VAT. Rates on the VAT can be high—for example, the basic rate in the United Kingdom is 17.5 percent.

The VAT has some important advantages. It is relatively easy to collect and, as a consumption tax, does not penalize savings. There are some potential difficulties. Since U.S. states already levy retail sales taxes, incorporating a VAT at the state level could be difficult and be seen to impinge on state taxing authority. In addition, some conservatives worry that it is too efficient and consumers will not notice all the taxes they pay. Liberals worry that the VAT, like all consumption taxes, could be regressive. An old joke goes that the time will come for the VAT when liberals recognize it is a money machine and conservatives recognize it is regressive.

Proponents of consumption taxes have tried to meet the challenge of fairness in different ways. The "flat tax" designed by Robert E. Hall of Stanford University and Alvin Rabushka of the Hoover Institute brings the personal income tax and corporate income tax into a single, unified tax system. Under the flat tax, one low, single tax rate applies to both businesses and individuals. Businesses deduct their wage payments before they pay taxes. In addition, they can deduct any investment spending they make from their income before the tax is calculated. Recall that in a simple economy, without government or the foreign sector, saving equals investment, $S = I$. Allowing a deduction for investment has generally the same effect as allowing a deduction for savings. So this flat tax is a type of consumption tax.

This version of the flat tax has an important feature that ensures that wealthy individuals (and other owners of corporations) still pay taxes. Suppose the corporation or business makes an extraordinary return on its investment. Consider, for example, the tremendous profit generated by Apple's iPod. Over 14 million iPods were shipped in fiscal year 2006. If the profit for each iPod were $100, Apple's total profit from iPods would be $1.4 billion. Under this version of the flat tax, these extraordinary gains would be taxed in full. Owners of a corporation or business may earn extraordinary gains, but if they do, they will pay taxes on them.

The projected federal deficit has led many policymakers to consider whether a European-style value-added tax (VAT) would make sense for the United States. Grafting a VAT on to the U.S. fiscal system would pose many challenges.

Summary

In this chapter we explored three topics that are the center of macroeconomic policy debates today. Here are the key points to remember:

1 A *deficit* is the difference between the government's current expenditures and revenue. The government debt is the sum of all past yearly deficits.

2 Deficits can be financed through either borrowing or money creation. Financing deficits through money creation is called monetizing the *deficit*. It leads to inflation.

3 Deficits can be good for the country. Automatic stabilizers and expansionary fiscal policy both work through the creation of deficits.

4 The national debt incurs two burdens on citizens: It can reduce the amount of capital in an economy, leading to lower levels of income; it can also result in higher taxes that future generations will have to pay.

5 A number of developed countries have recently changed their monetary policy to emphasize targeting the inflation rate or a range for the inflation rate.

6 Although targeting inflation can increase the credibility of a central bank, it does limit the tools left for active stabilization policy.

7 A *consumption tax* would increase the incentives for private saving. However, it is not clear that total savings would necessarily increase, and there would be concerns about the fairness of this form of taxation.

Key Terms

Capital gains, p. 322
Consumption taxes, p. 320
Monetizing the deficit, p. 313
Ricardian equivalence, p. 314

GLOSSARY

A

Absolute advantage A producer has an absolute advantage over another in the production of a good or service if he or she can produce that product using fewer resources.

Accelerator effect The tendency for investment to increase when aggregate output increases and to decrease when aggregate output decreases, accelerating the growth or decline of output.

Actual investment The actual amount of investment that takes place; it includes items such as unplanned changes in inventories.

Adjustment costs The costs that a firm incurs when it changes its production level—for example, the administration costs of laying off employees or the training costs of hiring new workers.

Aggregate behavior The behavior of all households and firms together.

Aggregate demand The total demand for goods and services in the economy.

Aggregate demand (AD) curve A curve that shows the negative relationship between aggregate output (income) and the price level. Each point on the AD curve is a point at which both the goods market and the money market are in equilibrium.

Aggregate income The total income received by all factors of production in a given period.

Aggregate output The total quantity of goods and services produced in an economy in a given period.

Aggregate output (income) (Y) A combined term used to remind you of the exact equality between aggregate output and aggregate income.

Aggregate production function The mathematical representation of the relationship between inputs and national output, or gross domestic product.

Aggregate saving (S) The part of aggregate income that is not consumed.

Aggregate supply The total supply of all goods and services in an economy.

Aggregate supply (AS) curve A graph that shows the relationship between the aggregate quantity of output supplied by all firms in an economy and the overall price level.

Animal spirits of entrepreneurs A term coined by Keynes to describe investors' feelings.

Appreciation of a currency The rise in value of one currency relative to another.

Automatic destabilizers Revenue and expenditure items in the federal budget that automatically change with the economy in such a way as to destabilize GDP.

Automatic stabilizers Revenue and expenditure items in the federal budget that automatically change with the state of the economy in such a way as to stabilize GDP.

B

Balance of payments The record of a country's transactions in goods, services, and assets with the rest of the world; also the record of a country's sources (supply) and uses (demand) of foreign exchange.

Balance of trade A country's exports of goods and services minus its imports of goods and services.

Balance on capital account In the United States, the sum of the following (measured in a given period): the change in private U.S. assets abroad, the change in foreign private assets in the United States, the change in U.S. government assets abroad, and the change in foreign government assets in the United States.

Balance on current account Net exports of goods plus net exports of services plus net investment income plus net transfer payments.

Balanced-budget multiplier The ratio of change in the equilibrium level of output to a change in government spending where the change in government spending is balanced by a change in taxes so as not to create any deficit. The balanced-budget multiplier is equal to 1: The change in *Y* resulting from the change in *G* and the equal change in *T* are exactly the same size as the initial change in *G* or *T*.

Barter The direct exchange of goods and services for other goods and services.

Base year The year chosen for the weights in a fixed-weight procedure.

Black market A market in which illegal trading takes place at market-determined prices.

Brain drain The tendency for talented people from developing countries to become educated in a developed country and remain there after graduation.

Budget deficit The difference between what a government spends and what it collects in taxes in a given period: $G-T$.

Business cycle The cycle of short-term ups and downs in the economy.

C

Capital Things that are produced and then used in the production of other goods and services.

Capital flight The tendency for both human capital and financial capital to leave developing countries in search of higher expected rates of return elsewhere with less risk.

Capital gain An increase in the value of an asset.

Capital market The input/factor market in which households supply their savings, for interest or for claims to future profits, to firms that demand funds to buy capital goods.

Capital-intensive technology A production technique that uses a large amount of capital relative to labor.

Cartesian coordinate system A common method of graphing two variables that makes use of two perpendicular lines against which the variables are plotted.

Catch-up The theory stating that the growth rates of less developed countries will exceed the growth rates of developed countries, allowing the less developed countries to catch up.

***Ceteris paribus*, or all else equal** A device used to analyze the relationship between two variables while the values of other variables are held unchanged.

Change in business inventories The amount by which firms' inventories change during a period. Inventories are the goods that firms produce now but intend to sell later.

Circular flow A diagram showing the income received and payments made by each sector of the economy.

Command economy An economy in which a central government either directly or indirectly sets output targets, incomes, and prices.

Commodity monies Items used as money that also have intrinsic value in some other use.

Comparative advantage A producer has a comparative advantage over another in the production of a good or service if he or she can produce that product at a lower *opportunity cost.*

Compensation of employees Includes wages, salaries, and various supplements—employer contributions to social insurance and pension funds, for example—paid to households by firms and by the government.

Complements, complementary goods Goods that "go together"; a decrease in the price of one results in an increase in demand for the other and vice versa.

Constrained supply of labor The amount a household actually works in a given period at the current wage rate.

Consumer goods Goods produced for present consumption.

Consumer price index (CPI) A price index computed each month by the Bureau of Labor Statistics using a bundle that is meant to represent the "market basket" purchased monthly by the typical urban consumer.

Consumer sovereignty The idea that consumers ultimately dictate what will be produced (or not produced) by choosing what to purchase (and what not to purchase).

Consumer surplus The difference between the maximum amount a person is willing to pay for a good and its current market price.

Consumption function The relationship between consumption and income.

Contraction, recession, *or* slump The period in the business cycle from a peak down to a trough during which output and employment fall.

Contractionary fiscal policy A decrease in government spending or an increase in net taxes aimed at decreasing aggregate output (income) (*Y*).

Contractionary monetary policy A decrease in the money supply aimed at decreasing aggregate output (income) (*Y*).

Corn Laws The tariffs, subsidies, and restrictions enacted by the British Parliament in the early nineteenth century to discourage imports and encourage exports of grain.

Corporate bonds Promissory notes issued by firms when they borrow money.

Corporate profits The income of corporations.

Cost shock, *or* supply shock A change in costs that shifts the short-run aggregate supply (*AS*) curve.

Cost-of-living adjustments (COLAs) Contract provisions that tie wages to changes in the cost of living. The greater the inflation rate, the more wages are raised.

Cost-push, *or* supply-side, inflation Inflation caused by an increase in costs.

Crowding-out effect The tendency for increases in government spending to cause reductions in private investment spending.

Currency debasement The decrease in the value of money that occurs when its supply is increased rapidly.

Current dollars The current prices that we pay for goods and services.

Cyclical deficit The deficit that occurs because of a downturn in the business cycle.

Cyclical unemployment The increase in unemployment that occurs during recessions and depressions.

D

Deadweight loss The total loss of producer and consumer surplus from underproduction or overproduction.

Deficit response index (DRI) The amount by which the deficit changes with a $1 change in GDP.

Deflation A decrease in the overall price level.

Demand curve A graph illustrating how much of a given product a household would be willing to buy at different prices.

Demand schedule A table showing how much of a given product a household would be willing to buy at different prices.

Demand-pull inflation Inflation that is initiated by an increase in aggregate demand.

Depreciation The amount by which an asset's value falls in a given period.

Depreciation of a currency The fall in value of one currency relative to another.

Depression A prolonged and deep recession.

Descriptive economics The compilation of data that describe phenomena and facts.

Desired, *or* optimal, level of inventories The level of inventory at which the extra cost (in lost sales) from lowering inventories by a small amount is just equal to the extra gain (in interest revenue and decreased storage costs).

Discount rate The interest rate that banks pay to the Fed to borrow from it.

Discouraged-worker effect The decline in the measured unemployment rate that results when people who want to work but cannot find jobs grow discouraged and stop looking, thus dropping out of the ranks of the unemployed and the labor force.

Discretionary fiscal policy Changes in taxes or spending that are the result of deliberate changes in government policy.

Disposable personal income *or* after-tax income Personal income minus personal income taxes. The amount that households have to spend or save.

Disposable, *or* after-tax, income (Y_d) Total income minus net taxes: $Y - T$.

Dividends The portion of a firm's profits that the firm pays out each period to its shareholders.

Doha Development Agenda An initiative of the World Trade Organization focused on issues of trade and development.

Dow Jones Industrial Average An index based on the stock prices of 30 actively traded large companies. The oldest and most widely followed index of stock market performance.

Dumping A firm's or an industry's sale of products on the world market at prices below its own cost of production.

Durable goods Goods that last a relatively long time, such as cars and household appliances.

E

Easy monetary policy Fed policies that expand the money supply and thus lower interest rates in an effort to stimulate the economy.

Economic growth An increase in the total output of an economy. It occurs when a society acquires new resources or when it learns to produce more using existing resources.

Economic integration Occurs when two or more nations join to form a free-trade zone.

Economic theory A statement or set of related statements about cause and effect, action and reaction.

Economics The study of how individuals and societies choose to use the scarce resources that nature and previous generations have provided.

Efficiency In economics, allocative efficiency. An efficient economy is one that produces what people want at the least possible cost.

Efficiency wage theory An explanation for unemployment that holds that the productivity of workers increases with the wage rate. If this is so, firms may have an incentive to pay wages above the market-clearing rate.

Efficient market A market in which profit opportunities are eliminated almost instantaneously.

Empirical economics The collection and use of data to test economic theories.

Employed Any person 16 years old or older (1) who works for pay, either for someone else or in his or her own business for 1 or more hours per week, (2) who works without pay for 15 or more hours per week in a family enterprise, or (3) who has a job but has been temporarily absent with or without pay.

Entrepreneur A person who organizes, manages, and assumes the risks of a firm, taking a new idea or a new product and turning it into a successful business.

Equilibrium The condition that exists when quantity supplied and quantity demanded are equal. At equilibrium, there is no tendency for price to change. In the macroeconomic goods market, equilibrium occurs when planned aggregate expenditure is equal to aggregate output.

Equilibrium price level The price level at which the aggregate demand and aggregate supply curves intersect.

Equity Fairness.

European Union (EU) The European trading bloc composed of 27 countries.

Excess demand *or* shortage The condition that exists when quantity demanded exceeds quantity supplied at the current price.

Excess labor, excess capital Labor and capital that are not needed to produce the firm's current level of output.

Excess reserves The difference between a bank's actual reserves and its required reserves.

Excess supply *or* surplus The condition that exists when quantity supplied exceeds quantity demanded at the current price.

Exchange rate The ratio at which two currencies are traded. The price of one country's currency in terms of another country's currency.

Exogenous variable A variable that is assumed not to depend on the state of the economy—that is, it does not change when the economy changes.

Expansion *or* boom The period in the business cycle from a trough up to a peak during which output and employment grow.

Expansionary fiscal policy An increase in government spending or a reduction in net taxes aimed at increasing aggregate output (income) (*Y*).

Expansionary monetary policy An increase in the money supply aimed at increasing aggregate output (income) (*Y*).

Expenditure approach A method of computing GDP that measures the total amount spent on all final goods and services during a given period.

Explicit contracts Employment contracts that stipulate workers' wages, usually for a period of 1 to 3 years.

Export promotion A trade policy designed to encourage exports.

Export subsidies Government payments made to domestic firms to encourage exports.

F

Factor endowments The quantity and quality of labor, land, and natural resources of a country.

Factors of production (or factors) The inputs into the process of production. Another term for resources.

Factors of production The inputs into the production process. Land, labor, and capital are the three key factors of production.

Fallacy of composition The erroneous belief that what is true for a part is necessarily true for the whole.

Favored customers Those who receive special treatment from dealers during situations of excess demand.

Federal budget The budget of the federal government.

Federal debt The total amount owed by the federal government.

Federal Open Market Committee (FOMC) A group composed of the seven members of the Fed's Board of Governors, the president of the New York Federal Reserve Bank, and four of the other 11 district bank presidents on a rotating basis; it sets goals concerning the money supply and interest rates and directs the operation of the Open Market Desk in New York.

Federal Reserve Bank (the Fed) The central bank of the United States.

Federal surplus (+) *or* deficit (–) Federal government receipts minus expenditures.

Fertility rate The birth rate. Equal to (the number of births per year divided by the population) × 100.

Fiat, *or* token, money Items designated as money that are intrinsically worthless.

Final goods and services Goods and services produced for final use.

Financial intermediaries Banks and other institutions that act as a link between those who have money to lend and those who want to borrow money.

Fine-tuning The phrase used by Walter Heller to refer to the government's role in regulating inflation and unemployment.

Firm An organization that transforms resources (inputs) into products (outputs). Firms are the—primary producing units in a market economy.

Fiscal drag The negative effect on the economy that occurs when average tax rates increase because taxpayers have moved into higher income brackets during an expansion.

Fiscal policy Government policies concerning taxes and spending.

Fixed-weight procedure A procedure that uses weights from a given base year.

Floating, *or* market-determined, exchange rates Exchange rates that are determined by the unregulated forces of supply and demand.

Foreign direct investment (FDI) Investment in enterprises made in a country by residents outside that country.

Foreign exchange All currencies other than the domestic currency of a given country.

Free enterprise The freedom of individuals to start and operate private businesses in search of profits.

Frictional unemployment The portion of unemployment that is due to the normal working of the labor market; used to denote short-run job/skill matching problems.

Full-employment budget What the federal budget would be if the economy were producing at the full-employment level of output.

G

General Agreement on Tariffs and Trade (GATT) An international agreement signed by the United States and 22 other countries in 1947 to promote the liberalization of foreign trade.

Goods market The market in which goods and services are exchanged and in which the equilibrium level of aggregate output is determined.

Government consumption and gross investment (G) Expenditures by federal, state, and local governments for final goods and services.

Government spending multiplier The ratio of the change in the equilibrium level of output to a change in government spending.

Gramm-Rudman-Hollings Act Passed by the U.S. Congress and signed by President Reagan in 1986, this law set out to reduce the federal deficit by $36 billion per year, with a deficit of zero slated for 1991.

Graph A two-dimensional representation of a set of numbers, or data.

Great Depression The period of severe economic contraction and high unemployment that began in 1929 and continued throughout the 1930s.

Gross domestic product (GDP) The total market value of all final goods and services produced within a given period by factors of production located within a country.

Gross investment The total value of all newly produced capital goods (plant, equipment, housing, and inventory) produced in a given period.

Gross national income (GNI) GNP converted into dollars using an average of currency exchange rates over several years adjusted for rates of inflation.

Gross national product (GNP) The total market value of all final goods and services produced within a given period by factors of production owned by a country's citizens, regardless of where the output is produced.

Gross private domestic investment (*I*) Total investment in capital—that is, the purchase of new housing, plants, equipment, and inventory by the private (or nongovernment) sector.

H

Heckscher-Ohlin theorem A theory that explains the existence of a country's comparative advantage by its factor endowments: A country has a comparative advantage in the production of a product if that country is relatively well endowed with inputs used intensively in the production of that product.

Households The consuming units in an economy.

Hyperinflation A period of very rapid increases in the overall price level.

I

Identity Something that is always true.

Implementation lag The time it takes to put the desired policy into effect once economists and policy makers recognize that the economy is in a boom or a slump.

Import substitution An industrial trade strategy that favors developing local industries that can manufacture goods to replace imports.

Income The sum of all a household's wages, salaries, profits, interest payments, rents, and other forms of earnings in a given period of time. It is a flow measure.

Income approach A method of computing GDP that measures the income—wages, rents, interest, and profits—received by all factors of production in producing final goods and services.

Indirect taxes minus subsidies Taxes such as sales taxes, customs duties, and license fees less subsidies that the government pays for which it receives no goods or services in return.

Industrial Revolution The period in England during the late eighteenth and early nineteenth centuries in which new manufacturing technologies and improved transportation gave rise to the modern factory system and a massive movement of the population from the countryside to the cities.

Infant industry A young industry that may need temporary protection from competition from the established industries of other countries to develop an acquired comparative advantage.

Inferior goods Goods for which demand tends to fall when income rises.

Inflation An increase in the overall price level.

Inflation rate The percentage change in the price level.

Inflation targeting When a monetary authority chooses its interest rate values with the aim of keeping the inflation rate within some specified band over some specified horizon.

Innovation The use of new knowledge to produce a new product or to produce an existing product more efficiently.

Input *or* factor markets The markets in which the resources used to produce goods and services are exchanged.

Inputs The goods and services that firms purchase and turn into output.

Inputs *or* resources Anything provided by nature or previous generations that can be used directly or indirectly to satisfy human wants.

Interest sensitivity *or* insensitivity of planned investment The responsiveness of planned investment spending to changes in the interest rate. *Interest sensitivity* means that planned investment spending changes a great deal in response to changes in the interest rate; *interest insensitivity* means little or no change in planned investment as a result of changes in the interest rate.

Intermediate goods Goods that are produced by one firm for use in further processing by another firm.

International Monetary Fund (IMF) An international agency whose primary goals are to stabilize international exchange rates and to lend money to countries that have problems financing their international transactions.

Invention An advance in knowledge.

Inventory investment The change in the stock of inventories.

Investment The process of using resources to produce new capital.

***IS* curve** A curve illustrating the negative relationship between the equilibrium value of aggregate output (income) (*Y*) and the interest rate in the goods market.

Interest The fee that borrowers pay to lenders for the use of their funds.

J

J-curve effect Following a currency depreciation, a country's balance of trade may get worse before it gets better. The graph showing this effect is shaped like the letter *J*, hence the name J-curve effect.

L

Labor demand curve A graph that illustrates the amount of labor that firms want to employ at each given wage rate.

Labor force The number of people employed plus the number of unemployed.

Labor force participation rate The ratio of the labor force to the total population 16 years old or older.

Labor market The input/factor market in which households supply work for wages to firms that demand labor.

Labor productivity Output per worker hour; the amount of output produced by an average worker in 1 hour.

Labor supply curve A graph that illustrates the amount of labor that households want to supply at each given wage rate.

Labor-intensive technology A production technique that uses a large amount of labor relative to capital.

Laffer curve With the tax rate measured on the vertical axis and tax revenue measured on the horizontal axis, the Laffer curve shows that there is some tax rate beyond which the supply response is large enough to lead to a decrease in tax revenue for further increases in the tax rate.

Laissez-faire economy Literally from the French: "allow [them] to do." An economy in which individual people and firms pursue their own self-interest without any central direction or regulation.

Land market The input/factor market in which households supply land or other real property in exchange for rent.

Law of demand The negative relationship between price and quantity demanded: As price rises, quantity demanded decreases; as price falls, quantity demanded increases.

Law of one price If the costs of transportation are small, the price of the same good in different countries should be roughly the same.

Law of supply The positive relationship between price and quantity of a good supplied: An increase in market price will lead to an increase in quantity supplied, and a decrease in market price will lead to a decrease in quantity supplied.

Legal tender Money that a government has required to be accepted in settlement of debts.

Lender of last resort One of the functions of the Fed: It provides funds to troubled banks that cannot find any other sources of funds.

Life-cycle theory of consumption A theory of household consumption: Households make lifetime consumption decisions based on their expectations of lifetime income.

Liquidity property of money The property of money that makes it a good medium of exchange as well as a store of value: It is portable and readily accepted and thus easily exchanged for goods.

***LM* curve** A curve illustrating the positive relationship between the equilibrium value of the interest rate and aggregate output (income) (*Y*) in the money market.

Lucas supply function The supply function embodies the idea that output (*Y*) depends on the difference between the actual price level and the expected price level.

M

M1, *or* transactions money Money that can be directly used for transactions.

M2, *or* broad money M1 plus savings accounts, money market accounts, and other near monies.

Macroeconomics The branch of economics that examines the economic behavior of aggregates— income, employment, output, and so on—on a national scale.

Marginal propensity to consume (*MPC*) That fraction of a change in income that is consumed, or spent.

Marginal propensity to import (*MPM*) The change in imports caused by a $1 change in income.

Marginal propensity to save (*MPS*) That fraction of a change in income that is saved.

Marginal rate of transformation (*MRT*) The slope of the production possibility frontier (ppf).

Marginalism The process of analyzing the additional or incremental costs or benefits arising from a choice or decision.

Market The institution through which buyers and sellers interact and engage in exchange.

Market demand The sum of all the quantities of a good or service demanded per period by all the households buying in the market for that good or service.

Market supply The sum of all that is supplied—each period by all producers of a single product.

Medium of exchange, *or* means of payment What sellers generally accept and buyers generally use to pay for goods and services.

Microeconomics The branch of economics that examines the functioning of individual industries and the behavior of individual decision-making units—that is, firms and households.

Minimum wage A price floor set for the price of labor.

Minimum wage laws Laws that set a floor for wage rates—that is, a minimum hourly rate for any kind of labor.

Model A formal statement of a theory, usually a mathematical statement of a presumed relationship between two or more variables.

Modern economic growth The period of rapid and sustained increase in real output per capita that began in the Western World with the Industrial Revolution.

Monetary policy The behavior of the Federal Reserve concerning the nation's money supply.

Monetary policy The tools used by the Federal Reserve to control the quantity of money, which in turn affects interest rates.

Money market The market in which financial instruments are exchanged and in which the equilibrium level of the interest rate is determined.

Money multiplier The multiple by which deposits can increase for every dollar increase in reserves; equal to 1 divided by the required reserve ratio.

Moral suasion The pressure that in the past the Fed exerted on member banks to discourage them from borrowing heavily from the Fed.

Mortality rate The death rate. Equal to (the number of deaths per year divided by the population) × 100.

Movement along a demand curve The change in quantity demanded brought about by a change in price.

Movement along a supply curve The change in quantity supplied brought about by a change in price.

Multiplier The ratio of the change in the equilibrium level of output to a change in some exogenous variable.

N

NAIRU The nonaccelerating inflation rate of unemployment.

NASDAQ Composite An index based on the stock prices of over 5,000 companies traded on the NASDAQ Stock Market. The NASDAQ market takes its name from the National Association of Securities Dealers Automated Quotation System.

National income The total income earned by the factors of production owned by a country's citizens.

National income and product accounts Data collected and published by the government describing the various components of national income and output in the economy.

Natural rate of population increase The difference between the birth rate and the death rate.

Natural rate of unemployment The unemployment that occurs as a normal part of the functioning of the economy. Sometimes taken as the sum of frictional unemployment and structural unemployment.

Near monies Close substitutes for transactions money, such as savings accounts and money market accounts.

Negative demand shock Something that causes a negative shift in consumption or investment schedules or that leads to a decrease in U.S. exports.

Negative relationship A relationship between two variables, *X* and *Y*, in which a decrease in *X* is associated with an increase in *Y* and an increase in *X* is associated with a decrease in *Y*.

Net business transfer payments Net transfer payments by businesses to others.

Net exports (*EX* – *IM*) The difference between exports (sales to foreigners of U.S.-produced goods and services) and imports (U.S. purchases of goods and services from abroad). The figure can be positive or negative.

Net exports of goods and services (*EX* – *IM*) The difference between a country's total exports and total imports.

Net interest The interest paid by business.

Net investment Gross investment minus depreciation.

Net national product (NNP) Gross national product minus depreciation; a nation's total product minus what is required to maintain the value of its capital stock.

Net taxes (*T*) Taxes paid by firms and households to the government minus transfer payments made to households by the government.

Nominal GDP Gross domestic product measured in current dollars.

Nominal wage rate The wage rate in current dollars.

Nondurable goods Goods that are used up fairly quickly, such as food and clothing.

Nonlabor, *or* nonwage, income Any income received from sources other than working—inheritances, interest, dividends, transfer payments, and so on.

Nonresidential investment Expenditures by firms for machines, tools, plants, and so on.

Nonsynchronization of income and spending The mismatch between the timing of money inflow to the household and the timing of money outflow for household expenses.

Normal goods Goods for which demand goes up when income is higher and for which demand goes down when income is lower.

Normative economics An approach to economics that analyzes outcomes of economic behavior, evaluates them as good or bad, and may prescribe courses of action. Also called policy economics.

North American Free Trade Agreement (NAFTA) An agreement signed by the United States, Mexico, and Canada in which the three countries agreed to establish all North America as a free-trade zone.

Not in the labor force A person who is not looking for work because he or she does not want a job or has given up looking.

O

Ockham's razor The principle that irrelevant detail should be cut away.

Okun's Law The theory, put forth by Arthur Okun, that in the short run the unemployment rate decreases about 1 percentage point for every 3 percent increase in real GDP. Later research and data have shown that the relationship between output and unemployment is not as stable as Okun's "Law" predicts.

Open Market Desk The office in the New York Federal Reserve Bank from which government securities are bought and sold by the Fed.

Open market operations The purchase and sale by the Fed of government securities in the open market; a tool used to expand or contract the amount of reserves in the system and thus the money supply.

Opportunity cost The best alternative that we forgo, or give up, when we make a choice or a decision.

Origin On a Cartesian coordinate system, the point at which the horizontal and vertical axes intersect.

Output growth The growth rate of the output of the entire economy.

Outputs Goods and services of value to households.

P

Per-capita output growth The growth rate of output per person in the economy.

Perfect substitutes Identical products.

Permanent income The average level of a person's expected future income stream.

Personal consumption expenditures (*C*) Expenditures by consumers on goods and services.

Personal income The total income of households.

Personal saving The amount of disposable income that is left after total personal spending in a given period.

Personal saving rate The percentage of disposable personal income that is saved. If the personal saving rate is low, households are spending a large amount relative to their incomes; if it is high, households are spending cautiously.

Phillips Curve A curve showing the relationship between the inflation rate and the unemployment rate.

Planned aggregate expenditure (*AE*) The total amount the economy plans to spend in a given period. Equal to consumption plus planned investment: $AE ; C + I$.

Planned investment (*I*) Those additions to capital stock and inventory that are planned by firms.

Plant-and-equipment investment Purchases by firms of additional machines, factories, or buildings within a given period.

Policy mix The combination of monetary and fiscal policies in use at a given time.

Positive economics An approach to economics that seeks to understand behavior and the operation of systems without making judgments. It describes what exists and how it works.

Positive relationship A relationship between two variables, *X* and *Y*, in which a decrease in *X* is—associated with a decrease in *Y*, and an increase in *X* is associated with an increase in *Y*.

Post hoc, ergo propter hoc Literally, "after this (in time), therefore because of this." A common error made in thinking about causation: If Event A happens before Event B, it is not necessarily true that A caused B.

Potential output, *or* potential GDP The level of aggregate output that can be sustained in the long run without inflation.

Price ceiling A maximum price that sellers may—charge for a good, usually set by government.

Price feedback effect The process by which a domestic price increase in one country can "feed back" on itself through export and import prices. An increase in the price level in one country can drive up prices in other countries. This in turn further increases the price level in the first country.

Price floor A minimum price below which exchange is not permitted.

Price rationing The process by which the market system allocates goods and services to consumers when quantity demanded exceeds quantity supplied.

Price surprise Actual price level minus expected price level.

Privately held federal debt The privately held (non-government-owned) debt of the U.S. government.

Producer price indexes (PPIs) Measures of prices that producers receive for products at all stages in the production process.

Producer surplus The difference between the current market price and the full cost of production for the firm.

Product *or* output markets The markets in which goods and services are exchanged.

Production The process that transforms scarce resources into useful goods and services.

Production possibility frontier (ppf) A graph that shows all the combinations of goods and services that can be produced if all of society's resources are used efficiently.

Productivity growth The growth rate of output per worker.

Productivity of an input The amount of output produced per unit of an input.

Productivity, *or* labor productivity Output per worker hour; the amount of output produced by an average worker in 1 hour.

Profit The difference between revenues and costs.

Proprietors' income The income of unincorporated businesses.

Protection The practice of shielding a sector of the economy from foreign competition.

Purchasing-power-parity theory A theory of international exchange holding that exchange rates are set so that the price of similar goods in different countries is the same.

Quantity demanded The amount (number of units) of a product that a household would buy in a given period if it could buy all it wanted at the current market price.

Quantity supplied The amount of a particular product that a firm would be willing and able to offer for sale at a particular price during a given time period.

Quantity theory of money The theory based on the identity $M \times V = P \times Y$ and the assumption that the velocity of money (V) is constant (or virtually constant).

Queuing Waiting in line as a means of distributing goods and services: a nonprice rationing mechanism.

Quota A limit on the quantity of imports.

R

Ration coupons Tickets or coupons that entitle individuals to purchase a certain amount of a given product per month.

Rational-expectations hypothesis The hypothesis that people know the "true model" of the economy and that they use this model to form their expectations of the future.

Real business cycle theory An attempt to explain business cycle fluctuations under the assumptions of complete price and wage flexibility and rational expectations. It emphasizes shocks to technology and other shocks.

Real interest rate The difference between the interest rate on a loan and the inflation rate.

Real wage rate The amount the nominal wage rate can buy in terms of goods and services.

Real wealth, *or* real balance, effect The change in consumption brought about by a change in real wealth that results from a change in the price level.

Realized capital gain The gain that occurs when the owner of an asset actually sells it for more than he or she paid for it.

Recession A period during which aggregate output declines. Conventionally, a period in which aggregate output declines for two consecutive quarters.

Recognition lag The time it takes for policy makers to recognize the existence of a boom or a slump.

Relative-wage explanation of unemployment An explanation for sticky wages (and therefore unemployment): If workers are concerned about their wages relative to other workers in other firms and industries, they may be unwilling to accept a wage cut unless they know that all other workers are receiving similar cuts.

Rental income The income received by property owners in the form of rent.

Required reserve ratio The percentage of its total deposits that a bank must keep as reserves at the Federal Reserve.

Reserves The deposits that a bank has at the Federal Reserve bank plus its cash on hand.

Residential investment Expenditures by households and firms on new houses and apartment buildings.

Response lag The time that it takes for the economy to adjust to the new conditions after a new policy is implemented; the lag that occurs because of the operation of the economy itself.

Run on a bank Occurs when many of those who have claims on a bank (deposits) present them at the same time.

Scarce Limited.

Services The things we buy that do not involve the production of physical things, such as legal and medical services and education.

Shares of stock Financial instruments that give to the holder a share in the firm's ownership and—therefore the right to share in the firm's profits.

Shift of a demand curve The change that takes place in a demand curve corresponding to a new relationship between quantity demanded of a good and price of that good. The shift is brought—about by a change in the original conditions.

Shift of a supply curve The change that takes place in a supply curve corresponding to a new relationship between quantity supplied of a good and the price of that good. The shift is brought about by a change in the original conditions.

Shock therapy The approach to transition from socialism to market capitalism that advocates rapid deregulation of prices, liberalization of trade, and privatization.

Slope A measurement that indicates whether the relationship between variables is positive or negative and how much of a response there is in Y (the variable on the vertical axis) when X (the variable on the horizontal axis) changes.

Smoot-Hawley tariff The U.S. tariff law of the 1930s, which set the highest tariffs in U.S. history (60 percent). It set off an international trade war and caused the decline in trade that is often considered one of the causes of the worldwide depression of the 1930s.

Social overhead capital Basic infrastructure projects such as roads, power generation, and irrigation systems.

Social, *or* implicit, contracts Unspoken agreements between workers and firms that firms will not cut wages.

Speculation motive One reason for holding bonds instead of money: Because the market price of interest-bearing bonds is inversely related to the interest rate, investors may want to hold bonds when interest rates are high with the hope of selling them when interest rates fall.

Stability A condition in which national output is growing steadily, with low inflation and full employment of resources.

Stabilization policy Describes both monetary and fiscal policy, the goals of which are to smooth out fluctuations in output and employment and to keep prices as stable as possible.

Stagflation A situation of both high inflation and high unemployment. Occurs when output is falling at the same time that prices are rising.

Standard and Poor's 500 (S&P 500) An index based on the stock prices of 500 of the largest firms by market value.

Statistical discrepancy Data measurement error.

Sticky prices Prices that do not always adjust rapidly to maintain equality between quantity supplied and quantity demanded.

Sticky wages The downward rigidity of wages as an explanation for the existence of unemployment.

Stock A certificate that certifies ownership of a certain portion of a firm.

Store of value An asset that can be used to transport purchasing power from one time period to another.

Structural adjustment A series of programs in developing nations designed to: (1) reduce the size of their public sectors through privatization and/or expenditure reductions, (2) decrease their budget deficits, (3) control inflation, and (4) encourage private saving and investment through tax reform.

Structural deficit The deficit that remains at full employment.

Structural unemployment The portion of unemployment that is due to changes in the structure of the economy that result in a significant loss of jobs in certain industries.

Substitutes Goods that can serve as replacements for one another; when the price of one increases, demand for the other increases.

Sunk costs Costs that cannot be avoided because they have already been incurred.

Supply curve A graph illustrating how much of a product a firm will sell at different prices.

Supply schedule A table showing how much of a product firms will sell at alternative prices.

Surplus of government enterprises Income of government enterprises.

T

Tariff A tax on imports.

Tax multiplier The ratio of change in the equilibrium level of output to a change in taxes.

Terms of trade The ratio at which a country can trade domestic products for imported products.

Theory of comparative advantage Ricardo's theory that specialization and free trade will benefit all trading parties, even those that may be "absolutely" more efficient producers.

Tight monetary policy Fed policies that contract the money supply and thus raise interest rates in an effort to restrain the economy.

Time lags Delays in the economy's response to stabilization policies.

Time series graph A graph illustrating how a variable changes over time.

Trade deficit Occurs when a country's exports of goods and services are less than its imports of goods and services in a given period.

Trade feedback effect The tendency for an increase in the economic activity of one country to lead to a worldwide increase in economic activity, which then feeds back to that country.

Trade surplus The situation when a country exports more than it imports.

Tragedy of commons The idea that collective ownership may not provide the proper private incentives for efficiency because individuals do not bear the full costs of their own decisions but do enjoy the full benefits.

Transaction motive The main reason that people hold money—to buy things.

Transfer payments Cash payments made by the government to people who do not supply goods, services, or labor in exchange for these payments. They include Social Security benefits, veterans' benefits, and welfare payments.

Treasury bonds, notes, and bills Promissory notes issued by the federal government when it borrows money.

U

U.S.-Canadian Free Trade Agreement An agreement in which the United States and Canada agreed to eliminate all barriers to trade between the two countries by 1998.

Unconstrained supply of labor The amount a household would like to work within a given period at the current wage rate if it could find the work.

Underground economy The part of the economy in which transactions take place and in which income is generated that is unreported and therefore not counted in GDP.

Unemployed A person 16 years old or older who is not working, is available for work, and has made specific efforts to find work during the previous 4 weeks.

Unemployment rate The percentage of the labor force that is unemployed. That is, the ratio of the number of people unemployed to the total number of people in the labor force.

Unit of account A standard unit that provides a consistent way of quoting prices.

V

Value added The difference between the value of goods as they leave a stage of production and the cost of the goods as they entered that stage.

Variable A measure that can change from time to time or from observation to observation.

Velocity of money The number of times a dollar bill changes hands, on average, during a year; the ratio of nominal GDP to the stock of money.

Vicious-circle-of-poverty hypothesis Suggests that poverty is self-perpetuating because poor nations are unable to save and invest enough to accumulate the capital stock that would help them grow.

W

Wealth *or* net worth The total value of what a household owns minus what it owes. It is a stock measure.

Weight The importance attached to an item within a group of items.

World Bank An international agency that lends money to individual countries for projects that promote economic development.

World Trade Organization (WTO) A negotiating forum dealing with rules of trade across nations.

X

***X*-axis** On a Cartesian coordinate system, the horizontal line against which a variable is plotted.

***X*-intercept** The point at which a graph intersects the X-axis.

Y

***Y*-axis** On a Cartesian coordinate system, the vertical line against which a variable is plotted.

***Y*-intercept** The point at which a graph intersects the Y-axis.